SOVIET FOREIGN POLICY

SOVIET FOREIGN POLICY

JAN F. TRISKA | DAVID D. FINLEY
Stanford University | *Colorado College*

THE MACMILLAN COMPANY, *New York*
COLLIER-MACMILLAN LIMITED, *London*

Library of Congress catalog card number: 68–12288

The Macmillan Company, New York
Collier-Macmillan Canada, Ltd., Toronto, Ontario

Printed in the United States of America

To our wives and students.

ACKNOWLEDGMENTS

We are deeply indebted to more individuals than we shall be able to enumerate here for whatever merits this book possesses. We absolve them from our sins and record our gratitude to them hereby.

The book largely owes its appearance to the Stanford Studies of the Communist System, a research and training program in the Stanford Institute of Political Studies, with which both authors have been associated since its inception in 1963. Our thanks go to our present and former colleagues in that program, all of whom in one way or another have contributed to our undertaking.

The library of the Hoover Institution on War, Revolution, and Peace, at Stanford University, has been a rich source of research materials for us. We would be remiss not to mention our gratitude for this splendid resource and for the friendly cooperation of the Hoover reference staff.

Special thanks go to our colleagues elsewhere, particularly Dr. Robert M. Slusser of Johns Hopkins University, Dr. Fred A. Sondermann of Colorado College, and Dr. David E. Clarke of Western Washington State College.

For very useful criticism of an earlier version of the manuscript we thank Dr. Oles M. Smolansky of Lehigh University. Mr. Robert J. Patterson has been our helpful and patient editor at The Macmillan Company. C. Bradley Scharf earns our sincere appreciation for carefully preparing the index. Lastly, but importantly, our gratitude for secretarial assistance goes to Mrs. Vivienne C. Burden and Mrs. Marie Kinzie.

We wish to acknowledge permission to reprint materials, the copyright for which is held by the following: *The Current Digest of the Soviet Press*, published weekly at Columbia University by the Joint Committee on Slavic Studies (copyright 1960 by the Joint Committee on Slavic Studies); *The Journal of Conflict Resolution*, University of Michigan; *Documents on International Affairs*, published by Oxford University Press under the auspices of the Royal Institute of International Affairs; *Law and Contemporary Problems*, Duke University; *The New Leader; Western Political Quarterly*, University of Utah, copyright owners; U.S. Naval Ordnance Test Station, China Lake, California; Stanford University Press, publishers of *The Theory, Law, and Policy of Soviet Treaties* by Jan F. Triska and Robert M. Slusser, © 1962 by the Board of Trustees of the Leland Stanford Junior University.

J. F. T.
D. D. F.

CONTENTS

A NOTE ON TRANSLITERATION

We have tried to follow the Library of Congress transliteration formula for Russian titles. We have, however, freely modified this formula in the case of proper names to conform with more popular usage in the United States. We hope the linguist's discomfort will be compensated by the nonlinguist's ease.

INTRODUCTION

This book is an experiment. We generally expect a textbook to be a systematic survey of the scholarly consensus in its area of coverage—a synthesis of existing knowledge laid out as a basis for the student to build upon. The scholarly consensus about Soviet foreign policy includes agreement upon most of the historical detail of what the Soviet Union has done in the international system, and very little more. But this is not a book of history. Our bibliography refers the reader to a considerable number of excellent histories covering intensively most of the activities of the Soviet Union in world affairs. Where does that leave us? The questions we address as political scientists are the *how* and *why* questions. On these the interpretations of Soviet foreign policy are widely divergent and even contradictory in the West, not to mention the diversity one finds if, as one should, one investigates non-Western opinion and communist as well as noncommunist views. One way we seek satisfaction is through experiment.

Because of the wide gamut of interpretations of Soviet foreign policy there is a limit to the useful synthesis we can perform. As the literature is filled with polemical contradiction, any effort to impose consensus where there is none would be fruitless. We therefore are more concerned to investigate and explain diversity than to reconcile it. Our book is an experiment because it poses questions that the student who has grasped the course of the historical events should pose for himself; it then seeks to answer some of these questions by means of empirical inquiry.

We have included some frankly experimental sallies among the following chapters out of another consideration as well. We want to open doors for the student and persuade him that new techniques of political analysis show some prospect for allowing more precise handling of the available data in a field still relegated by many to the occult arts. If the student feels that here is a vital subject matter filled with scholarly ferment, which permits and demands more work, we shall not be too chagrined to have some of our exploratory inclusions controverted. We have aspired to make a book that would be interesting to students of political science, who are concerned with the tools of the discipline, as well as bits of fact, and with the building of theory as well as its final outlines.

No modes of analysis have been rejected here per se. History, legal analysis of institutions, functional and content analysis all find some place.

We confess, however, that because frustrating differences occur from impressionistic interpretation, we were inclined to use quantitative indicators wherever we found them available and the relevant questions amenable to quantitative analysis. In this fashion we have sought to break through the formidable distortions that stem from cultural diversity.

As the reader will soon discover, the logic of our organization of the subject matter is not complicated. In the first chapter we provide a broad historical orientation. Chapters II, III, and IV are then devoted to the process of Soviet foreign policy decision-making, which is described in terms of the four complex variables of role structure, personality, the belief system, and events. Subsequently we turn outward from the decision-making process to some of the particular arenas in which Soviet foreign policy engages the rest of the international system. Approximating the Soviet categories specified at the XXth Party Congress, we examine first the Soviet Union and the international communist system; then the Soviet Union and the developing countries of Asia, Africa, and Latin America; then the Soviet Union and the capitalist countries of the Western world. We conclude with two chapters dealing with Soviet participation in the institutions of a common international order and a short effort to extrapolate current trends into future contingencies.

Problems of Analysis

We have already referred to the varied and sometimes contradictory interpretations of Soviet foreign policy. Let us now consider the dimensions of this problem as we see them.

The study of Soviet politics, and especially of Soviet foreign policy, has until recently been characterized by search for a skeleton key which used by itself might explain motivation and resultant action of the Soviet Union in the international system. Some analysts have identified the writings of Karl Marx together with the maze of their ambiguous interpretations and elaborations as the progenitors of all Soviet goals, expectations, and formulations of action. For instance, note the following passages from Gerhart Niemeyer and John S. Reshetar, Jr., *An Inquiry into Soviet Mentality:*

> The conviction of a Communist outcome of history renders the Soviet elite somewhat impervious to contradictions between their policies and experience, even experience relating to their own objectives. . . .

> Since the basic frame of Soviet reference is a future believed to be exclusively Communist, combined with a totalitarian regime supposed to be the present earnest of the future, Communists live in a world which they

will essentially hostile to the rest of the world. Consequently, Soviet rationality differs radically from that of the West, and bars any mutual intercourse. The relation between the two worlds is irrational, since premises are neither shared nor compared nor considered relevant to each other, but are conceived in mutual exclusiveness and hostility.[1]

Such analyses, *post factum*, may be persuasive; but it remains an open question whether they are made so by compelling empirical evidence or by the expansibility of the doctrinal formulations themselves—which like the Delphic Oracle seem amenable to a great variety of sometimes contradictory attributions of meaning.

Other analysts, unimpressed by the intangibles of this malleable "ideology," have cast most or all of it aside as camouflage and disingenuous rationalization or, at most, the vestige of long dead revolutionary zeal preserved, like Lenin's corpse, as a symbol of continuity which does not really exist. Instead of doctrine, they look to historical demands asserted by the Russian nation and bequeathed intact by a faltering nineteenth century despotism to a twentieth century successor. Hans J. Morgenthau may be quoted here as an example:

> The clamor for consistency in dealing with the different revolutions sailing under the flag of Communism is the result of that confusion which does not see that the real issue is Russian imperialism, and Communist revolution only insofar as it is an instrument of that imperialism.[2]

The era of Joseph Stalin and the intrigue within the Kremlin following that dictator's death persuade other commentators to discount both Marxist-Leninist doctrine and Russian nationalism and to interpret Soviet foreign policy as chiefly the by-product of interpersonal competition for possession of the paraphernalia of power in the Soviet Union. Perhaps the best example of this personal approach to the explanation of Soviet policy is to be found

[1] Gerhart Niemeyer and John S. Reshetar, Jr., *An Inquiry into Soviet Mentality* (London: Atlantic Press, 1956), pp. 39, 49–50. See also Nathan Leites, *The Operational Code of the Politburo* (New York: McGraw-Hill Book Company, Inc., 1951); John Foster Dulles, *War or Peace* (New York: The Macmillan Company, 1950); William H. Chamberlin, *Blueprint for World Conquest* (Washington, D.C.: Human Events, 1946). In recent years this outlook has been oversimplified and adopted by individuals of a very conservative political persuasion in the U.S. See, for instance, Fred Schwarz, *You Can Trust the Communists* (Englewood Cliffs, N.J.: Prentice-Hall, Inc., 1960); and Anthony T. Bouscaren, *Soviet Foreign Policy* (New York: Fordham University Press, 1962).

[2] *In Defense of the National Interest* (New York: Alfred A. Knopf, 1951), p. 80. See Nicholas Berdiaev, *The Origins of Russian Communism* (London: G. Bles, 1937) for an idealist counterpart to Morgenthau's "realism"; also, Arnold J. Toynbee, *The World and the West* (London: Oxford University Press, 1953), pp. 1–17.

in Robert Conquest's painstaking and valuable study, *Power and Policy in the U.S.S.R.* (New York: The Macmillan Company, 1961).

Other single-factor explanations credit perceived need to maintain the Soviet bureaucracy, or an inescapable concomitant of a totalitarian movement with driving the Soviet Union to an expansionist foreign policy. Thus Peter Meyer wrote in 1952 (before Stalin's death):

> Soviet imperialism is motivated neither by the interests of the 'Russian nation' nor by the interests of 'international communism.' Its driving force is the interest of the Soviet bureaucratic regime. For this reason, as the experience of all the satellite countries have shown, the mere expansion of Russia's power and influence is not sufficient—its peculiar social order must be imposed everywhere, replacing previous social forms; only this can satisfy the needs of the Soviet bureaucracy.[3]

Many variations on these themes may be found in the literature on Soviet foreign policy.[4] None of the proposals are without merit. Evidence can be adduced selectively to sustain the most exotic. But, as general theories, they seem to us to succumb to the lure of oversimplification—a temptation to explain the complex by imposing a single formula which relies upon a single "decisive" factor.

In recent years, however, the trend has been away from single-factor explanationsof Soviet foreign policy and toward an integration of a multiplicity of factors. The question has been rephrased. No longer is it, "What factor is the key to the Russian enigma?" Now we ask, "What is the operational mix of the factors which influence Soviet policy?"[5] The answers, far more sophisticated than any that could be given to the former question, are still dissatisfying to the extent that they remain almost entirely theoretical with empirical evidence used only illustratively.[6] It is our hope here to keep close

---

[3] "The Driving Force Behind Soviet Imperialism," *Commentary* (March, 1952), p. 217. The literature on totalitarianism is typified by Hannah Arendt, *The Origins of Totalitarianism*, rev. ed. (New York: Meridian Books, 1958), and Carl J. Friedrich and Zbigniew K. Brzezinski, *Totalitarian Dictatorship and Autocracy*, rev. ed. (New York: Frederick A. Praeger, Inc., 1966).

[4] For an extensive survey, see William A. Glaser, "Theories of Soviet Foreign Policy: A Classification of the Literature," *World Affairs Quarterly*, XXVII (July, 1956), 128–152.

[5] Examples of this trend include: Zbigniew K. Brzezinski, "Communist Ideology and International Affairs," *Journal of Conflict Resolution*, IV, No. 3 (September, 1960), 266–291; Adam B. Ulam, "Soviet Ideology and Soviet Foreign Policy," *World Politics*, XI (January, 1959), 153–172; and Alvin Z. Rubinstein, *The Soviets in International Organizations* (Princeton: Princeton University Press, 1964), pp. 318–48.

[6] See Daniel Bell, "Ten Theories in Search of Reality," *World Politics*, X (April, 1958), reprinted in Alexander Dallin, ed., *Soviet Conduct in World Affairs* (New York: Columbia University Press, 1960), pp. 1–36.

to an empirical base in identifying the various factors and trying to specify their relative influence and relationship to each other.

Another criticism which hindsight allows us to raise against the single-factor theories is that they are static rather than dynamic, while they attempt to explain a process which has been changing very rapidly. One might ask, though, why we should be skeptical of the old aphorism that the more things change the more they remain the same. Our answer is that Soviet motivation is a product of more fundamental elements; although the basic variables of personality, role, belief system, and events have, as building blocks, remained constant, their content and proportional combination have changed frequently. It is their content and combination at any one time that produces the motivation of the USSR as an actor in the international system. We shall try to show evidence for this conclusion in the historical survey which is Chapter I below.

Reacting to the inadequacy of single-factor explanations of Soviet foreign policy and to the absence of hard evidence from which to conclude the relationship of multiple factors at any one time, we have attempted in Chapters II, III, and IV to treat the Soviet Union as an organization and to look intensively at the major variables which are characteristic of any organizational behavior.

When we say that Soviet foreign policy is organizational behavior, we mean that it is the resultant of an ordered relationship of many individual behaviors. This does not preclude a disproportionate place for any one individual, nor even domination of the process by a single individual's will. It simply is to say that a variety of opinions enter the process of formulation. The Soviet Union is an abstract term by which we designate over 230 million people and their shared environment. The Soviet Union acts as a participant in an international transaction (whether a barter agreement with Afghanistan or a missile confrontation with the United States) with a single official voice. It acts as an organization, not as an individual. If one man should speak for it, he does so by some *consent*, however that consent may have been obtained. The maintenance of consent presupposes organization. Thus our conception allows for the possibility of empirical findings of any democratic or authoritarian pattern, but it insists that state action must be sanctioned in some way by discernible, ordered relationships.

The basic increment of a nation's international behavior, i.e., its relationship with other elements of the international system, is the *decision*. Thus we want to find out the way foreign policy decisions are made. We concern ourselves accordingly with the variables that condition decisions: the structure of roles and offices which demand policy-relevant choices by their occupants, the occupants themselves—the *men* who make Soviet foreign policy, the shared attitudes and beliefs which limit and otherwise condition choices, and the events which are changes in the domestic and international environment and which when perceived by the decision-makers also condition their policy choices. In the jargon of political science, we are engaged in *decision-making analysis,* and we employ as means to this end both *elite analysis* and *group analysis.*

Sources of Data

In this book we are asking the student to think along with us as we try to establish and refine a model of the Soviet Union as a participating element (a subsystem) of the larger international system. We utilize an approach described well by William H. Riker, applying it to a different context of research:

> The essential feature of this method is the creation of a theoretical construct that is a somewhat simplified version of what the real world to be described is believed to be like. This simplified version or model is a set of axioms (more or less justifiable intuitively) from which nonobvious general sentences can be deduced. These deduced propositions, when verified, become both an addition to the model and a description of nature. As more and more sentences are deduced and verified, greater and greater confidence in the validity of the axioms is felt to be justified. Conversely, the deduction of false or inconsistent sentences tends to discredit the axioms.[7]

We can go only a short way toward the sophisticated refinement of the model we would like to achieve. The careful reader will find it all too obvious that our model raises as many questions as it answers. We hope that at least a few readers will be stimulated to join us and carry the enterprise further.

How far can it fruitfully be carried? This is a fair question. On the one hand we may observe that prediction of Soviet action on the basis of the most elaborate and carefully verified model will always be limited by the concomitant prediction of contingent changes in the values and weights of partially independent variables. To this we may say only that the current crudity of the model leaves plenty of room for improvement before the point of diminishing returns is reached.

On the other hand we may question the scholar's ability to explore the relevant hypotheses simply because of the difficulty of acquiring data. We

[7] William H. Riker, *The Theory of Political Coalitions* (New Haven: Yale University Press, 1962), p. 7.

need biographical information about decision-makers, legal and theoretical definitions of role and role relationships, and detailed information on decision-makers' verbal commitments and physical actions. Admittedly we do not have access to all the sources of data we should like. One obstacle is the ephemeral nature or absence of records. Another obstacle is the closed society of the USSR and the relatively high rate of distortion in relevant data when it is permitted out of the Soviet system. However, we are optimistic, since the amount of relevant information which is preserved is a gold mine of evidence given modern techniques of analysis. Much, if not most, organizational decision-making is reflected in the written transcripts necessary to effective management and communication in a large bureaucracy. And the USSR is not nearly so closed a society today as it has been in the past. Indeed, growing Soviet appreciation for decision-making rationality and for social science in the service of such rationality shows promise of a day when traditional "kremlinology" will be rendered obsolescent. The scholar's most frequent problem may be rational selection and interpretation, not access.

Finally, verbal communications are being revealed as more fertile sources of a greater variety of relevant evidence than most of us—and most decision-makers as well—have ever imagined. Techniques of rigorous content analysis, often employing the assistance of modern computer technology, are revolutionizing the prospects of deriving valid and reliable inferences from publicly available materials. In some of the chapters that follow, we attempt to use a few of these techniques in a relatively rudimentary way; but we are only scratching the surface of the possibilities.

SOVIET FOREIGN POLICY

chapter
1
FROM SOCIALISM IN ONE COUNTRY TO SOCIALISM IN ONE REGION: An Interpretation of the Five Decades of Soviet Foreign Policy[1]

Communism, as revealed by the practice of those countries in which it is the official political philosophy, is undergoing continual and fairly rapid change. If the probable behavior of communist states in future situations is to be estimated, it is essential to assess the nature and rate of this change and to project it as accurately as possible.

To do this, one first should take a view of communism which embraces a long time span. Much of the Western difficulty in predicting the behavior of communist countries is due to the prevailing tendency to use a frame of reference which is too short in time and too narrow in context. Further difficulty is caused by the widespread belief that communism does not essentially change, that there is some peculiar quality about it which constrains it to remain the same. Such a belief is both false and dangerous.

Changes in communist thought, movements, and organization have been frequent and fundamental. Like all other social systems, communism contains the seeds of its own transformation. Indeed, these seeds have tended to produce changes which are disruptively rapid. Communist leaders such as Brezhnev, Mao Tse-tung, Hoxha, and Tito all perceive, on the one hand, the unavoidability of change and, on the other, the danger of change which is too rapid. With good reason, they fear the extremes of "revisionism" and of "dogmatism" or "talmudism," seeing these internal tendencies as even more dangerous to their systems than the external threat of "imperialism."

In this chapter we propose to examine Soviet communism over a long time span and in a broad international context. The international scene of the late 1960's is different from that of the mid-1920's, and the Soviet Union of today is a different one from that of forty years ago. We must study and understand these differences.

The body of revolutionary thought which inspired the 1917 Russian Revolution envisaged revolution throughout the world. For a number of

[1] This chapter is based in part on material drawn from Jan F. Triska, "Socialism in One Region," *New Leader,* XLIII, No. 50 (December 26, 1960), 10–13. By permission.

1

years, this dream remained the ideal of the Russian Communists. But the world revolution failed to occur, and the Russians soon found themselves on the defensive as a target of international hostility. This led to a major change in Communist goals and to the emergence, in Russia, of the policy of "socialism in one country." This policy was to prove dominant for a number of decades. Lately, Soviet theoreticians have been subjecting the policy of socialism in one country to the closest scrutiny; we shall do the same here.

By the mid-1920's it was becoming increasingly clear that the expected world revolution would not occur in the foreseeable future. This growing realization led to a complicated theoretical strife within the Soviet Union, focusing around the issue of what communist doctrine should be and how it should be applied. Those who still considered world revolution to be imminent claimed that the Russian Revolution was the first in a long series of revolutions that would transform all the states in the world. For them, the primary duty of the new Soviet state was to promote the spread of the revolution everywhere, by all possible means, and at once. Those who realized that world revolution was not an immediate possibility maintained that the first task was to achieve "socialism in one country," that is, to transform the Soviet Union into a strong, self-contained, modern and prosperous citadel of communism. Although in sharp disagreement as to immediate policy, these two groups agreed on the long-term goal of world communism.

When Lenin died, in 1924, the latent tension between these groups emerged as an open conflict in the struggle for succession. The "world revolution now" faction focused around the leadership of the intellectual and visionary Leon Trotsky, and the "socialism in one country" faction took its lead from the pragmatic and purposeful Stalin. Trotsky was doctrinally correct, but Stalin was more realistic; the fight between them was bitter. Because of its obviously greater realism, but more because of Stalin's organizational maneuvers, the Stalinist policy triumphed. Stalin was quick to assert that the consolidation of socialism in one country did not imply a fundamental departure from the ideological prescriptions of Marx and Engels, only a temporary retreat in order to ensure final victory. "Tactics," he said in 1924, "is the determination of the line to be taken by the proletariat during a comparatively short period of the ebb or flow of the movement, of advance or retreat of the revolution. . . ." Stalin won the power struggle, and therefore, according to the frequently repeated Soviet pattern, his doctrines dominated. Trotsky was driven into exile, first within the Soviet Union, and then abroad, finally to be murdered by Stalin's agents.

"Socialism in one country" was proposed as a short-range tactic. But as the world at large was far from ready for revolution, Stalin transformed the tactic into a strategy of indefinite duration. Preservation and building up of the USSR took first priority and became the goal on whose fulfillment the achievement of international communism would depend. Communists and Communist Parties abroad were constrained to serve this goal.

In effect, the interests of world communism became identified with the exclusive national interest of the Soviet Union. Not until the end of World War II would Soviet socialism emerge from the confines of one country to embrace an international system. Adoption of "socialism in one country" marked the end of an era of Soviet foreign policy and the beginning of another.

SOCIALISM IN ONE COUNTRY

"Socialism in one country" did not spring fully developed from Stalin's head. It was rendered necessary by the series of failures, calamities, and frustrations which occurred during the first few years of existence of the Soviet state and by the increasingly obvious hostility of many of the non-communist countries, which understandably had little patience for a policy admittedly directed at their destruction. Lenin had assumed that the survival of the Bolshevik revolution would depend on successful world revolution, and the early Bolsheviks were passionately committed to the policy of promoting such a revolution as soon as possible. The unreality of this policy had to be driven home by unmistakable events before Stalin's attack on it could succeed. By the early 1920's, however, this had happened, and the necesssity for coexistence with the established traditional states was becoming obvious to all but the most dogmatic.

Once in power Lenin and the Bolsheviks recognized that the powerful forces opposing their government could not be ignored and that compromises and concessions would be necessary. They recognized that patience would be needed and that, if their Communist government were to survive, some of its most cherished intentions would have to be modified or deferred.

The first event to impress the Bolsheviks with the unavoidability of com-promise was the Brest-Litovsk Peace Treaty of March 3, 1918, a temporary though traumatic surrender of their then raw revolutionary stand. A second event, setting internal limits to the speed with which they could implement their policies, was the costly civil war, which almost exhausted Russia's already severely depleted resources. Concurrently came the Allied inter-vention, an undeclared war which compelled the Bolsheviks to appeal to their enemies in the name of "economic advantages" of peace. When the allied intervention forces withdrew, the Bolsheviks were left face to face with complete economic chaos and widespread famine at home and with a governmental opposition abroad so concerted and universal that Moscow was virtually isolated. The feebleness of the foreign proletarian rising then dealt a final blow to the Bolshevik policy of world revolution. In some foreign countries proletarian revolutions were crushed, as in Finland, Bavaria, Poland, Slovakia, and Hungary; in others they were atomized to a degree which made them futile; and in still others the proletariat, ignoring Bolshevik exhortations, made no attempt at revolutions at all.

In 1919, in the middle of the civil war, the Bolsheviks got together with such foreign Social Democratic radicals as happened to be in Moscow at the time and founded the Comintern, the Third or Communist International. This was an ambitious attempt to establish a world-wide revolutionary organization capable of both formulating and enforcing fundamental principles on all questions of world revolution. The intention was to "fulfill the aim of the First International" of Marx and Engels by ensuring the speedy and complete victory of communism all over the world. Only two years later, in 1921, the leaders of the Comintern were reluctantly admitting that their hopes had been "temporarily" defeated and that their plans had been "temporarily" shelved.

The series of attacks and misfortunes which the young Russian Soviet Federated Socialist Republic (RSFSR) suffered in its first few years of existence brought about two developments, each of which sought expression in the doctrine and policy of "socialism in one country." In the first place, the attacks and misfortunes forced Lenin and the Bolsheviks to realize that to persist in the policy of world revolution would be suicidal and, therefore, coexistence with the capitalist enemies was a condition of survival. This policy of coexistence, already advocated by several Bolshevik leaders as early as 1920, was made official by Lenin at the IXth All Russian Congress of Soviets in 1921. He asked: "Is such a thing thinkable at all as that a socialist republic could exist in a capitalist environment?" Answering his own question, he went on to say: "This seemed impossible either in a political or in a military sense. That it is possible in a political and a military sense has been proved: it is already a fact."

In the second place, the "temporary" failure of world communist revolution brought about a change within the hierarchy of the Comintern. Initially all officials, Soviet and non-Soviet, had in practice enjoyed equal rank within the organization, but gradually the Soviet officials acquired seniority, since they represented the only country in which there had been a successful revolution. The more the issue of world revolution receded, the more the Russian Communists took over the leadership of the Comintern. The failure of world revolution brought about the supremacy of Soviet communism and the Soviet comrades began increasingly to shape both Comintern and communism in such a way that each would serve the new and only revolutionary country, the Russian Soviet Federated Socialist Republic.

In this way, the political climate in Soviet Russia became receptive towards the doctrine of "socialism in one country." In the original Bolshevik state, the Russian Soviet Federated Socialist Republic became the Union of Soviet Socialist Republics (USSR), now composed of four republics—the RSFSR and the Ukrainian, Belorussian and Transcaucasian Soviet Socialist Republics. The policy of coexistence with the bourgeois world had by then become an established guiding principle of Soviet foreign policy, and only two important Western nations remained firmly hostile to the new Soviet Union—the United States and France. The other Western nations had developed a working relationship with the Bolsheviks on the basis of bargaining and mutual expediency. The Bolsheviks had broken through to a workable foreign policy and a viable pattern of international relationships.

The political posture of the Bolsheviks at this state of their development rested on principles which were to be rendered explicit in the doctrine of "socialism in one country" as later defined by Stalin: temporary but active compromise with the "imperialist" enemies, and the increasing subordination of foreign comrades in the Comintern.

In the ensuing decade, bounded by Soviet entry into the League of Nations in 1934, the Bolsheviks attempted to pursue two conflicting policies: one which operated within the traditional rules of international relations and the other which was subversive of them. It was clear that successful active coexistence with the bourgeois states would require principles and procedures of a conventional sort in the field of foreign policy. The Bolsheviks saw that their diplomacy must be traditional, reliable, and respectable, especially in view of the unconventionality of their diplomacy at the beginning. Yet at the same time they did not want to sacrifice their original—and essentially subversive—instrument for world revolution. They therefore adopted a dual policy: one aspect, pursued chiefly by the Commissariat for Foreign Affairs, was open, official, and conventional; the other, pursued principally by the Comintern, was underground, clandestine, and revolutionary.

The short-term goals of both these policies were determined by the interest of creating socialism in the Soviet Union. If a strong and unassailable Soviet state could be constructed, revolutionary movements elsewhere could be promoted far more easily and effectively. If socialism in the Soviet Union were to fail, then, as Stalin emphasized, the cause of world revolution would be lost. The immediate task was therefore to build up in the Soviet Union the strongest possible base for world communism in the shortest time possible—a task which above all things required that the Soviet Union not become involved in war. Thus, in this period, the open side of Soviet policy was aimed at strengthening the Soviet Union through diplomacy while the secret side was aimed at undermining the capitalist and imperialist states through the Comintern. Both policies emphasized the need to defend the Soviet Union against all enemies and to avoid involvement in war.

The "Stalinization" of the Comintern, that is, its transformation from an instrument serving world communism into an instrument serving the Soviet Union, was formally promulgated at the VIth Comintern Congress in July, 1928, and it contributed to one of the worst disasters of world communist policy. In the 1920's, there were good prospects for establishment of a second revolutionary communist state in China. Stalin, acting through the Comintern, destroyed much of this potential. He insisted upon setting the timetable for the Chinese Communists and conforming their tactics to the dictates of Russian experience. Displaying at best an utter insensitivity to the dynamics of the Chinese situation, he led the Communist Party of China to massacre at the hands of Chiang Kai-shek, so weakening Chinese communism that it remained unsuccessful for more than twenty years. Paradoxically, this failure in China further strengthened Stalin's domestic position and reinforced his demand for continued support and defense of the Soviet Union—still the only Communist party-state in the world.

As time passed, the task of keeping the Soviet Union out of war grew more difficult. And it was evident that were an attack to come before a strong communist fortress could be built the Soviets would be unable to resist the reactionary tide. Communist achievements would be obliterated and the cause would be set back perhaps for decades. What was to be done? Local Communist Parties and the underground activities of the Comintern were having little success in their attempts to weaken and subvert the enemy bourgeois countries. It seemed without an increased Soviet participation in European diplomacy and without more vigor and initiative on the conventional side of foreign policy the chances of continuing to build a communist stronghold in the first socialist state would be poor. Therefore there must be skillful and energetic action on the diplomatic front, aimed not only at preserving peace for the USSR, but also at using the time thus gained to obtain from abroad such needed equipment and skills as were not yet available from domestic resources.

So, a dual policy for the diplomatic front was adopted; on the one hand advocating "peace" and on the other hand appealing to the capitalist countries to abandon their policy of "economic aggression" and to open up foreign trade with the Soviet Union. Accordingly, Foreign Commissar Litvinov expounded a policy of peace through disarmament in 1927 and 1928 before the Disarmament Preparatory Commission of the League of Nations and again at the World Disarmament Conference in 1932. He advocated the renunciation of war as an instrument of national policy, first in the vague and too comprehensive Kellogg-Briand Pact, then in the Litvinov Protocol that the Soviet Union concluded with its neighbors on the basis of this Pact, and later still in a series of bilateral nonaggression and neutrality pacts with these neighbors.

This policy of political peace was linked to a policy of economic peace. Speaking about the "Soviet Draft Protocol on Economic Non-Aggression" in Geneva in 1931, Litvinov said that economic peace was inseparable from general peace. Economic peace, that is, unrestricted foreign trade, was important to the Soviet Union as a means for accumulating the reserves of foreign currency needed to ensure the success of the Five Year Plans. The first Soviet Five Year Plan was highly ambitious, envisaging a forced program of rapid industrialization; its feasibility rested on the assumption that it would be possible to purchase considerable quantities of equipment and assistance from abroad. The construction of "socialism in one country" and a communist fortress depended on the success of the Five-Year Plans.

The rise of aggressive militarism in Japan and of Nazism in Germany was a serious double threat to the Soviet Union, a threat both from the East and from the West. After some initial blunders, especially with regard to Germany, Stalin responded by further emphasizing the conventional, diplomatic side of the dual Soviet foreign policy. At the time, that is, in the mid-1930's, the wisest course seemed to be for the Soviet Union to join the Western democracies, for they appeared logical allies against the rising danger of fascism. But these were the *status quo* powers, profoundly distrustful of the Soviet Union and its revolutionary past. If there were to be any chance of alliance, the Soviet Union ought to acquire a new image, suggesting a sharp break with its revolutionary past and a sense of identity with the Western democracies. Stalin therefore set about emphasizing Soviet similarities to the West and de-emphasizing the differences.

The resulting synthetic Soviet posture was initially successful. The Soviet Union was admitted to the League of Nations in 1934 and Soviet-French and Soviet-Czechoslovak mutual-assistance treaties were concluded in 1935. In order to facilitate further alliance with Western democracies and to add the finishing touches to the new look, the 1936 (Stalin) Constitution was adopted in the USSR. This ostensible marriage between Western constitutionalism and the Soviet system made the USSR, in Stalin's words, "the most democratic country in the world." Since the capitalist democracies had now become allies, the Comintern ordered the Communists in these countries to support and work for the capitalist governments rather than resist them. (In England, during World War II, this policy reached extremes of absurdity when, owing to the political truce, conservative candidates in by-elections found themselves vigorously supported by the local Communists).

This was the limit to which the pre-World War II rapprochement was carried. The danger of war seemed temporarily averted, and Stalin could turn his attention fully to the domestic side of his first objective, building up the Soviet Union. With this in mind, he gave orders that the Party and the state apparatus be "cleansed" of all those who, in his view, were the domestic equivalent of the Nazis and the Japanese imperialists and therefore a threat to socialism in the USSR. At the same time, and on the grounds that the state was threatened by reactionary saboteurs, Stalin intensified his dictatorship in the USSR.

But Stalin's new allies, the Western democracies, showed themselves to be irresolute and ineffective, just at the time when the extreme right in both Europe and Asia was becoming increasingly determined and aggressive. This development was discouraging to Stalin, and he began to doubt the soundness of his new foreign policy. He repeatedly saw what seemed to him to be evidence of vacillation and impotence on the part of the Western democracies. The League of Nations—a creature of the Western democracies —did not appear able to offer the collective security for which it had been set up. When the time came for it to act, it always proved to be paralyzed. Acts of aggression went unchallenged and unpunished. The Japanese imperialists waged war against a helpless China; Spain was rent by a civil war in which extreme left and extreme right fought with bitter determination, while the paralyzed democracies took a neutral position and looked on. Mussolini committed an act of flagrant aggression in invading Ethiopia, and members of the League of Nations could not even summon the resolution to apply economic sanctions to Italy. Hitler extended the territory of Germany by means of a series of increasingly insolent coups, and even this did not sting the democracies into action. Indeed, the whole process culminated in the Munich appeasement of 1938—an event which was to trigger a change in Soviet foreign policy.

For several years preceding this change, the cooling attitude of the Soviet Union towards the West had been paralleled by a corresponding Western disillusionment with the Soviet Union. If Stalin's "new look" had impressed the West, his Great Purge, which was taking place in the late thirties, largely destroyed the good impression and revived earlier hostility. Western confidence that the Soviet Union would prove an acceptable ally slowly but surely disappeared; the Great Purge massacres were too horrible even for many Western Communists. Although exposed to the same threat, the Soviet Union and the West sought different solutions and chose divergent paths. The rapprochement all but disappeared.

Stalin was disillusioned and frustrated. In his eyes the Western democracies had demonstrated both inability and lack of any real desire to stand up to the fascist menace. He felt that, in supporting collective security, he had let himself be both victimized and duped. His 1934–1938 policy had not paid off. Once again, the question faced him, what should be done? Germany, Italy, and Japan were determined, dangerous, and actively hostile. The Western democracies—ineffective, passive, and unenthusiastic about socialism—looked like liabilities rather than supports. At first, Stalin decided to isolate Soviet socialism from both sides: this course appeared wise after the partition of Czechoslovakia at Munich in 1938. The world seemed saturated with danger and any policy of involvement seemed riskier than a policy of isolation.

But the policy of nonparticipation in international relations proved in practice to be more dangerous than the previous policy of ineffective commitment. If, as seemed likely, the Fascists were planning to destroy socialism in the Soviet Union and if, as also seemed likely, the Western democracies were planning to let the Communists and the Fascists destroy each other, a policy of inaction could result in the Soviet Union becoming the victim of hostile intentions on the part of all the powers in the world. What steps could the Soviet Union take to protect itself against a totally hostile world?

After six months of the isolation policy, Stalin decided that his best chance lay in trying to play the Western democracies and the Fascists against each other. So he offered to cooperate with both sides, deciding to make a deal with whichever made the higher bid. Not unexpectedly, the higher bid came from Hitler. Stalin accepted it, and signed the now infamous nonaggression pact with Germany on August 23, 1939.

This new Soviet foreign policy appeared on the surface to be a sharp repudiation of the USSR's tradition of strong antifascism. In fact, it was a logical step in pursuit of the well-established Soviet policy of defending "socialism in one country" by any available means—a strategy which was already twenty years old. To keep its enemies of the moment divided, the USSR cooperated with Germany in the post-Rapallo period against the

West, switched to the West against Germany in the thirties, and switched again to Germany against the West when Hitler showed his strength. The apparent ease with which the new policy was carried out should therefore not have caused surprise. In 1939 the Fascists appeared to be the most powerful force in the world and the chances of preserving the USSR against them appeared quite limited. Perhaps, by joining them, the danger could be reduced if not removed.

The Nazi-Soviet nonaggression pact came as an abrupt shock to the Western democracies, some of whose statesmen had been hoping that a war between Germany and Russia would get them out of their international dilemma. They disliked both socialism and fascism with equal intensity though for different reasons. Their dilemma lay in the fact that they could not fight one system without, in practice, being compelled to endorse the other. But if the two systems were to attack each other, their conflict would bail out the West. The Nazi-Soviet nonaggression pact put an end to such hopes. Only a few days later Hitler invaded Poland and precipitated what Stalin called the *Imperialist War*. But even then the issue was not clear. For about a year the Imperialist War was a "phony war." Almost no fighting was going on, and the possibility of a dramatic realignment of international alliances was being rumored. The situation became somewhat clarified in the spring of 1941. The replacement of Chamberlain by Churchill ushered in a new and more decisive spirit in England, France was invaded and fell, and the Battle of Britain was joined. Hitler's forces were extended and Russia need no longer fear the full impact of undiminished German might.

But on June 22, 1941, with all France under his control and desperately little to stop him making a successful invasion of England, Hitler incredibly launched a surprise attack against the Soviet Union. For Russia, this transformed the "Imperialist War" into the "Great Patriotic War." The period of Nazi-Soviet alliance had been short, but while it lasted the Soviet Union had been able to win spoils which were to outlast both Hitler and Stalin. Indeed, apart from a piece of Finland won by the USSR in 1940 and returned, for the most part, in 1955, the Soviet territorial gains—Eastern Poland, Estonia, Latvia, Lithuania, Rumanian Bessarabia, and Western Bukovina— became, and remain to this day, integral parts of the Soviet Union. The Nazi-Soviet alliance thus had a dual pay-off: it brought the Soviet Union substantial and permanent territorial gains and it tipped the very delicate balance of international relations enough to precipitate a war between the Western democracies and the fascist countries.

When Hitler attacked the Soviet Union, all the ingenious overt and covert maneuvers to keep the Soviet Union out of war seemed to have been in vain.

In spite of the many switches in policy which the "socialism in one country" concept had dictated, the capitalist countries seemed to have embarked, as Lenin had predicted, on an "imperialist war" for "new markets," and this war had turned against the Soviet Union. Now, all available forces, both at home and abroad, had to be mobilized to save the only socialist state in the world from physical annihilation.

For this purpose, the dual policy was even less effective than it had been in the preceding period. Communists in the West were therefore urged to support their governments actively, as they had become the new Soviet allies in the war against fascism and Nazism. They were also urged to cement resistance and to become partisans and local patriots in the territories occupied by Nazi Germany. In 1943, the Comintern was dissolved because its continued existence, even on a purely formal level, harmed rather than helped the Soviet cause. Immediate Soviet needs were best served by an official state foreign policy on a single level.

After the battle for Stalingrad and the successful Soviet summer offensive in 1943, when the Red Army managed to recapture two-thirds of the territory it had lost, the outcome of the war for the Soviet Union ceased to be in doubt. These victories gave Stalin increased strength in bargaining with the Allies, so that at the subsequent Allied conferences in Teheran, Moscow, Yalta, and Potsdam, he was once again able to concentrate on spoils. He did so shrewdly and with remarkable success.

The increased international power which the Soviet Union gained from victory and territorial growth was enhanced by the disappearance or weakening of those international forces which had been most threatening to it. The world had changed a great deal since 1939. As international powers, Germany, Italy, and Japan, together with their various collaborators, had ceased to exist. The war had greatly speeded the disintegration of the nineteenth-century empire systems. To Stalin, the immediate postwar world presented a rosy vista of fresh opportunities for the Soviet Union—great new vacuums to be filled by the kind of human order for which the USSR stood. Freshly freed from traditional controlling influences, many parts of the world seemed ripe to receive the Soviet system. Soviet dual foreign policy, suspended during the war, was now swiftly reinstated. There was no time to lose.

As a result of the westward sweep of the Red Army toward Berlin and the belated but immensely rewarding Soviet entry into the war against Japan, the Carpatho-Ukraine (formerly part of Czechoslovakia), the Kuriles and southern Sakhalin, Tannu Tuva, East Prussia and Koenigsberg now were annexed to the USSR. Eight European satellite states "joined" the "socialist camp" in the immediate postwar period, mostly in response to the persuasive blandishments of Red Army bayonets and Soviet military occupation. North Korea followed; then as a product of the deep convulsions of China and Southeast Asia, the Chinese Peoples Republic and later the Democratic Republic of Vietnam were added to the "camp." Victory in the "Great Patriotic War" had consolidated and strengthened the Soviet Union as the world fortress of communism. It had brought unimagined territorial expansion. "Socialism in one country" had succeeded beyond even Stalin's expectations.

But socialism had also emerged from the confines of one country; and this event, pregnant with implications for the future of Soviet foreign policy, remained in the shadow of Stalin's triumphs, its dimensions completely escaping the aging dictator.

THE OBSOLESCENCE OF SOCIALISM IN ONE COUNTRY

To Stalin, the new "socialist allies" of the Soviet Union in Europe and Asia were all only satellites, to orbit obediently and remain dependent upon the Soviet Union. Their sole purpose was to serve the USSR, which by then had a highly developed socialist system, in order to strengthen it further. Pursuant to the "socialism in one country" policy, this was a logical and proper view. To milk the satellite economies, to subordinate their politics and to rearrange their social systems to fit the new role—all these were imperative to fulfill the Soviet principle.

Temporarily it worked. The more depleted the satellite economies, the stronger the Soviet economy; the more subjugated their politics, the more imposing the Soviet position; and the more streamlined their social systems, the easier their control by Soviet governors. In the long run, however, such simple justification of Soviet colonialism was untenable. The exhausted and impoverished satellite economies, dried up by incessant Soviet demands and beset with outworn and obsolescent industrial plants, were rendered constantly less efficient. Complete political subordination and dependence on the Soviet Union brought about such universal uneasiness in the satellite states that the abrupt Yugoslav defection in 1948, as we know from the East German, Polish, Hungarian, Chinese, and Albanian follow-ups, proved to be only a beginning—a manifestation of serious strain in Stalin's new empire.

If the social systems of the satellites now resembled the Soviet system, and if socialism had indeed emerged from the confines of one country, then the "socialism in one country" phase and all it stood for and all it justified as a phase of socialist development must be ended. The Soviet national interest could no longer be regarded as the only concern of the world's Communists, and the strategic goal of world communism to consolidate the dictatorship of the proletariat in one country was obsolete. A new stage of development had arrived: the Soviet Union had become merely one, although the most powerful, among several socialist states. The communist gain was a Soviet loss, just as thirty years before the communist loss had been a Soviet gain.

But Stalin apparently did not understand all this. Unable to perceive what was new in new situations, he dealt with them as if they manifested no change. To him, the satellite party leaders were "eidetic personalities" and he treated them as he had treated their predecessors in the Comintern. In fact, to remind the satellite Party leaders—now the new leaders of their respective governments within their own socialist countries—of their proper place within the communist hierarchy, Stalin in 1947 insisted on founding a new Comintern, rechristened the Communist Information Bureau or Cominform. Essentially the same organization, though limited now to the European satellites (less East Germany and Albania) plus the large nonruling Communist Parties of Italy and France, the Cominform was designed to tighten discipline within the new Soviet empire and consolidate Stalin's control there. The organization, however, was stillborn. Headquartered in Belgrade, it was enormously embarrassed by the defection of Tito (who was ceremoniously expelled *in absentia* from the first session). Subsequently, the organization simply withered, to be replaced in 1953 by the editorial offices of its monthly publication, *Problems of Peace and Socialism*, now emanating from Prague. Lenin's contemptuous old phrase, "a letter-box International," became an apt description.

Stalin's misunderstanding of the new situation had brought serious complications in the communist states of East Europe and resulted in the loss of one of them, Yugoslavia. If his shortsighted attempt to treat Communist China also as a Soviet satellite had been continued, even the East German Communist sycophant, Walter Ulbricht, admitted later, it would have meant an outright loss of China too, a catastrophe for Soviet foreign policy. But, fortuitously, Stalin died in March of 1953.

It appears in retrospect that his eventual successor, Khrushchev, recognized the danger and pressed for changes in Soviet foreign policy from the beginning of his decade in power. By attempts to eliminate the threatening schism between Moscow and Peking in the later 1950's, to effect a *rapprochement* with Tito, to revise the blatant economic exploitation of the satellites, and to introduce at least a semblance of political autonomy among the satellites,

Khrushchev not only modified past Soviet policies, but also repudiated Stalin's leadership of the world communist movement.

The immediate alterations introduced by Khrushchev in the Soviet policies vis-à-vis other communist states were radical and far-reaching. They affected the equilibrium of power in the communist world and subjected the system itself to a re-examination of fundamental assumptions. The resistance they evoked in many quarters was strong enough to deter and at times to unnerve even the determined Khrushchev. He carried Soviet foreign policy within the system of communist party-states all the way from "socialism in one country" to "proletarian internationalism in the Great Socialist Common-wealth of Nations." He acted under the pressure of events, and in the process he was forced to yield more than he anticipated, though less than enough to satisfy his "satellites." Khrushchev the ideologist had a difficult time catching up with Khrushchev the politician. And with increasing emphasis and frequency, his new Communist Chinese competitors leapt into the ideological gaps.

SOCIALISM IN ONE REGION

Khrushchev inherited Soviet power in an era, as Anastas Mikoyan put it, when it was "no longer certain who is encircling whom." For a price he broke with Stalin's isolationist traditions; for a price he transformed the dictatorship of the proletariat from a national into an international force again. The price was "socialism in one country," the identification of world communism exclusively with Soviet national interest and absolute Soviet primacy in the communist bloc. The USSR gradually came to accept and even urge "polycentrism" instead of centralization of all power in Moscow. It reluctantly gave ground while centrifugal forces of considerable dimension were being unleashed. The price was high but inevitable. The era in which Soviet will might be a surrogate for world communism had ended with the irresistible pressure to accommodate heterogeneous demands by undigested, nationally conscious elements of Stalin's unexpected empire.

Let us explain.

Under the Soviet Constitution of 1918, the RSFSR was a highly centralized political unit, the government of which was the culmination of a hierarchy of geographically differentiated Soviets guided by the Communist Party. In 1924, under the second Soviet Constitution, the RSFSR became the equally centralized Union of Soviet Socialist Republics (USSR), then composed of the original RSFSR plus the Ukrainian, Belorussian, and Trans-caucasian SSR's. In 1936, under the third (Stalin) Soviet Constitution, the

USSR consisted of eleven Union Republics: the RSFSR, the Ukrainian, Belorussian, Uzbek, Kazakh, Turkmen, Tadjik, Georgian, Azerbaijanian, Armenian, and Kirghiz SSR's. In form, the Soviet Union became a decentralized, federal state. Assimilation however was pursued by a constant attempt to infuse national forms with homogeneous socialist content. In 1940, the former Baltic states of Estonia, Latvia, and Lithuania became Soviet Socialist Republics. The same year, with the acquisition of Bessarabia and Western Bukovina from Rumania, the Moldavian Soviet Socialist Republic was created. And the Karelo-Finnish SSR (later partitioned and dissolved as an SSR) "joined" the Soviet Union after the Winter War of 1940. And, as we said earlier, the Carpatho-Ukraine, the Kuriles and southern Sakhalin, Tannu Tuva, East Prussia and Koenigsberg all were annexed to the USSR after World War II.

This Soviet growth by annexation and assimilation of successive geographic layers continued manifestly but informally with the acquisition of the eight European (Poland, East Germany, Czechoslovakia, Albania, Bulgaria, Hungary, Rumania and Yugoslavia) and four Far Eastern (China, North Korea, North Vietnam, and Outer Mongolia) party-states.

This rapid increase in Soviet governed territory and population unavoidably led to some relaxation of the original rigid pattern of all-encompassing centralization insisted upon by Lenin and, as best he could, by Stalin. But denial of autonomy in the USSR, and later on in the "satellite" states, appeared to have become incompatible with the continued Soviet growth. The formal though insincere homage paid by Stalin to administrative decentralization in 1936 and 1944 was far exceeded by the decentralization initiated by Khrushchev in 1957 and 1958 in the USSR and by his gestures toward "complete equality"—political, social, economic, and ideological— of all socialist states at the XXIst Party Congress in 1959 and thereafter.

The RSFSR of 1918 is now just one political unit within a system of states. Expansion of Soviet hegemony over this system demanded significant operational changes. Insistence upon the centralization of the 1930's today would imply such inefficiency and ineffectiveness that the dissolution of the system would threaten. "Autonomy" is the new catchword employed with progressively greater substantive meaning from Prague to Bucharest to Pyongyang—and in territorial as well as in functional terms.

Under Stalin, Moscow's central control not only achieved its maximum feasible intensity and extensiveness but passed these points. Stalin's very success in expanding the Soviet organizational control thus incurred its potential failure. Large organizations tend to ossify and stagnate. Incapable of self-modification of their control mechanisms, they become helpless.

With control dissipated, they disintegrate. While control devices might eventually be available which could sustain a Stalinist-type regime embracing as much as one-third of humanity living on one-fourth of the world's available space, Stalin's bite was far too big for his times. Modern science and technology as yet had not supplied effective instruments to permit further growth of the Soviet organization without far-reaching decentralization. Unlike Stalin, Khrushchev recognized that his job was not really one of patching up here and there, but a substantive overhaul of the whole organizational machinery of Stalin's empire.

The success of the Soviet organizational system under Stalin expanded it out of all proportions and threatened to incapacitate it. In dialectical formulation, the successful "socialism in one country" thesis brought about the antithesis of Yugoslavia, Poland, Hungary, Albania, and Communist China. The synthesis could be either a collective break into twelve hostile states or, with a skillful transformation of the organization embracing them, it could be a strong regional system of "socialist" but somewhat autonomous states. Khrushchev turned his abundant energies toward achieving the latter and avoiding the former.

Khrushchev knew from bitter experience in East Europe how attractive the national communism doctrine was for each individual member of the system. The ever-present danger of the potential "socialism in one country" position, which had brought the USSR such success, was threatening when adopted in the smaller party-states and critical when espoused by China. As a consequence, there was only one long-range alternative available to Khrushchev: to subordinate Soviet national interest to the interest of the communist party-state system as a whole. To preserve the system from fratricidal disintegration, the Soviet Union had to give up some of its prerogatives within it. The Soviet "socialism in one country" had to become regional socialism in and for the party-state system. There was no other way. The communist strategy which, as Stalin put it, provided "general direction along which the revolutionary movement of the proletariat should be directed with a view to achieving the greatest results" had ended its *Soviet* phase. In the past it provided for Soviet security because the Soviet Union was the "inspirer," the citadel of world communism. It was the only communist country. But this being no longer the case, the fact invalidated the form. A system of obedient satellites orbiting the Soviet sun was untenable. Given its organizational inadequacy, given the need for a unified socialist confrontation of the noncommunist world, a system pursuing "socialism in one region" had to replace a system serving "socialism in one country."

As a concomitant of "socialism in one region" came a new Soviet emphasis upon institutionalized interstate cooperation among the party-states to the relative neglect of interparty cooperation. Formal treaties and agreements among governments proliferated and were confirmed by expansion of the varieties of intercourse they sanctioned: commerce, group and personal travel, media of mass communication, cultural and educational interchanges to name a few of the more prominent. The emphasis on interstate cohesion through formal agreements promoted, by definition, a sense of nearer equality among the participants and a greater toleration of compromise and a greater concern for mutual interests.

The Soviet de-emphasis of interparty relations understandably accompanied the weakening of Marxist-Leninist doctrine as a compelling source of unity. The existence of diverse demands among the parties—manifested notably in the Polish and Hungarian party resistance to CPSU prescriptions in 1956, the second Yugoslav disaffection in 1958, the Chinese-Albanian party factionalism, and the ill-concealed disagreement which characterized both the 1957 and 1960 Moscow conferences—cast strong doubt upon the "scientific" utility of doctrine as a guide to a single "correct" course of policy for any given historical epoch. The formally agreed "unanimous" statements which emerged from the 1957 and 1960 conferences testified to the meager limits of ideological unanimity among the participants.

In an important speech to Soviet party elite on January 6, 1961 Khrushchev noted that it was "impossible" and "unnecessary" to "lead Communist parties from a single center" because "it spells no advantage to our party or other parties" and "it only creates difficulties." If cohesion was to be achieved at all, it was clear ideology would henceforth need strong support from other sources.

The tolerable limits of ideological divergence for a Communist Party seeking to remain in good favor of the USSR have not clearly been defined. There is good evidence in the course of Soviet-Rumanian relations in the mid-1960's that the East European parties continue to probe for those limits. The admission of Yugoslavia as an associate member of the *interstate* Council for Mutual Economic Assistance is one case which illustrates how far party diversity may be overlooked in the drive for state cohesion.

To summarize, under Khrushchev the Soviet policy of "socialism in one country" was discarded reluctantly as destructive to the Soviet interest of preserving a cohesive and functional socialist system. It was replaced by a policy of "socialism in one region," raising the interests of the party-state system as a whole above those of the Soviet Union and hence of any other individual state, although endeavoring to define specific system interests as compatibly with Soviet national interests as possible. Decentralization of the system's control mechanisms was recognized to be essential to maintenance of the system as now expanded. The accompanying diversity of ideological interpretation diminished the effectiveness of Marxist-Leninist doctrine as a cohesive force within the system. The Soviet Union, therefore, raised the relative emphasis placed upon interstate cooperation and lowered the relative emphasis placed upon party unanimity.

SOCIALISM IN ONE REGION AND SINO-SOVIET RELATIONS

Let us now examine the Sino-Soviet schism against this background of the development of the Soviet position within the system of party-states.

Half a century after its uneasy beginning, the Soviet Union is one of the world's greatest powers. Deploying enormous military capacity, economic assets, and political suasion, it has reached heights undreamed of by the revolutionary Bolsheviks. As a powerful national state its revolutionary zeal has been moderated. Even a casual visitor to the Soviet Union in the 1960's can not help observing the nonrevolutionary and "bourgeois" striving of all —citizens, officials and even Party elite—for regularity and stability. There seems to be almost a craving for routine, and, unlike communist ideology with its insistence upon permanent change and personal sacrifice, a demand for private gain, higher salary, shorter working hours, installment-buying, better television sets, and more family cars.

Conditions inside the Soviet Union have moderated Soviet attitudes abroad. Concepts of friend and foe, war and peace, victory and defeat have acquired new meanings. The Soviet Union now plays a vital part in a world balance of power which it helped to establish and which it respects in its own way as much as its bourgeois partners do, even if that means the recognition of neutralism and neutrals (including communist neutralism in Yugoslavia). The USSR has traveled a long way since 1917, is proud of its journey, and in many ways announces that it has "arrived." It is a powerful "have-nation," conscious that it has vested a great deal of its capital in what it has achieved in contrast to what it may achieve. It is unlikely today to take willingly any major risk which will endanger its present position in the world.

Within the communist party-state system, Communist China in contrast to the USSR is an underdeveloped "have-not-nation" whose very political existence remains unaccepted by the world's greatest power. Young as a communist party-state, its leaders are insecure, inexperienced in the world setting, and irresponsible; they are impatient, competitive, internationally maladroit, quarrelsome, and aggressive. As a potentially powerful state, however, Communist China demands and receives special attention. Friends and foes cannot but take its potential position into serious consideration. Its Soviet would-be friends, intimately associated along the world's longest land frontier, are especially well aware of China's potential strength.

The issues between the USSR and Communist China stem from the facts that while one has had time to develop its economy, the other has not; one is being satiated, the other is hungry; one has arrived, the other has barely departed; one is accepted, whereas the other is still rejected; one has matured, the other is an upstart; one shows healthy respect for the present order in the world which it has helped establish, the other challenges it; one wishes security, coexistence, and peaceful competition in the world, the other seems to need external insecurity in order to rally domestic cohesion. A shrewd strategist, Khrushchev knew that in order to achieve his domestic goals in the 1960's, he had to motivate the Soviet masses as well as the Soviet bureau-cracy less by Stalinist fear than by emphasis on rewards, incentives, and promotions. Khrushchev's successors have accepted this requirement as a truism. Mao Tse-tung, on the other hand, has utilized Stalinist methods more and more in China and cannot but disagree with the present regimen prescribed by Brezhnev and Kosygin in the USSR. While nuclear war (as a victorless affair) became an impractical prospect for one, it is speculated upon by the other as dangerous and drastic but in its effect far from fatal and perhaps therefore even desirable.

Khrushchev's early reappraisal of the Soviet position in the communist world in general, and of Soviet-Chinese relations in particular, led to his trip (with Nikolai Bulganin) to Peking in the fall of 1954. There he in-augurated a new era of Soviet policy concessions to China. Initially, the reasons for these concessions were clear and simple. The Soviet Union, realizing that in terms of power Tito was a pigmy next to Mao, abhorred the prospect of a defection *à la* Tito in the Far East. With time, however, the reasons became increasingly complex and inevitably took on ideological coloring.

It seems clear that current Soviet policy is more dependent upon China than vice versa. As developed above, Soviet policy within the communist system since Stalin had been constrained to give high priority to cohesion among the party-states, to adopt a goal of "socialism in one region" in order to promote material prosperity and harmony within the region, and to maintain the stability of the larger international order which it had taken a part in creating. Chinese radicalism not only withholds the largest party-state's cooperation, it also opens room for public debate for each issue among the other party-states, thus encouraging greater diversity and even less Soviet control. The Chinese dependence on the Soviet Union, on the other hand, is primarily material. China unquestionably needs the economic and technological assistance which the Soviet Union has progressively denied her since 1958. But by the mid-1960's China has become accustomed to the deprivation. She is still in a better position to modernize herself than was the USSR in the 1930's. China's second major reliance upon the Soviet Union is for military support should general war be incurred. In that event it is probably still reasonable for her to calculate that, forced to choose sides between "imperialism" and Chinese communism, the USSR would reluctantly take the latter.

When the struggle is translated into ideological terms, the Soviet Union is again at a disadvantage. The Chinese contend that only they are correct in analysis of the current international balance of forces and interpretation of ideological imperatives. The Soviet Union, differing, is heretical. While the Soviet Union, for its part, charges China with ideological deviation, past Soviet acceptance of ideological diversity among the European party-states has put her in the position of defending a limited ideological pluralism. Both philosophically (given the monist base of Marxism-Leninism) and practically this is difficult and has led, as already pointed out, to relative upgrading of state relations as a Soviet remedy. "Socialism in one region" cannot avoid the stigma of being a second postponement of the world revolution, replacing "socialism in one country" for similarly pragmatic considerations.

The Soviet Union is thus doubly on the defensive in her struggle with China. Her conduct at the Moscow party conferences of 1957 and 1960, seeking to patch up the quarrel with "unanimous" declarations of unity, sustains the judgment. So too does the long restraint exercised even by the ebullient Khrushchev while subjected to public berating by the Chinese press. The carefully preserved euphemisms of the polemical interchange were broken first by the Chinese, and Khrushchev's successors, as he himself, have endeavored vainly to eliminate unilaterally the public controversy. Both the XXIInd and XXIIIrd Congresses of the Communist Party of the Soviet Union were far more notable for their restraint in condemnation of China than for what criticism they did produce.

Like the analogous struggle between Stalin and Trotsky forty years ago, the present struggle between the conservative Soviet and radical Chinese elites is a struggle for power in the world communist system and will be decided less by dialectics than by organization. Here the challenged Soviet Union continues to hold the advantage over the challenger, China. While the Chinese call to active revolution is more emotionally appealing to the nonruling Communist Parties of the underdeveloped world, Chinese material aid has compared unfavorably in general to that from the cautionary USSR. And the experience of following the Chinese lead has proven disastrous in several cases, most notably Indonesia. The balance sheet at the XXIIIrd Congress of the CPSU, held in March of 1966, showed overwhelming preference for the Soviet Union. Only three parties, those of Japan, New Zealand, and Albania, demonstrated their support of China by following her boycott of the sessions. While the party-states (most notably Rumania) have exploited the unaccustomed independence afforded them by continuation of the conflict, only Albania has publicly embraced the substance of Chinese policies. By 1968 the Soviet policy of "socialism in one region" had been badly mauled by the struggle with China, but it had not been discarded; and the Chinese challenge for leadership within the world communist system appeared to have passed a crest and be in decline.

SOCIALISM IN ONE REGION AND SOVIET RELATIONS WITH THE NONCOMMUNIST WORLD

We have already taken note of some of the internal and external changes that have influenced dramatic shifts in Soviet foreign policy within the party-state system since the close of the "Great Patriotic War." The *embourgeoisement* of Soviet society and the inevitable participation of the Soviet Union in establishing the present configuration of forces in the larger international system have given Soviet policymakers a vested interest in conservation of that system which is not shared by all her fellow party-states. Let us again turn our attention beyond the party-states and pick up briefly the strands of postwar Soviet policy toward the Western democracies and underdeveloped countries of the world.

Stalin's resumption of the prewar dual foreign policy toward the capitalist West consolidated the territorial advances brought during the Second World War with striking initial success. Relieved of the fascist menace, Stalin's interstate collaboration with the Allies progressively diminished into intransigent obstinacy. Western will and persistent hopes for a continuation of the wartime cooperation were among the reasons the West tolerated Soviet seizure of the initiative. The emerging stalemate at the interstate level, which cloaked the covert arm of Soviet foreign policy, became the task of the Ministry of Foreign Affairs. Soviet parliamentary obstruction in the United Nations through use of the Security Council "veto," as well as her strained interpretations of wartime political commitments in Poland and elsewhere in East Europe, typified Foreign Ministry holding action; meanwhile, covert initiative subverted noncommunist administrations in "liberated" states, culminating with the Czechoslovak *coup d'etat* in February of 1948.

But the new tide of Soviet opportunity for external expansion, released by the convulsions of the Second World War, receded as it had a quarter century before. Stalin had managed to alarm the Western Allies to an unprecedented peacetime unity by his aggressive tactics. The beginnings of recovery from the social and economic prostration that was the legacy of war in Western Europe reduced the appeal of Communist Parties in France and Italy. The economic cooperation catalyzed by the Marshall Plan brought prospects of a new prosperity that challenged the Stalinist empire and helped stabilize Western democracies. The Soviet attempt to wrest Iran into satellite status in 1946, the Czechoslovak coup, the Greek insurgency of 1947, and finally the ominous effort to squeeze the West from Berlin in 1948–1949 prompted a comparable military cooperation. Thus NATO was formed as a shield against Stalin, from Norway southward and eastward to the Turkish-Iranian border. And NATO embodied the enormous military threat of atomic weapons, unmatched as yet in the Soviet arsenal.

Thus brought to a stalemate in Europe, effectively "contained" by the West, and threatened by disaffection within the party-states system, Stalin in his last years was forced to devote his attention to preserving what he had already achieved.

"Socialism in one country" had taken the wind from the Comintern's sails in the 1920's, and the successive prewar policies directed toward Soviet national security had further dissipated the subversive effect of the communist movement in the West. For a short time in the 1920's, the "colonial and semicolonial" countries, which we are now accustomed to call the *developing world*, seemed to offer an Eastern alternative for communist initiative. But as we have already noted, Stalin's insensitivity to Chinese conditions brought disaster there in 1928. Thereafter, "socialism in one country" so lowered the priority of efforts to stimulate revolution in Asia as to make insignificant this thrust of Soviet foreign policy.

After 1945, encouraged by the new complexion of China, the acquisition of North Korea, and the generally loosened grip of European colonialism throughout the underdeveloped world, Stalin renewed the effort to extend Soviet influence as far as possible southward and eastward in Asia. Thwarted in Iran in 1946, he moved into what appeared to be a gap in Western defenses by inspiring and supporting the attack on South Korea in June of 1950. This final Stalinist probe, blocked militarily by unexpected United States resolve, was still in process of being reduced when death ended the dictator's long tenure.

Stalin had been fond of conceptualizing international politics as the hostile confrontation of two armed camps. When he died in March of 1953 his policies had gone a long way toward establishing just such a dichotomous and inflexible configuration. The effect of the Korean War was to stimulate American efforts to replicate the shield of NATO in the East and thereby extend the instruments of containment, proven effective in Western Europe, to perform their function globally. The effort was only partially successful, but in response to Stalin's postwar threat an unprecedented anticommunist, anti-Soviet coalition confronted an empire of party-states.

We have already seen that seeds of dissolution had sprouted in Stalin's empire. On the other side of the "Iron" and "Bamboo" curtains the "capitalist coalition" was not as durable or all-embracing as Stalin's formulation might have presented it. The divisions in both camps would soon become much more apparent.

Khrushchev's accession to power in the Soviet Union marked the beginning of a re-examination of Soviet relationships with the noncommunist world which was every bit as profound as the re-examination of relations within the system of party-states. Subsequent departures from the Stalinist pattern of policy were no less dramatic or consequential. Unquestionably the prime factor inspiring the re-examination was the ominous "balance of terror" emerging from the Soviet-American nuclear arms race.

It was apparent to Khrushchev that the intensification of cold-war alignments, complemented by a sophistication of military weaponry that raised the prospect of mutual annihilation in any general war projected little opportunity and enormous intrinsic danger for the Soviet Union. The cohesion of NATO, and later its expansion to admit West Germany, the announced American policy of "massive retaliation," the American nuclear superiority and delivery-system lead, the experience of Western military resistance to Stalin's incursions—all underlined the futility and danger of more of the same. Recognition of the concurrent obsolescence of "socialism in one country" and the successful growth of Soviet military and economic power also caused reappraisal of Soviet policies toward the noncommunist world.

The XXth Party Congress of the CPSU in February, 1956, most widely celebrated for the momentous "secret speech" denouncing Stalin, was no less notable as an occasion for foreign-policy innovation. In his Central Committee Report to that gathering, Khrushchev reformulated his predecessor's concept of the world to include three camps instead of two. The "colonial and semicolonial" areas of Asia, Africa, and Latin America were explicitly separated from the capitalist camp and endowed with a unity of their own. In the same report, Khrushchev reinterpreted Lenin's pronouncements on war to conclude that in the present epoch general war between the imperialist and socialist systems was not "fatally inevitable" and in fact must be avoided.

The premises of Soviet foreign policy toward noncommunist countries, premises which were to pervade the Khrushchev decade and persist into the mid-1960's, were here revealed. Upon them was built the new theory of "peaceful coexistence of differing social systems"—the term *peaceful coexistence* having been extracted from its historical context and original connotation as an expedient tactic for survival in adversity and raised to the stature of a strategy of indefinite duration. Upon them was built the theory of "peaceful economic competition" or "competitive coexistence"—shifting some attention from the military to more flexible political and economic means for pursuing foreign-policy goals. Upon them also was built the theory of the isolation of world capitalism through recruitment of the third world of colonial, semicolonial, and former colonial peoples into the ranks of world socialism.

In relations with the Western democracies during the last decade an eratically broadening matrix of interstate associations have developed. Soviet diplomats gradually emerged from the stiff mold of automatons, which characterized Stalin's postwar emissaries, and the obstructionist holding action of these official representatives of the Soviet state gave way to active pursuit of Soviet interests. Strenuous efforts were made to increase trade and other economic interchanges with all capitalist states. Cultural exchanges and travel of private citizens from abroad in the Soviet Union were fostered with increasing enthusiasm. The Soviet Union took a more active and cooperative role in the work of United Nations specialized agencies. "Summit diplomacy" was espoused, and Soviet leaders, led by Khrushchev himself, made numerous pilgrimages abroad to spread the image of a peace-loving nation eager to promote all varieties of normal state intercourse. The argument advanced was that communism would be the wave of the future; that the Soviet Union's material success stood as a beacon to guide less-progressive societies; that time would prove the superiority of the socialist economic system as the Soviet Union under leadership of its Communist Party went about constructing the material abundance necessary to found a society governed by communist social relations.

The Soviet Union, under Khrushchev, supplemented its propaganda attacks on the foreign-economic-assistance programs of the "imperialist" states with a growing foreign-assistance program of its own during the years following the XXth Party Congress. Seeking to confirm the new image of "disinterested" friends to the peoples emerging from the oppression of Western imperialism, the Soviet Union expanded trade, granted economic credits, and selectively undertook conspicuous construction projects among the underdeveloped states: first in Asia, then the Middle East, and later in Africa south of the Sahara and in Latin America.

But the most fundamental premise of Khrushchev's foreign policy toward the noncommunist states was that of the possibility of avoiding general or nuclear war. The policies of economic competition and winning favor in the underdeveloped world rested upon this premise, and it also entailed some difficult differentiation of the acceptable and the unacceptable modes of struggle against world "reaction."

In brief, as the theory developed during Khrushchev's tenure, general war between socialist and capitalist nations was no longer inevitable because the military might of the socialist system had now been developed to the point that capitalist aggression could be deterred by the fear of socialist retaliation. If the socialist system remained vigilant, it might thus preserve the peace while economic competition proved its superiority and won converts by its persuasive example. General war must be avoided because it would inevitably induce the introduction of nuclear weapons of mass destruction by the side facing defeat and would thus lead to mutual catastrophe. It was not reasonable, Khrushchev once pointed out to the Chinese, to plan to erect the communist society upon a bed of nuclear cinders. In response to the charge that he was a *revisionist* of Leninism, Khrushchev replied that the material conditions had changed since Lenin wrote and that it was blind *dogmatism* to apply Lenin's principles by rote and not to interpret them in the light of these changed conditions.

This reformulation of the prospects for general war left undefined the acceptable limits for the use of violence in propagating world communism. The Soviet Union since 1956 has taken a very cautious position on this question. While it supports in theory "wars of national liberation" indigenously sponsored to overthrow reactionary regimes, it insists that such wars must also be indigenously inspired and that the revolution cannot be carried to a colonial country before the time is "ripe." With similar prudence, the Soviet Union eschews the prospect of local or regional wars between forces of socialism and "reaction" for fear of escalation into general war.

The delicate distinctions between acceptable and unacceptable uses of military force and the perceived necessity of maintaining a formidable military deterrent to possible capitalist aggression have understandably led to the most critical junctures in Soviet foreign relations, both with the West and within the party-state system during the years since 1956. It is on the issue of acceptable risk of escalation that much of the verbal controversy with the Chinese has taken place. It has been the same issue of escalation that has defined the power confrontations with the United States over Berlin in 1961, Cuba in 1962, and most recently Vietnam. The policy of nuclear intimidation has been moderated by successive professions of interest in various plans of arms reduction and disarmament. The multilateral Nuclear Test Ban Treaty, concluded in Moscow in the summer of 1963, establishes the credibility of some of these professions. The line between good faith and propaganda, however, is not clear to the West and in all probability is unclear and changing to the Soviet decision-makers themselves.

Throughout the past decade, we may observe finally, the Soviet Union has acted on the side of caution when pressed by circumstance to define her position on the use of military forces. Her actions have been more cautious than her words, and her words have become a notably moderate and responsible counterpart to the shrill professions of her erstwhile Chinese ally.

The pages above have been devoted to an interpretive overview of the course and concerns of Soviet foreign policy in the half century since the Bolshevik Revolution first obliged Lenin to balance his dreams of world revolution with his practical sense of self-preservation. We are concerned in this volume as a whole less with historical detail than with facts that can help us understand the determinants of contemporary Soviet foreign policy. Thus, in the chapters to come, we shall turn to certain integral aspects of this process and ask the reader to accompany us while we use a variety of means to explore the questions policymakers, already in possession of the historical narrative, might find consequential.

THE INSTITUTIONS OF
SOVIET FOREIGN POLICY

It may be persuasively argued that in no nation can foreign-policy decision-making be realistically separated from domestic decision-making except on an analytical plane—there is too much influence of the one upon the other. What is done domestically, what happens domestically, has an irrevocable impact beyond the geographical frontiers; and actions by a state in the international system set limiting conditions within which domestic life and policy must be maintained. Because the consequences of foreign and domestic policymaking for each other are inescapable, the institutions of any rational public-decision process must reflect the relationship. In the Soviet state especially, communist roots are international roots, and the conception of a socialist Soviet Union has been integrally enmeshed in the conception of a coming socialist world system of which the Soviet Union would be only the first element.

In examining the institutional relations of Soviet foreign policy, therefore, it is not feasible to draw a sharp line between those concerned with internal affairs and those concerned with foreign relations. We must begin our description of the institutions of the foreign-policy process with the institutions of Soviet public policy as a whole. The overarching function of the Communist Party will become evident as we proceed.

A. ADMINISTRATION

The Supreme Soviet

The first principle for the organization and activity of Soviet state organs, as acknowledged in Soviet constitutional law, prescribes responsibility of the "organs of state power" (at the national level the Supreme Soviet and its Presidium) to the Soviet people, who in law create them. *The Large Soviet Encyclopedia* and all authors on Soviet state law point to the virtual 100 per cent voter turnout for quadrennial elections to the Supreme Soviet (99.94 per cent in 1966) as evidence that this body really reflects the will of the people.

27

Constitutionally vested with state sovereignty, the Supreme Soviet exercises all rights in the jurisdiction of the USSR *insofar* as they do not fall under the jurisdiction of organs accountable to it. The qualification is all-important, for administrative charges have placed every significant responsibility under some such subordinate jurisdiction, leaving to the Supreme Soviet the passive role of maintaining accountability after the fact of action. The real importance of this accountability is greatly reduced too by the constitutionally recognized role of the Communist Party as guide to all Soviet organizational action—to include establishing criteria for the activities of nominally subordinate organizations accountable to the Supreme Soviet. In neither law nor theory then is the Supreme Soviet in a position to control foreign or domestic policy, and it has never done so in practice.

The frequently drawn conclusion that the Supreme Soviet is simply irrelevant for the Soviet policy process is, however, hasty. The Supreme Soviet must give *post factum* approval to the decrees of its own Presidium and to the decrees and policies of the Soviet government (Council of Ministers). In law, it has the prerogative of rescinding them. All changes in policies and policymakers must therefore be legitimized formally by the Supreme Soviet. As a result it is a forum for announcements of new foreign-policy directions, for justification and public defense of old policies (so used, for example, by Khrushchev in December, 1962 to defend and confirm his actions in the Cuban missile crisis), for elaboration and clarification of policies to a wide variety of audiences, for sampling public response, and for molding public opinion both at home and abroad.

Customarily, the short agenda for semiannual Supreme Soviet sessions includes one item labelled, "Concerning the International Situation and the Foreign Policy of the Soviet Union." Typically, the subject is raised on the last day of a three- to five-day session and is handled by a report on government foreign policy and analysis of the current international situation presented by the Foreign Minister. Having heard the report at a joint sitting, the two chambers separate for a period of "debate" in which deputies reiterate and approve with varying degrees of praise particular portions of the report. There follows in each chamber unanimous adoption of a decree formally approving the foreign policy of the government.

In law and theory it is the Presidium of the Supreme Soviet which acts in its place during the long intervals when the larger body is not in session. This Presidium's constitutional jurisdiction over foreign affairs therefore includes all the larger body's rights (subject to ratification) and is made more meaningful by proximity to the daily decision process. However, for the same two reasons—Party guidance and historical precedent the—Presidium has never played a powerful part in that process. Unlike the Supreme Soviet itself, whose infrequent sessions guarantee a focus of domestic- and foreign-audience attention, meetings of its Presidium have merely served to document a record of legitimacy for government and Party behavior. Some thirty-four individuals constitute the Presidium, including a Chairman who acts as head of state, a Secretary, fifteen Deputy Chairmen (one from each Union Republic), and seventeen other members, all elected by the Supreme Soviet for the four-year duration of its convocation. They are nominated as a slate, having, in practice, the explicit approval of the Party Central Committee.

After the initial session the Presidium convenes the Supreme Soviet sessions and, in the sphere of international relations, receives foreign ambassadors, ratifies and abrogates treaties, appoints and recalls plenipotentiary representatives of the USSR. In law it may rescind decrees of the government which it deems contrary to laws of the USSR, proclaim a state of war "in the event of an attack on the USSR, or when necessary to fulfill international treaty obligations concerning defense against aggression," appoint and remove members of the government, and in other, lesser ways influence or control Soviet foreign policy.[1]

In practice the Presidium of the Supreme Soviet has traditionally been composed of prestigious but politically weak personalities, and it has not been a source of initiative in the policy process. A break with this tradition began in 1960 with the election of Leonid I. Brezhnev to the chairmanship and has continued since with the succession of Anastas Mikoyan and then Nikolai Podgorny to that post. It seems feasible that given independently strong occupants together with its constitutional and bureaucratic potential, the office of Chairman may now be an active power locus for both domestic and foreign Soviet decision-making.

Both chambers of the Supreme Soviet—the Council of Union and the Council of Nationalities—elect Permanent Commissions on Foreign Affairs. In theory these two Commissions, now including thirty-one Deputies each, are charged with preliminary consideration of legislation proposed to their respective chambers. They are authorized to examine the government's foreign policy as reflected in the Foreign Minister's report and to debate and make recommendations concerning it.[2] In law, Commission members, as all Deputies of the Supreme Soviet, may direct questions to a Minister

[1] See F. I. Kozhevnikov, ed., *International Law* (Moscow: Foreign Languages Publishing House, n.d.), p. 289.

[2] A. Denisov and M. Kirichenko, *Soviet State Law* (Moscow: Foreign Languages Publishing House, 1960), pp. 224–228. Cf. Andrei Y. Vyshinsky, ed., *The Law of the Soviet State* (New York: The Macmillan Company, 1948), pp. 348–52; and Julian Towster, *Political Power in the USSR, 1917–1947* (New York: Oxford University Press, 1948), pp. 255–256. For recent appointments, see *Pravda,* August 4, 1966.

for an obligatory verbal or written reply within three days. When these rights are viewed in the company of the investigative prerogative mentioned earlier, it is apparent that there is considerable legal potential for Foreign Affairs Commission influence in Soviet foreign policy. Heretofore, that potential has been unrealized, but recently the submission of treaties and reports to the Commissions and their formal, unanimous action upon them have begun to build a precedent for involvement. When the Seventh Supreme Soviet met for its first session, in August, 1966, Chairman Nikolai Podgorny devoted his major address to plans for augmenting the size and role of all Supreme Soviet Permanent Commissions. The respective foreign-affairs contingents revealed a high incidence of familiar names from the Communist Party elite. Their Chairmen, M. A. Suslov and B. N. Ponomarev, were both veterans of long service in the foreign-affairs departments of the Party Secretariat.

It can not be overemphasized that the theoretical and legal potential for influence by the Supreme Soviet and its agencies in the foreign-policy process has not been realized. A typical illustration of their involvement in the past comes in the report of the first session of the Sixth Supreme Soviet in April of 1962. *Pravda* noted that after their election the two Foreign Affairs Commissions met in a joint sitting under the chairmanship of (Communist Party Secretary) M. A. Suslov and discussed the materials of Foreign Minister Gromyko's report on the international situation and on recent international talks held in Geneva (presented to the two chambers on the previous afternoon). The Commissions, according to *Pravda*, decided to recommend to the Supreme Soviet that it issue a decree approving the government's foreign policy. That afternoon, again in a joint sitting, the Supreme Soviet itself "debated" Gromyko's report. Various Deputies spoke in praise of the government, and a decree approving its foreign policy was proposed on behalf of the Commissions. It was passed unanimously.[3]

In Soviet state law a sharp distinction is drawn between the organs of *state power* (composed of Deputies to the Supreme Soviet who have been elected by the people) and the organs of *state administration* (the government, which is formed by and accountable to the organs of *state power*). By tradition both because of constitutional delegations of decision-making authority and because of the constitutionally recognized guiding role of the Communist Party, we have seen that the actual institutional function of the organs of *state power* in the foreign-policy process is either passive or potential, not active, influence. We turn now to the Council of Ministers, which is the Soviet government and the primary body charged with

[3] *Pravda,* April 25 and 26, 1962.

administering the affairs of state and answering for them to the organs of state power.

The Council of Ministers

In law and theory the Council of Ministers is appointed by and account-able to the Supreme Soviet and its Presidium. The forms of this prescribed relationship are observed in practice. In April of 1962, after the new Supreme Soviet had ratified its own leadership, Nikolai Podgorny, a member of the Party Presidium, took the floor and in the name of "a group of Deputies" praised the work of the Council of Ministers and of its Chairman, N. S. Khrushchev. His motion of confidence was approved unanimously, and the Deputies instructed Chairman Khrushchev to present a proposal concerning the composition of the new Council.[4] Khrushchev forthwith read out the composition of the Council, announced that it had been approved by the Central Committee of the CPSU, and asked the Deputies to confirm it. They did so, again unanimously.[5]

In August, 1966 Khrushchev's name was missing, but the ritual remained the same. Deputy N. G. Yegorychev, First Secretary of the Moscow Party organization, moved and received acceptance of the government's resignation and approval of its work. On behalf of the Party Central Committee, Deputy L. I. Brezhnev, General Secretary of the CPSU, then moved reappointment of Chairman Kosygin. He was confirmed. Kosygin later submitted a list of candidates having explicit approval of the Party Central Committee. They were unanimously elected as the new Council of Ministers.[6]

Ninety members were on the list which constituted the Council of Ministers in mid-1967. The number and the offices have changed frequently with successive reorganizations of the ministerial structure. Included in 1967 were the Chairman of the Council, two First Deputy Chairmen, nine Deputy Chairmen, sixty-three members of ministerial rank heading Ministries or State Committees or Specialized Agencies of the government, and fifteen Chairmen of the Councils of Ministers of the Union Republics of the USSR serving *ex officio.*

Long too large and amorphous a group for active collegial decision-making, the Council of Ministers has in practice been represented by its own Presidium, composed of the Chairman, his First Deputies, Deputies, and such other members as these wish to include.

[4] The old Council of Ministers customarily presents a formal resignation at the time the newly elected Supreme Soviet convenes.

[5] *Pravda,* April 26, 1962.

[6] *Pravda,* August 4, 1966.

Established as "the highest executive and administrative organ of the state power of the Union of Soviet Socialist Republics" in Article 64 of the Constitution, the authority of the Council is set out in general terms in Articles 68 and 69. Included here is the charge to exercise "general guidance in the sphere of relations with foreign states." Constitutionally this power is shared with the fifteen Union Republics, which may "enter into direct relations with foreign states and . . . conclude agreements and exchange diplomatic and consular representatives with them." But in practice this concurrent right of the Union Republics, which dates from 1944, has provided some flexibility but no diminution of the central government's prerogative to control the implementation of Soviet foreign policy.[7]

More specifically, the Council of Ministers is formally empowered: (1) to grant and withdraw recognition of states and governments; (2) to establish and break diplomatic relations with foreign states; (3) to order acts of reprisal against other states; (4) to appoint negotiators and supervise the negotiations of international treaties and agreements; (5) to accede to international conventions not requiring ratification; (6) to conclude agreements which do not require ratification; (7) to confirm all treaties and agreements which do not require ratification; (8) to examine preliminary international treaties and agreements which do not require ratification; (9) to supervise and direct Soviet diplomatic agents and organs; and (10) to appoint Soviet diplomats and accredit foreign diplomats below the rank of plenipotentiary as well as Soviet trade representatives abroad.[8] Embassy and consulate operation, the organization of overseas missions, the conduct of trade negotiations, and Soviet participation in the United Nations and its affiliated organizations—all these activities are directed by the Council of Ministers through its operating agencies. The Council also directs Soviet military affairs by establishing the organization of the Armed Forces, setting annual draft quotas, recommending the allocation of funds, providing for the training of military officer cadres, and submitting nominations for appointment of high-ranking military personnel.

[7] See Vernon V. Aspaturian, *The Union Republics in Soviet Diplomacy* (Geneva: Librairie E. Droz, 1960), pp. 195–200, 209–213.

[8] Kozhevnikov, *op. cit.* pp. 289–290. Treaties subject to ratification by the Presidium of the Supreme Soviet are peace treaties, treaties of mutual assistance against aggression, treaties of mutual nonaggression, and treaties that the concluding parties agreed were to be ratified. Only the organ that ratifies a treaty is authorized to abrogate it. This division of authority was established in 1938 and accounts for the formal as well as practical freedom of action which the nominally subordinate and accountable Council of Ministers possesses in this area. The practice of submitting even treaties which do not technically require specific Supreme Soviet action to the Foreign Affairs Commissions of that body has developed as part of the trend towards greater involvement of the Supreme Soviet in recent years.

Controlling in daily operations a wide variety of subordinate ministerial and nonministerial agencies, the leadership of the Council is theoretically, legally, and in fact the central institution for *administration* of Soviet foreign relations with noncommunist states. It draws together the chief administrators of both domestic and foreign policy. It draws together also the offices with access to factual information and technical expertise with the offices possessing authority to make binding administrative decisions. Through the persons of this dozen men, the discretionary judgment is exercised that gives continuity and substantive detail to the policy directions provided by the Party. Roles of the Presidium of the Council of Ministers are thus junctures into which informational and value inputs must pass and where they must be resolved into output directives.

The process of the Presidium of the Council of Ministers, like all organs of Soviet administration, incorporates two incompatible theoretical principles, which are reconciled in practice by a shifting compromise: the principle of collegiality (kollegial'nost) and the principle of one-man management (edinonachalie). The compromise between the two is closely related to the Leninist concept of "democratic centralism." In the words of a recent Soviet monograph devoted to the subject, "The essence of the collegial form of government leadership consists of the fact that the most important questions of direction in the popular economy and social-cultural construction in the USSR are decided not by one person but collectively."[9] But although the active participation of the collective is theoretically sought, one man must be responsible for each decision. At the ministerial level:

All ministries . . . are constructed and function on the basis of one-man leadership. At the head of the ministry . . . stands one individual—the Minister, appointed by the highest organ of state power.

The Minister individually directs as commissioned his branch of the government and carries for his activity personal responsibility before the Supreme Soviet, the Presidium of the Supreme Soviet and the Government, of which he is a member.[10]

The compromise is effected in law by obliging the Minister to consult with his collegium before arriving at any major decision. The Minister, however, is not obliged to concur with the vote or sense of his collegium, and he may countermand its judgment. Either way he is held responsible for the results

[9] E. V. Shorina, *Kollegial'nost' i edinonachalie v Sovetskom gosudarstvennoe upravlenii* (Moscow: Gosizdat. Iuridicheskoi literatury, 1959), p. 7.

[10] *Ibid.,* p. 79.

personally. If, in a case of serious conflict, the Minister is proven right by events, he may recommend that the Presidium of the Council change the membership of his collegium. If he is proven wrong, he may be charged with stubborness or disregard of the collegial process, or worse, and may be replaced. Members of the collegia have the right of appeal past the Minister to the Council itself and to the Party.

The principles are accorded general validity. Thus the ministerial model clarifies the formal relationship among members of the higher leadership. It also indicates the special place that success occupies as a criterion for an individual's performance in the Soviet system.

Although the Council of Ministers as a whole (in practice its Presidium) appoints the collegia of its ministries and their subordinate main administrations, the responsibility which is explicitly placed upon the Minister's shoulders carries with it a considerable freedom of action. It is clear, for example, that the appointment of the collegia and subordinate personnel is primarily determined by the Minister himself. It is he who nominates, but the Council and the Party organs have the power of approval or veto. Bureaucratic rationalization too requires that relatively minor decisions be made at the lowest level of authority capable of handling them. The demand that minor decisions not be delayed, the sheer volume of decisions that must be made, and the ready availability of information on which decisions must be based are all factors that operate to increase the discretion allowed and the resultant influence of subordinate government organs not only in the sphere of foreign policy, but also in that of domestic policy as well.

None of the multitude of Ministries and State Committees subordinate to the Council of Ministers can be completely excluded as having no effect on the foreign-policy process of the USSR. Most maintain advisory personnel who specialize in the international implications of their subjects. If in no other way, the interests of each agency compete for the allocation of funds in the national budget with the interests of the agencies directly concerned with the conduct of international affairs. Manifesting their demands through their representatives on the Council and its Presidium, they provide inputs which affect the output action of the USSR as an actor in the international system. In our examination of institutions, however, we shall focus on those agencies substantively concerned with foreign affairs—those which represent the USSR directly in transactions with the international system outside.

The following agencies subordinate to the Council of Ministers are directly involved in the conduct of Soviet foreign policy, and we shall look at them here briefly: the Ministry of Foreign Affairs, the Ministry of Defense, the Ministry of Foreign Trade, the State Committee for Foreign Economic

Relations, the State Committee for Cultural Relations with Foreign Countries, the Committee for State Security, and the Telegraph Agency of the Soviet Union (TASS). We shall close with an examination of the Soviet Mission Abroad.

The Ministry of Foreign Affairs

The People's Commissariat of Foreign Affairs was established by decree of the Congress of Soviets dated November 8, 1917. It was alleged to be an organ for administration of a "qualitatively new diplomacy, expressing the interests of the working class."[11] Diplomacy was officially conceived to be the "peaceful, day-to-day work of implementing the foreign policy of a State, carried on by the organs of the State for their international relations in the interests of the ruling class." The diplomacy of the Soviet state would be qualitatively new because it would not be based upon the class interests of the exploiter classes,[12] as that of all prior states, but upon the interests of the working class, as defined by their vanguard, the Communist Party.

The Ministry, basing itself "upon the need for the most careful consideration of the situation and of the prospects for the future development of international relations," would exercise day-to-day control over diplomatic missions and consulates, direct their work, submit all major questions of foreign policy for the consideration of the government, and defend the interests of the state and its citizens abroad. More specifically, under terms of a Statute adopted in 1923, the Ministry had and still has the following tasks:

(a) the defence of the foreign political and economic interests of the USSR, and also of Soviet citizens abroad;

(b) the execution of decisions regarding the conclusion of treaties and agreements with foreign States;

(c) control over the implementation of treaties and agreements concluded with foreign States and assistance to the appropriate institutions of the USSR and Union Republics in the exercise of their rights as laid down in these treaties and agreements;

---

[11] Kozhevnikov, *op. cit.,* p. 286.

[12] "The real nature of the diplomacy of exploiter states based on private ownership, the exploitation of man by man and national antagonism, was defined by the founders of Marxism-Leninism in the following manner: 'The incitement of people against people, the utilisation of one people to oppress another and thus to ensure the further existence of absolute despotic authority—that sums up the art and activity of all hitherto existing rulers and their diplomats.'" *Ibid.,* pp. 286–287, quoting Marx and Engels, *Sochineniia,* VI, 237.

(d) control over the fulfillment by the appropriate organs of power of treaties, agreements and other acts concluded with foreign States.[13]

The Minister directs all the day-to-day activity of his Ministry. He "conducts negotiations with the representatives of foreign states, receives diplomatic representatives, appoints diplomats, from attachés to chargés d'affaires, countersigns letters of credence and recall as well as consular patents, authorizes the publication of agreements concluded between the USSR and foreign states, and fulfills a number of other functions.[14]

The early impatience of the Soviet leadership toward the panoply of conventional European diplomatic practices gave way early to the force of circumstances. Trotsky, the first People's Commissar for Foreign Affairs, had hoped to "issue a few revolutionary proclamations to the peoples of the world and then shut up shop,"[15] an attitude apparently shared briefly by Lenin himself. But the appointment of George Chicherin as Trotsky's successor marked recognition that the new Soviet state existed in a persisting international system whose structure could not be wished away and would not immediately disintegrate. Any attempt to ignore the ground rules of that system could only operate to the disadvantage of Soviet Russia, which had interests as an actor, unwilling though it might be, in that system. A master of *Realpolitik* beyond his radical ideals, Chicherin, in his twelve years as People's Commissar placed a lasting stamp upon the form of the Ministry. The form became a mirror of other Western Foreign Offices. Pressed by the same demands for rationalization of the task as in other countries, the Soviet Foreign Office was drawn under Chicherin into the same institutional pattern.[16]

[13] *Bulletin of the Central Executive Committee, the Council of Peoples Commissars and the Council of Labour and Defence of the USSR*, No. 10 (1923), Article 300. See supplements of May 22, 1925 *The Code of Laws of the USSR*, No. 34 (1925), Article 233 and of May 4, 1927 *The Code of Laws of the USSR*, No. 25 (1927), Article 266. On February 1, 1944, the People's Commissariat of Foreign Affairs was changed from an All-Union to a Union-Republic Commissariat, bringing into existence foreign affairs commissariats in each of the Union Republics. In 1946 the Commissariats were redesignated Ministries in the course of general redesignation of the organs of state administration.

[14] Kozhevnikov, *op. cit.,* pp. 290–291.

[15] Leon Trotsky, *My Life* (New York: Charles Scribner's Sons, 1930), p. 341.

[16] See Theodore H. von Laue, "Soviet Diplomacy: G. V. Chicherin, Peoples Commissar for Foreign Affairs, 1918–1930," in Gordon A. Craig and Felix Gilbert, eds., *The Diplomats, 1919–1939* (Princeton: Princeton University Press, 1953), pp. 234–241. Cf. Louis Fischer, *The Soviets in World Affairs* (London: Jonathan Cape, 1930), II, 821–825. See also B. Kantorovich, "Organizatsionnoe razvitie N.K.I.D.," *Mezhdunarodnaia zhizn,* No. 15 (133) (November 7, 1922), 51–55; and Robert M. Slusser, "The Role of the Foreign Ministry," in Ivo J. Lederer, ed., *Russian Foreign Policy* (New Haven, Conn.: Yale University Press, 1962), pp. 197–239.

There were some clear differences in function: policy implementation was kept more distinct from policy formulation than in most other Western nations; foreign policy was pursued simultaneously by other agencies (chiefly by the Communist Party apparatus and the Comintern). Gradually, however, as the tenacity of the old international system became more and more obvious and then much later when Nikita Khrushchev elevated the tactic of "peaceful coexistence" into a strategy to meet the nuclear environment after Stalin's death, the form of the conventional Foreign Ministry embodied a more substantial content. Today it is indisputably the chief organ for *administering* foreign relations with the noncommunist industrial nations, and it has a major role in the *formulation* of policies toward those countries as well. Its role in Soviet foreign relations with the developing countries and with the communist system is more complex as we shall see later.

The structure of the Ministry of Foreign Affairs reflects a familiar rationalization of labor along both geographic and functional lines. One of the largest of Soviet Ministries, in 1967 it showed one First Deputy Minister (V. V. Kuznetsov), five Deputy Ministers, and seven nonministerial members of the collegium presided over by Minister Andrei A. Gromyko. In the words of a U.S. government report:

> Overall supervisory chores are divided among the Deputy Ministers, with the First Deputy acting in a general capacity as the Minister's right-hand man. The Collegium advises the Minister and, at the same time, serves as a co-ordinating board for the activities of the various components of the ministry. It helps translate policy directives into specific assignments, oversees their implementation, and assesses the results.[17]

Ten Administrations and Divisions are delineated by function: Protocol, Treaty and Legal, Press, Consular, Personnel, Diplomatic Corps, Archives, Economic, Administrative, and the "Special" Administration for Intelligence (operated by the KGB directly).[18] Two Administrations share responsibility for Soviet participation in international organizations, with one of these specifically oriented to international economic organizations.

Of the fifteen Main Administrations organized geographically, five are

---

[17] *National Policy Machinery in the Soviet Union,* Report to the Committee on Government Operations, U.S. Senate (Washington, D.C.: Government Printing Office, 1960), pp. 41–42.

[18] *Staffing Procedures and Problems in the Soviet Union,* Report to the Committee on Government Operations, U.S. Senate (Washington, D.C.: Government Printing Office, 1963), p. 31, chart 10; Aleksandr Kaznacheev, *Inside a Soviet Embassy* (Philadelphia: J. B. Lippincott Company, 1962), pp. 179, 184; *Directory of Soviet Officials,* pp. 22–24.

devoted to Europe, one to Scandinavia, one to the U.S.A., one to Latin American Countries, two to Africa, and one each to the Near East, Middle East, South Asia, Southeast Asia, and Far East. Directly subordinate to the collegium are the Soviet Mission to the United Nations and some eighty-two embassies abroad. A Secretariat of the Ministry, also directly subordinate to the collegium, completes the organization. Not surprisingly, examination of the prior career posts held by present members of the diplomatic corps indicates that successive reorganizations have altered this list over the years. Aside from a general trend toward greater differentiation, increased emphasis upon the developing areas of Asia and Africa is reflected in the recent changes.[19]

Within the Main Administrations the work of the Foreign Ministry is further broken down by divisions and sections, both in the functional and geographic areas. A geographic desk supervises the operations of diplomatic elements of the Soviet mission in each country, solves minor problems, and refers major problems to superiors. The desk also acts as an important element in the selection, consolidation, and forwarding of information about the country of its responsibility, drawn from diplomatic reports.[20]

The vast majority of personnel staffing the administrative subdivisions of the Ministry are career diplomatic personnel drawn into the service in their twenties and trained at the Institute of International Relations, an exacting six-year institution of higher education run by the Ministry itself in concert with the Party and Komsomol, the Committee for State Security, and the Ministry for Higher and Specialized Education. Promotions normally are made along a clear hierarchy within the service, with lateral entry rare except for certain special areas to be considered later. At the base of the hierarchy of diplomatic rank is the Probationer (Information Officer), followed in ascending order by Attaché, Third Secretary, Second Secretary, First Secretary, Minister/Counselor, and Ambassador. Second Secretaries and above are considered senior diplomatic staff; those in lower ranks are the junior diplomatic staff. Within the home ministry an Ambassador will normally fill the office of Director of an Administration or Division Chief. Other members of the senior diplomatic staff will be Deputy Chiefs of Division and Chiefs of subordinate sections.

---

[19] The second African Administration was established in February 1961 to specialize in Africa south of the Sahara, particularly the newly independent states and southwest Africa. The Latin American Administration was separated from that for the United States in February, 1962.

[20] I. N. Ananov, *Ministerstva v SSSR* (Moscow: Gosiurizdat, 1960), pp. 183–222; *National Policy Machinery in the Soviet Union*, p. 42.

The Ministry of Defense

Nikita Khrushchev once remarked that if the USSR's generals did not accept a political decision they would be replaced. The principle has teeth in it. The top Soviet military hero of World War II, Minister of Defense, and first career military officer to achieve either alternate or full membership in the Communist Party Politburo, Marshal G. K. Zhukov, was summarily relieved of his offices and publicly disgraced by Khrushchev in 1957, less than four months after he had been instrumental in securing Khrushchev's embattled leadership. There seems to be little doubt that now, as for most of the duration of Soviet power, the Soviet military establishment, highly centralized under direction of the Minister of Defense, occupies a well-checked subordinate role in the Soviet policy processes, both foreign and domestic.[21] This, however, does not enable us to say that the role is *insignificant* for the shape of Soviet foreign policy, but only that the Soviet military leaders are self-consciously subservient in their participation in the decision processes. The weight of their participation will be considered in the following chapter. The means of violence represented by the Soviet military establishment significantly affects the capability of the Soviet Union as an actor in the international system. This fact alone is sufficient to relate the making of decisions about the Soviet military establishment to the foreign-policy process.

The organization of the Ministry of Defense parallels that of other Soviet Ministries concerned with foreign affairs. A centralized hierarchy of authority is topped by the Minister, who is personally responsible for the Ministry's performance both to the Council of Ministers and to the Supreme Soviet, which must approve his appointment. The Minister's freedom of action is curtailed by the legal and theoretical requirements of *collegiality* in decision-making and by the legal and theoretical obligation to follow the guidance of Party organs. The Minister himself (Marshal A. A. Grechko replaced Marshal R. Ya. Malinovsky in April, 1967 following the latter's death) and the majority of his subordinates are customarily military professionals. They are considered to fuse in their persons the military and political interests of the Soviet people: "The leaders of the Soviet Armed Forces are representatives of the Communist Party and the Soviet government who carry out Party policy expressing the basic interests of the entire Soviet people,"[22] Embodying the same class interests as the rest of the people, the Soviet

[21] See Raymond L. Garthoff, *Soviet Military Policy* (New York: Frederick A. Praeger, Inc., 1966).

[22] V. D. Sokolovskii, ed., *Soviet Military Strategy* (Englewood Cliffs, N.J.: Prentice-Hall, Inc., 1963), p. 497.

military are said, by legal and theoretical definition, to be free of the professional biases that have led bourgeois countries to a dichotomy of military and civilian interests. That they are not and cannot be free of their own professional biases and sensitivities is amply documented by the continuing debate over Soviet economic and defense priorities and by ill-concealed military disenchantment with Khrushchev's diplomatic bluffs and "adventures" between 1958 and 1964.[23]

In addition to the necessary technical, logistical, and operational Directorates, the Ministry of Defense includes an Intelligence Directorate (the GRU), which impinges on foreign-policy processes as the parent organization for Soviet military attachés and covert military-intelligence activity abroad. We shall say more of the GRU below in the contexts of the Committee for State Security and the Soviet Missions Abroad. For now we may note merely that this Directorate is charged with operations against military, economic, technical, scientific, and political targets in all countries of strategic importance. It is responsible for setting up deep-cover networks for economic sabotage, guerrilla operations, and special military missions.[24]

The Ministry of Foreign Trade

All foreign trade of the Soviet Union is conducted through specially chartered state monopolies—export and import corporations—under the direct supervision and guidance of the All-Union Ministry of Foreign Trade in Moscow. Nationalization of foreign trade was the subject of an early Soviet government decree by which foreign-trade enterprises were expropriated by the Soviet state. The state-monopoly principle (there are now some thirty-four chartered state-trading corporations),[25] which established the Soviet government as intermediary for all commercial transactions between Soviet and foreign firms, has been maintained with little revision during the subsequent evolution of the Soviet state. Accordingly, foreign economic relations have been a mechanism for both economic and political foreign policy in the hands of the government acting under Party guidance. An organization reminiscent of the "mercantile" states of past centuries has produced a significant asymmetry with most Western democracies, which the Soviet leadership has exploited for political benefit.

---

[23] See Garthoff, *op. cit.*

[24] *Staffing Procedures and Problems in the Soviet Union,* p. 58. Cf. *Soviet Intelligence Systems* (Fort Holabird, Md.: U.S. Army, November, 1962).

[25] See the two-page advertisement by the Soviet American Trade Company (AMTORG) in the *New York Times,* January 16, 1967, pp. C–56–57.

The Ministry is divided into geographic and functional administrations, charged with directing all of the country's foreign-trade activity, working out and implementing measures for developing trade relations with foreign states, compiling and carrying out export and import plans, working out tariff policy and directing the customs service, guiding the work of its subordinate organizations, and exercising control over the trade-monopoly corporations.[26] Pursuant to these tasks, the Ministry:

(1) Prepares drafts of trade treaties, commercial and other economic agreements within the Ministry's competence between the USSR and other states, submitting them in the manner prescribed for consideration and conclusion; negotiates with foreign states trade treaties, trade, payment and other economic agreements, and signs them upon authorization by the USSR Government, exercising control over their execution.

(2) Works out measures covering imports, exports and re-exports and for improving the quality of export and import goods, and also of equipment; through the State Export Goods Quality Inspection Office, which is a component part of it, it exercises control over the quality of export goods both during the process of their production and at the time of shipment; it implements measures covering currency and other financial questions in the sphere of foreign trade and regulates receipts of payments accuring from foreign trade operations, establishes rules for the transit of foreign goods on USSR territory, and issues import and export permits.

(3) Works out measures for carrying out customs policy and administers the customs service through the Chief Customs Administration, which is a component of it.

(4) Directs the activity of the USSR's trade delegations and trade agencies abroad, and of trade counsellors at USSR embassies and legations abroad.

(5) Controls the activity of economic organizations possessing the right to conduct operations in the foreign market and guides the work of offices, organizations and enterprises under its jurisdiction, and sees to it that the laws, edicts and rules covering foreign trade are observed.[27]

The overseas representation of the Ministry of Foreign Trade is the Soviet Trade Delegation, a unique institution for which the USSR has sought diplomatic accreditation over the years with varying degrees of success. The place of the Trade Delegation as one part of the complex Soviet Mission Abroad will be considered more extensively below. Here it will suffice to

[26] K. K. Bakhtov, "Monopoliia vneshnei torgovli SSSR i razvitie ee organizatsionnykh form," *Vneshniaia torgovlia,* No. 10 (October, 1964), p. 48.

[27] *Ibid.*

indicate that under a decree of the Central Executive Committee and the Council of People's Commissars issued on November 13, 1933, and still in force, the Trade Delegation is charged with representing the interests of the USSR in the sphere of foreign trade, helping to promote and develop Soviet foreign economic relations, and regulating and carrying on the Soviet Union's foreign trade. Additionally, the Delegation studies the general economic conditions and market trends of the country to which it is accredited and keeps the Ministry of Foreign Trade informed on these conditions.[28]

The State Committee for Foreign Economic Relations

A Main Administration for Economic Relations with the People's Democracies was set up within the Ministry of Foreign Trade on January 6, 1955, allegedly in response to the pressure from expanded activity in connection with assistance to these countries to promote their technical-economic development. In 1957, this Administration was separated from the Ministry, reorganized, and became the State Committee for Foreign Economic Relations, focusing its attention upon the Soviet technical- and economic-assistance program for the developing countries as well as Soviet economic relations with the party-states of the communist system.[29]

The primary distinctions between the Ministry and the State Committee appear to be (1) the legal right to issue normative decisions binding on all state organizations, which is constitutionally vested in the Ministry and not in the State Committee, and (2) an emphasis upon coordinating activities by the State Committee (especially the relations among the State Bank, the Ministry of Finance, and the Ministry of Foreign Trade regarding foreign-assistance programs). Insofar as the Committee is directly responsible to the Council of Ministers (in practice its Presidium) for the foreign-assistance program, it is probable that in these matters it takes precedence over the Ministry of Foreign Trade. As will be illustrated, the Committee maintains its own representatives in countries abroad, with concentration in the developing countries that are participants in the Soviet assistance program. The Committee representatives oversee and coordinate foreign-trade-corporation personnel managers and technical specialists abroad in their work, setting up industrial enterprises and preparing local personnel for their operation and management.

[28] *Ibid.*, pp. 48–49. Cf. Kozhevnikov, *op. cit.*, pp. 305–310; P. A. Cherviakov, *Organizatsiia i tekhnika vneshnei torgovli SSSR* (Moscow: Vneshtorgizdat, 1962), pp. 46–49.

[29] Bakhtov, *op. cit.*, p. 48; Cherviakov, *op. cit.*, p. 58.

The State Committee for Cultural Relations with Foreign Countries

In law and theory the instruments of Soviet propaganda abroad are very closely supervised by the Communist Party's central organs. The expertise of the propagandist was long ago raised to a high level within the Party and has since been regarded as the special province of the Party technician. For this reason the fusion of Party and state "information" organs is greater than the fusion in other functional areas we have examined. The State Committee for Cultural Relations with Foreign Countries is in fact a coordinating body for various institutional efforts to project an attractive image of the Soviet Union abroad, i.e., Soviet propaganda programs.

The Committee was established without fanfare in 1957, apparently to coordinate, oversee, and promote Soviet exchanges with other countries in the arts, education, and sciences. The familiar geographic and functional structure was followed. According to a Soviet press release of February 4, 1960, the Committee was then elevated by the Presidium of the Supreme Soviet to become an integral part of the Council of Ministers. The new stature probably resulted from (1) intensification of use of "peaceful exchanges" as an instrument of foreign policy compatible with the peaceful-coexistence theme then ascendant and (2) the concurrent intensification of Soviet efforts to win favor in the developing countries through a stepped-up program of educational assistance. The first Chairman of the Committee was G. A. Zhukov, who, less than a month after his appointment, was also appointed as Chairman of the Soviet Commission in UNESCO.[30]

In regard to the capitalist countries, the Committee promotes agreements for the exchange of academic personnel and information on scientific achievements and for the exchange of performing artists and exhibitions of a cultural or scientific nature. In regard to the party-states of the communist system, the emphasis is on a functional integration of cultural activities, basic scientific research, and the education of administrative and technological specialists. This effort, too, is pursued on the basis of formal treaties and agreements. In regard to the developing countries, the Committee promotes and oversees a wide variety of programs running from the export of doctors and medical facilities to needy countries, through jointly undertaken scientific research expeditions and projects, to the importation of students for all sorts of technical education and training in the USSR.[31]

[30] *Pravda,* June 28, 1957, p. 6.
[31] See reports in *Moscow News,* No. 81 (1957); *Pravda,* February 23, 1964; S. K. Romanovsky in *Izvestiia,* April 28, 1964 and *Sovetskaia Kultura,* December 26, 1964, for examples.

Perhaps the most important institution whose activities are coordinated by the Committee for Cultural Relations is the Union of Soviet Societies for Friendship and Cultural Relations with Foreign Countries. The Union is a reorganized version of the All-Union Society for Cultural Relations with Foreign Countries (VOKS) and in law is a nongovernmental institution allegedly inspired by popular fervor among the Soviet people. The theory which calls for Communist Party guidance of all Soviet organizations and the tradition of especially close Party attention to propaganda instruments, however, effectively nullifies the distinction, and in practice the Union works under the supervision of the Committee as well as the direct control of various Party agencies. In 1964, the Union included forty-one affiliated associations for friendship and cultural relations with various countries and groups of countries; it maintained some sort of formal cultural ties with 118 different countries.[32]

When the vast distribution of cultural, political, and technical literature by these societies is considered along with the extensive Soviet program for educating the youth of the developing countries in the USSR, the long reach of the Committee for Cultural Relations with Foreign Countries may be appreciated.

The Telegraph Agency of the Soviet Union (Tass)

Information and the channels by which it enters and departs are integral to the operating processes of any organization. On December 1, 1917, Lenin, recognizing the usefulness of an international press agency as a "window on the world," continued the Petrograd Telegraph Agency of the Tsarist regime. He even carried on the agency's legal association with the government by attaching it to the Council of People's Commissars, retaining most of the bourgeois editors until the new Soviet regime could find its own. But ideologically suspect and challenged by Bolshevik purists, the PTA was complemented with a parallel "Press Bureau," established by and attached to the All-Russian Central Executive Committee. In the spring of 1918, Lenin merged the two agencies into the Russian Telegraph Agency (ROSTA) and charged it with both news and propaganda functions. Although the training and organizing of propagandists was very shortly transferred to the Party apparatus proper, ROSTA never was divested of the responsibility for political evaluation in its releases, and it bequeathed this responsibility

---

[32] Frederick C. Barghoorn, *Soviet Foreign Propaganda* (Princeton, N.J.: Princeton University Press, 1964), pp. 245–246; *Ezhegodnik bol'shoi sovetskoi entsiklopedii,* 1960, p 17; 1962, pp. 25–26; 1964, p. 22.

to its successor agency, the Telegraph Agency of the Soviet Union (TASS) in 1925 upon the ratification of the All-Union Constitution.[33]

Pravda, the primary Party newspaper in the USSR, has developed an extensive collection staff of its own (although it prints many TASS news stories) and, to a lesser degree, so has *Izvestiia*, the government spokesman. In 1961, an "unofficial" new press agency, *Novosti*, was established by the Union of Soviet Societies for Friendship and Cultural Relations with Foreign Countries. Today, *Novosti* has assumed some of TASS's role in distributing propaganda material abroad, serving as a "feature syndicate." Nevertheless, TASS remains the most extensive Soviet news-collection and distribution service, and herein lies its importance in the Soviet foreign-policy process.

There are two primary divisions: the Editorship of Foreign Information (INOTASS) and the Editorship of Union News (RSI). INOTASS, which employs the elite personnel of the agency,[34] is divided into geographic desks, with a special bureau to translate and distribute to these desks materials from a large variety of foreign newspapers and periodicals. The desk editors also maintain direct telephone, cable, and/or radio contact with their correspondents abroad. Information is funneled upward, to be distributed in part to RSI and in part to a daily mimeographed book intended to furnish background information (and thus affect decisions) for the Ministries, Party organs, and other dependent news editors. Under Party supervision the outgoing TASS World Service then distributes stories free to news media in all countries via teletype and radio.[35]

The Committee for State Security

Let us turn now to the institutional role of foreign intelligence in Soviet foreign policy. Large quantities of sensational literature have been published in the West about the activities of the Soviet Secret Police. Much that is said there is probably true, and much that is misleading probably results from an honest effort to recount memories which are distorted by horror. All the accounts suffer from one cause of distortion: they portray a complex bureaucratic activity from the limited perspective of a single participant, frequently a victim. The Soviet Union understandably furnishes little

[33] Theodore E. Kruglak, *The Two Faces of TASS* (Minneapolis; University of Minnesota Press, 1962), pp. 16–21.

[34] Most have an education paralleling that of junior diplomatic staff, and many have in the past been transferred to the Foreign Ministry, rising even to ambassadorial posts. (Kruglak *op. cit.,* pp. 45–46; Cf. Alexander Barmine, *One Who Survived* (New York: G. P. Putnum's Sons, 1945)).

[35] Kruglak, *op. cit.,* pp. 42–50

systematic information about this triply sensitive subject: sensitive for its legacy of past horror, sensitive for its impact on the internal and external images of the Soviet state, and sensitive for its close connection with perceptions of current state security. Our picture of the Soviet foreign-policy process would not be complete without taking account of the institutions of state security, however. They must be pieced together from fragmentary information publicly accessible.

The historical evolution of these institutions sheds light on their theoretical place. In the tumultuous early weeks following the Bolshevik seizure of power, on December 20, 1917, specifically, the "Extraordinary Commission for Combating Counter-revolution, Speculation, Sabotage and Malfeasance in Office" (Cheka) was formed, on Lenin's order, as the primary means of dispensing "revolutionary justice." In theory, justice was defined by the interests of the working class, and these were defined by the leadership of the Bolshevik party, the vanguard of the working class. In theory, the infant revolution must be threatened by the bourgeois and feudal-class remnants in Russia and by every bourgeois foreign state, and the apparent confirmation of theory was abundantly manifest in the events of those early months. The hold of the Bolsheviks on the Russian state was tenuous; it seemed clear that the Cheka must be uncompromising and ruthless in protecting the new party-state against its enemies, dispensing "justice" thereby. This was the charge to the Cheka; it has remained, with little modification, the theoretical and legal rationale for the organs of the Secret Police through the subsequent evolution of the Soviet regime. In the years since Stalin, in consideration of a changed environment, the political burden of outraged human sensibilities, and a still indeterminate matrix of competing personal ambitions, a new emphasis upon the "principles of socialist legality" has moderated the freedom of action of the Secret Police. Its institutions still, however, reflect more closely than others the maxim that the end justifies the means.

We are not directly concerned here with the Secret-Police institutions for internal security of the Soviet state against its enemies. The institutions that are directly involved in the foreign-policy process are those concerned with foreign espionage. These have been a part of the Secret Police throughout its history. Despite numerous bureaucratic reorganizations, the basic pattern has remained the same. The theoretical rationale, simply embodied in law, is the same: protection of the Soviet state against its enemies. These institutions have gathered and evaluated information abroad for the use of the Soviet-government organs and the Party. There is no indication that in this work (where socialist legality is rather irrelevant) there has been any major reorientation in the years since Stalin's death. As for implementation of Soviet foreign-policy directives, the tasks of subversion and sabotage vary with geography and policy; but organization shows little change.

The Committee is composed of subdivisions of three varieties: Main Administrations distinguished by function, Service Sections, and Special Sections. The latter two may be dispensed with quickly. The Service Sections perform logistical and common technical-support functions. The Special Sections are devoted to specialized intelligence and security techniques. The First Main Administration merits our most careful attention. Commonly known as the *Foreign Directorate*, it is primarily responsible for espionage. Other Main Administrations include Counterintelligence, the Secret Political Directorate, Military Counterintelligence, the Partisan Directorate,[36] and three Guards Administrations—one for protection of government and Party leaders, one for plant and installation security in the USSR, and one for the Border Troops.[37]

The First Main Administration (Foreign Directorate) is charged with five continuing tasks: (a) collection of strategic intelligence regarding foreign countries; (b) manufacture and dissemination of long-range propaganda; (c) surveillance of Soviet citizens abroad; (d) penetration and neutralization of anti-Soviet organizations (principally *émigrés*) abroad; and (e) supervision of intelligence efforts of other Soviet intelligence organizations.

The Administration is divided into an Operations Branch, charged with collection and other field activities, and an Information Branch, charged with processing the information and publishing it as intelligence to user agencies. The Information Branch also determines information-collection requirements, which become requests to be filled by the Operations Branch and by other intelligence agencies. Both the Branches are subdivided into geographical and functional departments composed of varying numbers of case officers. In addition to these two branches, the Administration contains three additional sections for the fulfillment of its remaining tasks. One is devoted to penetration of *émigré* organizations abroad (it has sponsored the "unofficial" Committee for the Return to the Fatherland), with a view both to their destruction and to engineering redefections. Another is concerned

[36] Peter Deriabin and Frank Gibney, *The Secret World* (Garden City, New York: Doubleday & Company, Inc., 1959), p. 187, consider the Partisan Directorate a portion of the Foreign Directorate.
[37] The Border Troops totalled 270,000 men in early 1965 according to a research memorandum issued by Radio Free Europe (Munich) on Feburary 18, 1965.

with the supervision of intelligence and security organs in other party-states of the communist system. A third gives its attention to surveillance of Soviet citizens abroad. A fourth is the control agency for deep-cover intelligence operatives abroad. Last comes the *Spetsburo,* or special section for carrying out unusual tasks. It is the latter section that reportedly arranged the assassination of Trotsky in 1940.[38]

The Soviet Mission Abroad

The organizations thus far described account for the administration of Soviet foreign policy in diplomatic, military, economic, and psychological dimensions plus the acquisition of necessary information. The arm of Soviet foreign-policy administration abroad is the Soviet Mission, in which all of these functions are represented. The Soviet Mission Abroad is distinguished from most of its Western counterparts both by its size and its lack of administrative integration. We have reliable information on the Mission in Burma to provide an example.

Here, in a relatively small country to which the USSR was not devoting a particular emphasis, the Mission included over one hundred Soviet officials in 1959. Only some thirty-six of these were Foreign Ministry personnel under the direct administration of the Ambassador. The representatives of other Soviet foreign-policy agencies, reporting independently to their parent organizations in Moscow, made up the remainder. The division of labor within the Embassy proper (those nominally under the direct administration of the Ambassador) included three major parts: one concentrating upon analysis and reporting of the Burmese domestic political situation (the Internal Section), one concentrating upon the Burmese government's economic policy (the Economic Section), and one concentrating upon Burmese foreign relations and foreign policy (the External Section). Each Section was headed by a senior diplomatic staff officer with his subordinates assigned two or three specific subjects to monitor and report upon. Periodic reports were submitted to the Foreign Ministry with the purpose of providing

---

[38] Much of the organizational material above has been drawn from *Soviet Intelligence Systems,* unclassified material published by the U.S. Army Intelligence School, Fort Holabird, Maryland, November 1962. Cf. Deriabin and Gibney, *op. cit.,* Chapters 15, 27, and Appendices; *The Kremlin's Espionage and Terror Organizations,* Testimony of Petr S. Deriabin, Hearing before the Committee on Un-American Activities, House of Representatives (Washington, D.C.: Government Printing Office, 1959); E. A. Andreevich, "Structure and Functions of the Soviet Secret Police," in Simon Wolin and Robert M. Slusser, eds. *The Soviet Secret Police* (New York: Frederick A. Praeger, Inc., 1957), pp. 96–179; Vladimir and Evdokia Petrov, *Empire of Fear* (New York: Frederick A. Praeger, Inc., 1956), Chapter 18; Kaznacheev, *op. cit.*; and *Report of the Royal Commission on Espionage* (Sydney: Commonwealth of Australia, 1955).

information and, through the Ambassador, suggesting lines of action.[39]

Complementing the senior and junior staffs were a support staff of non-diplomatic personnel for clerical and service functions. Because of an extensive bifurcation of roles, owing to cover designations for four separate intelligence groups, the make-up of the mission must be considered in two ways: by its official surface constituency and by its *sub-rosa* constituency.

Officially, aside from the Foreign-Ministry personnel proper, there were: a *Trade Mission* (next largest), concerned with securing the Burmese market for Soviet products, whose chief officers, although clothed with diplomatic rank and immunity, reported directly to the Ministry of Foreign Trade in Moscow; an *Economic Mission*, concerned with the Soviet economic-assistance program and reporting to the State Committee for Foreign Economic Relations; and a *Cultural Mission*, concerned with exchanges and the guidance of the Burmese-Soviet Friendship Society, responsible to the State Committee for Cultural Relations with Foreign Countries. The *Military Attaché's office*, though officially an integral part of the Embassy, reported directly to the Ministry of Defense. Four other parts of the Soviet Mission operated autonomously in the official organization: *Soviet Film Export* (*Sovfilmeksport*) and *International Book Representatives* (*Mezhkniga*), which worked directly with the Ministry of Foreign Trade, and the *Soviet Information Bureau* and *TASS*, which worked directly with their parent agencies in Moscow. The top members of each, except the TASS correspondents, were protected by diplomatic rank.[40]

The Soviet mission as just described contains no official intelligence component distinguished from the official information gathering and reporting function charged to all the mission's elements. Intelligence personnel, however, actually included a large number of those filling the official roles described above. Apart from their official positions they were organized into four groups: Military Intelligence (GRU), Economic Intelligence, the Foreign Ministry's Tenth (Special) Administration, and Political Intelligence. The chief members of each of these groups were professional intelligence officers who spent little time in their cover roles or else used them directly for intelligence purposes and who owed no accountability to the Ambassador

[39] Kaznacheev, *op. cit.,* pp. 79–95. The reports were highly formalized and ranged from conversation and essay reports dealing with a single event, through political letters and regular monthly chronicles of events, to elaborate semiannual and annual reports which summarized and synthesized the information contained in prior reports and included the Ambassador's conclusion and suggestions.

[40] *Ibid.,* pp. 96–107.

or other official superiors. Junior members retained their primary status in the official organizations but devoted all or most of their time to intelligence functions. Finally, each group had its own technical personnel, sent abroad in the guise of technicians for the official organization. Military Intelligence, numbering five men directed by the Chief Intelligence Directorate of the Soviet General Staff in Moscow, was headed in Burma by the official Military Attaché and had both espionage and operational functions.[41] The Economic Intelligence group operated in Burma from within the Economic and Trade Missions[42] and was directed by the Committee for State Security (KGB) in Moscow. Its operational responsibility was subversion of the Burmese governmental economic offices, business circles, and foreign firms. Its espionage was designed to provide the economic information which would be the basis for long-range Soviet policy planning for this area.

The "Tenth Department" group in Burma numbered eight and operated under direction from the parent organization in the Foreign Ministry in Moscow, which itself is dually subordinate to the Ministry and to the KGB. In Burma, it was charged with the technical security of the Embassy's work, surveillance of all Embassy personnel on the job and in their living quarters, and occasional operational intelligence missions as requested by the Ambassador.[43]

The Political Intelligence group in Burma was the largest (eleven members) and most authoritative. It was directed and staffed by the Political Intelligence Service (of the Foreign Section) of the KGB and was primarily an operational agency. Its primary objective was penetration and subversion of the local political regime through active participation in the domestic party struggle. Analysis and gathering of information was secondary. The chief of the group, who held the rank of colonel in the KGB, operated under the cover of First Secretary and later Counselor of the Embassy. The Cultural Mission, Sovfilmeksport, the Soviet Information Bureau, and TASS all provided cover roles for Political Intelligence agents and their operations.[44]

The diversity of organizational roles exhibits the Soviet penchant for double-checking not only outside information, but also the behavior of Soviet representatives themselves. It further demonstrates the complicated fusion of overt and covert methods in both the gathering of information for, and the implementation of, Soviet foreign-policy decisions. It is clear that

[41] Primarily subverting the Burmese army: *Ibid.,* pp. 180–181.

[42] More in the Economic Mission than in the Trade Mission. The latter appeared to Kaznacheev to have more regular business in trade matters, p. 183.

[43] *Ibid.,* pp. 179–187.

[44] *Ibid.,* pp. 188–202.

none of the policy decisions themselves are made in the mission. These emanate from Moscow, from the government parent organizations, or, probably in most cases, from the Party leadership.

Party organizations exist within the missions themselves,[45] of course, but seldom function there as transmission belts for policy directives. Including Party and Komsomol members from the variety of organizational matrices described above, they could not conceivably be compatible with both the diplomatic and intelligence hierarchies. Thus, they have become agencies for occupying off-duty time and endeavoring to raise the morale, reliability, and political alertness of the entire Soviet colony, all of whom belong to one or the other group (90 per cent Party members in Burma) and all of whom have been investigated and cleared for overseas assignment by their respective Departments of Cadres.

Some account should be taken of the context in which the Soviet Mission Abroad has been described here. The circumstances both of time and place undoubtedly mean that some of the specifics are applicable only to Burma, a developing country in Southeast Asia, in 1959. It is to be expected that different environments would reveal different organizational emphases. The general structure, however, is representative.

The Soviet Mission to the United Nations

The Soviet Union is represented in the United Nations by three delegations, since Belorussia and the Ukraine have qualified for full membership as a product of negotiations at the end of World War II. Stalin had contended that each Union Republic should be represented, and the constitutional reorganization to give the Union Republics some legal authority to participate in the international system (February 1, 1944, *supra*) was undertaken largely with this end in view. In practice, the legal prerogatives of the Union Republics are carefully circumscribed, and custom has completely subordinated their "Foreign Ministries" to Moscow's will.[46] There are no instances on the record that show the slightest deviation by the Ukraine or Belorussia in the debates and votes of any United Nations organs.

The extensive Soviet representation in the United Nations was headed in the mid-1960's by Ambassador Nikolai Fedorenko as Permanent

[45] Kaznacheev reports that in Burma the mission Party group was known as the *Trade Union Organization* and the Komosmol as the *Physical Culture Organization*. Both held frequent obligatory meetings and sponsored study groups. *Ibid.,* p. 55.

[46] Foreign Ministries have been identified in most of the Union Republics; Mikhail Menshikov returned from serving as Soviet Ambassador to the U.S. in 1960 to become Minister of Foreign Affairs for the RSFSR.

Representative in both the General Assembly and Security Council. Besides Ministers from Belorussia and the Ukraine, he was supported by a Deputy Permanent Representative of ministerial rank and ten Counselors distributed among the major UN organs. In Geneva, the USSR maintains a permanent delegation headed by a Minister and five Counselors, and it has recently sought a larger quota of personnel for the UN Secretariat. The USSR is represented in the International Court of Justice and a wide variety of UN commissions and affiliated international organizations, including UNESCO, the International Labor Organization, the Economic Commissions for Europe and the Far East, and the International Atomic Energy Agency.[47] It refuses to participate in those in which it judges "the influence of the major imperialist agencies is particularly pronounced (for example, the International Bank for Reconstruction and Development, the International Monetary Fund, etc.)."[48]

Consideration of Soviet Missions brings to an end our examination of the state institutions for Soviet foreign-policy decision-making. Later, we shall endeavor to relate them to one another in the context of various types of decision situation. Meanwhile, we turn to another group of institutions, whose functions constitute an essential complement to those of the Soviet state agencies: the various organs of the Communist Party of the Soviet Union.

B. PARTY INITIATIVE AND CONTROL

Throughout our discussion of state institutions in the Soviet foreign-policy process, we have returned repeatedly to the observation that in theory, law, and practice—all three—each of these institutions must defer to and seek the guiding initiative of the Communist Party of the Soviet Union.

In theory this obligation follows directly and indisputably from acceptance of the most fundamental doctrines of Marxism-Leninism. These contain an exclusive explanation of the process of history—material, dialectical, inevitable—and they present an exclusive epistemological instrument, allegedly scientific, by which the observed world may be analyzed and the observer thus enabled to conform consciously to the historical demands of the system of which he is a part. The members of the CPSU are by definition the custodians and enlightened implementors of the policies entailed by scientific application of Marxism-Leninism to the current epoch. As such, they are

[47] See Kozhevnikov, *op. cit.,* pp. 348–361.
[48] *Ibid.,* pp. 348–349.

the vanguard of the people. They can purport to say with scientific authority what the objective interests of the people are in any context at any time. and they cannot authoritatively be contradicted. The central organs of the Party, embodying its collective wisdom, must therefore be regarded officially as the guiding institutions for the country and the key to objectively correct policy decisions, both foreign and domestic.

In Soviet law, the distinction between the state organs and the Party is carefully emphasized. The Party is held to be a voluntary, militant union of like-minded people. The state embraces the whole population; it subordinates all citizens to the will of organs of state power which represent the interests of the people as a whole. The Party is the leading core of all public organizations and carries out its decisions through them; but it must not, in law, supplant them. Rather, the source of Party authority must be the confidence of the people, won as a result of correct policies and persuasion.[49]

The basic legal formulation of this relationship is to be found in the Constitution, Article 126, which states in part that "the most active and politically-conscious citizens in the ranks of the working class, working peasants and working intelligentsia voluntarily unite in the Communist Party of the Soviet Union, which is the vanguard of the working people in their struggle to build communist society and is the leading core of all organizations of the working people, both public and state."[50]

In 1961, a Soviet treatise reports, 828,000 Party members were also members of state soviets at all levels. They made up 45.4 per cent of the soviets' total membership.[51] At the XXIInd Party Congress in October, 1961, Party membership was reported at a total of 9,716,005 (8,872,516 full members, 843,489 candidates), or about 4 per cent of a total Soviet population in the vicinity of 215 million, and about 7 per cent of the potentially eligible adult population. By the time of the XXIIIrd Congress in April, 1966, there were a total of 12,471,079 (11,673,676 full members and 797,403 candidates) in a population of about 230 million, still below 6 per cent. The disproportionate size of the Party groups within the organs of state power when compared to the Party group in the total Soviet population is clearly evident here. Precise data for Party membership among the officials of state administrative organs are unavailable. However, biographical compilations indicate a

---

[49] Denisov and Kirichenko *op. cit.*, pp. 142–144; V. A. Karpinsky, *The Social and State Structure of the USSR* (Moscow: Gosizdat, 1950), pp. 123–124; A. I. Luk'ianov and B. M. Lazarev, *Sovetskoe gosudarstvo i obshchestv'ennye organizatsii,* 2nd ed. (Moscow: Gosizdat Iuridicheskoi Literatury, 1961), p. 215.

[50] See also the *Rules of the Communist Party of the Soviet Union* (1961), Preamble.

[51] Luk'ianov and Lazarev, *loc. cit.*

probable fraction far in excess of the 45.4 per cent in the soviets. Among agencies directly involved in foreign affairs, the authors have yet to find an individually identified official who is not either a member of the Komsomol or Party. At the XXIIIrd Party Congress in April of 1966, the late Minister Malinovsky proudly announced that the proportion of Communists and Komsomol members among Soviet military officers was approximately 93 per cent and that among all Armed-Forces personnel the figure was over 80 per cent.[52] Such domination of state offices by Party and Komsomol members is not surprising in light of the close control the Party exercises over the educational institutions through which aspirants must progress in order to attain the ranks of the state bureaucracy (see Chapter III).

The legal and theoretical relationship of Party and state organs and the fact that there exists a high concentration of Party members in state offices are nothing new in the Soviet system. They are validated by tradition that shows no prospect of decline. They account not only for effective arrogation of policy *initiative* to the top Party organs, but also for close Party control over the instruments of policy *implementation*.

Let us turn now to the composition of these top Party organs and their involvement in the foreign-policy process.

The All-Union Party Congress

"The supreme organ of the CPSU is the Party Congress." So begins Article 31 of the Party Rules as adopted at the XXIInd Party Congress in October of 1961. Convened at least once every four years by call of its Central Committee, the Congress:

(A) hears and approves the reports of the Central Committee, of the Central Auditing Commission, and of the other central organizations;
(B) reviews, amends and endorses the Program and the Rules of the Party;
(C) determines the line of the Party in matters of home and foreign policy, and examines and decides the most important questions of communist construction;
(D) elects the Central Committee and the Central Auditing Commission.[53]

The Party Congress is thus formally empowered as the supreme institution for exercising Party guidance over the foreign policy of the USSR. Historically, the Congress has seldom performed this function. Even in the early

[52] *Pravda,* April 3, 1966.
[53] *Rules of the Communist Party of the Soviet Union* (1961), Article 33.

years of the Soviet regime the Congress devoted most of its time to domestic concerns, and more unanimity was displayed on foreign policy than on any of the other items considered. The early Congresses, smaller in size and called more frequently than under Stalin or even since his death, took a more active part in discussion of foreign policy. Never arenas for the formulation of policy, they did provide advice and varying degrees of ratification for specific policies.

On occasion they were called upon, in effect, to arbitrate disagreements among the members of the Central Committee and its leadership. But after 1930 Stalin only called three Congresses over the remaining twenty-three years of his life. Those that were called were larger and less suitable to real debate. The number of subjects on the agenda diminished; debate became ritual praise. The Congress overall became merely an additional prop of Stalin's propaganda, an infrequently used sounding board, and an instrument for ceremonial legitimation of the record of action. Like the Supreme Soviet, it listened politely, applauded vigorously, and approved unanimously.

Since Stalin's death, the statutory requirement of one Congress every four years has been approximated (the XXIst in 1959 was an Extraordinary Congress and the XXIIIrd, in 1966, was about five months overdue), but the Congress has not by any means become an organ for policy formulation. Until 1961, membership remained stabilized at the level of the last Congress of Stalin's life; then, for the XXIInd and XXIIIrd, attendance was nearly quadrupled (see Table II-1).

Table II-1   Recent Congresses of the CPSU

Congress	Year	Duration	Voting Delegates	Nonvoting Delegates	Approximate Ratio Delegates/ Membership
XIX	1952	10 days	1,192	167	1/5000
XX	1956	11 days	1,349	81	1/5000
XXI (Extra)	1959	9 days	1,269	106	1/6000
XXII	1961	14 days	4,394	405	1/2000
XXIII	1966	11 days	4,620	323	1/2400

The increase in size is indicative of a changed role. The Congress remains a sounding board for the leadership and an instrument for the ritual legitimation of the leadership's past action. But additionally it is a transmission belt between the formulators and implementors of policy—a communications device for elaboration and clarification of leadership demands in both direct and esoteric language. The Congress is carefully orchestrated to leave a record which may be studied thereafter as a guide to action by Communists at home and abroad.[54]

The Congress is also a gigantic rally. Aside from domestic Party officials from every level,[55] the delegates of eighty-six fraternal Communist and Workers' Parties and a few other sympathetic groups were prominent at the XXIIIrd Congress. Most of these got a chance to be associated with a special speech of greeting and dedication. The involvement was nourishment for continuing effort and sacrifice and enthusiasm among Communists throughout the world after the Congress closed.

The Central Committee

One action required of the Party Congress is ratification of the Party Central Committee. Lenin once said, "Not one important political or organizational question is decided by any one State institution in our republic without guiding instructions from the Central Committee of the Party."[56]

In practice the Central Committee does not take the initiative in formulating the instructions that it passes on to various state organs. It is called upon to discuss and confirm general policy directions proposed by its own leadership. Required by the Party Rules to meet in plenary session not less than once every six months, the Central Committee is much closer to daily decisions than the Congress and may in practice modify before the fact the programmatic elements of Party (hence national) foreign policy. It is a manageable group for deliberation and is mostly composed of individuals whose full-time jobs give them power to make their will felt in the Soviet system—the elite who administer the agencies of both Party and state. From its ranks will come the successors to the present Party Politburo and Secretariat.

While its formal authority, like that of the Party Congress, is greater than

[54] The stenographic record of the XXIInd Congress was quickly published in a large edition. Its phraseology is quoted copiously with and without attribution by every Soviet author; a new edition of the basic ideological manual was prepared to include Congress materials.

[55] The Congress delegates are elected at Oblast Party Conferences in the RSFSR, Belorussia, and the Ukraine and at Republic Party Congresses in each of the other twelve Union Republics. All party members are eligible to be elected. The number depends on the size of the constituency party and is based on a delegate/membership ratio established by the Central Committee when the Congress is announced. The slate of nominees in each constituency is, in practice, carefully prepared in advance by the Oblast or Republic leadership, probably with the advice and consent of Moscow. The Oblast Conference or Republic Congress merely ratifies the slate. *National Policy Machinery in the Soviet Union,* p. 10.

[56] V. I. Lenin, *Sochineniia,* 3rd ed. (Leningrad: Gosizdat, 1935–1937), XXV, 192.

what it customarily has exercised, the Central Committee can not be dismissed as performing only legitimating functions. The Party Rules (1961) stipulate:

> Between congresses the CC CPSU directs the activities of the Party, the local Party bodies, selects and appoints leading functionaries, directs the work of central government bodies and social organizations of working people through the Party groups in them, sets up various Party organs, institutions and enterprises and directs their activities, appoints the editors of the central newspapers and journals operating under its control, and distributes the funds of the Party budget and controls its execution.
>
> The Central Committee represents the CPSU in its relations with other parties.
>
> The CC CPSU shall keep the Party organizations regularly informed of its work.
>
>   *   *   *   *   *   *   *   *   *   *   *
>
> The CC CPSU elects a Presidium to direct the work of the CC between plenary meetings and a Secretariat to direct current work, chiefly the selection of personnel and the verification of the fulfillment of Party decisions, and sets up a Bureau of the CC CPSU for the Russian Soviet Federated Socialist Republic (RSFSR).
>
> The CC CPSU organizes the Party Control Committee of the CC.[57]

The size of the Central Committee is set by the Party Congress which elects it. This determines in part the role it may play in the foreign-policy process. With increasing size, the likelihood of initiative diminishes and consensus is achieved by an increasing generalization of decisions and by firmer leadership. Since the VIth Congress met on the eve of the Bolshevik Revolution in August, 1917, the Central Committee has been increased from 22 members to 360 members and candidates. Today the 360 often meet jointly with the 79-member Central Auditing Commission and customarily invite the participation of additional technical or administrative specialists.

Stalin first took the initiative in enlarging the Central Committee, probably as a part of his effort to dilute any authority which might challenge his personal freedom of action. Later, after he had consolidated his personal

---

[57] *Rules of the Communist Party of the Soviet Union* (1961), Articles 35–40. In 1966 at the XXIIIrd Congress these Rules were amended to change *Presidium* to *Politburo*, to delete the Bureau for the RSFSR, and to distinguish the election of a General Secretary from election of the Secretariat as a whole. *Pravda*, April 9, 1966.

dictatorship, Stalin "hardly ever" called CC meetings.[58] Since Stalin's death the Central Committee has grown still further, probably in response to a leadership desire to accentuate the advisory and ratifying role while avoiding an institutional challenge to its prerogative for initiative. Its growth is also a recognition of the increased dimensions of the Soviet bureaucratic task and apparatus. But while the growth trend has continued, the post-Stalin leadership has seen to it that the Central Committee has met as required, thus increasing the extent of its involvement in the policy process.

Table II-2 Recent Plenums of the Central Committee, CPSU

DATE CONVENED	DURATION	AGENDA
January 10, 1961	9 days	Soviet agriculture; XXIInd Congress
June 19, 1961	1 day	XXIInd Congress
October 14, 1961	1 day	XXIInd Congress
March 5, 1962	5 days	Soviet agriculture
April 22–23(?), 1962	1 day	Formation of new Supreme Soviet and government personnel changes in Party organs
November 19, 1962	5 days	Party leadership in industry, construction, agriculture; Party organization; Party personnel changes
June 18, 1963	4 days	Sino-Soviet relations; Artistic expression in USSR
December 9, 1963	5 days	Expansion of chemical industry to increase farm yields
February 10, 1964	5 days	Soviet agriculture; Sino-Soviet rift
October 14, 1964	1 day	Dismissal of Khrushchev
November 16, 1964	1 day	Personnel and structural changes in Party organs
March 24, 1965	3 days	Soviet agriculture; Personnel changes in Party organs
September 27, 1965	3 days	Planning, management, incentives in Soviet industry; XXIIIrd Congress
December 6, 1965	1 day	Economic Plan and Budget for 1966
February 19, 1965	1 day	New Five-Year Plan for USSR
December 12, 1966	2 days	Sino-Soviet relations; 1967 National Economic Plan and Budget

[58] Khrushchev made this report during his famous "secret" address to the XXth Congress, February 20, 1956. He added:

"It should be sufficient to mention that during all the years of the Patriotic War not a single Central Committee Plenum took place. . . . Stalin did not even want to meet and talk with Central Committee members. . . .

"Of the 139 members and candidates of the Party's Central Committee who were elected at the Seventeenth Congress [in 1934], ninety-eight persons, i.e., seventy percent, were arrested and shot (mostly in 1937–38)."
Crimes of the Stalin Era (New York: The New Leader, 1956), pp. 19–20.

Under General Secretary Leonid Brezhnev, as throughout the Khrushchev decade, Central Committee plenums usually have avoided direct consideration of questions of foreign policy (see Table II–2). Their most apparent impact on foreign policy has been indirect, through confirmation of personnel who would make foreign-policy decisions in both the Party and government. Brezhnev's report on Sino-Soviet relations to the December, 1966 Plenum was a departure from custom which emphasized the importance of the subject matter.

Although the autocratic tradition, well established by Stalin and nurtured also by Marxist-Leninist decision-theory, has operated to preclude initiative or independence for the Central Committee, several incidents during the Khrushchev decade may have set precedent for more influential Central Committee participation in the formulation of policy in the future. In 1955, Molotov's disagreement with Khrushchev over policy toward Yugoslavia was brought to the Central Committee for discussion (Molotov's stand was condemned).[59] In 1957, when a majority of the Party Presidium voted to oust Khrushchev from his post as First Secretary, Khrushchev successfully appealed to the Central Committee to overrule its nominally subordinate organ.[60] Finally, in 1964, Khrushchev was deposed only after an apparently unanimous Presidium (less Khrushchev of course) was sustained by a non-unanimous Central Committee plenum following lengthy debate.[61] These events showed Central Committee influence both upon policy and policy-makers. The Committee's statutory position in relation to its Presidium and Secretariat sustains what is now a minor but potentially more significant influence over both.

The Politburo of the CC CPSU

The Central Committee, after its election at the Party Congress, meets to elect some of its own members to four nominally subordinate organs, two of which, the Politburo and Secretariat, are of utmost importance in the foreign-policy process.

The Politburo (so renamed in 1966 after fourteen years as the Presidium) is clearly the paramount collegial organ for the formulation of Soviet foreign

[59] Robert Conquest, *Power and Policy in the U.S.S.R.* (New York: The Macmillan Company, 1961), pp. 264–266. See particularly the footnote on p. 266, drawing on information provided by Mr. Seweryn Bialer. Cf. Wolfgang Leonhard, *The Kremlin Since Stalin* (New York: Frederick A. Praeger, Inc., 1962), pp. 100–109.

[60] Roger Pethybridge, *A Key to the Soviet System* (New York: Frederick A. Praeger, Inc., 1962), *passim*. Cf. Leonhard, *op. cit.*, pp. 243–248 and Conquest, *op. cit.*, pp. 309–321.

[61] *The New York Times,* October 17, 1964 and *Manchester Guardian,* October 19, 1964. Cf. *Pravda,* October 16, 1964.

policy. In the Party Rules, it is charged merely with directing the work of the Central Committee between plenary meetings. It is legally accountable to the Central Committee, but there is no further statutory regulation of its activity.[62] In practice, the Politburo meets regularly about once a week to consider and decide all major issues of public policy, foreign and domestic. It publishes decrees in the name of the Central Committee which are absolutely binding on all other Party organizations and all Party members. In cases for which government organs will be the direct executors of the decisions, they are often couched as joint decrees of the Central Committee and the Council of Ministers. This form, however, is incidental to their authority.

The composition of the Politburo has been irregular, and as much of its procedure as we can infer with confidence has been the product of historical prescription and the insistent logic of the task. Stalin's Politburo (Presidium) in 1952 was inflated to include twenty-five full and eleven candidate (nonvoting) members. Immediately after Stalin's death, the organ was reduced to ten full and four candidate members. In the subsequent years of Khrushchev's challenge, consolidation, and control, the membership was stabilized at about twelve full members and four candidates. At the XXIIIrd Party Congress in April of 1966, eleven full members and eight candidates were elected.

At the height of his control, Stalin apparently liked to divide the Politburo into specialized subgroups and to meet with each subgroup independently, thereby forestalling the possibility of a personal challenge to his own authoritarian control. Only he coordinated the various subgroups. In the Khrushchev years, the Politburo (Presidium) regularly met in bloc, but the volume and variety of policymaking that had to be discharged understandably required continuation of some division of responsibility. A little later we shall examine the nature of this division more closely. For now we may observe that influence in the foreign-policy process may be directly correlated with a Politburo member's personal and official spheres of competence.

The Politburo customarily includes men whose personal influence is based in full-time offices of the state organs, as well as men whose influence is based in full-time Party offices. The Chairman of the Council of Ministers, the Chairman of the Presidium of the Supreme Soviet, and the General Secretary of the Party are all members by prescriptive custom. Usually economic planning, construction, and management are represented by Party leaders who hold full-time offices in these state agencies. Regional and Republic Party organizations are accorded a voice, and it has become customary to

[62] A personnel renewal principle applies now to the Politburo as to all Party organs. Three consecutive terms are the normal limit. However, the XXIIIrd Congress amended this rule to make renewal only a guiding principle and not a binding and inflexible directive.

recognize the major nationalities among the candidate members if they are not already represented. Thus, several elite hierarchies are drawn together in the Politburo membership, with top Party rank their common denominator and Party doctrines their rationale for claiming legitimate authority.

Rarely have the professional foreign service or the professional military been represented directly on the Politburo. Since the 1953 downfall of Beria, representatives from the Secret Police have been absent. The chief administrative officers of these three hierarchies are customarily brought in as technical advisers and briefing officers for the Politburo rather than being included in its deliberations.[63]

We thus see the Politburo as an institution at the focus of all the major information networks in the Soviet system. This fact alone would be strong evidence of its primacy in the process of policy formulation, even if we did not have the historical record and the theoretical justification. All the perceptor agencies, whose reports of the international and national environment are collected and filtered and synthesized in their respective Party or state bureaucracies, funnel information in the direction of the Politburo. Only in the Politburo is there access to all of the information relevant to foreign-policy decisions, subject only to temporal and personal limitations of its members.

DICTATORSHIP

Nominally the Politburo is subordinate and accountable to the Central Committee. In practice this has rarely been the case. The crucial factor in determining the limitations, if any, upon the Politburo's sovereignty is its unanimity. History has shown that where the Politburo members were agreed on policy and policymakers, no other organ could challenge it. The Central Committee has been able to exercise a decisive influence over it only when Politburo unity has given way to deep antagonism over proposed policy or personal ambitions. In those cases the Central Committee's weight has supported one or another of the contending factions within the Politburo; it

[63] For detailed surveys of the evolution of the Politburo membership, see Merle Fainsod, *How Russia is Ruled,* rev. ed. (Cambridge, Mass.: Harvard University Press, 1963); Leonard Schapiro, *The Communist Party of the Soviet Union* (London: Eyre and Spottiswoode, 1960); Conquest, *op. cit.*; Leonhard, *op. cit.*; George K. Schueller, *The Politburo* (Stanford: Stanford University Press, 1951). Khrushchev's "Secret Speech" at the XXth Party Congress (See *Crimes of the Stalin Era, op. cit.*) and his subsequent random remarks are our best guide to current Politburo process. See also *National Policy Machinery in the Soviet Union,* pp. 18–22, and Sidney I. Ploss, "Recent Alignments in the Soviet Elite" (Center of International Studies, Princeton University, Occasional Papers on Soviet Politics, No. 6, March 16, 1964), pp. 6, 23.

has never displayed independent initiative. In 1918, Lenin successfully appealed to a divided Central Committee for approval of the Brest-Litovsk capitulation, threatening to resign from the Sovnarkom and the Central Committee if not supported. We have already mentioned Khrushchev's successful appeal to the Central Committee against Molotov's objections to reconciliation with Tito in 1955 and his successful 1957 appeal to the Central Committee when a majority of the Politburo (Presidium) sought to depose him as First Secretary. In these cases the Politburo had forfeited sovereignty by failing to achieve internal agreement.

The crucial need for unity has been conducive historically to dictatorship within the Politburo. Agreement on both personnel and policy may be achieved by coercion, volition, or some combination of the two. The principle of collegiality demands emphasis on volition, but personal ambitions and the clash of strong wills have fostered recourse to coercion. Democratic centralism and the official stature of Marxism-Leninism as an objective science (entailing uniquely correct policies at any one time) have been used as justifications for coercion. Just as they have sustained the practice of Central Committee domination of the Party Congress and Politburo domination of the Central Committee in spite of statutory provisions to the contrary, Politburo members have sustained domination of the Politburo itself by a dictator—the ultimate in centralization.

Although there is no dispute about Lenin's primacy in the formulation of Soviet policy, foreign and domestic, the evidence indicates that, in power, he relied less upon coercion than upon the cooperation granted him within the Party as its brilliant organizer and successful leader. The sentiment among his colleagues, even in times of policy disagreement, that Lenin was indispensable, allowed him to prevail by recourse to the threat that if not supported he would resign.[64]

Stalin, however, did not enjoy Lenin's intellectual domination of the Party or Lenin's reservoir of voluntary authority, and he faced greater personal and policy challenges. He chose therefore to rely more upon coercion and less upon volition. Successful, he eventually neutralized Politburo influence almost as much as Central Committee influence. A former Soviet diplomat who attended several Politburo meetings in 1933 testifies to Stalin's dictatorship:

A thin appearance of collective work is still kept up at Politburo meetings. Stalin does not "command," he merely "suggests" or "proposes." The

---

[64] Robert C. Tucker, "Autocrats and Oligarchs" in Ivo J. Lederer, ed., *Russian Foreign Policy* (New Haven: Yale University Press, 1962), p. 180.

fiction of voting is retained. But the vote never fails to uphold his "suggestions." The decision is signed by all ten members of the Politburo, with Stalin's signature among the rest. Yet everyone knows that there is only one boss. The phrases used, the forms of address, follow the traditional Party terminology; but behind them all Comrade Stalin's word is law. . . . Stalin not only is generally called "the Boss" by the whole bureaucracy, but *is* the one and only boss.[65]

This judgment is corroborated by Stalin's successor himself. Khrushchev in his "secret speech" at the XXth Party Congress said:

After the war . . . Stalin became even more capricious, irritable, and brutal; in particular his suspicion grew. His persecution mania reached unbelievable dimensions. . . . Everything was decided by him alone without any consideration for anyone or anything. . . .
Sessions of the Political Bureau occurred only occasionally. . . . Many decisions were taken by one person or in a roundabout way, without collective discussion. . . .
The importance of the Political Bureau was reduced and its work disorganized by the creation within the Political Bureau of various commissions. . . . The result of this was that some members of the Political Bureau were in this way kept away from participation in reaching the most important state matters.[66]

During the years of Khrushchev's consolidation and control, when great public emphasis was placed upon the need for collegiality and the "cult of the personality" was damned as wanton distortion of Marxist-Leninist principles, it was clear that procedures within the Politburo (Presidium) changed. Nevertheless there were multiple indications that Khrushchev himself was the paramount formulator of Soviet foreign policy, more than *primus inter pares* in the collegial Politburo. The apparent contradictions raise the question of where and what limitations restricted Khrushchev's freedom to make Soviet foreign policy. To what extent could he be regarded as the dictator *over* the Politburo?

In support of Khrushchev's great personal role we note his near monopoly as spokesman for Soviet foreign policy, his disparagement of his top state officials and use of them as props for effect,[67] his frequent reliance upon

[65] Barmine, *op. cit.*, p. 213.

[66] *Crimes of the Stalin Era*, pp. 46, 61–2.

[67] E.g., Khrushchev's often cited treatment of Foreign Minister and Central Committee member Andrei Gromyko in the presence of Averell Harriman and his use of Defense Minister and Central Committee Member Rodion Malinovsky at the abortive 1960 Paris summit conference.

personal diplomacy, and his willingness to make long extemporaneous statements on complex international issues. We note further his personal arrogation of offices and his reliance on few advisors in time of international crisis.[68] Finally, we note that the logic of circumstance demands more centralization of foreign-policy formulation than of domestic policy. Response to unforeseen events and foreign initiatives, where time is of essence, requires abrupt resolution of issues and undercuts collegiality.

On the other hand, both the narrowly unsuccessful effort to unseat Khrushchev in 1957 and the successful effort in 1964 showed that if he could not command voluntary allegiance and his opposition could remain united in the determination to replace him, Khrushchev's vast power could be shorn away with startling ease and a minimum of organizational disruption. Policy success and the ability to divide both personal and policy opposition seem to have been the supports of his power. Once these were lost and allegiance fell away the structural advantages of his position were inadequate to preserve him. The power of a dictator in today's USSR appears to be informally available to the man who can concert the law and theory of the system with success in attaining the system's goals. Unsustained formally, failure to utilize the power of dictator successfully may lead to its evaporation. Neither Brezhnev nor Kosygin has clearly arrogated or sought the role of dictator over the Politburo, although few would deny Brezhnev's advantage if a struggle between them should develop. Apparent agreement on vital questions has enabled "collective leadership" to survive. Deep disagreement could still necessitate another recourse to the dictator.

The Secretariat of the CC CPSU

The Party Rules state only that the CC CPSU elects a Secretariat "to direct current work, chiefly the selection of personnel and the verification of the fulfillment of Party decisions. . . ." Since 1922, when Stalin utilized the post of General Secretary (previously considered chiefly a clerical chore) to begin his drive for domination of the entire Party and state apparatus,

---

[68] Khrushchev occupied the posts of First Secretary, Chairman of the Bureau for the RSFSR, and Chairman of the Council of Ministers in addition to his Presidium membership between 1958 and his fall in October, 1964. At the height of the Cuban missile crisis in 1962, Khrushchev reportedly met repeatedly with Mikoyan, Kosygin, Suslov, Brezhnev, and Kozlov, failing to call in the entire Presidium (*Staffing Procedures and Problems in the Soviet Union,* p. 25). On the relationship of Khrushchev to his leadership colleagues, see Carl A. Linden, *Khrushchev and the Soviet Leadership, 1957–1964* (Baltimore: Johns Hopkins Press, 1966).

the Secretariat has been the second most influential institution for Soviet decision-making. Its foreign-policy importance lies first in its control over the appointment and dismissal of personnel who make substantive decisions, second in its responsibility for the formulation of issues and alternatives which will constitute the agenda for Politburo sessions, and third in its responsibility for the elaboration, execution, and audit of Party decisions already taken by the Politburo.

Today, the Party Secretaries (eleven since the XXIIIrd Congress) administer a sizable central bureaucratic apparatus which controls all the paid Party officials in the USSR (probably between 200,000 and 250,000 individuals). A functional parallel may be found between the Secretaries of the Central Committee and the Presidium of the Council of Ministers. Although the former administer a numerically smaller bureaucracy, their reach is no less ubiquitous in Soviet society and abroad, and their authority is greater than that of their state counterparts both in theory and practice.

The post of General Secretary has, since the struggle for power after Lenin's death, been the key to achieving the position of dictator. It affords its occupants what thus far has been an insuperable advantage over any competitor: constant communication with subordinate officials and control over appointment, promotion, and demotion of the Secretaries of all Party organizations. Statutorily, subordinate secretaries and bureaus are elected by their respective Party Conferences or Congresses, subject to confirmation by the next higher Party organization. In practice this amounts to nomination by the higher secretariat and approval by the Conference or Congress. The resultant descending chain of command extends to the composition of subordinate central committees and the CC CPSU, for the slates of candidates are prepared for Conference or Congress approval by the respective secretariats. By exercising this means of control, the General Secretary is thus not only able to ensure that full-time Party organizations at all levels are favorable to him and dependent on his pleasure, but he may also be able to pack the Central Committee with men he can count upon.

In theory, Party Secretaries, unless they concurrently sit on the Politburo, are providers of information and advice and the executors of Politburo directives. In practice, aside from the influence over policy decisions derived from these prescribed activities, additional obligation for policy initiative is inescapable. Soviet decision theory inherently tends to centralize initiative at the highest level. But efficiency demands that discretion be applied to avoid an unmanageable overburden for the Politburo. The inevitable consequence of this situation is skeletal guidance from the Politburo, to be filled in for routine decisions by the administrative discretion of individual Secretaries and their subordinates, with only unusual cases or cases of conflict taken back to the Politburo. We can only conjecture from logical extrapolation of fragmentary information what criteria for competence at various levels exist.[69] It is clear, however, that Marxist-Leninist theory supports a much greater prerogative for initiative in the lower echelons of the Party hierarchy than in the state hierarchy.

The Central Apparatus of the CC CPSU

The staff agencies immediately responsible to the Secretariat are usually referred to as the *Central Apparatus*. The latest of a long succession of structural revisions (following Khrushchev's dismissal) consolidated a number of functionally related departments of the Central Apparatus. Khrushchev had divided the organs concerned with industrial progress in the USSR from those responsible for agriculture. Here we shall confine our attention to those agencies in the new Central Apparatus which are closely associated with Soviet foreign policy: the Commission for Party Organizational Questions, the Agitprop Department, the International Department, the Department for Liaison with Communist and Workers' Parties of the Socialist Countries, the Department for Travel Abroad, and the Chief Political Directorate of the Soviet Army and Navy.

The Commission for Party Organizational Questions, the Department for Travel Abroad, and the Chief Political Directorate are all concerned with staffing other agencies and enter the foreign-policy process only as they screen and select the individuals who themselves will participate directly in the decision process. The Commission, headed by Party Secretary I. V. Kapitonov, has primary responsibility for the assignment of personnel in both Party and government offices, including the other departments of the Central Apparatus. Thus it acts as a selective filter through which all personnel who will administer Soviet foreign policy must pass. It maintains personnel records of the Party; it also exercises a supervisory control over the central, interregional, and Republic Party schools, which prepare personnel for responsible Party, government, and trade-union assignment (see Chapter III). It is likely that personnel selection for government agencies is not initiated by the Commission in the normal course of its operations. It controls the pool of candidates by virtue of controlling admission to prerequisite educational institutions,

---

[69] See Leonhard, *op. cit.*, pp. 3–5, 9; Cf. Conquest, *op. cit.*, pp. 159–163.

and it must pass on the Party acceptability of the proposed appointees.[70]

The final agency of the Central Apparatus concerned with personnel related to foreign policy is the Chief Political Directorate of Soviet Army and Navy. We have mentioned this agency earlier in its alter ego as a Main Administration in the Ministry of Defense. Charged with political education and the maintenance of political reliability in the armed forces, the Department is obliged to coordinate its activity with the Minister of Defense, but its chief (in the mid-1960's former Ambassador A. A. Yepishev) owes primary responsibility to the Party Secretariat.[71]

The foreign departments of the Central Apparatus may be compared functionally with the Foreign Ministry under the Council of Ministers. Indeed under Stalin there was a single department that dominated the information gathering, planning, and execution of Soviet foreign policy, leaving the Foreign Ministry severely limited in scope. While the Department's formal concern was the relationship among Communist Parties and the development of the world communist movement—not state relations between the Soviet Union and foreign governments—the distinction was a fine one and generally ignored in practice. Party guidance for the Foreign Ministry justified any amount of Apparatus intervention in state diplomacy. The Department had been a guiding force behind the Comintern. With the latter's formal dissolution in 1943, its Moscow leadership was absorbed into the foreign department of the Apparatus.[72]

After World War II, the proliferation of party-states produced a new type of international relationship for the Soviet Union, and the Foreign Department became the chief agency for its conduct. This relationship between the Soviet party-state and the other party-states of the communist system became the province of the Department for Liaison with Communist and Workers' Parties of the Socialist Countries, under the supervision of Party Secretary Andropov (until mid-1967 when Andropov moved to the chairmanship of

[70] *Staffing Procedures and Problems in the Soviet Union,* pp. 13–14; *Problemi e Realta dell' U.R.S.S.* (Rome, 1958), extracts in Conquest, *op. cit.,* Appendix VIII, pp. 464–465. See also John Armstrong, *The Soviet Bureaucratic Elite* (New York: Frederick A. Praeger, Inc., 1959), p. 3, Chapters II–III; David T. Cattell, "Formulation of Foreign Policy in the U.S.S.R." in Phillip W. Buck and Martin W. Travis, eds., *The Control of Foreign Policy in Modern Nations* (New York: W. W. Norton & Company, Inc., 1957), p. 674. Louis Nemzer, "The Kremlin's Professional Staff: The 'Apparatus' of the Central Committee of the Communist Party of the Soviet Union," *American Political Science Review,* XLIV, No. 1 (March, 1950), 64–85.

[71] See Boris Kuban, "Politics in the Soviet Air Force," in Asher Lee, ed., *The Soviet Air and Rocket Forces* (New York: Frederick A. Praeger, Inc., 1959), pp. 201–15.

[72] David J. Dallin, *Soviet Foreign Policy After Stalin* (Philadelphia: J. B. Lippincott Company, 1961), p. 43.

the KGB). In these relations the Foreign Ministry still remains of secondary importance.

The International Department today, under Party Secretary Ponomarev, is responsible for CPSU relations with the Communist and Workers' Parties of non-party-states and currently places its emphasis on the developing countries of Asia, Africa, and Latin America, cooperating closely with but not supplanting the Foreign Ministry in these areas.

Both foreign departments are subdivided geographically and include among their activities the gathering of intelligence through agents' contact with native Communists and sympathizers abroad, the organization of bilateral and multilateral exchanges of delegations and conferences, and the transmission and execution of policy decisions of the Secretariat and Politburo with regard to foreign parties. Reliable data on the size of these departments is unavailable, but according to a U.S. government estimate in 1960, there were then between 100 and 150 officials employed in each of the Central Apparatus departments.[73]

Finally, in considering the agencies of the Central Apparatus engaged in the Soviet foreign-policy process, we must give our attention briefly to the Department of Agitation and Propaganda (Agitprop). "Agitation and Propaganda" includes the media and content of mass communications, education, literature, and art. In all of these areas Agitprop is responsible for carrying out Politburo directives. Bearing directly on foreign policy are the Party control of educational materials and curricula for institutions training future foreign-policy decision-makers (see Chapter III) and the control of content and dissemination of domestic propaganda on foreign affairs and Soviet foreign propaganda. Both *Pravda*, the CPSU CC official daily spokesman, and *Kommunist*, the CC's chief theoretical journal, have the status of Sections under Agitprop.

The chief editors of many other Soviet publications, including for example, *Izvestiia, Komsomolskaia Pravda,* and *Problems of Peace and Socialism* (the Prague-based organ of the Communist system) are collegium members.

Aside from their activity as disseminators of Soviet propaganda under direction of the Secretariat and Politburo of the Party, the mass-communications organs act as channels for acquisition of information. We have already examined TASS as such a vehicle. The extensive network of correspondents maintained abroad by *Pravda* serves as an overlapping function, and the Party personnel of all mass media are expected to report continuously on popular attitudes as they encounter them.

[73] *National Policy Machinery in the Soviet Union,* p. 24.

The supervision of Agitprop over Soviet foreign-propaganda instruments projects into every Soviet agency maintaining contact with countries abroad. The Commission is the central instrument for transmission of Politburo directives concerning agitation and propaganda practice. Aside from press and publishing agencies, the state radio and the vast array of "unofficial" associations for education, science, culture, and patriotic activity look directly or indirectly to Agitprop for instructions.

At this point we have completed a sort of physiological description of the institutions of Soviet foreign policymaking. What is equally important for an understanding of role structure as an influence in the foreign-policy process is the operating relationships among them. We turn to that subject more explicitly in the following section.

C. RELATIONSHIPS AMONG THE INSTITUTIONS OF SOVIET FOREIGN POLICY

Drawing upon organization and decision theory, we may identify a number of analytically distinct functional requisites for national foreign-policy decision-making. We make the assumption, which we believe to be sound, that a self-maintaining system must preserve a synoptically rational decision process. This is not to deny that individual decisions may fail to meet, or even intentionally approach, standards of synoptic rationality. Nor is it to deny the existence of a variety of institutionalized short cuts in the decision process, e.g., the cognitive and effective premises afforded by doctrine, to be considered in Chapter IV. It is, however, to reason that a system whose maintenance depends upon rational decisions must *customarily* operate according to the synoptic model.

Making this assumption, the following functional requisites must be provided for:

1. *Information selection and collection:* it is necessary to decide what sort of informational premises will be relevant to foreign-policy decisions and to collect and communicate information perceived to meet these selection criteria.
2. *Formulation of purpose:* this function must be performed successively within the bounds set by the prescription of higher authority, along a continuum from a pole of few or no "givens" to almost complete higher prescription of purpose.
3. *Information interpretation:* it is necessary to analyze and evaluate the technical significance of new information which has been collected as relevant to foreign-policy decisions.

4. *Formulation of alternatives and advice on their relative desirability:* possible choices of courses of action to achieve purposes must be formulated and compared for advantages and disadvantages.
5. *Selection or innovation of a course of action:* a commitment must be made binding the state to expend its resources on a particular course of action.
6. *Elaboration, explanation, interpretation of the selected course of action:* the implications of the commitment must be decided and clarified for the multiplicity of agents which will implement the commitment.
7. *Reiteration, confirmation, ratification of the selected course of action:* both the selected course of action and the selector must be approved explicitly in order to maintain organizational support for the commitment.
8. *Dissemination and implementation of the selected course of action:* the course of action as understood and supported at each subordinate level of the apparatus must be specified for each unique operational context in which it is perceived to be relevant and the appropriate verbal or physical action must be carried out.

There are three gross chronological phases of the decision process defined by these eight functions: first, the establishment of the setting for the commitment to particular course of action—functions 1 through 4 above; second, the commitment—function 5; and the third, the carrying out of the commitment—functions 6 through 8.

Table II-3   Chronological Phases of Foreign-Policy—Decision Process

TIME	PHASE I	PHASE II	PHASE III
	(1) (3) (4) (2)	(5)	(6) (8) (7)

Drawing upon the descriptions of Soviet institutions above, we find the following correlations of institution and primary function in the foreign policy decision process prescribed by Soviet theory, law and practice:

1. *Information selection and collection:*
   All Diplomatic Missions Abroad
   Foreign Ministry Departments and Administrations
   Sections of the Central Party Apparatus Departments
   KGB, Foreign Directorate Agents (Covert)
   GRU (Overt: Attachés; and Covert: Agents)
   Special Delegations and offices abroad of State Committees for Foreign Economic Relations and Cultural Relations
   INOTASS correspondents and geographic desks

2. *Formulation of purpose:*
   Politburo leadership (minimum circumscription)
   Politburo of the CC, CPSU
   Secretariat of the CC, CPSU
   Presidium of the Council of Ministers (maximum circumscription)
3. *Information interpretation:*
   Foreign Ministry Departments and Administrations
   Departments of the Central Apparatus of the CC, CPSU
   KGB, Foreign Directorate
   Collegia of the Ministries of Foreign Affairs, Foreign Trade, Defense
4. *Formulation of alternatives and advice on their relative desirability:*
   Secretariat of CC and individual Secretaries
   Department Heads of Central Party Apparatus
   Ministers of Foreign Affairs, Defense, Foreign Trade
   State Committee Chairmen
   Presidium of Council of Ministers
   Members of the Politburo of the CC, CPSU
5. *Selection or innovation of a course of action:*
   Politburo leadership
   Politburo of the CC, CPSU
6. *Elaboration, explanation, interpretation of the selected course of action:*
   Members of Politburo of the CC, CPSU
   Secretaries of the CC and Department Heads of the Central Apparatus
   Members of the Presidium of the Council of Ministers
   Ministers of Defense, Foreign Affairs, Foreign Trade
   Chairmen of state committees
   Chief propaganda agencies (*Pravda*, TASS)
7. *Reiteration, confirmation, ratification of the selected course of action:*
   Central Committee, CPSU
   Members of Politburo of CC, CPSU
   Secretaries of the CC, CPSU
   All subordinate supervisory levels of Party and government
8. *Dissemination and implementation of the selected course of action:*
   Missions Abroad
   KGB Agents
   GRU Military Intelligence Agents
   Operational units of Armed Forces
   Sections of Central Party Apparatus Departments

It is apparent that not every input which prompts an output from the Soviet foreign-policy apparatus progresses the same chronological course (or decision trajectory). The same institutions do not participate in the same way or to the same extent in every decision sequence as it goes through the three chronological phases described above. Bureaucratic rationalization (necessary to the maintenance of the system) must assure that some criteria of importance are established, disseminated, and applied in order to ensure that issues of perceived great importance and intricacy receive the attention and priority they warrant and that issues of lesser importance and less intricacy are dispatched at the lowest level of authority competent to resolve them rationally. In operation the authority relationships are arranged in two closely related hierarchies organizationally distinct below the Party Politburo. Figure II–1 portrays the relationship.

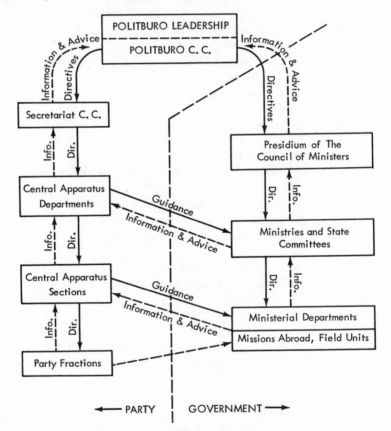

FIGURE II–1   Institutionalized Authority Relationships

Juxtaposing the hierarchy of authority of the Soviet foreign-affairs institutions with the chronological order of the ideal-type decision process, we produce a field in which we can graphically represent a typology of rational foreign-affairs decision trajectories. In response to perceptions of the relative gravity of decision consequences, the trajectory will arc higher or lower through the institutional hierarchy. In response to perceptions of the relative pressure of time, Phases I–III may be drawn out or compressed.

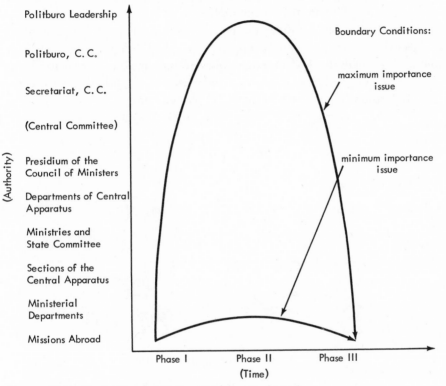

FIGURE II–2   Soviet Foreign Policy Decision Trajectories

In the latter part of Chapter IV we shall return to the process of Soviet foreign-policy decision-making again at this point. First we think it necessary, however, to turn to two other considerations without which further development of the rational model of Soviet foreign policy-making might become misleading. These two considerations are the *individual personalities* which enter the role structure thus far described and the *attitudes* which these men inject into the decision-making process.

While our discussion so far has been based upon what we feel to be the sound assumption that a self-maintaining, decision-making apparatus must incorporate a high order of synoptic rationality in its customary processes, the assumption of such rationality must be qualified to make way for real men and real attitudes. As we noted in the introduction, rationality is relative, and it must be analyzed in the frame of reference possessed by the decision-makers.

Thus we turn now, in Chapter III, to the men who make Soviet foreign policy, to investigate the predictable impact of personal background and group membership on the foreign-policy decision process. Thereafter, in Chapter IV, we shall consider the place of the belief system in relation to "objective" conditions of environment. We shall bring Chapter IV and our assessment of the Soviet foreign-policy decision-making process to a close with some consideration of doctrine and events as conditioners of foreign-policy decisions in the field we have established here.

THE MEN WHO MAKE
SOVIET FOREIGN POLICY

In Chapter II we described the legal and theoretical structure of Soviet foreign policymaking and the operational relationships of the decision process. Now we turn to the men themselves, the human individuals who perform in the roles of Soviet foreign-policy decision-making.

There is a thesis about Soviet politics as a whole which has aptly been described as *kto-kgo* (who-whom): Who is influencing whom, who is deferring to whom, who is an accomplice of whom, who is trying to eliminate whom? It reflects a conviction that personalities are all-important in the USSR, that Soviet policy, both foreign and domestic, can properly be regarded as the by-product of perceived expediency in the interpersonal maneuvering among the elite for positions of personal power and advantage.

Robert Conquest in his study of Soviet "dynastics" characterized the Soviet elite as follows:

> The assertion that the struggle for power is a permanent feature of Soviet politics is in itself a general theory of their nature. . . .
> In fact this [struggle] *is* Soviet political life, the real arena in which disputes on policy such as must inevitably arise in any political system are solved. All the rest is simply either the echo of what is decided at the top, or else social pressure which can find political expression only at the focus of the power struggle.[1]

No reasonable man can doubt that personality and personal aspirations have played a great part in shaping the course of the Soviet Union both domestically and as a part of the international system. This is even acknowledged readily by Soviet leaders when they revere Lenin for his perceptive recognition of the correct course in a particular historical epoch and when they condemn Stalin for his personal corruption in perverting the sacred mission of the Party.

---

[1] Robert Conquest, *Power and Policy in the Soviet Union* (New York: The Macmillan Company, 1961), pp. 11–12.

But a danger lies in the temptation to exclude the other plausible factors while interpreting Soviet policy as the product of personal wills in conflict over personal goals. Let us, therefore, look closely at the men in the Soviet foreign-policy elite and try to gather some knowledge that will sustain a judgment of their place relative to institutional structure and doctrine and events in making Soviet foreign-policy behavior what it is.

Who are the men who make Soviet foreign policy? We have previously identified their offices—the elite foreign-affairs roles—in conjunction with the investigation of institutions and role relationships in Chapter II. Very little about their private lives is available for any but the most prominent Soviet leaders.[2] However, the courses of public careers are well documented and can collectively be correlated with role analysis to reveal some interesting patterns.[3] Below the top echelons of the policymaking hierarchy we can examine the recruitment and training processes that condition today's bureaucratic subordinates and tomorrow's leaders.

A. FOREIGN-POLICY ELITES

There are a number of popular propositions about the men who make Soviet foreign policy which the biographical data at our disposal tends to

[2] Even for the most prominent leaders, reliable information is extremely scarce and narratives must be reconstructed from scattered fragments. In the books in English concentrating on Khrushchev, very little of his personal and family data could be gleaned. Victor Alexandrov, *Khrushchev of the Ukraine* (New York: Philosophical Library, Inc., 1957); Edward Crankshaw, *Khrushchev: A Career* (New York: The Viking Press, Inc., 1966); Konrad Kellen, *Khrushchev, A Political Portrait* (New York: Frederick A. Praeger, Inc., 1961); G. Paloczi-Horvath, *Khrushchev: The Road to Power* (London: Martin Secker and Warburg, Ltd., 1960); Lazar Pistrak, *The Grand Tactician* (New York: Frederick A. Praeger, Inc., 1961); and Myron Rush, *The Rise of Khrushchev* (Washington, D. C.: Public Affairs Press, 1958).

[3] Official biographies which imply credit and blame for public service are subject to rewriting with changes in a leader's public stature. These are always selective and must be recognized as such. See for example the pamphlet *Nikita Sergeevich Khrushchev, on the Occasion of His Visit to the United States* (N.Y.: International Arts and Sciences Press, 1959). The vital statistics and record of offices held, however, are usually available because, to some extent, the authority of Soviet leaders depends on their visibility. Our most useful sources have been Heinrich E. Schulz and Stephen S. Taylor, eds., *Who's Who in the U.S.S.R., 1965–66*, rev. ed. (N.Y.: Scarecrow Press, 1966); Wladimir S. Merzalow, ed., *Biographic Directory of the U.S.S.R.* (N.Y.: Scarecrow Press, 1958); Hans Koch, ed., *5000 Sowjetköpfe* (Cologne: Deutsche Industrieverlags, 1959); *Bolshaia Sovetskaia entsiklopediia*, 2nd ed. (Moscow, Gosudarstvennoe Nauchnoe Izdatelstvo, 1954–1958); *Ezhegodnik bol'shoi Sovetskoi entsiklopedii* (Moscow, 1957–1966); A. A. Gromyko *et al.*, eds., *Diplomaticheskii slovar'*, rev. ed. (Moscow: Gosizdat. Politicheskoi Literatury, 1960–1964). The first two of these were compiled from the resources of the Institute for Study of the U.S.S.R. in Munich. Unless otherwise indicated, data used in this section are drawn from a cross-checking of all these sources.

illuminate. The first of these propositions is that the men who make Soviet foreign policy are all "Party career" men and that the state and government apparatus is merely a shadow organizational hierarchy whose members have their real influence on Soviet international behavior, if any, in their alter-ego capacities of Party officials. We cannot simply reject this proposition, nor can we totally confirm it. But what we can say is that a fusion of roles in a single individual is increasingly rare. We find it only at the very top level, that is, in the Politburo leadership and at three points in the lower echelons of authority: among propaganda specialists, diplomatic representatives in the communist party-states, and the foreign-intelligence control apparatus.

Since the ouster of Nikita Khrushchev, the "interlocking directorate" of Soviet decision-making reflected in the Politburo has become less interlocked. The list of members emerging from the XXIIIrd Party Congress in April, 1966 shows the Politburo rather as a collegium of men representing distinct constituencies, whose collective authority is legitimated by common Party rank. Party penetration of all non-Party bureaucracies continues. But a reverse penetration of high Party organs by individuals of primarily technical competence and little or no professional Party job experience is an increasingly common phenomenon.

The prime institutional authority of the Party is theoretically unquestioned, and, as we discussed in Chapter II, the critical decision function of policy innovation remains uniquely in the Politburo. In the case of most other roles which impact directly on foreign relations, there also remains an indirect effect of Party status upon government function, but there is no fusion of roles. In the case of state relationships with the "imperialist camp" and most of the "third world," the personnel of the Foreign Ministry stand on their own feet, perform a usually decisive function in the policy process, and definitely do not constitute a shadow organization. Likewise, the Ministry of Defense and the government agencies concerned with foreign economic relations contribute substantially and independently in the foreign-policy process. The indirect effect consists in the stature within the Party which role players in these government agencies possess. The greater that stature, e.g., incidence of Central Committee membership, the more likelihood that the agency participates in the policy process at levels of goal formulation or elaboration rather than in merely providing information and implementing decisions.

Some notable remaining instances of Party-government role fusion deserve enumeration. As will be made clear in the following section, the training of propaganda personnel has always been and continues to be a Party responsibility in the USSR. The theory by which the CPSU guides as a vanguard

Table III-1 The Politburo of the Communist Party (April, 1966)
(alphabetical order)

Name	Other Major Party Positions	Major Government Positions
a. MEMBERS (11)		
BREZHNEV, Leonid I. (6/57)*	General Secretary, Central Committee of CPSU	Chairman, Constitutional Commission; Member Presidium of USSR Supreme Soviet
KIRILENKO, Andrei P. (4/62)	Member, CPSU Secretariat	Member, Presidium of RSFSR Supreme Soviet
KOSYGIN, Aleksei N. (5/60)		Chairman, USSR Council of Ministers
MAZUROV, Kirill T. (3/65)		First Deputy Chairman, USSR Council of Ministers
PELSHE, Arvid Ye. (4/66)	Chairman, CC-CPSU Party Control Committee	
PODGORNY, Nikolai V. (5/60)		Chairman, Presidium of USSR Supreme Soviet
POLYANSKY, Dmitriy S. (5/60)		First Deputy Chairman, USSR Council of Ministers
SHELEPIN, Aleksandr N. (11/64)	Member, CC-CPSU Secretariat	
SHELEST, Petr E. (11/64)	First Secretary, Ukrainian CP	
SUSLOV, Mikhail A. (7/55)	Member, CPSU Secretariat	Chairman, Foreign Affairs Commission, Council of the Union, USSR Supreme Soviet
VORONOV, Gennadiy I. (10/61)		Chairman, RSFSR Council of Ministers
b. CANDIDATE MEMBERS (8)		
DEMICHEV, Petr N. (11/64)	Member, CC-CPSU Secretariat	Member, Presidium of USSR Supreme Soviet
GRISHIN, Viktor V. (1/61)		Chairman, Presidium of All-Union Central Council of Trade Unions
KUNAYEV, Dinmukhamed A. (4/66)	First Secretary, Kazahk CP	
MASHEROV, Petr M. (4/66)	First Secretary, Bellorussian CP	
MZHAVANADZE, Vasiliy P. (6/57)	First Secretary, Georgian CP	
RASHIDOV, Sharaf F. (10/61)	First Secretary, Uzbek CP	
SHCHERBITSKY, Vladimir V. (12/65)		Chairman, Ukrainian SSR Council of Ministers
USTINOV, Dmitriy F. (3/65)	Member, CC-CPSU Secretariat	

* Date in parenthesis represents date on which individual assumed this position.

and the appreciation of communications media as the primary means of such guidance suffice together to eliminate in the mind of the Soviet leadership any serious need to differentiate Party and non-Party journalism and other mass-media activity. Here more even than in the Party Politburo fusion exists. The career patterns of Soviet editors, public-information officers and cultural-affairs officers bear evidence to this integration, and their impact on foreign affairs is important.

Similarly, there is a fusion of Party and government roles in the personnel assigned to diplomatic representation in other Communist party-states. That this should be so is readily understandable. In many of the party-states of the communist system, there is not yet a socialist state apparatus which is more than a shadow of the Party. Thus, it is really a representation to a fraternal party and not another state that the Ambassador within the system performs. As *state* relations develop within the communist system (and there is evidence of their gradual emergence and their cultivation by Moscow), we may expect this pattern to change, to find the Soviet Foreign Ministry's career diplomats as Ambassadors. Such a trend would, incidentally, be good evidence that state and Party apparati in the party-states were becoming dichotomous.

The fusion of foreign-intelligence agencies of the Party and government is the final example of role integration. Again this fusion is not surprising. So long as the perceived threat from abroad is a threat to the Communist Party rather than a threat to the national existence of USSR, and the "imperialists" are at pains to thus define their opposition, it is reasonable to suppose foreign espionage will be a Party-dominated function. Additionally, the availability of indigenous assistance abroad for *communism* is not matched by potential assistance for the USSR as a national entity. Recruitment therefore benefits from continued fusion of foreign intelligence.[4]

On the other hand, the independent significance of most of the Foreign Ministry and diplomatic personnel and of the economic establishment are attested by the lack of Party activism to be found among them. In the all-important relations with the "imperialist camp," the discourse is being carried on primarily by men in the Foreign Ministry who have been trained in and have largely accepted the existing structure of the Western nation-state system. The CPSU relies upon them for this function. In a real sense we may say that it is the nature of the adversary that has determined the independent

[4] Aleksandr Kaznacheev, *Inside a Soviet Embassy* (Philadelphia: J. B. Lippincott Company, 1962), pp. 179–218.

life of the Foreign Ministry and the various other agencies of the government involved in foreign affairs. It has been impossible for the CPSU to deal with the United States as a Communist Party abroad; yet, it must deal with the United States. The Foreign Ministry under Khrushchev took on a stature of increased importance because the fundamental foreign-policy line which Khrushchev was forced by circumstances to adopt was the *state* policy of coexistence. So long as Khrushchev *qua* Party leader insisted that there could be no *ideological* coexistence, and Khrushchev *qua* government leader insisted there must be indefinite *state* coexistence, relative independence of the foreign-affairs agencies of the government and the non-Party, foreign-affairs decision-makers were assured. The years since 1964 have brought no change.

The semantic shift in designation of the Armed Forces from "Red Army" to "Armed Forces of the Soviet Union" reflected a similar independence from Party for the personnel of the Ministry of Defence. When the official mission of this force changed from the propagation of communism abroad to state defense of the borders of the USSR, it became inevitable that the Armed Forces and their leading cadres were no longer only agents of the Party but had assumed a position quite independent of, and in some cases antagonistic to, Party goals. As in the case of the Foreign Ministry, the career lines of the Soviet military elite confirm this independence. They are military professional first, Party members secondarily.

To summarize, at the top echelon of the Soviet foreign-policy, decision-making apparatus—leadership in the Party Politburo—Party and government roles are frequently fused in the persons who dominate the formulation of broad goals and the selection of specific courses of action for important international engagements. At the subordinate but highly influential echelons of foreign-policy decision-making in which information is gathered and interpreted and alternatives formulated and in which less-important engagements are prosecuted, fusion of roles is the exception. The personnel of the Foreign Ministry, the economic agencies, and the military who operate at this level perform influentially in their respective government roles and not in their Party alter-ego capacities. At these levels, Party membership is primarily a clearance for occupancy and performance in important non-Party roles.

A second and closely related popular proposition about the men who make foreign policy for the Soviet Union is that whether identified in Party roles or government roles, their background will show a common experience of recruitment, training, and job experience—there is just one mold for Soviet foreign-affairs officials. This we find is most misleading—more and more role differentiation and more and more differentiation in experience and training is evident. In the Party Politburo, the top foreign-affairs roles, we find today three distinctive career patterns represented: the Party "line officer" who has achieved his status in domestic Party administration and, projected into the top decision-making echelon, necessarily assumes direct responsibility for foreign-policy decisions; secondly, the Party "staff officer" whose specialization in foreign affairs has carried him up via the Party Central Apparatus and Secretariat to a seat in the Politburo, where he continues to be responsible for his field of technical competence and experience; thirdly, the production specialist, successful in managing the Soviet economy and coopted into Party ranks at a relatively high level. Leonid Brezhnev typifies the first category; Mikhail Suslov the second; Aleksei Kosygin epitomizes the third.

Table III-2 indicates the educational background of men who have been members or alternates in the Politburo since the XXIInd Party Congress. Almost all have experienced some higher education, and in most cases that higher education has been in a field of engineering, directly and practically associated with the building of the new Soviet economy. Few of these men, and even fewer of the incumbents, have built their careers primarily upon revolutionary dedication.

In the government foreign-affairs agencies we find that the men in top positions are in most cases career government professionals. Examination of the Foreign Ministry, down through the heads of Administrations, shows that over two-thirds of these men, including Foreign Minister Andrei Gromyko, have spent their entire careers in non-Party roles.

The exceptions to this pattern are mostly accounted for by the fusions of role discussed above in regard to propaganda personnel, diplomats in the party-states, and foreign-intelligence personnel. Because the distinction between Party and government function itself breaks down in these areas, the substitutability of personnel is not surprising. One other exception, the use of government roles as a "dumping ground" for Party officials fallen from Party favor is discussed later. It should be noted particularly that Party rank, such as membership in the Central Committee, is definitely not evidence that a man is primarily a Party career professional. The career patterns of Foreign Ministry personnel show that such a badge of status is frequently a recognition of long and meritorious state service.

A third general proposition about the men who make Soviet foreign policy, which is confirmed by our data, is that among the elite of both Party and government those who are directly concerned with foreign affairs have a greater familiarity with domestic problems than those directly concerned with domestic affairs have with foreign-policy problems. The staff specialists

Table III-2   Politburo of the Central Committee, CPSU : Education

*BREZHNEV†	Graduated from Kursk Technicum for Land Utilization and Reclamation (1927); graduated Dneprodzerzhinsk Metallurgical Institute as Metallurgical Engineer (1935).
*DEMICHEV	Graduated Moscow Chemical-Technical Institute (1944).
*GRISHAN†	Graduated Moscow Technicum of Railroad Economy (1937).
KHRUSHCHEV†	Studied in Workers Faculty, Donets Industrial Institute, Stalino (Donetsk) (1922–1925); studied in Stalin Industrial Academy (1929–1931).
*KIRILENKO	Graduated professional-technical school (Voronezh?); graduated Rybinsk Aviation Institute (1936).
*KOSYGIN†	Graduated Leningrad Cooperative Technicum (1924); graduated Leningrad Textile Institute (1935).
KOSLOV	Studied in Workers Faculty, Leningrad Mining Institute (1928); graduated Leningrad Polytechnical Institute (1936).
*KUNAYEV	Graduated Moscow Institute of Non-Ferrous Metallurgy (1936).
KUUSINEN†	Graduated Historical and Philological Faculty, Helsinki University (1905).
*MASHEROV	Graduated Vitebsk Pedagogical Institute (1939).
*MAZUROV	Graduated Gomel Highway Technicum (1933); graduated Higher Party School, CC, CPSU (1947).
MIKOYAN†	Graduated Armenian Theological Seminary, Tiflis (1915).
*MZHAVANADZE	Graduated Goergian Military School (1927); graduated Lenin Military-Political Academy, Leningrad (1937).
*PELSHE	Graduated Moscow Institute of Red Professors (1931).
*PODGORNY†	Graduated Workers Faculty (Kiev?) (1927); graduated Kiev Polytechnical Institute of Food Industries (1931).
*POLYANSKY	Graduated Kharkov Agricultural Institute (1939); graduated Higher Party School, CC, CPSU (1942).
*RASHIDOV	Graduated Dzhiak Pedagogical Technicum (1936); graduated Philological Faculty, Uzbekistan University, Samarkand (1941).
*SHCHERBITSKY	Graduated Dnepropetrovsk Chemical-Technical Institute (1941).
*SHELEST	Graduated Mariupol Evening Metallurgical Institute (1935).
*SHELEPIN†	Studied at Moscow Institute of History, Philosophy and Literature (1936–1939).
SHVERNIK	Completed four-year city elementary school, St. Petersburg (1900).
*SUSLOV†	Graduated Workers Faculty, Moscow (1924); graduated Moscow Institute of National Economy (1928); studied and taught in Moscow Economic Institute of Red Professors.
*USTINOV†	Graduated professional-technical school (1927); graduated Leningrad Military-Mechanical Institute (1934).
*VORONOV	Studied in Tomsk Industrial Institute (1931); studied in Novosibirsk Institute of Marxism-Leninism (1936).

* Indicates incumbents, June, 1967.

† Indicates a major foreign-affairs orientation. Incumbents with a major foreign-affairs orientation are underlined.

in the Party have generally entered foreign affairs after early experience in domestic Party work, often of a "line" nature. And the Party "line officers" who have acceded to the top foreign-affairs positions have spent most of their careers concerned primarily with domestic work. Only the career diplomatic personnel and military leadership show a lack of career familiarity with domestic problems. On the other hand, of the top elite concerned

Table III-3 Members and Alternates of the Politburo, Central Committee, CPSU, since 1962
Career Patterns

(1) Never has held a full-time, non-Party position.
(2) Achieved high elite status in Party; has held important non-Party positions subsequently.
(3) Began career in Party work; career accelerated through non-Party positions.
(4) Began career in non-Party work; career accelerated through Party positions.
(5) Achieved high elite status in non-Party work; has held important Party positions subsequently.

NAME	(1)	(2)	(3)	(4)	(5)
BREZHNEV				*	
*DEMICHEV		*			
*GRISHIN†			*		
KHRUSHCHEV†		*			
*KIRILENKO				*	
*KOSYGIN†				*	
KOZLOV	*				
*KUNZYEV				*	
KUUSINEN†	*				
*MASHEROV	*				
*MAZUROV		*			
MIKOYAN†		*			
*MZHAVANADZE				*	
*PELSHE	*				
*PODGORNY†				*	
*POLYANSKY		*			
*RASHIDOV			*		
*SHCHERBITSKY		*			
*SHELEPIN†			*		
*SHELEST					*
*SUSLOV†	*				
SHVERNIK		*			
*USTINOV†					*
*VORONOV			*		

* Indicates incumbents, June, 1967.
† Indicates a major foreign-affairs orientation. Incumbents with a major foreign-affairs orientation are underlined.

Table III-4 Representation of Various Groups of Soviet Society in the CPSU Central Committees and Central Auditing Commissions Elected by the XXth, XXIInd and XXIIIrd Congresses*

	XXTH CONGRESS	XXIIND CONGRESS	XXIIIRD CONGRESS
Central Party Apparatus	24 = 7.5% ⎫ 44.6%	45 = 11.4% ⎫ 45.1%	44 = 10.0% ⎫ 41.2%
Regional Party Apparatus	118 = 37.1% ⎭	133 = 33.7% ⎭	137 = 31.2% ⎭
Central Government Bureaucracy	58 = 18.2% ⎫ 28.3%	48 = 12.2% ⎫ 24.9%	72 = 16.4% ⎫ 26.4%
Regional Government Bureaucracy (including industrial managers)	32 = 10.1% ⎭	50 = 12.7% ⎭	44 = 10.0% ⎭
Armed Forces	21 = 6.6%	34 = 8.6%	35 = 8.0%
Ministry of Foreign Affairs	17 = 5.3%	20 = 5.1%	22 = 5.0%
KGB, MVD, Justice	4 = 1.3%	4 = 1.0%	4 = 0.9%
Supreme Soviet Apparatus	17 = 5.3%	18 = 4.6%	24 = 5.5%
Trade Unions (including Cooperatives)	6 = 1.9%	10 = 2.5%	11 = 2.5%
Komsomol	3 = 0.9%	3 = 0.8%	3 = 0.7%
Scientists, Academicians, and so on	3 = 0.9%	7 = 1.8%	7 = 1.6%
Writers, Artists and Public Figures	7 = 2.2%	10 = 2.5%	9 = 2.1%
Leading Workers, Farmers and so on	5 = 1.6%	13 = 3.3%	19 = 4.3%
Unidentified	3 = 0.9%	—	8 = 1.8%
TOTAL	318 = 100%	395 = 100%	439 = 100%

* Analysis by Christian Duevel, "The Central Committee and Central Auditing Commission Elected by the XXIIIrd CPSU Congress," Radio Liberty Research Paper, No. 6 (1966).

only peripherally with foreign affairs, few if any have extensive career experience with foreign affairs.

One impact of this situation would seem to be insulation of a very small foreign-affairs elite with a correspondingly high degree of personal influence. The career background of the majority of the Soviet elite shows a lack of experience with, and, hence, we may presume a lack of technical competence for dealing with, the details of Soviet *foreign* policy.

A further related proposition confirmed by our investigations is that the Party Central Committee and Central Auditing Commission are essentially domestically oriented. In our consideration of structure and role relationships, we posited for these agencies a limited arbitral and veto function and thus a normally passive power of restraint upon its "leading cadres." Only about 70 of the 439 members and candidates hold foreign-affairs associated positions. It is a reasonable conclusion, therefore, that the already limited power of veto possessed by the Central Committee is even less of a restraint upon the foreign-affairs elite among the "leading cadres" than upon those concerned with domestic matters. This is a further indication of the insulation of the small foreign-affairs elite from external restraints and points to the consequently greater opportunity for personal influence among this select group.

Table III-5 Probable Foreign-Affairs Responsibilities, June 1967

Politburo	
Brezhnev, Leonid I.	General responsibility; CPSU relations abroad
Grishin, Victor V.	Trade Union relations abroad
Kosygin, Aleksei N.	General responsibility; Soviet State relations abroad
Podgorny, Nikolai V.	Soviet State relations with nonsocialist countries
Shelepin, Aleksandr N.	Soviet relations with Asian States
Suslov, Mikhail A.	World Communist movement
Ustinov, Dimitry F.	Soviet defense economics
Secretariat	
Andropov, Yuri V.	CPSU relations with Communist and Workers' Parties of socialist countries
Ponomarev, Boris N.	CPSU relations with Communist and Workers' Parties of nonsocialist countries
Council of Ministers	
Grechko, Andrei A.	Minister of Defense
Gromyko, Andrei A.	Minister of Foreign Affairs
Lesechko, Mikhail	Chairman, Commission of Pres. C.M. for CMEA
Patolichev, Nikolai S.	Minister of Foreign Trade
Semichastny, Vladimir Ye.	Chairman, Committee for State Security (KGB)

Both the third and fourth propositions here testify to the predominance of domestic political experience and orientation among the Soviet decision-making elite. Foreign policy, it should be stressed, is institutionalized as a relatively secondary and dependent part of the overall Soviet decision process. From the point of view of traditional Marxist internationalism, this is paradoxical indeed. But it is true. The proportion of foreign-affairs experience in the uppermost elite emphasizes the dependent relationship. Table III-5 identifies the leading foreign-affairs responsibilities in mid-1967 as well as we can reconstruct them from individual assignments and activities.

The Soviet Diplomats

Soviet diplomats play a crucial role among the selectors of information relevant to formulating and administering Soviet foreign policy. They likewise play a crucial role among agents for implementing Soviet policy abroad. They thus constitute an essential link between Soviet policy formulation and the external environment. Though supplemented and corroborated institutionally by additional channels of information gathering and agencies of policy implementation, Soviet diplomatic personnel are central to important functions of the decision process. Let us therefore look briefly at the composition of the Soviet diplomatic elite.

As we have mentioned earlier, most of the Foreign Ministry staff and representatives abroad who deal with the Western nonsocialist countries are career diplomats. In contrast, personnel dealing with the socialist countries are predominantly Party career men coopted into diplomatic service. Diplomatic professionals outnumber Party men in the "third world," but there, a third career pattern is also recognizable. That is the technological specialist, trained for example in agronomy, industrial engineering, or economic planning rather than as a Party professional or in conventional diplomatic skills.

In the case of Ambassadors to the large Western capitals, seniority in the diplomatic service (usually at least twenty-years service) is the rule, and this background is frequently complemented by the badge of Central Committee or Central Auditing Commission rank in the Party. At home these men may expect assignment as Deputy Foreign Ministers or Heads of Geographic Administrations and may receive collegium status.

The ambassadorial posts seem to carry rather indefinite tenure. Career men, who spend about 60 per cent of their service abroad and the rest in geographically analogous positions of the Ministry, shift assignments on an average of about every $2\frac{1}{2}$ years until they reach ambassadorial rank. Thereafter, reassignment becomes less frequent.

Since the educational qualifications for entry into the diplomatic service are high and the training program arduous (see the following section), a professional diplomatic career usually begins in a man's late twenties. The most competent apprentices emerge into ambassadorial positions some twenty to twenty-five years later. Of the ambassadorial corps as constituted in 1966–1967 (sixty-two careers available), only three had served with the Ministry before 1938. Most (thirty-eight) had entered the service just before or after World War II. The remaining twenty-one began their service after 1946. Of the latter, most fell into the category of Party career men posted in the socialist states; a few were technological specialists coopted for service in the "third world."

Perhaps the most notable feature of the careers of Foreign Ministry personnel concerned with the Western nonsocialist countries is the prevailing absence of Party activism. Membership is apparently universal, although no record of Party association is noted in official biographical sketches unless the individual has achieved the status of Central Committee or Central Auditing Commission membership. The latter distinctions are common at the collegium level. In special cases they reflect personal rank, but usually they are closely matched to seniority within that bureaucratic hierarchy.

Geographical-area specialization is the most common differentiation of technical competence among the diplomatic elite, but a functional specialization (e.g., economics, public information, international law) is not uncommon.

An interesting and difficult question is the extent of horizontal recruitment between the foreign departments of the CPSU Central Apparatus and the Foreign Ministry. One Deputy Foreign Minister, A. L. Orlov, shows such Party work interspersed with Ministry assignments. Party Secretary Yuri Andropov served in the Foreign Ministry in 1953 and as Ambassador to Hungary from 1954 to 1957. Leonid Ilichev, Khrushchev's favorite ideologue, was demoted from the Communist Party Secretariat to a post as Deputy Foreign Minister in 1964. Valerian Zorin, now Soviet Ambassador in Paris, spent his early career in Komsomol and Party staff agencies.

This pattern seems more and more to be an exception to the rule however. Where it does appear, one or two other conditions seem concurrent: the diplomatic work relates to the socialist countries or the individual is a propaganda specialist. On the whole, the composition of the Soviet diplomatic elite supports the earlier proposition that instances of Party and Government career fusion are increasingly infrequent exceptions. In the following section on recruitment and training of foreign-policy elites, we shall examine in some detail the careers of two representative Soviet diplomats.

Finally, we turn to the "dumping-ground" proposition that government foreign-affairs roles have been a convenient place for the "exile" of personnel who have lost favor with the Party leadership. The career data we have indicate that important roles in the Ministry of Foreign Trade may be staffed with men of this sort. It is clear that the Minister, Patolichev, was suddenly dropped from a top position of Party influence after a highly successful Party career.

The Foreign Ministry has harbored some formerly high-ranking Party officials. Ambassador Aristov in Poland is one current example, as is the earlier mentioned Deputy Minister Leonid Ilichev. Molotov's initial banishment to Ulan-Bator was another celebrated case.

There seems to be good evidence that in particular cases government roles provide an opportunity to truncate the Party influence of a man who falls afoul of the leadership without the inconvenience of immediate formal condemnation. The ambassadorships in party-states have already been observed to be Party-filled positions. They are tailor-made for depriving the occupant of the opportunity to maneuver for Party support at home. But the instances of such "dumping" are relatively rare in comparison to the number of rising stars found in such roles. The general rule has been that mistakes drop a man completely from the visible Soviet elite, both Party and government. When "dumping" into government roles occurs, it represents an effort to continue to benefit from an individual's technical competence while eliminating his domestic political influence, or, in a minority of cases, to put the individual into limbo while a final resolution of his status takes place.

We close this section on the elite individuals who make Soviet foreign policy by reiterating the narrowness of that elite and the apparent consequence of great personal influence. In its upper echelons, in contrast to the authority pyramid for domestic policymaking, the burden of judgment and responsibility is fixed heavily on very few shoulders. At the lower echelons of bureaucracy, especially on the government side, which we conceive to be important in providing the informational premises for decisions and for interpreting and implementing decisions, the pyramid broadens abruptly. But only a minority of the Politburo of the Party, the Secretariat, and the Central Committee are foreign-affairs oriented. Among the government role players, a few of the ministerial personnel oriented toward foreign affairs hold high party rank but virtually none hold simultaneous Party offices. Thus Brezhnev, Kosygin, Podgorny, Suslov, Shelepin, Ustinov, and Grishin, with Party technical collaboration from Ponamarev and Andropov and with government technical collaboration from Lesechko, Gromyko, Grechko, Semichastny and Patolichev, may be considered the dominant personalities of Soviet foreign policy. Among them today we find the molding experience of a Party-line officer's career predominant, but also represented are the professional specializations of Party theoretical and propaganda work and state diplomatic, military, and economic technologies. There is no doubt that it is the "business-like," domestically oriented "builder of communism" who now has greatest freedom of action. But the inputs from the other professional orientations limit and condition the decisions of this select group.[5]

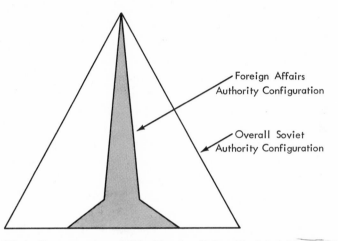

Foreign Affairs
Authority Configuration

Overall Soviet
Authority Configuration

DIAGRAM III-1 Concentration of Elite Foreign-Policy Decision-Making Authority

B. RECRUITMENT AND TRAINING

As helpful as the career background of the current top echelon of the Soviet foreign-affairs elite are, it touches only a small fraction of the total personnel drawn into the foreign-policy process as we have conceptualized it. Assessment of the "men who make Soviet foreign policy" requires some attention to the largely anonymous middle and lower echelons who furnish up the information upon which decisions are taken and who interpret decisions in the course of their implementation. We cannot look at them as individuals, but we can distinguish them as groups.

Let us turn first to the training of the Party elite. In Stalin's classic formulation of 1937, he divided the Party's leading cadres into 3,000–4,000 "first-rank leaders whom I would call our Party's corps of generals," about

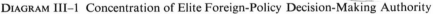

[5] For interesting comparisons between Soviet and East European foreign-policy elites, see R. Barry Farrell, "Foreign Policy Formation in the Communist Countries of Eastern Europe," *East European Journal,* I, No. 1 (March, 1967), 39–74.

30,000–40,000 "middle-rank leaders who are our Party's corps of officers," and about 100,000–150,000 of the "lower-rank Party command staff who are, so to speak, our Party's non-commissioned officers."[6] In late 1961, the Party claimed one-third as many paid officials per 1,000 Party members as there had been in 1940.[7] From these and other fragmentary bits of information, we might estimate the leading cadres at the time of the XXIIIrd Party Congress as 5,000–6,000 "generals," 50,000–60,000 "officers," and 200,000–220,000 "non-commissioned officers." A little over a quarter million paid Party professionals is a reasonable supposition in the mid-1960's.[8]

It is from these Party "officers and non-commissioned officers" that the top foreign-affairs elite is in large measure recruited, and it is in these ranks that attitudes are molded which later will condition the foreign policy of the country.

From our earlier examination of the top elite, we found two basic types of Party workers channeled into the foreign-affairs roles: line officers of the Party who have acceded to the top leadership positions in the Politburo and by that role necessarily into major foreign-affairs influence and responsibility; and staff officers of the Party who, by virtue of their technical competence (such as "ideological work") or specialized staff experience (such as liaison with the Communist Party of a particular country), have gained influential roles in the Departments of the Central Apparatus and thence in the Secretariat.

Armstrong notes that in 1939 only 40 per cent of the Raikom and Gorkom Committee Secretaries had completed their secondary education and that only eighteen of forty-eight Obkom Secretaries had attained this level. At that time, 65 per cent of the Obkom Section Directors—staff officers with technical functions—had completed secondary schooling. In that postpurge period after emasculation of the best brains in the Party, strenuous efforts were made to raise the educational level of Party officials to enable them to cope with the ever more complex business of socialist construction. After the dislocation of the Great Patriotic War, these efforts were renewed and

[6] Joseph Stalin, *Mastering Bolshevism* (*Report to the Plenary Session of the Central Committee of the Communist Party of the Soviet Union, March 3, 1937*) (N.Y.: Workers' Library Publishers, 1937), p. 36.

[7] P. Pigalev, "Sovershenstvovat' rabotu mestnykh partiinykh organov," *Partiinaia zhizn,* No. 24 (December, 1961), p. 12.

[8] Soviet data on total cadres is not available. For estimates see Merle Fainsod, *How Russia is Ruled,* rev. ed. (Cambridge, Mass.: Harvard University Press, 1963), pp. 205–207. See also John A. Armstrong, *The Soviet Bureaucratic Elite* (New York: Frederick A. Praeger, Inc., 1959), Chapter I; and Leonard Schapiro, *The Communist Party of the Soviet Union* (London: Methuen, 1963), p. 573. Two useful Soviet articles are Pigalev, *op. cit.,* and "KPSS v tsifrakh (1956–1961)," *Partiinaia zhizn'* (1962), pp. 44–54.

a rapid rise in educational level ensued. In the Ukraine by 1951 37.5 per cent of "directing cadres" had some higher education and this number had gone up to 56.4 per cent by 1955.[9]

It is safe to say that among the men drawn from Party staff roles especially, the self-educated Communist *apparatchiki* are virtually gone. The sort of bootstrap educational system by which today's leaders have tried to ensure the better preparation of tomorrow's leaders means that the poorest formal education in the Soviet leadership today belongs to those in the upper-elite strata. Each successive lower echelon reflects more thorough formal training as prerequisite for admission and advancement.

Insofar as the line officers of the Party prevailed in the top leadership positions of the Khrushchev system, the top roles reflected less formal education than their immediate staff subordinates. But as the survey of the Party Politburo shows (Table III-3), the relatively uneducated Bolshevik—in his position because of revolutionary record and Party allegiance alone—is becoming an anachronism in the decision hierarchy. The difference between incumbents and ex-Politburo members over the past five years testifies to the speed of the old Bolsheviks' departure. What is of primary interest beyond this elementary fact is the character of the education the future foreign-policy-leadership member possesses.

There has been no abrupt shift in the pattern of Party education since the 1930's. Changes have been quantitative rather than qualitative. The senior decision elite of today, who were recruited into the Party between 1920 and 1940, received their formal education before World War II in the atmosphere of privation and foreign threat that dominated the 1920's or the domestic terror and the new Nazi threat of the 1930's. The major difference in their formal training compared with the young men who are trained today for tomorrow's leadership is that they got less and they got it at an older age.

The Party official is repeatedly trained and retrained in intensive courses provided by Party schools. The major cities offer Evening Universities of Marxism-Leninism to provide elementary courses for local officials. Officials being considered for advancement into middle leadership positions are selected for full-time training at especially designed Party schools running from the Oblast level to the Higher Party School of the Union Republic and its parent institution the Higher Party School of the Central Committee of the CPSU in Moscow. At the top of the hierarchy is the Academy of Social Sciences, also directed by the Central Committee.[10]

[9] Armstrong, *op. cit.,* p. 32.
[10] Nicholas DeWitt, *Education and Professional Employment in the USSR* (Washington, D.C.: National Science Foundation, 1961), especially pp. 32–33, 300.

The curriculum of the full-time, Inter-Oblast Party School—four years of intensive instruction leading to a diploma that certifies completion of higher education—is available to us as it was constituted in 1957.[11] Just over 40 per cent (1,330 hours) of instruction time was devoted to "political and general social science subjects."[12] Fifteen per cent (480 hours) was devoted to "economics and planning subjects." The rest (1,390 hours) was reserved for "applied-technical managerial subjects." Optional electives included foreign languages. Courses provided for Party staff specialists, for example journalists and other "ideological workers," contain less applied-technical and economic material in the staff specialty area.

These Inter-Oblast Party Schools, of which there are about thirty in the USSR, are apparently subordinate branches of the Higher Party Schools of the Republics and the Central Higher Party School in Moscow. All are supervised by the Ideological Department of the Central Apparatus. Although curricula for the higher branches are not available, the piecemeal evidence suggests they follow the same general content but include instruction at a higher level of sophistication. Admissions criteria for all include Party membership, a completed secondary education, and a maximum age of thirty-five years which may be waived in particular cases.[13]

During the decade 1946–1955, the Party claimed 55,000 Party functionaries (including 6,000 correspondence students) were trained in these schools, indicating an average enrollment at any one time of some 22,000 officials.[14] In 1956, the Higher Party School in Moscow had 200 students enrolled in its regular division and 3,000 in its four-year correspondence course.[15]

The Ukrainian Republic Higher Party School (in 1956) was divided into two faculties: a Soviet faculty for students oriented toward general state administrative activities and a larger Party faculty for those oriented toward Party and Komsomol organizational work.[16] Such a separation may or may not exist at the Higher Party School in Moscow. The latter has been identified as containing thirteen departments, some of which award the Candidate

---

[11] V. N. Malin *et al.,* eds., *Spravochnik partiinogo rabotnika* (Moscow, Gosudarstvennoe Izdatelstvo Politicheskoi Literatury, 1957), p. 415. See also Armstrong, *op. cit.,* p. 35.

[12] Including: history of the CPSU (250 hours); dialectical and historical materialism (200 hours); political economy (300 hours); history of international workers' and national liberation movements (180 hours); history of the USSR (150 hours); Party and government affairs and procedures (150 hours); and foundations of Soviet jurisprudence (100 hours).

[13] DeWitt, *op. cit.,* pp. 222, 300.

[14] Malin *et al., op. cit.,* p. 410.

[15] I. N. Shumilin, *Soviet Higher Education* (Munich: Institute for the Study of the USSR, 1962), p. 78.

[16] Armstrong, *op. cit.,* p. 37.

degree to graduates. It seems probable that there is progressively more course differentiation at the parent institutions.

Finally, the Central Committee operates the Academy of Social Sciences (*Akademiia Obshchestvennykh Nauk*) in Moscow for the preparation of high-level Party theoreticians and especially for the staffing of Central Apparatus institutions. It offers a two-year advanced-degree program in political studies (especially "philosophy") which continues the function of the pre-World War II Institute of Red Professors.[17] The Academy recognizes the following fields of specialization: political economy, economics and politics of foreign countries, theory of state and law, international law, history of the USSR, general history, international relations, history of the Communist Party, dialectical and historical materialism, history of Russian and Western philosophy, logic and psychology, theory and history of literature, theory and history of art, and foreign languages. Aside from theorists for full-time Party staff positions, the Academy prepares instructors in the social sciences for institutions of higher learning and theoretical personnel for scientific-research institutions and scientific journals.[18]

The Academy's orientation toward foreign affairs is indicated by its specialized divisions and no less by the fact that its Rector since 1958, Yuri P. Frantsev, was formerly Director of the Institute of International Relations of the Ministry of Foreign Affairs and is a frequent analyst of foreign affairs in theoretical journals.

Admission to the Academy of Social Sciences is limited to Party members of not less than five years standing who are under forty years of age. They must be graduates of an institution of higher learning, have had experience in Party propaganda, instructional, or literary work, and possess a demonstrated talent in scientific activity. Candidates take competitive examinations (after being recommended and making initial application) in their chosen specialty, in the foundations of Marxism-Leninism, and in foreign language.[19]

From this short survey of Party education, we may conclude that the Party official at the middle echelon of the structure who has a direct foreign-affairs professional concern (probably as a staff specialist) has been through an intensive formal higher-education process which has given him a grasp of a great body of factual material all within a rigid doctrinal framework. His interpretations have been made for him. All of his considerable study of the international system and of politics in general has been presented

[17] DeWitt, *op. cit.,* p. 34, 435; Shumlin, *op. cit.,* p. 79.

[18] George S. Counts, *The Challenge of Soviet Education* (New York: McGraw-Hill Book Company, Inc., 1957), pp. 281–282.

[19] *Ibid.,* p. 282.

within the guidelines of doctrine. His personal experience does not match this received material. If he is primarily domestically oriented and only peripherally concerned with foreign affairs (a line officer who may eventually succeed to the Politburo and thus to direct foreign-affairs responsibility), he has less grasp of factual material but the same often-repeated doctrinal framework in which to form his conclusions about the international system. We may sum up by saying that this anonymous man who influences Soviet foreign policy by providing information to his superiors and implementing their directives today possesses a rich substantive sophistication constrained within a simple and rigid Party-given structure of values and priorities.

Government Administrators

If the Party man is becoming more urbane and sophisticated through more extensive formal education, the same is even more apparent for the government administrator. For him, Party membership is a stamp of clearance in most cases; his elite status depends upon his technical competence, and that to a very great extent is a product of his formal training.

A good Komsomol record and demonstration of outstanding intellectual accomplishment in secondary school are the two keys to successful passage through the political and academic screening process and admission to a department of one of the state universities or specialized institutes run by the government Ministries under general coordination by the Ministry of Higher and Specialized Secondary Education. Individuals are not drafted into a specific field of study. Quotas for the various specialties are decided by the planning organs, and then individuals compete for the available openings. Admissions committees generally consist of the institution Director and his deputies, several senior professors and department chairmen, and representatives of the CPSU, Komsomol, Trade Union, and perhaps other "social organizations."[20]

Applications for admission must include character-recommendation certificates from Party, Komsomol, management and trade-union organizations. These are screened by the committee before the applicant is allowed to take the competitive examinations. There is clear indication that "social class" is an additional factor in weighing applications and favors the children of the present Soviet elite. This is apparently prevalent especially in such high-prestige and privileged career fields as the diplomatic service. There is an official criterion of "social worthiness" to which character recommendations

[20] DeWitt, *op. cit.*, pp. 243–244.

are obliged to address themselves. Its ambiguity offers a place for "social class" to take effect.[21]

Graduation from a university faculty or specialized institute (usually a matter of five or six years of intensive and tightly programmed study) generally assures the student of an initial assignment in his specialty and obligates him to remain in that post for several years. Order of merit in one's graduating class in some cases affords the student choice among a variety of more and less desirable appointments.

Courses in political indoctrination are understandably a feature of all Soviet higher-education curricula, not just Party schools. Thus the prospective trade expert or diplomat is exposed to smaller[22] but qualitatively comparable doses of the studies which make up so large a proportion of Party higher education. A Central Committee decision of June 18, 1956 made separate courses in political economy, dialectical and historical materialism, and the history of the CPSU obligatory for all students in higher education.[23] The training is supervised by the Ministry of Higher and Specialized Secondary Education, Central Administration on the Teaching of Social Sciences.[24]

Total enrollment figures indicate that in 1960, 1,156,000 Soviet students were studying full time in all Soviet institutions of higher education (including Party schools), with some 1,240,000 more attending in an evening or extension-correspondence capacity. Of the total, the vast majority were pursuing engineering-industrial or education (teacher-training) programs, with somewhat less than 10 per cent engaged in socioeconomic studies.[25]

An important implication here is that for the large majority of the Soviet population with higher education, the political indoctrination courses, as dry and unloved as they may be, constitute the sole formal study of politics in general and international relations in particular. This would seem to reinforce the pattern of a practically oriented society of builders, who accept

[21] *Ibid.*, pp. 245–246; Kaznacheev, *op. cit.*, Chapters II and III. See also Kaznacheev, *Conditions in the Soviet Union*, Testimony before a Subcommittee of the U.S. Senate Committee on the Judiciary, January 22, 1960 (Washington, D.C.: Government Printing Office, 1960).

[22] Usually at least 8 per cent of instructional time: DeWitt, *op. cit.*, p. 312.

[23] Text available in Malin *et al.*, *op. cit.*, p. 320; cited in DeWitt, *op. cit.*, p. 312. Standard texts currently include Kuusinen *et al.*, *Fundamentals of Marxism-Leninism*, rev. ed. (Moscow: Foreign Languages Publishing House, 1963) and the new edition of the *History of the Communist Party of the Soviet Union* (Moscow: Foreign Languages Publishing House, 1960).

[24] Reports of exchange students and defectors indicate that much of this training is passively tolerated by most students and enthusiastically received only by a minority of Komsomol or Party activists.

[25] DeWitt, *op. cit.*, pp. 317–319.

rather uncritically the rudimentary simplicities of the Communist world view and eschew further concern with politics. Accordingly, it confirms the proposition put forward earlier that in the Soviet Union foreign affairs is the province of a very narrow elite—both Party and state—with a correspondingly low degree of popular restraint upon its maneuvering. Figures for 1959 graduations from Soviet higher-education institutions, for example, show 108,600 engineering graduates, 138,000 education graduates, and just 25,000 graduates in all socioeconomic categories including the graduates of the Party institutions of higher education. This is out of a total graduation of some 338,000.[26]

Particular attention is warranted and fortunately is possible for the training of Foreign Ministry personnel. As is the case with other government work, young men and women are not drafted into foreign-affairs careers. Indeed the desirability of such work, offering the possibility of travel abroad, makes the Institute of International Relations, run under the supervision of the Foreign Ministry, one of the most competitive schools in the USSR.[27]

Application for admission to the Institute is not, in contrast to most government institutes, open to all aspiring students who have graduated from secondary school. The initiative must be taken by one's Oblast Party Committee, thus providing at the outset a high assurance of political reliability. If admitted by a committee which further examines his political qualifications meticulously, the student must pursue the specialized curriculum prescribed for him by the Institute.

The Institute is governed by the Ministry of Foreign Affairs in conjunction with the KGB, the Party Central Committee, and the Ministry of Higher and Specialized Secondary Education.[28] Its Director is appointed by the Foreign Ministry, but he is closely restrained by the Institute's collegium, which consists besides the Director and his three deputies, of two deans and a group of department chairmen. He is also significantly restrained by the Institute's powerful Party and Komsomol committees. All must confirm the collegium's decisions.[29]

The 2,000 student complement for the six-year program of study is drawn from three groups. First and most numerous are the specially advantaged

---

[26] *Ibid.,* p. 328.

[27] Soviet Ambassador Dobrynin has complained to American associates that this claim to choice candidates is now being weakened by the increasing attractiveness of scientific-technical careers which offer as great material reward and in some cases also the possibility of travel abroad. Max Frankel, "Moscow's Man Intrigues Washington," *New York Times Magazine,* July 29, 1962, p. 14.

[28] Kaznacheev, *op. cit.,* p. 28.

[29] *Ibid.,* p. 29.

children of the ruling elite, whose secondary education in closed and privileged schools gives them an advantage in preparation, particularly in foreign languages. The second group consists of experienced KGB officers, older than the former group—in their middle and late thirties. The third group is made up of Komsomol activists of high demonstrated ability. Although outstanding intellectual ability and discipline are apparently essential for admission to and success at the Institute, they must in most cases be accompanied by one of these three background patterns. Additionally, about 10 per cent of the students customarily come to the Institute from the other party-states of the communist system.

The lives of the students are thoroughly permeated by the demands for participation placed upon them by Party and Komsomol organizations. About 30 per cent of them are Party members (notably the KGB students) and the rest invariably Komsomol members. When the time comes for graduation, the order of merit and hence some priority in choice of assignment depends at least as heavily upon Party and Komsomol recommendations as upon academic distinction.[30]

The student body is divided into two divisions, Western and Eastern, according to geographic area of specialization. The fixed course of study (no optional courses) is divided into general subjects which both divisions take,[31] area subjects which all students in one division take,[32] and highly specialized subjects which students concentrating in a particular country (ten to twelve per group) take.[33]

About 40 per cent of the curriculum is devoted to language training, with the requirement that a graduate have a thorough knowledge of two foreign languages (i.e., that of his country of specialization and the foreign language most frequently used there). Depending upon the country of specialization, three languages may be required in some cases.[34]

Upon graduation from the Institute, some 30 per cent of the most outstanding (by Party and Komsomol criteria as well as by academic distinction) are accepted for careers in the Foreign Ministry or the foreign-intelligence divisions of the KGB. A 1957 graduate estimated that with the new emphasis on the underdeveloped "third camp" in Soviet foreign policy, about half of

[30] *Ibid.,* pp. 33–34, 39.

[31] General subjects include history of international relations, international law, philosophy, and Marxism-Leninism among others.

[32] Eastern area courses include history of the Orient, economic geography of the Orient, philosophic schools of the Orient, etc.

[33] Specialized subjects include history, geography, economy, administration, politics, art, literature, and music of the country involved.

[34] Kaznacheev, *op. cit.,* pp. 29–32.

the Soviet diplomats, propagandists, and interpreters to be found in this area in 1962 were graduates of the Institute.[35]

The remaining 70 per cent of the graduates remain in the USSR and go to work in the propaganda field or as interpreters and consultants in the various other Ministries and State Committees which have foreign interests. Some take up again their earlier careers in the Komsomol or Party. Five to 6 per cent go on to postgraduate courses at the Institute or other political institutions and become professional teachers.[36]

A graduate who is selected for service in the Foreign Ministry is customarily sent abroad in the area of his specialty as an Information Officer in an embassy. This is a probationary assignment. For two years he will be watched for reliability, morale, and general ability in relatively menial diplomatic work. Those of his colleagues who do not come from the IIR are probably graduates of the Military Foreign Language Institute, the Special Interpreters' Department of the Moscow Foreign Language Institute, or Moscow University's Special School of Economics.[37] Acceptable performance in the probationary period (the Ambassador makes the final decision, and about one-half of the probationers reportedly are found acceptable) normally results in promotion to Attaché rank. Five to six years of service may achieve Third Secretary status, top rank in the junior diplomatic service. A two-year course in the Foreign Ministry's Higher Diplomatic School in Moscow seems to be a prerequisite for further promotion into the ranks of the senior diplomatic service: Second and First Secretaries, Counselors, Ministers, and Ambassadors.[38]

While the junior diplomatic service is customarily composed of career diplomats, there is an influx of noncareer personnel from the middle ranks of the Party and other government agencies at the juncture between the junior and senior services.[39] In the mid-1960's, approximately one-third of the Soviet ambassadors abroad had been "rerouted" into diplomatic careers, either temporarily or permanently, after substantial service and achievement in nondiplomatic work—principally in Party Secretary roles. If the pattern at the ambassadorial level is preserved at the lower ranks of the senior diplomatic service, as seems to be the case on the basis of sparse evidence, the proportion of horizontal entries at the Second Secretary level is probably considerably greater than one-third. There is indication of considerable

[35] *Ibid.*, p. 36.
[36] *Ibid.*
[37] *Ibid.*, pp. 41–42.
[38] *Ibid.*, pp. 38–39, 41–43.
[39] Kaznacheev, *op. cit.*, p. 42; confirmed by examination of ambassadorial career lines.

attrition of men unable to make the career transition even with the help of the Higher Diplomatic School training.[40]

The foregoing material on foreign-service training has been drawn almost entirely from the testimony of Aleksandr Kaznacheev, a junior Soviet diplomat, who defected from the Soviet embassy in Rangoon in 1959 when he was twenty-seven and who thereafter received political asylum in the United States. It is difficult to compare his testimony with other sources, for it goes well beyond what is elsewhere publicly available. But with this caveat, we may observe that there is no contradiction of prior information in his statements, and there seems to be no reason to question their validity.

After accepting Kaznacheev's account as an accurate description of the recruitment and training—the shared personal experience of the Soviet junior diplomatic service today—we must still remind ourselves that the confusion of World War II and the very different environment of the Soviet Union in the 1930's from that of the Soviet Union today mean a considerable measure of difference between the molding experience of men like Kaznacheev and of today's senior career diplomats.

Fortunately we have relatively extensive information on the background of Anatoliy F. Dobrynin, since 1961 the Soviet Ambassador in the United States. Examining it reveals some contrasts between his generation of Soviet diplomats and that of Kaznacheev.

Dobrynin was born in Moscow in 1919, two years after the Bolshevik Revolution, into the family of an architect. His higher education, as that of his wife, was as an aircraft engineer. He was working on the design of military aircraft during World War II when he was drafted for special work, possibly because of the knowledge of both German and English with which he complemented his engineering proficiency in a critical field. He was specially schooled in foreign-trade principles, then for work helping Soviet officials buy engineering products in the West which would be needed in the postwar period of reconstruction. This job led in turn to his forsaking engineering entirely to take up a career in the Foreign Ministry in 1946 at the age of twenty-seven. His posts are well accounted for after 1949 but not in the period from 1946 to 1949. As Dobrynin holds the Candidate degree in historical sciences, presumably in his specialty, the U.S.A., it seems probable that a good portion of these three years were spent in an academic environment, perhaps at the Academy of Social Sciences. He is known to be a member of the CPSU, but no Party activity is on the record.

From 1949 to 1952 Dobrynin served as an assistant to the Foreign Minister,

[40] *Ibid.*

then Andrei Vyshinsky. Next he began the first of three tours of duty abroad, each in the United States. He served in the Embassy in Washington as Counselor and then as Counselor-Minister, the second-ranking post. He returned to Moscow from 1955 to 1957 to serve again as an adviser to the Foreign Minister, this time Dimitri Shepilov, and he was an active participant at a number of United Nations meetings. In 1957, he was sent as an "international civil servant" to become Undersecretary to United Nations Secretary-General Dag Hammarskjold. In New York, he reportedly ran the Office of Political and Security Council Affairs efficiently and served as an interested broker between Hammarskjold and the Soviet delegation.

In 1960, Dobrynin was recalled early from his UN assignment by Foreign Minister Andrei Gromyko and became Chief of the American Department and a member of the collegium of the Ministry of Foreign Affairs. Two years later he replaced foreign-trade specialist Mikhail Menshikov as Ambassador in Washington.

As Ambassador, he has shown urbanity and personal charm in contrast to some of his predecessors and especially to the Stalinist stereotype of the stolid robot-like Bolshevik diplomat. He apparently has been ready to discuss the subtleties of international relations with his official counterparts and to conduct reasoned discourse without resort to the formulations of *Pravda* editorials. His manner and his words have impressed American associates, and they communicate well except in the area of economics. Here Dobrynin seemed at first to lack a sophisticated grasp of the United States. For what it may be worth, he himself acknowledged that he felt a lack of understanding of the American economy personally and that embassy economics experts upon whom he must rely similarly lacked the ability to interpret critically nuances of the U.S. economy.[41]

In Dobrynin's career we see a contrast with that described by Kaznacheev for the present generation of junior Soviet diplomats. Dobrynin's formal training was not in diplomacy; he was conscripted into diplomatic work after World War II almost by accident, and much of his diplomatic training has been on the job. He thus possesses a more varied educational background and consequently less uniformity with his peers' molding experiences. Entirely a product of the Soviet environment and a man who was just emerging from

[41] Data on Dobrynin taken principally from Max Frankel, "Moscow's Man Intrigues Washington," *The New York Times Magazine,* July 29, 1962, pp. 10, 14, 16. See also Gromyko *et al., op. cit.,* Vol. I, 470; and Schulz and Taylor, *op. cit.,* p. 181. Drew Middleton, "The New Soviet Man in Diplomacy," *The New York Times Magazine,* December 7, 1958, pp. 23, 107–10 provides some interesting contrasts between the post-Stalin Soviet diplomats and their predecessors.

adolescence during the Great Purge of the 1930's, he has nevertheless served closely and successfully with the old Bolshevik *apparatchik*, Vyshinsky, then the ill-fated "anti-party careerist" Shepilov, and finally with Khrushchev's Foreign Minister, Gromyko. Changes of doctrine and policy have inescapably required him to adapt abruptly in the transition from Stalinism to Khrushchev's peaceful coexistence. It has been one key to his success that he has evidently been adept at such adaptation.

In common with the career diplomats described by Kaznacheev, he is a member of the Party, thus establishing his political reliability and his credentials for unhindered advancement based upon technical competence. But also like the later career diplomats he has never worked full time at being a Party man.

KGB Men

We have regrettably little information on the recruitment and training of Soviet specialists in foreign espionage who staff the foreign affairs–oriented offices of the KGB and Military Intelligence. Much more is available on the operations of these colorful and notorious organizations.[42]

We do know, however, that the KGB operates a network of schools at the specialized secondary level and a few in which students may receive credit for "partial higher education." Schools providing "militia" type training have been identified in Minsk and in Alma Ata. The school in Minsk (which offers a two-year course of instruction) accepts only candidates who have been discharged from the Armed Forces and have completed a ten-year school. Its graduates are commissioned as lieutenants in the KGB.[43]

Personnel drawn from these schools and others like them provide cadres for the domestically oriented divisions of the KGB and the Border Troops. At least a portion of foreign-intelligence agents and their technical-support personnel are drawn from this sizable manpower pool, but it is certain that those who go on in this fashion receive much additional training.

KGB officers are also drawn from among the graduates of a special KGB Institute (or Higher School) which provides a four-year course in internal security, a variety of shorter specialized courses, and incorporates a faculty of foreign languages formerly known as the Leningrad Institute of Foreign Languages. Graduates of the internal-security program receive the equivalent

---

[42] See particularly the *Report of the Royal Commission on Espionage, 22nd August, 1955* (Sydney: Commonwealth of Australia, 1955); Simon Wolin and Robert M. Slusser, eds., *The Soviet Secret Police* (New York: Frederick A. Praeger, Inc., 1957); and Oleg Penkovskiy, *The Penkovskiy Papers* (Garden City: Doubleday & Company, Inc., 1965).

[43] DeWitt, *op. cit.*, pp. 29-30.

of a law degree. Personnel who will operate in the Main Directorate of Foreign Intelligence receive two years additional training in intelligence subjects at the Higher Intelligence School, which is maintained by the Directorate exclusively for its own personnel.[44]

From Kaznacheev's account of the Institute of International Relations, we can calculate that from 500 to 600 of that Institute's normal student body probably has prior KGB service.[45] Presumably many if not all these students continue to serve the KGB and particularly its Main Directorate of Foreign Intelligence after graduation.

The extensive reorganization of the KGB apparatus in the last decade has undoubtedly had some impact on the character of personnel recruited and trained for foreign-intelligence work. In an effort to eliminate the KGB as a potentially independent power base for political aspirants, Khrushchev promoted Party and Komsomol control of its cadres. Aleksandr Shelepin, Chairman of the KGB from 1958 through 1961, told the XXIInd Party Congress in October, 1961:

> State Security organs have been reorganized, considerably reduced, released from functions not pertaining to them, cleansed of careerist elements. The party has directed a great number of party, administrative, and Komsomol workers to work in them. The State Security Committee and its local organizations now have cadres who are well-trained, intelligent, and boundlessly devoted to the party and the people, capable of successfully solving the complex tasks of state security in our country. The entire activity of the agencies of state security is now under the continual supervision of the Party and Government. . . .
>
> An exceptionally large role in the work of organs of the State Security Committee is played by party organizations, which have occupied a worthy and proper place in all our work. The Chekists can now look the Party and Soviet people in the eye with a clear conscinece.[46]

While the impact of the reorganization is incomparably greater for domestic operations of the KGB, it is probable that there is some carry-over into the Foreign Intelligence Directorate. We may infer that recruits are screened and assigned by the Komsomol and Party and that these organizations play as large a part in the training of KGB personnel today as they do in the lives

[44] *Staffing Procedures and Problems in the Soviet Union,* Report to the Committee on Government Operations, U.S. Senate (Washington, D.C.: Government Printing Office, 1963), pp. 58–60.

[45] Kaznacheev, *op. cit.,* pp. 32–33.

[46] *Pravda,* October 27, 1961, p. 10.

of students at the Institute of International Relations. Shelepin and his successor, Vladimir Semichastny, both former First Secretaries of the Komsomol and Chiefs of the Department of Party Organs in the Central Apparatus, are in their persons indication of thorough Party penetration of the formerly insulated KGB apparatus.

Officers of the Military Intelligence counterpart of the KGB's Foreign Directorate, that is, the GRU, receive their training at the Military-Diplomatic Academy. This school, which admits only commissioned officers who are graduates of an institution of higher education, is the key to advancement to responsible positions in Military Intelligence abroad. About seventy-five officers a year, reportedly almost all Russian by nationality, enter the three-year course of instruction provided. The curriculum emphasizes general political studies, geographic area studies, language, and technical procedures of espionage. Additional schools are maintained by the GRU for translator and interpreter training and for the special training of undercover agents.[47]

Soviet Military Leaders

The background of recruitment and training which molds Soviet military officers who rise to influence in the foreign-policy process is in most cases clear-cut and uniform. The Ministry of Defense maintains its own hierarchy of schools from the secondary level through advanced study. At the secondary level, Suvorov (army) and Nakhimov (navy) schools provide precareer training in addition to a regular secondary education for the privileged group of children admitted to them (mostly the sons of the current officer corps). Graduation here assures admission to a three-year officer-training school leading to a commission in the Armed Forces and credit for "partial higher education." Promising company-grade officers are assigned to one of about twenty branch-oriented military academies which prepare them for field-grade appointment in a four- to six-year course of study. At these academies they receive professional leadership and staff training, but also they receive a high-quality scientific and technical education in fields relevant to their military specialties. Finally, the Voroshilov Higher Military Academy provides two years of advanced command and staff study for those officers picked for advancement into the top echelons of military authority.[48]

This hierarchy of service training seems to be uniform and little changed since the early 1930's. There is a distinctive continuity and lack of horizontal entry which implies a high order of intellectual uniformity and even isolation

---

[47] *Staffing Procedures and Problems in the Soviet Union,* pp. 58–59.

[48] See George Schatunowski, "The Training of Personnel," in Asher Lee, ed., *The Soviet Air and Rocket Forces* (New York: Frederick A. Praeger, Inc., 1959).

among the Soviet officer corps—a professional military orientation toward problems of international relations. After the removal of Zhukov in 1957, Khrushchev made the same effort here as with the KGB to penetrate the natural insulation of military careers with Komsomol and Party organizational allegiances. It is evident that these agencies operate in the military schools and units in a manner comparable to what we have observed in the cases of the Foreign Ministry and the KGB.[49] But it is also evident that the functional requisites of the Soviet military establishment foster a powerful self-reinforcing cohesion of collective outlook in this elite.

Information and Propaganda Specialists

Finally in this survey we turn to the recruitment and training of personnel in the information and propaganda elite, whose stature has always been high in the Soviet Union. Their function as brokers of information between Soviet decision-makers and both the domestic population and the world beyond Soviet frontiers significantly involves them in the foreign-policy decision process. Their management of information channels is a frequently overlooked factor.

Recruitment and training of these personnel is frankly a function of the Party Organs and Ideological Departments of the Party Central Apparatus. It has been evident that there is a thorough integration of Party and non-Party work in all Soviet communications media. The normal distinctions between Party and non-Party roles break down completely, and individuals simultaneously fill offices in both hierarchies. It is all "ideological work." No effort is expended to persuade anyone that there is or should be any freedom from Party control in any of the Soviet communications media.

The integration is also evident in alternation by career journalists between offices in the Party Apparatus and offices nominally in the government hierarchy. The careers of holders of leading editorial positions testify to this flexibility. Armstrong has documented numerous cases of the same pattern in the lower echelons of government and Party in the Ukraine.[50]

The same integration is evident in the schooling of journalists. Party schools at all levels, charged with courses in "party-theoretical work," are a principal training ground. These operate under the supervision of the Agitprop Sections of regional Party organizations. Students are drawn from

---

[49] See the speeches by Malinovsky and Golikov to the XXIInd Party Congress stressing this penetration and condemning Zhukov's resistance to it: *Pravda,* October 25, 1961, pp. 4–5 and October 30, 1961, p. 3. See also Schatunowski, *op. cit.,* p. 190 and Boris Kuban, "Politics in the Soviet Air Force," in Lee, *op. cit.,* pp. 201–209.

[50] Armstrong, *op. cit.,* pp. 88–102.

among Komsomol activists with a demonstrated verbal facility; their education follows the general curriculum outlined above for other Party officials, with a special tailoring to emphasize journalistic skills.

Journalism faculties in the state universities, closely supervised by Agitprop are apparently becoming more important as sources of personnel for domestically oriented reporting and editing jobs.[51] Students of these faculties undergo considerable on-the-job training as apprentices in the editorial offices of Soviet newspapers and journals as a part of their higher education. In Moscow they perform under the supervision of editors who, for the most part, are simultaneously affiliates of the Agitprop Department in the Party Central Apparatus.

The foreign correspondents and foreign editorial staff members of INOTASS, *Pravda*, and *Izvestiia*, elite journalistic positions in the USSR, are all graduates of institutions of higher education and most frequently are the product of faculties of law, history, political economy, or foreign languages in the state universities. Their qualifications are generally comparable to those of members of the Soviet diplomatic service.[52]

Responsible personnel of Soviet communications media, editors of local and regional papers, news agency workers, radio and television workers, and so on regularly receive leaves of absence to attend special agitation/propaganda seminars and short courses on current Party practices and policies.[53] These are the same courses and seminars attended by agitation/propaganda officials of the Party organizations throughout the Soviet Union,[54] and they assure alert sensitivity to variations of the current Party line.

In brief conclusion to this examination of the development of cadres for the Soviet foreign-affairs elite, it is appropriate to point out some consistent characteristics of the recruitment and training process. First, there is striking evidence that the present Soviet leadership is firmly convinced of the critical importance of formal training of cadres to the decisions they will make in their later careers. Stalin's words in 1937 still epitomize this outlook:

> I think that if we are able, if we succeed in giving ideological training to our Party cadres from top to bottom and steeling them politically so

[51] Theodore E. Kruglak, *The Two Faces of TASS* (Minneapolis: University of Minnesota Press, 1962), p. 45.

[52] *Ibid.*

[53] Armstrong, *op. cit.,* pp. 94–95.

[54] See *Pravda,* September 13, 1961 for a report on the Central Committee decree of May 5, 1961, "Concerning Measures for Improving the Selection and Training of Propaganda Personnel."

that they can find their bearings with ease in the internal and international situation, if we succeed in making them fully mature Leninists and Marxists capable of solving the questions of the leadership of the country without making serious mistakes, then we can thereby solve nine-tenths of all our tasks.[55]

Political maturity is demanded of all cadres and is pursued cautiously, unimaginatively, and intensively through repetitive and uniform application to history, philosophy, and political economy all as Soviet apologetics. There is no pluralism of values to be tolerated, no dilemma to be explored. Political education thus becomes mastery of given principles and acquisition of intellectual facility in their application and their defense against a variety of predictable challenges. There is no doubt about the thoroughness of the foundation which is given to prospective foreign-affairs cadres. The approach is Jesuitical, with generally corresponding results.

Of equal importance though, political reliability and uniformity of political training are the only common denominators of the various Soviet foreign-affairs cadres. Their respective professional specialization is narrow and intensive and is undertaken at an early age. This specialization becomes more pronounced with each passing year as an environment of dislocation and rapid change characteristic of a revolutionary society gives way more and more to a relatively stable, highly bureaucratized social environment in which professional expertise is the single clear ladder to the personal rewards of a successful career.

The Soviet training and recruitment policies are thus directed toward the twin goals of professional competence and unquestioning political reliability. One may perceive the clear accord of these policies with the needs generated by Marxist-Leninist theory in the context of the present Soviet state. But one may also perceive the likelihood that increasing professional compartmentalization will be conducive to concommitant growth of professional parochialism in the USSR. This, in turn, may be expected to lead to greater group allegiances, barriers to communication and differences of perception. The implied development of conflicting definitions of group interest will surely produce new strains within the decision-making process, within the organizations which formulate and administer Soviet foreign policy.

One of the indicators of relative unanimity or divergence of outlook among the Soviet decision elite is the extent of influence which shared doctrinal reference points render in their decision-making processes. It is to this question that we turn in the next chapter.

[55] Stalin, *loc. cit.*

DOCTRINE AND EVENTS IN SOVIET FOREIGN POLICY

In foregoing chapters we have examined the role structure of Soviet foreign policymaking and the individuals and groups who occupy the roles and perform within them. This chapter will be devoted to the place in Soviet foreign policy of the belief system, specifically, its Marxist-Leninist doctrinal component. No issue of Soviet studies has generated more discussion or more division of opinion than that of "ideology" as a motivating force behind Soviet conduct in international affairs. Unfortunately, there has been little concern for precise definition of the terms under discussion, and, not infrequently, the argument has been reduced to the polemics of competing prejudices.

Let us refer to the standard Soviet manual on Marxism-Leninism for a short statement of what this body of doctrine is:

Marxism-Leninism regards the world such as it actually is, without adding an invented hell or paradise. It proceeds from the fact that all nature, including man himself, consists of matter with its different properties.

And nature, as well as all its individual phenomena, is in constant process of development. The laws of that development have not been ordained by God and do not depend on man's will. They are intrinsic in nature itself and are fully knowable. There are no inherently unknowable things in the world; there are only things which are still unknown, but which will become known through science and practice.

The Marxist-Leninist world outlook stems from science itself and *trusts* science, as long as science is not divorced from reality and practice. It itself develops and becomes richer with the development of science.

Marxism-Leninism teaches that not only the development of nature, but the *development of human society* too, takes place in accordance with objective laws that are independent of man's will.

By revealing the basic laws of social development, Marxism raised history to the level of a genuine science capable of explaining the nature of every social system and the development of society from one social system to another.[1]

We lay aside the question of the validity of these claims. What concerns us here is their operational significance for Soviet foreign policy, not their accuracy.

A. THE NATURE AND FUNCTIONS OF MARXIST-LENINIST DOCTRINE

In the course of a 1961 address to the XXIInd Party Congress, Frol R. Kozlov—then heir apparent to Khrushchev—said, "Marxist-Leninist theory, the mighty ideological weapon of cognition and revolutionary transformation of society on communist lines, is the lodestar in the party's activities."[2] The statement is a typical public formulation by the Soviet elite of the influence that Marxist-Leninist theory wields upon Soviet behavior.

There are two aspects to this influence, according to Kozlov, stated here as *cognition* and *transformation*. That is, Marxist-Leninist theory is a science by which the Communist creates knowledge of phenomenological relationships; and it is also a "lodestar," or a guide to action—a tool by use of which the Communist promotes the "revolutionary transformation of society."

Bourgeois nations are perceived as fundamentally different. *Kommunist*, the chief theoretical journal of the Communist Party of the Soviet Union, reflected some first principles of the communist world view in the course of a 1962 contrast between a Communist's ideology and the ideology it attributed to the bourgeois West:

Politics and ideology are in general understood subjectively in the bourgeois world. . . . Arbitrary rule is the basis of politics; the limits of the possible and the impossible in politics are determined by brute force. As far as ideological activities are concerned, the concept of "ideology," like the concept of "propaganda," is employed by bourgeois theorists in

[1] O. W. Kuusinen *et al., Fundamentals of Marxism-Leninism* (Moscow: Foreign Languages Publishing House, n.d. [1960]), pp. 16–19.
[2] *Pravda*, October 29, 1961, p. 4.

the sense of a completely arbitrary association of ideas, subject solely to a person's intentions and will. . . .

Such a concept of politics, ideology and propaganda is far removed from reality. The bases of politics are completely objective and realistic; they are dictated by economics, by the class interests of particular social groups. Ideological struggle is directly linked with political struggle—they are distinct but closely interrelated forms of class struggle. To hold that class struggle was dreamed up by someone, that it can be ended at will or by agreement, is to become enmeshed in the sticky web of bourgeois idealist views about the nature of social relations.

Indelibly stamped in the political consciousness of people today are two objectively existing lines of world development: the path of the socialist system and the path of capitalism. Social developments are perceived today precisely from this standpoint, taking on political implications. . . .[3]

The Communist's "objective" ideology rejects the influence of personal arbitrariness in the sweep of human history. Any formulation involving such personal intentions and will is therefore either the incorrect conclusion of ignorance or purposefully deceitful propaganda.

Here is the first of the two functions of Marxist-Leninist theory acknowledged by Kozlov—that of *cognition*. Marxist-Leninist theory provides an objective description of the relationship of forces in human society and of their predictable development. It provides the epistemological framework needed for attributing significance to observed occurrences.

The 1958 edition of the authoritative *Political Dictionary* defines Marxism-Leninism as "the science of the laws of development of nature and of society, of the revolution of the exploited masses, of the victory of socialism, of the construction of communist society; the ideology of the working class and its Communist Party."[4] Under the entry *ideology*, it goes on to illuminate Marxism-Leninism as the "guide to action" leading to a revolutionary transformation of society:

Ideology—the aggregate of political, legal, moral, and religious, aesthetic and philosophical views, expressing the interests of one or another class. Originating as the reflection of the material conditions of the life of society and the interests of certain classes, ideology itself renders

[3] G. Frantsov, "Chto skryvaetsia za lozungom 'ideologicheskogo razoruzheniia'," *Kommunist*, No. 13 (September, 1962), p. 114.

[4] B. N. Ponomarev, ed., *Politicheskii slovar'*, 2nd ed. (Moscow: Gosudarstvennoe Izdatelstvo Politicheskoi Literatury, 1958), p. 337.

an active influence on the development of society, accelerating or impeding it. The character of influence of ideology on the overall course of social development is determined by the role which its class plays at the time. Ideology which defends a moribund base, interests which are departing from the class stage, plays a reactionary role and holds back the development of society. Such, for example, is the role of contemporary bourgeois ideology. The ideology of the working class and its party is Marxism-Leninism—the revolutionary weapon in the struggle for overthrow of the exploiting system and for the construction of communism.[5]

Finally, we refer again to the Soviet manual of Marxism-Leninism for a synthesis of these two aspects of *ideology:*

By revealing the laws governing the operation and development of the forces of nature and society, genuine science can always foresee the new. The Marxist science of the laws of social development enables us not only to chart a correct path through the labyrinth of social contradictions, but to predict the course events will take, the direction of historical progress and the next stages of social advance. . . .

The Marxist-Leninist theory is not a dogma but a *guide to action.* But one has to learn to apply it correctly.

It illumines the path ahead. Without Marxism-Leninism, even progressively-minded people have to grope in the dark, without a genuine and profound understanding of the events taking place around them.

Marxist-Leninist theory provides a scientific basis for revolutionary *policy.* He who bases his policy on subjective desires remains either a futile dreamer or risks being thrust into the background of history. For history does not conform to man's wishes if these are not in accordance with the laws of history. That is why Lenin emphasized the need for a sober scientific analysis of objective situations and the objective course of evolution as the basis for defining the political line of the Party and for subsequently carrying it out with all revolutionary determination.[6]

So much for the official Soviet attribution of the function of Marxist-Leninist theory. The noncommunist scholarly world (not to mention the popular commentators) is divided in agreement or disagreement. On the one hand it is contended that the Soviet elite are "true believers" and that the injunctions derived from Marxist-Leninist theory do indeed undergird Soviet

---

[5] *Ibid.,* pp. 199–200. Cf. Mark M. Rozental, ed. *Kratkiy filosofskii slovar'* (Moscow: Gosudarstvennoe Izdatelstvo Politicheskoi Literatury, 1954), p. 186.

[6] Kuusinen *et al., op. cit.,* pp. 17, 19. Emphasis in the original.

conduct domestically and in the international system.[7] If occurrences seem frequently to confound prediction of Soviet actions on the basis of doctrine, that is because of the ambiguous conclusions to which this pseudoscience is amenable and not because of any disregard for it in Soviet planning. Analogy is sometimes drawn to the alleged impulse of competing Christian orthodoxies in the sanguinary religious wars of sixteenth-century Europe.

On the other hand, Marxist-Leninist theory is frequently perceived in the West as at best a lifeless utopian scheme which may once have inspired revolutionary zeal but today is simply irrelevant both as a "science of cognition" and as a "guide to action." It is preserved only as a convenient verbal structure to give a useful semblance of continuity to otherwise grossly inconsistent pragmatic actions. In fact, the argument goes on, the cognitive process of the Soviet elite does not differ significantly from that of the Western elites, and motivation is alternatively provided by personal aspirations or bureaucratic self-preservation or pragmatically conceived national interests.[8]

The controversy revolves about the place of Marxism-Leninism as an active ingredient in policy deliberations. Less subject to dispute is the contention that the body of Marxist-Leninist doctrine has a *passive*, less direct function for Soviet foreign policymaking. This function may readily be inferred from our earlier theoretical and legal description of the institutions and roles of the process. Before we go on to the more difficult question of Marxism-Leninism as an active input into the considerations of foreign-policy decision-makers, let us acknowledge its importance for justifying their authority. Both the role relationships and the appointment of personnel to fill the roles are sustained by a rationale based on Marxist-Leninist propositions, which to all indications is acceptable to the vast majority of the Soviet population and is adhered to by the elite itself. As Alfred G. Meyer has said, "Ideology

---

[7] One extreme of this contention is to be found in the literature of the American radical right; for example, see the widely sold volume, Fred Schwarz, *You Can Trust the Communists* (Englewood Cliffs, N.J.: Prentice-Hall, Inc., 1960), pp. 1–16. A more intellectually cogent application of this contention is reflected in Gerhard Niemeyer, "The Ideological Motivation of Communists," *Modern Age,* V (1961), 389–396. In *The Operational Code of the Politburo* (New York: McGraw-Hill Book Company, Inc., 1951), Nathan Leites derives canons of Soviet policy directly from the "sacred texts of Bolshevism."

[8] See the discussion of theories of Soviet foreign policy in our introduction. Robert V. Daniels, *The Nature of Communism* (New York: Random House, Inc., 1962), pp. 191–92, 205, 351–53, 372 sees Marxist-Leninist revolutionary doctrine as denuded of meaning and no longer an active guide for Soviet policy. In this belief he speaks for an impressive number of his fellow scholars. The view is perhaps even more prevalent among statesmen than academicians. See, for example, Chester Bowles, "Is Communist Ideology Becoming Irrelevant?" *Foreign Affairs,* XL (1962), 553–565.

functions as a legitimation device. It is to convince the citizenry that the Party and its leaders have a legitimate claim to rule them. More broadly, it is to convince the people that the entire system of government is legitimate."[9] Robert Conquest notes further that in the USSR "The supremacy of political criteria, the idea that a Party decision overrides all others, is firmly established. It remains a basic principle of the Party of Stalin and Khrushchev, of Brezhnev and Kosygin, and of their probable successors."[10]

Force may or may not have accompanied the installation of a particular elite or the establishment of a new political system. But the maintenance of authority, the stability of that system (as Machiavelli recognized long ago), depends upon the cultivation of a voluntary grant of authority. Whether or not its component propositions are intellectually understood and supported by the population, or even by the elite itself, becomes irrelevant for the function of the rationale once it achieves acceptance. This function is undeniably one aspect of the place of Marxism-Leninism in the Soviet decision process. The variables of personality and role structure, of which policy itself is a function, are to this extent functions of doctrine.

We are inclined to reject the concept of "ideology" as giving rise to too many imprecise perceptions to be analytically useful for our study. In its place we shall try to distinguish more operational concepts of the *belief system* and of *doctrine* instead. We define the belief system to include the totality of personally experienced and otherwise learned attitudes and preconceptions which an individual brings to the task of solving new problems —brings not necessarily with conscious intent but brings inevitably because he has no way to avoid them.

With the belief system thus broadly construed, any particular cluster of specific doctrinal propositions about values or about the relationships of phenomena must occupy a subordinate or lesser included position. Such is the position of the cluster of doctrinal propositions that constitute Marxist-Leninist theory.

The belief system may be conceptualized as a pair of mental maps one superimposed on the other. The first is the cognitive map which the individual constructs in order to orient himself in a system of phenomenological relationships. The second is an "affective" map, constituted of the individual's relative value preferences. When the latter is superimposed upon the former,

[9] Alfred G. Meyer, "The Functions of Ideology in the Soviet Political System" (Paper prepared for the Mid-West Political and Social Science Association meeting, Bloomington, Indiana, April 1965), pp. 10–11.

[10] Robert Conquest, *Russia After Khrushchev* (New York: Frederick A. Praeger, Inc., 1965), p. 20.

the two maps together provide an individual with his expectations of future occurrences, a set of categories for classifying new perceptions, and a guide to formulation and evaluation of goals.[11] It is very probable that all of us harbor contradictions within our individual belief systems, contradictions which we can tolerate without tension so long as they are not brought into conjunction in a context requiring resolution.[12] There may be contradictions between bodies of simultaneously accepted doctrine, or between doctrine and inferences from experience, or between inferences from different perceived experiences; and there may be such contradictions in the cognitive or the affective parts of the belief system. Similarly there will probably be areas of overlap and multiple reinforcement of doctrines and experiences. Both the cognitive map and the affective map are continually compiled and revised through the individual's life, the first from accretion and conflict of perceptions of fact[13] and the other from accretion and conflict of successive perceptions of value.

Discussions of Marxism-Leninism and Soviet foreign policies are usually cast in terms of a hypothetical contrast between "ideology" and "national interest." What is implied is that Soviet decision-makers are motivated by a mixture of desires to reach an international communist millenium and/or to maximize the national security, prosperity, and influence of the Soviet Union, with the relative proportions of the mixture remaining open to argument.

We are inclined to regard the long-ensuing debate as arid and misleading. In the first place, the terms are usually left inadequately defined, or the definitions of the alternatives are not mutually exclusive. Indeed, virtually all communist leaders after 1917 have acknowledged the power of the Soviet Union as a necessary condition for the successful spread of communism. Since then no behavior demonstrably aimed at preserving or advancing the welfare of the USSR has been subject to unambiguous condemnation as antithetical to the interest of world communism, a situation Stalin recognized and fully exploited. Now, with a record of fifty years of Soviet policy before us, one can objectively say only that preservation of the Soviet Union as a

[11] See Robert C. North, "Two Revolutionary Models: Russian and Chinese," in A. Doak Barnett, ed., *Communist Strategies in Asia* (New York: Frederick A. Praeger, Inc., 1963), pp. 35–36; Christian Bay, *The Structure of Freedom* (Stanford: Stanford University Press, 1964), pp. 355–359.

[12] See Leon Festinger, *A Theory of Cognitive Dissonance* (New York: Harper & Row, Publishers, Inc., 1957), pp. 1–31; C. E. Osgood and P. H. Tannenbaum, "The Principle of Congruity in the Prediction of Attitude Change," *Psychological Review,* LXII (1955), 42–55.

[13] Festinger, *op. cit.,* pp. 33–83. Each decision faced by the individual tends to set up some degree of dissonance, which usually is reduced by modification of predecision attitudes.

nation has remained the most basic canon of Soviet foreign policy. The rest is relative. Attribution of motive, on the basis of objective historical activity, depends upon the observer's subjective assessment of the Soviet leaders' subjective assessment of the degree of Soviet influence necessary to sustain an international advance of communism.

By looking at events, then, we cannot say with any confidence that the internationalist millenial goals or the doctrinal principles upon which they are founded are either disbelieved or serve only as a cynical propaganda device to rally support abroad. Nor can we assert that they are the daily determinants of Soviet policy. The polemics and counterpolemics lead to no satisfactory conclusion, for the arguments are constructed upon sand.

The "national interest" at any time, for any nation, is in operational terms a subjective evaluation by the collective decision-making elite who can commit the nation to a course of action. Depending upon the perceptions of fact and value among these people, Soviet national interest may be served by the aggressive pursuit of power by Communist Parties in all countries. Or, Soviet national interest may not be served by such a course at all. The national interest is a *conclusion*, derived logically from premises of fact and value, some of which may have been drawn from, or conditioned by, the precepts of Marxism-Leninism.

The relevant questions, then, concern the nature and extent of these Marxist-Leninist precepts in the intellectual and emotional make-up of the effective Soviet decision elite. These are very difficult questions to investigate and answer. We cannot psychoanalyze the subjects. Even if we could, we would still face the problem of translating our conclusions about the individual to the behavior of the organization. But the questions will not go away, and important policy decisions depend upon the answers we give. Let us be as rigorous as we can in seeking tentative answers.

What are the logical possibilities for influence on behavior by a cluster of such doctrinal propositions in one's belief system? Referring back to our introductory discussion of rationality, we expect the belief system to enter all rational decision processes as the learned preconceptions of the decision-makers. But as only those believed propositions which are perceived to be relevant to the subject of a new decision will consciously be introduced as premises by the decision-makers, it seems unlikely that a particular body of doctrine would be reflected at all times to the same extent. One might, however, expect that because of the all-encompassing scope of Marxist-Leninist doctrine, it would, if operative at all, make itself manifest in the choices of its believers more frequently than narrower bodies of doctrine.

One would certainly expect that affective propositions of Marxist-Leninist doctrine would find a strong place in the conscious formulation of goals for any political effort, especially in the formulation of long-range and general goals. Goal formulation is the most conspicuous place for Marxist-Leninist doctrine in Soviet-elite verbal behavior. Note for example the summary of objectives with which Khrushchev concluded the foreign-affairs section of his Central Committee Report to the XXIInd Party Congress:

> What tasks emerge from the present-day international situation for the Soviet Union's foreign policy? We must continue to implement steadily and constantly the principle of peaceful coexistence of states with different social systems as the general course of the Soviet Union's foreign policy; strengthen the unity of the countries of socialism on the basis of fraternal co-operation and mutual aid; make our contribution to the cause of strengthening the might of the world socialist system; develop contacts and co-operate with all fighters for peace throughout the world; act with all those who want peace against those who want war; strengthen the proletarian solidarity with the working class and the working people of the whole world; give comprehensive moral and material aid to peoples who are fighting for their liberation from imperialist and colonial oppression and for the consolidation of their independence; develop in the broadest way international business contacts, economic co-operation, and trade with all countries, wishing to maintain the same relations with the Soviet Union; pursue an active and flexible foreign policy striving for the settlement of urgent world problems by negotiation; expose the intrigues and maneuvers of warmongers; and establish business-like co-operation with all states on a reciprocal basis.[14]

Both the cognitive and affective aspects of Marxist-Leninist doctrine were reflected here, and tasks were formulated in relation to a doctrinaire view of the historical process.

Aside from goal formulation, it appears necessary that Marxist-Leninist doctrine as a cognitive science, if operative in the elite's belief system, must strongly influence expectations of historical development and the consequences of its own actions. The cognitive propositions of Marxist-Leninist doctrine must be drawn upon to define the forthcoming situation in which action is contemplated. They should also affect judgments of the relative viability of perceived alternatives.

We would expect recourse to doctrine for definition of the preaction

[14] *Pravda,* October 18, 1961, p. 5.

situation to be inversely related to the availability of empirical evidence to describe that situation. Because the doctrine is prospective, generalized, and abstract, whereas empirical evidence is retrospective and specific, one might expect the latter to be preferred where readily available. That is to say, we would expect the premises available in the doctrinal component of the belief system to be called upon to fill up the gaps in the empirical evidence.

But aside from the provision of substantive premises to fill up cognitive gaps in the evidence of empirical observation, doctrine may be expected to have an unconscious but influential place insofar as it provides categories for classifying and then understanding and interpreting the significance of environmental conditions and observed occurrences. We would expect it, in this capacity, to alert the decision-maker to doctrinally important pheno- mena and thus act as a filter of his perceptions. We should expect stereo- typed categories and impressions to have a greater inertial influence in the perceptual ordering of relatively obscure or ambiguous occurrences—such as empirical indicators of national capacity for performing future acts, or unconfirmed indicators of attitudes on the part of others, or general clusters of events possibly evincing trends—than in the ordering of more tangible and unmistakable observations such as specific acts or expressions of attitude.

Similarly, because of the greater extent of abstraction required of the decision-maker to arrive at generalizations than to arrive at specific con- clusions, we would expect more doctrinal premises and more doctrinal inter- pretation in analyses which lead to generalized conclusions.

An Experimental Examination of Some Propositions about Marxism- Leninism as an Active Ingredient in the Soviet Foreign-Policy Process

To try to throw some light on the validity of this conceptual framework and to make of it an analytically useful tool, we have endeavored to test some specific hypotheses. We selected some quantitative content-analysis techniques to do this.

Quantitative content analysis of public statements is one imperfect but promising method by which modern social scientists seek to overcome the obstacles to investigating motivation in human behavior. Basically, quanti- tative content analysis discovers the frequency of use of selected verbal symbols and semantic formulations and uses this information as one ground for concluding some of the attitudes or beliefs of the speaker. There are pitfalls to such analysis. It would be misleading to think of it as a panacea. But its use can take us part way toward the answers we seek. And it sharpens our thinking, cuts through our cultural biases, and identifies our assumptions in a systematic fashion.[15]

DATA

The records of the XXIInd CPSU Congress in October, 1961 provide a unique opportunity to examine the carefully considered formulations of most of the top Soviet elite (at a time when the membership of this elite was relatively stable) in exactly the same environment. All of the speeches placed the authors in the same position of personal responsibility before a primary audience of their elite colleagues, subordinate CPSU officials, and foreign communist leaders. They were similarly facing a secondary audience of the lower Soviet bureaucratic echelons, the Soviet public, and all strata of the international public simultaneously, making the orchestration of propaganda themes and deceptions very difficult. The context was primarily one of analysis of long-range plans and expectations, with approximately one-third of the floor time devoted to foreign affairs. Innovations of policy were not being debated; the Congress was not a deliberative body. But, choices were elaborated and justified, interpreted, ratified, and disseminated at the Congress. And, as noted earlier, we have Khrushchev's own word for what we

[15] The following quotation expresses our attitude toward content analysis as a research tool:

Content analysis should begin where traditional modes of research end. The man who wishes to use content analysis for a study of the propaganda of some political party, for example, should steep himself in that propaganda. Before he begins to count, he should read it to detect characteristic mechanisms and devices. He should study the vocabulary and format. He should know the party organization and personnel. From this knowledge he should organize his hypotheses and predictions. At this point, in a conventional study, he would start writing. At this point, in a content analysis, he is, instead, ready to set up his categories, to pretest them and then to start counting.

This may seem like a long and expensive procedure. It is; but it is short and cheap compared with what has sometimes been called 'a fishing expedition.' (Harold D. Lasswell, Daniel Lerner, and Ithiel de Sola Pool, *The Comparative Study of Symbols* [Stanford: Stanford University Press, 1952], p. 65.)

The following works on the methodology and potential of content analysis techniques have been particularly helpful in the development of methodology compatible with the purposes and resources of this study: Bernard Berelson, *Content Analysis in Communication Research* (New York: The Free Press, 1952); Harold D. Lasswell and Nathan Leites, *Language of Politics* (New York: George W. Stewart, Publisher, Inc., 1949); Charles E. Osgood, George J. Suci, and Percy I. Tannenbaum, *The Measurement of Meaning* (Urbana: University of Illinios Press, 1957): Ithiel de Sola Pool, ed., *Trends in Content Analysis* (Urbana: University of Illinois Press, 1959); Robert C. North, Ole R. Holsti, M. George Zaninovich, and Dina A. Zinnes, *Content Analysis, A Handbook with Applications for the Study of International Crisis* (Evanston: Northwestern University Press, 1963); J. David Singer, *Soviet and American Foreign Policy Attitudes: A Content Analysis of Elite Articulations* (China Lake, California: U.S. Naval Ordnance Test Station, January, 1964).

might have inferred anyway—that subject matter and approach of each speech was preplanned with an eye both to immediate impact and to posterity.

Several of our propositions involve comparison of the place of Marxism-Leninism in different contextual settings. The data for comparison of the long-range planning context with that of routine, short-range conduct of Soviet foreign affairs and with crisis situations were taken from Khrushchev's statements only. For the routine material, his statements and public communications with British Prime Minister Macmillan and American President Kennedy in regard to the eighteen-nation Arms Control and Disarmament Conference in Geneva were chosen to reflect verbal conduct before an exacting primary audience and, nearly simultaneously, before a very broad secondary audience in regard to a subject of perceived grave consequence but little time pressure. For the crisis material, Khrushchev's statements at the time of the two Cuban crises of 1961–1962 were chosen. Both of these occasions were clearly perceived to be crises by Khrushchev within the definition we have suggested for "crisis," that is, a situation in which the decision-makers involved perceive their choices to have irrevocable and grave consequences and also perceive time to be of so much essence that an unmistakable commitment is immediately necessary. These once again were statements made before an exacting primary audience and, nearly simultaneously, before a very diverse secondary audience.

METHODOLOGY

A careful reading of the materials of the XXIInd Party Congress discovers numerous instances of verbal formulation which might be cited to sustain conceptually plausible propositions about the place of Marxism-Leninism. But other examples could be collected to support a contradictory argument in almost every case. One advantage of quantitative methods of analysis is that they offer some protection against our own biases.

Two techniques were applied to the data. First, the representational technique of counting instances of words or phrases prejudged to have a high doctrinal loading was used. A word/phrase list for this purpose was developed and amended during the analysis. Terminology was included or rejected according to our prior judgment as to whether or not it constituted a short-hand symbol for a concept or relationship or characteristic property clearly derived from Marxist-Leninist theoretical formulation.[16] The results of this analysis were then expressed by a fraction representing the number

---

[16] See Ithel de Sola Pool *et al.*, *The "Prestige Papers"* (Stanford: Stanford University Press, 1952), pp. 88–90; R. N. Carew Hunt, *A Guide to Communist Jargon* (New York: The Macmillan Company, 1957).

of doctrinally stereotyped words or phrases in proportion to the total number of words in the statement analyzed. We called this fraction a *Doctrinal Stereotype Quotient* (DSQ).

The second technique of content analysis used was instrumental. The statements were examined for the presence of explicit, related premises and conclusions. Where the text indicated that its author perceived a causal or contingent relationship between two propositions, the pair (premise and conclusion) were extracted. These pairs were categorized according to the nature of the premise and its interpretation as reflected in the conclusion. Premises were classified as (1) furnished in their substance by Marxist-Leninist doctrine or (2) furnished by empirical observation. If furnished by empirical observation, we took note whether the observation was of a specific or general occurrence, condition, or attitude. Regardless of whether the premise was attributed to doctrine or empirical observation, each pair was coded as to whether the conclusion drawn was general or specific. Finally, if the premise was an empirical observation, it was coded as to whether or not the occurrence was given a markedly doctrinaire interpretation.

PROPOSITIONS AND FINDINGS

1. The proportion of premises taken entirely from doctrine will be greater in the context of analysis leading to a conclusion of general trends or general expectations for the future than will be the proportion of such doctrinal premises in the context of narrowly focused analysis leading to specific causal relationships or expectations of specific events. (More intellectual abstraction required of the decision-maker.)

This proposition was clearly confirmed in the materials we analyzed. Over three-quarters of all doctrinal premises led to conclusions of general trends or general expectations.

2. The proportion of premises taken entirely from doctrine will be greater in context of analysis of long-range planning and expectations than it will be in the context of routine, short-range analysis and decision. (Less clearly ascertainable empirical evidence available.)

Clearly confirmed in our materials.

3. The proportion of premises taken entirely from doctrine will be greater in the context of a perceived crisis situation than it will be in the context of routine, short-range analysis and decision. (Lack of time prevents collection of all normally available empirical evidence which is perceived relevant.)

We were surprised to find this proposition rejected in the materials we examined. Virtually no doctrinal premises were explicitly invoked by Khrushchev in either context.

4. The proportion of premises taken from empirical observations which

have a marked doctrinal interpretation will be greater in the context of analysis leading to a conclusion of general trends or general expectations for the future than in the context of narrowly focused analysis leading to specific causal relationships or expectations of specific events. (More intellectual abstraction required of the decision-maker.)

The pattern of our results was inconsistent. We could neither confirm nor reject this proposition.

5. The proportion of premises taken from empirical observations which have a marked doctrinal interpretation will be greater in the context of analysis of long-range planning and expectations than it will be in the context of routine, short-range analysis and decision. (Less clearly ascertainable empirical evidence available.)

Clearly confirmed in our materials.

6. The proportion of premises taken from empirical observations which have a marked doctrinal interpretation will be greater in the context of a perceived crisis situation than it will be in the context of routine, short-range analysis and decision. (The belief system tends to rigidify and screen out dissonant stimuli under pressure.)

The proposition could not be confidently confirmed because of great variation among the materials we analyzed.

7. The interpretation of vague or general perceptions of conditions, occurrences, or attitudes will more frequently be markedly doctrinaire than will interpretation of specific conditions, occurrences, or attitudes. (More leeway for interpretation by the decision-maker.)

Overall, the evidence is inconclusive here; it follows the proposition for the long-range and routine, short-range contexts, but there is a reversal in the crisis context. Specific conditions, occurrences, and attitudes are most likely to be interpreted doctrinairely in the long-range context, but they are more likely to be interpreted doctrinally in the crisis context than in the routine, short-range context. Vague or general conditions, occurrences, or attitudes are most likely to be interpreted doctrinairely in the long-range context, but they are less likely to be so interpreted in the crisis context than in the routine, short-range context. The proposition thus remains unconfirmed.

8. The impact of doctrine will be greater in the context of analysis of long-range planning and expectations than it will be in the context of routine, short-range analysis and decision. (Combines Propositions 2 and 5.)

Clearly confirmed in our materials.

9. The impact of doctrine will be greater in the context of a perceived crisis situation than it will be in the context of routine, short-range analysis and decision. (Combines Propositions 3 and 6.)

Unconfirmed in our materials. Again we found too great a variation to warrant confident conclusions.

Going beyond the premises for conclusions in the subject area of foreign affairs to the mere presence or absence of doctrinal stereotypes in the verbal formulation of international problems and their solutions by Soviet decision-makers, we can add the following propositions and findings.

10. There will be a greater density of doctrinal stereotypes present in the context of analysis of long-range planning and expectations than there will be in the context of routine, short-range analysis and decision. (Lack of clearly ascertainable empirical evidence available.)

Clearly confirmed in our materials.

11. There will be a greater density of doctrinal stereotypes present in the context of analysis of a perceived crisis situation than there will be in the context of routine, short-range analysis and decision. (The belief system tends to rigidify and screen out dissonant stimuli under pressure.)

As was the case with our other expectations in regard to the crisis context, this proposition remains unconfirmed in our materials.

12. There will be greater density of doctrinal stereotypes present in the foreign-affairs formulations of elite members whose primary role involves them only peripherally in foreign affairs than in the foreign-affairs formulations of elite members whose role involves foreign affairs directly and

Table IV-1

DECISION-MAKERS: ELITE CONCERNED WITH FOREIGN AFFAIRS (DECREASING ORDER OF INVOLVEMENT)	DSQ (FOREIGN AFFAIRS)	DSQ (OVERALL)
Khrushchev	.045	.033
1. Gromyko	.013	.013
2. Malinovsky	.010	.012
3. Kuusinen	.041	.044
4. Mikoyan	.036	.039
5. Ponomarev	.063	.051
6. Adzhubei	.007	.008
7. Pospelov	.049	.042
8. Suslov	.050	.065
9. Brezhnev	.029	.025
10. Grishin	.058	.032
11. Shelepin	.020	.019
12. Satiukov	.064	.043
	Range .007 — .064 Median .039	Range .008 — .065 Median .036

extensively. (There is a relative lack of exposure to relevant empirical stimuli.)

Clearly confirmed in our materials (see Table IV–1).

13. There will be a greater overall density of doctrinal stereotypes present in the verbal formulations of elite members directly and extensively involved in foreign affairs than in the formulations of elite members whose role involves primarily domestic affairs. (More comprehensive empirical evidence is available to the domestic decision-maker.)

Clearly confirmed in our materials (see Table IV–2).

Table IV-2

FOREIGN-AFFAIRS PERIPHERAL (DECREASING ORDER)	DSQ (FOREIGN AFFAIRS)	DSQ (OVERALL)
1. Kozlov	.055	.032
2. Polyansky	.034	.010
3. Kosygin	.058	.015
4. Podgorny	.044	.020
5. Ilichev	.051	.043
6. Ignatov	.050	.018
7. Kirilenko	.053	.018
8. Voronov	.087	.009
9. Shvernik	.044	.027
10. Mazurov	.075	.012
11. Mzhavanadze	.030	.023
12. Demichev	.039	.019
13. Golikov	—	.018
14. Rashidov	—	.018
15. Spiridonov	—	.024
	Range .030 — .087	Range .009 — .043
	Median .051	Median .018

14. The density of doctrinal stereotypes in the verbal formulations of older members of the Soviet foreign-affairs elite will be greater than that among the younger members. (There is a perceived decrease in utility of Marxist-Leninist doctrinal propositions in a nonrevolutionary epoch for the Soviet Union.)

Clearly confirmed in our materials.

Both the premise-analysis and doctrinal-stereotype findings showed a striking contrast between doctrinal impact in short-range statements by Khrushchev and statements by Khrushchev and other Soviet elite members at the XXIInd Party Congress. It occurred to us that intervening variables might be distorting the apparent results. It seemed plausible to suggest that the relatively high DSQ in Khrushchev's Congress statements might follow

Table IV-3 Soviet Foreign Affairs Elite at Time of the XXIInd Party
Congress*

RANKED IN DECREASING ORDER OF OVERALL DSQ	
1. Suslov	.065
2. Ponomarev	.051
3. Kuusinen	.044
5. Satiukov	.043
5. Pospelov	.042
6. Mikoyan	.039
7. Khrushchev	.033
8. Grishin	.032
9. Brezhnev	.025
10. Shelepin	.019
11. Gromyko	.013
12. Malinovsky	.012
13. Adzhubei	.008

* Underlining indicates individuals remaining in the foreign-affairs elite in mid-1967.

from a perceived need to rationalize long-range outlooks and plans for Soviet foreign policy in terms of doctrine for purely propagandistic purposes. The Soviet leader was, after all, speaking here in his role as Party First Secretary and Presidium member, whereas in the non-Congress material he was speaking as Chairman of the Council of Ministers. Also, at the Congress, Khrushchev's primary audience consisted of Soviet Party and government colleagues—the Soviet elite—whereas in the non-Congress material his primary audience consisted of foreign, noncommunist elites.

We made two checks to try to clarify the probabilities of distortion resulting from such intervening variables. First, the text of Khrushchev's three major statements at the Congress was broken down according to whether the subject matter concerned relatively long-range and general or short-range and specific material. The DSQ were computed separately for each category. While both DSQ were appreciably higher than those found in the non-Congress material, the contrast in DSQ here confirmed the sharp break when the context of analysis changed from the long-range and general to the short-range and specific.

Secondly, comparative DSQ were sought from a further sample of Khrushchev's foreign-affairs statements in which the context of analysis was short-range and specific but in which the primary audience more closely approximated that of the Congress.

On June 15, 1961, and again on August 7, 1961, Khrushchev went before the Soviet people directly on radio and television for major speeches. In the first case his 8,900-word statement was devoted entirely to the current foreign-affairs issues which he had just discussed with the American President at Vienna. The context was therefore relatively short range and specific, consisting primarily of questions of disarmament and arms control, Germany and the status of Berlin. The DSQ for this statement was very low (.006). In the second case, eight weeks later, Khrushchev began his statement with a discussion of the recently published Draft Program for the CPSU, saying that he would speak briefly of domestic affairs and then dwell at greater length on the international situation. By way of transition from discussion of the Draft Program to the current issues of foreign affairs (again chiefly the German question and disarmament), he devoted some 1,150 words (12 per cent of the statement) to a description of general trends in the international system. Here his DSQ was relatively high (.049). Thereafter, he turned to the aforementioned specific and short-range issues for some 5,800 words. Here his DSQ dropped sharply to (.007).

We concluded from these two checks that the two intervening variables which it was infeasible to hold constant in this study, the primary audience and the official role from which statements were made, were not of sufficient importance to significantly alter our earlier findings or invalidate the conclusions they sustain. We would propose as plausible though unverified explanations of the insignificance of these variables first, the growing futility of segregating the primary and secondary audiences of public statements as a result of modern communications developments, and, secondly, the practical fusion of Khrushchev's two roles of Party leader and government leader.

What have our content-analysis findings entitled us to say about the place of Marxist-Leninist doctrine as an active ingredient in the process of Soviet foreign-policy decision-making?

We have distinguished among the Soviet decision elite and found that Marxism-Leninism is not a constant in their verbal formulations but varies with different individuals. In general, it is more evident in the formulations of older members of the elite and those whose elite status has been achieved chiefly in Party work. It is less evident among the younger elite and those who have pursued primarily government careers.

We have found that the evidence of Marxism-Leninism is also correlated with the decision-makers' substantive competence: more in the area of foreign affairs than in that of domestic construction of socialism. Here, however, we also observed that when a chiefly domestic decision-maker considered foreign affairs he was prone to adopt very doctrinaire referents and exhibit a higher DSQ than the foreign-affairs professionals.

We have found Marxism-Leninism strikingly correlated with the time span under consideration by the decision-maker. In the context of analysis of long-range planning and expectations, the evidence of doctrinal impact is far higher than in the context of relatively short-range analysis and expectations. In the latter context, the impact of doctrine has been found very small indeed, and no significant variation has been observed for crisis behavior, although this remains an open question in some respects.

Next, we have found that the visible evidence of Marxism-Leninism seems to be directly correlated with the level of abstraction in the conclusions arrived at by the decision-makers: more doctrine in the case of broad generalization and less in the case of specific conclusions. More evidence of doctrine is also apparent where empirical perception by the decision-maker has been vague or general and where extensive leeway for interpretation has existed.

Finally, we must note that the content analysis performed here definitely rejects the possibility that Soviet foreign-policy decision-makers draw all their premises from Marxism-Leninism or even that all empirical premises are doctrinally distorted in their perception. Doctrinal interpretation of empirical observations is considerably more frequent than occasions where premises were taken entirely from doctrine. But in all cases, even where the presence of doctrine was most clearly evident, empirical observations without identifiable doctrinal refraction were also utilized as premises. In the section which follows we shall examine directly the functions of events in Soviet foreign policy. After that we shall have a better basis for assessing the *interaction* of the two variables.

The major unexpected result of our analysis is the lack of distinction between doctrinal influence in short-range, routine-decision situations and crisis-decision situations. Although some difference is indicated in the likelihood of doctrinaire interpretation of specific as opposed to generalized observations in these cases, the bulk of our findings reject any difference in overall doctrinal influence between these two contexts. We had expected to find greater recourse to doctrine under the time pressure of a crisis.

Looking closely at the statements taken from the crisis context, it is apparent that in the 1962 Cuban Missile Crisis, in particular, Khrushchev perceived a collision course of events which seemed to be slipping from his control and acquiring a dynamic energy of their own. It was almost in desperation that he appealed to President Kennedy to recognize the imminence of catastrophe and the fact that he, Khrushchev, did not want this catastrophe to occur but was incapable of acting to prevent it. He perceived himself to be boxed in by past commitments which seemed irrevocable, so that he had to depend upon an initiative from Kennedy to avert the calamity. We note particularly Khrushchev's pained expression of perceived predicament in his open letter to Bertrand Russell of October 24: "We have no other way out."[17]

The constriction upon perceived alternatives in a crisis situation seems here to repeat a pattern documented for the pre-World War I crisis of 1914, particularly in the behavior of the German Kaiser.[18] But there is no clear indication here that doctrine became a more critical component of the perceptual field of the decision-maker under such pressure. To the contrary, it seems plausible to conclude from the findings here that doctrine really became irrelevant to the Soviet foreign-affairs leadership after once playing its major part in setting the cognitive pattern of general relationships in human society and in formulating long-range expectations and plans. This should not be construed to discount the latter functions, for their legacy is a train of perceptions and policies leading to such occasions when the decision-maker may perceive, with the most pragmatic intent, that "we have no other way out." The finding here, however, may be construed optimistically: it indicates that there was no increase in recourse to doctrine by Khrushchev in crisis situations and thus no added barrier to communication. One conclusion from this finding might be that signals clearly delivered by noncommunist national actors will probably be understood as intended by the Soviet leadership.

On the other hand, we should take note that the unit of analysis for all of our experimental comparisons of crisis and short-range verbal formulations was Khrushchev. The clear possibility arises that the impact of the belief system may vary with personality or, more likely, that while the belief system does uniformly tend to rigidify and gain importance in the face of a perceived crisis, doctrine did not make up a large enough part of Khrushchev's belief system to bring about an identifiable change in his crisis verbal behavior. Either way the relative DSQ of the individuals who have replaced Khrushchev becomes a point of considerable interest. It is thus noteworthy that both Brezhnev and Kosygin trail Khrushchev in that respect.

The empirical analysis in this section does not itself preclude the logical

[17] *The New York Times,* October 25, 1962, p. 22.

[18] See Dina A. Zinnes, Robert C. North, and Howard E. Koch, Jr., "Capability, Threat and the Outbreak of War," in James N. Rosenau, ed., *International Politics and Foreign Policy* (New York: The Free Press of Glencoe, 1961), pp. 469–82; also Ole R. Holsti, "The 1914 Case," *American Political Science Review,* LIX, No. 2 (June, 1965), 365–378.

possibility that in the long-range planning and analytical context the high DSQ results from cynical use of doctrinaire terminology to mask non-doctrinaire perceptions. Quite probably, insofar as the bureaucratic impulse of organizational conservatism is concerned, self-seeking personal aspirations and chauvinistic pragmatism condition Soviet foreign-policy premises and disingenuous use is made of the convenient Marxist-Leninist formulations. Our analysis does reveal, however, the following general correlations: (1) doctrinal influence and the subject under consideration, (2) doctrinal influence and the categories of decision context, and (3) doctrinal influence and professional role and career experience of elite members. Some consistent and unmistakable relations have been indicated in our sample.

The impact of linguistic formulation by itself upon human thought patterns has been persuasively demonstrated in other studies.[19] Thus, even if total cynicism were posited for the Soviet elite's recourse to doctrinal stereotypes and premises (and this "noise level" is hardly compatible with the effective and efficient accomplishment of the bureaucratic task facing that elite today), the pervasiveness of the doctrinal formulations may safely be inferred to guarantee Marxist-Leninist doctrine a strong and variable influence as an active ingredient of Soviet foreign policymaking.

B. THE NATURE AND FUNCTIONS OF EVENTS

The process of Soviet foreign-policy formulation and execution occurs in a context of *events*, i.e., changes in the environment. The institutions of Soviet foreign policy are the outcome of past events and they are reshaped in response to an environment which continues to change. The men who make Soviet foreign policy are affected by events they perceive; their opportunities for influence, as well as their goals and expectations, are largely determined by their location in relation to events. Formal systems of belief are molded and repeatedly challenged or reinforced by perceptions of events. And, in their turn, institutions and men and doctrines leave their own imprint on the course of events.

For example, when we consider institutions we recall that the first People's Commissar for Foreign Affairs proposed to preside over the demise of the Soviet Foreign Office. Trotsky, and apparently Lenin too, felt confident in

---

[19] See, for example, S. I. Hayakawa, *Language in Thought and Action* (New York: Harcourt, Brace & World, Inc., 1949), pp. 18–22, 24–33, 165–185, 253–266. For consideration of this phenomenon in the context of Soviet politics, see Barrington Moore, Jr., *Soviet Politics—The Dilemma of Power* (Cambridge, Mass.: Harvard University Press, 1950), pp. 414–418.

1917 that a unique concept of international relations would enable them to change radically the format of international transactions that had become entrenched during the century since the Congress of Vienna. But Soviet achievement over the next five years was largely the story of relinquishment of this early enthusiasm and of institutional adaptation to a persistent environmental condition that could not be wished away. Soviet Russia adopted the institutions of conventional "bourgeois" diplomacy. Conversely, the dual institutions of Foreign Office and Communist International—the configuration imposed on a reluctant Soviet Russia by the international system—so disconcerted the Allies that they could not resolve the question of whether they should accept the anomaly, attack it, or ignore it in hopes it would disappear. A significant portion of international relations in the decade following the Bolshevik Revolution was the story of efforts by the Western powers to find ways to adapt their own institutions for the dual confrontation with both a Soviet state and, concurrently, the agent of international communism.[20]

Considering individual men, we note that the failure of "collective security" to restrain Hitler brought on both the replacement of Maxim Litvinov by Viacheslav Molotov as Soviet Foreign Minister and the Nazi-Soviet Pact in 1939.[21] In later years, no less spectacularly, the events of "Barbarossa" and U.S. commitment to war in Korea each abruptly deflected Stalin's foreign policy.[22] And it was Stalin's apparent inability to cope successfully with the impact of the Marshall Plan and Tito's defection that foretold the disruption of the Soviet system of domination in Eastern Europe after 1953. More recently, it would be hard to deny the role of the 1956 Polish and Hungarian uprisings in Khrushchev's foreign policy in Eastern Europe, or for that matter, the continued disintegration of Soviet hegemony in East Europe as a factor in Khrushchev's 1964 political demise.

A dramatic impact of events upon doctrine, confirmed in 1956 at the XXth Party Congress, cannot be mistaken: the clear and candidly acknowledged

[20] See Louis Fischer, *The Soviets in World Affairs* (London: Jonathan Cape, 1930), particularly Volume I, 279–299; George F. Kennan, *Russia and the West Under Lenin and Stalin* (Boston: Little, Brown & Company, 1961), pp. 165–107; and the documentary surveys, Xenia Joukoff Eudin and Harold H. Fisher, *Soviet Russia and the West, 1920–1927* (Stanford: Stanford University Press, 1957); and Xenia Joukoff Eudin and Robert C. North, *Soviet Russia and the East, 1920–1927* (Stanford: Stanford University Press, 1957).

[21] See Max Beloff, *The Foreign Policy of Soviet Russia, 1929–1941* (London: Oxford University Press, 1947–1949), II, 120–166, 211–319.

[22] See Marshall D. Shulman, *Stalin's Foreign Policy Reappraised* (Cambridge, Mass.: Harvard University Press, 1963), pp. 139–175; J. M. Mackintosh, *Strategy and Tactics of Soviet Foreign Policy* (N.Y.: Oxford University Press, 1963), Chapter 4.

changes in the Soviet doctrine of war, wrought by recognition of the destructive potential of nuclear energy.

But all of these cases merely lead to the conclusion that, yes, there is a reciprocal relationship between events on the one hand and institutions, men, and Marxist-Leninist doctrine on the other. The interesting and unanswered questions remain: What is the nature of the relationship? How do events enter the foreign-policy decision process of the Soviet Union?

The function of events has sometimes been counterposed to the function of doctrine in Soviet foreign policy, with the assumption that where one was operative the other would not be. The controversy over "ideology versus national interest" has frequently followed this path. Our analysis in the preceding section urges the fallacy of such a dichotomy, suggesting that Marxist-Leninist internationalism and Soviet national welfare can never be wholly separated. The priority of national survival was established by March, 1918 and has not been seriously questioned since. Because of the relatively few occasions when a premise for decision can be identified as taken entirely from propositions in the "sacred texts" of Marxism-Leninism, if this were the only entry of doctrine into the decision process it might be dismissed as of little practical import. Much more frequently we find that doctrine enters as an interpretive modifier to which perceived events are subjected. It is a set of symbolic referents by which a specific national interest in any one case can be subjectively formulated. In the vast majority of cases, the statement of fact which furnishes the premise for a subsequent conclusion draws upon the perception of an event or condition of the real world, whether or not doctrinally interpreted. The abstractions of doctrine are seldom called upon by themselves. National interest, we repeat, is a conclusion drawn from perceptions of fact and value; some of these perceptions are evaluated with reference to Marxist-Leninist abstractions and some of them are not.

Given this mutual dependence, let us try to explain the function of events not only in relation to doctrine but as a typology of conditioners of the foreign-policy process with distinguishable differences in impact. Our first step will be to describe the outlines of Soviet foreign policies for the 1960's, trying to assume the vantage point of Soviet decision-makers.

Borrowing from Stalin, we might call the general analysis of the international situation presented by Khrushchev and his colleagues at the XXIInd Party Congress an assessment of the "permanently operating factors" of the 1960's. Public propositions about the international system and the position of the Soviet Union within it reflected the perceived background conditions against which Soviet leaders could set finite events for evaluation.

These Soviet-perceived background conditions may be presented concisely.

The same themes repeatedly emerge in the speeches of the Congress, frequently in identical phraseology with variation only in the supporting and qualifying material. Their first appearance came in Khrushchev's formulation of the Central Committee Report. It is not surprising that resolutions on the international situation later adopted by the Congress assiduously followed Khrushchev's themes. According to the First Secretary himself, the report had been scrutinized and approved by each member of the Politburo. The Central Committee had presumably inspected and ratified the text when meeting for that purpose the week before the Congress opened.

There were five major Soviet themes, under each of which several subthemes might be subsumed. The following formulations are our summaries and condensations, using so far as possible the words of the original: "Report of the Central Committee of the Communist Party of the Soviet Union to the XXIInd Party Congress—Report by Comrade N. S. Khrushchev."[23]

1. The main content of the period after the XXth Party Congress [February, 1956] has been the competition of two world systems—the socialist and the capitalist.

2. Socialism has been consolidated into the framework of a growing and strengthening world-wide commonwealth.

3. The capitalist system has been declining in internal power and international influence.

4. The disintegration of the colonial system continues.

5. The campaign of socialist and peace-loving elements against the preparation of a new aggression and war constitutes the main substance of contemporary world politics.

Let us take each of these main themes about the international situation and examine its component parts.

Under (1), the competition of the two world systems, we find the following contentions:

(A) The socialist system is one of harmony, arising from the common interests of the socialist countries oriented toward social progress, peace, creative activity.

(B) The capitalist system is one of conflict, arising from the contradictions within and between capitalist countries; but, the system is united by its opposition to the socialist system. It represents reaction, aggression, war.

[23] *Pravda* and *Izvestiia,* October 18, 1961, pp. 2–11 as translated in Charlotte Saikowski and Leo Gruliow, eds., *Current Soviet Policies IV* (New York: Columbia Universtiy Press, 1962), pp. 42–77.

(C) Bourgeois political leaders nourish the thought that the socialist system will fail and distintegrate, and they devise provocations and diversions to foster this.

(D) The socialist system demonstrates to the masses that only socialism can solve their pressing problems.

(E) There is competition between the socialist and capitalist systems in the area of social/cultural progress.

(F) There is competition between the socialist and capitalist systems in the area of economic production.

(G) There is competition between the socialist and capitalist systems in the area of scientific production.

(H) There is competition between the socialist and capitalist systems in the area of military strength.

Under (2), the consolidation, growth, and strengthening of the socialist system, we find the following:

(A) The rate of development of material production in the socialist system surpasses that in the capitalist system.

(B) Industrial productivity is increasing faster in the socialist system.

(C) Total production in the socialist system is 36 per cent of total world production, but the socialist share is steadily increasing.

(D) The military strength of the socialist system is sufficient to defend against or reliably deter capitalist military threats.

(E) The People's Democracies have liquidated multistructural elements of their economies and are completing the building of socialism. Their strength assures the stability of future development.

(F) Over 90 per cent of the socialist system's agricultural production is now on a cooperative base.

(G) The living standard throughout the socialist system is being raised.

(H) Fraternal aid and cooperation among the countries of the system are being fully developed: consolidation of plans through COMECON, military consolidation through WTO.

(I) The rapid growth of trade within the system continues.

(J) Communist parties throughout the world are increasing in number and size overall: twelve new parties, 7 million new Communists in recent years.

(K) The world-wide socialist system is becoming the decisive factor in the development of world society.

(L) The Albanian leaders have departed from the commonly agreed course for the communist movement.

Under (3), decline of internal power and international influence of the capitalist system, we find:

(A) Contradictions in the capitalist countries are sharpening: the U.S. economy has suffered repeated recessions since World War II; the achievements of science only aggravate capitalist contradictions, as exemplified by the effect of automation on employment.

(B) Capitalism is suffering a moral defeat throughout the world. The masses are becoming convinced that it cannot solve their problems, that the only solution lies along the roads of socialism.

(C) Monopolist capital is losing its influence, as indicated by more frequent recourse to intimidation and oppression of its subjects.

(D) Capitalism can still postpone its doom by resorting to localized repression, but such action unmasks its true nature and hastens its eventual demise.

Under (4), the continuing disintegration of the colonial system, we find:

(A) The national liberation movement is defeating remaining colonial regimes.

(B) There is a continuing upsurge of revolutionary struggles for national liberation throughout the countries which have been the victims of the colonial system of imperialism: twenty-eight states have gained their political independence in the past six years.

(C) Increasing class consciousness among the peoples of the newly independent countries favors the development of socialist forms there.

(D) The peoples of Asia, Africa, and Latin America are turning more frequently to the socialist countries for the benefit of their experience in political and economic development and for protection and support against the imperialists.

(E) Neocolonial forms are being utilized by the imperialist countries to try to recoup their declining position in Asia, Africa, and Latin America. These forms include unequal treaties and military alliances.

Under (5), the primary importance of the campaign against the preparation of new war and aggression, we find:

(A) In the past few years, the forces of war and aggression have repeatedly threatened universal peace by resorting to brute force, e.g., the 1956 attack on Egypt, the 1957 intervention in Jordan and Lebanon, the 1961 invasion of Cuba, the 1961 effort to subjugate Laos.

(B) The preponderance of the forces of socialism has frustrated the imperialists' efforts to unleash a world war.

(C) The forces of war and aggression are not abandoning their efforts to bring the world to the brink of war. This is exemplified by threats of force in response to Soviet efforts to conclude a German peace treaty and normalize the status of West Berlin.

(D) Imperialist foreign policy is determined by the class interests of monopoly capital, in which aggression and war are organically endemic.

(E) When pressure from the masses enables moderate forces to take the upper hand in capitalist countries, international tension and the threat of war somewhat abate. When pressure from the masses relaxes and those who profit from war and the arms race take the upper hand, the international tension becomes more acute.

(F) The forces of aggression are becoming more insolent, as indicated by the attempt of the West German Bundeswehr to become the major military force in Western Europe today.

(G) The imperialist countries really do not want disarmament; they have brought talks on nuclear weapons to an impasse.

(H) Wars between states are not inevitable; peaceful competition can lead to socialist victory.

Taken together, these themes outline the Soviet leaders' public definition of the condition of the international system at the time of the XXIInd Party Congress. Two sources of distortion from their true assessment should be considered. First, because the Congress was intended to fulfill a rally function as well as a communicative function, there is a constant optimistic distortion (both by selection and interpretation). The Sino-Soviet conflict, for instance, was not explicitly mentioned in the survey of relations within the socialist system. Secondly, because the primary audience for Mr. Khrushchev's report was the Party elite of world communism, there is probably a self-conscious overuse of Marxist-Leninist terminology—the product of an intentional matching of audience and symbols. Our comparative tests of Khrushchev's use of doctrinal stereotypes in the last section confirm this likelihood. With these qualifications held in mind, we may accept the framework as presented, subject to comparison with Soviet behavior.

The Central Committee Report not only described the international environment but located the Soviet Union within it and identified tasks for the Soviet Union with regard to it. The position of the USSR included the following cluster or propositions:

1. The Soviet Union has entered the period of all-out building of communism, in which the material prerequisites for communist forms of societal relations are to be created.

2. The Soviet economy and culture are progressively more prosperous and the country militarily stronger than ever before.

3. Although the period since the XXth Congress has not been a simple one for which to formulate policy—we are pioneers over unexplored paths— the years have shown that the Party-Line set at the XXth Congress is correct.

It has been of great importance in pursuit of the goals of unity in the communist movement, preservation of peace and prevention of a new world war.

4. The relations of the Soviet Union with countries of different social systems are governed by the policy of peaceful coexistence with peaceful competition. The relations of the Soviet Union with countries of the socialist system are governed by the policy of fraternal collaboration. These policies are intended to avoid world war and to foster the eventual victory of the socialist system.

5. In carrying out these policies the Soviet Union continues to expose and frustrate the persistent machinations of imperialist elements who take recourse to violence. It also provides a bulwark of support to the peoples of the colonial and semicolonial countries in their struggle for independence and freedom.

Based upon this description of the international environment and the Soviet position within it, the Soviet leaders *professed* the following more specific lines of foreign policy:

1. to seek a program of general and complete disarmament which would bring an end to the arms race and a universal rejection of arms as a means of solving disputes between states.

2. to seek a peace treaty with Germany consolidating the German frontiers defined by the Potsdam Agreement.

3. to seek on the basis of a German peace treaty to normalize the status of West Berlin as a free, demilitarized city, to which international access must depend upon agreements with the German Democratic Republic.

4. to seek representation for the Chinese People's Republic and both German states in the United Nations.

5. to seek full equality of rights in the United Nations for the three groups of states: socialist, neutralist, and imperialist.

6. to seek the final liquidation of colonialism in all its forms.

7. to liquidate the consequences of colonialism by offering newly independent states friendly economic and cultural assistance and support against all forms of imperialist encroachment.

8. to seek recompense by the former colonial powers to their former possessions.

9. to seek atom-free zones in Europe and the Far East.

10. to seek a nonaggression pact between the countries of the WTO and NATO.

11. to seek a zone of disengagement of Armed Forces of military blocs and reduction of Armed Forces stationed abroad.

12. to seek the dissolution of all military alliances and the withdrawal of all Armed Forces stationed abroad.

13. to improve mutually advantageous economic and cultural ties with the socialist countries on the basis of long-term coordinated plans.

14. to develop cooperation with the great powers of Asia: India and Indonesia on a business-like basis.

15. to develop similar relations with the newly independent countries of Asia, Africa, and the Middle East.

16. to offer assistance to the people of the Congo to help them liquidate the consequences of colonial oppression.

17. to help the people of young independent states gain strength and take their place in international affairs.

18. to seek normalized relations with the U.S., built on principles of peaceful economic competition and renunciation of war to settle disputes.

19. to expand trade and cultural relations with West European countries.

20. to seek improved relations with neighbouring states: Austria, Sweden, Afghanistan, Finland, Norway, Denmark, Turkey, Iran, Pakistan, and Japan —which may be friendly and mutually advantageous despite differences of social and political systems.

21. to seek a Soviet-Japanese peace treaty.

22. to seek a greater volume of trade with the nonsocialist countries and the reduction of obstacles to such trade.

23. to seek continuing expansion of cultural relations with all countries.

24. to seek continuing direct contacts between leading figures of other countries and leading figures in the Soviet Union.

The foregoing pages have described the international environment and the relation to it and intents of the Soviet Union, all from the Soviet perspective presented at the XXIInd Party Congress. The only way to sort the policies adopted as purely psychological appeals from those adopted in substance as well is to compare the subsequent record of Soviet physical action with this verbal behavior.

The record of Soviet international activity in the five years following the XXIInd Congress cast considerable doubt upon the more altruistic gloss of these professions. Our purpose in identifying the verbal commitments here, however, is neither exposé nor absolution. The record of action is given our attention in Chapters V to XI. The point now is that whether undertaken as diversionary or expiating ploys or as bona fide commitments, these policies reflect intrinsically a reaction both to events and to the imperatives of Marxism-Leninism.

It is clear from these professed policies that the targets and respondents[24]

---

[24] The target and the respondent may be but are not necessarily the same. For example, a Soviet transaction with the U.S. as respondent may have as its Soviet target popular attitudes in Latin America.

for Soviet representations abroad as well as the content of the representations are in large part conditioned by the analysis of the international system and the place within it occupied by the USSR—as formulated by the Soviet leadership and abstracted from their statements. This formulation included the identification of *adversaries* (the imperialists and primarily the U.S.), of *collaborators* (the socialist countries), and more or less passive *subjects* to be manipulated (the newly independent and industrially backward countries) in a tripartite world. It also specified the scope and content of such policies as "support for the newly independent states to liquidate the consequences of colonialism," "conformity with the principles of proletarian international-ism," and "frustration of imperialist plans."

It is worth emphasizing at this point that when the setting is understood from the Soviet perspective, the designation of adversaries, collaborators, and subjects and the content of these policies as professed by Soviet officials follow rather logically. It is only when evaluated by non-Soviet standards with a different perspective of the setting that many actions seem either enigmatic or inconsistent with professions.

Thus, for example, in the specifications above, most American readers would make the following definitional translations:

1. "deterrence or frustration of imperialist encroachments against the Soviet Union" means "a convincing show of force and determination, or mobilization of pressure abroad in response to alleged threats to the USSR from U.S., British, French, and West German governments."
2. "liquidate the consequences of colonialism by offering support against imperialist encroachments" includes "reduce or eliminate U.S., British, French, Dutch, West German influence in Asia, Africa, and Latin America."
3. "seek socialist conformity with the principles of proletarian inter-nationalism" means "seek acceptance in all socialist countries of the main foreign and domestic lines of policy specified by the CPSU."

These are merely indicative of the general necessity to read Soviet policy specifications using Soviet definitions for Soviet terminology.[25] External value loadings must be self-consciously held in abeyance in order to grasp the implications for the policymaking process.

Implementation of the enumerated Soviet policies fell to the institutional structure and its staff as described in earlier chapters. Taken *in toto*, the policies may be usefully conceptualized as a system of programs, their

[25] For a partial guide to Soviet definitions, see R. N. Carew Hunt, *A Guide to Communist Jargon* (N.Y.: The Macmillan Company, 1957), *passim*.

content conditioned by long-range goals and perceptions of the setting and each operating in the larger international system: influencing and influenced by that environment. Graphically we have the following incomplete model of this system in Diagram IV-1.

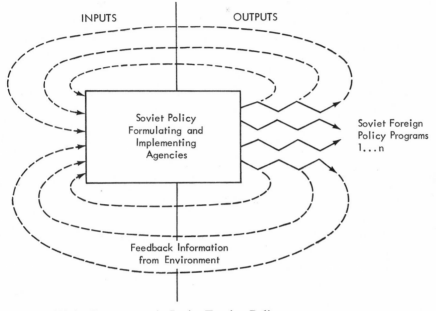

INPUTS   OUTPUTS

Soviet Policy
Formulating and
Implementing
Agencies

Soviet Foreign
Policy Programs
1...n

Feedback Information
from Environment

DIAGRAM IV–1   Programmatic Soviet Foreign Policy

In what ways do events become *inputs* for these programs? In the first place, some events (changes in the environment) are the indicators observed by the Soviet decision-makers to assess effectiveness and efficiency of the programs. In this fashion, they provide periodic reinforcement or doubts. As feedback information, they become inputs for subsequent decisions to modify or continue programs.[26]

But the question raises more complex relationships too. The pursuit of some Soviet foreign-policy programs engages the Soviet Union with relatively passive respondents in cases which admit assessment of policy success or failure without concern for many independent and intervening variables. But it also engages the Soviet Union with adversary respondents. On

[26] An excellent example of this feedback function of events is the survey of the Soviet foreign assistance program in Marshall I. Goldman, "A Balance Sheet of Soviet Foreign Aid," *Foreign Affairs*, XLIII, No. 2 (January, 1965), 349–360. On the same subject, see Janos Horvath, "Moscow's Aid Program: The Performance So Far," *East Europe*, XII, No. 11, 8–20.

occasion, Soviet programs are directly counterposed to antagonistic programs undertaken by independent national actors. Such, for example, was the case of the effort to achieve a status of military superiority over the United States to serve the policy of "deterring or frustrating imperialist encroachments against the USSR." The United States sought the same goal in reverse, and the result was a direct confrontation of antagonistic programs. While the abstract goals held much in common, the derivative programs held little.

On other occasions, Soviet programs collide obliquely with similar programs undertaken by other nations, usually adversaries. Such, for example, were the cases of competitive Soviet and American propaganda directed to the uncommitted countries and competitive economic assistance to the same countries. The events are stimulated by these collisions are hard for the Soviet Union to foresee, especially when the same target is shared by two adversary programs. Depending upon the immediate circumstances, the issue which is joined might erupt in a sequence of events or incidents with a dynamic logic of its own.

The finite events, or incidents, of Soviet foreign relations during the first half of the 1960's were in most cases the outgrowth of such collisions of Soviet programs with the programs of other countries. Soviet perceptions of these incidents then became inputs—in some cases radically influential inputs—in foreign-policy decision-making.

Incidents of this sort are easy to detect for any period. They furnish the stuff of newspaper headlines. As conditioners of subsequent foreign-policy decisions they differ from the simple success-failure program feedback already discussed. Once a collision of policy programs has occurred, the course of events is seldom more than 50 per cent under the control of any one national actor, often considerably less. The 1961 civil war in Laos is a case in point. Here, a collision of "imperialist" efforts to oppose the growth of "communist" influence in a newly independent country collided with Soviet efforts to reduce or eliminate "imperialist" influence and supplant it with socialist influence. But the immediate circumstances of the collision, involving a complex of personal ambitions and loyalties in Laos, reduced the extent of Soviet control over the course of events just as it reduced "imperialist" control. Thus loosened from the control of the original adversaries, the events that their colliding programs had stimulated became the basis for perceived threats and perceived opportunities, entering subsequent foreign-policy decision-making in these forms as well as object lessons for formulating new efforts to achieve the original program's goals.

Still other finite events may be of importance for Soviet foreign-policy decision-making. Incidents may arise from the collision of policy programs of third states, collisions which are tenuously related or even unrelated to Soviet programs. These incidents may sufficiently disturb the international environment to become intervening variables which can not be ignored by Soviet decision-makers. Such, for example, was the case of the Sino-Indian conflict in late 1962 or the malice-laden course of Arab-Israeli relations at various times since 1947. Both threats and opportunities for Soviet foreign policies may be the perceived impact of such incidents. Either way they become inputs for the Soviet decision process. Domestic events likewise, both within the decision-makers' own state and within other states, become inputs for national foreign-policy decisions when they are perceived to furnish opportunities or threats to national policy programs. Examples are Soviet perceptions of Chinese economic difficulties in 1959–1960, or the great Proletarian Cultural Revolution of 1966–1967, or the U.S. presidential election results in 1960 and 1964.

Now let us examine individually the nature and effects of some sequences of events in the early 1960's. Each emerged from major international issues, and each threw some light upon the functions of events in the Soviet foreign-policy process. The fifteen cases we have picked are classified roughly in the Table IV-4 according to a number of salient and significant characteristics.

One-third of the fifteen sequences found the United States and Soviet Union primarily respondents at the outset. Of these, the Cuban Bay of Pigs affair of April, 1961, the establishment of the Berlin Wall that August, and the Cuban missile confrontation of October, 1962 were of the high-stakes, short-decision-time form common to all severe *crisis* situations.[27] The immediate acts which occasioned the common sense of crisis here were once (Berlin) Soviet initiated, and twice American initiated.[28] Of lower perceived consequence, the unresolved issue of nuclear-test cessation (subsumed beneath the larger question of general disarmament) afforded much greater decision time. Between these poles, both in perceived consequences and decision time, was the Loatian civil war, a conflict which was moderated and contained by the long Geneva negotiations leading to new, formal neutralization in June, 1962. It is easy to find the programmatic Soviet-policy background for each of these sequences of events in the policies specified earlier in this section.

Three of the remaining sequences (the Sino-Soviet and Soviet-Albanian

[27] See Figure II-2 above. The crisis decision trajectory is characterized by maximum importance and minimum time.

[28] We deal with the bases of criteria for these judgments in Chapter IX. It is action started by a respondent who perceives an intolerable level of risk to himself from inaction that engages the crisis.

estrangement and the COMECON integration effort of 1961–1963) were products of progressive disagreements between the Soviet Union and its socialist "collaborators." Another followed from a Soviet initiative to modify relations with its neighbor Finland. The sporadic Congo civil war and the Sino-Indian war of late 1962 were third-party policy collisions which did not at their outset involve the USSR as either initiator or respondent. The three conflicts pitting Western European nations against their former colonies (Bizerte, the Algerian war, and the Netherlands-Indonesia controversy over West Irian) similarly erupted without the initial participation of the USSR. Finally, the Soviet Union in 1962 began to perceive the accelerating success of Common Market economic integration as a factor which must be reckoned with.

The Berlin Wall, Cuban missile, Sino-Soviet, Soviet-Albanian, and COMECON sequences are all cases of antagonistic collision of Soviet policy programs with programs of other countries. The events which erupted were perceived as direct threats to the attained position of the USSR. While elements of perceived opportunity for policy gains may perhaps be found in these cases, perception of threat unquestionably predominated, and each response was defensive action. The Laotian civil war and the Cuban Bay of Pigs sequences are also cases of antagonistic collision of Soviet policy programs. But in these two instances the USSR perceived itself threatened indirectly, in terms of its objectives in distant geographic areas. Thus the elements of threat are complemented by a larger proportion of opportunity.

Bizerte (where violence erupted over French retention of the naval base), the Congo civil war, the Algerian war, and the controversy over West Irian all were products of the collision of third-parties' policy programs. In each case, the Soviet Union recognized the opportunity to serve policies of "liquidation of colonialism" and "support for newly independent countries against the imperialists." The policy programs of one party to each of these collisions were perceived to converge with Soviet programs. The Sino-Indian war, on the other hand, was perceived as a collision of third-parties' policy programs, neither of which converged with Soviet programs and which in collision posed an unmitigated and severe threat to Soviet policies.

The Common Market progress and the sequence with Finland over military cooperation were not the outgrowth of programmatic collisions. The Common Market was perceived as a qualitatively new threat to the USSR (economic discrimination through imperialist cooperation) materializing abroad; conversely, pressure upon Finland to collaborate in the military sector was perceived as a qualitatively new opportunity for policy gain by the USSR.

Table IV-4 Some Selected Aspects of Major International Sequences of Events Affecting Soviet Foreign Policy in the Early 1960's

SEQUENCE OF EVENTS	USSR ENGAGED AT OUTSET	SOURCE OF INITIATIVE	DECISION TIME	DANGER OF GENERAL WAR	SOVIET PERCEPTION OF THREAT/OPPORTUNITY
1. Laotian Civil War	Yes	Pathet Lao/USSR/DRV	Medium	Medium	Opportunity
2. Congo Civil War	No	Lumumba	Medium	Low	Opportunity
3. Nuclear Tests	Yes	U.S./USSR altern.	Long	Low	Opportunity/Threat
4. Cuban Conflict (Bay of Pigs)	Yes	U.S.	Short	High	Threat
5. West Irian Conflict	No	Sukarno	Medium	Low	Opportunity
6. Bizerte Conflict	No	Tunisia	Medium	Low	Opportunity
7. Berlin Wall	Yes	GDR/USSR	Short	High	Threat
8. Soviet-Finnish Conflict	Yes	USSR	Medium	Low	Opportunity
9. Soviet-Albanian Conflict	Yes	USSR	Medium	Low	Opportunity/Threat
10. Soviet-Chinese Conflict	Yes	Chinese People's Republic (CPR)	Long	Low	Threat
11. Algerian War	No	Front of National Liberation (FLN)	Medium	Low	Opportunity
12. Common Market Issue	No	European Economic Community (EEC)	Long	Low	Threat
13. Cuban Conflict (Missiles)	Yes	U.S.	Short	High	Threat
14. Chinese-Indian Conflict	No	Chinese People's Republic (CPR)	Medium	Medium	Threat
15. COMECON Issue	Yes	USSR	Long	Low	Opportunity/Threat

Lastly, within the issue of nuclear tests, joined with the U.S., the Soviet Union recognized a degree of convergence for Soviet and American policy programs. Both harbored fears (or perceived threat) of the results of continued indiscriminant atmospheric nuclear explosions and of the proliferation of nuclear-weapon capability. There was thus a possibility for agreement to become effective. The problem was how to reflect the real agreement formally without adversely affecting either party's position on closely related issues about which there was disagreement. The technical problem was at least partially resolved and a degree of consensus confirmed by the Test-Ban Treaty concluded in 1963.

The question, "In what ways did events become inputs for programmatic pursuits of Soviet foreign policy?" has now led us past feedback information to a multifaceted variety of perceptions of threat and opportunity. They permit construction of a rough typology of events which Soviet decision-makers have given consideration.[29]

1. Events resulting from programmatic Soviet foreign policy efforts:
   a. from collisions with adversary programs directed toward the USSR as target/respondent (e.g., Cuban missile confrontation).
   b. from collisions with adversary programs directed toward a mutual target/respondent (e.g., Cuban Bay of Pigs Invasion).
   c. effect of programmatic efforts on a collaborator or passive subject without intervening adversary program (e.g., efforts to coordinate economic plans within COMECON in 1963).
   d. effect of programmatic efforts on adversary without intervening adversary program (e.g., Finnish military cooperation bid).
   e. from convergence with another country's program (e.g., West Irian controversy, nuclear-test cessation).
2. Events resulting from other countries' programmatic policy efforts:
   a. from collisions with Soviet programs where USSR is target/respondent—identical case with 1.a.
   b. from collisions with Soviet programs where there is a mutual target/respondent—identical with 1.b.
   c. from collision or convergence with a third country's program (e.g., CPR-India war).

[29] The typology is analytical rather than strictly descriptive. Thus the categories are not entirely mutually exclusive. For example, categories 1.e and 2.c clearly overlap. Those entries under 2.c which include perceived opportunities usually also include perceived convergence. It is some degree of perceived convergence which in any real case sustains negotiations. Likewise, the categories 2. a, b, and f, though needed for logical symmetry, are eliminated practically because of their identity with 1. a, b, and e respectively.

   d. effect on USSR of unreciprocated program directed toward USSR as target/respondent (e.g., Common Market).

   e. effect on collaborator or passive subject of program without intervening Soviet program (e.g., Marshall Plan in 1947—no clear case in early 1960's).

   f. from convergence with Soviet program—identical with 1.e.

The diagram first presented in incomplete form (Diagram IV-1) may now be expanded in Diagram IV-2:

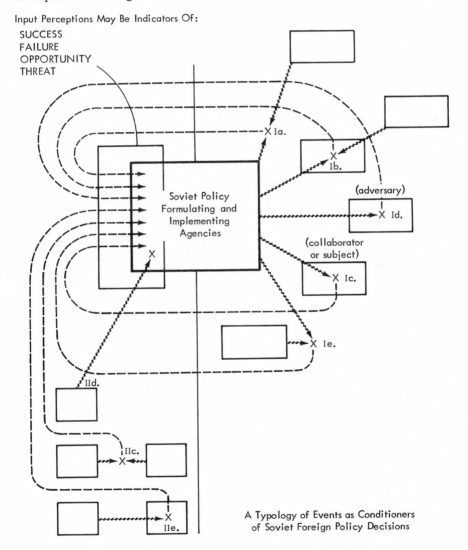

Input Perceptions May Be Indicators Of:

SUCCESS
FAILURE
OPPORTUNITY
THREAT

A Typology of Events as Conditioners
of Soviet Foreign Policy Decisions

To conclude from this analysis, events which, on the basis of subsequent policy outputs, appear to have a major impact in the Soviet foreign-policy decision process are indicators of change in the international environment. Discontinuities are perceived and their perception stimulates response. Also on the basis of subsequent policy outputs, it is the events that mark change in the relations among states of the international system that occasion visible Soviet response. While it is quite logical to expect domestic events to result in national change and this national change to affect a country's capabilities as an actor in the international system, Soviet commitments in the early 1960's infrequently demonstrate a direct relation to such occurrences. One of the few examples was the emphasis placed by Khrushchev on the policy of peaceful competition with the United States at the outset of the Kennedy administration in 1961. The release of two U.S. RB-47 crew members, held as violators of Soviet airspace and espionage agents, and later the willingness to release the U-2 pilot, Powers, in return for U.S. return of the convicted Soviet spy-runner, Colonel Abel, were obvious overtures in response to the domestic change in the U.S. In the absence of firsthand observation of Soviet decision-making, we may speculate that domestic events are usually a step removed from international change and that therefore the input for the decision process normally occurs later, in direct response to the international change.

Before they can be included in the Soviet decision process, the various sorts of events must of course be perceived by Soviet foreign-policy decision-makers. From the subsequent outputs of Soviet policy, it appears that the input perceptions may be classified as indications of (1) *success,* (2) *failure,* (3) *threat,* or (4) *opportunity.* The effects of Soviet programs which are unencumbered with the intervening variables of adversary programs provide the purest practical example of indicators of success or failure. An example mentioned above is the effect of Soviet efforts through COMECON to substitute a single integrated East European economy for the aggregation of autarchic national economies left over from Stalin's postwar East European policy. The collision of third parties' programs provides a relatively pure instance of an indicator of threat or opportunity. The USSR, a bystander to the collision, is not initially in a position to perceive success or failure for its own programs. The two dimensions are distinct analytically but rarely so in practice. A single sequence of events will usually contain elements of both success-failure and threat-opportunity.

An input perception of success is unlikely to impel change in Soviet policy. It will be regarded as a reinforcement of current policy. The same is true in the case of perceived opportunity with the exception that the opportunity may induce initiation of qualitatively new programs. Perceptions of failure and threat, on the other hand, are more likely to induce abrupt changes in Soviet foreign-policy outputs. They constitute a demand for response which is more psychologically compelling and show that current programs are not adequate. The relative intensity of the Soviet perceptions might be expected to determine whether the induced change would persist and become a change of programmatic policy or merely alter Soviet tactics with respect to this particular sequence of events. Thus, relatively few of the event sequences of the past few years can be said to have clearly resulted in changed Soviet programmatic policies. The likeliest case for such an effect was the high-threat Cuban missile confrontation with the United States. It is still a matter of debate whether Soviet policy programs directed toward achievement of military advantage over the U.S. have undergone any lasting alteration.

Over the longer time span, programmatic Soviet policy is noteworthy for its stability. A comparison of the Resolutions on Soviet Foreign Policy and the International Situation for the XXth, XXIst, and XXIInd Party Congresses shows that the international events of the intervening years had relatively little persisting effect. Much more significant in impelling programmatic change can be change in elite foreign-policy leadership within the USSR. The differences between the Resolutions of the XIXth and XXth Party Congresses testify to this. On the other hand, the differences between those of the XXIInd and XXIIIrd Congresses were slight.

The requirement that events be conveyed into the Soviet decision process as *perceptions* links our concern with events with our earlier examination of the functions of doctrine. We concluded that the most extensive influence of Marxist-Leninist doctrine as an active ingredient in Soviet foreign-policy decision-making was its operation as a guide to selective perception and interpretation. How much doctrinal impact was there in Soviet perception of events in the early 1960's? Or, metaphorically, how much refraction occurred in the doctrinal lenses through which the Soviet elite perceived events?

We found the greatest impact of doctrine in the context of long-range and general Soviet planning. Looking at the evidence of doctrinaire interpretation of observed events, we found in the long-range-planning context that slightly over one-third of the event-based premises were free of identifiable doctrinal interpretation; the rest showed explicit doctrinaire interpretation. For the short-range and crisis contexts the fraction of premises free of identifiable doctrinaire interpretation rose abruptly (to above three-fourths of the premises in our materials). The doctrinaire interpretation in both cases was much greater than the use of premises taken in substance from Marxist-Leninist doctrine.

By far the greatest impact of doctrine occurs in assessment of the condition of the international system, and these conditions go a long way in setting the boundaries of policy programs—by defining adversaries, collaborators, and passive subjects and by defining long-range expectations for the future condition of the international system. This is significant for the course of day-to-day policy, since there is a close relationship of programmatic policy to the eruption of the finite sequences of events (the conflicts of which headlines are made) which then tend to get out of the control of any single national actor involved, regardless of their genesis.

Definition of a country as "imperialist" or "socialist," with the inherent presumption of harmony or conflict,[30] the tripartite definition of the international system, the Marxist-Leninist analysis of class structure in the developing nations—all of these directly undergird the long-range programs of Soviet foreign policy specified earlier. Interpretation of the process of "imperialist neocolonialism" as qualitatively different from "distinterested Soviet aid and support," for example, is more important than just a propagandistic rationale. It is an attribution of motives which in turn gives shape to abstract expectations and provides some of the inarticulate premises for policy conclusions. Accordingly, the tenacity of programmatic Soviet foreign policy may be understood as a function of persistent definitions of the elements and process of the international system, for which Marxist-Leninist doctrine is the only logical originator.

It is a separate question whether or not Soviet responses to finite, discrete events in the course of international relations are significantly changed because of doctrinal interpretations. Our experimental evidence is inconclusive on this point, and we cannot measure the effective change the hypothetical distortion might have on action. Our findings suggest very little impact of this sort. The outstanding conclusion to be emphasized is the effect of doctrine as a major factor in setting up and reinforcing the courses of programmatic Soviet policy, whose subsequent collisions with non-Soviet programs result in the day-to-day demands for action facing Soviet (and foreign) decision-makers.

It is equally important not to overdo doctrinaire interpretation as a conditioner of the Soviet elite's foreign policy. It is clear that the unambiguous instances of doctrinaire interpretation of events are radically reduced when

---

[30] Stress is always placed by Soviet spokesmen on the impossibility of "ideological coexistence." The CPR is no more vehement than the USSR on this score.

the context changes from long-range, general planning to short-range and even crisis situations. It is equally clear that the contention that Soviet Communists and Western non-Communists cannot agree sincerely upon the immediate portent of many commonly perceived events is false.

Let us take up the separate question of doctrine as a perceptual lens modifying the events which become inputs for Soviet foreign-policy decision-making for the short-range and crises. The possibility that the lens does not exist in perception of these events seems highly unlikely. It is incompatible with our entire treatment of doctrine as a part of human belief systems that it could be avoided or consciously cast aside. Its lack of visible importance, therefore, in the interpretation of events for short-range or crisis conclusions would seem more reasonably attributable to a lack of significant meaning for interpretation of these events provided in the canons of doctrine. The events simply do not stimulate the application of doctrinal propositions. This hypothesis is supported by recognition of the ambiguity, historically, which Marxist-Leninists have encountered in regard to specific events. The power of Marxism-Leninism as a scientific tool by which to conduct daily action has been discredited repeatedly since the days of Marx himself. A good Marxist may preserve the faith by logic-chopping defensive sophistries (such as practised at the present time by Yevsei Liberman and his economist colleagues), or he may find fault with the scientist rather than with the science. Either way the effect is to give the doctrine little operative significance in formulating Soviet short-range or crisis expectations differently from the expectations of a non-Marxist. Even where doctrinal canons are applied, the current official status of Marxism-Leninism does not include much pretension to predict tactical responses in sequences of events of short duration.

The career data in Chapter III, which attested to the existence of a high degree of professional specialization in the Soviet elite and the discrimination among the elite found by calculating "doctrinal stereotype quotient," together with material found earlier in this chapter make it clear that the present limited impact of doctrine in the short-range and crisis contexts of Soviet foreign-policy decision-making could change radically with a change of elite personalities. The personalization of Soviet foreign policy as revealed both by our institutional and elite analyses supports this conclusion. If an "ideological purist" were to attain "dictator" status in the USSR, we might expect an abrupt rise in the application of doctrinal propositions, especially in the crisis context. For the present this seems an unlikely prospect. As we have shown, the men with the higher DSQ's are in general the older members of the Soviet elite, and time operates against them (see Chapter III, Table

III-3). A more likely contingency would be the accession of a man of pre-dominantly domestic orientation to the position of dictator. Such an individual, we have seen, tends to define the international situation more strictly in doctrinal terms than the individual who has long been directly concerned with foreign relations. Operating to neutralize this tendency is the demon-strated prejudice in favor of observed, "hard data" on the part of the pragmatic Soviet elite who have risen to prominence through domestic economic management. The impression created by three years of the Brezhnev-Kosygin leadership is that the latter force is the stronger.

THE SOVIET UNION AND THE WORLD COMMUNIST SYSTEM

In this chapter,[1] we submit that within the universe of global international relations, the communist world may be conveniently analyzed as a system of Communist Parties. This approach is helpful for several reasons. First, it permits description, ordering, and classification of interacting units—the Communist Parties—according to their functions. Gradually, generalizations about functions may be reached, and on this basis analytical models may be constructed. Second, political science and, in particular, comparative politics have developed a refined set of functions which offer uniform categories— socialization, recruitment, communication, and so on—for comparisons, as well as ready-made comparative hypotheses which may be tested in the complex, real world of Communist Parties. Third, the patterned, interactional activities, supportive as well as conflictual, which the Communist Parties have displayed in the last fifty years, have produced important reciprocally influential effects on the Parties as well as on the movement; the system approach permits us to relate interaction to effects in a meaningful way. And fourth, while the system approach focuses attention upon interaction and change, it does not prejudice the content of relations or the direction of change; the terms *Communist bloc, camp,* or *movement,* on the other hand, tend to emphasize solidarity within and antagonism outside the group of Parties. Also, as George Modelski points out, one cannot understand the structure of communist states without understanding the Communist Parties which rule in these states. Here the Communist Parties perform basic political functions, since "they facilitate communications against the background of common culture, guard solidarity, legitimize the rule . . . and serve as justification for claims to universality." On the other hand, while communist states could not exist without Communist Parties, Communist Parties could,

---

[1] This chapter is based in part on Jan F. Triska with David O. Beim and Noralou P. Roos, *The World Communist System,* Research Paper No. 1 (Stanford: Stanford Studies of the Communist System), 1963. We also wish to thank Henry S. Bienen and Julian K. Phillips for able research assistance.

and in fact have, existed without the states (there were seven national Parties with 400,000 members in 1917 and fifty-six national Parties with 4,200,000 members in 1939). This is why Communist Parties "deserve separate attention as an independent phenomenon of world politics."[2]

Communist Parties are either *ruling* Parties, that is, Parties which have succeeded in capturing control of government within their respective states —we call such states the Communist party-states—or *nonruling* Parties, which have not succeeded in this objective. The distinction between the two categories is important, because the ruling Communist Parties, with their monopoly of effective governmental control, have displayed interactional activities within the system which have been greatly superior in scope, frequency, and intensity to those of the nonruling Communist Parties. The nonruling Parties either share political power with other Parties, compete with them or with other political organizations for rule, or are outlawed and thus outside the legitimate political process in their states. Because of the heterogeneous or even hostile national environment in which they operate, much of the nonruling Parties' energy is exhausted locally, in collaboration, competition, and conflict with other national political organizations and groups. For this reason, their internal conversion processes have tended toward the unorthodox, and their maintenance and adaptive characteristics toward the flexible. The nonruling Parties' contribution to system performance has been secondary to that of the ruling Parties. In terms of functional categories, they may be perceived as the secondary-system units, whereas the ruling Communist Parties may be viewed as the primary or key units.[3]

THE COMMUNIST SYSTEM'S GOALS AND GOAL ACHIEVEMENT

In terms of the system goals, the functional distinction between the ruling and the nonruling Parties is even more striking. Like all political systems, the communist system has goals which are encompassing rather than specific. First among its major goals is *system maintenance*—the preservation of the integrity and inviolability of the system, so that the respective Communist Parties can maintain their achievements. The far-reaching changes which have taken place in the communist system since the death of Stalin bear

[2] George Modelski, "The Communist International System." To be published in *International Encyclopedia of the Social Sciences* (ms. pp. 9–10, 1966). See also his *The Communist International System* (Princeton, N.J.: Center of International Studies, Research Monograph No. 9, 1960).

[3] See "For Marxist-Leninist Unity of the Countries of Socialism," *Pravda*, February 10, 1963, p. 2 (hereafter called "For Marxist-Leninist Unity"); A. Chernyaiev, "Socialism Is the Main Force of World Revolutionary Development," *Pravda*, August 3, 1963, pp. 5–6.

evidence of efforts made to attain this goal, and the Sino-Soviet conflict provided eloquent testimony to significant failure in its pursuit.

The second major goal, *system advancement and development*, aims to make the communist party-states as economically advanced and modern as possible in the shortest possible time, by building into the economy socialist patterns of production, distribution, and consumption, as well as patterns of ownership and control. The recent spectacular miscarriage of the socialist economy in Czechoslovakia proved again that although the Stalin-Lenin model of economic development may have been suitable for pastoral, backward societies, it is patently not suited to advanced societies. The Czechoslovak economists finally discovered this hidden, dark side of the Lenin-Stalin model—as did earlier the Yugoslavs, and the Russians with their Liberman plan of profit and incentive schemes.

The third major goal is *system expansion*—a communist world. Intermediate stages are involved, but ultimately this goal means the conjoining of all national Communist Parties—as ruling parties—into one world-wide communist system. But, on the basis of the overall experience of the non-ruling Communist Parties during the last ten years, this goal today tends to be viewed as illusory.

In addition, the goal of system expansion is related to and dependent upon the other two major goals; failure in either adversely affects and even precludes system expansion. Because all three goals are mutually exclusive in the sense that the system has a finite amount of resources which it must apportion among the three goals by taking from one that which it grants the others, the first goal, system maintenance, is becoming too costly. In fact, the greater the system success in moving toward the third major goal, system expansion, the greater has appeared the deprivation in the pursuit of the first goal, system maintenance. Judging from the mushrooming conflict patterns within the Communist party-states, the goal of communist expansion could be achieved, if at all, only by sacrificing the movement as a system. This built-in paradox greatly reduces the system's investment in the goal of expansion, thus further reducing the functions of nonruling Communist Parties and widening the abyss between them and the ruling parties more than ever. The inverse relationship between the number of successful units—the ruling Parties—within the system and the system's solidarity and cohesion would require an allocation of resources to system maintenance that is entirely out of proportion to the other two goals. System advancement and development process tends to deviate from the costly Lenin-Stalin socialist model and goals, and system expansion, via the nonruling Parties, has slackened almost to zero. The gradual but increasing abdication of these two major goals, rather than the reinforcing of the third one, has tended to make the goal of system maintenance more precarious than ever before. The system's progress toward all its three major goals has been consistently slowing down. The communist system now shows the limits the movement has reached—and perhaps transgressed—on its way toward expansion, socialist development, and self-maintenance.

THE COMMUNIST SYSTEM'S ORGANIZATIONAL PROBLEMS

To sustain development and growth, large-scale political organizations must continually adapt their organizational structure to the new demands, responsibilities, opportunities, and challenges imposed by their very development and growth. In particular, they must constantly relate their *modus operandi* to the increasing ratio of responsibility, influence, and power which their development entails. Failure to do so, whatever the reason, is bound to lead to a series of reversals which, increasing in significance with time, result in a general slowdown, followed by serious breakdowns in the organizational structures which the frantically squeezed controlling valves barely manage to check. By then, not only is further development dangerously threatened, but also the actual existence of the organization is in danger. Continuous accommodation and checking of new stresses as they recur within the organization is an enormous but imperative task. The process of disintegration, which reduced and ultimately destroyed all large political organizations in the world in the past, has a tendency to creep in during times of stagnation, and frenzied insistence on preserving the *status quo* becomes incompatible with the very dynamism and vitality on which large-scale political organizations depend for their life.

As we pointed out above, in Chapter I, in 1918, the Russian Soviet Federated Socialist Republic was a highly centralized body politic, the government of which was the pinnacle of a hierarchy of Soviets—central, territorial, regional, area, district—and the Party. In 1923, 1936, 1940 and 1945 successive geographical layers were formally added. After World War II the Soviet growth by osmosis continued, in both Eastern Europe and Asia.

But the expansion under Stalin was both success and failure. The Soviet organization was beginning to move beyond its own saturation point, where this large-scale political organization ceased to be controllable, with the given safeguard mechanisms, within a framework now inadequate for its operation. Although control, enforcement, and conditioning devices to sustain a Stalinist-type regime, capable of controlling as much as one-third of humanity living on one-fourth of the world's available space, might eventually become available, under the circumstances the Soviet bite was far too big.

The problem is how to construct a rational organization which would produce a minimum of undesirable side effects but achieve a maximum of satisfaction compatible with the aims of the organizers. To use the Marxist pattern of logic, the successful Soviet "socialism in one country" thesis, at a time when great cost to the organization in human terms was thought necessary, brought about the polarization and antithesis of Yugoslavia, Poland, Hungary, China, Albania, and Rumania. The subsequent synthesis could take the form of a collective break into fourteen hostile Yugoslavias, Albanias, Chinas, or worse—undoubtedly worse, once the process of disintegration started in earnest—involving as well the loss of the nonruling Communist Parties; hopefully, by means of skillful surgery, there could be created an organization of "socialist" but autonomous states, supported by and supporting the nonruling Communist Parties in the world.

Since the demise of the Cominform, however, there has existed no institutionalized association of the Communist Parties, ruling or nonruling. The Parties do have extensive informal relations and communication networks, but these are seldom reliable or binding.

The several institutionalized associations of the Communist party-states—the Council of Mutual Economic Assistance, the Warsaw Treaty Organization, the Danube Commission, the Joint Institute of Nuclear Research, the Organization for the Collaboration of Railways, the International Broadcasting Organization, and the multilateral functional (and, in most cases, *ad hoc*) conferences on health, fishing industries, plant protection, cultural affairs, and so on—are at best utilitarian agencies that show increasing signs of ossification and retardation. So also are the multitude of other ties among the governmental agencies of Communist party-states, between trade unions, youth or women's groups, and other associations.

Historically, the principal instrument which the leaders of the communist system have utilized toward the fulfillment of system goals have been the nonruling Communist Parties—and these may have gained the assistance, in their respective countries, of other parties or groups disposed toward their goals, their belief system, or, perhaps, their tactical objectives. The nonruling Communist Parties may also have developed military forces of their own, either paramilitary or guerilla. Or they may have worked through numerous other methods and organizations, either communist or affinitive, such as trade unions, youth and women's groups, peace movements, street riots, and demonstrations. But this instrumentality has proved increasingly defective, unreliable, and imperfect. The conglomeration of pressures and conflicts among the ruling Communist Parties has made an impressive and sustained impact on the operational codes of the nonruling Parties, upon their orientation, and upon their composite relations with their several environments, especially the national. It is only to be expected that, in turn, the nonruling Parties were bound to impress deeply the ruling Parties with their new demands and expectations, based upon their changed perceptions of mutual relations with the ruling Parties.

More recently, the Communist party-states have turned their attention to what might be called *affinitive regimes.* These are ruling elites of countries which seem to exhibit empathy, for one reason or another, for the system. Rather than trying to replace the respective regimes with nonruling Communist Party elites, the attempt has been to win gradually the ruling regimes to the communist system, or, at least, to bind them so closely to the system that they would find extricating themselves difficult. Where they have decided to follow this strategy, the party-states have been willing to abandon the national nonruling Communist Parties to their own fate: Egypt under Nasser may serve as an example. The overwhelming evidence, however, again shows that the cost of this sustained attempt has exceeded the expectations—the effort has not paid off.

Finally, the communist system has either utilized existing international confederations of national front organizations or created new ones (e.g., the World Federation of Trade Unions, World Peace Movement, International Association of Democratic Lawyers) in an attempt to influence the national organizations to bolster the nonruling Communist Parties in their countries or to swing an affinitive regime closer to the communist system. These organizations still meet, attract attention, and pass resolutions. But since they are known for what they are—which had not been often the case in the past—their significance for the communist system goals is limited.

The problem of constructing a rational organization with a minimum of undesirable side effects and maximum satisfaction along the lines posed by the communist system goals has not been solved. The Communist Parties are becoming more autonomous, but less integrated, and they have no new structures to serve their desirable but complex system functions.

THE COMMUNIST SYSTEM IN SEARCH OF A THEORY

If there is no adequate system organization, is there an adequate association theory upon which such an organization could be built? Is there a communist-produced set of ideas linking the several units of the communist system which may be called a theory?

A *theory* may be defined as a generalization asserting that two or more things—activities, situations, or events—co-vary under specified conditions:[4] its acceptance depends on its precision and its verifiability. If a theory is well confirmed, it is called a *law*, if it is not yet confirmed it is known as a *hypothesis*. The formulation of *concepts* and their linkage into frameworks— just as the construction of *paradigms* or patterns of mutually related questions, propositions, and variables—is an analytical exercise which, while useful, may or may not lead to the building of coherent, formal theories.

To start with, the Communists have not made claims to possessing a theory linking the several units of the communist movement together. The closest they come to describing the mental underpinning of the world communist system is their talk of *proletarian internationalism*, a set of "principles" which dates back to the Communist Manifesto and the Marxian programmatic postulate, "Workers of the world, unite."[5]

Setting aside for the moment the several definitions—which are stochastic, normative, and hortatory rather than definitional (such as that "proletarian internationalism is the ideology and policy of the brotherhood and friendship of the whole working class")—proletarian internationalism, "the antithesis of bourgeois, capitalist nationalism" is a mental construct of considerable historical significance. Nationalism had no place in Marx's scale of values: the emancipation of labor was a social, rather than a local or national, problem which embraced all advanced countries. Nationalism was irrelevant to the common interest and objectives of the proletariat, which were above any limits imposed by nationalism.

Marx's theory, international in origin, character, and purpose, drew upon the elements of national experience, which it perceived as universal and historically repetitive. It postulated an international or nationless world, but it was not concerned with the in-between developmental stage—the period of transition from the nation to the no-nation level.

As a consequence, before the Bolshevik Revolution, Lenin's proletarians had no homeland. Their class enemy was international; hence, the conditions for their liberation were international.[6] In this period, only the class solidarity

[4] David Easton, *A Systems Analysis of Political Life* (New York: John Wiley & Sons, Inc., 1965) p. 7.

[5] "When a Marxist speaks of proletarian internationalism, the first thing that comes to his mind is the militant revolutionary appeal advanced by Marx and Engels: 'Workers of the world, unite.' " A. K. Azizian, "Proletarskii internatsionalism," *Znanie* (Moscow: Gospolitizdat, 1957), p. 98. See also Evgenii L. Korovin, "Proletarskii internatsionalizm i mezhdunarodnoe pravo," *Sovietskii ezhegodnik mezhdunarodnogo prava* (1958), p. 51.

[6] Lenin, *Sochineniia,* XXXI, 126, cited by T. Timofeyev, "Certain Aspects of Proletarian Internationalism," *International Affairs,* V (May, 1957), 46.

of the proletariat in several countries could express proletarian internationalism, the progress in uniting workers of all countries under the banner of the Communist Manifesto.

After the Bolshevik Revolution, the "toilers" had a homeland. But now, as Lenin put it, "the most important thing, both for us and from the point of view of international socialism, is the *preservation* of Soviet Russia."[7]

Stalin completed the hiatus: "An internationalist is he," he stated, "who unreservedly and without hesitation and without conditions is prepared to defend the USSR because the USSR is the base of the world revolutionary movement, and to defend and to advance this movement without defending the USSR is impossible."[8]

Ending with "the emergence of socialism from the confines of one country," the Soviet stage of development witnessed the testing of proletarian internationalism both horizontally and vertically: *Abroad*, the world movement of workers supported the first Communist party-state and in turn, "the toilers of the USSR supported the . . . movement";[9] *in the USSR*, proletarian internationalism was employed as "a national policy" vis-à-vis nationalities and minorities among and within the Union Republics. The Soviet Union, then, was the first political system to demonstrate empirically the possibilities of developing the model and setting the pattern for the future, Soviet theorists maintain.[10] An ideal proving ground, the USSR fulfilled its historical mission by bringing to its nationality and minority groups all the fruits and advantages of unity and solidarity on the basis of equality and self-determination. The Soviet pattern was thus "bound" to become a model of international and intergroup cooperation for the post-World War II community of Communist party-states.[11]

The short-lived Hungarian Soviet Republic of 1919 and the aborted Bavarian communist role provided little opportunity for the Soviet government to indulge in socialist international relations. Although a somewhat

[7] *Ibid.,* XXVI, 410. Italics added.

[8] Stalin, *Collected Works* (Moscow: Foreign Languages Publishing House), X, 51.

[9] Potelov, "Razvitie sotsializma i proletarskii internatsionalizm," *Kommunist,* No. 1 (January, 1957), p. 18.

[10] N. P. Vassil'iev and F. R. Khrustov, *O Sovetskom patriotizme* (Moscow: Gos. Pol. Literatury, 1952), p. 142, cited by Wladyslaw W. Kulski, *Peaceful Coexistence* (Chicago: Henry Regnery Company, 1959), pp. 34–35.

[11] G. I. Tunkin, "Socialist Internationalism and International Law," *New Times* (October-December, 1957), p. 5; "Novyi tip mezhdunarodnykh otnoshenii i mezhdunarodnoe pravo," *Sovetskoe gosudarstvo i pravo,* No. 1 (1959), pp. 81–94. See also S. Sanakoyev, "The Basis of the Relations between the Socialist Countries," *International Affairs* (July, 1958), p. 161; Potelov, *op. cit.,* p. 19; and Liu Shao-Chi, *Internationalism and Nationalism* (Peking: Foreign Language Press, 1949), p. 9.

greater scope for the testing of proletarian internationalism was furnished in relations between Soviet Russia and Mongolia and the Soviet districts in China, it was only after the Second World War that proletarian internationalism could be tested among the several Communist party-states and between them and the nonruling Communist Parties.

As long as Stalin was alive, the alternatives available to the new ruling Parties were limited: either they conformed, or, like Tito, they were expelled. Had Khrushchev not condemned Stalin as clearly as he did in 1956, the Soviet ability to impose its own rule on others would not have been curtailed so rapidly and so dramatically. But the Soviet quarrel with Peking and the ensuing indiscretions of both adversaries became community property. The increasing reluctance of many ruling as well as nonruling Parties to take sides and support either of the contestants has been striking evidence of the growing looseness and slackness of relationships among *all* parties.

In any event, this development could not have been entirely prevented, suppressed, or greatly retarded. But without Khrushchev's speech before the XXth Party Congress in Moscow in 1956, it probably could have been better and more discreetly controlled. Khrushchev's subsequent attempts to patch up matters here and there was not the kind of substantive overhaul of the organizational machinery that was needed.

The "new type" of international relations, which emerged with Khrushchev's prescription for "the Commonwealth of Socialist Nations," was formulated in 1955, *after* the April Bandung Conference. Like the Bandung Conference, the Commonwealth was said to stand for mutual assistance and cooperation, genuine friendly relations, world peace, and security for all. In particular, following the Bandung Declaration, the principles of mutual respect for territorial integrity, nonaggression, nonintervention in domestic affairs, sovereign equality, and mutual assistance were said to link all the Communist party-states "headed by the Soviet Union." The domestic construction of socialism in the USSR was essential for the development of the Commonwealth "because such construction involved a continuous search for theoretical principles which would guide development and bind socialist states in true proletarian internationalism."[12] But, in effect, the emphasis has been put on the *Communist party-states*, not on the world movement.

The historical term *proletarian internationalism* has denoted relations among all units as well as subunits of the world system; it has extended from relations among *individuals*, such as members of different parties, to relations

[12] *Kommunist*, No. 14 (October, 1955), pp. 4–7. See also, "On the Principles of Development and Further Strengthening of Friendship and Cooperation between the Soviet Union and Other Socialist States," *Pravda*, October 31, 1956, p. 1.

among the organizations of several *states,* such as the Warsaw Pact or Comecon. The category subordinated to it, both in time and space, has been *socialist internationalism,* the "new type" of relationships which pertains exclusively to the Communist party-states.[13] To use taxonomic categories: if general international relations is the class, then proletarian international relations is the order, and social international relations the family, the latter two being governed by the principles of proletarian internationalism and socialist internationalism respectively. As a consequence, proletarian internationalism, while continuing to remain the guiding principle of the world communist movement, has been the principal foundation from which evolve inter–party-state relations: this subsystemic superstructure is called *socialist internationalism.*[14]

But socialist internationalism, in contradistinction to, and as a result of, the lesson of the Soviet "socialism in one country" concept, means socialism in each Communist party-state as reduced by the existence of several socialist countries. While constructing their own socialisms in their own single countries and thus following the Soviet historical model, the members are also utilizing the advantages of membership in the common economic, ideological, political, cultural, and military system, thus enhancing the socialist community. The Communist party-state system is thus *not* perceived as a mere sum total of a group of states; it is viewed as an economic, ideological, political, cultural, and military community, counterposed to the capitalist system. Each party-state, while an independent sovereign entity, is also a component part of a broader social community.[15]

The *substance* of socialist internationalism is determined by the nature of the social system prevailing in the Communist party-states. The liquidation of private property and of capitalists produces conditions which are presumed to be ideal for interstate economic ties and relations. The public ownership of the means of production should preclude exploitation of man by man and create conditions for the close association of different peoples with a common purpose—the victory of socialism and communism in their respective countries by members of one political, social, and economic system. The resulting "community of equal and sovereign nations marching along the path of socialism and communism" has been proclaimed an achievement —a fulfillment of a promise and a victory.[16]

[13] Korovin, *op. cit.,* p. 52.
[14] Tunkin, *op. cit.,* p. 10.
[15] I. Dudinsky, "A Community of Equal and Sovereign Nations," *International Affairs,* No. 11 (November, 1964), p. 4.
[16] Sanakoyev, *loc. cit.*

SOCIALIST INTERNATIONALISM: COMMUNIST PARTY-STATES

The principal unifiers the Communist party-states are assumed to possess are (1) common aims, (2) common enemies, (3) common interests, and (4) common accomplishments. Respectively, the Communist party-states (1) all struggle for socialism and communism; (2) all seek to defend themselves against imperialism; (3) all are closer to each other than to any heterogeneous outsider because of their similar political, economic, social, and cultural systems; and (4) all participate in building socialism and communism through mutual assistance and cooperation. Hence, the party-states are bound together by the socialist international division of labor, the socialist world market, and close political, cultural, and military relations. In other words, the fact that these states are ruled by Communist Parties establishes basic similarities among them, creating a presumption of common interests and goals and therefore military and economic interdependence. It follows then that the substantial amounts of sustained transactions rationally conducted among all the party-states should mutually help them all, individually *and* collectively. The 1957 Declaration of Communist Parties, while emphasizing equality, territorial sovereignty, and noninterference in domestic matters of individual party-states, considered the "most striking" expression of socialist internationalism to be "fraternal mutual aid."[17]

Proletarian internationalism, in its socialist internationalism category, has thus been adapted to the realities of "modern" international relations as they are perceived by the communist theoreticians.[18] In the process, socialist internationalism has been deprived of its most forceful ingredient. The language of conventional and traditional international relations and, in particular, the growing insistence on state sovereignty as the only basis for mutual relations among Communist party-states imply not only formal equality, nonintervention in domestic affairs, independence, and integrity of the party-states in their mutual relations, but also a very important deviation from and contradiction to the commitments of proletarian internationalism. Thus, several problems are created: first, when, under the impact of 1956 and the Hungarian revolution, Khrushchev implicitly coupled proletarian internationalism with the principles of Bandung, he had to include a strong disclaimer that proletarian internationalism had anything to do with the simple concept of *peaceful coexistence* between socialist states. Had he not done so, the concept of dichotomous worlds would have been rendered meaningless:

[17] Dudinsky, *op. cit.,* pp. 5 and 6.
[18] Made available by TASS to *The New York Times,* November 7, 1964, p. 8.

From the denial of the fact that the world is split into two antagonistic systems and consequently into two camps the conclusion has been deduced that socialist states allegedly cannot make a distinction in their foreign policy between the socialist and the bourgeois states. This is a point of view alien to proletarian internationalism; it amounts in fact to undermining the unity among the brotherly socialist countries.[19]

Second, after the debacle of the Cominform, with the increasingly unsuccessful and therefore fewer system-wide Party meetings and reduced communication, the emphasis on state relations over Party relations among the Communist party-states made, indeed, for less fuss and strain. But the retrogressive deviation from proletarian internationalism that was implied when state sovereignty was proclaimed as the foundation of socialist internationalism marked an un-Marxian return to the Marxian nineteenth-century world in more ways than one.[20]

In fact, some Soviet authors even suggest that differences of views among the ruling Parties harmful to socialist internationalism should not be carried over to relations among the party-states!

For each socialist country, possible differences notwithstanding, can make its contribution to the overall victory of socialism if it strictly observes all its commitments to other socialist countries, extends economic, scientific, technological, and cultural cooperation with them, builds up their joint defense capabilities against imperialism, and joins with them in a united front in the international arena.[21]

Moreover, the Bandung principles, praised on the state level, are beginning to enter the *party* level as well. As the Central Committee of the Rumanian Workers' Party put it in April, 1964, there were no "parent" and "son" Parties—Parties that are superior and inferior—but only a family of *completely equal* Parties. Hence, parties must *respect* each other and must not *interfere* in each other's business, and no Party has a

---

[19] Potelov, *loc. cit.*

[20] M. Atrepetian and P. Kabanov, "Leninskie printsipy vneshnei politiki Sovetskogo gosudarstva," *Sovetskoe gosudarstvo i pravo* (1957), p. 65, cited by John N. Hazard, "Soviet Socialism as a Public Order System," *Proceedings of the American Society of International Law* (1959), p. 41; Potelov, *loc. cit.*

[21] L. Zieleniec and A. Charakchiev, "Milestone in the March of History," *World Marxist Review*, VIII, No. 5 (May, 1965), 22.

privileged position nor can it impose its line on opinions of other parties.[22]

Third, serious differences exist within the world communist movement and, in particular, among the Communist party-states on several issues, and "it would be unwise to close our eyes to the differences."[23] The Communist party-states are still economically unequal: there is a discrepancy between the development of relationships within the various party-states and between different parts of the Communist system; there are wide opportunities for multiform ties among the party-states which are not utilized; there are contradictions among them caused by the divergence of specific interests; there is a lack of experience in the imaginative shaping and evolving of multilateral economic and political ties; and there is a nationalistic climate of hatred and mistrust under which the various peoples have been brought up and which has not as yet completely disappeared.

For these reasons, search has been under way for more flexible and effective forms of cooperation that would conform to both "international interests" and "national aspirations" of the nations involved. Programs for such activity have included the Council for Mutual Economic Assistance, the Warsaw Treaty Organization, within which Soviet nuclear and missile capabilities have been of particular significance, meetings of leaders, exchange of information, coordination of foreign policies, and cultural exchanges. "But because it is being carried out and tried and tested for the first time in the history of mankind," socialist internationalism, "an exceptionally intricate undertaking," requires new skill, wisdom, and energy to accomplish the task of strengthening the unity of the party-state system.[24]

Fourth, socialist internationalism cannot develop "automatically." Socialism in the several countries may be creating a foundation on which socialist relations among the party-states can develop, but how this opportunity is used depends on the leadership in the several ruling Communist parties. The implementation of the principles of proletarian internationalism in the setting of the Communist party-states depends especially on the party-states'

---

[22] "Statement on the Stand of the Rumanian Workers' Party Concerning the Problems of the World Communist and Working-Class Movement, Endorsed by the Large Plenum of the Central Committee of the Rumanian Workers' Party Held in April 1964," *Rumania, Documents, Articles and Information Supplement* (1964), p. 50. See also S. Sanakoyev, "Internationalism and Socialist Diplomacy," *International Affairs* No. 5. (1965), p. 22.

[23] "Unity of Action of the World Communist Movement," *World Marxist Review*, VIII, No. 4 (April, 1965), 4, 5. An editorial.

[24] B. N. Ponomaryov (Secretary of the Central Committee of the CPSU), "Proletarian Internationalism Is the Revolutionary Banner of Our Epoch," *Pravda*, September 29, 1964; also, *Information Bulletin No. 25, World Marxist Review Publishers*, Prague (Toronto: Progress Books. November 16, 1964), p. 28; Dudinsky, *op. cit.*, p. 6; Zieleniec and Charakchiev, *op. cit.*. p. 21.

attitude toward nationalism in their midst. As Palmiro Togliatti, Secretary-General of the Italian Communist Party, stated:

> A fact worrying us and one we do not succeed in explaining fully is the manifestation among the socialist countries of a centrifugal tendency. . . . Without doubt there is a revival of nationalism. However, we know that the national sentiment remains a permanent factor in the working class and socialist movement for a long period, also after the conquest of power. Economic progress does not dispel this, it nurtures it. Also, in the socialist camp *perhaps* (I underline this perhaps because many concrete facts are unknown to us) one needs to be on one's guard against the forced exterior uniformity and one must consider that the unity one ought to establish and maintain lies in the diversity and full autonomy of the individual countries.[25]

The nationalist disunities, contradictions, and centrifugal tendencies among the Communist party-states that challenge socialist internationalism are assumed, however, to be transient and temporary phenomena. Of the three major dangers to socialist internationalism—the novelty of the transition to socialism of countries with differing social, economic, cultural, and historical backgrounds, the cult devoted to the personality of Stalin, and the "erroneous" policy of China based on nationalist distortions and deviations—the third, the pseudoleft, nationalist dogmatism, is depicted as the principal one. Chinese leaders are said to counterpose their divisive nationalist line to both socialist and proletarian internationalism. And now, years later, Lenin is quoted, with tongue in cheek: "One who has adopted nationalistic views naturally desires to erect a Chinese wall around his nationality, his national working-class movement . . . unembarrassed even by the fact that by his tactics of division and dismemberment *he is reducing to nil* the great call for the rallying and unity of all nations, all races and all languages."[26]

For this reason, the most compelling task for all believing in socialist internationalism is to assist in the healing of the breach and in the establishment of contacts and cooperation with the Chinese Communists. Marx and Engels had held regular congresses of the International, and Lenin considered it important systematically to hold congresses of the Comintern. To strengthen

[25] Translated from the Italian and with an introduction by Luigi Longo, Togliatti's successor, *The New York Times*, September 5, 1964, p. 2; Dudinsky, *op. cit.*, p. 5.

[26] Lenin, *Collected Works* (Moscow: Foreign Languages Publishing House, 1961), VI, 520–521, cited in Dudinsky, *op. cit.*, p. 5; Z. Zhivkov, "People's Democracy—Tried and Tested Road to Socialism," *World Marxist Review*, VIII, No. 6 (June, 1965), 25; Ponomaryov, *op. cit.*, pp. 34–35.

both proletarian and socialist internationalism, a new international communist organization would, perhaps, be the best means of overcoming the differences. But under no condition could the present split in the movement serve as a basis for severing relations with, or even excommunicating, any member.[27]

The Chinese version of the issue of nationalism versus proletarian internationalism and its consequences is somewhat different. True, the Chinese Communists support "progressive nationalism," "national independence," and "people's democracy" and oppose "reactionary nationalism" and "domestic reaction."[28] But, their view of proletarian internationalism changed with changed conditions. Earlier, it meant support of the USSR; now it means support of all the Communist party-states in the camp, their unity, and "the policies which the socialist countries *ought to pursue*."

It is under new historical conditions that the Communist and Workers' parties are now carrying on the task of proletarian internationalist unity and struggle. When one Socialist country existed and when this country was faced with hostility and jeopardized by all the imperialists and reactionaries because it firmly pursued the correct Marxist-Leninist line and policies, the touchstone of proletarian internationalism for every Communist party was whether or not it resolutely defended the only Socialist country. Now, there is a Socialist camp consisting of 13 countries, Albania, Bulgaria, China, Cuba, Czechoslovakia, the German Democratic Republic, Hungary, the Democratic People's Republic of Korea, Mongolia, Poland, Rumania, the Soviet Union and the Democratic Republic of Vietnam. Under these circumstances, the touchstone of proletarian internationalism for every Communist party is whether or not it resolutely defends the whole of the Socialist camp, whether or not it defends the unity of all the countries in the camp on the basis of Marxism-Leninism and whether or not it defends the Marxist-Leninist line and policies which the Socialist countries ought to pursue.[29]

Fifth, coercion is not an end but a means to an end. Still, the Communists would not use it if the classes departing from history would give up without recourse to violence. But they do not. The reactionaries have tried to cause troubles in several party-states—they tried to unleash civil war in Poland,

---

[27] "For Marxist-Leninist Unity of the Communist Movement, for Solidarity of the Countries of Socialism," *Pravda*, February 10, 1963, p. 3.

[28] Zieleniec and Charakchiev, *op. cit.*, p. 16.

[29] A letter sent on June 14 by the Central Committee of the Chinese Communist Party to the Central Committee of the Soviet Communist Party, as printed in the Chinese weekly *Peking Review. The New York Times,* Western Edition, July 5, 1963, p. 4.

to engineer a *putsch* both in Hungary and Czechoslovakia, and to organize counterrevolutionary armed actions in Rumania. They failed only because the means of coercion were now in the hands of the socialist governments in these countries and, in particular, in the new party-state security bodies, the armies, and the people's militias. These enabled the Communists to build up the preponderance of strength, limiting the opportunities of the capitalists for counterrevolutions.[30]

Coercion is inexcusable if used against fraternal parties and states. Thus, in the past, it became increasingly obvious that the Comintern as an international organization and center no longer suited the needs of the communist movement. Its interference with the internal matters of Communist Parties "went as far as the removal and replacement of leading party cadres and even of entire central committees, as far as the imposing from without of leaders, the suppression of distinguished leading cadres of various parties, and as far as the censure and even disowning of communist parties."

These unfortunate coercive practices were again employed in the Cominform. Yugoslavia's party was condemned and excluded from the Cominform, and Yugoslavia, a Communist party-state, was expelled from the party-state system. Thus, evil practices were extended from party to state relations, "rendering their consequences the more serious," and there occurred "numerous cases of expulsion from the party, arrests, trials and suppressions of many leading party and state cadres." Hence, the Central Committee of the Rumanian Workers' Party deemed the "sharp divergencies now prevailing in the communist movement" of the utmost gravity, as "the danger could arise of a repetition of the methods and practices" of the past.[31]

Lenin's original sentiments are now approvingly cited:

We want a *voluntary* union of nations—a union which *precludes any coercion* of one nation by another—a union founded on complete confidence, on a clear recognition of brotherly unity, on *absolutely voluntary consent*. Such a union cannot be effected with one stroke; we have to work towards it with the greatest patience and circumspection, so as not to spoil matters and not to arouse distrust and in order that the distrust inherited from centuries of land owner and capitalist oppression, centuries of private property and the enmity caused by divisions and redivisions may have a chance to wear off.[32]

---

[30] "Statement on the Stand of the Rumanian Workers' Party," pp. 48–49.

[31] *Ibid.*

[32] Lenin, *Selected Works* (Moscow: Foreign Languages Publishing House, 1961), III, 342, cited by Dudinsky, *op. cit.,* p. 6.

Sixth, the new inclusiveness, stratification, and particularization of proletarian internationalism, while responding to new needs, creates new difficulties. Proletarian internationalism stands now for the formation of a broad front of political alliance embracing four principal forces: (1) the Communist party-states; (2) the nonruling Communist Parties; (3) the Parties and organizations united in the national-liberation movement in developing nations; and (4) all peoples and organizations everywhere fighting against imperialism and for peace.[33] The line between the world communist system —the Communist party-states and nonruling Communist Parties—and the rest of the world is elusive and even irrelevant: "In the first half of our century, socialism has been a broad stream that attracts ever more countries and social forces."[34] United by the principles of proletarian internationalism, these countries and social forces are interrelated. For example, the *national liberation movement* would not have reached its present level were it not for the advances made by the Communist *party-states*. At the same time, however, the struggle of the Communists against capitalism would have taken place under much more difficult conditions were it not for *deprivation of imperialism of its colonial positions*. The *nonruling Parties* in the capitalist countries aided by the USSR and the other communist party-states significantly contributed to the progress made by the party-states. And the *nonruling Communist Parties* benefited greatly in their own development from the assistance rendered to them by the Communist party-states.[35]

The significance of proletarian internationalism rests then on its quadruple roles: (1) it is a model of unity among the Communist party-states; (2) the development of national-liberation movements in terms of their most important needs, economic development and defense of national independence, depends on the help of all Communists; (3) it unites all, even "the most diverse detachments" engaged in the revolutionary struggle everywhere in the world; and (4) it joins all peoples of good will in their struggle against war and reaction and for peace.

Proletarian internationalism is thus expected to strengthen the world socialist system "as the main factor in present day revolutionary development"; to synchronize the building of socialism and communism by each Communist party-state; to defend the unity of the international communist movement against reactionary nationalism, factionalism, and schism; to defend and creatively develop Marxism-Leninism as the ideological

---

[33] Ponomaryov, *op. cit.,* p. 30.
[34] *Pravda,* August 15, 1965, p. 1.
[35] "Unity of Action of the World Communist Movement," p. 4. An editorial.

foundation of the international communist movement; and to unite all progressive forces everywhere.[36]

This set of assumptions, explicitly broadening proletarian internationalism, led to the next apostate round within the communist movement, a profound disagreement concerning not the breadth but the purpose, rank-ordering, and relationships within the concept. The CPSU, supported by its friends, stipulated that all-world (all-state) communism would be achieved *because of the great successes of the Communist party-states*. Their economic, social, political, and scientific achievements must and would be so impressive that all mankind will be persuaded that only communism is the way of the future. Thus, the primary purpose of proletarian internationalism must be the victory and consolidation of communism in the several party-states. Hence, the world proletariat must support all the states which construct socialism (while, in turn, the socialist construction in the Communist party-states can proceed only in close association and in cooperation with the world revolutionary movement).[37]

The Chinese Communist Party and its friends, on the other hand, maintain that primacy belongs not to the Communist party-states but to the key area in the struggle for ultimate communist victory, namely, the oppressed people of Asia, Africa, and Latin America. All progressive forces everywhere, including the ruling Communist Parties, have a duty, which is primary and nonmutual, to support these peoples in their open, revolutionary struggle for liberation from imperialist oppression:

> The national democratic revolutionary struggles of the people in Asia, Africa, and Latin America are pounding and undermining the foundations of the rule of imperialism and colonialism, old and new, and are now a mighty force in defense of peace. In a sense, therefore, the whole cause of the international proletarian revolution hinges on the outcome of the revolutionary struggles of the peoples of these areas who constitute the overwhelming majority of the world population. Therefore, the anti-imperialist revolutionary struggle of the people in Asia, Africa, and Latin America is definitely not merely a matter of regional significance but one of over-all importance for the whole cause of proletarian world revolution.[38]

---

[36] Ponomaryov, *op. cit.*, pp. 28–29.

[37] Azizian, *op. cit.*, p. 98; Korovin, *op. cit.*, p. 71; S. Sanakoyev, *op. cit.*, p. 161.

[38] A letter sent on June 14 by the Central Committee of the Chinese Communist Party to the Central Committee of the Soviet Communist Party, as printed in the Chinese weekly *Peking Review. The New York Times,* Western Edition, July 5, 1963, p. 4.

Those who consider the significance of the national-liberation movement secondary to that of the Communist party-state system not only "cater to the needs of imperialism," but try to create a new "theory" to justify the continued rule of "superior nations" over "inferior nations." This is not proletarian internationalism, but a serious departure from it, and the theory is "fraudulent."

Not socialist internationalism and the Communist party-states, nor even the international communist movement, then, but the national-liberation movement is the principal social revolutionary force today. It leads the other forces as "the storm center of world revolution dealing direct blows to imperialism." This is why the future of proletarian internationalism as a world-wide international format and model hinges on the outcome of its struggle.[39]

In addition to these problems—denial of simple, peaceful coexistence among the socialist states; sovereignty of national Communist Parties; the party-state dichotomy; revival of nationalism; condemnation of coercion; watering down of the proletarian internationalism concept to include "all men of good will," and the employment of traditional international forms— there are many other issues and ideas on which there is disagreement and which at least tangentially affect the general consensus on proletarian internationalism. These include the inevitability of war, the involvement in an armed revolution, the impact of nuclear weapons on communist strategies, the possibility of disarmament, the economic relations among party-states, the involvement in local wars (among and with developing nations), and the lack of peaceful coexistence among the nations of the world. The kind of system climate which results is quite adverse to the building of a unified theory of international relations.

The growing national independence of the ruling Communist Parties, brought about by the reluctant Soviet emphasis on "complete" equality, nonintervention in domestic matters, and respect for the state sovereignty of the Communist party-states, largely eliminated the ruling Parties' subordination to the "victorious" CPSU. The end of rule by coercion and condemnation, initiated among the Communist party-states by Khrushchev, with his emphasis on voluntarism principally on the state level, was carried over to the party level and extended to the nonruling Parties. True, the Sino-Soviet split was bound to affect all the Parties, and pro-Chinese factions were bound to emerge both because of the seriousness of the conflict and the open and sustained challenge to the CPSU by the CCP. But the fact

[39] *Ibid.*

remains that in the process of deciding the issue for themselves, many Parties used this opportunity to assert their own growing independence of *any* Party. Being able to select from among more than one Party gained for them the freedom of formulating their own views and policies and brought home the opportunity of perhaps influencing the movement merely by deviating from the announced policies.

But then, perhaps, the dialectics of the international and national aspects of the communist movement are such that true unity of the movement's units in the long run can be achieved only when this unity is based on the units' independence and equality. This is what some Communists claim, urging that the present stage of development, characterized by disagreements, disharmony, and diversity, is, indeed, both unavoidable and necessary and will lead to a new synthesis of more perfect unity.[40]

Others disagree. Adherents of the Soviet wing in the movement complain that to state that discords and splits, both without and within the Communist party-states and Communist Parties, are necessary and unavoidable and that the dialectics of the development of the international working-class movement involves such disunity as well as unity on a new basis, means to endow the existing Sino-Soviet disharmony with "a theoretical foundation." This is profoundly dangerous—it is, in fact, "a call for a split," they maintain.[41]

But in their replies, the Chinese Communists emphasize that, on the contrary:

The leaders of the CPSU have themselves undermined the basis of the unity of the international communist movement and created the present grave danger of a split by *betraying Marxism-Leninism and proletarian internationalism* and pushing their revisionist and divisive line. . . . They have thus made a mess of the splendid socialist camp . . . [and] pursued a policy of great-power chauvinism and national egoism.[42]

It was the Soviet leaders who "arbitrarily infringed the sovereignty of fraternal countries, interfered in their internal affairs, carried on subversive activities, and tried in every way to control fraternal countries"; it was they who "openly called for the overthrow of the party and government leaders of Albania"; it was they who "violated the Sino-Soviet Treaty of Friendship,

---

[40] Sanakoyev, *op. cit.,* p. 21: Dudinsky, *op. cit.,* p. 7.

[41] Statement on the Stand of the Rumanian Workers' Party, p. 50.

[42] Editorial in *Hung Chi,* as published in *Yenmin Jih Pao,* February 5, 1964, *The New York Times,* February 7, 1964, p. 8. Italics added.

Alliance and Mutual Assistance"; and it was they who "provoked incidents on the Sino-Soviet border and carried out large-scale subversive activities in Sinkiang."[43]

Proletarian internationalism may be a true acid test or test supplied by history; it may be a slogan or a motto ("unity, unity, and, once again, unity of the world communist movement"); it may be a reliable tool, an instrument, a keystone, a bond, and a thesis; it may be a set of principles, an outlook and even a policy; *but it is not a theory.* As a generalization, asserting that two or more things co-vary under specified conditions ("proletarian internationalism is a unity of all progressive forces based on their common struggle against imperialism and for peace"), it is neither precise, systematic, nor verifiable. The premise of the identity of interests on a class basis no longer obtains. In fact, the concept is now so broad that it has little meaning. The subsequent limitation of the generalization designed for "the most advanced detachment" of the movement, i.e., the Communist party-state, the learning model for the future, the consequent greater concern for relations among states rather than among parties, and the Chinese denial of both these latter propositions and their disagreement on the rank-ordering of the revolutionary forces makes even this limited conceptual framework questionable. The fact that some kind of broad, theoretical presuppositions underly the crude empirical search for an overall unity and association does not bring the remote ideal any closer. The very hortatory and stochastic nature of the postulate and the history of the theorizing on the subject suggest that the concept has emerged not so much to analyze conditions as to make them and to persuade all of their great value. But a wish for unity without provision of an adequate theoretical base for it is irrelevant. It is not theory-building—it is at most a mechanistic continuation of a well-established habit.[44]

The conclusion is that there exists no formal theory of association in the world communist system. There is a great deal of theorizing about it, though, which occurs in the form of inductive reviews of *ad hoc* predictions for individual assumptions. This theorizing emanates from normative observations, case studies, and various nontechnical sources. Writings on the subject have often raised interesting questions but have not arrived at a theory of relations. Proletarian internationalism is, *at best*, two rival conceptual frameworks differing both in rank-ordering and in emphasis laid on particular

[43] *Ibid.*

[44] See *Pravda,* June 20, 1965, pp. 3–5. An editorial; G. Shanshiev, "Under the Banner of Proletarian Internationalism," *World Marxist Review,* VIII, No. 8 (1965), p. 60, citing R. Palme Dutt, *The International* (London: Terrence and Wishart, 1964).

principles; *at worst*, it is several hortatory speculations—unverified, imprecise, and unsystematic.

Or, to borrow their own language, the communist theoreticians have failed to develop creatively Marxist-Leninist teaching on internationalism in keeping with the conditions of the time, with the relations among socialist countries, and with the conditions in the world communist movement.

With obsolete organizational structure and without an association theory upon which a modern, rational organization could be built, the communist-system organizers are doomed to patching up, temporizing, and holding operations, which, in their sum total, are inadequate even for system maintenance, let alone for socialist development and system development of the Communist party-states. Politically stagnating and economically inactive, the system becomes increasingly vulnerable to adversities at home and abroad.

THE ALLIANCE SYSTEM OF RULING COMMUNIST PARTIES

To analyze the Communist party-states' alliance system, it may be convenient to describe first those major properties and propensities of the party-states which pertain to their alliance.

The fourteen states ruled by Communist Parties (where the CP's are at the helm) are the USSR, Chinese People's Republic, People's Republic of Albania, People's Republic of Bulgaria, Hungarian People's Republic, Democratic Republic of Vietnam, German Democratic Republic, Korean People's Democratic Republic, Heroic People of Cuba, Mongolian People's Republic, Czechoslovak Socialist Republic, Polish People's Republic, Rumanian Socialist Republic, and Socialist Federal Republic of Yugoslavia.[45] Whereas both the CPSU and the Chinese Communist Party recognize Cuba as one of the party-states, China excludes Yugoslavia.

A position "at the helm" is most influential for *Party membership*. Of about 43.9 million Communists in the world, organized in eighty-seven Communist Parties, more than 41 million, or more than 94 per cent, populate

---

[45] "Party Central Committee's Slogans for May 1, 1963," *Pravda,* April 8, 1963, pp. 1–2; *Pravda,* April 14, 1964, pp. 1–2; *Izvestiia,* April 15, 1964, pp. 1–2. Cf. "For Marxist-Leninist Unity," pp. 2–3. In the original 1963 *Pravda* listing of April 8, cited above, the Socialist Federal Republic of Yugoslavia was introduced as the Federal People's Republic of Yugoslavia. Three days later, the mistake was corrected. See "Correction," *Pravda,* April 11, 1963, p. 1.

the fourteen ruling Communist Parties.[46] Outside the party-states, Party membership is on the decline. In the last three years, the nonruling Communist Parties lost over one-third of their members.

The largest party in the world is the Chinese Communist Party, with some 18.5 million members. The Communist Party of the Soviet Union has 13 million members; the Communist Parties of Czechoslovakia, East Germany, Poland, North Korea, and Yugoslavia have over one million members each. If we project the Communist Party membership against the total population, then North Korea and Czechoslovakia lead (12 per cent), followed by East Germany (10.1 per cent), Bulgaria (6.5 per cent) and the USSR (5 per cent). The ratios for Communist Party members to adult population are available for all but North Korea and China. The ratio for Czechoslovakia, where 18.4 per cent of all adults are Communist Party members, seems virtually unequalled anywhere.[47] (See Table V-1.)

The *population* of the Communist party-states accounts for "more than one-third [of] the population of the world."[48] China, the most populous state in the world, with some 700 million people, is followed by the USSR, the third most populous state in the world, with about 221 million. The other party-states are much smaller.[49] (See Table V-2.)

The *geographical area* of the party-states accounts for about 26 per cent of the world's territory. The USSR is the largest state in the world (22.4 million km^2 or almost 8.6 million square miles) and China the third largest (9.56 million km^2 or 3.76 million square miles). Only one other state unit

[46] For example, 80 per cent or 13.5 million, of the 1963 Communist Chinese Party members had joined the party after 1949 (70 per cent after 1953). *China Quarterly*, No. 7 (April-June, 1961), p. 16.

[47] U.S. Department of State, Bureau of Intelligence and Research, *World Strength of the Communist Party Organizations* (Washington, D.C.: Government Printing Office, January, 1966); See also U.N., *Demographic Yearbook, 1961* (New York: U.N., 1962), Table 5, pp. 138–161. The figures in the text were calculated from population data based on censuses which, where available, gave the age group breakdown as provided by UN publications. ("Adults" are persons 20 years of age and older.) As the figures given by the State Department publication on CP membership are for 1965, the census data on total and adult population was adjusted by using the UN figures for average annual growth rate (Table 1, pp. 101–119).

[48] "For Marxist-Leninist Unity," p. 2. In mid-1960, the party-states had an estimated 984.5 million people (almost 1.3 billion in 1963). *Demographic Yearbook, 1962* (New York: U.N., 1962), Table 1, pp. 106–123.

Unless specific, particular sources are given, the statistical data below are from a supplement to the *Problems of Peace and Socialism,* No. 8 (August, 1963) (published in Prague in Russian language) entitled "The Economic Development of the Socialist Countries."

[49] U.N., *Compendium of Social Statistics, 1963*, Statistical Papers, Series K, No. 2 (New York: U.N., 1963), Table 1, pp. 22–30.

possesses more than 1 million km² of territory, namely, Mongolia (1.53 million km²). All other party-states are small.[50] (See Table V-2.) However, when these area figures are translated into *cultivated-land* area figures, i.e., the proportion of arable land and land under permanent crops to the total area, they present an entirely different rank-ordering of the party-states. Moreover, the economies of the party-states still depend a great deal upon agriculture. In these terms, the Eastern European party-states, with the exception of Albania, rank highest among the party-states.[51] (See Table V-2.)

The *density of population* of the party-states (with average value 75.14 km², i.e., seventy-five people live on 1 km²) is relatively high (world average value is 22 km²). East Germany has a considerable lead (with 159 people living on 1 km²) over other party-states, Hungary (with 108 km²) is second, and Czechoslovakia (with 107 km²) is third.[52] (See Table V-2.)

This population is predominantly *rural*—only 23.18 per cent of the Communist party-states' population live in cities with 20,000 or more inhabitants (37.85 per cent in Western Europe)[53]—and is still chiefly *dependent upon agriculture.* Sixty-nine per cent of the Chinese, 75 per cent of the Yugoslavs, 60 per cent of the Rumanians, 50 per cent of the Soviet citizens, 55 per cent of the Bulgarians, and 80 per cent of the Albanians are employed in agriculture.[54]

---

[50] U.N., *Statistical Yearbook,* 1962 (New York: U.N., 1963), Table 1, pp. 24–39. Cuba has 0.12 million km².

[51] The party-states' average (29.8 per cent) is well above the world average (10.41 per cent), but somewhat below the Western European average (31.03 per cent). Eastern Europe (but not the USSR) is thus well above the Western European average. *Production Yearbook, 1961* (Rome: FAO, 1961), Table 1, pp. 3–7.

[52] U.N., *Statistical Yearbook,* 1962, *op. cit.,* Table 1, pp. 24–39. These figures, however, do not divide the respective territories into effective and ineffective areas; they are based on the whole state area including mountains, deserts, climatically severe regions, etc.

[53] U.N., *Compendium of Social Statistics,* 1963, Table 5, pp. 70–80. Only the USSR, Cuba, East Germany, and Hungary (with 35.5, 34.7, 34.6, and 31.5 per cent of their respective populations living in cities of 20,000 or more inhabitants) have more than 30 per cent of urban population. The rest of the party-states rank from high of Bulgaria and Czechoslovakia (24.7 per cent and 21.6 per cent respectively) to low of Mongolia (13.0 per cent) and China (8.3 per cent).

[54] None of these figures are recent, however. No data are available for Mongolia, North Korea, and North Vietnam, all predominantly agricultural states. Only East Germany (21.7 per cent), Czechoslovakia (25 per cent), Hungary (36 per cent), Poland (38 per cent) and Cuba (42 per cent) have less than 50 per cent of their populations dependent upon agriculture. FAO, *op. cit.,* Table 5A, p. 19.

The party-states' *population growth* is somewhat slower (with an average 1.6 per cent annual rate of increase) than the world population growth (average 1.8 per cent). As may be expected, it is more rapid in the Far East and slower in Eastern Europe.[55]

The party-states' *population is relatively young* (especially in the Far East). Children between the ages of five and fourteen account for 21.6 per cent of the total population (whereas there are only 14.6 per cent children of the same age in Western Europe).[56] The party-states' *infant-mortality* rate is still relatively high (particularly in the Far East), however; it almost doubles that of Western Europe.[57] The *number of physicians and dentists* in proportion to the populations for which they care is quite high and well above the world average in the USSR and Eastern Europe.[58] Communist China has only

[55] The party-states' population growth is the most rapid in the Far East, where the annual rate of population increase oscillates between high of Mongolia (3.0) to low of North Vietnam (2.1) with North Korea (2.6) and China (2.4) in between. The much slower-growing Eastern European party-states are led in the annual population increase by the USSR (1.8) and Poland (1.4). Czechoslovakia (0.7) and Hungary (0.5) show the smallest annual population increase; Cuba (2.1) is in the middle between the Communist Far East and Eastern Europe. (The single exception to this pattern is Albania, which has the highest annual rate of population increase of all the party-states, namely (3.3). *U.N., Statistical Yearbook, 1962,* Table 1, pp. 22–39.

[56] U.N. *Demographic Yearbook, 1961,* Table 5, pp. 138–161. As a consequence of the uneven population growth in economically accelerated Eastern Europe, the Far Eastern sector is younger in population composition and has many more children than Eastern Europe. Unfortunately, no data are available for three party-states, Mongolia, North Korea, and Albania, and the only available age breakdown expressed in the percentage of the total population as compared with the young is five to fourteen years of age. On this basis, the four states leading the party-states in youthfulness of population are the USSR, North Vietnam, Cuba, and China with 37.4 per cent, 26.6 per cent, 23.7 per cent, and 20.6 per cent of the population in the five to fourteen years age bracket respectively. Czechoslovakia (17.9 per cent), Bulgaria (17.7 per cent), Hungary (17.2 per cent), and East Germany (11.98 per cent) have the fewest children of five to fourteen years among the Communist party-states. UNESCO, *World Survey of Education, II: Primary Education* (Paris: UNESCO, 1958).

[57] No data are available for the Far Eastern party-states, where the infant deaths under one year of age per 1,000 live births may be expected to be the highest among all the party-states. Still, in Eastern Europe (and Cuba) the indexes of value oscillate considerably from the high of Yugoslavia (32.2 infant deaths per 1,000 live births), Albania (76.5), and Rumania (71.0) to the low of Czechoslovakia (22.7), the USSR (35.0), East Germany (38.8), and Cuba (38.9). *U.S. Demographic Yearbook, 1961,* Table 12, pp. 222–235.

[58] In East Germany there is one dentist or physician for every 166.4 persons; in Czechoslovakia the ratio is 1:250.7; in Poland 1:241.9; in the USSR 1:511.9; in Bulgaria, 1:615.3; in Hungary, 1:655.6; and Rumania, 1:736.6. However, the ratios of Yugoslavia and Albania are 1:1365.4 and 1:3411.0 respectively. *U.N. Statistical Yearbook, 1962,* Table 175, pp. 603–609.

21.9 physicians for 100,000 population, and North Vietnam's ratio is 1.8 physician or dentist for 100,000 people.[59]

Table V-1 CP Membership for Year Ending December, 1965 (includes candidate members when applicable)

RANK	TOTAL	RANK	CP MEMBERS/ POPULATION (IN PER CENT)	RANK	CP MEMBERS/ ADULT POPULATION (IN PER CENT)
1. China	18,500,000†	13	2.4	not available	
2. USSR	13,000,000†	8	5		8.0
3. Poland	1,725,521***	9	4.8	7	8.0
4. Czechoslovakia	1,684,416	2	12.0	1	18.4
5. East Germany	1,610,679***	3	10.1	2	14.4
6. North Korea	1,600,000†	1 about	12		n.a.
7. Rumania	1,450,000****	4	6.6	3	10.1
8. Yugoslavia	1,030,041	6 about	5.5	5	9.0
9. North Vietnam	700,000	11 about	3.7	10	6.6
10. Bulgaria	550,384	5	6.5	4	9.5
11. Hungary	540,000***	7	5.2	8	7.6
12. Cuba	60,000†	14 about	1.0	12	1.3
13. Albania	about 53,000**	12	3.0	11	5
14. Mongolia	46,000***	10	4.5	9	7.2

† Estimated figures.
** 1962 claim.
*** 1963 claim.
**** 1964 claim.
Source: U.S. Department of State, Bureau of Intelligence and Research, *World Strength of the Communist Party Organizations* (Washington, D.C.: Government Printing Office, January, 1966).

In terms of *literacy and education* of population, Eastern Europe (again, with the exception of Yugoslavia and Albania) and the USSR stand high above the world average. East Germany and the USSR report only 2 per

[59] The last two figures are somewhat dated, however. The first comes from the 1958 *Chinese People's Handbook* (Peking) and the second from the U.N. *Statistical Yearbook* (New York: U.N., 1956), both cited in Norton Ginsburg, *Atlas of Economic Development* (Chicago: University of Chicago Press, n.d.), p. 28. The rest of the figures come from the U.N. *Statistical Yearbook, 1962,* Tables 1 and 175. No data are available for North Korea and North Vietnam. Cuba has one physician or dentist for every 677.1 persons.

cent of their population over fifteen years of age who are illiterate, Czechoslovakia and Hungary 3 per cent, Poland 5 per cent, Rumania 11 per cent, and Bulgaria 15 per cent. (The Western European average, not including West Germany and Great Britain, is 16.3 per cent.)[60] The Far Eastern party-states, on the other hand, are well below the world standard in this respect.[61] This overall pattern will be subject to changes before long, however. The available figures giving percentage of population enrolled in primary and secondary schools (but especially in primary schools) in the party-states suggest that radical steps are being taken to combat illiteracy in several of the units, especially in China, Yugoslavia, and Albania.[62] With reference to higher education (and excluding North Vietnam and Outer Mongolia, for which no data are available), the party-states' average (513.1 students per 100,000 population are enrolled in higher education) is above that of Western Europe (465.7).[63]

In terms of *mass-media communication*, the population of the party-states is relatively well taken care of. In fact, East Germany and Czechoslovakia have more radio receivers per thousand population than has the average Western European country (242)—East Germany has 323 and Czechoslovakia has 278. East Germany's daily newspaper circulation (456 per 1,000 population) is above and Czechoslovakia is just below (236) the Western European average (266.38). The party-states' average[64] is 173.4 for the radio receivers (as compared with the Western European average of 242) and 154.5 for the newspaper circulation per thousand population (as compared with 266.38 for Western Europe). The Far Eastern party-states are well below this standard.[65]

[60] U.N., *Compendium of Social Statistics,* 1963, Table 59, pp. 303–312.

[61] Eighty per cent of the North Vietnamese, 60 per cent of the North Koreans, 50 per cent of the Chinese, and 40 per cent of the Mongolians are illiterate. However, these are 1957 or older figures. See UNESCO, *World Illiteracy at Mid-Century* (Paris: UNESCO, 1957), Table 7, p. 39 and Table 10, p. 43.

[62] No figures are available for North Korea, Outer Mongolia, and North Vietnam. Still, the party-states' average (61.8 per cent of population aged five to nineteen enrolled in primary education) appears to compare favorably with the Western European average of 65.39 per cent. Czechoslovakia (71 per cent), Poland (69 per cent), Hungary (66 per cent), and Bulgaria (66 per cent) lead the list. U.N. *Compendium of Social Statistics,* 1963, Table 61, pp. 323–328.

[63] *Ibid.,* Table 62, pp. 329–331.

[64] This average excludes North Korea, North Vietnam, and Outer Mongolia, for which no figures are available and which would bring the party-states' average considerably below the average figure given.

[65] Here, again, the advanced Eastern European party-states (and the USSR) lead the field, whereas Yugoslavia, Albania, and China trail behind on the average, only 45 people out of 1,000 have radio receivers and 49 out of 1,000 receive newspapers daily there). U.N. *Compendium of Social Statistics,* 1963, Table 65, pp. 343–348.

Table V-2

| POPULATION (IN THOUSANDS,* ESTIMATED) | | AREA | | | | DENSITY OF POPULATION (PERSONS/KM²) | |
| | | TOTAL (IN MILLION KM²; 25/64 × KM² = SQ.MI.) | | CULTIVATED (PER CENT OF TOTAL AREA) | | | |
Rank		*Rank*		*Rank*		*Rank*	
1. China	738,500	1. USSR	22.4	1. Hungary	61.3	1. E. Germany	159
2. USSR	223,500	2. China	9.56	2. Poland	52.04	2. Hungary	108
3. Poland	30,750	3. Mongolia	1.53	3. E. Germany	46.8	3. Czechoslovakia	107
4. Yugoslavia	18,960	4. Poland	0.31	4. Rumania	43.6	4. N. Vietnam	103
5. Rumania	18,860	5. Yugoslavia	0.26	5. Czechoslovakia	42.4	5. Poland	96
6. N. Vietnam	17,600	6. Rumania	0.24	6. Bulgaria	41.7	6. N. Korea	89
7. E. Germany	16,000	7. N. Vietnam	0.159	7. Yugoslavia	32.7	7. Rumania	77
8. N. Korea	15,700	8. Czechoslovakia	0.128	8. N. Korea	19.3	8. China	73
9. Czechoslovakia	13,970	9. N. Korea	0.122	9. Cuba	17.2	9. Yugoslavia	71.5
10. Hungary	10,100	10. Cuba	0.12	10. N. Vietnam	16.9	10. Bulgaria	71
11. Bulgaria	8,080	11. Bulgaria	0.111	11. Albania	16.3	11. Albania	56
12. Cuba	7,210	12. E. Germany	0.108	12. China	11.2	12. Cuba	49
13. Albania	1,790	13. Hungary	0.093	13. USSR	9.9	13. USSR	10
14. Mongolia	1,020	14. Albania	0.0287	14. Mongolia	0.03	14. Mongolia	0.5

Source:
* Figures adjusted to 1963 by UN statistics on annual rate of increase: UN, *Demographic Yearbook, 1963*, pp. 123–141, and, for China, UN, *Demographic Yearbook, 1962*, p. 114.

In terms of *economic output*, the party-states are said to account for over one-third of the world's industrial output. According to official communist data, the Communist party-states produced in 1962 about 37 per cent of the world's industrial goods. However, this figure is not supported by the available statistics concerning key commodities and their total party-state production.[66]

For the purpose of comparing overall figures, data are, in fact, hard to come by, and the available statistics are frequently unreliable and/or obsolete. Per capita gross national product (or income, which is essentially similar), when available, tends to be both grossly understated for the less developed states and distorted even as a relative index of societal well-being because of the cultural differences among states. Nevertheless, as per capita national income is perhaps the best available measure of economic development, it may be convenient to use it, together with other data, as a useful comparative economic profile of the party-states, individually as well as collectively.

The *per capita gross national income* figures for nine of the party-states are available. Of these, eight rank above the world mean of $200 per capita, but well below that of the United States ($4,343), Canada ($1,667), most of the Western European countries (e.g. France $1,046), New Zealand $1,249, and Australia $1,215. China is at the bottom of the list, as are probably Mongolia, North Vietnam, and North Korea. East Germany, on the other hand, probably falls close to the USSR and Czechoslovakia.[67] (See Table V-3.)

The 1961 indexes of *industrial production* are available for seven of the fourteen party-states, all located in economically accelerated East Europe. (See Table V-3.) Their average industrial production index, 188.57, falls well above the average for the rest of Europe—141.46.[68] The 1961 crude-steel production data are available for ten Communist party-states. The USSR here leads with almost twice as much steel production as the rest of the party-states combined (70.7 million metric tons). Together, the ten party-states are responsible for about one-third, or about 32.22 per cent, of the world production of steel.[69] (See Table V-4.) The party-states' cement

---

[66] *Problems of Peace and Socialism,* Supplement, p. 4.

[67] Most of the data are for 1955 or earlier; consequently, due account is not taken of the changes that have taken place since then. Ginsburg, *op. cit.,* p. 18. See International Labor Organization, *Yearbook of Labor Statistics,* 21st Issue (Geneva: 1961), pp. 6–9.

[68] *Annual Bulletin of Transportation Statistics for Europe, 1961* (New York: United Nations, 1962), Table 2, p. 3.

[69] U.N., *Statistical Yearbook,* 1962, 1963, Table 109, p 257.

Table V-3

Per Capita Gross National Product (1955 or earlier)		World		Indexes of Industrial Production (1961)	Crude Steel Production (1961) (in thousands metric tons)	
Rank	$	Party-States	Rank	Rank	Rank	Total
1. USSR	682	1	18	1. Bulgaria	230	1. USSR	70,700
2. Czechoslovakia	543	2	20	2. N. Korea	217	2. China	15,500
3. E. Germany		not available		3. Yugoslavia	200	3. Poland	7,234
4. Poland	468	3	25	4. Rumania	194	4. Czechoslovakia	7,043
5. Hungary	387	4	27	5. Czechoslovakia	181	5. E. Germany	3,444
6. Cuba	361	5	31	6. USSR	179	6. Rumania	2,126
7. Rumania	320	6	35	7. Poland	176	7. Hungary	2,053
8. Yugoslavia	297	7	40	8. Hungary	160	8. Yugoslavia	1,532
9. Bulgaria	285	8	42	9. E. Germany	n.a.	9. N. Korea	780
10. China	56	9		10. China	n.a.	10. Bulgaria	340
11. N. Korea		n.a.		11. Cuba	n.a.	11. Cuba	n.a.
12. Albania		n.a.		12. Albania	n.a.	12. Albania	n.a.
13. N. Vietnam		n.a.		13. N. Vietnam	n.a.	13. N. Vietnam	n.a.
14. Mongolia		n.a.		14. Mongolia	n.a.	14. Mongolia	n.a.

Source:

Economic and Statistical Information on North Korea (January 15, 1960). JPRS 901–D.

Table V-4

Gross Energy Consumption (1961)

Rank	Total	Rank	kg per cap.
1. USSR	636.84	4	2,921
2. China	197.35		n.a.
3. Poland	95.39	3	3,182
4. E. Germany	84.66	2	4,942
5. Czechoslovakia	70.64	1	5,125
6. Rumania	26.62	7	1,433
7. Hungary	25.04	5	2,496
8. Yugoslavia	16.83	8	904
9. Bulgaria	12.43	6	1,565
10. Cuba	6.01	9	366
11. Albania	0.56	10	337
12. N. Korea	n.a.		n.a.
13. N. Vietnam	n.a.		n.a.
14. Mongolia	n.a.		n.a.

Installed Capacity Of Electrical Energy (1961) (in 1000 kilowatts)

Rank	Total
1. USSR	74,098
2. China	11,594
3. E. Germany	8,268
4. Poland	6,768
5. Czechoslovakia	6,372
6. Yugoslavia	2,681
7. Rumania	1,863
8. Bulgaria	1,046
9. Cuba	932
10. Albania	31
11. Hungary	n.a.
12. N. Korea	n.a.
13. N. Vietnam	n.a.
14. Mongolia	n.a.

Wheat Yields (in 100 kg per hectare)

Rank	Yield
1. E. Germany	34.8
2. Czechoslovakia	23.3
3. Bulgaria	19
4. Yugoslavia	17.3
5. Poland	16.9
6. Hungary*	15.7
7. China	13
8. Rumania	12.2
9. USSR	10.6
10. Albania	9.8
11. Cuba	n.a.
12. N. Korea	n.a.
13. N. Vietnam	n.a.
14. Mongolia	n.a.

Source:

* *FAO Production Yearbook, 1961* (New York: UN, 1962), XV (Rome: 1959). 1960–1961 yield.

output amounted to about 104 million metric tons in 1962, which was slightly less than one-third of the world output.[71] Petroleum production, put at 208 million metric tons, amounted to about one-fifth of the world output.[71]

Figures pertaining to *consumption of energy* are also available. They relate to the energy equivalents, measured in a common unit, of the consumption of coal and lignite, crude petroleum, natural gas, and hydroelectric power. The Communist party-states account for less than one-third (27.08 per cent) of the world energy consumption and produce more energy than they consume. The total *energy-production* ratio of the party-states to world production is about 1.4 to 4.4 thousand million metric tons of coal equivalent, or 33.48 per cent of the total world production.[72] (See Table V-4.)

In terms of the 1961 installed *capacity of electric energy* (i.e., normal end-of-year capacity of all generators available for simultaneous operation in both thermoelectric and hydroelectric plants), eleven of the party-states for which information is available constitute more than one-fifth of the total world production of electricity. Again, the USSR is responsible for almost two-thirds of the total party-states' production of electricity (74.1 million kilowatts annually), whereas China produces only 11.6 billion kilowatts.[73] (See Table V-4.)

Thus, the USSR is the largest party-state, possessing about twice as much territory as all the other party-states combined, and China has the greatest population—more than double that of the other party-states combined. The estimated Soviet gross national product (GNP), $270 billion, is second

---

[70] *Ibid.,* Table 107, p. 254.

[71] *Ibid.,* Table 105, pp. 245–252; see also *Problems of Peace and Socialism,* Supplement, p. 8.

[72] U.N., *Statistical Yearbook,* 1962, Table 122, p. 290; Y. L. Wu, *Economic Development and Uses of Energy Resources in Communist China* (New York: Frederick A. Praeger, Inc. [published for the Hoover Institution, Stanford], 1963), pp. 192–193.

[73] U.N., *Statistical Yearbook,* 1962, Table 124, pp. 302–309; Y. L. Wu, *op. cit.,* p. 18; *Problems of Peace and Socialism,* Supplement, p. 8. In the 1958–1963 period, the rate of economic growth of the fourteen party-states had declined by more than one-half. While the total party-state rate of growth in 1958 was 17.1 per cent, the 1962 industrial output rose only by 0.5 per cent, the slowest growth rate reported since the establishment of the party-state system. [*Ibid.,* p. 6. See also *The New York Times,* Western Edition, August 17, 1963, p. 2 (the average rate of growth for Western Europe in the 1950–1960 decade was 3.53 per cent). U.N., *Compendium of Social Statistics,* 1963, Table 100, p. 167.] The chief reason indicated as responsible for the slowdown was the failure of Chinese industry to recover fully from the disastrous consequences of the "leap forward" program and to grow according to the plan. However, Albanian, East German, North Korean, and Czechoslovak industrial rate of growth declined as well. Only Cuba, Rumania, and North Korea increased their industrial production in the period reported. (*Problems of Peace and Socialism,* p. 6.)

largest in the world after the United States ($553.9 billion). It is more than four times that of China and almost two-thirds of the total GNP of all party-states.[74] In terms of natural resources, the USSR and China have an over-whelming lead over the other party-states.[75] In terms of military might, the USSR's absolute eminence among the party-states is well established.

Clearly, then, in terms of size or weight, the USSR and China are the giants among the party-states. Together they control over 91 per cent of the total party-states' territory, contain 86 per cent of the party-states' popu-lation, and produce over three-fourths of the total GNP. Their share of the party-states' weight approaches monopoly proportions. The other twelve party-states are pigmies in comparison.

Should one member or unit of a coalition of states contain more than 50 per cent of the coalition weight or size, there would be virtually no pro-bability of a rebellious winning coalition of the smaller units without outside assistance, according to William H. Riker in his study of political coalitions.[76] This describes the Stalinist period. With two large units containing an over-whelming proportion of the party-states' weight, however, the temptation for each to increase its pay-off by attempting to form a winning coalition is very hard to resist. Their alliance becomes unstable. They are too large, relative to the alliance, to maintain a winning coalition.

When translated into relative or per capita figures, however, neither of the two giants lead the other party-states. In terms of advancement or moderni-zation, i.e., industrialization, urbanization, literacy and enlightenment, com-munication system, affluence and wealth, well-being of the population, and so on, the USSR and China are surpassed on the per capita basis by several small party-states, principally East Germany, Czechoslovakia, and Poland (and, in several respects, also by Hungary, Yugoslavia, Rumania, Bulgaria, and Cuba). The considerable quantitative asymmetry between the two principal and the twelve supporting actors among the party-states is thus greatly aggravated by the qualitative asymmetry between the two large and several of the small party-states.

Since modernization and advancement is a professed major party-state goal, the least advanced party-states might be expected to stand to profit

[74] Ginsburg, *Ibid.,* p. 16: *The New York Times,* Western Edition, July 15, 1963, p. 1.

[75] The USSR is first in the world in iron-ore deposits, manganese ore, and timber and second in bauxite reserves, gold, lead, and zinc; China, however, has more bauxite reserves than all the other party-states combined, twice the antimony reserves of the rest of the world, 21.3 per cent of the world's coal reserves, etc. (But the USSR has 26 billion barrels of proved petroleum reserves while China has virtually none.) *Oxford Economic Atlas,* 2nd ed. (New York: Oxford University Press, 1959).

[76] *The Theory of Political Coalitions* (New Haven: Yale University Press, 1962).

most from membership in the alliance. The backward party-states should be enthusiastic members, whereas the advanced members ought to be recalcitrant. The available empirical evidence, however, fails to support this proposition. East Germany and Czechoslovakia, relatively the most advanced party-states, show more enthusiasm for the alliance than the relatively most backward members, namely Albania, China, and North Korea.[77] This is the case, perhaps, because the advanced members assist the other less fortunate party-states. They thus play a positive, contributary, awarding role for which they are valued, rewarded, and placed close to the top of the alliance hierarchy. The advanced members have, thus, a considerable stake in this kind of an alliance, and their desire to maintain and develop it is not necessarily shared by the backward members.

The alliance organizer, the USSR, is bestowing respect and prestige on its industrial, industrious members and is assigning them the prestigious role of modernizers of the alliance. If the coalition organizer indeed succeeds in assigning and supporting specific, particular roles to members—a big *if*—then they are bound to profit from their assigned role of heavy industrial supplier and supporter of others. This is why the advanced party-states have a vested interest in the communist system's maintenance. The benefits which have accrued to them to date have been of limited significance; but, they might become tangible and significant in the future, for these advanced party-states have been permitted to maintain and develop a heavy industrial base— a supranational privilege denied most other members.

The backward members appear to play hardly any positive role in the goal of system advancement. The advanced party-states do not value the backward party-states' condition, and the backward party-states, in turn, appear to value negatively the advanced party-states. The differences in advancement are so great that "fraternal mutual assistance" could hardly overcome them in the intermediate run. It would impoverish the USSR and Eastern Europe to contribute rapidly and significantly to China's advancement, and China tells the other party-states, rather huffily, that "each Socialist country must rely mainly on itself for its own construction."[78]

China, the other major party-state and would-be organizer, is also one of the least advanced members of the alliance. It thus provides a rallying point

---

[77] F. Bruce Dodge, "Comparative Enthusiasm at the International Level: A Research Design and an Application to Eastern Europe." (Honors Thesis, Stanford University, 1964), *passim.*

[78] Letter sent on June 14, 1963 by the Central Committee of the Chinese Communist Party to the Central Committee of the CPSU. *The New York Times,* Western Edition, July 5, 1963, p. 4.

for the other less advanced members, who, like China, stress system goals *other* than economic development and maintenance, namely, ideological purity and world revolution.

If we consider additional contributing and analytical factors such as degree of social stability, ethnic differences, degree of internationalization, historical experiences, mode of joining the system, and degree of independence of the Communist Parties, we obtain multiple stratified and hierarchical rank orderings of alliance members. The two leading members, the USSR and China, because of their wide differences in achievement and economic progress, prescribe essentially different goal values for the alliance and for the communist system, and the alliance between them, too large relative to the coalition, thus becomes unstable and is in danger of splitting into two separate suballiances.[79]

Aside from the Sino-Soviet conflict, but principally as a consequence of the above-mentioned factors, some party-states appear to be more isolated from, and less cohesive with, the rest of the party-states. Some have stable and others unstable, or even no alignments with other members. Many disputes and conflicts arise, chiefly over boundaries and minorities, which help to perpetuate the many presystem suspicions and national jealousies. The European-Asian boundary (the USSR appears to consider itself principally a European, rather than Asian or Eurasian, power)[80] is politically, socially, economically, and ideologically more significant than the respective boundaries among member units (Mongolia in Asia and Albania in Europe being symmetrical exceptions), although the latter boundaries are better guarded against fraternal neighbors than are any boundaries in the West.

The three alliance organizations—the Joint Institute of Nuclear Research, the International Broadcasting Organization, and the Organization for the Collaboration of Railways—are useful agencies, with little or no political overtones, as are the multilateral functional and *ad hoc* conferences on health, fishing industries, plant protection, and so on. Both the ambitious Council of Mutual Economic Assistance and the military Warsaw Treaty Organization are Eastern European organizations (Outer Mongolia in Comecon is

[79] Cf. Morton A. Kaplan, *System and Process in International Politics* (New York: John Wiley & Sons, Inc., 1957), pp. 36ff.

[80] See "For Unity in the Struggle for Peace, Freedom and National Independence," *Pravda*, May 5, 1964, p. 1: "Every educated person knows that the Soviet Union is not only the biggest European power but the biggest Asian power as well. Approximately 40% of the territory of Asia falls within the boundaries of the Soviet Union. The Asian part of the USSR is almost twice as big as the territory of the whole of China. Furthermore, such major Asian countries as China, India, Indonesia, Pakistan, Burma and Japan taken together could be accommodated in the expanses of the Asian part of the USSR!"

a recent exception), whereas the membership of the Danube Commission, countering the flow of the river, is spilling over from Eastern into Western Europe and includes not only Yugoslavia, but Austria and, tentatively, West Germany as well.

In terms of *internationalization*, i.e., the volume and dimension of transactions of the party-states with the outside world, the party-states also differ a great deal. A simple index of internationalization (see Table V-5)—based on subindexes of (A) participation in the United Nations, (B) participation in other international organizations, (C) per capita imports of foreign goods, and (D) "communications" (the number of foreign tourists and the number of local citizens traveling abroad; the flow of nongovernmental mail in and out of the country; and the percentage of translated books to native-language books)[81]—where 1.00 is the average amount of internationalization[82] and

[81] A. *UN Participation.* Ten of the fourteen party-states are members of the United Nations (the three divided states and China are not members), but they participate in varying degree in its activities. Assuming that a nation has eighteen major ways of participating in the UN, we have devised the following index of participation (half a point is given for "observer" or "associate" status):

Yugoslavia	14.5	(1.55)
Cuba	12	(1.29)
Poland	11.5	(1.23)
Czechoslovakia	10	(1.07)
USSR	9	(.96)
Bulgaria	9	(.96)
Hungary	9	(.96)
Rumania	9	(.96)
Albania	8	(.86)
Mongolia	1	(.10)

The index in parenthesis was calculated by dividing the first figure by the average of all first figures. Amos Peaslee, *International Governmental Organizations* (The Hague: Martinus Nijhoff, 1956).

All countries, whether members of the UN or not, are free to submit documents to it. How many documents each country submits provides some measure of the role it sees for itself in directing international affairs through the UN. In 1961, the party-states submitted the following number of documents:

USSR	166	(5.07)
Czechoslovakia	64	(1.95)
Yugoslavia	61	(1.86)
Poland	56	(1.71)
Cuba	39	(1.19)
Bulgaria	23	(.70)
Hungary	15	(.45)
Rumania	13	(.39)
Albania	10	(.30)
Mongolia	7	(.21)
North Korea	3	(.09)

the index is the average of A, B, C, and D produces the following hetero-geneous results (in several cases, information for C and D was not available):

Table V–5

INDEX OF INTERNATIONALIZATION		A.* UN	B.* INT. ORGS.	C.* IMPORTS	D.* COM-MUNICATIONS
1. Czechoslovakia	1.75	1.51	1.63	1.74	2.14
2. Yugoslavia	1.45	1.70	1.90	.57	1.63
3. USSR	1.25	3.01	1.42	.31	.26
4. Poland	1.18	1.47	1.83	.67	.77
5. Cuba	1.13	1.24	1.08	1.63	.57
6. Bulgaria	1.07	.83	1.42	1.00	1.06
7. Hungary	1.06	.70	1.63	1.21	.70
8. Rumania	.85	.67	1.70	.51	.53
9. East Germany	.62	.02	.27	1.37	.82
10. Albania	.56	.58	.51	.58	n.a.
11. Mongolia	.54	.15	.13	(1.35)	n.a.
12. North Vietnam	.09	0	.17	n.a.	n.a.
13. North Korea	.08	.05	.10	n.a.	n.a.
14. China	.07	0	.13	n.a.	n.a.

* The A and B figures denote principally governmental activities while the C and D figures refer principally to nongovernmental activities.

East Germany	1	(.03)
North Vietnam	0	(0)
China	0	(0)

The two indexes are averaged to give the figure under (A). Note that only in the cases of the USSR and Czechoslovakia is there a broad discrepancy between the two measures of UN participation.

B. *International Organizations.* Listed below are the numbers of international organizations of which the various party-states are members. As under (A), half a point is given for "observer" or "associate" status. All organizations counted have permanent consultative bodies, except the Bandung Conference, which was included because of its unique im-portance. (The data are, again, from Peaslee's two-volume work, *International Governmental Organizations.*)

Yugoslavia	28	(1.90)
Poland	27	(1.83)
Rumania	25	(1.70)
Czechoslovakia	24	(1.63)
Hungary	24	(1.63)
USSR	21	(1.42)
Bulgaria	21	(1.42)
Cuba	16	(1.08)
Albania	7.5	(.51)
East Germany	4	(.27)

Finally, multilateral meetings and communications of Communist Parties, ruling as well as non-ruling, separately or jointly, have been increasingly unsuccessful and therefore fewer. In this matter, the Communist Parties cannot be viewed as possessing either legislative or executive authority, essentially because of the preference—perceived as system necessity—for unanimity and solidarity. A unanimous vote, given the pronounced heterogeneity of the Communist Party's national environments as well as their growing propensity for conflict, has produced only watered-down joint proclamations, declarations, and statements of principles. Judicial or arbitration function of the Communist Parties has never been taken seriously either.

At most, what the Communist Parties share are *hybrid and plurilateral*

North Vietnam	2.5	(.17)
Mongolia	2	(.13)
China	2	(.13)
North Korea	1.5	(.10)

C. *Imports.* A country's total imports are less significant—as a measure of internationalization—than the ratio of these imports to the size of the population, i.e., a given quantity of imported goods has a greater internationalizing effect on a small country than on a large one. Ideally, we should take the ratio of imports to gross national product; but, since GNP figures are not available for most Communist countries, we use the ratio of imports to population instead.

The first figure in the table below gives the party-states' imports in 1961 in millions of dollars. The second figure is the ratio of the first figure to the population in millions, i.e., the per capita imports. These ratios are then averaged to form an index:

Czechoslovakia	2024	148	(1.74)
Cuba	808	139	(1.63)
East Germany	2019	117	(1.37)
Mongolia	97	115	(1.35)
Hungary	1026	103	(1.21)
Bulgaria	666	85	(1.00)
Poland	1684	57	(.67)
Albania	81	50	(.58)
Yugoslavia	910	49	(.57)
Rumania	815	44	(.51)
USSR	5832	27	(.31)

U.N., *Statistical Yearbook,* 1962, Table 147. Note that this list, the first of the "society" indexes, presents quite a different typology from the "state" indexes considered thus far.

D. *Communications.* This is the most difficult factor to quantify. Data are hard to obtain, and it is not clear which of the many possible measurements are the most significant. Our calculations are based on four separate quantities, insofar as they were available:

i. Ratio of the annual number of citizens traveling abroad to total population. Travelers returning from foreign countries, it seems, are one of the most powerful internationalizing forces in a society.

ii. Ratio of annual foreign visitors visiting country to total population. The presence of foreign visitors, although probably less important than local citizens who have been abroad, is still an important factor in internationalizing the society.

coalitions which fluctuate from issue to issue (Yugoslavia, the 1956 Polish problem, Cuba, the inevitability of war with imperialism) and in which the respective exercise of influence by the two major Communist party-states, the USSR and China, demands or permits realignment and side-taking by other members. Even the *World Marxist Review: Problems of Peace and Socialism*, a monthly magazine printed in nineteen languages (and differing in content from one geographical target area to another), is essentially a Soviet and a European "cultural" tool of communication cohesion (the Chinese withdrew in the spring of 1963).

Stratification, segmentation, and diversity are thus prevalent among the Communist party-states on both Party and state levels. There is no single

---

iii. Ratio of letters sent abroad and received from abroad to domestic letters. The ratios for "sent" and "received" are averaged. Unfortunately, data are available for only three party-states.

iv. Ratio of foreign book translations to domestic book publication may be viewed as another important way in which a society is internationalized.

The table below omits the raw data, showing only the index number for each of the four categories and the average index:

	I	II	III	IV
Czechoslovakia	2.14	2.90			1.39
Yugoslavia	1.63	1.93	2.69	.81	1.12
Bulgaria	1.06	.59			1.16
East Germany	.82	.78		.86	
Poland	.77	.67	.35	1.31	.78
Hungary	.70	.85			.54
Cuba	.57	.57			
Rumania	.53	.61	.31		.67
USSR	.26	.59	.20		.51
(Albania)					(1.82)

U.N., *Statistical Yearbook,* 1962, Tables 146, 147, 148, 178, and 179. No data are available for Albania except under iv, book translations. Albania publishes very few books, only about four hundred titles per year, and about a quarter of these are foreign translations. All other Eastern European countries publish between 3,000 and 8,000 titles per year; so, Albania is still only slightly internationalized in this respect. The figure 1.82 is deceptively large and not included in the final index. Note that Czechoslovakia, more than any other party-state, sends an extraordinary number of citizens abroad each year. This typology is quite different from (C) but closer to (C) than to either of the state typologies (A) and (B).

[82] To compute the "average," take, for instance, the figures of membership in UN agencies. Ten of the party-states are shown to belong to between 1 and 14.5 agencies. Adding the column for all ten party-states yields 93.0, or an *average* (dividing by ten) of 9.3 agencies per party-state. The average party-state, then, belongs to just 9.3 agencies, so that Czechoslovakia is a little above average and the USSR is a little below average in this respect. To get the index, we simply divide each membership figure by the average membership figure, 9.3. For instance, 14.5/9.3 = 1.55 for Yugoslavia. If there were a hypothetical state between Czechoslovakia and the USSR which belonged to exactly 9.3 agencies, it would have an index of 1.00, showing it was a completely average case.

state rule-making or policy-articulating organ, although there are contenders for the role. Rule implementation, segmented and compartmentalized in the several party-states' organizations, such as the Council for Mutual Economic Assistance, is carried out principally on state rather than on Party levels. Although there are several state arbitration boards to resolve or contain anticipated functional or economic conflicts, there is no machinery to deal with Party or political conflicts. The party-states, the principal and key units of the communist system, possess no institutionalized leadership formula except on *ad hoc*, weight, or size basis. Even a simple conflict containing mechanism which would routinely deal with outstanding dissension among the party-states is entirely missing. As a consequence, there is no legitimate automatic coercive agency to enforce decisions of party-states either within the alliance or within the system as a whole.

The party-states (as well as the system as a whole) depend for their common endeavor on *agreement and persuasion*, which oscillates from various degrees of assertion to tentative consultative or advisory assistance, depending on the particular actors involved. Increasingly, the two major alliance organizers deny the other members the right to participate and share in community endeavors and benefits, rather than forcing obligations on them as Stalin did.

The principal unifiers and solidifiers of the party-states alliance on the other hand, are said to be: (1) the Communist Parties ruling the fourteen states, creating thereby fourteen similar or "socialist" political, economic, social, and legal systems (on the basis of this essential element of similarity, the CPSU includes Yugoslavia, which possesses the three elements of unity as well within the subsystem. The Chinese Communist Party—arguing on the basis of Solidifier No. 2, that Yugoslavia is not a socialist state— disagrees); (2) the acceptance by the fourteen Communist Party elites of the "Marxist-Leninist" belief system as a common source of present and future political, economic, and social means-and-goals orientation (the revisionist- dogmatist disagreement thus adversely affects a principal unifier of the party-states); (3) the Soviet military might, especially its thermonuclear weapons and delivery systems, almost symmetrical in weight to the military capability of the principal and most powerful party-states' opponent, the United States, but overwhelmingly asymmetrical in weight within the coalition (in terms of military weight, the USSR is *absolutely* the alliance- dominant party-state; and (4) the geographical contiguity of the member- units—an ecological prerequisite for recruitment and original membership, and an element which makes the initial Soviet-Chinese sponsorship of Cuban membership in the alliance questionable—helps to explain both the successful Albanian resistance to de-Stalinization after the Yugoslav defection and the hesitant Soviet recognition of the Ho Chi Minh regime in North Vietnam before contiguity with China was established in 1950.

The last-named is perhaps the weakest of the four elements of cohesion. On balance, it facilitates logistic extension of assertive control better than it fosters consensual entry. Over time, given the conditions prevailing among the party-states and the shrinking of the international system, geographical contiguity may prove to be an element of secondary importance.

With the absence of an organization of the parties, and only partial, functional, and segmented organizations of the states, the chief propensity of the party-states is now toward greater independence, function, utility, and complexity, a disposition leading further away from the initial achievement-oriented paternal hierarchy. The assertion of greater independence by some members has been successfully tested—by Yugoslavia, China, Albania, and Rumania. The integrating coercive forces of the USSR which initiated and perpetuated the Soviet bloc have much less to do with the present (but, again, Soviet-sponsored) utilitarian phase of communist community building in Eastern Europe. Still, the essential conflict-orientation of the members, coupled with the absolute lack of automatic conflict-containment machinery, does not make coercion as yet entirely obsolete.

However, the issue is no longer one of simple possession of means of coercion—superior weapons and delivery systems—but how to utilize the possession most effectively in order to reach the desirable goals *without* applying the means. This, in the last analysis, is the moot problem.

The Chinese challenge, which opened up new alternatives for the Communist party-states—a challenge which the Soviet Union has not been able to subdue—raised the cost of coalition maintenance for the Soviet Union. The coalition members are in a stronger position vis-à-vis the USSR because of the implied possibility of their defection to China, the frustrated candidate organizer. Given the present stalemate between the two powers, the more the coalition members ask, the more they get; their bargaining position is increasing in direct proportion with the increasing polycentrism in the coalition. This new doorway is bound to become irresistible even to the smaller, more docile Communist party-states once they discover the key. Sustained, however, this process has tended to escalate the cost of coalition maintenance for the organizer, the USSR, because the price, the autonomy of members, may become so inflated that the USSR will not be able to afford it unless goals are altered. Coalition containment is then bound to mean not only containment of anarchy in the coalition, but also the progressive alienation of all Parties, ruling and nonruling, in the communist system.

The progressive erosion of the Communist party-state alliance is bound to spread to the nonruling Communist Parties and affect adversely their system participation and maintenance.

THE STRATEGIES OF NONRULING COMMUNIST PARTIES

The fourteen Communist party-states have Party and state relations with virtually every corner of the globe. The ruling Parties relate to nonruling Parties and the governments of the party-states relate to governments of non–party-states. State relations are easier to define than are Party relations, although even here there is ambiguity.

The nonruling Communist Parties are aspirationally perceived by the Communist party-states as *potential ruling parties* within their state units. They are viewed—and rewarded—as outposts, as well as supporters, of the "socialist community." At the same time, they constitute tangible evidence of the present "world" extension of the communist system. The sustained interaction between the party-states and the Parties is thus mutually supportive.

The nonruling Communist Parties' rapport with the ruling Parties mirrors the ruling Parties' principal problems, stresses, expectations, setbacks, and advances. But, the local culture and social change requirements, totally different from those of the party-states' microcosms, impose upon local Parties demands for varied, imaginative, and seldom pretested operational codes. This flexibility creates misunderstandings with the party-states, misunderstandings which are often compounded by the party-states' overt and sometimes generous material support of the very governments hostile to their local Communist Parties.

The nonruling parties vary in size, local effectiveness, degree to which they are tolerated by their governments, discipline vis-à-vis the ruling Parties, "inner democracy," and so on. Aspirationally, they play the roles of the Czechoslovak, Yugoslav, Polish, or Chinese Communist Parties before the entry of those states into the party-states subsystem. In fact, they act and have acted as the legitimate native representatives of the party-states. Historically, because they depended for recognition, legitimacy, and support upon the party-states, their interdependence with the party-states was lopsided. Without the existence of the party-states, they would have been simply local Parties, equal in status to other parties within their respective states. This lopsidedness has been decreasing in direct proportion to the conflict orientation of the party-states, however. With the party-states coalition becoming progressively more unstable, the nonruling Parties' value as system allies to the ruling Parties, and especially to the two coalition organizers, the USSR and China, has been on the upswing.

As the national orientation of the nonruling Communist Parties tends to increase with their decreasing system orientation, they become subject to growing interaction with their operational environment. This interaction in turn tends to make an impressive and sustained impact on their operational codes and goals. They become subject to the same persistent national pressures which brought about the disunity among the ruling Parties in the first place. As a consequence, the less the nonruling Parties are willing to sponsor locally the interests of the ruling Parties and the more they deviate from their system functions and from their system goals, the more influential they tend to become locally. In fact, this deviation can lead to success: the greater the means-and-ends coincidence between the national environment and the respective nonruling Party, the stronger the Party. In those countries where the hostility between the Party and the national environment persisted—as in Ireland, Canada, or the United States—the nonruling Parties declined. They have gained or held their own in those countries—such as France or Italy—where they became, for all practical purposes, national electoral parties.

In developing nations, the nonruling Communist Parties tend to be revolutionary. Here they follow the traditional Leninist concept of dynamic revolutionary forces in societies which are not yet integrated and often not politicised. The nonruling Parties perform, in addition to their system objectives, the function of socializers toward modernity. They feed the aspirations and ambitions of those frustrated by the inability of the developing society to use their skills. The resulting high want/get ratio brings into the Communist Party all those wishing to mobilize and transform their society rapidly into modernity.

In developed nations, where there is no legitimate function for a revolutionary, deviant Party, the Communist Parties either persist and go underground, or they give in, conform, and become *electoral parties*. The former alternative tends to mean failure and the latter, success. The electoral Parties compete for votes with other national parties, and the competition forces them to reduce greatly, both structurally and functionally, their differences from other parties. They therefore tend to be pragmatic, nonheretic, and non-ideological, and their ties and interaction with the communist system tend to slacken. The Italian and French Communist Parties are good examples of this type of nonruling Party.

As for in-between nations, where segments of the population have not been incorporated and integrated into their social and political systems, the nonruling Parties tend to become Parties of protest. By defending and articulating the negative interests and dissatisfaction of isolated and alienated sections of society, they tend to integrate more into social than political Parties. In postwar France, when the French Communist Party left the protest field and entered the government as an electoral Party, the Party members and leaders found the transition difficult. "Denunciation and demagogy were easier and more enjoyable than responsibility."[83] Just as revolutionary Communist Parties, the Parties of protest tend to function principally as *communist system parties*, with all that this function implies.

In addition, the nonruling Communist Parties are *political parties*, because they seek, in competition with other local parties, to control their respective governments. They thus differ from the ruling Communist Parties, which are by definition without competition for rule, and hence are not in this sense Parties at all. This difference has important consequences in terms of social composition of the nonruling Parties, their structures and strategies, and their relations with other Communist Parties.

The Soviet press spoke of seventy-five Parties (ruling and nonruling) in 1958,[84] eighty-seven in 1960,[85] and eighty-eight in 1962.[86] One could list as many as eighty-nine Parties, but several of these receive little acknowledgment from the party-states.

What constitutes a Communist Party? Some Parties identify themselves as Communist, whereas others, such as the Irish Workers' League, are communist, although their names do not indicate it. Still others, such as the Mexican Workers' and Farmers' Party, have strong communist leanings, although they exist independently of, and sometimes compete with, the local Communist Party. Some countries have both a Communist party-states'-oriented Party and a "national" Communist Party; some countries have these plus a Trotskyite party. Where communism is illegal, numerous left-wing parties may preach Marxist slogans but maintain few connections with the Communist party-states.

We count here only those Parties which perceive themselves to be a part of the system and are so perceived by the party-states. This automatically excludes all Trotskyite and "national" Communist Parties, as well as those

[83] Hugh Seton-Watson, *From Lenin to Khrushchev* (New York: Frederick A. Praeger, Inc., 1961), p. 320.

[84] B. N. Ponomarev, "Communist Parties—Decisive Weapon of the Working Class," *Pravda,* April 28, 1958, p. 4.

[85] "Solidarity Under the Banner of Marxist-Leninism," *Pravda,* November 23, 1960, p. 1. An editorial.

[86] V. Tolstikov, "The Great Strength of the Contemporary Situation," *Sovetskaia Rossiia,* October 16, 1962, p. 3.

left-wing parties which do not acknowledge the party-states' leadership. Furthermore, we count only one Party per country, selecting that Party most closely identified with the communist system.[87]

These criteria yield eighty-seven Communist Parties. Omitting the fourteen ruling Parties, Table V-6 lists the seventy-three nonruling Communist Parties of the world, identified by country rather than by official name, as of 1966.[88]

Table V-6 Nonruling Communist Party Membership

Country	Estimated Membership (1965)	Per Cent of Adult Population	Legal Status (1965–1966)	Trend (1953–1965)
1. Italy	1,350,000	3.92	legal	even
2. France	280,000	.90	legal	down
3. Japan	137,500	.24	legal	up
4. India	125,000	.54	legal	even
5. Indonesia	more than 100,000	.19	illegal	down
6. Argentinia	65,000	.46	semilegal	up
7. Finland	50,000	1.73	legal	even
8. Austria	35,000	.80	legal	down
9. Great Britain	33,734	.10	legal	even
10. S. Vietnam	31,000	n.a.	illegal	up
11. Chile	30,000	.66	legal	even
12. Brazil	23,000	.06	illegal	down
13. Venezuela	20,000	.54	illegal	down
14. Sweden	20,000	.38	legal	even
15. Greece	20,000	.36	illegal	even
16. Belgium	13,000	.20	legal	down
17. Colombia	12,000	n.a.	legal	even
18. Netherlands	12,000	.16	legal	down
19. Cyprus	10,000	3.07	legal	up
20. Uruguay	10,000	.60	legal	even
21. W. Germany	10,000	.03	illegal	down
22. Sudan	8,000	1.22	illegal	up

[87] We do, however, count separate parties for Northern Ireland and the French overseas departments of Réunion, Guadeloupe, and Martinique, for the Communists do not acknowledge these areas to be actually part of the countries concerned and advance separatist claims.

[88] The figures were drawn largely from the 1966 edition of the State Department's publication, *World Strength of the Communist Party Organizations,* Bureau of Intelligence and Research, U.S. Department of State (Washington, D.C.: Government Printing Office, January, 1966), and UN, *Demographic Yearbook,* Statistical Office of the UN (New York: U.N., 1966), pp. 208–229.

Table V-6   Nonruling Communist Party Membership

Country	Estimated Membership (1965)		Per Cent of Adult Population	Legal Status (1965–1966)	Trend (1953–1965)
23. Nepal		6,000	n.a.	illegal	even
24. Mexico		5,250	.025	legal	down
25. Peru		5,000	.10	illegal	down
26. Denmark		5,000	.11	legal	down
27. Australia		5,000	.08	legal	down
28. Burma		5,000	n.a.	illegal	down
29. Spain		5,000	.05	illegal	even
30. Paraguay		5,000	.62	illegal	up
31. Bolivia		4,500	.62	legal	up
32. Lebanon		4,000	n.a.	illegal	down
33. Switzerland	fewer than	4,000	.10	legal	even
34. Canada		3,500	.03	legal	down
35. Pakistan		3,250	.006	illegal	even
36. Syria		3,000	.15	illegal	down
37. USA		3,000	.002	semilegal	down
38. Malaysia		2,700	.008	illegal	down
39. Ceylon		2,600	.01	legal	down
40. Norway		2,500	.10	legal	down
41. Equador		2,500	n.a.	illegal	even
42. Israel		2,000	.15	legal	even
43. Portugal		2,000	.04	illegal	down
44. Iraq		2,000	.04	illegal	down
45. Philippines		1,750	.01	illegal	even
46. Dominican Republic		1,700	n.a.	illegal	even
47. Iran		1,500	.01	illegal	down
48. Honduras		1,300	.16	illegal	even
49. Turkey		1,250	.08	illegal	even
50. Guatemala		1,000	n.a.	illegal	down
51. Guadeloupe		1,000	n.a.	legal	even
52. Algeria	fewer than	1,000	n.a.	illegal	down
53. Iceland		975	.95	legal	even
54. Martinique		700	.49	legal	even
55. Morocco		500	.03	illegal	even
56. Luxemburg		500	.21	legal	even
57. Jordan		500	.06	illegal	down
58. Panama		500	.096	illegal	even
59. New Zealand		400	.24	legal	even
60. Costa Rica		400	.063	illegal	even
61. Tunisia		250	.06	illegal	down
62. Nicaragua		200	.048	illegal	even
63. El Salvador		200	.02	illegal	down
64. Ireland		125	n.a.	legal	even
65. Cambodia		100	n.a.	legal	down
66. South Africa		100	.012	illegal	down
67. Malagasy Republic	fewer than	100	.003	legal	down

Table V-6   Nonruling Communist Party Membership

Country	Estimated Membership	Per Cent of Adult Population	Legal Status (1965-1966)	Trend 1953-1965
68. Basutoland	fewer than 100	.03	legal	even
69. Thailand		n.a.	illegal	n.a.
70. Laos		n.a.	legal	n.a.
71. Réunion		n.a.	legal	n.a.
72. Haiti		n.a.	illegal	n.a.
73. Tanzania		n.a.	legal	n.a.

The list of countries is perhaps most interesting in its omissions. Communist Parties do not exist in several states of the Middle East (e.g., Afghanistan, Egypt, Saudi Arabia, Libya). None of the three Guianas has an organized Communist Party, although the French overseas departments of Guadeloupe, Martinique, and Réunion all do. There are almost no Communist Parties in Africa south of the Sahara. Marxist influence certainly exists in African states and their ruling non-Communist Parties, but there is only one African Communist Party of any standing: that of Sudan. A Malagasy Communist Party claims 1,500 members but probably has less than 100.[89] Communist Parties were founded in Nigeria, Basutoland, and Zanzibar; needless to say, little is known of these Parties except that they are small. The Zanzibar (Tanzania) Party has probably flourished since the coup in January, 1964, but membership statistics for it are not available. The Soviet press has alleged that there are more than 40,000 Communists in "Equatorial Africa,"[90] but this claim seems greatly exaggerated.

International meetings of Communist Parties give one indication of how many countries have Communist Parties accredited by party-states. Eighty-one Parties met in Moscow in November, 1960; the Soviet press named seventy-eight of them, and the remaining three were probably those of the U.S., Iceland, and Pakistan. Delegations from seventy-nine foreign Communist Parties were acknowledged at the XXIInd CPSU Congress in 1961. Absent or unacknowledged at both meetings were the Communist Parties of the Philippines, Cambodia, Laos, South Vietnam, and Egypt, as well as the four marginal African Parties of Malagasy, Nigeria, Basutoland, and Zanzibar.

[89] *World Strength of the Communist Party Organizations*, p. 123.
[90] *Ibid.*, pp. 113–137.

In terms of membership, as may be expected, there are many more small Parties than large ones. Because many of the small Parties are illegal and many of the large ones are legal, it appears that governmental supervision at least partly causes the skew. But a distribution of legal parties still centers only on the lower ranges, as Table V-7 indicates:

Table V-7 N R C P's : Membership Distribution

CP MEMBERSHIP	0–2,000	2–4,000	4–6,000	6–8,000	8–10,000	10–12,000	12–14,000
For All Communist Parties:* Number of CP'S in each range	32	11	9	1	3	2	1
For Legal Communist Parties Only:** Number of legal CP's in each range	14	5	4	0	2	2	1

* Out of seventy-three Communist Parties, fifty-eight or eighty per cent of the Communist Parties have fewer than 14,000 members.

** Only ten of the thirty-four legal Communist Parties had more than 14,000 members in 1966.

The two classifications have seven entries each. These would have to be extended to nearly a thousand entries to include all Communist Parties. If we distribute the Parties not by membership but by logarithm of membership, we get something approaching a normal distribution.

Another way of viewing membership distribution is to calculate the ratio of Communist Party membership/population. Some small countries as, for example, Cyprus, have relatively small Parties, yet these Parties constitute a significant percentage of the population and wield more influence than their size would suggest. Conversely, a large Party such as that of Japan comprises only a tiny percentage of the population, and its influence is therefore less than its size indicates.

The ratio of Communist Party membership/adult population is even more relevant. Children do not normally join Communist Parties, so this ratio more accurately reflects the Party-membership appeal. Furthermore, underdeveloped countries have many more children in the total population. The ratio of adults to total population varies from a low of 43 per cent in Sudan to a high of 75 per cent in Luxemburg.

The distribution of Parties according to the ratio of Communist Party/adult population is skewed, just as were the previous distributions:

Table V-8 N R C P's Ratio of Membership to Adult Population for all Communist Parties, legal and illegal (except for the countries for which adult population figures were unavailable).

CP membership per cent of adult population	0–.1	.1–.2	.2–.3	.3–.4	.4–.5	.5–.6	.6–.7
Number of CPs in each range	27	6	5	2	1	2	2

CP membership per cent of adult population	.7–.8	.8–.9	.9–1	1.22	1.73	3.07	3.92
Number of CPs in each range	2	1	2	1	1	1	1

We thus have two measures of a Party's strength: membership in absolute terms and membership as a percentage of adult population. It is difficult to balance these two measures in assessing a Party's overall influence. Probably, the first figure measures the Party's weight in the system as a whole, the second figure its weight in its own country. There is no obvious way of combining the two figures to produce a single meaningful index with which to rank the Parties.

The fourth column in the Table V-6 indicates the legal status of the Communist Parties in 1965–1966. Of the seventy-three Parties, only thirty-five were consistently permitted to operate legally in this period. Forty have been outlawed.

Where Communist Parties are legal, election results give probably the best single measure of a Communist Party's influence in the country. Despite the size of the party, its composition, organization, or propaganda line, all of which are inputs into the electoral process, the most telling statistic is the single output: How many people, given the choice, select the Communist Party delegates as their representatives?

Free elections do not prevail in some of the countries in question, but, for forty-one of the seventy-three parties, we have at least some measure of the Communist Party's electoral success. In most cases, this is a percentage of seats held in the national legislature. The distribution of these percentages is wide and erratic, with no apparent pattern except, again, a general preponderance of parties in the lower ranges.

The most successful parties are Guadeloupe (33.7 per cent), Italy (25.3 per cent), Martinique (23.4 per cent), Finland (22 per cent), France (21.8 per cent), and Iceland (16 per cent). The least successful parties are those of Canada (0.04 per cent), Ireland (0.02 per cent), and at the very bottom, the U.S. (where the Communist Party's Earl Browder won only 0.01 per cent of the vote in 1940, the last presidential election in which the Communists participated). It must be remembered, however, that variation in electoral systems complicates these comparisons. Comparisons are most meaningful in elections for a single national candidate, usually a presidential candidate, or in a legislative election with a system of proportional representation. Where single-member districts prevail, the Communists may only put up candidates in a fraction of the districts and the total vote for communist candidates thus underestimates the appeal of the Communist Party in the country as a whole.

Twenty of the seventy-three parties hold seats in their national legislatures, and five of these hold them through a front organization, rather than in their own name. In only four countries do the local Communist Parties hold more than 10 per cent of the seats: Italy (27.5 per cent), Finland (23.5 per cent), Iceland (15 per cent), and Chile (10.4 per cent). Thus, in only four countries has the Communist Party achieved significant influence in the government through direct popular election. In most democratic countries, the Communists have had little success at the polls.

It is interesting to compare a Communist Party's membership with the number of votes it receives. In the U.S., for instance, Browder received 48,579 votes in the 1940 presidential election, but this was approximately the membership of the Party. Apparently no one but Party members voted for Browder. But in most other relevant countries there exists a broad periphery of voters who do not belong to the Party. The Israeli Communist Party gets votes about twenty times in excess of its membership. In Nepal, the Communist Party got forty times more votes than it had members. The ratio has risen to 95 in India and 165 in the Malagasy Republic (although the latter was a vote for a front organization, not for the CP).

In some countries, notably the democratic ones, this local support factor remains fairly stable. In Denmark, for instance, where Party membership has declined from 16,000 in 1953 to 5,000 in 1965, the number of votes for the Communist Party has declined proportionately, so that the ratio has remained about 6 to 1. In Japan, Communist Party membership has been rising, but electoral support has been rising even faster, so that the ratio has increased from 8 (1953) to 14 (1958) to 17 (1962). But in most countries, this factor jumps about erratically, as governmental suppression causes large changes in Party membership or local issues inflate or depress the Communist Party's electoral popularity.

The final column of Table V-6, which is somewhat arbitrary, is an estimate of each Party's trend over the twelve-year period from 1953–1965. It is based on both membership changes and on electoral results. In some cases, the indications are ambiguous. In Uruguay, for example, Communist Party membership has fallen, but electoral success has doubled. In India, the fortunes of the Party rose during the first half of the period and have been falling since. All such dubious cases are labelled *even*. These criteria indicate that of the seventy-three parties, thirty-one have been falling, thirty have remained even, and only seven have risen during the twelve years. Of these seven, two are medium-sized and five are large (over 10,000 members). To these latter five parties could perhaps be added large parties whose fortunes over the twelve-year period remained about even, but which enjoyed some electoral gains, namely, Italy and Chile. Table V-9 contains a list of parties both large and rising which might be described as *statistically impressive*.

Table V-9   Successful N R C P's

	1964
1. Italy	1,350,000
2. Japan	137,000
3. Argentina	65,000
4. S. Vietnam	31,000
5. Chile	30,000
6. Cyprus	10,000
7. Sudan	10,000

But these parties are exceptions. Ninety per cent of all nonruling Communist Parties have been either declining or holding about even. In particular, all European parties except Cyprus are in this category. The American Communist Party seems to have been declining faster than any other Party in the world.

Almost all Communist Parties reached peaks of membership and popularity during World War II, but the trend since the early 1950's has been toward smaller parties. This can be seen in Table V-10.

Table V-10   Membership N R C P's: Trends, 1953–1965

	1953	1963	1965
Small Parties (0–2,000)	20	36	32
Medium Parties (2–20,000)	34	27	29
Large Parties (over 20,000)	20	15	12
Total	74	78	73

A decline in size alone, however, does not necessarily indicate failure of the Party. The Cuban Communist Party had 30,000 members in 1953, but only 12,000 in 1957; it rose again after the revolution to 27,000 in 1960 and numbered 35,000 by 1964. Similarly, the Laotian Communist Party had 3,500–3,800 members in 1957, but had a cut back to 100 members by 1960; its membership has remained at this extremely low level since then, but its paramilitary arm, the Pathet Lao, has expanded from 1,800 in 1960 to 20,000 in 1964.[91]

In 1953, there were seventy-four nonruling Communist Parties with about 3,200,000 members; in 1965, there were seventy-three parties with about 2,600,000 members (including splinter groups). In 1953, those Communist Parties commanded some 20,000,000 votes; in 1965, about 27,000,000. Thus, while Communist Party voters have grown by almost 30 per cent over the twelve years, the Communist Party members declined by about one-fifth, and the ratio between them has almost doubled—from slightly more than six voters per party member to more than ten voters per party member. World population has grown by more than 20 per cent over the same period and this accounts for part of the electoral gain.

Nearly half the nonruling Party members used to be Indonesians. Indeed, until 1965, the entire growth in Communist Party membership could be credited to the phenomenal expansion of the Indonesian party (PKI). But the great majority of the new PKI members were simple peasants who joined because they were promised land. When the Party staged an uprising in October, 1965, they simply ignored the Party's call to rise and the communist coup collapsed. During the eight months of anticommunist terror which followed, some 400,000 Communists (including the Party leader Aidit) were reported slaughtered; the PKI was apparently virtually wiped out. This drastic development in Indonesia negatively affected the membership figure of the nonruling Communist Parties. Even though the nonruling Communist Parties minus Indonesia lost membership during 1953–1965 period, the loss now is absolute, in membership as well as in legislative seats.

The trends in Communist Party membership have fluctuated greatly from one area of the world to another. Summarized, the 1953–1965 trends can be seen in Table V-11.[92]

Beyond Asia, Communist Party membership is on the rise only in Africa, but the meaning of this increase is minimal. And so, in spite of the more than 20 per cent world-population growth in the last twelve years, the

[91] Our survey has used Pathet Lao figures to represent Laos, but the distinction between the two organizations and the opposite trends in membership are worth bearing in mind.

[92] Figures for Latin America include Cuba; Cyprus is counted as part of Europe.

Table V-11   N R C P's Membership Trends, 1953–1965, in Areas of the World

AREA	CP MEMBERSHIP, 1953	CP MEMBERSHIP, 1964–1965	CHANGE
Asia	178,000	415,600	+233.5%
Europe	2,582,000	1,867,109	−28%
Latin America	247,000	179,250	−27.5%
	(does not include Cuba)		
Middle East	80,000	38,450	−51%
U.S.A. and Canada	50,000	6,500	−87%
Australia and New Zealand	6,500	5,500	−15.5%
Africa (sub-Sahara)	3,100	9,000	+290.3%

nonruling Communist Party membership actually declined by about one-fifth.

In summary, it may be said that those nonruling Communist Parties which essentially abdicated their communist-system aspirations and functions and became responsible national electoral Parties have either slightly gained in membership or held even. But, then, they have tended to be Communist Parties in name only. Their differences from other national parties have been reduced almost to zero because of their responsible participation in the national political process. Those nonruling Communist Parties which have functioned as *protest* or even *revolutionary* parties, on the other hand, have been subject to strong adversities both at home and within the system. The home governments often take hostile attitudes towards them, especially in one-party states, and outlaw them; or they turn into amorphous movements and become victims of the "objective conditions" of the social environment which they were supposed, but failed, to change, as in Ceylon or Southern Italy; or new local parties have emerged, left of the Communist Parties, more modern, responsive, and suitable to the particular unhappy social conditions that prevail, as in some Latin American countries. Within the communist system, the rapidly growing conflict orientation of the ruling Communist Parties has produced strains and pressures which further weaken the nonruling Communist Parties, especially the protest and revolutionary types. Deprivation, isolation, and the need to make a choice between the organizers, the USSR, and China have not proved conducive to the maintenance, let alone growth, of the nonruling Parties.

CONCLUSION

The world communist movement has been analyzed here as an international system of Communist Parties. The system approach appeared convenient not only because it afforded a general examination of the movement's means and goals, organization, association theory, alliance system, and strategies, but also because it has served as a basis for subsequent studies which center principally on the comparison of an interaction among the Communist party-states. Poorly equipped to cope with complexities of the modern world, the communist system has been described, in this study as well as in the subsequent research, as being in a sustained and fairly rapid decline. Drastic alterations of the system priorities, goals, organization, and strategy seem inevitable.

To implement and to add to these findings, further data is needed, and a more extensive, systematic "second round" research is called for. We need to know more about the structures of nonruling Communist Parties and their changing interaction with their social and political environments, with other parties, and with other systems. We need to know more about the Parties' changing ideological orientation and the degree of system cohesion this orientation provides. But most of all, we need an adequate causal explanation of the respective Communist Parties' emergence and strength: Why have the nonruling parties been vigorous in some national states and not in others?[93]

[93] Bearing these questions in mind, the Stanford Studies of the Communist System has prepared a comparative paradigm of the nonruling Communist Parties, the major focus of which is on the *varieties* of Communist Parties in the world and on the *causes* and the *consequences* of the variations. At the present time, six studies based on the paradigm are being written—on the Communist Parties of Brazil, Italy, Japan, Argentina, Cyprus, and Austria. The investigators plan to follow with studies of the Communist Parties of India, France, Chile, and Laos. Over the next five years, the investigators hope to provide comparative monographs on as many of the almost eighty Communist Parties as is reasonably possible, aiming toward a gradual, overall comparative analysis of all the units of the communist system.

chapter VI

PROCESSES AND INSTITUTIONS IN THE WORLD COMMUNIST SYSTEM[1]

We propose in this chapter to argue that, from the time of Khrushchev's consolidation in power, the policy of the Soviet Union toward the countries of Stalin's empire—the satellites—has been based upon the desire to maintain Soviet hegemony in circumstances which made Stalin's policy of empire obsolete and ineffective. Recognizing the inadequacy of Stalin's concepts and instruments of control, the Soviet leadership has sought to transform the institutional format and nature of authority in its hegemony and thus to maintain and stabilize its influence in the face of growing centrifugal forces.

Khrushchev's policies were only partially successful—decreasingly so after 1960. His removal from power in the fall of 1964 has frequently been attributed to this imperfect achievement. But the post-Khrushchev leadership has been singularly unable to revise the directions or the consequences of their predecessor's policy. The tempo has slowed; the same centrifugal forces tug persistently; polycentrism continues to advance as a discomfiting but tangible reality.

In the pages that follow, we examine some of the processes and institutions through which Khrushchev and his successors have pursued Soviet interests among the Communist party-states.

THE PROCESS AND CONDITION OF INTEGRATION

We shall use the term *integration*. We use it to describe cooperative behavior in an action system, where *cooperation* means joint action toward a common goal. Effective cooperation usually presupposes *coordination*, which includes synthesis of information and adjustment of courses of action among the coordinated parties. A decision-making approach to behavior is useful

[1] This Chapter is based in part on material drawn from David D. Finley, "A Political Perspective of Economic Relations in the Communist Camp," *Western Political Quarterly,* XVII, No. 2 (June, 1964). Reprinted by permission of the University of Utah, copyright owners.

for clarifying the concept. If the informational inputs for a decision commiting all the acting units of the system to act toward a common goal are drawn from all relevant units of the system, then the decision represents integrated behavior. A system in which most decisions are so based and do commit the system as a whole is extensively integrated. It follows that a system may be integrated or not in a variety of substantive contexts which may be broad or narrow in the scope of decisions they subsume.

It also follows that a system may be integrated in different institutional forms. For example, if the institutionalized decision-making process for the system is unified only at the top level of the pyramid of authority, but most decisions are made there and bind the system as a whole, we will have a highly integrated system with what we may call *top-level institutional integration*. If the institutionalized decision-making process for the system is instead unified far down into the subordinate levels of the authority pyramid, and decisions made on these levels still bind the system as a whole, then we still have a highly integrated system with what we may call in contrast *institutional integration in depth*.

We have not yet examined the basis of authority in an integrated system. Proceeding from the definitions above, one can conceive of highly integrated systems of both institutional forms (or any intermediate variety) in which authority is based upon coercion. But it is just as easy to conceive of such forms in which authority is based upon voluntary consensus derived from a community of values. Therefore, the institutional form of integration in a system does not determine either the extent of integrated behavior in the system or the basis of its authority. It remains to be seen whether or not one institutional form is in practice more or less conducive to integrated behavior and to a particular sort of authority.

It follows from this discussion that integration is a condition in which we may find a system. We frequently use the term in speaking to refer as well to a *process*—that of becoming integrated. The intensive propagation of a single value system, for instance, may be conducive to the development of a consensus which will sustain cooperation in a system institutionally integrated in depth. The demonstration of unanswerable military force may foster resignation which will sustain extensive cooperation in a system integrated institutionally by a single dictator.

Below we address our attention to Soviet efforts since 1945 to achieve and maintain an integrated hegemony over the Communist party-states. We consider first the processes and condition of integration in the allocation of economic values and focus upon the Council of Mutual Economic Assistance (COMECON). Thereafter we shift our attention to the simpler story of military integration and the Warsaw Treaty Organization, and thence briefly to a lesser but potentially important integrating institution, the Joint Institute for Nuclear Research.

COMECON: AN OVERVIEW

Formed in 1949 but of very minor importance until after Stalin's death, COMECON has been steadily increasing in stature to the point of becoming the major organizational instrument in the Soviet effort to retain control in spite of East European desires for more initiative. Often called the communist counterpart of the West European Common Market, COMECON consists of numerous economic coordinating groups in which representatives of each member state participate, allegedly on a basis of sovereign equality, in order to facilitate rapid economic progress for the region as a whole as well as for each member. COMECON provides both the carrot of mutually desired economic goals and the stick of coercive economic pressure for members to concert their energies under Soviet guidance. In these ways, COMECON today signifies a major alteration of Stalinist policy. It means a shift from top-level (Kremlin) integration of the USSR and East Europe toward the direction of institutional integration in depth. While the basis of authority in COMECON thus far remains in part the threat of Soviet coercion, a partially successful attempt has been made to shift the basis toward a community of Soviet inculcated values. The trends reflected by COMECON are compatible with Khrushchev's expressed preferences to advance communism by economic means and to de-emphasize the terror that characterized the regime of his predecessor. The trends also are entirely compatible with Marxist doctrinal thinking as currently developed in the USSR.

One need not conceive the world in Marxist terms in order to accept the intimate relationship between economic interdependence and political interdependence. The much heralded economic side of COMECON as a cooperative association of sovereign states is thus inseparable from the unpublicized aspects of COMECON as a political instrument. Few can doubt that for the forseeable future the Soviet Union will remain far and away the most economically powerful country in the communist system. This status enabled Khrushchev, and enables his successors, to talk about an association based upon the sovereign equality of its members, and even to allow some real equality in procedural matters, without fear of losing the economic leverage that seems to be a means for effective Soviet control. Unhindered by the Marxist doctrine that politics is only economic superstructure, we in the West may see a latent but potentially dangerous element within this "organization of equals" that could bring trouble for the Soviet Union. The *form* of participation as equals may encourage a taste for more real equality in decision-making influence. The impact of form upon content is less likely to be perceived as a serious threat by a convinced Communist.

Before World War II, the Soviet Union was in effect conterminous with the communist system, and there was no practical obstacle to equating the welfare of the Soviet Union with the welfare of the world communist movement. Stalin, of course, did just this when he imposed the doctrine of "socialism in one country" and destroyed Trotsky. But when, after World War II, "socialism in one country" succeeded beyond even Stalin's expectations—when communism became the ruling myth in twelve countries instead of one—the facile old equation became inadequate. Each country could perceive its own needs distinct from those of the Soviet Union, and each was loath to give the Soviet Union priority. "Socialism in one country" had made itself obsolete through success.[2] Stalin's remedy was to employ armed force accompanied by appeal to the precedent of Soviet success as proof that he was right. But this solution proved inadequate. The satellite states of East Europe continued to covet initiative for themselves; and Communist China, untrammeled by conventional satellite bonds, began to assert itself independently. The specter of polycentrism posed a severe threat to the primacy of the Soviet Union, the more so as the ambiguous doctrinal history of Soviet communism continued to provide opportunity for discord and little support for any distinct "orthodoxy."

In the latter 1950's, political primacy by virtue of economic predominance of the USSR within the communist system became an advisable alternative to political primacy by virtue of armed force and terror, rationalized by alleged infallibility of doctrine. Because of the existing economic imbalance of the twelve core countries the system, economic advantage could apparently be maintained by the USSR. COMECON could translate this economic advantage into Soviet political control of its members. COMECON's deepening institutional integration of the member countries' decision-making processes could then be used to foster a sense of community, while economic predominance would enable the USSR to choose policy for the whole.

To summarize, the Soviet Union under Khrushchev appeared to be trying to strengthen its political control within the communist system by shifting the base of its control within the core. There are three aspects to this shift: first, a shift of the institutional form of integration from top-level integration toward institutional integration in depth; second, a shift of the basis of

---

[2] Jan F. Triska, "Socialism in One Region," *New Leader,* December 26, 1960, pp. 10–13.

Soviet authority to include a larger consensual component in proportion to the coercive component; third, a shift in the nature of the coercive component of Soviet authority from the threat of armed force and terror, rationalized by proclaimed infallibility of doctrine, toward greater reliance on economic leverage. The Soviet Union is trying to create a single, deeply integrated decision-making apparatus for the economies of the member states of COMECON. Although the procedures of the apparatus provide formal equality for all the members in the decision-making process, the economic advantage enjoyed by the USSR permits it to control the process. Khrushchev seemed to believe that a binding economic interdependence of the political units that are members of COMECON would foster binding political interdependence and that if the Soviet Union could control the supranational economic organization, it could thereby control the political units.

In selecting the economic battlefield for his major effort against Western capitalism, Khrushchev and his successors have shown great confidence in their own economic system. It is not surprising, therefore, that they should rely more and more upon economic leverage to retain the Soviet position within the world communist system. But one should not jump to the conclusion that they have freely chosen the course represented by COMECON. The factors which have advised it have not been pleasant for the USSR, and the future course will be a difficult one. The multiplication of socialist states has been a burden as well as a triumph for the Soviet Union in the cold war with the West. Continued economic dissatisfactions and recurrent economic emergencies in the "people's democracies" of Eastern Europe have forced the Soviet leadership to search for new ways to improve economic efficiency among them. There is no doubt that economic survival of the core, as well as the opportunity for more subtle and effective Soviet political control, has played a large part in the evolution of the present program. That the two purposes appear to be compatible, at least in the Marxist-conditioned perception of Soviet leaders, is doubtless the persuasive appeal of Khrushchev's vision.

It is by no means certain that the Soviet Union will succeed in this undertaking. There are severe technical as well as attitudinal obstacles which must be overcome, and the early 1960's showed that they will not be overcome easily. Although the obstacles vary from country to country, enough commonality exists to permit formulation of a rough balance sheet and some cautious contingent statements on that basis. A later section of this chapter is devoted to these tasks.

The intervening sections of the chapter are concerned with filling in this overview, by describing the post-World War II evolution of the political-economic relations in the party-states of the communist system and then by presenting characteristics of COMECON and the directions in which that organization seems to be moving. Attention is then shifted to some comparisons with the Warsaw Treaty Organization and the Joint Institute for Nuclear Research. Three appendices supplement the text.

DERIVATION OF THE PRESENT POLICY OF ECONOMIC INTEGRATION

There have been six discernible phases of political-economic relations among the countries of the communist system since 1945. They are not sharply defined; frequently some of the distinguishing trends of one phase overlap another. However, each is sufficiently distinct from both its predecessor and successor to make the categorization useful as a framework within which to understand the course of events.

The first phase covered the years 1945 to, roughly, mid-1948. In it the USSR gained and consolidated control over the governments and economies of Eastern Europe. Although the process differed somewhat in each state, Soviet objectives gave them all a general similarity. Once in control, Stalin exploited the economic capabilities of these states for the single-minded purpose of reconstructing the war-devastated Soviet Union. General treaties of commerce and navigation, aptly described as *hunting licenses*, were concluded by the Soviet Union with most of the Eastern European countries, then appropriately characterized as *satellites*. These remain the legal basis for bilateral economic relations between these states and the USSR.[3] Within their framework, annual bilateral trade and payments agreements supplemented by short-term delivery protocols established the terms and substance of trade.[4] The testimony of subsequent defectors and inference from later developments indicate that during these years there was no equality in the negotiation of Soviet-satellite relationships.[5] Important characteristics of the period were effective Soviet dictation of trade terms to each of the satellites and dominance of Soviet demands in shaping the redevelopment of each.

[3] Summaries and references are available in Robert M. Slusser and Jan F. Triska, *A Calendar of Soviet Treaties, 1917–57* (Stanford: Stanford University Press, 1959); legal analysis is available in the companion volume, Jan. F. Triska and Robert M. Slusser, *The Theory, Law and Policy of Soviet Treaties* (Stanford: Stanford University Press, 1962).

[4] See Nicholas Spulber, *The Economics of Communist Eastern Europe* (New York: John Wiley & Sons, Inc., 1957), pp. 425–426 and 455–457.

[5] See, for instance, Fritz Schenk and Richard Lowenthal, "Politics and Planning in the Soviet Empire," *New Leader*, XLII, Nos. 1–3 (January 5, 12, 19, 1959), Part I.

Soviet credits provided economic leverage,[6] and Party allegiance or Soviet military intimidation maintained political compliance. The concept of "reparations" partially covered the USSR's preferred position in the cases of Hungary, Bulgaria, Rumania, and East Germany; otherwise, little concern was evidenced for any rationale to screen blatant exploitation. Each East European state tended to become a useful appendage of the USSR. Interaction among the East European states was de-emphasized, and the bulk of intercourse was conducted bilaterally between each satellite and the USSR.[7]

The Yugoslav defection in 1948 bore evidence to growing restiveness in East Europe as the national populations became aware that the product of their reconstruction effort was not being reflected in a better living standard at home but was being siphoned off for the benefit of the USSR.[8] The Marshall Plan, launched to promote economic recovery in Western Europe, also challenged the USSR to reconsider its relations with the remaining satellite states. A second phase of these relations thus began in late 1948 and continued to the death of Stalin in March, 1953. Ever tighter bonds imposed by Moscow characterized this phase, as Stalin determined that no more countries would go the way of Yugoslavia. Tighter control of foreign trade was implemented by extending the period of trade and payments agreements first to three and then to five years.[9] Circumstantially aided by the embargoes and restrictions placed upon trade with the communist nations by the West, the USSR directed an increasingly large proportion of the total East European foreign trade toward itself, thus increasing those states' dependence on Soviet markets and imports.[10]

Early in 1949 the Council of Mutual Economic Assistance (COMECON) was created in Moscow. COMECON was heralded as an association of equal,

[6] A summary of credit arrangements between the USSR and the countries of Eastern Europe may be found in United Nations, Economic Commission for Europe, *Economic Survey of Europe in 1957* (Geneva: United Nations, 1958), Chapter VI, Table VI–R, pp. 55–58.

[7] See Zbigniew K. Brzezinski, *The Soviet Bloc,* rev. ed. (New York: Frederick A. Praeger, Inc., 1961), pp. 122–125 and Spulber, *op. cit.,* pp. 303–305.

[8] Schenk and Lowenthal, *op. cit.,* Part I.

[9] See V. Klochek and K. Viriasov, "Economic Co-operation of Free Peoples," *Pravda,* April 16, 1953, pp. 3–4 (translated in *Current Digest of the Soviet Press,* V, No. 15, 13–15) for a discussion of the change from short- to long-term agreements. Discussions of specific agreements of the long-term type are in "Novoe dolgosrochnoe torgovoe soglashenie mezhdu Soiuzom SSR i Vengerskoi narodnoi respubliki," and "Novoe piatiletneie torgovoe soglashenie mezhdu Sovetskim Soiuzom i Chekhoslovatskoi respublikoi," *Vneshniaia torgovlia,* No. 6 (June, 1960), pp. 3–4.

[10] Spulber, *op. cit.,* pp. 409–424. For the growth of trade within the Communist Camp 1948–1952, see *Economic Survey of Europe in 1957,* Chapter VI, Table VI–A, pp. 35–36.

sovereign states for the purpose of facilitating "broader economic cooperation of the countries of people's democracy and the USSR." Bulgaria, Rumania, Hungary, Czechoslovakia, Poland, and the USSR took part from the beginning.[11] Albania sought admission and was received within a few months, and the German Democratic Republic (GDR) brought the membership to eight in early 1950. The apparent purpose for COMECON at its outset and during the remainder of Stalin's life was more thorough domination of the East European states' foreign economic relations. Bilateral trade relations with the USSR continued as in the past, but, in addition, COMECON "encouraged" the conclusion of similar long-term trade and payments agreements among the satellites themselves in order to bind the group closer together. There was no effort to make the various East European economies complementary, but the foreign trade of each state was largely redirected from the traditional channels to the West to new channels within the system. It has been suggested that one immediate purpose of COMECON was to enforce the economic embargo against Yugoslavia and thus bring Tito to heel. Whether or not this motive existed, it is apparent that in spite of the claims to sovereign equality the organization was created by Stalin only to ensure continuation of his dictatorial control over the member states in order that his economic and political goals might be served. Coerced conformity was still the rule.

The main economic need of the USSR still was capital goods, and the development of the satellite economies was redirected from prewar patterns to help fulfill this need. The model of single-minded industrialization and attempted self-sufficiency in the prewar development of the USSR also impelled each satellite to plan its economic development so as to emulate the Soviet Union. The ideal in the period of "socialist construction" that began in 1949 seems to have been multiple autarky—an array of economic miniatures of the USSR.[12] The presence or absence of appropriate natural resources or existing production facilities mattered little. Each satellite would

[11] *Izvestiia,* January 25, 1949, p. 1. This chapter will not attempt to present a comprehensive history of COMECON's activity. See Frederic L. Pryor, "Forms of Economic Co-operation in the European Communist Bloc," *Soviet Studies,* XI (1959), 173–194, and the same author's subsequent book, *The Communist Foreign Trade System* (Cambridge: M.I.T. Press, 1963); Andrzej Korbonski, "The Evolution of COMECON," *International Conciliation,* No. 549 (September, 1964); Michael Kaser, *COMECON* (London: Oxford University Press, 1965); and Kazimerz Grzybowski, *The Socialist Commonwealth of Nations* (New Haven: Yale University Press, 1964). The most thorough coverage of COMECON's early history from the Soviet viewpoint is N. Siluianov, "Bratskoe sotrudnichestvo i vzaimopomoshch' sotsialisticheskikh stran," *Voprosy ekonomiki,* No. 3 (March, 1959), pp. 22–40.

[12] Spulber, *op. cit.,* pp. 289–305.

have its own industrial economy based on its own production of iron and steel. Although an increase of trade among the satellites was implemented under the auspices of COMECON, this autarkic ideal persisted. There was no planned specialization of production, but each country's course was dictated by the USSR through the extension of selective credits. Hybrid industries duplicated one another in environments naturally unconducive to their support.[13]

During this second phase of relations Stalin instituted the Soviet-satellite joint-stock company, a legal device whereby Soviet management and satellite labor were combined to exploit a major resource in a satellite state. Disliked intensely from their inception in the satellites concerned, these companies rationalized Soviet economic domination and a preferred position for the Soviet Union in the distribution of production.[14]

Stalin considered the creation of the "second world market" his most significant postwar accomplishment.[15] However, the precarious equilibrium of the economic system he created was preserved only by the unanswerable military power of the USSR. As might be imagined, the hybrid industrialization and particularly the artificial emphasis placed on capital goods in Eastern Europe was accompanied by a corresponding neglect of the extractive industries and agriculture, not to mention consumer goods.[16] The area as a whole, which had been a net exporter of foods and raw materials prior to World War II, saw its surpluses in these categories decline and turn into a net import balance with the USSR a reluctant supplier.[17] The indications of crisis multiplied, and the dissatisfactions of the societies grew. Stalin would brook no relaxation and answered signs of resistance with physical repression. Tensions in East Europe rose, and it seems unlikely that even Stalin could have contained the situation much longer. But fate intervened, and Stalin died in March of 1953.

Before going on to the third phase of postwar system relations, we should

[13] For examples of uneconomical measures since required to support hybrid industries in Eastern Europe, see *Economic Survey of Europe in 1957,* Chapter VI, p. 26 and George Kemeny, "Hungary and COMECON," *Survey,* No. 40 (January, 1962), p. 167.

[14] Most joint-stock companies were dismantled in 1954–1955; only the uranium industry continues to be controlled by the USSR through this device. See George Ginsburgs, "Soviet Atomic Energy Agreements," *International Organization,* XI, No. 1 (Winter, 1961), pp. 49–65.

[15] Joseph Stalin, *Economic Problems of Socialism in the USSR* (New York: International Publishers, 1952), pp. 26–27.

[16] See Schenk and Lowenthal, *op. cit.,* Part I, p. 6 and Brzezinski, *op. cit.,* pp. 138–150.

[17] *Economic Survey of Europe in 1957,* Chapter VI, p. 5. See also G. Rubinstein, A. Pokin, and V. Azov, "Vneshniaia torgovlia Sovetskogo Soiuza posle vtoroi mirovoi voiny," *Vneshniaia torgovlia,* No. 4 (April, 1958), pp. 18–32.

note that 1945–1953 saw a gradual broadening of the scope of formal treaty ties between the USSR and the satellites of Eastern Europe. At first, such ties were generally of a bilateral nature, emphasizing the lack of cohesion among the satellites themselves and their unique dependence on the USSR. For example, joint scientific and technical commissions were created to direct research and training within each satellite and to disseminate the information of useful innovations.[18] As Soviet emphasis was more and more directed toward binding the separately developing East European states closer to a socialist world market independent of the West, these functional relationships were multilateralized. Regulatory commissions with multiple membership proliferated and have steadily expanded their province in the ensuing years in spite of subsequent shifts in the direction of economic policy among the party-states. They remain an integral part of the current Soviet-sponsored program whose evolution we are tracing.

Another aspect of current Soviet policy, closely related to the development of multilateral functional relations, has been the centralization of education and training within the communist system. A subject given consistent attention by the USSR since the early days of the Comintern Party Schools, the scope of this effort greatly expanded after World War II. Ostensibly, the Soviet Union generously gives the benefit of its experience and advanced techniques to facilitate the rapid building of socialism in the other countries. Although there is some truth in this contention, it is also true that centralized training of scientists, technicians, economists, and administrators is a powerful force for instilling attitudes toward the socialist system compatible with the ideals of the USSR. Future sources of friction at least theoretically may be eliminated by the uniform indoctrination of the future decision-makers of the member units of the system.[19]

Let us return to the chronology of our derivation. The economic crisis in Eastern Europe in 1953 at the time of Stalin's death required immediate measures to avoid overt rupture of the Soviet empire. Such measures were

[18] Bilateral commissions to implement measures of scientific and technical collaboration were established between the USSR and the other members of the Communist system, beginning with an agreement with Poland concluded March 5, 1947. Each commission was to meet semiannually in Moscow and the partner's capital alternately. References to the meetings of the commissions are to be found in Slusser and Triska, *op. cit., passim.*

[19] See O. W. Kuusinen *et al., Fundamentals of Marxism-Leninism* (Moscow: Foreign Languages Publishing House, n.d.), pp. 824–836 on Soviet sensitivity to techniques of education to advance Soviet ends. Part II, Section 5 of the Program adopted by the Communist Party of the Soviet Union at the XXIInd Party Congress (*Pravda,* November 2, 1961, p. 8) emphasizes the need to "mold the new Soviet man." It may safely be assumed that such molding is not limited to the Communist system, as the activities of Moscow's Patrice Lumumba Friendship University testify.

taken with unceremonious haste by Stalin's immediate successors, Malenkov and the industrial managers. The interlude of Malenkov during 1953 and part of 1954, before the rise of Khrushchev to prominence, must be considered a third distinct phase of postwar system relations. The Malenkov solution may be easily underrated. It did avoid major violence, and it brought at least temporary alleviation of acute dissatisfaction in most of the East European states. However, in the longer run, the Malenkov solution was no solution at all. It was a relaxation of capital goods production and a re-channeling of investment capital into consumer goods.[20] No generic change was made in the Stalinist ideal of a group of industrialized, self-sufficient states dominated by the USSR and existing for the benefit of the USSR. The pursuit of the ideal merely slowed down, while the pattern and, with it, the source of earlier tensions remained. In one way the Malenkov program compounded the problem. New emphasis on consumer goods in the USSR left the East European states with a surfeit of capital goods. The reduction in the Soviet demand, and the consequent diminution of this market, was a severe blow to their economic balance.[21] The abrupt attempt to rechannel investment in the East European states also brought frequent instances of waste and dislocation in its wake.[22]

Among the party-states, China occupied a unique position. From the establishment of the Chinese People's Republic in October, 1949, a new dimension had been added to the communist system. In the economic sphere it meant an insistent demand upon the USSR for economic, technical, and scientific aid. Whatever the political considerations, these demands were unwelcome. The USSR had already stripped Manchuria of all removable capital goods, and, unlike Eastern Europe, China now offered little economic advantage to compensate for its demands. Thus Soviet response to the Chinese demands remained minimal.[23] On China's part there was never any "satellite" subservience in her attitude toward the USSR.

The strongly independent orientation of China toward party-state affairs and later its challenge to the Soviet Union for doctrinal leadership have affected the status of other Asian members of the system. Economically

[20] See Schenk and Lowenthal, *op. cit.,* Part I; also, see Brzezinski, *op. cit.,* pp. 155–165 for a discussion of the reception of the Malenkov New Course in some of the individual satellite states.

[21] *Economic Survey of Europe in 1957,* Chapter VI, pp. 23–24.

[22] Schenk and Lowenthal, *op. cit.,* Part I, p. 6.

[23] The structure of formal agreements between the USSR and the Chinese People's Republic has been similar to that between the USSR and Eastern Europe satellites; see Robert F. Dernberger, "The International Trade of Communist China," in C. F. Remer, ed., *International Economics of Communist China* (Ann Arbor: University of Michigan, 1959), pp. 163–169.

insignificant, they have become objects of political competition between China and the Soviet Union. With the reception of the Mongolian People's Republic (MPR) into full membership in COMECON in mid-1962 the Soviet Union gave notice of victory in one tug of war. Mainly because of geography, China appeared predominant in the Korean People's Democratic Republic (KPDR) and the Democratic Republic of Vietnam (DRV). By 1966, the allegiance of both these states was in doubt.

The strictly European composition of COMECON at its inception continued during its first twelve years. The 1962 acceptance of territorially contigual Mongolia bears evidence to COMECON's role as a political instrument of the Soviet Union. China and the other Asian system members attended COMECON plenary sessions as "observers" between 1957 and 1961; but, with the aggravating doctrinal rupture in the system, attendance at the fifteenth session in Warsaw (December 1961, following the XXIInd Party Congress in Moscow) revealed a Chinese boycott. The boycott extended in June, 1962 to the KPDR and DRV, while the MPR was won over. Subsequently, nonmember Asian attendance has been sporadic.

Let us turn back to the emergence of COMECON as an institution of economic and political import in 1954. The conditions of this emergence seem to be primarily economic. As the long term inadequacy of the Malenkov measures impressed itself in 1954, Khrushchev developed an alternative which was to carry relations among the party-states into a fourth postwar phase. That year we find the first serious break with the goal of an economic system of multiple autarky in Eastern Europe. Khrushchev's ideal from the beginning seems to have been a supranational economic system embracing the USSR and Eastern Europe that would replace autarkic development with mutual dependency based upon economic production according to comparative national advantage. From late 1954 we find increasing attention being given to the possibilities of a rational division of labor and specialization of production among the satellites. The Council of Mutual Economic Assistance, dormant since serving Stalin's purpose of more thorough Soviet control over the member states in 1949 and 1950, was resurrected as the formal decision-making structure to implement this new concept.[24]

[24] A permanent Soviet Deputy to COMECON, N. Siluianov, explains the resurrection of the organization in 1954 by contending that the unprecedented success of separate economic development in each of the Eastern European People's Democracies had brought about a need for closer economic cooperation and even interstate specialization to take full advantage of the new material base that had been achieved. In his view, it was runaway progress that, operating dialectically, brought a qualitative change and demanded a new formal arrangement to recognize the material situation. No failure was acknowledged in past policy, only growing pains. See Siluianov, *op. cit.,* p. 27.

When COMECON was convened in Moscow on March 26th and 27th, 1954, it was to present to the delegates the idea of a unified five-year plan for the whole group of states and to initiate an examination throughout the satellites of available productive capacity. The results of this survey revealed that the total industrial capacity of the area as a whole considerably outstripped the currently available supplies of raw materials and fuels.[25] Khrushchev must have welcomed the discovery of this discrepancy, for it buttressed the economic desirability of coordinated economies to maximize progress, and it pointed up the inadequacy of multiple autarky for this purpose. But after the faltering Malenkov program had been abandoned, a dynamic, spectacular new program was needed for psychological as well as for practical reasons. As a result the Sixth Soviet Five-Year Plan and its East European counterparts were imposed from Moscow without thorough low-level planning and coordination. In the haste and wishful thinking with which they were drawn up, norms were established according to estimates of total industrial capacity without full consideration of the lack of necessary raw materials and fuels to support such levels. Thus, even while coordinated planning machinery was being set up within COMECON, the Plans began running into trouble. Strenuous attempts to meet impossibly high quotas in Eastern Europe resulted in a lowered standard of living, food shortages, and, inevitably, popular disaffection.[26] Poland, with other states dependent upon it for increased coal deliveries, fell behind her quotas rapidly.[27] Appeal to the USSR for help brought merely the advice to "discover hidden reserves."[28] Citizen uprisings ensued and were followed in the fall by the Hungarian Revolution, attributable in no small measure to the economic strictures caused by abrupt and ill-prepared imposition of a joint five-year plan on the member states of COMECON by the USSR.

The Hungarian Revolution in October and November of 1956 brought an end to the fourth phase of postwar system relations. The Sixth Five-Year Plan and its counterparts were scuttled and a new effort undertaken to find a solution for the difficulties originally incurred under Stalin's regime. Some of the characteristics of the fifth phase, which began in 1957 and continued into 1960, were already taking shape while the fourth phase was running

---

[25] Schenk and Lowenthal, *op. cit.*, Part II, pp. 16–17. See also, "Integrating the Satellites: The Role of COMECON," *East Europe*, VIII, No. 11 (November, 1959), p. 8 and compare with Siluianov, *op. cit.*, p. 29.

[26] Schenk and Lowenthal, *op. cit.*, Part I, p. 17.

[27] *Ibid.*, p. 18; "Integrating the Satellites: The Role of COMECON," p. 4.

[28] Schenk and Lowenthal, *op. cit.*, Part II, p. 18.

into trouble. The idea of an interdependent economy based upon comparative advantage was retained and elaborated. But the concept of imposition of such a program, virtually ready-made in Moscow, was discarded. Instead, a gradual program of deep integration was instituted, built upon mutual participation in coordinated planning from the lowest level on upward and stressing specific cooperative economic-development projects among the member states of COMECON.

The ideal-type then adopted can be characterized as a single economic community disregarding old national boundaries, highly industrialized as a whole but with each region producing only what its natural resources dictate can be most efficiently produced there. Comparative advantage would not be restricted to a narrow view of comparative costs; that is to say, different levels of pre-existing industrialization and their consequences for the costs of production would not be assumed as a starting point. Nor would the present distribution of population and labor skills be a major detriment. Rather, each branch of the economic system would be centrally planned for the most efficient long-term utilization of resources to meet socially determined needs, and all other factors would be brought artificially into line with the resulting pattern. In his widely publicized article of August, 1962 on needs for future development of the communist system, Khrushchev pointed in this direction:

> Lenin foresaw the future collaboration of socialist nations as taking place in a single world-wide cooperative in which the economy would be conducted according to a common plan. . . .
>
> The various economies, supplementing one another will gradually merge into a single streamlined complex. . . .
>
> The socialist world system is not just a socio-political union of countries, it is a world economic system. It follows then that the coordination should be pursued not within the restricted limits of each socialist country but on the scale of the socialist world economy, which means overcoming the national exclusiveness inherited from the past.[29]

The deep institutional integration to be realized through the COMECON organization would eventually rest upon a consensual authority base, after the Soviet Union had inculcated the desired value consensus. Meanwhile, Soviet goals could still be maintained as the goals of cooperative action through the exercise of Soviet economic leverage.

[29] Khrushchev *op. cit.*, pp. 2–11.

It should be unnecessary to say that such an ideal economy could not be implemented among the members of COMECON in 1957; nor could it in 1967. The attempt would run afoul of the distribution of existing production facilities, availability of skilled and manual labor forces, and many varieties of national and cultural allegiances, to mention only a few of the most obvious difficulties. In spite of the practical difficulties, it would be hard to overestimate the importance of Khrushchev's rejection of an aggregation of autarkic state economies and his substitution of a supranational economic community as an ideal.

Since 1957, there has been a slow approach toward the new ideal, with step following step only as the material base is achieved through careful planning and negotiations among the states concerned. From 1957 to 1960, emphasis was placed upon the coordination of foreign trade among the COMECON member states, the reduction of duplication in the production of particular items within sectors of industry being developed concurrently in two or more member countries, and cooperative efforts of several member countries to expedite specific projects of mutual advantage. After 1960, in the sixth and latest stage of post-World War II relations, primary emphasis was shifted to the coordination of both short- and long-term national plans among member countries in order to approach the goal of a single, deeply integrated economy.

Before elaborating on the activities of these latest two phases of planned integration, we should look closer at the organization at their base. The organizational structure and the scope and significance of COMECON's activity have steadily expanded since 1956. Until then, the organization consisted primarily of a Council, with representatives from member countries that met irregularly in plenary session to consult and make "recommendations" to their respective governments on matters involving mutual economic cooperation. There was no public charter or constitution; all activity was undertaken pursuant to the brief original treaty signed in 1949 and to the rather vague spirit of "proletarian internationalism." Supplementing the Council, which, after 1954, began convening at approximately semiannual intervals, was a Conference of Deputies and a Secretariat. While Council sessions were held alternately in the capitals of the member countries, both the Secretariat and Conference of Deputies were located permanently in Moscow.

In 1956, while the Sixth Five-Year Plan and its made-in-Moscow counterparts still ostensibly governed the cooperation of the members, a number of temporary specialized Commissions were established by the Council to consider particular difficulties arising among members. Soon accepted as a useful innovation, the Commissions became permanent organs of COMECON. More have since been established to cover each major branch of the "camp" economy and a number of functional areas requiring continuing attention. Since 1960 they have become the site for efforts to coordinate the COMECON economy, providing unifying directions for guidance of separate national plans over the short range and for the fifteen- to twenty-year perspective.

In accord with the increasing prominence of COMECON, its increased activity, and its frequent public association in the Soviet press with the developing unity of the "socialist commonwealth," the Twelfth Session of the Council in December, 1959, by then relegated to the function of sounding board rather than working organ, adopted a formal Charter for COMECON and an accompanying Convention to specify its legal status. The Charter was ratified by all members and took effect in April, 1960, forging another formal element in the burgeoning supranational bureaucratic apparatus.[30]

Later additions to the organizational structure and authority of COME-CON are the very important Executive Committee, created in June, 1962, and a faltering International Bank for Economic Co-operation, opened in January 1964.

From 1957 to 1960 the coordination of trade between pairs of member countries was facilitated by recommendations arrived at in the COMECON Commissions. A rapid increase in volume transfer between nearly every pair testifies to a considerable measure of success. However, all efforts to escape from the restrictions of bilateral barter relations and to put COMECON trade on a multilateral payments basis were stymied.

Perhaps the biggest obstacle faced between 1957 and 1960 was the reluctance of the Eastern European states to accept any specialization of their production or division of labor that would reduce what self-sufficiency they had achieved. Although Khrushchev frequently insisted that only the USSR and perhaps China among the communist states could validly pursue a policy

---

[30] See V. I. Morosov, "Pravovye aspekty deiatiel'nosti organov soveta ekonomicheskoi vzaimopomoshchi," *Sovetskoe gosudarstvo i pravo,* No. 10 (October, 1961), pp. 146–155. The implications of Morosov's discussion of the legal aspects of COMECON are given perceptive consideration by Robert S. Jaster in "CMEA's Influence on Soviet Policies in Eastern Europe," *World Politics,* XIV, No. 3 (April, 1962), 505–518. The texts of both Charter and Convention are included below as Appendix VI–1 and Appendix VI–2.

of fully diversified production,[31] he remained temporarily content with a compromise. That compromise was advertised as the "international socialist division of labor." According to this principle, no satellite state is expected to give up production in any basic branch of the economy. However, duplication of production of similar items is prevented by bilateral specialization agreements within each industrial subdivision. The advantages of mass production through automation may conceivably be achieved this way, although the principle of comparative advantage is partially thwarted.[32] Specialization of this limited degree was apparently best achieved in the machine equipment sector of industry. Soviet writers frequently point with pride to a series of specialization agreements covering over a thousand specific varieties of machine parts, negotiated bilaterally with COMECON.

Little if any objection has been raised to the idea of joint projects among the member countries of COMECON, although a certain amount of rivalry for the allocation of scarce resources has been evident. The most frequently

[31] Khrushchev, in an interview with a group of Hungarian journalists printed in *Nepszbadsag* (Budapest), July 21, 1957, and reprinted in translation in *Economic Survey of Europe in 1957,* Chapter VI, p. 31, note 45:

"We already said a long time ago that a better co-operation should have been established between our two countries. It is impossible to have developed everything everywhere simultaneously. Unfortunately we have too often spoken in vain. Hungarians, Poles, Rumanians, and also others have tried to build up everything by themselves. Perhaps it is only little Albania which has not attempted this. . . . In the Soviet Union this is naturally not the same problem as elsewhere since Soviet industry produces for a vast demand. The same applies to China with its immense population. But for small countries this creates very great problems, for which solutions cannot be found within national boundaries. . . .

Capitalist experts have found out that it is mass production which renders production cheap and economic. We Marxists, too, have to see the importance of this problem. The sooner and the better we develop the division of labour between our countries, the greater our economies will be. Each socialist country has to succeed in producing a great part of its products in large quantities, and at low cost."

The model of autarky is condemned in the new Program of the Communist Party of the Soviet Union as follows (*Pravda,* November 2, 1961, p. 2):

"The line of Socialist construction in isolation, detached from the world community of Socialist countries, is theoretically untenable because it conflicts with the objective laws governing the development of Socialist society. It is harmful economically because it causes waste of social labour, retards the rates of growth of production and makes the country dependent upon the capitalist world. It is reactionary and politically dangerous because it does not unite, but divides the peoples in face of the united front of imperialist forces, because it nourishes bourgeois-nationalist tendencies and may ultimately lead to the loss of the Socialist gains."

[32] *Pravda,* June 17, 1962, published a manifesto on the basic principles of the internationalist socialist division of labor just adopted by the sixteenth session of COMECON. It is available in translation in *Current Digest of the Soviet Press,* XIV, No. 24 (July 11, 1962), 3–8.

used example of the success of this sort of integrated activity is to be found in the "Friendship Pipeline," which allegedly reduces appreciably the cost of fuel oil in Eastern Europe by connecting the COMECON countries there with the Soviet oil fields. A single electric-power grid (the "Peace Power Grid") now integrates the energy systems of East Europe and the Ukraine, with a multilateral directorate established in Prague in 1962. Further examples of joint projects include Czech-Polish cooperation in exploiting lignite and copper resources in Poland, the Danube-Oder Canal, "Intermetall," development of a cellulose complex in the Danube delta, and other, lesser undertakings.

The first efforts of Khrushchev's policy of deep integration—that is, coordination of trade among the member countries of COMECON, reduction of duplication in production of specific items within various branches of industry, and jointly expedited projects of mutual appeal—brought acceptable progress without serious opposition on the part of member countries. Thus far, there was little real threat to the all-round industrial development of each state, no sacrifice of achieved economic independence, and no perception of severe conflicts of interest. But after 1960, with steady prodding by the USSR toward radical specialization of production, considerable resistance began to manifest itself. It was evident in the apathy characterizing implementation of measures which had been approved or recommended by COMECON. The degree to which the East European members have been bound legally to observe recommendations reached by COMECON organs is open to some question, probably as much among the member states themselves as among Western observers. Certainly a tacit obligation to conform exists, although the Charter provides an opportunity for members to ratify or not ratify at their discretion.[33] The ambiguity is consistent with the view that a form of elaborate protection for member sovereignty is to be maintained while Soviet economic pressure operates *sub rosa*. In theory, conflicts of interest between COMECON as a whole and its member units were not a problem to the Marxist ideologue, who could not justify a conflict of national interests within world communism once the situation had been correctly analyzed. But, in practice, these conflicts of interest became the foremost obstacle to COMECON's progress.

Both the Soviet desire to overcome this reticence and the Soviet determination to expand COMECON as the basis for party-state unity were confirmed by events surrounding the Sixteenth Council Session. Just prior to the Session an important meeting was called of First Secretaries of the

[33] See Morosov, *loc. cit.*

Communist Parties from each member country except Albania. At this meeting a new Executive Committee for COMECON was established, to consist of Deputy Premiers from each member country charged with taking "concrete measures" to implement decisions of COMECON directed toward more thorough economic integration.[34] While not specifically so empowered, it appears certain that this Executive Committee represented a step toward the sort of single authoritative planning organ for COMECON as a whole, which Khrushchev called for earlier.[35]

Since mid-1962, priority for coordination has been given to the development of fuel- and power-production facilities within COMECON over the period until 1980. This topic reportedly occupied a major portion of the agenda at both the Sixteenth and Seventeenth Council Sessions in 1962, at relevant Permanent Commission meetings in 1962 and 1963, and at several of the bimonthly Executive Committee meetings during 1963 and 1964. Public communiqués assert that some agreement has been achieved in this area, but obviously the progress has been difficult. In 1963, Rumanian (and some Czech and Hungarian) disaffection with COMECON's alleged infringement of sovereignty became increasingly evident. And over the following three years progress toward greater economic integration has stagnated.

From this sketch of the development of political-economic relations among the member states of the communist system since World War II, it remains for us to summarize eight salient characteristics of the current economic program as they have evolved from the mistakes and demands of the preceding years:

1. Trade among member countries of COMECON is governed by five-year bilateral agreements negotiated in accord with COMECON recommendations for emphasis of economic development in each country, which in turn are guided by the principle of comparative advantage. These agreements provide for an increasing amount of intermember trade and the gradual increase of interdependency because of it.

2. All economic relations among the member countries, and to a growing degree the course of domestic development, are being coordinated in the alleged interest of the region as a whole through the device of fifteen- to twenty-year "perspective agreements" negotiated bilaterally according to the recommendations of the Permanent Commissions of COMECON.

[34] See the communique issued at the conclusion of this meeting and printed in *Pravda,* June 9, 1962.

[35] Referred to in N. Ptichkin, "Ravitie sotrudnichestva v ramkakh SEV," *Vneshniaia torgovlia,* No. 1 (January, 1963), p. 5.

3. Specialization of production according to the "international socialist division of labor" represents a compromise between production according to comparative advantage and a "well-rounded" economy for each member state. Such specialization is making slow progress against East European resistance.

4. Strong emphasis is being placed upon cooperative plans for multilateral development of economic resources within Eastern Europe. Numerous projects are under way which point toward freer international flow of investment capital among the COMECON countries and the creation of more mutual economic interests.

5. The trend to expand the sphere of functional coordination between member countries of COMECON and to place this coordination on a multilateral formal treaty basis continues as it has since shortly after World War II.

6. Centralized training for economists, administrators, scientists, and technicians continues to receive emphasis among the member countries of COMECON.

7. The program represented by the above six characteristics is generally limited at present to the USSR, the party-states of East Europe, and the Mongolian People's Republic, and its organizational basis is the Council of Mutual Economic Assistance. The Chinese People's Republic, the Korean People's Democratic Republic, and the Democratic Republic of Vietnam, though party-states, cannot be considered participants. They are not members of COMECON, and they enter into only selected aspects of the program, if at all.

8. The origin of this program and the pressure for its acceptance is Soviet. Motivation for its creation certainly came from the course of political-economic development of the communist states of Europe and Asia, but its form and concept were developed by Khrushchev. East European acceptance has been reluctant and has forced compromise in the Soviet ideal.

This program adds up to an effort to create eventually an integrated supranational economy embracing the USSR and East Europe, based upon consensus rather than coercion, by progressing through a transitional period of economic federalism. Through COMECON, which holds up the criterion of "welfare of the Socialist System" as a unifying concept, the Stalinist model of Soviet dictatorship over a group of economic microcosms of the USSR has given way to an organizational system stressing economic interdependency and mutual participation in centralized economic planning. At present, the basis of authority still is largely Soviet economic coercion. The ideal of a community of values is a long way off.

THE POLITICAL APPEAL OF ECONOMIC INTEGRATION

The preceding chronological derivation of the present political-economic program for COMECON countries has emphasized the immediate economic influences that molded it. We contended earlier, however, that one appeal of this program to Khrushchev had been the apparent convergence of economic advisability and political opportunity. Let us now draw back in perspective a little and consider directly the latter half of this appeal.

Considered strictly in economic terms, such deep institutional integration seems to be of undeniable political advantage to the USSR. The implementation of a single economic unit based on comparative advantages promises to eliminate waste from duplication of production and support of hybrid industries. It offers to eliminate national boundaries as barriers to restrict economic intercourse by substituting the welfare of the whole for narrowly conceived national welfare as the goal for all economic activity. The multilateralization of functional activities, too, offers to eliminate practical obstacles to maximum cooperation. In the same way that free trade improved upon eighteenth-century mercantilism, a single economic and functional system could be expected to give East Europe an economic boost, allowing the whole party-state system to benefit from the material prosperity.[36] With such an economic rationalization of the area, the proportions of agricultural production and of the extractive industries in relation to the production of capital and consumer goods could be centrally planned according to some criterion of social need, and thus the source of numerous Soviet headaches in the past could be removed. The political advantage of such economic rationalization for Khrushchev's avowed purpose of burying the noncommunist world through the competition of parallel economic systems need not be spelled out further.

Secondly, the states of Eastern Europe were a springboard for Khrushchev's economic offensive in the underdeveloped and uncommitted world. A unified approach to these relationships would facilitate the communist ability to meet the economic needs and aspirations of these peoples.[37]

A third advantage to the USSR of such an integration may be found in the rationale it provides for shifting the insistent and unwelcome economic

[36] The often drawn parallel between the Common Market and integration in Eastern Europe seems valid here. Many of the same economic advantages should be obtainable in both systems.

[37] See "Eastern Europe Overseas," *East Europe*, X, No. 10 (October, 1961), 12–15, Robert L. Allen, *Soviet Economic Warfare*, pp. 110–128; and Jan Wszelaki, *Communist Economic Strategy: The Role of East-Central Europe* (Washington, D.C.: National Planning Association, 1959), p. 91.

demands of the Chinese People's Republic from the USSR to the East European states. Overall welfare of the Commonwealth of Socialist Nations makes a more reasonable appeal for the acceptance of unpalatable responsibilities than does an arbitrary requirement dictated by the Soviet Union.[38]

In the fourth place, the increased participation of the smaller members of COMECON in the planning process for the area as a whole promises to mitigate the unpleasantness of the satellite image for countries outside the communist system. If the aura of participating junior partners can be established about the European party-states, and if the program can be economically successful at the same time, the negative aspects of joining the Commonwealth in order to achieve the benefits of a short cut to satisfaction of elementary material aspirations may well be moderated to the considerable political advantage of the USSR.

Finally, and probably most important of all, the establishment of shared economic goals through the interdependency of the parts of a supranational system must offer the advantage to the USSR of a counterforce to nationalistic tendencies in East Europe. This is the carrot provided by COMECON, an incentive for cohesion that must grow with the increasing scope of the program and thus become harder and harder to resist. A corollary to this advantage is the prospect that the opportunity to participate in the decision-making process of area-wide economic planning, coupled with more and more centralized training of the planning personnel will serve further to subordinate national differences to collective unity. What we may term mutual self-interests may be set up to override potentially divisive tendencies. The expanding bureaucratic apparatus of COMECON provides a strong, formal cohesive bond.

These seem to be advantages for the USSR of economic integration pursued through COMECON. The program is not without important disadvantages too. In the first place, as the senior partner in the integrated system, the USSR may expect to be called upon to rescue other members whose plans fail. There is already precedent for this in the large shipments of grain from the USSR to Eastern Europe during 1957 and 1959 because of poor harvests—this at a time when the USSR could have made good use of the grain at home.[39] Another example of the same Soviet obligation is observable in the round of credits it proffered in 1956 and 1957 after the

---

[38] See Wszelaki, *op. cit.,* pp. 86–90 for an indication of the heavy Chinese trade with Eastern Europe.

[39] For the Soviet statistics, see *Vneshniaia torgovlia SSSR, statisticheskii obzor* (Moscow Vneshtorgizdat, 1956–1965).

failure of the Sixth Five-Year Plan and its satellite counterparts.[40] A second, related disadvantage for the USSR is the reasonable expectation that in a so-called *community of peers*, where the collective good is paramount and all member states are to march shoulder to shoulder into communism, it will be very difficult for the USSR to justify continued priority for the perceived economic needs of the relatively advanced Soviet Union.

The most formidable disadvantage of the system as viewed from the interests of the USSR, however, is the potential for development of unacceptable particular goals and methods among the COMECON member states when granted the opportunity for autonomous participation in the planning process. There remains the danger that there really is no effective substitute for tyranny in the communist system and that such an opportunity extended to the countries of East Europe will open a Pandora's box out of which nationalistic differences will proliferate beyond control. The current Albanian and Rumanian cases may be examples.

On the other hand some of these disadvantages may have their compensation. The prospective economic demands upon the USSR—emergency reserves and investment capital—are inevitable whether there is integration or not. They may be turned into political advantages while being offset as economic disadvantages by the leverage they afford. Deep integration will establish "camp welfare" as the criterion for economic policy. The state that can define "camp welfare" will exercise a more subtle but more persistent influence over the camp than one which must rely on physical repression. The USSR may be challenged in the realm of ideological orthodoxy, but there is little doubt that its prestigious position and its economic superiority within the camp will allow it to define "camp welfare" to dependent nations. Participation by all members of COMECON may well be a useful and relatively harmless concession by the USSR. The analogy may be drawn of a corporation in which one party owns more than 50 per cent of the stock. Although the other owners may participate in decisions, the majority stockholder retains ultimate control. The two most formidable advantages the Soviet Union holds within the communist system are in the areas of economic and military superiority. The military advantage is intrinsically greater, but it is also less flexible as a political instrument. The ramifications of Soviet

[40] The extensive credits proffered by the USSR in 1956–1957 are generally considered to have had more to do with alleviating economic difficulties in Eastern Europe from that time through 1959 than the new measures for coordination of production. United Nations, Economic Commission for Europe, *Economic Survey of Europe in 1959* (Geneva: United Nations, 1960), Chapter III, p. 47.

economic power reach somehow into every aspect of daily life in every member country of the system.

The crux of the problem seems to be whether or not there really can be a substitute for direct dictatorship in a practical (as opposed to theoretical) communist system. For the present, the political dangers opened up by such a formal alteration of Stalin's empire seem to be counteracted adequately by Soviet control of the integrated decision-making structure of the system— the Council of Mutual Economic Assistance. The formal right of all member states to participate in the decision process as equals is moderated by a number of practical safeguards for Soviet primacy. Soviet officials occupy many of the critical positions in COMECON today and probably will continue to do so. The Secretariat is permanently domiciled in Moscow, recalling the precedent of the Comintern. Most important, however, is probably the formal assumption that only the USSR may indefinitely follow a course of full diversification of economic production.[41] The prospective economic interdependence thus will not affect the USSR nearly as much as the other members of COMECON. The leverage retained in these circumstances seems adequate to maintain political as well as economic control over the economically integrated system. Enough autonomy will be granted to relieve the pressure of persistent national proclivities and to facilitate the old Soviet remedy of finding a scapegoat in case of errors. Meanwhile, centralized training, sharing of experience—all sorts of measures for "mutual aid among independent countries"—may be expected in time to weaken the particular and divergent inclinations of nationally minded groups within the member states. These old patterns of thought and action will be replaced gradually with new, "enlightened" Soviet ways.

In summary, this integration of economies and economic decision-making structure seems theoretically well suited to maintain the practical communist axiom about varieties of equality. The Soviet Union stands to remain considerably "more equal" economically and therefore politically. Thus, Khrushchev expected to seek steadily deeper integration, promoting an organization that encourages member participation in the formal decision-making process and, at the same time, reserves practical direction for the USSR. In this way the Soviet Union under Khrushchev wielded a more subtle, more viable instrument than Stalin fashioned for exercising Soviet control of the communist camp. It seemed to offer both economic prosperity and political control.

[41] See the Khrushchev quotation in footnote 30. It is interesting to note, though perhaps coincidental, that Siluianov, *op. cit.,* writing later, in 1959, seemed to exclude China too from all-around diversity, leaving only the USSR in this category.

We have looked at economic integration from the Soviet perspective. How does the prospect seem to impress the other party-states? In advocating the idea the USSR has made two appeals, both directed to the self-interests of Eastern Europe without much ideological embroidery. First is the argument that economic and functional integration is the best way to bring about each member country's own economic development. Second, it is maintained that such a system will equalize the progress of each country to the point where all will be able to march shoulder to shoulder into the communist epoch approximately together.

Aspects of this case are strongly attractive to the Eastern European states. Memories of the oppressive Stalinist policy, followed by the shortages and imbalances that resulted during the Malenkov relaxation, reinforce the impression that economic integration through coordinated planning and a division of labor probably is the fastest way to economic prosperity. In theory, the purely economic argument is persuasive. Secondly, the promise of a formal equality in the decision-making process of the supranational organization is exceedingly attractive. The lip service to sovereign equality in what we have called *economic federalism* is hard to resist. Lastly, both Party men and economic planners may find that the prospect of this kind of integration enhances their personal position as members of an international communist elite.[42]

In spite of these attractions, there are some very disquieting aspects. Marxist economics are reinforced by the precedent of the USSR under Stalin to indicate that the proper course for a developing revolutionary socialist state includes establishment of a strong heavy-industry base and as much self-sufficiency as possible. The former has the political connotation of promoting the growth of a true industrial proletariat; the latter claims the support of a stereotyped idea that is reinforced by the tendency of interstate deliveries within the system to be unreliable in the absence of a profit motive.[43] Deep integration destroys each country's image of itself as an industrialized, self-sufficient entity.

Another, and probably the most important, disadvantage perceived by

[42] In the latter regard see Schenk and Lowenthal, *op. cit.*, Part III, pp. 20–21.

[43] See Alfred Zauberman, "Economic Integration: Problems and Prospects," *Problems of Communism* (July-August, 1959), p. 23. When unforseen difficulties endanger Plan fulfillment, export deliveries tend to lag well before any domestic norms are revised. For a receiver country, dependent upon the exported goods, this characteristic lag can be economically frustrating and possibly disastrous. See, for example, the strictures caused by Polish failure to fulfill coal deliveries to the other satellites in 1956. The incentive of direct profit and the onus of private responsibility for failure to make good give the capitalistic Western contract a higher reliability than has been found among the socialist state monopolies.

the Eastern European satellites is the prospect of political dependency engendered by economic dependency. Critically examined, the propaganda of sovereign equality comes to mean only subordination to the supranational needs of the system. Then too, the prospect of equalization of progress, although it might be supposed to be attractive to a backward state like Bulgaria, can hardly seem attractive to men interested in the progress of the relatively advanced Czechoslovakia first and the other states later. Finally, the long-term economic requirements of a deeply integrated system run afoul of national identity in the satellites. International specialization of labor and production, based upon regional comparative advantage, arouses the prospect of redistribution of the labor force without regard for cultural and ethnic lines.[44] Such homogenization does not strike a responsive chord in an area noted for its sharp prejudices and national pride.

The sum of these unattractive features produces a strong resistance to any integration that goes beyond cooperative development projects and generally coordinated long-range planning on a basis of equal representation of national interests. Soviet leverage, however, and the fact that the East European states had even less autonomy in the past generally allow Soviet will to prevail. Severe tests are presently observable in progress in Albania and Rumania. We shall consider these briefly a little later.

So far, we have restricted consideration of the political impact of integration to the East European members of the system. There remain the MPR, KPDR, DRV, and, by far the most important, the Chinese People's Republic (CPR). As has been mentioned earlier, it is apparent that present concepts of integration are not focused toward Asia in the same way as toward Europe. The minor socialist countries of Asia, like the nonruling Communist Parties, offer no significant economic *quid pro quo* and are important only as showcases or bases for expansion. Within the system today, they represent trophies in the struggle between China and the Soviet Union. China itself is another matter. Aside from its threat to Soviet hegemony, its growth to power was a major stimulus to the USSR to devise a new and effective means to control the spread of polycentrism.

As has been made unmistakably evident by the XXIInd Congress of the Soviet Union and subsequent events, it is only with the greatest difficulty that

[44] Efforts have been made in this direction in the special case of labor shortage in the Polish coal mines. It has been suggested that Czechoslovak labor should be relocated to ease the stricture, although little publicity has been given the idea. See Schenk and Lowenthal, *op. cit.*, Part III, p. 20.

the USSR maintains any influence over Chinese actions at all, the remaining levers being Soviet nuclear weapons and Chinese need for Soviet products and financial credits. The course of the Soviet program described in this chapter indicates a long-range Soviet hope to enlist East Europe in a successfully integrated system to which China will eventually be forced to seek admission in order to keep apace of the advancing mainstream of world communism. There has been no effort by the USSR to include China in the construction stage of this system, and for its part China shows no eagerness to enmesh itself in such a supranational structure. Instead, China apparently desires to take part or refrain in particular aspects of the program according to its own perception of Chinese national interests. Mao Tse-tung is eager to win for China its own group of satellites independent of the USSR. Not a member of COMECON, China does not intend to specialize its economic production but rather seeks autarky on the old Stalinist model. It refuses to acknowledge the USSR as the fount of Marxist doctrinal authority, and it insists on implementing independent approaches to problems of socialist development. Finally, it has reached its present stature as a communist power independently, feels little political debt to the USSR, and has not been exploited by the USSR. China thus does not crave equality of participation in the decisions that will mold its future. It has already effectively asserted that sort of equality.

History shows little precedent, in the absence of a pre-existing community of values, for effective extension of national power without an initial, forceful subordination of new territory to a conqueror. The process of transformation from an empire based upon coercion to a community based upon legitimacy and voluntarily accepted authority (which we have inferred to have been an important part of Khrushchev's program for the COMECON countries) seems to have required that the empire originally be clearly established. That the CPR has never been so subordinated to the USSR is undeniable, and the fact would seem to militate against the probability of incorporation of the CPR into a value community, even if integration in East Europe progresses successfully toward the Soviet ideal.

ALBANIA, RUMANIA, AND THE FUTURE OF INTEGRATION THROUGH COMECON

The prospects for Soviet success in the economically based program to strengthen political control within the communist system as described above, as well as the obstacles which threaten success, may well be considered by briefly appraising the Soviet-Albanian rift and the lesser disaffection of Rumania from the perspective of our thesis.[45]

Albania presents a case in which a member of COMECON had openly defied Soviet guidance and refused to accept Khrushchev's diagnosis of the current international epoch and the methods by which world communism should seek to advance its cause. Polycentrism had apparently come close to separating one member of COMECON from all semblance of unity with the rest. Both the Stalinist devices to secure subordination were neutralized at the outset—armed force by virtue of Albania's inaccessible position, and the pontifical infallibility of Moscow's doctrine by virtue of a defiant and strongly entrenched national dictator who took advantage of a major division of ideological thinking within the system to assert himself against the prevailing arbiter in Moscow.

Since then, mutual economic interest has proven insufficient to lure Albanian cooperation. In large part this fact appears due to replacement of Soviet economic support by the fellow dissident in the system, China. It is quite plausible to suggest that a shared resentment by China and Albania toward Soviet preference for domestic advancement instead of aid to less developed system members stimulated the open opposition to the Soviet course. National self-interest in both cases appears to have exerted a strong centrifugal force. We must conclude that, at this stage of the development of the integrated system, COMECON's carrot has shown itself inadequate for its purpose.

The positive incentive having failed, Khrushchev resorted to various forms of state coercion in his capacity as a member of the COMECON economic community, assuring meanwhile the comparable action of other members. In 1961, Enver Hoxha, the Albanian dictator, said:

This process started in the second half of last year, that is, after the Bucharest meeting. . . . Thus, in the economic sphere all credits granted by the USSR to our country for its third five-year plan were cut with the aim of sabotaging the economic plan of our country; without any reason at all, the Soviet specialists working in Albania and whom our economy greatly needed were withdrawn in a unilateral way, although we had asked them officially to stay. By demanding the repayment of old

---

[45] For detailed discussion of the background and development of the Soviet-Albanian rift, see William E. Griffith, "An International Communism," *East Europe*, X, No. 7 (July, 1961), pp. 3–9, 41–45; the same author's subsequent book, *Albania and the Sino-Soviet Rift* (Cambridge: M.I.T. Press, 1963); and J. F. Brown, "Albania, Mirror of Conflict," *Survey*, No. 40 (January, 1962), pp. 24–41. On the Rumanian disaffection see J. F. Brown, "Rumania Steps Out of Line," *Survey*, No. 49 (October, 1963), pp. 19–34.

credits starting this year—although according to existing documents this should start in 1970—the Soviet side has almost completely broken off trade relations. All the Albanian students, civilian and military, who were studying in the USSR, were deprived of their scholarships and so forth, and economic pressure was accompanied by restrictive measures in the military sphere. In these anti-Marxist and hostile actions toward the Albanian people, Nikita Khrushchev was also followed by certain leaders of the socialist countries of Europe.[46]

Khrushchev himself, speaking at the XXIInd Party Congress, categorized Albania's disaffection as deviation from the "fraternal family of the Socialist Commonwealth, the path of unity with the whole international Communist movement." He assured the Congress that the Soviet Party would "continue, in keeping with its internationalist duty, to do everything it can so that Albania may march shoulder to shoulder with all the socialist countries."[47] Khrushchev's First Deputy, Mikoyan, noting that the Albanian leaders were "departing from internationalist positions and backsliding onto the path of nationalism," echoed the diagnosis of his chief.[48]

Although Soviet-sponsored pressures against Albania have been severe in the effort to bring the recalcitrant member back into line, it may be noted that none of the formal links that established the Albanian state as a member of the community has been completely severed. It may seem paradoxical that the customary foreign-trade protocols between Albania and other states of COMECON, including the USSR, have been solemnly concluded as usual in the lee of Party invective, until one realizes that these are the transmission belts which allow pressure to be increased or relaxed and Soviet state purposes thus pursued. With regard to her economic ties, Albania has been constrained to admit:

> The greater development of economic and trade relations with the countries of the socialist camp has been, and still is, the first and main task for our foreign trade. This task has its origin in the nature of our socialist economy, in our country's participation in the socialist camp and in its membership in COMECON.[49]

[46] Speech by Enver Hozha, November 7, 1961 (twentieth anniversary of the founding of the Albanian Workers' Party and the forty-fourth of the November Revolution); excerpt quoted in *East Europe*, X, No. 12 (December, 1961), p. 37.

[47] *Pravda*, October 18, 1961, p. 10, translated in *Current Digest of the Soviet Press*, XIII, No. 42 (November 22, 1961), 5.

[48] *Pravda*, October 22, 1961, p. 8, translated in *Current Digest of the Soviet Press*, XIII, No. 51 (January 17, 1962), 13.

[49] *Zeri i Popullit* (Tirana), March 29, 1962, on the occasion of the signing of a new trade protocol with the GDR; as quoted in *East Europe*, XI, No. 5 (May, 1962), p. 40.

Since the XXIInd Party Congress, Albania has not attended sessions of COMECON, but it has remained a member and there have been no indications of formal expulsion. In the official communiqué following the fifteenth plenary session in Warsaw in December, 1961, the Chairman announced Albania's absence in terms of regret such as might be used in the case of a wayward and headstrong child:

> As far as the last session is concerned, Albania did not come to Warsaw at all. One is forced to conclude that the Albanian leaders, in shunning co-operation with the Council on Mutual Economic Aid, are pursuing a course of worsening relations with the socialist countries, which will harm only the Albanian people.[50]

It would seem that Albania has been censured but not exiled. This is a sharp contrast to what we might have expected from Stalin. The more recent and milder case of Rumanian obstructionism to the progress of specialization and coordination in national plans through COMECON likewise reveals a course of Soviet action markedly different from that taken, for example, in the case of Yugoslav resistance twenty years ago. Both Albania and Rumania are being handled carefully and subtly on the state level, in spite of vitriolic but ineffectual invective at the level of Party disputation. Brezhnev and Kosygin probably believe that Rumania and perhaps even Albania too can be brought into line again by such state action, particularly in view of the domestic difficulties of China. Should they succeed, it would be a triumph for the policy of emphasis upon economic leverage to direct the behavior of other political units in the communist system.

The very facts of Albanian and Rumanian disaffection, however, point out the most formidable political pitfall the policy hazards. National independence is still attractive, and the procedural equality of an organization like COMECON encourages a desire for more. Thus, while devising an organizational instrument to allow political deviation but to contain it within the limits set by economic needs, Khrushchev and his successors risk starting a progressive process they cannot stop. This is the danger that must haunt them. We suggested earlier that the course of political primacy through control of a deeply integrated COMECON economy was not a free choice for Khrushchev's Soviet Union. It was rather the only viable alternative available, given the particular economic problems of the COMECON countries and the new inadequacy of terror or faith to serve the political purpose.

[50] *Pravda,* December 17, 1961, p. 4, translated in *Current Digest of the Soviet Press,* XIII, No. 50 (January 10, 1962), 32.

It does offer a tempting rationale for success; but only time will tell whether the theory can be converted into reality.

THE WARSAW TREATY ORGANIZATION

Soviet efforts to maintain hegemony among the party-states through the development of an integrated regional economy display, as we have seen, a complex pattern of institutional innovation in conflict with historical inertia. Penetrating to the homely determinants of livelihood for each human individual, there is little doubt that the influence of economic policy is paramount in the Soviet attempt to change the basis of popular authority and establish a stable hegemony. At once a complement and counterpoint to the Soviet economic effort, however, is the Soviet policy for military integration of the party-states. The latter has, since 1955, been reflected in the evolution of the Warsaw Treaty Organization. In much shorter compass we can examine this effort, seeking by way of comparison to highlight the patterns revealed in our study of the processes and conditions of economic integration.

After the termination of World War II (for the USSR the "Great Patriotic War"), the U.S., in January, 1946, offered a four-power mutual-assistance proposal to guarantee the disarmament of Germany and the collective security of Europe. The Soviet Union, philosophically ill at ease with the principle of general and indefinite collective agreements across ideological frontiers, and with eyes open to her opportunities in war-prostrated Western Europe, was unenthusiastic. Stalin preferred bilateral military alliances with the Eastern European states. The precedent for these bilateral treaties of "friendship, co-operation and mutual assistance" had been set by the pact concluded during the war (1943) with Czechoslovakia. In the postwar period, similar treaties were concluded with all the satellites except Albania. The Chinese People's Republic was included in 1950, the German Democratic Republic (over Western objections) in 1964. Pursuant to the Soviet vision of an interrelated matrix of autarchic states in the latter forties and the early fifties, similar, supplementary treaties of alliance were concluded among many satellite pairs in Eastern Europe.

As various Western analysts, and indeed Soviet spokesmen too, have emphasized, the military purposes of the Soviet Union were probably as well provided for by this matrix of bilateral agreements as by the alternative of a unified collective-security organization. System integration had already been achieved—an assertive top-level integration—through unquestioned Soviet military control. No integration in depth, for instance, through multilateral coordination among satellite Armed Forces had been attempted nor was it perceived desirable by Stalin.

When collective-security arrangements came to Eastern Europe, they came in response to the Western incorporation of the Federal German Republic into the North Atlantic Treaty Organization. From 1952 to 1955, American efforts to draw the Federal Republic into a military partnership proceeded first through the abortive European Defense Community, then to fruition through the Paris Agreements and entry of the Federal Republic into NATO. Soviet protests against this course of events, voiced most specifically at the Moscow Conference of December, 1954, culminated in the conclusion in Warsaw, on May 14, 1955, of a multilateral Treaty of Friendship, Co-operation and Mutual Assistance, which mirrored in its provisions many of the articles of its Western counterpart. The parties to it (the USSR, Albania, Bulgaria, Czechoslovakia, the German Democratic Republic, Hungary, Poland, and Rumania) acted in concert, according to the Preamble:

> Taking into consideration the situation obtaining in Europe as a result of ratification of the Paris agreements, which provide for the formation of a new military grouping in the shape of the "Western European Union" together with a remilitarized West Germany in the North Atlantic bloc, which increases the threat of another war and creates a menace to the national security of the peace-loving states. . . .[51]

An additional convenience afforded by the Treaty to the USSR was a timely new rationale for continued presence of Soviet troops in Hungary and Rumania. The old explanation, support for the Soviet garrison in Austria, was to be made obsolete by the conclusion of the State Treaty neutralizing Austria, signed in Vienna the very next day.

The themes of the Warsaw Conference were set by the Soviet Premier, Nikolai Bulganin in his speech of May 11. "German militarism" was re-emerging with the help of the Paris Agreements. "West German militarists" had received the right to recruit a standing army and to equip it with all modern weapons. West Germany was being "turned into a bridgehead for the deployment of large aggressive forces." The Soviet government believed "the peace-loving countries of Europe must, in these new conditions, see to the safeguarding of their security." The participants at Warsaw must therefore unify their defense efforts through the proposed Treaty of Friendship, Co-operation and Mutual Assistance.[52]

---

[51] *Soviet News,* May 16, 1955.
[52] *Soviet News,* May 18, 1955, reprinted in Royal Institute of International Affairs, *Documents on International Affairs* (N.Y.: Oxford University Press, 1958), pp. 189–90.

The Treaty, which was signed on May 14th and promptly ratified by the eight participants, pledged the signatories to render immediate assistance as considered necessary, including armed force, in the event of an armed attack in Europe upon any other signatory. In such an event, immediate consultations would be undertaken to determine appropriate joint measures for restoring and upholding international peace and security. Additionally, the signatories agreed to refrain in their international relations from the threat or use of force and to work for the adoption of effective measures toward arms reduction and the prohibition of weapons of mass destruction. Assistance to members who might be the victims of aggression would be provided within the purview of Article 51 of the United Nations Charter and would cease as soon as the UN Security Council had taken measures to ensure peace. The signatories agreed to consult among themselves on all important international questions relating to their common interests and to cooperate in strengthening their economic and cultural relations, meanwhile observing principles of mutual respect for independence and sovereignty and non-interference in internal affairs. The Treaty was declared to be binding on all members for a period of twenty years, with an additional ten years in force for those who did not denounce it within a year of expiration. Additional members might accede to the Treaty and participate in its implementation with the consent of the original parties. A final provision declared that the Treaty would automatically cease to be effective on the date a general European treaty of collective security might come into force.[53]

The structure arising from the Warsaw Treaty was a simple one. For the purpose of holding the consultations provided for and for considering problems arising in connection with implementation of Treaty provisions, a Political Consultative Committee was formed and vested with the paramount authority. It was composed of governmental ministers of the member nations or other, specially appointed representatives. The Committee was granted authority to establish such auxiliary organs as it felt necessary. Secondly, a Joint Command was created for the members' Armed Forces, which were to be assigned to this command by agreement among the states and would function on the basis of jointly defined principles to guarantee their frontiers and territories and defend against possible aggression. A separate statement on the formation of the Joint Command provided that Marshal I. S. Konev of the USSR would become commander-in-chief of the joint Armed Forces as allotted by the members. The Ministers of Defense

---

[53] See text of Treaty, included as appendix below.

of the member countries were designated Deputies to the Commander-in-Chief, and a joint staff composed of permanent representatives of the members' own general staffs was to be established at the organization's headquarters in Moscow. The deployment of joint forces on the territory of member states was to be governed by "the requirements of mutual defense, in agreement among these states."[54]

When the Political Consultative Committee first formally met the following January in Prague, it established two subordinate organs: (1) a Permanent Commission to handle recommendations in the fields of foreign policy for the bloc of member states, and (2) a unified Secretariat, to be headquartered in Moscow and to include representatives of all the members. The Committee decided to meet whenever necessary but in any event not less than twice a year. Also, at this meeting, a statute providing for the organization of the Joint Command was approved, and the inclusion of East German Armed Forces, a proposal deferred the previous spring in Warsaw, was agreed upon.[55]

A declaration concerning international security was issued following the two-day meeting which called for (1) a major power agreement to exclude nuclear weapons among forces stationed in Germany; (2) continuation of efforts toward general disarmament; (3) a European collective security system and conclusion of bilateral nonaggression pacts; and (4) limitation and control of arms and troops in a zone to include all of Germany.[56]

During the first decade of the Warsaw Treaty Organization, the pattern set in these initial meetings in Warsaw and Prague was reinforced with little change. The Political Consultative Committee continued to be a sounding board for enunciation of Soviet cold-war policies and helped give an aura of collective unanimity to Soviet foreign propaganda. The semiannual schedule of meetings was not adhered to; they have occurred irregularly about once a year. Even then, as *The New York Times* Correspondent A. M. Rosenthal once described it, they proved a rather ceremonial shadow of their NATO counterparts:

> When the Western military alliance meets it hands out military information and the inside story on political squabbles. When the Communist military alliance meets it hands out smoked salmon. . . .
> Three and a half hours were enough for a review of the world situation,

[54] *Soviet News,* May 16, 1955.

[55] Robert M. Slusser and Jan F. Triska, *A Calendar of Soviet Treaties* (Stanford: Stanford University Press, 1959), p. 348; *Izvestiia,* January 29, 1956.

[56] *New Times* (Moscow), No. 6 (1956), pp. 33–36; see also *International Organization,* X (May, 1956), 337.

the exchange of pleasantries and the approval of a communique. Then everyone was ready for the toasts and the buffet table.[57]

The Hungarian Revolution of October-November, 1956, by all odds the most severe crisis to face the WTO, did not even occasion a meeting of the Political Consultative Committee. The Nagy government's repudiation of the Warsaw Treaty was met by Soviet armed intervention, which violated explicit Soviet legal interpretation of the Treaty clauses, but no formal meeting of the Committee took place until 1958.

The second meeting (in May, 1958) gave formal approval to the withdrawal of Soviet troops from Rumania; publicized the Rapacki Plan for an atom-free zone to include West and East Germany, Poland, and Czechoslovakia; and called for a nonaggression pact between NATO and the WTO. The third meeting, in Moscow on February 4, 1960, served as a sounding board for Khrushchev's announcement of proposed Soviet Armed Forces reductions of 1,200,000 men and issued a declaration which repeated old demands for a German Peace Treaty, cessation of "war propaganda," a NATO-WTO nonaggression pact, bilateral East-West nonaggression pacts, and the establishment of nuclear- and rocket-free zones. A year later in March of 1961, the communiqué released, following the Committee's meeting, reiterated the conclusions arrived at the preceding November by the Moscow Conference of World Communists and Workers' Parties about peaceful coexistence. The meeting in January-February of 1962, following the XXIInd Party Congress of the CPSU, was distinguished only for the exclusion of Albania from further active participation. The official communiqué released following the meeting on February 28, 1963 in Warsaw followed the same format as its predecessors, reiterating Soviet policy lines, and then mentioned that the meeting had reviewed the status of members' combat readiness and problems in coordination of military training. No record was made of a meeting in 1964. The next formal communiqué, following a January, 1965 meeting, was largely devoted to strong but redundant protestations against a proposed NATO Multilateral Force which, according to the Committee, would endanger peace and raise international tensions by giving West German *revanchists* access to nuclear weapons.

On the Warsaw Treaty's tenth anniversary, in May of 1965, its commander-in-chief, Marshal of the Soviet Union, Andrei A. Grechko, wrote a long article for *Pravda* which celebrated the organization's accomplishments (preservation of the peace), described its continuing indispensability (the

[57] "Contrasts Noted between Two Pacts (NATO and Warsaw Pact)," *The New York Times,* December 17, 1959, p. 3.

imperialist threat), and propounded once again the Soviet foreign-policy themes which have persisted over the decade: the need for a German peace treaty, for "normalization" of the status of West Berlin, for renunciation by both German states of nuclear armaments, for a central European atom-free zone and a NATO-WTO nonaggression pact, and for a general conference on collective security for all European states.[58]

What beyond a multilateral propaganda forum has the Warsaw Treaty Organization been since 1955? As a symbolic response to the perceived challenge of the West in drawing West Germany into NATO, the WTO has clearly served usefully as a political playing card for the Soviet Union. Regardless of what its substantive addition to the military capability of Eastern Europe and the Soviet Union may be, it represents negotiating capital that a series of bilateral agreements did not. But what else? According to Marshal Grechko, it has brought about a significant standardization of military equipment and training in Eastern Europe, and it has established a unified military doctrine and common view of the nature of a future war which are reflected in the common statutes and directives for training.[59]

There is little reason to doubt Grechko's claims. Since about 1961, it has sponsored joint maneuvers and other military exercises of increasing size and multilateral scope. In September of 1964, for example, amphibious landings, airborne drops, and artillery defensive operations were carried out in Bulgaria and included Bulgarian, Rumanian, and Soviet troop elements.[60] In the summer of 1963, some 40,000 Soviet, Polish, Czech, and East German troops participated in combined air and land exercises in the GDR. Similar exercises were held in a large area west of Berlin in the spring of 1965. In October, 1965, large-scale exercises, again involving Soviet, Polish, East German, and Czech units, were conducted in the GDR near the Baltic coast.[61]

The communiqués describing such joint exercises usually note that they have been undertaken as "a component of a general plan for the combat preparation of the armies of the socialist commonwealth"[62] or "in accordance with the plan of combat readiness of the Combined Armed Forces of the member countries of the Warsaw Treaty." A critical juncture such as

[58] "Militant Alliance of Fraternal Peoples," *Pravda,* May 13, 1965, p. 3 (condensed translation in *Current Digest of the Soviet Press,* XVII, No. 19, 24).

[59] *Ibid.*

[60] *Izvestiia,* September 22, 1964, p. 2.

[61] *Izvestiia,* October 22, 1965, p. 1.

[62] General N. I. Batov, then Chief of Staff of the Warsaw Treaty Forces as quoted in *Izvestiia,* October 22, 1965, p. 1.

the Cuban Missile Crisis in October-November, 1962 produced an announcement in Moscow that the Deputy Commanders-in-Chief of the Warsaw Treaty countries had been summoned there to consider implementing mobilization plans for their respective forces. It seems reasonable to conclude then that the WTO has also led to the existence of formal contingent military plans which integrate the fighting and logistical capabilities of the members' defense organizations.

Estimates of the number and distribution of forces within the Warsaw Pact Joint Command in the middle 1960's must be patched together from a variety of sources. As some of these differ, the figures we give here should be treated cautiously. The Soviet Group of Forces in East Germany is clearly the core of the offensive military capability of the WTO and consists of some twenty first-line divisions, half of them armored and all averaging a strength of about 10,000 men each. These are augmented by support troops to produce a total of about 250,000 men. Two other Soviet Groups of Forces are located in Eastern Europe, the Northern Group of two divisions and a total of about 25,000 men in Poland, and the Southern Group of four divisions and about 55,000 men in Hungary. These latter two groups primarily serve to provide communications and logistical support for the group in Germany. According to Marshal Sokolovskii in a press conference on February 17, 1965,[63] the total Soviet Armed Forces strength at that time had been fixed by the Fourth Session of the Supreme Soviet at 2,423,000. If this figure is accepted as reliable, it indicates a probable total active Army and Home Air Defense Force of about 1,660,000 men, allowing some 400,000 for the Air Force, and about 350,000 for the Navy and Naval Air Force. Additionally, it is estimated that in 1965 Security and Border Guard Forces numbered about 270,000. These totals indicate the probable equivalent of fifty active and full-strength Soviet divisions in early 1965, about half of them deployed in Eastern Europe within the WTO Joint Command.

In contrast to the USSR all elements of the East European Armed Forces are in WTO jurisdiction. These states deployed at this same time armies totaling slightly in excess of one million men, organized into about sixty-seven divisions. Their air and relatively small naval forces added about 180,000 more. Active Security Forces in this area, who would undoubtedly be called upon in the event of hostilities, numbered about 260,000 in all.

In the north, Czechoslovakia deployed an army of some 230,000 and fourteen divisions, followed by Poland with 215,000 and fourteen divisions,

---

[63] Sokolovskii's statements were carried over Radio Moscow and in a TAAS release on February 17, 1965. See Radio Free Europe, *Communist Area Report*, USSR, February 18, 1965.

and East Germany with about 200,000 and eight divisions. Hungary sustained an army of about 80,000 organized into six divisions. Rumania's 200,000-man army with thirteen divisions and Bulgaria's 125,000-man army with twelve divisions complete the Joint Command.[64]

In the Stalinist years immediately following World War II, Soviet military policy in Eastern Europe, like Soviet economic policy, had as its chief aim the domination of occupied satellites and their exploitation for the purposes of the USSR. This aim was facilitated by the sovietization of the Armed Forces of the countries of Eastern Europe. All Western-oriented and anti-communist personnel were eliminated from positions of responsibility, Soviet officer cadres were introduced into critical positions far down into the chain of command, and local Secret Police were virtually fused with their Soviet counterpart to augment Stalin's control of the puppet Party elites.

When the Warsaw Treaty was concluded in 1955, there was no immediate change in the condition of the "sovietized" East European Armed Forces. Indeed, one author reports a number of demanding secret stipulations as part of the original treaty: Soviet troops to be assigned in Eastern European countries with the mission of preserving internal order; "host" governments to pay the expenses of maintenance for Soviet elements but to relinquish all legal jurisdiction over them; and Soviet troops to remain by right in Eastern European countries other than Czechoslovakia and Bulgaria for a period of twenty years.[65] If, as we have argued, the Warsaw Treaty Organization was established primarily as a political response to the incorporation of West Germany into NATO, there is no reason to suppose there was any alteration envisaged in the master-satellite conception of authority between the USSR and the other members.

However, the national resentment of Soviet control which developed in Eastern Europe as a product of economic irrationality, popular disillusionment over Soviet idealism, and Soviet vacillations in economic policy following Stalin's death apparently spilled over into resentment of Soviet military supervision of the satellites. When this resentment was catalyzed by "destalinization" in the Soviet Union and burst into open revolt in both Poland and Hungary, Khrushchev found it expedient to change to more subtle means of military control in Eastern Europe than that afforded by sovietization. The WTO provided an alternative bureaucratic structure.

---

[64] Figures drawn from Richard F. Staar, "The East European Alliance System," *United States Naval Institute Proceedings,* XC, No. 9 (September, 1964), 32, updated where possible by reference to *The Statesman's Year Book, 1965–66* (London: St. Martin's Press, 1965).

[65] Staar, *op. cit.,* p. 30.

Between December, 1956 and June, 1957 new "status of forces" agreements were negotiated by the Soviet Union with Poland, East Germany, Rumania, and Hungary which increased the authority of the satellites with respect to Soviet troops on their territories. Subsequently, as the departure of Marshal Rokossovskii from Poland indicated, sovietization was to be de-emphasized. Since this time, however, Soviet control has been steadily if less obtrusively maintained through the WTO command structure. Command authority runs directly from the Soviet commander-in-chief (a First Deputy Defense Minister of the USSR) down through the East European Ministers of Defense to all of their respective military echelons. WTO Missions are accredited to each member state except Poland, and these Missions, reporting back to headquarters in Moscow, are, in effect, instruments of Soviet control to replace the old Soviet officer cadres in the respective Armed Forces.[66] In the event of war, current Soviet strategic thinking makes quite clear that this chain of command would be even less ambiguous. Warsaw Treaty Forces would be under the direct command of the Supreme High Command of the Soviet Armed Forces.[67]

It is time now to draw back in perspective again and focus upon the similarities and differences of COMECON and WTO as integrating instruments for Soviet foreign policy among the party-states. It is clear, first of all, that neither organization was created consciously for the purpose it later came to serve. COMECON, as conceived in 1949, had the limited purpose of isolating Yugoslavia and fostering a matrix of bilateral satellite dependencies. The WTO was created in 1955 as a political response to the Western incorporation of the Federal Republic into NATO. But in subsequent years, as the old integrating mechanisms failed, both COMECON and the WTO provided alternatives for maintenance of Soviet control. COMECON offered in-depth institutional integration of economic decision-making and an authority pattern based upon consensus rather than coercion, thus appealing to economic rationality and also, at least in the short run, to sentiments of national heterogeneity in Eastern Europe. Yet it gave the Soviet Union the opportunity to take recourse to economic coercion in the event consensus opposed her national aims. The WTO, on the other hand, after the crisis of the Hungarian Revolution, offered an alternative to sovietization of East European Armed Forces which was less offensive to national sensibilities but retained an assertive top-level integrated configuration. Military coordination of the members of WTO was achieved by Soviet dictate still.

[66] Staar, *op. cit.*, pp. 35–36.
[67] V. D. Sokolovskii, ed., *Soviet Military Strategy* (N.Y.: Frederick A. Praeger, Inc., 1963), pp. 367–68.

For two reasons the assertive, top-level configuration of the WTO was acceptable, whereas such a configuration for economic integration was unacceptable. First, military capabilities were more easily discerned from Moscow despite the absence of low-level institutional integration. The questions were less complex. And achievement of coordinated action in military matters was also less complex because of the relatively fewer occasions for military than for economic coordination. Thus, whereas an attempt to impose from Moscow a joint economic five-year plan (as happened in 1954) failed, the imposition of a joint military-readiness plan could succeed.[68]

Secondly, the relative economic capacities of the Eastern European members of COMECON are sizable enough that they need not feel wholly at the mercy of the USSR. Although the USSR has a great economic advantage which can be used coercively or as a lure, most of the other member states are sufficiently developed economically and possess sufficient resources that they are not totally dependent. Thus, they can and do demand a share in the supranational decision-making which only institutional integration in depth can offer. The relative military capacities of Eastern Europe, given conditions of an age of nuclear weapons, have appeared so unbalanced in favor of the USSR that through the first decade of the WTO the Eastern European countries have been resigned to total military dependence upon the USSR. The Soviet "nuclear umbrella" appeared desirable in the face of perceived "imperialist threat," and even when there may have developed some doubt about the virulence of the "imperialist threat," that Soviet "nuclear umbrella" has seemed inevitable. Thus there was continuing consent for the assertive, top-level configuration of WTO integration during a decade in which consent for that sort of economic integration broke down.

COMECON, representing the economic goal of consensual, in-depth institutional integration, has however run into the obstacle of national reluctance to forego the old aspirations for autarky. In the case of Albania, and more clearly in the present case of Rumania, the carrot of economic prosperity has seemed to become insufficient lure for acceptance of the Soviet vision of the future. We have already analyzed the roots of this current stalemate.

Recent reports from Eastern Europe now show unmistakable evidence

---

[68] The fact that the economic plan was put to the test immediately and the military plan has only been tested by partial simulation may account for some of the contrast here. It is not really established whether or not such top-level military integration could succeed or not. It was rather conclusively shown in Eastern Europe that that sort of economic integration could not.

that sentiments of nationalism are beginning to destroy in a like fashion the authority base for the WTO. It is quite evident that a theoretical conflict exists between Eastern European national identity and assertive military integration through the WTO. Consent has heretofore been maintained by perception of an outside threat ("imperialism") combined with resignation to the fact of overwhelming Soviet military superiority. But in 1965 and 1966 doubts have crept into this rationale. The socialist-imperialist dichotomy no longer seems so simple. The "nuclear umbrella" seems to pose as much danger as security. Uncertainties in WTO military policy toward the West have been exposed by the Sino-Soviet conflict and the American war in Vietnam. The constabulary function of Soviet Warsaw Treaty Forces is an odious suspicion still. Most of the same disintegrating forces that have beset NATO may in fact be observed at work among the members of the WTO.

The replacement of Warsaw Treaty Forces Chief of Staff N. I. Batov by another Soviet general, M. I. Kazakov, in November of 1965[69] may or may not reflect cross pressures within the organization. Certainly the outspoken challenges of Rumanian Communist Party General Secretary Ceausescu to Soviet leadership in the WTO do. As early as the spring of 1964 the Rumanian objections to economic specialization in COMECON spilled over publicly into dissatisfaction with Soviet hegemony through the WTO. In disregard of her WTO obligations, Rumania unilaterally reduced her Armed Forces from 240,000 to 200,000 and cut down the term of service for conscripts by one-third. Since his succession to the late Gheorghiu-Dej in March, 1965, Ceausescu has repeatedly asserted Rumanian opposition to all military blocs and to the stationing of troops at bases abroad. A report circulated in the spring of 1966 that Ceausescu had sent confidential notes to fellow East European members of the WTO asking that consideration be given to changing the WTO statutes. Finally, in May, 1966 Ceausescu challenged Soviet Party Secretary Brezhnev's call for a strengthened Warsaw Pact by delivering a strong speech to Rumanian Party elite calling military blocs and military bases abroad "an anachronism incompatible with the independence and national sovereignty of the peoples and normal relations between states."[70] The speech immediately preceded a visit by Brezhnev to Bucharest and probably occasioned the latter's criticism of Rumania later in Prague. Notably there were no voices raised against Ceausescu's stand elsewhere in Eastern Europe.

[69] *Pravda*, November 24, 1965, p. 6.

[70] Quoted in David Binder, "Ceausescu of Rumania, Man Battering at the Kremlin Wall," *The New York Times Magazine*, May 29, 1966, p. 45.

THE JOINT INSTITUTE FOR NUCLEAR RESEARCH

In the immediate postwar years, when the Soviet Union was hastening to match the challenge of Western possession of atomic weapons, the resources of nuclear material available in Eastern Europe were unsurprisingly commandeered to support that effort. "Joint-stock" companies, the device widely used at this time to implement Soviet economic control in Eastern Europe, were established to harness East European capital and labor, under Soviet direction, to produce fissionable uranium for export to the USSR.

The uranium, even from the richer sources in Czechoslovakia and East Germany, probably was secondary to the Soviet nuclear effort. For our purposes here it is important to note that the effective Soviet monopoly of prospecting, extracting, and processing nuclear raw material gave the Soviet Union a total monopoly upon developmental applications of nuclear energy (defense, industry, medicine) and gave her unchallenged leadership in all aspects of nuclear research as well. There were no obstacles to the total integration of all aspects of atomic energy. Of the party-states, only the Soviet Union was significantly involved, and because of its unmistakable military and political importance all the Soviet effort was tightly integrated at the highest echelon of authority.

Following Stalin's death and the establishment of some balance to the East-West nuclear-weapons race, the Soviet leadership sought to draw upon the scientific talent of Eastern Europe and to explore the peaceful potential of nuclear energy without losing the total integration which had heretofore existed through the policy of exclusiveness. In January, 1955 the Soviet government announced that it would assist in organizing experimental centers outside the USSR for research into the peaceful uses of nuclear energy. The announcement was addressed to China, East Germany, Poland, Rumania and Czechoslovakia; but the door was explicitly left open to inclusion of other interested states.[71] Over the subsequent five months, bilateral agreements to implement the January announcement were concluded with Rumania, Czechoslovakia, Poland, China, Hungary, and East Germany in that order. Yugoslavia followed in January of 1956. In these agreements the Soviet Union undertook to furnish each partner an experimental atomic pile and cyclotron, necessary equipment and fissionable material, technical assistance, and technical and scientific documentation. Finally, the Soviet Union undertook to provide facilities for training scientific personnel from the partner states in Soviet scientific institutions.[72]

---

[71] *Pravda,* January 18, 1955, p. 1.
[72] Slusser and Triska, *op. cit.,* pp. 326–348; Grzybowski, *op. cit.,* pp. 145–146.

The cooperative behavior solicited through these Soviet-initiated bilateral agreements with other party-states was broadened in scope later in 1956 and 1957 to include industrial applications. Agreements with East Germany, Czechoslovakia, and Hungary provided for assistance to these states in construction of atomic power plants. Poland, in addition to a power plant, was promised a second atomic pile.[73]

By opening up an opportunity for other party-states to participate in development of the uses of atomic energy, the Soviet Union stood to benefit materially from employment of an enlarged pool of scientific talent. It might also benefit politically from the propaganda impact of shared nuclear technology. But, at the same time, the Soviet Union risked planting the seeds of eventual challenge to its nuclear leadership and control among the party-states. The Joint Institute for Nuclear Research was the Soviet response to the latter problem. The JINR reflected the Soviet effort to integrate the new field of atomic energy for the party-states and to integrate it in the service of Soviet policy.

The JINR was created by a multilateral agreement (paralleling COMECON and the WTO) signed in Moscow on March 26, 1956 by all the party-states except North Vietnam.[74] Pursuant to this agreement a first session of representatives from each signatory met in Dubna, near Moscow, the following September for a week-long convocation. Statutes were adopted to endow the Institute as a legal entity and establish its purpose to organize international research in the field of nuclear physics and the peaceful uses of atomic energy.[75]

The Statutes provided that the Conference of Representatives Plenipotentiary should be the supreme organ of the Institute. The Conference would elect a Director (three-year term) and two Deputy Directors (two-year terms), adopt amendments to the Statutes as recommended by the Director, approve the budget, admit new members and hear reports by the Director. Action was to be by 2/3 vote, with each member represented equally. The Director would preside over a Scientific Council, composed of three scholars designated by each member state and charged with formulating work proposals for approval by the Conference. A Finance Commission, with membership designated by participating states, would apportion the

[73] Grzybowski, *op. cit.,* p. 146.

[74] *United Nations Treaty Series* (New York: United Nations Secretariat, 1957), CCLIX, 125–143; CCLXXIV, 377.

[75] M. M. Lebedenko, "Ustav ob'edinennogo instituta iadernykh issledovanii," *Sovetskoe gosudarstvo i pravo,* No. 2 (February, 1957), pp. 116–118.

assessments of members, which would underwrite the Institute's activity.[76]

The first session of the Conference admitted the remaining party-state, North Vietnam, to the JINR, distinguishing the Institute from COMECON (Mongolia is the only non-European member) and the WTO (entirely European). Members are statutorily authorized to resign from the JINR by giving notice of intent three months before the end of a fiscal year. Thus far none has done so publicly, but there is no current Albanian or Chinese participation. Empowered to associate with other institutes and research organizations on the territory of member states, the center of JINR activity remains its laboratory complex (formerly operated by the Soviet Academy of Sciences) at Dubna.

Thus in brief, we have the structure of JINR. It is worth noting with respect to authority that Article 22 of the Statutes explicitly states that "The Institute's directorate is guided in its activities only by the decisions of the Conference of Representatives Plenipotentiary and the Scientific Council, and accepts no instructions whatsoever from single member states."[77] As Conference decisions are made by a two-thirds vote, there is greater supranational authority and less Soviet control provided by the formal structure of the JINR than is the case in COMECON, and the contrast is even greater with the WTO.

How does the JINR compare with our other two institutions? In scope it is narrowest of all in the mid-1960's. Proportionately, far fewer decisions in the party-state system deal with peaceful uses of atomic energy than deal with military problems. An even smaller fraction must be envisaged when atomic-energy decisions are compared with the totality of economic decisions within the purview of COMECON. But this assessment of the present should be qualified by noting that no field of human effort promises to ramify more rapidly than that of atomic energy. As a contributor to the *process*, as distinguished from the *condition* of integration among the party-states, the JINR thus appears to possess importance disproportionate to its present role.

In formal depth and differentiation of decision-making role structure, the JINR more closely resembles COMECON than WTO. It is technologically oriented, differentiated by scientific subdisciplines, and draws its information from the breadth of its membership rather than from a single political source as does the WTO. Today in fact, however, residual Soviet leadership in all

[76] The original agreement to set up the JINR contained a schedule of contributions which obligated the Soviet Union to pay 47.25 per cent of the total, China 20 per cent, and the other party-states radically lower amounts. Grzybowski, *op. cit.*, p. 148. See also Modelski, *Atomic Energy in the Communist Bloc*, pp. 134–138.

[77] Quoted in Grzybowski *op. cit.*, p. 149. See Lebedenko, *op. cit.*, p. 118.

phases of nuclear research and continued Soviet control of the available fissionable material (outside China) mean that most premises for decision are furnished by the USSR. The monopoly of fissionable material also means that in spite of procedures which underline the majority rule, the Soviet Union may exert a coercive leverage considerably more effective than in COMECON. Centralized training and research planning for the party-states, however, probably fosters the creation of a highly integrated community of values.

Finally, the extent of integration within its narrow purview must be assessed as greater for the JINR than for either that of the WTO or COMECON. Today it appears that that integration approaches 100 per cent.

What may we say on the basis of the exploratory comparisons we have made here about the achievement and potential of these three institutions as vehicles for integration of the party-states? Regarding achievement, we may observe that the WTO and JINR have been more effective within their purviews than has COMECON as presently organized. Based upon present knowledge we may tentatively attribute this greater effectiveness to narrower scope or more coercive authority or both together. The authority base appears the more decisive of the two explanatory factors in these cases if we consider the relatively extensive economic integration achieved in Eastern Europe by Stalin utilizing coercion.

When we consider the *condition* of integration, as well as the *process*, however, we have grounds for suggesting that while a coercive authority base has shown itself feasible for developing extensive integrated behavior (COMECON before 1956, and the WTO), it has shown itself weak for maintaining the integrated condition. The experience of COMECON shows that until a conscious effort was made toward a consensual authority base, the integrated behavior achieved in the system came at the cost of steadily rising, explosive interstate tensions. The recent dissension in the WTO appears to confirm this experience of the economic sector.

Likewise, we can predict that a top-level institutional structure, over time, will be destructive to an integrated system. The recent difficulties COMECON has faced in moving toward greater integration leave open the question whether a structure delegating significant decision-making authority far down into a well-differentiated bureaucratic structure can be expected to enhance integration when confronted with the need to cope with conflicting values. But it is clear that both in COMECON before 1956 and in the WTO more recently, top-level institutional structures have exacerbated dissatisfactions among those members excluded from participation.

The foregoing pages have been devoted to examining some of the institutions and processes central to the conduct of Soviet foreign policy among the party-states of the world communist system. In the course of this examination we have argued the thesis that the Soviet Union since Stalin has sought to alter the institutional forms and bases of authority in Stalin's old empire, in order to preserve Soviet hegemony under changing circumstances. We would have to conclude that in general the attempt has been a losing effort, that Soviet control in Eastern Europe has suffered a relatively steady decline and shows little evidence of reversing that trend. The dominant fact of the first half of the 1960's in the system of Communist party-states, as in the larger international system as a whole, has been the re-emergence of pluralism and neonationalist sensibilities in reaction to the post-World War II era of nationalism's eclipse by polar ideological allegiances.

THE SOVIET UNION AND
THE DEVELOPING AREAS

At the XXth Congress of the Communist Party of the Soviet Union in February, 1956, First Secretary Nikita Khrushchev defined the international position of the USSR by reference to three categories of states: those of the "socialist camp," the "imperialist camp," and the "nonaligned" states of Asia, Africa, and Latin America. This tripartite categorization marked a departure from Stalin's dichotomous perception of the two polarized political "camps" which harked back to the Revolution of 1917 and the years in which the Soviet Union conceived itself as the sole state fortress of Marxian socialism, beset on all sides by the malevolent bastions of international finance capitalism.

Khrushchev described the nonaligned states as follows:

The forces of peace have been considerably augmented by the emergence in the world arena of a group of peace-loving European and Asian states which have proclaimed non-participation in blocs as a principle of their foreign policy. The leading political circles of these states rightly hold that to participate in closed military imperialist alignments would merely increase the danger to their countries of becoming involved in the aggressive forces' military gambits and being drawn into the ruinous maelstrom of the arms race.

As a result, a vast "peace zone," including both socialist and non-socialist peace-loving states in Europe and Asia, has emerged in the world arena. This zone embraces tremendous expanses of the globe, inhabited by nearly 1,500,000,000 people—that is, the majority of the population of our planet. . . .

The present disintegration of the imperialist colonial system is a post-war development of world-historic significance. Peoples who for centuries were blocked by the colonialists from the highway of progress followed by human society are now going through a great process of regeneration. . . . The complete abolition of the infamous system of colonialism has now been placed on the order of the day as one of the most acute and pressing problems.

The new period in world history, predicted by Lenin, when the peoples of the East play an active part in deciding the destinies of the whole world and have become a new and mighty factor in international relations, has arrived. In contrast to the prewar period most Asian countries now act in the world arena as sovereign states or states which resolutely uphold their right to an independent foreign policy. International relations have spread beyond the bounds of relations among countries inhabited chiefly by peoples of the White race and are beginning to become genuinely world-wide relations.[1]

The new formulation by Khrushchev was not to be dismissed as a rhetorical device. It confirmed a fundamental shift in the strategy of Soviet foreign policy which has persisted and grown in importance over the subsequent decade. It also reflected a pragmatic new flexibility in post-Stalin Soviet policy which offered both fresh opportunity and grave challenge to the USSR's "imperialist" competitors. Lastly, it acknowledged the independent political significance of the developing areas as a coherent factor in international relations.

The shift in Soviet strategy may be compared to the shift by a military commander from a strategy of intensive attack against the core of his enemy's strength to an effort to isolate and weaken his enemy by denying him peripheral resources. The confrontation of blocs was perceived to have reached a stalemate—Berlin, NATO, Korea—and "containment" had raised cumulatively a stubborn obstacle. Further frontal attack promised little success, great cost, and the danger of mutual nuclear annihilation.

But there seemed to be other ways to skin the cat. Lenin's tactic of "peaceful coexistence" could be resurrected as a long-range strategy rather than a short-range retrograde expedient. The Soviet model of rapid industrial development could be used to appeal to newly independent countries yearning to close the material gap between their perceptions of the possible good life and their perceptions of a degrading and miserable present reality. Half the population of the world might thus be wooed to the "socialist camp," not only weakening the imperialists by loss of resources they heretofore relied upon but strengthening the "socialist camp" by the addition of these resources.

Post-World War II history was replaying post-World War I history. When

---

[1] "Report of the Central Committee of the Communist Party of the Soviet Union to the 20th Party Congress—Report by Comrade N. S. Khrushchev, First Secretary of the Communist Party of the Soviet Union," *Pravda,* February 15, 1956, pp. 2–3. Translated in *Current Digest of the Soviet Press,* VIII, No. 4 (March 7, 1956), 6–7.

the bright prospect of carrying the revolution westward to Warsaw, Berlin, and thence Paris and beyond flickered and died, the Comintern was re-oriented eastward in the 1920's. When the post-World War II drive westward to expand socialist war gains in Eastern Europe resulted in a rigid East-West standoff, the USSR again turned toward the East. The failure of military force employed conventionally across international frontiers (as demonstrated in Korea) dictated a revision of strategy. This time that revision was a switch to a new dimension of conflict, not a resigned withdrawal such as followed the 1927 debacle in China. The "revolution from above" would be sought by economic and diplomatic tactics resting on the appeal of the successful Soviet socialist economic model as contrasted with the discredited model of Western imperialism.

This willingness to re-examine conditions and to discard disproven tactics and strategy has characterized the new flexibility of Soviet policy ever since. Its pragmatism has been demonstrated by willingness both to rethink ideo-logical rigidities in the context of new perceptions of events and to demand that new policies should be sustained by the logic of events first, rather than solely by verbal authority drawn from the past.

Fresh opportunity was offered the USSR's "imperialist" competitors because the success of "containment" had now forced a departure from the rigid military nexus toward economic and psychological dimensions of con-flict along which the capacity of Western liberal democracy had not hereto-fore been fully employed. Dealing with the Soviet Union now became a variegated enterprise with a host of new unknown quantities to be investi-gated—the Western diplomat's role took on a new interest and new potential. But these new dimensions also posed the West with a challenge, for now the West no longer advanced the unique demonstrated path for successful conversion of twentieth-century technology to the service of man. The achievements of the USSR's economic development, and especially their speed, offered an apparently viable alternative. Recognition and acceptance of the new dimensions of conflict thus imposed stringent new demands upon Western liberalism.

Soviet perception of the developing areas as possessing together a coherent, manipulable force of independent significance in international relations had the effect of reinforcing that significance. In a way, it was a self-fulfilling prophecy; saying so made it so. By identifying these areas as a unit and attempting to deal with them as such, the USSR committed its prestige to the possibility of eliciting a coherent, unified response from them. Failure to elicit such a response would henceforth mark a serious defeat for the USSR as a state within the international system and a personal discreditation of the Soviet leadership which had, allegedly scientifically, advanced the new tripartite formulation of international forces.

THE NATURE OF THE TARGET

To analyze Soviet foreign policy toward the developing areas we are first obliged to take brief note of the target's characteristics. What homogeneity does it manifest? What demands does it emit? To what stimuli does it respond?

When the term *developing areas* is used, either in Washington or in Moscow, it is almost always followed by a ritualistic recital of the trinity: "of Asia, Africa, and Latin America." Clearly there is no geographic unity to be found here. The term *developing* itself is imprecise and conveys little. What is meant is an inoffensive reference to a relatively backward socioeconomic system, backward by the standard of economic modernization and social advancement established by the industrialized nations of Europe and North America with their concommitant urbanization and advanced technology. The developing countries are widely divergent in richness of cultural heritage. They present an array of political systems ranging all the way from autocratic rule claiming divine right to parliamentary democracy. In short, they are aggregated under one heading solely because of a shared socioeconomic condition. Insofar as they make common demands upon the rest of the international system and insofar as they respond similarly to stimuli from the rest of the international system, their behavior is a function of their common socioeconomic status.

The people of the developing areas constitute half the population of the earth and occupy more than half of its land area. They share a low standard of living indicated by per capita annual income as low as $40. They are malnourished, poorly housed, poorly educated, and beset by disease. They are also dissatisfied and frustrated. And they are growing in numbers at a rate approaching 2 million a month.[2]

These countries, which we aggregate by a socioeconomic criterion, share also, in most cases, the experience of colonialism. For many it is an old memory, as in Latin America. For a few, as in the belt across southern Africa, it is a present fact. But for the majority, it is a personal experience in the recent past. As calculated by a Soviet statistician in May of 1965,

[2] See Barbara Ward, *The Rich Nations and the Poor Nations* (New York: W. W. Norton & Company, Inc., 1962).

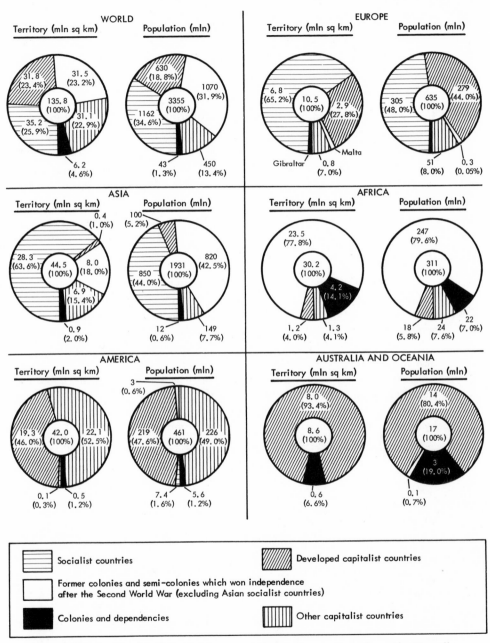

FIGURE VII–1   The World's Territory and Population as Seen from the Kremlin, May 1965[3]

[3] Reprinted from *International Affairs* (Moscow), No. 5 (May, 1965), p. 106.

Fifty-five countries, with an aggregate population of more than 1,800 million, have broken free of their colonial chains and proclaimed independence since the end of the Second World War—13 from 1945 to 1950, three in the subsequent five years, 24 from 1956 to 1960, and 15 since then.[4]

For most of these millions, their colonial overlords were Western Europeans. From this shared experience springs an antipathy toward the whole congeries of behavior summed up in the term *imperialism*, an antipathy closely associated with the noncommunist, industrialized West. From it also stems a heightened sense of national identity which draws no distinction among external dangers and is hypersensitive to them all.

The major common demands placed on the international system by the people of the developing areas can thus, we submit, be enumerated as follows:

1. Provision of the means to attain material prosperity, including an economic model for the modernizing process by which the living standards of the West may be attained quickly by a labor-intensive, capital-poor, rural economy.
2. Recognition of the political independence and political equality of each new nation-state.
3. Provision of a model of political institutions which will enable concerted national action to meet internal demands and foster political socialization and communication at the national level (the model to be accompanied by a rationale legitimating its allocations of authority).
4. Provision of assistance to the governing elite in preserving the political order they have established against both internal and external threats as they perceive them.

These are the basic demands of the target which Soviet foreign policy-makers assay as the nonaligned peoples of Asia, Africa, and Latin America, demands to which they must tailor their policies in the service of Soviet interests.

FORMULATION OF SOVIET GOALS

Soviet goals in the developing areas have been formulated within a maximum-minimum range of prospects since the early days of the Russian Bolshevik regime. At the maximum end of the continuum, the optimum

---

[4] "The World in 1965," compiled by K. Ilyina of the USSR Central Statistical Board, in *International Affairs*, No. 5 (May, 1965), p. 105.

outcome for the Soviet Union, stands conversion of the peoples and incorporation of the developing areas into the communist party-state system. At
the minimum end of the continuum stands depriving the imperialists of the
assets of these areas. In between are the promotion of socialist political and
economic regimes and active support for the Soviet international posture
vis à vis the "imperialist" West. There is nothing new in this continuum of
goals. What has changed over the years is the immediate priority awarded
them and the strategy and tactics by which they are pursued.

A fundamentally important issue which has divided Communists since at
least 1920 has concerned the role of the national bourgeoisie in the developing
countries. At the IInd Congress of the Comintern in 1920, Lenin took the
position that Communists should collaborate closely with the national bourgeoisie while pursuing national liberation from imperialist control. After
independence was achieved and the class struggle matured further, the
bourgeoisie would disintegrate and the communist leadership could be
purged of reactionary elements.[5]

An opposing position was advanced by a young Indian revolutionary
named M. N. Roy, whose theses on the "colonial question" were destined
to persist forty years later in the Sino-Soviet disagreement. Roy insisted that
the indigenous Communists must maintain sole leadership of the revolution
in its national-liberation stage as well as later, that the national bourgeoisie
could not be relied upon and must be confronted immediately.[6]

The issue remained unresolved, with both Lenin's and Roy's theses adopted
by the Comintern. But Stalin, after pursuing Lenin's course in his direction
of the Chinese Communists' disastrous collaboration with Chiang Kai-shek
in the later 1920's, reverted to a cautious, noncollaborative position which
reinforced the Comintern's ineffectual decline prior to the Second World
War. Alone, the Communists were incapable of mobilizing the national
liberation. Even after the war, Stalin, as shown by his attacks upon Gandhi,
Nkrumah, and others as bourgeois stooges, was unable to utilize the tide of
national opposition to colonialism for the purposes of Soviet policy.

Stalin's reversion to noncollaboration and insistence upon party control
of national liberation struggles had the effect of defining all noncommunist
elements in the developing areas—which included the vast majority of the
anti-imperialist activists—as a part of the "imperialist camp." Denying them,
in spite of themselves, an essential distinction from the imperialist bourgeoisie, he maintained his dichotomous view of the world and preserved the

[5] See Xenia Joukoff Eudin and Robert C. North, *Soviet Russia and the East, 1920–1927*
(Stanford: Stanford University Press, 1957), pp. 63–65.
[6] *Ibid.*, pp. 65–67.

image of a capitalist encirclement. In adamantly insisting upon the maximum Soviet goal, he denied himself the advantages open for pursuit of lesser goals.[7] His successor, Khrushchev, redefining the balance of forces to discriminate between noncommunist national forces in the developing areas and the Western imperialists, provided a base for reassessing the "encirclement" and reopened the field for Soviet activity which Stalin had closed to a stalemate.

The outcome of Khrushchev's new flexibility was to readopt Lenin's emphasis upon national liberation first, as an essential step in the right direction. This was a modest but more feasible goal and one which would use the noncommunist national fervor for independence to assist the communist movement. Between 1954 and 1960 Soviet policy moved consistently to reinforce this limited goal, achieving noteworthy success and, incidentally, exacerbating Soviet-Chinese policy differences. In the early 1960's there was a period of re-examination, as we shall see later; thereafter the same policy appears to have been resumed.

In his Central Committee Report to the XXIIIrd Party Congress in March of 1966, General Secretary Leonid Brezhnev concluded his section devoted to the developing areas by succinctly restating Soviet policy:

Comrades, the CPSU sees its internationalist duty in continuing to do its utmost to support the struggle of the peoples for final liberation from colonial and neo-colonial oppression. Our party and the Soviet state will continue to: render utmost support to the peoples fighting for their liberation and strive for the immediate granting of independence to all colonial countries and peoples; develop all-round cooperation with countries that have won national independence and help them to advance their economy, train national cadres, and in the struggle against neo-colonialism; strengthen the fraternal links of the CPSU with the communist parties and revolutionary democratic organizations in Asian, African, and Latin American countries.

The successes of the national liberation movement are inseparably bound with the successes of world socialism and the international working class. The firm and unbreakable alliance of these great revolutionary forces is the guarantee of the final triumph of the cause of national and social liberation of the peoples.[8]

---

[7] Stalin's viewpoint in the case of Africa is discussed well by Alexander Dallin, "The Soviet Union: Political Activity," in Zbigniew Brzezinski (ed.), *Africa and the Communist World* (Stanford: Stanford University Press, 1963), pp. 8–11.

[8] *Pravda,* March 30, 1966.

PROGRAMMATIC SOVIET FOREIGN POLICY

Thwarted in his postwar expansion first in Iran and later in Korea, and increasingly occupied with problems within his empire, Stalin expended relatively little Soviet effort in Asia, and virtually none in the Middle East, Africa, and Latin America in the period from 1948 to 1953. Meanwhile, the United States sought to replace the crumbling colonial basis of resistance to communism with an extension of the military-alliance matrix which had proven effective in Western Europe. The consequences were fortuitous when Khrushchev began to reactivate Soviet interest in the developing areas. Soviet colonialism was not viewed as a tangible threat by most of these peoples; such perception required abstraction from the experience of others (in this case, the states of Eastern Europe and of the USSR itself[9]). But Western colonialism was a recent memory restirred by the persistent and suspect U.S. efforts to organize resistance to the unseen threat. The U.S. was easily associated with West European imperialism, not only by historical ties but by present and continuing alliances. The inevitable American economic presence could readily be construed as only a new contrivance of Western finance capital, a "neo-colonialism."

In representing itself as the champion of national liberation, the Soviet Union had all the cards stacked in its favor; Khrushchev's astute propaganda campaign made the most of them. Asia and the Middle East received first attention. In the late 1950's and early 1960's Africa received an increased emphasis. Latin America, although trailing far behind (probably because of Soviet perception of entrenched American economic power as well as its geographic inaccessibility), received steadily growing attention. In 1965, the important journals of international propaganda appeal, *New Times* and *International Affairs*, for example, divided their coverage almost equally among the three continental areas. During that year, *International Affairs* devoted thirty-five articles to Asia, thirty-six to Africa, and thirty-five to Latin America.

The expansion of Soviet propaganda efforts in the developing areas may also be suggested by some figures on its international radio broadcasting and its distribution of books and periodicals abroad. In 1948, Soviet broadcasts, totaling some 334 hours weekly, were directed primarily to Western Europe (40 per cent); 14 per cent went to the Near East, South Asia, and Africa combined and 17 per cent were beamed to the Far East. But the Latin American effort was negligible. By 1959, Western Europe received only 27 per cent of a vastly increased total effort, with the Near East, South Asia,

[9] See Walter Kolarz, *Communism and Colonialism* (New York: St. Martin's Press, 1964).

and African areas taking over first place at 30 per cent in thirteen languages. During that decade broadcasts to the Far East dropped to 12 per cent; and in 1959 Latin America still received minimal attention. In the early 1960's, broadcasting to Africa in a variety of African languages was greatly increased. Competing with China now, the USSR also increased its broadcasts to Latin America (to sixty-three hours in 1961).[10]

A shift in target areas took place in April, 1964. While broadcasts to the developing areas continued, broadcasts to Western Europe were further reduced by 16 per cent and those to North America by 10 per cent. During the first half of 1964, the USSR added six new languages to its international broadcasting: Malayam (India), Lingala (Congo), Zulu (South Africa), Thai, Cambodian, and Uighur (Sinkiang). Soviet broadcasts to Latin America in Spanish were augmented by addition of a "second program" emanating from Soviet Far Eastern transmitters. In the summer of 1964, two more languages were added: Laotian and Malagasay.[11] By then total weekly broadcast hours by Soviet stations had mounted to 1,350. Most of these hours were coordinated with the broadcasts of the party-states of Eastern Europe.

Table VI-1[12]   Weekly Hours of International Broadcasting by Communist Countries (June 30, 1964)

USSR	1350
Eastern Europe	1367
Communist China	909
Far East Orbit (Pyongyang, Hanoi and Ulan Bator)	399
Cuba	350
Total	4375

As Frederick C. Barghoorn puts it:

Certainly in terms of weekly broadcast hours, the Soviet effort in the use of radio as an international propaganda instrument is the largest in the

[10] Frederick C. Barghoorn, *Soviet Foreign Propaganda* (Princeton; Princeton University Press, 1964), pp. 279–281.

[11] *Developments in International Broadcasting by Communist Countries in the First Half of 1964.* Prepared by The United States Information Agency (Washington, D.C.: Government Printing Office, September, 1964), pp. 1–3.

[12] *Ibid.,* p. 4.

world. It also has the most powerful transmitting equipment of any international radio system. The advantages enjoyed by Radio Moscow in terms of numbers of hours, strength of signal, and ability to exploit developing situations may at times be of considerable political importance.[13]

Some idea of the scale of Soviet export of printed propaganda materials abroad may be gained from the single item that in 1963 over 47 million copies of books in non-Soviet languages were produced in the USSR. *Mezhdunarodnaia Kniga*, the international book publishing and distributing firm, dates back to 1923 and deals with outlet firms throughout the world. In addition to books on all subjects, it exports some two hundred different periodicals (see Table VII-3). Among its books in 1963 were over 1,300 titles. Although some were designed for a domestic Soviet audience, the language breakdown (see Table VII-2) indicates almost 700,000 copies were probably destined for the Near East and South Asia, with some 50,000 for Africa. The Foreign Languages Publishing House in Moscow put out 1,800,000 copies of 117 titles in Spanish, most undoubtedly directed to a Latin American audience. Almost two million books were published to explain Soviet foreign policy alone. The prices charged for these books varied from about one-third of the U.S. equivalent for scientific works down to virtually nothing for the more blatant propaganda. In 1964, five-volume collections of Khrushchev's speeches reportedly could be purchased in Cairo, Beirut, and Khartoum for 4 cents per volume.[14]

Mezhkniga is supplemented by the Lenin Library and the Library of the Academy of Sciences in Moscow, which conduct book-exchange programs with several thousand institutions throughout the world. *Sovfilm*, exporting Soviet films, and the All-Union Chamber of Commerce, sponsoring diverse trade fairs and exhibitions, are two additional foreign-propaganda agencies.[15] Chapter II makes note of the TASS international free-news service and the extensive matrix of Friendship Societies and professional front organizations which pursue propaganda activities through personal contact. Since 1956, the primary focus of all these agencies has been support of the Soviet propaganda program in the developing areas.

[13] Barghoorn, *op. cit.,* p. 285.
[14] *USSR Foreign Language Book Publishing Program: 1963,* U.S. Information Agency, Research Report R–101–64 (Washington, D.C.: Government Printing Office, July 21, 1964), pp. 1–5.
[15] Barghoorn, *op. cit.,* pp. 286–93.

Table VII-2[16] Soviet Foreign Language Book Publishing—1963

AREA LANGUAGES	LANGUAGE	NO. TITLES	COPIES
African languages	Amharic	9	24,000
	Swahili	10	28,800
Totals		19	52,800
"Bloc" languages	Albanian	2	1,000
	Bulgarian	3	172,000
	Czecho-Slovak	8	312,250
	Hungarian	52	451,100
	Macedonian	1	3,500
	Mongolian	2	1,000
	Polish	36	415,100
	Rumanian	4	108,000
	Serbo-Croat	5	53,300
Totals		113	1,517,150
Western European languages	Dutch	4	22,000
	Finnish	45	269,550
	German	251	20,668,450
	Italian	2	50,000
	Norwegian	2	14,000
	Swedish	4	19,500
Totals		308	21,043,500
Far Eastern languages	Chinese	7	29,950
	Indonesian	3	14,000
	Japanese	1	2,300
	Korean	13	99,201
	Tibetan	1	2,500
	Vietnamese	13	183,700
Totals		38	331,651
Near Eastern and Southeast Asian languages	Afghan	1	6,000
	Arabic	24	233,700
	Bengali	9	59,600
	Farsi	3	30,000
	Greek	3	5,600
	Hindi	14	111,000
	Kurdish	10	7,000
	Marathi	4	30,750
	Persian	4	29,000
	Singhalese	3	70,000
	Tamil	3	34,600
	Telugu	5	25,500
	Turkish	1	1,500
	Urdu	2	6,000
Totals		86	640,550

[16] *USSR Foreign Language Book Publishing Program: 1963*, pp. 8–9.

Table VII-2 Soviet Foreign Language Book Publishing—1963 (cont'd.)

AREA LANGUAGES	LANGUAGE	NO. TITLES	COPIES
International languages	English	412	17,243,686
	French	227	4,698,000
	Portuguese	2	17,200
	Spanish	117	1,776,150
Totals		758	23,735,036
Dead languages	Latin	11	54,220
Grand Totals All Languages		1314	47,374,907

Table VII-3[17] Total Annual Circulation of Soviet Magazines in Various Languages (Selected Years)

	1956 (in 1,000)	no. of mags.	1959 (in 1,000)	no. of mags.	1963* (in 1,000)	no. of mags.
Arabic	286	(1)	320	(2)	168	(2)
Chinese	1,468	(2)	4,395	(3)	1,294	(2)
English	2,008	(9)	1,940	(10)	3,481	(12)
French	1,158	(6)	917	(7)	981	(13)
German	2,744	(6)	2,916	(6)	3,270	(10)
Hindi	71	(2)	65	(2)	668	
					All Indian } (3)	
Urdu	33	(2)	33	(2)	Languages	
Japanese	186	(2)	130	(2)	134	(2)
Korean	540	(2)	568	(2)	112	(2)
Serbo-Croat	11	(1)	9	(1)	15	(1)
Spanish	420	(6)	1,043	(7)	1,717	(9)
Swedish	104	(1)	73	(1)	none	

* These figures include *Soviet Union*, published in seventeen languages in 650,000 copies.

[17] *Periodicals Exported by the Communist Countries in 1964,* U.S. Information Agency, Research Report R–15–65 (Washington, D.C.: Government Printing Office, February, 1965), p. 5.

Table VII-4[18] Communist Propaganda Activities in Africa, 1960–1963

Activity	12/31/60	12/31/61	12/31/62	12/31/63
Broadcasts to Africa				
Weekly hours to Africa (except Arabic)	96	200	298	333
Weekly hours partly to Africa	66	10	10	10
Weekly hours in Arabic	166	166	180	183
No. of languages (including Arabic)	5	6	10	11
No. of African languages (excluding Arabic)	1	2	4	5
Films				
Communist films produced on African subjects (yearly totals)	4	18	13	31
African countries about which communist films produced (yearly totals)	4	13	6	n.a.
No. of African film festivals staged by or participated in by communist countries	2	4	5	6
News Services				
African countries with communist news services	n.a.	6	11	16
Total no. of communist news service installations in Africa	6 (est.)	18	31	42
Local Communist Newspapers and Periodicals				
No. of countries in which published	5	5	6	7
No. of publications	19	20	16	22
Total estimated circulation	53,000	64,000	90–100,000*	100–120,000
Cultural Agreements				
African countries involved (cumulative)	4	7	10	13
Total agreements—cumulative (new agreements, renewals, and old agreements presumed still in effect)	11	30	37	58
Cultural Presentations				
Communist *Performing Arts* in Africa				
No. of different African countries	7	5	11	11
Total countries programmed by all groups**	10	5	13	21

Table VII-4[18] Communist Propaganda Activities in Africa, 1960–1963 (cont'd.)

ACTIVITY	12/31/60	12/31/61	12/31/62	12/31/63
Communist Athletic Teams				
No. of different African countries	7	6	9	16
Total countries programmed by all teams**	9	9	18	34
Communist Cultural Gifts to Africa				
African countries involved	n.a.	n.a.	8	8
No. of cultural gifts	n.a.	n.a.	24	33
Exhibits (in Africa)				
Total African countries involved	9	11	12	13
Total exhibits shown	32	43	68	78
No. of essentially cultural and propaganda (yearly totals)	3	11	33	47
No. of essentially economic and technical (yearly totals)	29	32	35	31
Students				
Estimated African students in communist countries (mostly full-time academic)	1,166	3,044	4,714	6,135
Diplomatic				
African countries with communist representation	11	13	18	22
Cumulative communist accreditations (or agreements)	44	72	99	122*
Communist Parties				
Number of parties in Africa	6	8	9	9
Estimated party membership	Under 10,000	Under 10,000	11,000	11,000
Communist Fronts and Friendship Societies				
No. of African countries involved	10	12	11	13
No. of fronts and friendship societies	35	42	43	44

263

Table VII-4[18]   Communist Propaganda Activities in Africa, 1960–1963 (cont'd.)

ACTIVITY	12/31/60	12/31/61	12/31/62	12/31/63
Credits and Grants (excluding military aid)				
Countries accepting economic aid	4	7	8†	9
Cumulative aid extended in $ million (much of it not drawn)	279	602	678‡	856

* Part of this increase from 1961 was a paper increase, since in earlier years the sizable circulation of an Algerian paper was not included in the African totals.

** A touring troupe or athletic team which played in more than one country is counted once for each country visited.

† Includes five instances in which agreements were reportedly concluded in 1962 as well as nine more in 1963, although representatives had not arrived as of December, 1963.

‡ These figures refer to June 1962.

[18] *Communist Propaganda Acitivities in Africa, January, 1963–June, 1964*, U.S. Information Agency, Research Report (Washington, D.C.: Government Printing Office, November, 1964), pp. 36–39.

SOVIET ECONOMIC POLICIES

The major thrust of Soviet foreign policy in the developing areas since Stalin has, however, met the economic demands of the peoples in economic terms. It has consisted of the Soviet aid and trade programs.

The Soviet Union frequently aggregates Soviet trade with the developing countries along with loans and commercial credits, exchanges of personnel and information, and grants both in cash and kind as "aid" or "disinterested assistance." We provide in this chapter some figures which suggest the scope and extent of several of these programs in the recent period (see also Appendix VII-1). Here, excluding for the moment international trade figures but including all the other items customarily grouped as aid by the Soviet Union, let us examine the trends substantiated by the record.

The theory of games provides a framework for understanding the international relationships which result from the post-World War II phenomena of large-scale foreign-aid programs. We need to consider the whole of these relationships in order to assess the Soviet part. Drawing heavily upon a perceptive article by David Beim,[19] we conceptualize foreign aid in the mid-1960's as a four-player, nonzero-sum game. The four players are the United States, the Soviet Union, China, and the "developing nations." By nonzero sum we mean that one player's loss is not necessarily another player's proportionate gain, that there may be strategic interaction from which the sum of pay-offs, in terms of both political influence and economic growth, may not be balanced by deprivations. Aid agreements may be mutually profitable—the game is in part a cooperative one. But the differing goals of, for example, the Soviet Union and the United States assure that it is also in part a conflictual game.

The game was initiated by the United States. Growing out of the wartime U.S. Lend-Lease Program and the American support of the immediate postwar rehabilitation programs of the United Nations, it reflected the "enlightened self-interest" of the United States in restoring the self-sustaining prosperity of mixed economies in the parliamentary democracies of Western Europe and in the promotion of political stability and peaceful change throughout the world. The primary pay-offs sought by the United States were a strengthened resolve among aided nations to resist the efforts of the Soviet Union to spread communism and a renewed domestic confidence in noncommunist political and economic alternatives. Two shifts of emphasis became evident in the American aid programs during the 1950's: (1) they

[19] David Beim, "The Communist Bloc and the Foreign Aid Game," *Western Political Quarterly,* XVII, No. 4 (December, 1964), 784–799.

moved from primary stress upon military hardware to economic tools; (2) they moved from primary stress upon the mature economies of the industrialized West to the developing areas.

In terms of game theory, the Soviet Union participated in foreign aid only negatively and symbolically until after Stalin's death. The Soviet Union did not commit appreciable material resources, but contented itself with a propaganda campaign which stressed the "neo-colonial" intent of American assistance. It was upon this ground that the USSR condemned and refused to participate in the Marshall Plan in 1947. That line did not change during the succeeding six years. Beginning in 1954, however, the Soviet Union committed increasing funds in the effort to neutralize Western achievements and then to take advantage of the new world balance of forces perceived by Khrushchev in 1956.

Until the late 1950's, China could be conceived as a part of the "Soviet bloc" in analyzing the foreign aid game. With the rapid exacerbation of the Sino-Soviet conflict thereafter, competition in foreign aid distinguished China as a player in her own right. The other communist party-states, who were significant in the game, may still be considered as adjuncts of the USSR.

In some ways the "developing areas" as a player in the game refers to a passive target. That is to say, the U.S., USSR, and CPR are bidding competitively for favorable responses from the developing areas. But the capacity of the target thus to accept or refuse bids and to demand a price for continuity of policy means in effect that in the mid-1960's the target, adopting a strategy of its own, can and in large part does determine the course of the game. The "game," too, may be broken down into as many separate games as there are developing countries. In each case the other three players remain the same.

From the point of view of the developing countries, we agree with Beim: the stakes of the game are economic development, political stability, and political independence. They are faced with minimizing the dependence which may be engendered by accepting the material aid to maximize stability and speed of development.

The other three players may be motivated to extend aid by the desire to: (1) promote good will and solidify friendly relations; (2) promote economic and hence political dependence of the target country upon the donor; (3) cultivate an ideological ally; and/or (4) obtain military advantage versus another player.[20] Additionally, these players may be motivated by either short-term tactical, or long-term strategic considerations. Promoting good

[20] *Ibid.*, pp. 785–88.

will seldom amounts to more than a tactical achievement, whereas the cultivation of ideological alliance assumes a strategic dimension. The other two purposes may be pursued either tactically or strategically.

Examining the nature of Soviet foreign assistance, we find that early Soviet commitments can generally be classified as tactical efforts for temporary victories to balance American achievements. Soviet aid was concentrated in spectacular projects, such as stadiums and hotels, which appealed to the target regimes but accomplished little more. In subsequent years, most of Soviet aid apparently sought strategic economic dependence. Beim, analyzing all communist party-state aid through 1961, comes to the conclusion that 85 per cent was devoted to establishing and maintaining economic dependence, with all but 1 per cent of it employed strategically.[21]

The Soviet Union, following upon the heels of American efforts to prevent the expansion of communism through the employment of foreign economic assistance, was able on several occasions to exploit American mistakes. Playing upon the developing areas' susceptibility to charges of Western-imperialist intent and taking advantage of the timely opportunity, the Soviet Union, for example, offered to build the Aswan Dam for Egypt (after American refusal), to finance the Bokaro Steel Mill for India (after American refusal), and to send aid to Tunisia (after French bombing of Bizerte). Coordinating her aid with propaganda campaigns, the Soviet Union exploits her contributions at least three times: when the commitment is made, when the aid is first extended, and when the project is completed. Personal visits by Soviet leaders have been used skillfully to draw maximum international attention to each commitment.[22]

But the advantage to the Soviet Union which accrued from following chronologically behind American proffers of aid and promising a more satisfactory arrangement for the target "with no strings attached" has subsequently become a Soviet disadvantage to be exploited by a still later entry in the competition for developing areas' favor, namely, China. A significant source of economic aid only since 1956, with her greatest effort dating after 1962, the Chinese appear to have contributed to the Soviet decision in 1963 to resume large-scale foreign aid after a two-year period of reappraisal.

It appears that the Soviet effort to foster economic dependency in the late 1950's was supported by the expectation of steady growth of ideological compatibility. To the discomfiture of the USSR, the anti-imperialist dynamics which afforded early Soviet-aid success did not extend to adoption of Soviet

[21] *Ibid.,* p. 794.
[22] Marshall I. Goldman, "A Balance Sheet of Soviet Foreign Aid," *Foreign Affairs,* XLIII, No. 2 (January, 1965), p. 351.

Table VII-5[23] Estimated Communist Country Credits and Grants Extended to Less Developed Countries of the Free World, as of December 31, 1964 (millions of U.S. dollars)

AREA AND COUNTRY TOTAL	USSR 4,268	EASTERN EUROPE 1,368	CHINA 786	TOTAL 6,422
Africa	*758*	*223*	*255*	*1,236*
Algeria	229	22	52	303
Central African Republic	0	0	4	4
Congo (Brazzaville)	9	0	25	34
Ethiopia	102	12	0	114
Ghana	89	82	42	213
Guinea	70	25	27	122
Kenya	44	0	18	62
Mali	55	22	20	97
Morocco	0	17	0	17
Senegal	7	0	0	7
Somali	57	6	22	85
Sudan	22	0	0	22
Tanzania	30	18	45	93
Tunisia	28	19	0	47
Uganda	16	0	0	16
Asia	*2,061*	*566*	*385*	*3,012*
Afghanistan	541	7	0	548
Burma	14	1	84	99
Cambodia	21	5	50	76
Ceylon	30	10	41	81
India	1,022	255	0	1,277
Indonesia	369	260	107	736
Nepal	20	0	43	63
Pakistan	44	28	60	132
Latin America	*100*	*187*	*0*	*287*
Argentina	100	4	0	104
Brazil	0	183	0	183
Middle East	*1,346*	*392*	*146*	*1,884*
Cyprus	0	1	0	1
Iran	39	21	0	60
Iraq	184	34	0	218
Syria	151	48	16	215
Turkey	8	8	0	16
UAR (Egypt)	899	278	85	1,262
Yemen	65	2	45	112
Europe—Iceland	*3*	*0*	*0*	*3*

[23] *The Communist Economic Offensive Through 1964*, U.S. Department of State, Bureau of Intelligence and Research, Unclassified Research Memorandum RSB–65 (Washington, D.C.: Government Printing Office, August 4, 1965), p. 6.

economic or political forms or even, on many occasions, to support for Soviet international positions. For example, while Nasser was eager to accept Soviet assistance at Aswan and Soviet arms to match Israel's perceived military threat and Soviet markets for Egyptian cotton, he was not willing to take a benevolent attitude toward domestic Communists. Quite the contrary— he suppressed the Communist Party in Egypt. Iraq, also cultivated by Soviet economic aid, similarly turned resistant toward a perceived internal communist threat. The list of disappointments could be extended. Suffice to say, in late 1960, the Soviet Union abruptly suspended any new aid commitments while evaluating the returns on its investment.

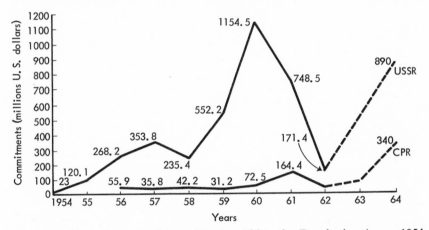

FIGURE VII–2[24]   Soviet and Chinese Foreign Aid to the Developing Areas, 1954–1964

The Chinese competition and the inertia of expectations generated over the past five years now told upon the USSR. Suspension of aid was perceived as punishment and rebounded against Soviet popularity. The specter of Chinese replacement briefly loomed. Most significantly, the Soviet leadership was asked to decide whether the minimal Soviet objective among the developing areas—denial of these areas to the imperialists—was worth the investment, when the maximal objective—their incorporation into the communist system—would be indefinitely deferred.

Upon the answer to this last question depends Soviet foreign policy in the developing areas. It was answered negatively in the late 1920's by Stalin

[24] Maurice D. Simon, "Communist System Interaction with the Developing States, 1954–1962: A Preliminary Analysis" (Stanford Studies of the Communist System, Research Paper No. 10, January, 1966), pp. 78, 84; *The Communist Economic Offensive Through 1964, op. cit.,* pp. 1–20.

and brought a withdrawal of Soviet effort. It has been answered in the negative by the Chinese Communists with a different conclusion; the Chinese, denigrating the policy of collaboration with national bourgeois regimes, actively call for a "second wave" of revolution among the newly independent states. But after a period of re-evaluation the Soviet answer to this crucial question became "yes." The statement compromised upon by the eighty-one Party leaders meeting in Moscow in November of 1960 acknowledged that the bourgeoisie in the developing areas might play a "progressive" role in the struggle against imperialism and feudalism.[25] This proposition was reiterated in the Program of the CPSU, adopted at the XXIInd Party Congress in October of 1961, and again by Brezhnev in his Central Committee Report to the XXIIIrd Party Congress in March of 1966. Articles in the Soviet press in the mid-1960's repeatedly emphasize the acceptability of independent courses of political and economic development among these countries. Rather than calling for socialist systems, Soviet authors increasingly use the term *noncapitalist* in prescribing the best course for the developing areas. Recent articles stress the complicated economic and political residue of the colonial period and the consequently long period of domestic adjustment before the socialist path may be undertaken. For example, K. Ivanov begins one of a cycle of articles on "the national-liberation movement and non-capitalist path of development" with the following tolerant paragraph:

> The picture of the historical process as a straight and continuous ascent from the lower to the higher stages belongs to the realms of fantasy. History is made by people, moreover, flesh-and-blood and not imaginary, "ideal", people. Zigzags, sudden twists and turns, outbursts of contradictions, occasional advances and retreats, steps forward and steps back are all interwoven in the live fabric of every people's history. This is especially manifest in the national-liberation movement of countries where the working class is only emerging and has not yet crystallized into the determining force and social features inherent in peasant movements are the most telling. Here nothing is automatically certain in advance, every step forward has to be won in battle and progress is often attained at the price of bitter disappointments, mistakes and searches.[26]

Although other, similar statements abound to confirm current Soviet acceptance of the minimal goals of policy in the developing areas, and

[25] Text of the statement reprinted in *The New York Times,* December 7, 1960, pp. 14ff.
[26] K. Ivanov, "The National-Liberation Movement and Non-Capitalist Path of Development," *International Affairs,* No. 2 (February, 1966), p. 12.

although they lead to analyses of conditions which are refreshingly free of the rigid old stereotypes, it is clear that the Soviet leadership still regards the tripartite world as a transitional stage. It will take time, the argument goes in effect, and patience, but "the revolution deepens as independence is won," and the superiority of socialist political and economic forms will eventually assert themselves. Time and conditions in the developing areas are on the side of socialism; the capitalist way, still present as a complicating factor, is in history's backwash.

To refer once again to our game-theory framework, the target countries of Soviet (and American and Chinese) foreign-aid strategy have gained the initiative because of the competition and basic inability to concert among the aid donors. Bargaining to secure maximum economic advantage at least political cost, they demand continued Soviet aid in return for maintaining neutrality. The Soviet Union concedes to this extortion because it is hopeful that time will move today's noncapitalist neutrals the full socialist way.

Following their optimistic estimate, the Soviet leadership resumed making new aid commitments in the latter half of 1963. A peak of $1,154.5 million had been committed by the USSR in the developing areas during 1960 (a commitment which in terms of the Soviet GNP matched the U.S. foreign-aid commitment). In 1961 and 1962 the totals dropped precipitously (to $171.4 million in 1962). But by 1964 the Soviet Union again announced extensions of $890 million.[27]

We have largely ignored Soviet military policy in the developing areas thus far. The neglect stems in part from the extensive consideration to be given the use of military force in Chapter IX, under the heading of Soviet risk-taking behavior. But it also stems from our conviction that the military dimension is relatively submerged in current Soviet policy toward the third world. The reader will recall that it was the ineffectiveness of Stalin's efforts in Korea that helped bring Khrushchev's 1956 revision of the Soviet view of the developing areas and Soviet strategy therein. Coupled with Soviet hesitancy to embark upon a course which would bring further direct military confrontation with the United States (a position reinforced by the current Soviet leadership's desire to prove its policy in the face of the Chinese challenge), this strategy has left Soviet military assistance primarily a

[27] See sources for Figure VII–2. Soviet credits are normally repayable over a ten- to fifteen-year period at interest rates between 2 and 3 per cent, in the currency of the receiver state. Availability of the credits is customarily spread over several years, depending upon the economic plans of both the USSR and the receiver. *The Communist Economic Offensive Through 1964*, pp. 1–3.

verbal-contingency promise. Doubtless sizable quantities of arms have been delivered piecemeal to rebellious factions in countries as yet unfreed from "colonial bondage." But this has not formally involved the Soviet state. Arms deliveries have been made to Syria, Egypt, Iraq, Indonesia, Afghanistan, and Yemen,[28] with generally poor returns. But Soviet military policy in the developing countries currently appears to be restricted to the assurance that *in the event* they should be attacked or their independence otherwise threatened they may be confident of Soviet assistance (of carefully unspecified nature). While much of the third world remained to be liberated, the Soviet Union rightly acquired the image of purveyor of arms to revolutionaries. Today the encouragement of social disorder contradicts Soviet efforts to woo nascent and insecure regimes; this gambit is left to the Chinese.

Soviet trade figures are closely related to Soviet-aid commitments. They reflect purchases made in the USSR with commercial credits extended under the heading of "aid." Accordingly, the tables in Appendix VII-2 show the same general trend of expansion in interchange with the developing areas in recent years. A typical statement of Soviet trade policy follows:

The Soviet Union has substantially broadened its economic ties with the newly-independent countries. It has concluded trade and payments agreements with 35 developing countries. Trade with these former colonies increased ten times over from 1953 to 1963. It is based on non-interference in domestic affairs, respect for national sovereignty, mutual benefit and full equality. The USSR does not seek any concessions or privileges. And that is especially important for the developing countries, for their foreign trade is badly impeded by exclusive economic groups of the capitalist states which dictate prices and seek to retain developing countries as their raw-material appendages and markets for their manufactures.[29]

The concentration of Soviet trade and aid volume with relatively few selected countries of the developing world and the customary refusal of the USSR to take in trade the output of infant industries (insisting instead on basis raw-materials) belie the disinterested and unique nature of the opportunity it professes to extend. There can be no doubt, however, that the residue of Western colonialism provides a fertile field for such propaganda.

[28] Beim, *op. cit.*, p. 793; cf. Uri Ra'anan, "Tactics in the Third World," *Survey*, No. 57 (October, 1965), pp. 30–34.
[29] "Soviet Foreign Trade," *International Affairs*, No. 6 (June, 1965), p. 86.

SOME RETURNS ON SOVIET ECONOMIC POLICIES

We have presented the Soviet argument for sustained economic assistance to certain developing countries; and we have assessed receptivity of these countries to Soviet assistance, in terms of the game-theory framework. We said that post-Stalin Soviet decision-makers have viewed their assistance as means first to deprive the imperialists, secondly to gain allies against the imperialists, then to woo socialist associates, and in the long run, perhaps, members of the world communist system. For their part, the developing countries have demanded and accepted Soviet assistance in return for maintaining neutrality. Let us now tentatively examine the more specific question of short-run returns, the *quid pro quo* delivery from the recipient countries, in terms of the Soviet expectations: How much support from the recipients of its assistance has the USSR received against its capitalist adversaries?

We have selected twenty states for analysis.[30] The two criteria for our selection were (1) aid or trade dependence on the party-states and (2) geographic contiguity to the party-state system. The twenty states satisfying one or both of these criteria, listed alphabetically, are: Afghanistan, Burma, Cambodia, Ceylon, Cyprus, Ethiopia, Finland, Ghana, Guinea, Greece, India, Indonesia, Iran, Iraq, Nepal, Pakistan, Thailand, Turkey, United Arab Republic, and Yemen. (Laos and South Vietnam were not included because the state of confusion there has created an instability which makes meaningful analysis well-nigh impossible.) In order to measure the relationships between the USSR and these states, we utilized three indices: (1) similarity of *voting records at the United Nations* on issues reflecting East-West differences; (2) *economic aid* in the form of credits and grants from the USSR and other party-states; and (3) the flow of *trade* between the countries and the USSR.

We decided that a state's voting record in the United Nations on cold-war issues is as objective an indication of its political attitude towards the USSR as can easily be found. On the floor of the General Assembly each member delegation expresses its position on East-West issues almost daily, voting against one side or the other. Even an abstention may reveal a stance. We recognized that other factors besides a state's political position in the cold war might influence its voting behavior (for example India's vote for Communist Chinese membership in the world body reflects a belief in the principle of universal representation more than it does a procommunist attitude),

[30] This portion of Chapter VII is based on Jan F. Triska with David O. Beim and Noralou P. Roos, *The World Communist System*, Research Paper No. 1 (Stanford: Stanford Studies of the Communist System), 1963.

but these influences are almost impossible to pinpoint and to weigh. We found that member nations do not always explain their votes and decided it would reduce the objectivity of our study to weigh votes on the basis of statements of government spokesmen or press editorials and interpretations.

We selected nineteen votes during 1961 and 1962 in the UN General Assembly and Standing Committees which we judged most relevant to a description of cold-war alignments. The subjects dealt with in 1961 included the Congo, Tibet, Hungary, Korea, China, Mauritania, Cuba, and nuclear testing. Each vote exhibited definite characteristics of the cold-war split, i.e., the West (meaning at least the U.S.A., Great Britain, and France) voting one way, the Communist party-states voting the other, and the votes of the remaining states scattered.

The votes are tabulated in Table VII-6. Total votes with the West are subtracted from total votes with the party-states, and the difference divided by the total votes cast—which may be less than twelve or seven, but which includes the abstentions:

Table VII-6   Key Votes at the United Nations[31]

	Votes with Party-States (A)	Votes with the West (B)	Total Votes (N)	Index: (A–B)/N
1961				
Guinea	9	1	12	.67
Indonesia	7	1	12	.50
Afghanistan	5	1	12	.33
UAR	5	1	12	.33
Yemen	5	1	12	.33
Iraq	5	1	12	.33
Ceylon	6	3	12	.25
Ghana	5	2	12	.25
India	5	3	12	.17
Cambodia	3	2	11	.09
Burma	5	5	12	.00
Ethiopia	4	4	12	.00
Nepal	4	4	11	.00
Finland	2	4	12	−.25
Cyprus	0	7	11	−.64
Pakistan	1	8	11	−.64
Iran	0	9	11	−.82
Greece	1	11	12	−.83
Thailand	0	11	12	−.92
Turkey	0	12	12	−1.00

[31] United Nations, General Assembly, 15th, 16th, and 17th Sessions, *Official Records, Plenary Meetings* (New York: UN, 1961 and 1962).

Table VII-6   Key Votes at the United Nations (cont'd.)

VOTES WITH PARTY-STATES (A)	VOTES WITH THE WEST (B)	TOTAL VOTES (N)	INDEX: (A–B)/N
1962			
Indonesia	3	0	7	.43
Ghana	3	0	7	.43
Ceylon	3	0	7	.43
Cambodia	3	0	7	.43
Ethiopia	3	0	7	.43
Nepal	3	0	7	.43
Guinea	2	0	6	.33
UAR	2	0	6	.33
Afghanistan	2	0	7	.28
Iraq	2	0	7	.28
Burma	2	0	7	.28
Finland	1	1	7	.00
India	2	3	6	−.17
Cyprus	1	3	7	−.28
Yemen	0	3	7	−.43
Pakistan	1	4	5	−.60
Greece	0	6	7	−.86
Iran	0	7	7	−1.00
Thailand	0	7	7	−1.00
Turkey	0	7	7	−1.00

Table VII-6 provides a clear division of the twenty states into three categories for 1961: nine inclined toward the USSR, four neutral (we arbitrarily designated the range from .10 to −.10 as neutral), and seven inclined toward the West. For 1962, the breakdown was: eleven inclined toward the USSR, one neutral, and eight inclined toward the West. The table arranges the states in order, according to the degree of alignment.

From the recipient state's point of view, UN voting on East-West issues is an "output": a favorable action directed from the state to the USSR (or to the West). We shall next consider what we expected to be the corresponding "input": a favorable action directed from the Communist party-states (or from the West) to the recipient states. We selected economic aid in the form of credits and grants, and constructed an index analogous to that in the previous table.

Table VII-7[32] Economic Aid from 1954–1962* (Grants and Credits)
(in millions of U.S. dollars)

	AID FROM PARTY-STATES (A)	AID FROM THE WEST (B)	INDEX: (A − b)/(A + B)
Iraq	218.0	18.0	.85
Guinea	125.0	13.4	.80
Afghanistan	514.0	193.0	.45
Yemen	44.0	22.8	.32
Indonesia	638.0	393.1	.24
Burma	97.0	75.3	.19
Ghana	196.0	156.0	.11
UAR	716.0	575.9	.10
Nepal	54.0	47.6	.06
Ethiopia	114.0	111.3	.01
Ceylon	69.0	79.4	−.07
India	982.0	3533.3	−.56
Cambodia	65.0	250.7	−.59
Cyprus	1.0	16.9	−.89
Turkey	17.0	1251.3	−.97
Iran	6.0	657.3	−.98
Pakistan	33.0	1733.1	−.99
Greece	0	444.8	−1.00
Thailand	0	308.3	−1.00

* Figures for Finland are unavailable.

This table was also divided into three groups. During the 1954–1962 period, seven countries received significantly more aid from the Communist party-states than they did from the West, four states received roughly equal assistance from the West and the communist countries, and eight countries received the bulk of their grants and credits from the West.

A strong relationship between a positive index number for economic aid and a procommunist voting record in the United Nations emerged. Six countries (Iraq, Guinea, Afghanistan, Indonesia, Burma, and Ghana) out of the seven which received significantly more aid from the Communist party-states than from the West for 1954–1962 also strongly supported the communist doctrines in the UN as is shown by their positive index numbers. Yemen was the exception, registering a +.32 index number for economic

[32] Data for the party-states' aid was found in "Sino-Soviet Bloc Credits and Grants, Jan. 1, 1954–March 31, 1961," *East Europe*, XII, No. 2, 5; and "Economic Aid Commitments and Expenditures, 1954–1962," *East Europe*, XII, No. 11,13. Figures for Western aid were taken from Agency for International Development, Statistics and Reports Division *United States Foreign Assistance, July 1, 1945–June 30, 1962* (Washington, D.C.: Government Printing Office, 1962).

aid, but a − .43 percentage for UN voting record. It should be noted that Yemen received 6.7 million dollars in new Western aid in 1962. This may well explain the discrepancy.

The third set of data we used concerned neither an output nor an input, but both. The following table sets forth the manner in which each country's *trade* was divided between the West and the party-states in 1961–1962; the West here means the United States, Great Britain, and France:

Table VII-8   Percentage of Trade with the West and the Party-States[33]

	PER CENT WITH PARTY-STATES (A)	PER CENT WITH THE WEST	INDEX: (A − B)/(A + B)
1961			
Yemen	17	2	.79
Afghanistan	47	24	.32
Guinea	35	20	.27
United Arab Republic	31	20	.19
Burma	16	16	.00
Finland	18	28	−.22
Ceylon	12	33	−.47
Greece	10	28	−.47
Indonesia	7	27	−.59
Turkey	8	40	−.67
Iran	4	24	−.71
India	7	46	−.73
Iraq	4	32	−.78
Cambodia	5	41	−.78
Pakistan	3	34	−.84
Ghana	4	48	−.86
Ethiopia	2	34	−.88
Cyprus	3	46	−.88
Thailand	1	22	−.91
1962			
Yemen	15	2	.75
Afghanistan	42	22	.31
Guinea	29	25	.07
United Arab Republic	28	28	.00
Burma	15	15	.00
Finland	20	28	−.17
Ceylon	14	33	−.40
Greece	11	28	−.43
Cambodia	12	38	−.52
Indonesia	7	27	−.59

[33] *Directions of Trade, A Supplement to International Financial Statistics Annual 1958–1962*, International Monetary Fund, International Bank for Reconstruction and Development.

Table VII-8   Percentage of Trade with the West and the Party-States
(*cont'd.*)

	PER CENT WITH PARTY-STATES (A)	PER CENT WITH THE WEST	INDEX: (A — B)/(A + B)
India	10	43	—.62
Iraq	6	30	—.67
Ghana	7	47	—.74
Turkey	6	40	—.74
Ethiopia	4	36	—.80
Iran	2	25	—.85
Cyprus	4	48	—.85
Pakistan	2	54	—.93
Thailand	1	21	—.95
Nepal	no data	no data	

Table VII-8 indicates the United States' overwhelming superiority over the party-states in the realm of trade relationships with the nonaligned countries. It also casts great doubt upon trade patterns as a reliable indicator of political alignment. In 1961, only four of the countries (Yemen, Afghanistan, Guinea, and the United Arab Republic) did more trade with communist countries than with the West; in 1962, only two countries (Yemen and Afghanistan) remained in this category. Our data generally indicate that economic aid is much more closely correlated with UN voting than is the flow of trade. We might cynically hypothesize that nonaligned countries are more fearful that their votes in the UN may provoke U.S. congressional efforts for withdrawal of aid programs than they are that government and private trade will decrease in retaliation for unfavorable votes in the UN.

As a final step, we took an average of the three indices of affinity and responsiveness in order to examine how they correlated with each other. Our results are summarized as follows:

Six countries (Greece, Pakistan, Cyprus, Iran, Turkey, and Thailand) were negative according to all three indices. Finland was negative in both the indices for trade and voting record in 1961 (no aid figures were published and it was assumed that Finland received no aid from either side, giving it an .00 index number in this area). India had a negative index number in all three criteria in 1962. During these years these countries were in no sense allies of the communist system, and we accordingly omitted them from further consideration.

In 1961, four countries (Guinea, Yemen, Afghanistan, and the United Arab Republic) were positive in all criteria; only three countries (Guinea, Afghanistan, and Nepal) had positive index numbers in all criteria examined in 1962. We think that these states may be termed the *allies* of the communist system in the 1961–1962 period and should be examined for additional inter-actions with the system. The extent of their affinity or responsiveness may be seen from Table VII-9:

Table VII-9   Indices of Affinity*

COUNTRY	INPUT (AID)	INTERACTION (TRADE)	OUTPUT (UN)	AVERAGE
1961				
1. Guinea	.93	.27	.67	.62
2. Yemen	.46	.79	.33	.53
3. Afghanistan	.17	.32	.33	.27
4. UAR	.26	.19	.33	.26
1962				
1. Guinea	.80	.07	.33	.40
2. Afghanistan	.45	.31	.28	.35
3. Nepal	.06	—	.43	.25

* 1.00 means total commitment; .00 means total neutrality.

This typology is of course transient: membership and rank in the matrix may, and in fact does, change considerably from one year to the next. In 1961, the UAR had a +.26 index of alliance; in 1962, it received an increase of economic aid from the West and its positive trade index number of +.19 dropped to .00. Thus, the UAR had an index of alliance of only +.14 in 1962. It is interesting to note that Guinea's +.62 index in 1961 dropped to +.40 in 1962; Yemen also dropped from +.53 to +.21. The reasons are probably not difficult to guess: the communist embrace can be rather tight and possessive. The more stable friendships with the party-states may be those maintained from a distance.

Another consideration is that the West, and especially the United States, becomes alienated and estranged from countries which lean too far toward the Communists, leaving them little alternative but total dependence on the party-states. It would be possible to argue that Fidel Castro did not intend to make Cuba a Communist party-state but simply could not withstand the pressures generated around the level of 80 per cent commitment to the Communists. It will be interesting to see whether states which reach a level of commitment of more than 50 per cent (halfway between neutrality and commitment to the party-states) in the future can remain stable at this plane and resist becoming a slow-motion Cuba.

Some states demonstrated mixed tendencies which made them quite diffi-cult to classify. In both 1961 and 1962, Iraq, Indonesia, and Ghana were heavily dependent on the West for trade, received more economic assistance from the party-states than the West, and provided the communist countries with considerable support in the UN. Burma and the United Arab Republic received more aid from the party-states than the West and traded equally with both sides in 1962 but strongly backed the communist countries in the world body. Ethiopia received a shade more economic assistance from the party-states, was almost completely dependent on the West for trade, and voted strongly in favor of the communist countries in the UN. Ceylon in 1961 and 1962 and Cambodia in the latter year were dependent on the West in both the areas of trade and economic assistance; yet, they followed the party-states' lead in the UN. It would be erroneous to call these countries neutrals in the light of their strong support of the party-states in the world organization; but, can we reasonably term them allied states when they depend very much on the West for either aid or trade or both?

Obviously, economic assistance is among the principal influences which determine the nonaligned states' political stance in the cold war. It does not, however, tell us everything.

Two other facets of Soviet policy in the developing countries should occupy us briefly before we close this chapter—the formation of a sizable body of positive treaty law linking the developing countries and the USSR, and the training of youth from the developing areas in the Soviet Union.

Table VII-10 shows the quantitative expansion of Soviet treaty commitments with developing countries through 1962. Much of the expansion is clearly the product of the formation of new countries during this period, not of any change in Soviet policy. The latter has remained relatively constant since 1956. Agreements have been sought to pave the way for expanded economic and cultural interchange, to enhance the influence of the Soviet way through enhancing its accessibility. The USSR has assiduously sought early diplomatic arrangements with each newly formed country from this same motivation. Beyond these rather unremarkable observations, we should note that the USSR has applied itself particularly to treaty relations with its immediate neighbors (of the developing world as well as the West). The formation of a reliable buffer zone, or *cordon sanitaire*, about Soviet borders long has taken priority over perceived disagreements on political systems. Thus Soviet relations with the kingdom of Afghanistan, anticommunist Turkey, neutral Pakistan, and anticommunist Iran explicitly emphasize cordiality and cooperation across differing social and economic systems. We shall examine Soviet treaty policy in greater detail in a later chapter of this book.

Table VII-10[34]   Treaties Concluded between the Soviet Union and 26 Developing States, 1954–1962

	1954	1955	1956	1957	1958	1959	1960	1961	1962	TOTAL
Afghanistan	5	6	6	3	4	8	9	2	6	49
Burma	0	5	3	2	0	1	3	1	2	17
Cambodia	0	0	2	4	4	3	4	1	1	19
Ceylon	0	0	1	0	5	1	0	1	6	14
Ethiopia	0	0	1	0	0	4	2	3	2	12
Ghana				0	1	2	5	11	2	21
Guinea					1	5	7	5	4	22
India	1	6	4	2	4	7	9	6	6	45
Indonesia	0	0	4	1	0	6	10	9	3	33
Iran	4	4	1	6	6	0	1	1	2	25
Iraq	0	0	0	0	2	6	3	1	3	15
Israel	1	1	0	0	0	0	0	0	0	2
Jordan	0	0	0	0	0	0	0	0	0	0
Lebanon	3	1	2	0	0	1	0	1	0	8
Mali							0	4	4	8
Morocco			0	1	3	2	2	1	2	11
Nepal	0	0	1	0	1	3	2	1	1	9
Pakistan	0	0	1	1	0	0	1	1	0	4
Somali Republic							1	5	2	8
Syria	0	2	4	5				1	3	15
Sudan			1	0	0	2	1	6	1	11
Thailand	0	0	1	0	0	0	0	0	0	1
Tunisia			0	1	1	1	2	2	3	10
Turkey	0	0	0	0	0	0	1	2	3	6
UAR (Egypt)	4	2	5	3	9	2	7	0	6	38
Yemen	0	1	3	1	0	1	2	1	1	10
TOTALS	18	28	40	30	41	55	72	66	63	413

Table VII-11 suggests the continuing emphasis placed upon education of the youth of developing areas in the Soviet Union. Supplemented by the other Communist party-states (with the harmonious effort now torn asunder by the conflict with the Chinese), Soviet policy in this regard has not altered from the days of Stalin except to expand in scope with the new emphasis on winning noncommunist friends. Friendship University, opened in Moscow in the fall of 1960 for the special purpose of training students from the developing countries, has an extensive genealogy going back to the Comintern's University for the Toilers of the East, among whose alumni are many of the ranking officials of the nonruling Communist Parties today.[35] In the

[34] Simon, *op. cit.,* p. 92.
[35] "Friendship University—The Early Versions," *Survey,* No. 39 (July, 1961), pp. 18–23.

past decade the Party qualifications for prospective students have disappeared, and the propaganda and political training are no longer advertised as such; it would be naive to conclude that the education dispensed by Friendship University is any the less politically motivated. It is difficult to obtain reliable and up-to-date statistics on the numbers of students from developing countries studying in the Soviet Union. U.S. State Department estimates for the 1960–1961 academic year showed 100 students from Latin America (excluding 100 more from Cuba), 441 from Africa, 664 from the Middle East (including Egypt), and 362 from other Asian countries enrolled in Soviet institutions of higher education.[36] Figure VII-5 shows a rapid increase in the number of African students studying in the party-states between 1960 and the end of 1963. It is probably safe to assume that the number in the USSR kept pace proportionately. Figures at the close of 1963 showed 443 Latin Americans (excluding Cubans) then enrolled in the USSR, more than quadrupling the 1960 total. We may conclude from these incomplete data that there has been a general increase in the student training program of the Soviet Union to correspond with the increases of other facets of Soviet interaction with the developing countries over the past decade.

The burden of this chapter has been to explicate the changes in Soviet policy toward the developing areas of the world in the decade dominated by Khrushchev's formulations at the XXth Party Congress. We have suggested the extent of the shift wrought in prior Soviet policy toward these areas and in so doing we have illuminated the new pragmatism adopted by the Soviet decision-makers. The extent to which the new policies challenged the West and loosened the rigid stalemate into which the cold war had been drawn in the early 1950's has become apparent in examination of Soviet programs, each of which finds competitive American and Chinese efforts arrayed against it. We conclude with the proposition that in commiting their state to the new strategies, Khrushchev and his successors have committed themselves irrevocably. Wagering time to be on the side of socialism and counterposing the Soviet economic model to the industrialized West, they have disavowed Stalin's unimaginative reliance upon opportunistic employment of force. Were they to have second thoughts, they would not only have to discard a vast corpus of ideological rationalization and incur great hostility in the developing states, but they would find the Chinese occupying their former ground and unwilling to allow a graceful retreat. The struggle

[36] *Sino-Soviet Bloc Exchanges with the Free World in 1960,* U.S. Department of State, Bureau of Intelligence and Research, Unclassified Report No. 8401 (Washington, D.C.: Government Printing Office, February 1, 1961), pp. 11–14.

Table VII-11[37]   Student Exchange between the Communist System and the Developing States, 1956–1962

	TOTAL NO. STUDENTS SENT TO COMMUNIST SYSTEM 1956–1962	AVERAGE ANNUAL NO. STUDENTS TO SYSTEM 1956–1962*	STUDENTS IN HIGHER EDUCATION 1956**
Afghanistan	80	11.4	1,503
Burma	70	10.0	12,695
Cambodia	80	11.4	822
Ceylon	45	6.4	6,322
Ethiopia	60	8.6	827
Ghana	420	70.0	2,700
Guinea	580	116.0	5,285
India	200	28.6	1,044,848
Indonesia	830	118.6	44,802
Iran	less than 40	counted as 0	18,805
Iraq	2,755	393.6	12,000
Israel	less than 40	counted as 0	15,272
Jordan	less than 40	counted as 0	1,345 (1962)
Lebanon	less than 40	counted as 0	5,676
Mali	280	93.3	3,106 (1960)
Morocco	150	21.4	3,388
Nepal	110	15.7	4,387
Pakistan	less than 40	counted as 0	144,848
Somali Republic	450	150.0	294 (1960)
Sudan	290	41.4	3,144
Syria	555	79.3	10,126
Thailand	less than 40	counted as 0	50,833
Tunisia	40	5.6	2,333
Turkey	40	5.7	54,069
UAR (Egypt)	775	110.7	97,730
Yemen	400	57.1	696 (1958)

* Preindependence years not counted in deriving the average.
** Secondary students had to be counted for Guinea, Mali, and Yemen, since no statistics on students in higher education were available. The number of students for the Somali Republic in higher education was so small that its secondary students were also counted.
Sources: United Nations Social and Economic Council, *Statistical Yearbook*, 1963.

with China, the struggle for socialism in the developing areas, and the peaceful competition with "imperialism" all rest heavily upon the validity of the premises of 1956.

[37] Simon, *op. cit.*, pp. 93–94.

Escalation, deterrence, fear of "gaps," reduction of tensions, balance of terror—these expressions, describing processes and attitudes which were largely unknown fifteen years ago, are becoming clichés today. The context is the cold war, but the issue is the potentially hot thermonuclear war which "will destroy us unless we do something about it." Disagreement on the "us" that will be destroyed has been less acute than disagreement on who the "we" are and what the "something" is that must be done. Who are, or ought to be, the "we," and what is, or ought to be, that "something"? In this chapter we would like to offer a fresh perspective for assessing these concerns.

DUPRÉEL'S THEOREM

In 1948, Professor Eugene Dupréel of the University of Brussels published a lengthy study entitled *General Sociology.*[2] In a chapter on the "Evolution of Extended Conflicts" he proposed that, "While the character of the aggressor and defender intermingle and merge, the opposing forces tend to balance each other. They take the same forms to meet and neutralize each other more completely."[3] In a protracted conflict, the opponents must employ the same means (*moyens mis en d'oeuvre*); if they do not, that side which fails to modernize these particular means to match those of the other side,

---

[1] This Chapter is based in part on material drawn from Jan F. Triska and David D. Finley, "Soviet-American Relations: A Multiple Symmetry Model," *Journal of Conflict Revolution,* IX, No. 1 (March, 1965), 37–53. By permission.

[2] Eugene Dupréel, *Sociologie general* (Paris: Presses Universitaires de France, 1948). Cf. also Andrew M. Scott, "Challenge and Response: A Tool for the Analysis of International Affairs," *The Review of Politics,* XVIII, No. 2 (April, 1956), pp. 207–226; George Liska, *International Equilibrium* (Cambridge: Harvard University Press, 1957).

[3] Dupréel, *op. cit.,* p. 151.

other things being equal, is doomed. The moral issue of aggressor versus defender become irrelevant and immaterial for the outcome of the conflict, which is maintained or decided by the balance or imbalance of the mutual means.[4]

Few would deny that Dupréel's theorem describes the symmetry of *weapons-systems* build-up in the cold war of the past fifteen years. The two opposing forces have done their utmost to surpass—and as a consequence they continually meet, balance, and neutralize—each others' weapons systems. In the process of the cold war these weapons systems become deterrents of the hot war. Should either side's perceptions of equilibrium or near equilibrium of deterrents be sufficiently disturbed, a precipitous response might ensue. Given this alternative, the prolonged cold-war conflict, sustained in part by mutual images of military-hardware symmetry, is certainly preferable. (We will return later to a concommitant of maintaining this dynamic symmetry—the inherent danger involved in the inexorable escalation of deterrents.)

Thus, on the *micro* level of specific-weapons systems,[5] the American development of atomic-fission weapons first and then thermonuclear weapons led to feverish Soviet scientific research and capital investment in this area— and resulted in atomic and thermonuclear parity or near-parity. Conversely, the 1957 Sputnik caused consternation in the U.S. before eurythmy was once again restored. Similarly, missile-delivery systems have absorbed much of the military development on both sides.

On a *macro* level, too, in the military confrontation, the operation of Dupréel's proposition is observable. The establishment of the North Atlantic Treaty Organization (in itself a Western response to the postwar Soviet

[4] Charles A. McClelland has observed the tendency of nations in conflict to engage in "trade-off sequences" and to develop parallel "counterpart structures": "The Acute International Crisis," *World Politics,* XIV (October, 1961), 182–204. The related concept of "mirror images"—a psychological tendency of opponents in a conflict situation to perceive each other's motives and actions similarly and to be guided in their own actions accordingly—is presented by, *inter alia,* Urie Bronfenbrenner, "The Mirror Image in Soviet-American Relations: A Social Psychologist's Report," *Journal of Social Issues,* XVII, No. 3 (1961), 45–56.

Strategic use of the latter tendency by one party in a conflict situation is explored by Paul Linebarger, "Taipei and Peking: The Confronting Republics," *Journal of International Affairs,* XI, No. 2 (1957), 135–142.

[5] Within the military sector of the spectrum of East-West interaction we conceive specific weapons systems, e.g., the U.S. Polaris, to occupy a subordinate place to international military alliances, such as NATO. The specific weapons system is just one part of the hardware which serves the military alliance. We thus distinguish along a continuum of complexity within the military sector by saying the weapons system occupies a *micro* level and the alliance a *macro* level.

military threats in Europe)—a supranational military agency designed to reshape the role, scope, and organization of the U.S. and Western Europe vis-à-vis the USSR and its bloc—prompted in turn a similar Soviet and bloc reaction. Formally, at least, the Warsaw Treaty Organization presents a near mirror-image of NATO—a concept of unified military resources rationalized as a Soviet-East European defense system against the NATO threat.

Dupréel's theorem, axiomatic in the weapons-deterrents sector of the cold war, appears to have validity in other sectors as well. In fact we submit that the stimulus-response sequence, upon which Dupréel's theorem is founded, is a basic propensity of most interactions encompassed in the East-West dialogue to which we conveniently refer as the *cold war,* a propensity by now so well established that any stimulus inserted into the process by one of the opponents may be expected to bring about a *proportionate response in kind* from the other. If the multiple-symmetry model we are about to construct is indeed a simplified description of reality, it should fit not only the military subsystem at two different levels, but into other subsystems within the conflictual-interaction process as a whole.

Diplomacy, an essential subsystem of interaction between states, serves as a convenient example and a testing ground. In a broad sense, "diplomacy" includes three further subsystems—or types of diplomacy—characteristic of the cold war, namely *conventional, open,* and *covert diplomacy.* All of these originated with the West. *Conventional diplomacy,* negotiation of international differences and demands outside the public eye by officially accredited diplomatic representatives, has been practiced along the lines established by the European powers at the Congress of Vienna in 1815. *Open diplomacy,* the conduct of international negotiations in public, has been with us at least since the League of Nations. And *covert diplomacy,* i.e., foreign intelligence and espionage activity, the time-honored left hand of conventional diplomacy, is exemplified far back in the Old Testament.[6] All three types, however, have been modernized in application by the Soviet Union. They have been elaborated and intensified to such a degree that, taken together, they represent a new and qualitatively different diplomacy— one which has had to be matched in all its aspects by opponents of the Soviet Union, because it has been made a critical instrument in the cold-war dialogue. Historically, the Soviet Union had to adopt the methods of Western diplomacy, and, in turn, the diplomatic asymmetry which the Soviet Union evoked by its thorough exploitation of the three types of diplomacy generated an irresistible pressure upon the West to re-establish equilibrium

[6] Allen Dulles, "The Craft of Intelligence," *Harper's* (April, 1963), p. 133. See also Dulles' book, *The Craft of Intelligence* (New York: Harper and Row, Publishers, Inc., 1963).

as soon as possible. The Western perception of disadvantage prompted by the Soviet-initiated disequilibrium led to a series of Western responses designed to restore balance to the whole diplomatic sector.

SOVIET DIPLOMACY: CONVENTIONAL, OPEN, AND COVERT

Soviet Russia was not initially inclined toward the practice of *conventional diplomacy*. But it was one thing for Leon Trotsky, the first People's Commissar of Foreign Affairs, to proclaim that he would not deal with the discredited professional diplomats of capitalism and to engage instead in direct and immediate support of communist revolutions abroad; it was another thing for the young, inexperienced, revolutionary Soviet state to survive in an established and hostile world until the next round of revolutions came about—especially since the next round of revolutions took a long time in coming. The resulting incongruous, contradictory situation demanded, on the one hand, acceptance of the means of intercourse used by the enemy, making the embrace of conventional diplomacy imperative for Soviet Russia. On the other hand, the impossibility of giving up the objectives of world revolution, without which there would have been no Soviet Russia—and without which there would be no communist support for the Soviet government abroad—demanded the retention of an unconventional and revolutionary diplomacy designed to overthrow the old world. Unable to survive without conforming to the universally accepted diplomatic conduct but unwilling to sacrifice their unique strength for it, the Bolsheviks decided, after much soul-searching, to do both—to conduct their diplomacy on both levels at the same time. To make this combination palatable to their capitalist opposites, they not only pushed the ideological, revolutionary, and subversive diplomacy underground, into the realm of *covert diplomacy*, but they hopefully covered it up by sustained verbal exhortations "to all governments" to terminate the traditional and "discredited" diplomacy of the past and to replace it by an *open diplomacy* of the future. They called for an elected diplomatic corps representing the people—replacing the professional diplomatic representatives of governments—meeting in open forums for all to see, hear, and judge. Such a democratic diplomacy, they reiterated, was the only way to conduct foreign affairs. The 1917 Decree on Peace, the first act of Soviet foreign policy, which called for "open negotiations . . . in full view of all the people," was just such an "enlightened" proposal.

Forced by their opposition, the Communists accepted conventional diplomacy (the story of Chicherin at Genoa in 1922 is too familiar to need retelling here); in turn, however, they not only forced their enemies to accept a greatly modernized system of covert diplomacy, but they succeeded in considerably broadening both the conventional diplomacy and the open diplomacy of the League of Nations and the United Nations as well. It appears that Dupréel's theorem was being borne out in this sector too.

In *conventional diplomacy*, the sustained Soviet insistence that the agents of its foreign-trade monopoly, as a state monopoly, must be accorded special, nonreciprocal rights and privileges abroad has paid off handsomely. In most of the countries of the world which trade with the USSR, there are now permanent Soviet trade delegations, which, as the sole Soviet business representatives, enjoy the same diplomatic privileges and immunities as accredited Soviet diplomats, namely personal immunity, extraterritoriality, immunity from taxation, and so on, entirely without benefit of precedent, custom, and tradition. They are thus doubling the Soviet diplomatic corps in these countries. The persistent demands of other governments to equal and thus neutralize this Soviet diplomatic advantage have not proved too successful. It is true that, on a bilateral level, some *quid pro quo* arrangements have usually been found and employed on an *ad hoc* basis. On other levels and in general, however, no acceptable formula has ever been discovered.

In *open diplomacy*, also, Soviet Russia accepted a challenge and then returned it in kind. The Soviet advocacy of "open negotiations" as the most democratic kind of diplomacy was at first verbal. With time, however, the advantages to be had through actual application of open diplomacy for the Soviet cause were recognized. In international organizations, agencies, and conferences the Soviet representatives, in their minority position, have relied on "bold minority" tactics. Originally elaborated by Lenin as a tactic for the Party in a parliamentary situation, the Soviet "fraction"—a solid-core unit endeavoring to achieve and maintain minority control of the forum— became an effective device to turn the Soviet minority position into advantage. The Party's long minority experience afforded a wealth of information and techniques valuable for such purposes. In the United Nations, for example, Soviet "bold minority" tactics have proved effective enough to permit the USSR and its fraternal socialist allies frequently to neutralize and balance the numerically superior Western position.[7]

Carrying open diplomacy to "its logical conclusion," namely, the "people to people" level, the Soviet Union established a number of Soviet-sponsored international organizations and conferences which, like the World Peace Council, "are truly universal and represent . . . not the governments but the peoples themselves. In this is (their) particular strength and indisputable

[7] See Chapter X.

moral authority."[8] The Soviet World Federation of Trade Unions, the International Union of Students, the International Federation of Resistance Movements, the International Association of Democratic Lawyers, the World Federation of Scientific Workers, and other similar organizations and agencies illustrate the Soviet endeavor on this level.

The major Soviet advantage in open diplomacy appears to rest, however, in the personal diplomacy practiced on the highest levels, the much publicized summit diplomacy of heads of governments. Khrushchev may not have been the head of state, as is the American or the French president or the British queen, but like Adenauer or Macmillan he was the chief of his government and thus the most important Soviet executive officer. As he was the Chairman of the Council of Ministers, principal member of the Party Presidium, and First Secretary of the Party (as well as Chairman of the Party's special Bureau of the RSFSR), Khrushchev was the principal Soviet decision-maker. This was the key to his effectiveness in summit diplomacy; he could verbally commit the whole of Soviet power on the spot, openly and publicly. This his opposite numbers, whether heads of state or heads of government or both, could not do. This is why summitry was attractive to Khrushchev (and to Stalin before him). Certainly his considerable freedom of action facilitated the dramatic act, the play to world public opinion, that has recurrently characterized Soviet diplomacy.

But perhaps the major Soviet innovation rests in covert diplomacy, the third subsystem of its diplomacy, which includes *foreign intelligence and espionage*. If ever difference in degree led to differences in kind, or as Lenin put it, citing Marx, if "quantity turned into quality," Soviet intelligence activities abroad would qualify; through sheer numbers, scope, and volume, this Soviet realm of endeavor qualitatively changed modern diplomacy. The veritable armada of Soviet spies, intelligence agents, and counterintelligence agents has permeated international relations as never before. Judging from individual accounts of escapees and defectors from Soviet diplomatic and intelligence services over the last twenty years, their numbers, operating throughout the world, is in the tens of thousands.

Soviet foreign-intelligence agents are either attached to the Soviet diplomatic mission in a country or operate outside the Soviet embassy and unknown to it. Although little is known about the latter group, which apparently has several branches responsible to and operating under the guidance of parent intelligence organizations in Moscow, the former group has been

---

[8] S. V. Molodtsov, *Sovetskoe gosudarstvo i pravo*, No. 7 (1951), p. 23; cf. also *The Supplement, New Times*, No. 28 (July, 27 1956).

identified and described by Kaznacheev and others before him.[9] It includes the Political Intelligence Service, the military intelligence, the economic intelligence, and the Tenth or Special Department of the Ministry of Foreign Affairs.

The core of Soviet foreign-intelligence personnel operating from Soviet embassies abroad is the *Political Intelligence Service*, the foreign branch of the Soviet security police (KGB), which is in practice directly subordinate to the Party's Central Committee. Its officers have diplomatic rank and thus enjoy diplomatic immunity. They are the professionals. With them work selected members of the local Soviet diplomatic corps recruited on the spot as "associate members" on a part-time basis while retaining their full diplomatic staff membership. Additionally, there are code clerks, messengers, typists, drivers, and other technical personnel attached to the Political Intelligence Service who have normally only service passports and do not enjoy diplomatic immunity. The *military-intelligence* officers are directly subordinate to the intelligence branch of the Soviet general staff and operate through the Military Attaché's office. The *economic-intelligence* officers are subordinate both to the KGB and either the Ministry of Foreign Trade or the State Committee for Foreign Economic Relations. And officers of the *Tenth or Special Department of the Ministry of Foreign Affairs* enjoy, because of their mission—overall security of personnel—an unusual degree of autonomy within the Foreign Ministry and within the embassies. A watchdog, technical agency, the Tenth Department is in fact the KGB section in the Foreign Ministry.

This Soviet intelligence apparatus attached to the respective Soviet Missions Abroad is further amplified not only by the Soviet intelligence groups operating outside the Soviet embassies, but also by satellite intelligence personnel, organized along the same lines as the Soviet establishment; native-born agents, recruited in the respective countries either for general and continuing service or functionally and *ad hoc* for the job they know best;

[9] Aleksandr Kaznacheev, *Inside a Soviet Embassy* (Philadelphia: J. B. Lippincott Company, 1962). See also Walter Krivitsky, *In Stalin's Secret Service* (New York: Harper & Row, Publisher, Inc., 1939); Alexander Orlov, *The Secret History of Stalin's Crimes* (New York: Random House, 1953); Igor Gousenko, *The Iron Curtain*, 1st ed. (New York: E. P. Dutton & Co., Inc., 1948); Vladimir Petrov (with Evdokia Petrov), *Empire of Fear* (N.Y.: Frederick A. Praeger, Inc., 1956); V. Petrov, *My Retreat from Russia*, trans. by David Chavchavadse (New Haven: Yale University Press, 1950); Peter Deriabin (with Frank Gibney), *The Secret World*, 1st ed. (Garden City, N.Y.: Doubleday & Company, Inc., 1959); Nikolai Khokhlov, *In the Name of Conscience*, trans. by Emily Kingsberry (N.Y.: David McKay Company, Inc., 1959); Joseph Swiatlo, *Behind the Scene of the Party and Bezpieka* (New York: Free Europe Committee, 1955); Pawol Monat (with John Dille), *Spy in the US*, 1st ed. (New York: Harper & Row, Publishers, Inc., 1962).

and members of local Communist Parties who offer a welcome reservoir of talent, skill, and enthusiasm.

U.S. RESPONSE: THE CIA

The Soviet diplomatic system, carried simultaneously on the three levels or subsystems, unbalanced the post-World War II East-West diplomatic relations. The chief Western antagonist, the United States, could not afford to let the Soviet stimulus go unanswered. Perceiving less "challenge" in conventional[10] and open diplomacy, where bilateral reciprocity, if not multilateral equilibrium, could be maintained by updated traditional responses without much innovation, the United States assessed the covert-diplomacy "gap" as a critical threat to the United States and the West within the diplomatic sector of the cold war. "In order to meet and neutralize" the Soviet-generated asymmetry, the U.S. responded in kind to the Soviet stimulus.

The publicly available data today not only confirm the existence of an elaborate U.S. intelligence organization but seem to indicate that the number of U.S. intelligence personnel, the scope and volume of their activities, as well as the techniques they use, quite effectively match their Soviet counterparts.

The U.S. foreign intelligence has grown from insignificance to formidable

[10] The Soviet monopoly of foreign trade, a Soviet innovation in conventional diplomacy, caused many headaches but no real consternation among foreign governments and businessmen: "The demands of the Soviet trade treaty partners to equalize and thus neutralize the considerable Soviet advantage in foreign trading are almost as old as the Soviet foreign trade monopoly. In the late 1920s, a number of European businessmen, especially in Germany, sought to establish a centralized and uniform Office of the European Business World, which, like the Soviet foreign trade monopoly, would engage in foreign trade on an organized, collective, central basis and become a clearinghouse for all existing European trade with the Soviet Union." (See Zaitless, "Sowjetrussland in völkerrechtlichen Verkehr," *Osteuropa*, VII, No. 12 (1931–1932), 709–718.) This attempt has been severely rebuked by the Soviet officials and Soviet press. (See, for example, L. B. Krasin, *Problemes de commerce exterieur* (Moscow-Leningrad: Gosizdat., 1928), p. 258.)

In 1954, a similar plan was considered by the Council of Europe. Based on the assumption that East-West trade should be viewed as "part of the general policy of the West toward the Soviet bloc countries," the West, forming its own foreign trade monopoly, would through such a common action preserve the freedom of engaging in trade with the communist countries and increase the profitability of such trade to the West as a whole. "If the Communist countries value trade most for political purposes, the West should form its own monopoly. It should in fact form a Trading Corporation through which all trade with Soviet bloc countries would be channeled. The organization for European Economic Cooperation provides the framework within which such a corporation could function. Profits, which might be considerable in the case of commodities and equipment whose scarcity value is great in Soviet bloc countries, insofar as they were not needed to offset proportions. The crucial push in the present direction was administered by the outbreak of the cold war; there was no Central Intelligence Agency before 1947. In the years just prior to U.S. entry into World War I, Army Intelligence—the only formal U.S. foreign-intelligence service—consisted of four people: two officers and two clerks. On the eve of World War II, the U.S. foreign intelligence again was understaffed, uncoordinated, and starved for funds. Congress was loath even to sustain military attachés abroad, as it considered the job a rather useless vacation for the officers involved. The formally designated intelligence division of the State Department included only eighteen persons as late as 1943. President Roosevelt is said to have told Major General (then Colonel) William J. Donovan, who was to set up the OSS, in 1941, "You will have to begin with nothing. We have no intelligence service."[11] It is true that during both world wars the U.S. intelligence services grew rapidly—to over twelve hundred persons in World War I and to around twelve thousand in World War II. But cutbacks after both wars appear to have been speedy and far-reaching.

While U.S. intelligence efforts were reduced progressively during the inter-war years, after World War II President Truman established a National Intelligence Authority consisting of the Secretaries of State, War, and Navy

losses deliberately incurred, could be used for the benefit of underdeveloped countries." ("The Political Aspect of East-West Trade: The Soviet Approach," *World Today,* XII, No. 10 (1956), 416.)

Would not such a concerted move "remove the element of propaganda which at present distorts the true significance of many deals between Soviet bloc countries and those of the Middle and Far East, at the expense of the West, by combating more successfully than hitherto economic penetration and increasing the volume of funds available for investment in underdeveloped countries?" (*Ibid.,* p. 417.)

"A high official of the United State government," reported James Reston in *The New York Times* on December 2, 1958, "discussing the problem of meeting the Communist (trade) offensive, commented this afternoon: 'It is politically impossible for us to discuss in public the radical changes we shall have to make to deal effectively with the Soviet economic offensive. They control all of their foreign trade. They can use it as a political instrument regardless of cost. They can take losses to drive competition out of a given market precisely as large producers once were able to do to eliminate small competitors in this country.

" 'We have been discussing quietly inside our own Government for six months *the need to establish an overseas trade monopoly to compet. with the Soviet monopoly on equal terms,* but this is so foreign to our normal way of doing business that we dare not mention it in public' " (italics added). But, said Reston, "the Administration was just as divided on less radical policies than the creation of a monopoly for the sake of United States products overseas." Jan F. Triska and Robert M. Slusser, *The Theory, Law and Policy of Soviet Treaties* (Stanford: Stanford University Press, 1962), pp. 327–328.

[11] Quoted by Harry H. Ransom, *Central Intelligence and National Security* (Cambridge: Harvard University Press, 1958), p. 58.

and including the Presidential Military Advisor. The National Intelligence Authority founded the Central Intelligence Group as its operational arm, which Congress replaced in 1947 with the Central Intelligence Agency. The CIA was set up as an independent organization functioning under the National Security Council and coordinating all U.S. foreign-intelligence agencies and activities—State Department, Army, Navy, Air Force, Atomic Energy Commission, FBI, and National Security Agency. The CIA became a remarkably similar organizational counterpart of the Soviet Foreign Intelligence Directorate of the KGB.

Responding to cold-war demands, the agencies coordinated by the CIA as well as the CIA itself (in its role as an information-gathering and evaluating organ) have grown greatly since 1947. Educated estimates put the total number of personnel serving the U.S. intelligence community, at least part-time, at somewhere between twenty and thirty thousand persons.[12] The CIA budget, separate from other, subordinate intelligence agencies, is usually estimated at between one-half and one billion dollars annually.[13] And the CIA headquarters, second largest office building in the Washington area (the largest is the Pentagon), can house 10,000 employees. What we can gather from the rarely publicized activities of the U.S. intelligence services— e.g., the U-2 incident, information on Soviet activities in Cuba, apprehension of Soviet intelligence agents in the U.S., the Penkovsky affair, and so on— indicates that the U.S. intelligence community is now well equipped to meet the challenge introduced by the USSR in this third realm of diplomacy. The cold war in this area is an active one. It is a largely unknown, undercover, secret war waged by full-time, highly skilled professionals—the intelligence agents, spies, and counterspies—on both sides.[14] An expert assessment of the activities on both sides, data for which are not publicly available, would be necessary before saying confidently that symmetry has in fact been restored. The former director of the CIA, however, strongly implies that this is now the case.[15]

THE BERLIN BLOCKADE

Let us turn briefly to two dramatic sequences of post-World War II Soviet-American interaction which provide some further evidence for an analysis

[12] *Ibid.,* p. 82.

[13] Allen Dulles indicates that it is considerably below a billion. *Op. cit.,* p. 132.

[14] For recent additions to the voluminous literature, see Christopher Felix (pseud.), *A Short Course in the Secret War* (New York: E. P. Dutton & Co., Inc., 1963); and Sanche de Gramont, *The Secret War* (New York: G. P. Putnam's Sons, 1962).

[15] See Dulles, *op. cit.,* p. 174.

of reciprocity in conflict. First, the Berlin Blockade of 1948–1949.[16]

At a conference in London in the spring of 1948, the Western powers and the USSR tried to work out an agreement for the future of Germany. They were unable to do so; and the West decided to act alone. At a later meeting, the U.S., Great Britain, France, Belgium, the Netherlands, and Luxemburg determined to convene a West German assembly to draw up a constitution. The Communist party-states delivered a violent protest to this move. Marshal Vasili Sokolovsky, the Soviet Military Occupation Governor, walked out of the Allied Control Council, and the USSR began to tighten control of Western traffic across its German frontiers. The final blow, in the eyes of the Soviets, was the reform of West German currency. German economic reconstruction was hampered by the lack of stability of the old reichsmark, but the Big Four had never come to terms over the distribution of a new currency. As an economically unsound Germany was viewed as dangerous, the Western powers finally decided to issue a new currency for their zones. Official notice was given to Marshal Sokolovsky on June 18, 1948. On that day the Soviets began the blockade steps against western Berlin— ostensibly to prevent a flood of devalued currency from entering East Germany.

The USSR first halted passenger traffic between its zone and West Germany; later it extended the prohibition to include all foot and road traffic "for technical reasons connected with the repair of bridges." Pressure was put on West Berlin by curtailing the supply of electricity generated in the Russian sector and by stopping food deliveries. Marshal Sokolovsky announced to the Berlin population that the four-power city *Kommandatura* had ceased to exist.

In its response, the West reaffirmed its authority in Berlin. Could the material needs of the $2\frac{1}{4}$ million civilians and the military personnel in West Berlin be met by an extended aid operation? If so, the blockade could be defeated. Great Britain and the United States determined to attempt an airlift and also began a counterblockade which stopped movement by rail

---

[16] The events of this period as seen from several different points of view are recorded, *inter alia,* in the following publications: Lowell Bennett, *Berlin Bastion: the Epic of Post-War Berlin* (Frankfurt am Main: F. Rudl, 1951); Lucius D. Clay, *Decision in Germany* (New York: Doubleday & Company, Inc., 1959); Max Charles, *Berlin Blockade* (London: A. Wingate, 1959); W. Phillips Davidson, *The Berlin Blockade: A Study in Cold War Politics* (Princeton: Princeton University Press, 1958); Curt Riess, *The Berlin Story* (New York: The Dial Press, Inc., 1952); Robert Rodrigo, *Berlin Airlift* (London: Cassell, 1960); Bruce L. Smith, *The Governance of Berlin* (New York: Carnegie Endowment for International Peace, 1959); and *The Soviet Union and the Berlin Question* (Moscow: USSR Ministry of Foreign Affairs, 1948).

through their zones to and from the Soviet zone. By August, the blockade and counterblockade sealed off road, rail, and water routes between East and West Germany, thus isolating Berlin and making the airlift essential.

It was not certain at the time that the Soviet blockade could be overcome by flying supplies into Berlin. Soviet fighter planes were making occasional excursions into the Western air corridors in July making flying there dangerous for the Western pilots. The USSR also issued warnings about the air-traffic rules, alleging that the West was violating them and saying that planes found outside the 20-mile corridors might be forced down. A first announcement to this effect was made in July. When the warning was repeated in November, Western officials were worried that bad weather would cause planes inadvertently to stray outside the limits. The United States therefore warned in turn that the Russians would be held responsible for injuries to American flyers or damage to their planes. The British issued a similar warning, and in spite of Soviet threats and occasional interference, the airlift carried an enormous tonnage. Accidents occurred. Between June 26, 1948 and May 12, 1949, sixty-one persons were killed. (In ten American crashes, thirty-two military personnel and one civilian lost their lives, in seven British crashes, sixteen RAF men, six British civilians, and six German civilians lost their lives.) But in spite of these losses, the airlift was successful in overcoming the blockade, and Soviet interference with it was ineffectual.

Meanwhile, the struggle over the currency issue continued. Though the West did not keep to the agreements to treat Germany as one economic unit, they still hoped to do so for Berlin. But on June 23 the Soviets issued their own currency, announcing that it was to be used in the East zone and *all* of Berlin. The Big Three then proceeded to block the Soviet move by introducing the Western currency into their respective Berlin sectors. The Berlin city government decided that Sokolovsky's order would apply only to the Soviet sector and that the two currencies would circulate side by side as legal tender within the city.

Negotiations for settling the blockade crisis were frustrated by the opposing positions of the East and West. The Western powers said they were willing to discuss Berlin questions provided that free traffic was established in Germany. The Soviets insisted on discussing Berlin only as part of the larger German problem, as Berlin lay entirely in the Soviet zone. Concerning currency, Foreign Minister Molotov insisted that the bank of issuance for Berlin be located in the Eastern sector. This was agreeable. But four-power supervision of the bank, since it would mean control by the West, was unacceptable to the USSR. It was finally decided that the bank would be subject to a four-power commission, and that the four military governors would work out the regulations. At the meetings for this purpose, however, Sokolovsky would not confine himself to the subjects agreed on for discussion. The Western negotiators even had two interviews with Stalin, but no compromise resulted from the discussions at any level.

The Western governments became convinced that the "Soviet attitude" would not change and refused to continue negotiating. On September 26, 1948 they referred the problem to the UN Security Council. The USSR insisted that the UN did not have competence, but it did not interfere with the voting and subsequent discussion. The neutrals tried strenuously to work out a compromise, there being a widespread fear of war. Secretary General Trygve Lie suggested a four-power conference; a committee of experts was set up, but it dissolved itself after failure to reach any agreement.

A breakthrough finally came at the end of January, 1949. At an interview with an American journalist, Stalin made no mention of the troublesome currency question when giving his views of the German situation. This was taken to be a hopeful sign. Discussion and clarification of positions followed. On May 5, 1949, after ten and a half months of blockade, the four powers announced in New York their decision to lift the restrictions on May 12 and to hold a Foreign Ministers' meeting in Paris later that month. The meeting itself brought no settlement on Germany, but the blockade episode was over.

THE 1962 CUBAN CRISIS

The second dramatic sequence we include here covers the tense days of the Kennedy-Khrushchev confrontation over Soviet missiles in Cuba.[17]

After Fidel Castro assumed control of the Cuban nation on January 1, 1959, the United States viewed events in that country with mounting alarm. Expropriation of American property and closer ties between Cuba and the communist system served to confirm American fears. To quell a possible Soviet-inspired, Marxist-oriented engine of revolution in this hemisphere, the CIA-aided Bay of Pigs invasion was carried out with Cuban-exile manpower in April of 1961, an ill-conceived project which proved a total failure and highly embarrassing to the United States.

Early in 1962, the Soviet Union announced an agreement to supply arms and military technicians to Cuba. In April, President Kennedy warned that the United States would employ "whatever means may be necessary" to

[17] For a full account, see Elie Abel, *The Cuban Missile Crisis* (Philadelphia: J. B. Lippincott Company, 1966); and *The Cuban Crisis: A Documentary Record* (New York: Foreign Policy Association, 1963).

prevent aggression by Cuba against any part of the American hemisphere—stating at the same time, however, that the current build-up in Cuba showed no "significant offensive capability."

The situation gradually grew more tense, and the Soviet military build-up in Cuba gave rise to increasing disquiet in the United States. Early in September, Kennedy asked Congress for authority to call 150,000 reservists to active duty should the international situation make it advisable. A few days later, the USSR warned that any United States attack on Cuba or Soviet ships bound for Cuba could mean war. On September 13, Kennedy said the United States would move swiftly against Cuba if and when necessary. The Kennedy Administration still had not moved from its position that the Cuban weapons were only defensive, and it was resisting mounting pressure from Congress and other quarters to act against Cuba. On September 25, Castro announced that the USSR would collaborate in building a Cuban port as headquarters for a joint fishing fleet. The next day the House approved a Senate resolution for putting Congress on record as serving notice that the United States would use military force if necessary against a Cuban threat to United States security. The tension continued to grow, and on October 12, the USSR expelled the First Secretary of the United States Embassy in Moscow on spy charges, the second United States diplomat to be expelled in one week. Although the Kennedy Administration continued to maintain its public standpoint that the weapons in Cuba were only defensive, photographic evidence of offensive weapons had been received.

The crisis became acute on October 22, when President Kennedy announced a "quarantine" of Cuba by air and sea to exclude further shipments of offensive weapons. The surprise generated by his announcement was considerable, both in the USSR and in the United States. On the following day, Soviet officials challenged the right of the United States to institute such a blockade and asserted that such an action was risking nuclear war. The Warsaw Pact countries were alerted. Meanwhile, the Organization of American States, hitherto only lukewarm in support of the Kennedy Administration's Cuban policy, unanimously voted to authorize the use of armed force to prevent shipments of offensive weapons to Cuba. Kennedy's action received widespread and rapid support from the West.

On October 24, the blockade became effective; the first confrontation between Soviet and American ships was awaited with anxiety. It was widely recognized that a truculent challenge of the blockade by a Soviet ship could lead to its sinking, an act of war which could trigger a full-scale nuclear exchange between the United States and the USSR. The United Nations Secretary-General, U Thant, intervened, suggesting a two- or three-week cooling-off period and advising that the Soviet ships avoid challenging the blockade. Whether or not this helped alleviate the immediate situation is a moot question, but the Russian ships did avoid challenging the blockade. On October 25, a spectacular televised confrontation between U.S. Ambassador Stevenson and Soviet Ambassador Zorin occurred in the United Nations. Mr. Stevenson angrily asserted that existing offensive weapons in Cuba must be removed.

Direct correspondence ensued between Krushchev and Kennedy, and unorthodox channels of communications were called into service as the Soviet Union sought a bargained resolution of the impasse. On October 28, a key letter from Khrushchev arrived, stating that work on the bases had been stopped and that the weapons would be crated and shipped back to the USSR under United Nations supervision in return for a United States pledge not to invade Cuba. Although there was some doubt about whether any such United States pledge had been given, and although Castro refused to allow any UN supervision, this letter virtually marked the end of the crisis. Tension, of course, remained very high, but a series of events in the succeeding weeks reduced it to a more normal level. A tense moment occurred on October 31 when Castro refused to permit UN inspection unless the United States evacuated the naval base at Guantanamo. But President Kennedy declared himself provisionally satisfied with aerial inspection and stated that, on the evidence of such inspection, Soviet missiles were being crated and the bases dismantled. On November 9, United States Navy ships intercepted Soviet cargo vessels but did not board them, contenting themselves with photographing the deck cargoes. The Soviet crews were cordial. On November 10, the Kennedy Administration announced that all the offensive weapons appeared to have been removed. On November 20, the United States blockade of Cuba was lifted, after assurance had been received that Soviet jet bombers would be removed within thirty days. According to the U.S. air reconnaissance, the bombers were in fact removed within the stipulated period.

RESPONSE IN KIND

To summarize the argument thus far, we suggest that unilateral initiation of a novel course of action which effectively unbalances the conflict between antagonists, novel either in nature or in magnitude, must elicit a compensating response from the target if the system of which the opponents are part is to recover its previous equilibrium. It should be made clear that we do not posit any historical inevitability in the process of reciprocity leading to successive re-establishments of equilibrium. On the contrary, it is quite possible that one nation or another in a bilateral conflict system will fail to take the unilateral steps necessary to re-establish the equilibrium and, as a result, that the conflict may be resolved to the advantage of its opponent. We do contend, however, that maintaining and perhaps modifying the nature of the conflict system obliges a nation to meet and match its opponent in some fashion along every dimension into which the conflict is carried.

We should also remind the reader at this point that we do not by any means intend to imply that *only* external stimuli determine or should determine international behavior by states. The attention to the decision process in Chapters II, III, and IV should be sufficient to impress our conviction that *both* domestic and external factors are operative. Here we give our consideration to the demands imposed by external stimuli.

But once a new stimulus has been inserted into the system, must the response always occur in *kind*? Dupréel's theorem appears to make it mandatory by stipulating that the "means," i.e., the stimulus-response chain, in order "to meet and neutralize each other more completely, take the same forms." The data we have thus far brought forward seem to support the proposition. Indeed, the most rapid, simple, reciprocal, and proportionate response to correct an asymmetry tends to be the routine response in the East-West relationship.

But in the process of equalization of means, the introduction of a stimulus in a generically new sector, or at least a different dimension of the old sector, of the conflict system may change the ground rules governing that system to the extent of the reciprocal investment of resources it prompts. The new dimension tends to alter the relative value of the older ones, and this in turn may lead to a newly perceived asymmetry demanding compensation. In the development already described, the Soviet Union successfully introduced what amounted to a novel utilization of foreign intelligence and espionage. The American response in kind confirmed foreign intelligence and espionage as an important dimension of the conflict system. It does not seem too much to say that the increased importance of covert diplomacy altered the value of conventional diplomacy in the same conflict system, and that the altered value of conventional diplomacy provoked mutual adjustment in its use by both the U.S. and the Soviet Union. Similar conclusions may be drawn from the two Soviet-American crisis sequences just recounted.

There is a reasonable corollary to the proposition that a novel stimulus may change the ground rules of the system by prompting a diversion of both parties' resources. The ground rules may also be changed to the extent that the added investment by one party in a particular means of conflict changes how he sees the potential destruction that can be brought about: the maintenance of a symmetry of nuclear-weapons systems has obviously changed the Soviet perception of the value of the weapons dimension for pursuit of the East-West conflict. The ground rules of the conflict seem to be tending toward tacit renunciation of active use of this class of military hardware and a correspondingly increased role for competition along the dimensions of the economic sector of the system.

All this suggests that the various dimensions cannot properly be regarded as independent of one another. Thus it may not be ineffective to switch dimensions when responding to a given challenge. Historical evidence, however, indicates that such diversionary tactics are not adequate of themselves to re-establish equilibrium in the system. Each dimension must be maintained symmetrically, and this demands response *in kind*, along the same dimension in which the challenge occurs.

To illustrate, let us refer to the *economic* sector of the East-West conflict system. The European Economic Community (EEC), originally a stopgap in despair, has become a formidable economic force. The repercussions of Secretary Marshall's speech at Harvard University in June, 1947 changed the economic relations of the Western world irretrievably. They also posed a novel challenge which the Soviet Union was not slow to recognize. In fact, the Soviet Union saw the import of the new challenge before Britain did (the latter finally sought to restore equilibrium within the West first, via the European Free Trade Association [EFTA], and, failing that, by seeking membership in EEC). One Soviet response, in September, 1947, was inauguration of the Cominform as a device to promote cohesion of the socialist countries against the perceived threat of a possible new North Atlantic Community. Perhaps the doctrinal impossibility of economic collaboration between capitalist nations in the "epoch of imperialism" led to mistaken perceptions and brought a response on the political rather than on the economic level. At any rate, when the basic nature of the challenge was recognized to be indeed economic, it was met by economic response—the Council of Mutual Economic Assistance COMECON. It is COMECON, a supranational economic counterpart of EEC, that has absorbed increasing Soviet energy in recent years while the Cominform, inapplicable in the new context, withered and died. How compelling was the demand for a response *in kind* is accented when one recalls that this supranational economic organization directly contradicted the well-established Stalinist principles of economic autarchy, dating from the isolation of Soviet Russia by the West after the Bolshevik Revolution.

This case seems to sustain the contention that response in kind is mandatory to re-establish equilibrium disrupted by a novel challenge. It also sustains the contention that the system may be modified unilaterally by recourse to challenges along new dimensions of conflict.

RESPONSE IN DEGREE

If more space were available we could go on and describe, both in magnitude and diversity, the East-West and Soviet-U.S. symmetry-maintaining dynamic. Additional sectors would include: education;[18] competition for the allegiance of the uncommitted nations in Africa, Asia, and Latin America;[19] information and propaganda agencies abroad;[20] scientific research; and so on. Suffice it to say that we know of no significant example in East-West relations where a challenging initiative, if perceived as disturbing the pre-existing harmony within a relevant sector, has not brought about an attempted response in kind to redress the balance. The evidence is strong, and the model relatively simple. But to proceed further, it appears that the response to be effective, must match the stimulus in *magnitude*

[18] Should the United States establish a special institute providing advanced training in modern diplomacy, a national academy of foreign affairs? Such a proposal was put forth by Dr. James Perkins, the head of a special advisory board to the President (and now president of Cornell University). It would have high-level professional faculty and a select student body recruited from the Departments of State, Commerce, Defense, and Treasury, the United States Information Agency, the International Development Agency, and trained to serve therein. Its study program would bring about "deeper understanding of the nature of the problems of modern diplomacy." The new academy would be headed by the Secretary of State, assisted by a board of regents appointed by the President and subject to confirmation by the Senate. President Kennedy promptly endorsed the proposal, stating that he planned to send a bill to Congress proposing the institution of such an academy.

But even if the proposal were realized, the fact remains that no precedent in international-relations training will be thereby established, no unique school of diplomacy created. Such an advanced training institution already exists, a going concern with some 2,000 students, a high-level professional faculty and a program of study which is stiff as anyone could ask for. This is Moscow's highly secret Institute of International Relations, already described in Chapter III above.

In providing U.S. diplomats with advanced training in modern international relations and diplomacy, perhaps it matters little whether the single institution recommended by Dr. Perkins answers the need, or whether students would be sent to recognized universities offering the requisite courses. The requirements of diplomacy have become so complex, and the role of diplomacy in foreign affairs so vital and demanding, that the education of the professionals needs constant refurbishing. The United States must match the training of its opposite numbers on the international-relations chessboard.

[19] David O. Beim, "The Communist Bloc and the Foreign Aid Game," *Western Political Quarterly*, XVII, No. 4 (December, 1964). See Chapter XII.

[20] Cf. *19th Report to Congress, July 1–December 31, 1962,* United States Information Agency (Washington: Government Printing Office, 1963) and other reviews of the USIA operations in this series.

as well as in kind. Let us examine this proposition for a moment.

At the elementary level of conflict it is obviously a truism: having more men under arms than one's opponent, other things being equal, provides a significant military advantage for conquest or credible threat of conquest. At more sophisticated levels of conflict the assessment of significant advantage is a great deal more difficult, for the indicator of balance or symmetry— mutual capacity to inflict intolerable deprivation on the opponent—becomes less closely identifiable with the more easily measured surrogates for capacity. Nevertheless, the proposition that a response must match the challenge in degree in order to preserve equilibrium remains a truism. It merely demands recognition, not proof.

The sum total of the East-West conflict system is a combination of many stimulus-response chain processes which, ideally constructed, appears as a multiple-symmetry-maintenance model. So long as the balance is maintained in each sector or dimension, the model, although a conflict rather than a harmony construct, is essentially in a state of equilibrium. It is dynamic rather than static equilibrium, because the locus of the center of gravity of the model is continually changing as the symmetry in each sector or dimension is successively re-established.

Figure VIII-1 is an effort to clarify graphically the concept of multiple symmetry as a description of the maintenance of a bilateral conflict system between national actors. Dimensions (e.g., military, economic, diplomatic) of the conflict system are represented as planes intersecting along the Y axis,

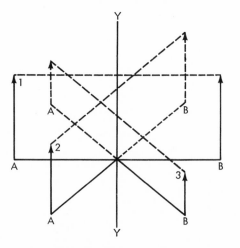

Figure VIII-1   Schematic Representation of Three Hypothetical Dimensions (1,2,3) of Conflict with Means in Each Symmetrically Balanced between A and B.

which is also the locus of the center of gravity of the entire system if symmetry is maintained in all dimensions. The level or degree of sophistication at which balance is maintained in each dimension is indicated by the length of the vertical arrows designated A and B to represent the conflicting parties.

The absolute magnitude of the means mutually possessed in any one dimension of conflict cannot itself disrupt the equilibrium of the system. It can and does alter the potential consequences of disruption (as when both sides have atomic and thermonuclear weapons). But the system may be severely destabilized in two general ways. First, it may be disturbed by a conscious failure of one party to re-establish symmetry in a relevant dimension. Some unilateral disarmament proposals would fall into this category. Paradoxically, efforts to stay ahead of the opponent also fall into this category—calculated attempts to surpass the opponent by responses which, because of their magnitude, are really new stimuli. The latter practice is especially common in the U.S.-Soviet weapons-systems build-up, where both opponents maintain that parity is not enough. The only way to preserve peace, they both argue, is to surpass the military capabilities of the other side. This sustained and conscious attempt to surpass each other's capabilities results in continuously emerging "gaps" on both sides which, in being removed, escalate the means in the military dimension. Figures VIII-2 and VIII-3 graphically illustrate these two courses of the system. In each, A and B represent the conflicting parties, and the vertical arrows at each of these poles represent the magnitude of investment or degree of sophistication in a single dimension of the conflict system.

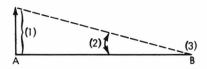

Figure VIII-2   Conscious failure of B to respond to A's challenge: disruption of equilibrium. (1) stimulus; (2) stimulus perceived by B; (3) conscious failure to respond.

The second general way in which stability may be disrupted is misperception on the part of either or both partners of either or both partners' actions. The misperception may result from a lack of accurate information about the opponent because of secrecy and inept intelligence. One side may misperceive either the *kind* or the *magnitude* of the opponent's challenge. If the kind of challenge is misperceived, the response will be in a different dimension and will therefore not meet and match the challenge (see Figure VIII-4). In this case, however, the response may introduce a new dimension

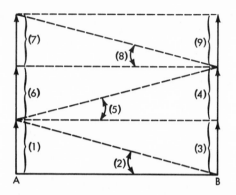

FIGURE VIII-3   Efforts by both A and B to meet and then surpass each other: equilibrium successively disrupted and reestablished with escalation of mutual capacity. (1) stimulus; (2) stimulus perceived by B; (3) B responds in kind and degree; (4) B attempts to surpass A; (5) stimulus perceived by A; (6) A responds in kind and degree; (7) A attempts to surpass B; (8) stimulus perceived by B; (9) B responds in kind and degree. . . .

into the conflict and thus start a challenge-response chain of its own, e.g., Brussels Pact, Cominform, USIA. If the magnitude of the challenge is misperceived, the response may be either disproportionately small or disproportionately large and hence fail to restore equilibrium, e.g., the initial COMECON response to ERP, EEC, and the Soviet threat, NATO, WTO sequence respectively. Figure VIII-5 illustrates this case.

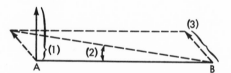

FIGURE VIII-4   Error in B's perception of the kind of A's challenge: equilibrium disrupted. (1) stimulus; (2) stimulus misperceived by B; (3) B responds in different dimension, failing to meet A's stimulus.

Alternatively, misperception leading to disrupted equilibrium may result from a rapid or accelerating growth of capacity in one or more dimensions of the system. With rapid growth there is (1) increasing difficulty or misperception in assessing the capacity gain associated with new technical achievements and (2) increasing fear of "falling behind" engendered by recognition of just this difficulty of assessment. The more misperceptions, the less the chance of a real balance being re-established and (what is of more practical importance) the less the chance of *mutually perceived* balance being achieved (see Figure VIII-6). This threat could also be stated as the danger

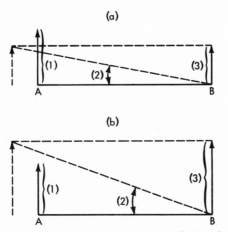

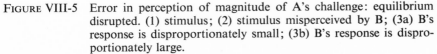

FIGURE VIII-5   Error in perception of magnitude of A's challenge: equilibrium disrupted. (1) stimulus; (2) stimulus misperceived by B; (3a) B's response is disproportionately small; (3b) B's response is disproportionately large.

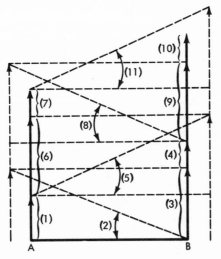

FIGURE VIII-6   Efforts by both A and B to meet and then surpass each other, combined with mutual overestimates of each other's actions: equilibrium disrupted, rapid escalation of mutual capacity. (1) stimulus; (2) stimulus misperceived by B; (3) B's response in kind and degree; (4) B's effort to surpass A; (5) stimulus misperceived by A; (6) A's response in kind and degree; (7) A's effort to surpass B; (8) stimulus misperceived by B; (9) B's response in kind and degree; (10) B's effort to surpass A; (11) stimulus misperceived by A. . . .

of progressively less objective rationality in the decision processes of the parties of the system.[21]

We suggest on the strength of this analysis that disruption of the multiple equilibrium is a danger signal and that stable equilibrium is desirable. A failure to re-establish symmetry in a relevant sector results in a progressively greater gap which invites the opponent to utilize the asymmetry; the accelerating escalation leads to progressive breakdown of standards of perception on the part of the opponents, and this in turn leads to increasing misperceptions on both sides with reference to both kind and degree of stimuli. There is less and less chance of resumption of equilibrium positions.[22]

It should be stressed that no conclusions are to be drawn from the physical analogies. They serve merely to clarify the verbal descriptions. Nor do the diagrams exhaust the possible varieties of relationship of the bilateral system. In particular it should be noted that, in reference to the real world, the conflict system involving two parties conceptualized here must be considered only a subsystem of a multination system of interaction. To take Communist China into account, for example, one would have to think in terms of three such bilateral subsystems: Soviet-American, Chinese-American, and Soviet-Chinese. The concurrent effect of particular stimuli and responses in two or more such subsystems of which the actor is a party would seriously complicate the technical difficulties of policy implementation.

"HARD DETERRENCE" AND "PEACEFUL ACCOMMODATION"

The multiple-symmetry model as a conceptualization of the East-West or Soviet-American conflict system is a device for orientation and provides a framework for analysis. Having tested the model's applicability in various dimensions of Soviet-American relations, we are confident that it approximates in gross terms, but fairly, the reality of the ongoing conflict system. We hope that it may provide not only a fresh insight into the behavioral pattern of the cold-war parties, but also a common denominator and meeting ground for both the "hard-deterrence" and the "peaceful-accommodation" theorists. Both groups, from the point of view of this model, resemble the proverbial blind man theorizing about the elephant; they seem to approach the same problem from opposite sides, each perceiving only part of the whole.

[21] See Dina A. Zinnes, Robert C. North, and Howard E. Koch, Jr., "Capability, Threat and the Outbreak of War," in James N. Rosenau (ed.), *International Politics and Foreign Policy* (New York: The Free Press of Glencoe, 1961), pp. 469–482.
[22] *Ibid.*

An illustration can be offered here. We have observed that nation A can, by unilateral initiative, establish a syndrome of interaction with its opponent, nation B—a syndrome which, while tending to be self-sustaining, alters the ground rules for the conflict system of the two nations. The initiative is open to either nation; the other must respond in kind in order to restore symmetry and equilibrium. When nation A offers a stimulus, nation B must respond if it perceives that the former symmetry has been disturbed. Thus, for example, when Henry Stimson disbanded the code section of the U.S. State Department in 1919 "because gentlemen don't read each other's mail," he was engaging in wishful thinking and making potentially catastrophic policy. Other people were reading U.S. "mail" and the U.S. could not, in the long run, afford to disregard the challenge. Similarly, when the hard-deterrent advocate insists that the Soviet military challenge to the United States must be met in kind, he is on sound ground.

On the other hand, recognizing that the stimulus-response process works both ways, nation B will observe that nation A cannot expect to ignore B's initiatives with impunity but must respond in kind, too. Thus when the peaceful accommodator seeks to have the U.S. eschew the military dimension of conflict and turn instead to dimensions in which reciprocal activity will not increase the potential consequences of disrupted equilibrium, he too is on sound ground; he is recognizing the availability of other dimensions and the possibility of changing the ground rules of the conflict system. (That the Soviet Union is not immune to such challenges has, we think, been thoroughly demonstrated both by Soviet adoption of conventional diplomatic paraphernalia in the 1920's and by Soviet recourse to supranational economic organization in the 1950's.)

Thus we have two contentions that are compatible and not mutually exclusive: (1) that the U.S. ought to *meet* the Soviet military challenge in *kind* and *degree* and (2) that the U.S. ought to *change the ground rules* of the conflict by supplying *new stimuli* and thus opening *new dimensions*. But the hard-deterrent advocate often goes on to assess the military dimension as the *decisive dimension*—a vital sector where the U.S. must not only meet but surpass challenges; where mere parity is dangerous in itself. He thus advocates the process described in Figure VIII-3 for conflict in the military sector—a process which tends to perpetuate escalation (demanding reciprocal investment of resources that might otherwise be devoted to different dimensions) and runs the risk of lapsing into the kind of escalation described in Figure VIII-6 if mutual misperceptions of stimuli occur. The peaceful accommodator, on the other hand, as part of his policy of opening new and less inherently dangerous dimensions, often recommends that we ignore Soviet stimuli in the military sector as self-defeating. This amounts to a rejection of Dupréel's theorem—a course for which precedent perhaps might be found in Allied activities vis-à-vis the USSR at the end of World War II. On the basis of our model, such a course could be justified only by the contention that the Soviet Union had initiated no military stimulus at all—a wishful and unrealistic thought.

And so the radical among the "war hawks" in fact advocate nuclear war as surely as if they advocated pushing the button on the doomsday machine, while the naïve among the "peace doves" in fact recommend an outright surrender. Yet both groups might agree, upon reflection, that the challenge-response, symmetry-maintenance model we have constructed suggests that their positions are not mutually exclusive. They both claim they opt for peace, although advocating opposite means; the model helps suggest the consequences of each attitude if each *excludes* the other.

CONCLUSION

The crux of the problem facing the United States seems to be the difficulty of combining both policies: (1) realistically perceiving and then meeting the Soviet challenges without striving to surpass them in such dimensions as that of military-weapons systems and (2) devoting at the same time a sufficient portion of scarce resources to the initiation of its own challenges in more acceptable sectors. This is not the place to go into a detailed prescriptive program for American foreign policy based upon the multiple relationships we have described; we make no claim to having a simple answer for such a complex task.[23] The technical difficulty of assessing a stimulus realistically and making decisions aimed at parity instead of superiority is formidable indeed. As a sustained *policy*, however, parity would not be impossible, dangerous in itself, nor, we submit, ineffective vis-à-vis the USSR.

What we do think to be indicated is *the necessity for acceptance of a conflict*

---

[23] Charles E. Osgood has offered some imaginative ideas for U.S. initiative as part of his GRIT proposal; for instance, the establishment of international universities overseas. Osgood advises that U.S. initiatives should be pointed toward construction of the prerequisites for democratic as opposed to totalitarian life. See Charles E. Osgood, *An Alternative to War or Surrender* (Urbana: University of Illinois Press, 1962), pp. 9, 123–124. This suggests to us a general guideline for selection of new dimensions of conflict that are inherently advantageous to the U.S.

Charles A. McClelland has suggested that just the expansion of the variety of sectors and dimensions of interaction offers opportunity for constructive consequences through establishment of new and broader communications. See Charles A. McClelland, "General Systems in the Study and Control of Conflict," in Elton B. McNeil (ed.), *The Nature of Human Conflict* (Englewood Cliffs, N.J.: Prentice-Hall, Inc., 1965).

system such as we have described at the outset, and then an effort *gradually to change the ground rules of that system* in such a way that there is both *lowered threat of disruption of equilibrium and lowered consequence of a disruption.* We do not aspire to the removal of conflict but rather to its understanding, regulation, and containment within bounds compatible with survival. *Unilateral stimulus can and does result in bilateral change—as long as it is perceived by the target as adversely affecting a relevant conflictual dimension.* If both the theorists of hard deterrence and those of peaceful accommodation can find some common ground in this conceptualization, we think that a useful step forward will have been taken.

THE SOVIET UNION:
Reckless or Cautious?

It is important that our assumptions about Soviet behavior in a given crisis of known dimensions be tested empirically, so that our assessments of this behavior be as accurate as possible; upon such assessments a great deal may depend. This chapter is an attempt to test systematically one set of such assumptions. Its purpose is to examine and analyze the principal syndromes of militancy vs. manipulation in Soviet crisis behavior in order to assess the level and pattern of Soviet risk-taking.[1]

The *time* within which the research is located is the 1945–1963 period, which spans such significant events as the cold war; the coming into existence of "the socialist system" and "polycentrism"; transformations in Soviet society since Stalin's death; "peaceful coexistence"; the new Soviet approach to developing countries; and changes in the world communist movement. In a sense, the impact of these events, individually as well as cumulatively, on the risk-taking propensity of the USSR came due in the individual international crises which involved the Soviet Union during this time period.

We have examined significant *events* in this period in order to isolate situations where the Soviet Union either did or might have been expected to take a risk. The list of crises we have selected includes four different types

[1] This chapter is a shortened and somewhat altered version of a final report, "Pattern and Level of Risk in Soviet Foreign Policy-Making: 1945–1963," submitted on September 10, 1964 to Dr. Thomas W. Milburn, Head, Behavioral Sciences Group, U.S. Naval Ordnance Test Station, China Lake, California by Jan F. Triska under Contract N123 (60530)34324A. We are grateful to Dr. Milburn for permission to publish this study; neither he nor the U.S. Naval Ordnance Test Station, however, should be linked to the views expressed here. At the same time, we wish to acknowledge with pleasure the collaboration and research assistance rendered by Murray L. Adelman, David E. Clarke, John D. Heyl, Kuan Lee, Joseph Levy, James G. Pattillo, Dorothy K. Reilly, Leslie L. Roos, Jr., Andrew Rossos, George E. Spink, William S. Tuohy, and Patricia Weiss, Research Assistants; and Gregory H. Davis, Jr., Coordinator of Research. And we are indebted to Lt. William C. Parker, Military Assistant for Strategic Studies, N.O.T.S., who patiently read and edited the final copy of the report. In addition, Professors Vernon V. Aspaturian, David T. Cattell, K. J. Holsti, Fred Warner Neal, and Nish Jamgotsch, Jr. kindly commented on the paper at two public conferences on the West Coast.

of situations: (1) direct East-West crises; (2) Communist party-states crises; (3) indirect East-West crises; and (4) crises involving Communist China and a third party. Some of the crises included could have been omitted as intrinsically unimportant (e.g., Finland in 1961 and Tibet in 1959); we included them so as to provide a variety of situations from which additional data could be obtained. On the other hand, we have omitted significant crises (such as the Algerian war, the Biserte issue, the Dutch-Indonesian conflict, and the U.S.-Guatemalan crises) as nonessential to our principal objectives.

We decided to include all cases and situations where: (1) the U.S. and the Soviet Union directly opposed one another and threatened recourse to force (Berlin and Cuban blockades); (2) a major ally of the USSR was involved in a quarrel (and a threat of recourse to force had been made) with the U.S. (Quemoy, Formosa) or with another power (India); (3) a civil war took place with covert or overt aid from the USSR (Korea, Indochina, Laos, Greece); (4) a diplomatic move by either a Western power or a Communist party-state was perceived as a threat to the political status of the USSR (NATO, Yugoslavia, China); (5) the Soviet Union was threatened with uprising in a dependent Communist party-state (Poland, Hungary); (6) neither the Soviet Union nor its ally was directly involved, but the USSR was confronted with an opportunity in the changed international political universe to make either political or ideological gains (Suez, Bay of Pigs, Jordan-Lebanon, Congo). In each of these situations there was a rise in international tensions, gradual and anticipated in some cases, rapid and unexpected in others. Each situation or case either provided the Soviet Union with an opportunity to act in the interest of furthering its own foreign-policy objectives or placed it in a position where it felt that it was compelled to act. As a result, tensions in international relations were either heightened or lessened. In all, twenty-nine situations were chosen as being appropriate for the purpose of the study. Listed chronologically, they are as follows:

Iranian crisis, 1946; Greek crisis, 1947; Marshall Plan, 1947; Czechoslovak coup, 1948; Berlin blockade, 1948; Soviet-Yugoslav crisis, 1948; Korean war, 1950–1953; invasion of Tibet, 1950; Formosa Straits, 1950; Indo-China, 1950–1954; East Berlin riots, 1953; NATO, 1955; Polish revolt, 1956; Hungarian revolution, 1956; Suez crisis, 1956; Lebanon-Jordan crisis, 1958; Quemoy crisis, 1958; proposal on Berlin, 1958; revolt in Tibet, 1959; Laos crisis, 1959–1962; U-2 incident, 1960; Congo, 1960; Bay of Pigs invasion, 1961; Berlin Wall, 1961; Soviet-Albanian dispute, 1961; Russo-Finnish relations, 1961; Sino-Indian dispute, 1962; Cuban crisis, 1962; and Sino-Soviet conflict, 1963.

Although our research procedures were intended to scale Soviet risk-taking behavior in terms of low-to-high risk alternatives without prejudging the matter in each case, our initial expectation was that the Soviet Union would probably display a preference for low-risk ventures in foreign policy. The following general assumptions based on relevant literature, recent history, internal structure, and international position of the Soviet Union contributed to this expectation:

1. All successive Soviet decision-makers, believing in the ideological inevitability of the victory of socialism in the world, have tended to prefer low over high risks. Lenin, Stalin, and Khrushchev were all essentially low risk-takers in international relations.

2. The asymmetry (dysfunction) between the Soviet state and Soviet society makes the Soviet system more static-protective, cautious, and defensive (e.g., the Berlin Wall) and less dynamic-offensive and aggressive (e.g., Hungary in 1956, Czechoslovakia in 1948, and the Cuban crisis in 1962). As a *state system*, the USSR is indeed a great power. It has a first-rate, formidable weapons systems and an outstanding capability for both conventional and nuclear war; it is a modern, advanced, effectively organized world power with an efficient and extensive communication system, at home and abroad. It has a high level of state (political) stability, a steady rate of economic growth, and a decisive influence in international relations. Soviet *society*, however, is underdeveloped, poor, backward, agricultural (50 per cent of its population are peasants forcibly turned into inefficient farmers),[2] where the general and chronic lack of consumer goods and facilities is periodically aggravated by administrative disorders, famines, natural disasters, bureaucratic chicaneries, and direct Party pressures.

This extensive societal underdevelopment within the heart of one of the most modern state systems is bound to restrict those opportunities in which the resources for modernization can be used to promote the external interests of the Soviet Union. As a consequence, the golden opportunities abroad must often be left begging, even if the effort would not take much sacrifice (e.g., Latin America, Congo, Iraq, Algeria).

Viewed from the point of this assumption, the Soviet *advances* in the world since 1945 demanded at best low-level risk-taking.[3] They were the result of

---

[2] "An agricultural problem drastically reduces both the Chinese and Russian proneness to foreign adventure," Ithiel de Sola Pool, "Deterrence as an Influence Process" (Cambridge: M.I.T., Center for International Studies, 1963), 60 pp. Mimeographed.

[3] Slusser and Triska described this low-risk propensity on the part of the USSR with respect to its treaty policy as follows: "Basing our opinion on the study of Soviet treaty policy, and especially on its three basic determinants—time, partners and subject matter—we believe that improvement upon, rather than a risky challenge of, the *status quo* characterizes current Soviet treaty policy." Jan F. Triska and Robert M. Slusser, *The Theory, Law, and Policy of Soviet Treaties* (Stanford: Stanford University Press, 1962), pp. 376–377.

(1) the collapse of underdeveloped, unstable, weak systems such as China, Vietnam, Cuba; (2) the correct Soviet assessment of mild Western and U.S. reaction (Czechoslovakia); (3) the incorrect Soviet assessment of Western and U.S. reaction (Korea, one year after the mild U.S. response to the 1949 Communist Chinese take-over); (4) wartime occupation (East Germany, Poland, Hungary, Rumania, Bulgaria); and (5) the submissiveness of local Communist Parties controlling their systems (Yugoslavia, Albania). The successful Soviet advances were bargains, required taking few chances, and were in part the result of Western errors. They were well balanced by Soviet *retreats*, forced by effective resistance abroad to Soviet pressures which might have escalated into high-level risk-taking by the opponent, e.g., Iran, Greece, Berlin, Yugoslavia, Cuba. (The example of Yugoslavia in 1948 is especially illuminating: Stalin threatened as punishment for Yugoslav defection from the Cominform to close the Danube waterway to Yugoslav shipping. Tito countered by threatening to close the Yugoslav part of the Danube, in the area of the Iron Gates, to Soviet and satellite shipping. Stalin retreated and the escalation was averted.)

3. The Soviet Union has successfully completed its "take-off" as an industrial state, and with its industrial infrastructure nearly complete, some leisure and affluence has been achieved. Increased attention has been given to consumer demands. A revolutionary program tends to exhaust itself through fulfillment, and a relatively comfortable population is less willing to accept high risks than a population suffering the hardships of an early revolutionary period.

RESEARCH STRATEGY

Rather than focusing on general objectives of the Soviet Union, we set out to catalog the similarities and regularities of Soviet behavior in crises (e.g., Soviet troops have not been normally employed except in crises within the Communist party-states system; economic interests and demands and economic determination have not been the major Soviet bone of contention in crises; the USSR has appeared more sensitive to crises in the Communist party-states in Eastern Europe than anywhere else in the world; increasingly it appears more important for the USSR to contain the influence of its opponents in the Communist party-state system than to expand and advance its own interests; and so on). The Soviet strategy of controlled risks is based on flexible tactics adapted to requirements of particular situations. An empirical taxonomy of Soviet tactics should help us clarify and classify Soviet-perceived alternatives and assist us in understanding and anticipating

Soviet preferences and choices selected from the alternative courses of action.

The Soviet Union may have displayed low risk-taking behavior in the eighteen years under investigation; but we wish to know what its risk-taking index has been and what did it depend on in individual crises. Can Soviet risk-taking be quantified on a linear scale? How much risk is the USSR prepared to take in order to achieve *what* actual gains or to avoid *which* tangible losses? And how much in the way of losses sustained or gains foregone would the USSR accept in order to eliminate high risks? Soviet decision-makers may not be gamblers, preferring short odds and low level of investment;[4] but the active amassing of an immense and up-to-date war machine can be assumed to complement such a low risk-taking profile. These problems and questions are the heart of this chapter.

Survey of Available Literature

In the course of our preliminary investigation, we have perused both theoretical literature on risk and risk-taking as well as specific literature on risk and risk-taking in Soviet foreign policy. Both efforts were illuminating, rewarding, and stimulating; their utility for our study, however, was close to marginal, and for good reasons: *Economic theories of risk*, based on the expectation of probable gain as a statistical function of history, were found to be generally inapplicable. In the first place, we collected only a limited number of crises. Second, the United States and the Soviet Union found themselves soon after World War II on unfamiliar ground—engaged in a nuclear–electronic-age power struggle in a world where Europe had lost its moral authority and technological supremacy and where ex-colonial nations were discarding their old political masters and embarking on systematic attempts to organize politically in order to benefit from modernization. The U.S. and the USSR were thrust into leadership in an age which, as the French poet René Char put it, was "without history." The United States and the Soviet Union had to make up the rules as they went along; most of the twenty-nine crises had limited historical precedents.

Decision-making theory, as in the case of psychological studies in laboratory-stimulated situations where individual actors make decisions while confronted with uncertainty of outcome, was for us a rather barren source of possible theoretical schema applicable to the specific problem of risk at hand. First, we were able to look at the Soviet Union only from the *outside*. Second, we wanted to know *what* the Soviet Union did in a particular instance more than *how* it arrived at a particular decision.

---

[4] Dean G. Pruitt, "Psychological Aspects of Foreign Policy Making" (Newark: University of Delaware, Center for Research on Social Behavior, 1964), p. 5. Mimeographed.

Game theory provided no ready-made conceptual scheme which could be suitably applied to our research either, although it was useful to the extent that it characterized the external actions of nations in tense situations as "bids" in a cooperative bargaining process where neither party wanted to lose—i.e., be blown up in a nuclear holocaust in crises involving the United States and the Soviet Union (Thomas C. Schelling). Furthermore, the game-theory literature is still based on very limited empirical research. Some experimental work has been done (e.g., Marquis, Pruitt and Coombs, J. W. Atkinson, M. Deutsch, Festinger), but it has not been applied as yet. Anatol Rapoport and his associates have carried out perhaps the most extensive experimental study of nonzero-sum gaming via the mathematical approach. And Thomas Schelling has applied game theory directly and successfully to the political arena. To us, Schelling's work, which links the world of the laboratory and that of political reality, was perhaps the most relevant; still, he appears to be more at home in the former than in the latter world. We thus found the game-theory literature more inspiring than applicable.[5]

As to the literature on *Soviet* risk-taking, we found little theory but a

[5] Michael A. Wallach, Nathan Kogan, and Daryl J. Kam, "Group Influence on Individual Risk Taking," *Journal of Abnormal and Social Psychology,* LXVI, No. 2, 75–86; D. G. Marquis, "Individual and Group Risk-Taking," *M.I.T. Industrial Management Review* (Fall, 1962); D. G. Pruitt, "Three Experiments on Decision-Making Under Risk" (Department of Political Science, Northwestern University, 1961), mimeographed; C. N. Coombs and D. G. Pruitt, "Components of Risk in Decision Making: Probability and Variance Preferences," *Journal of Experimental Psychology,* LX, 265–277; D. G. Pruitt, "Some Characteristics of Choice Behavior in Risky Situations," *Annals of the New York Academy of Science,* XXCIX (1962), 784–794; D. G. Pruitt, "Pattern and Level of Risk in Gambling Decisions," *Psychological Review* (1961); Y. Rim, "Personality and Group Decisions Involving Risk," *Psychological Review,* XIV, No. 1 (1964); John W. Atkinson, ed., *Motives in Fantasy, Action, and Society* (Princeton: D. Van Nostrand Company, Inc., 1958), pp. 322–339; Leon Festinger, "A Theory of Social Comparison Processes," *Human Relations,* VII (1954), 117–140; M. Deutsch, "The Effect of Motivational Orientation upon Trust and Suspicion," *Human Relations,* XIII, No. 2 (1960), 123–139; M. Deutsch, "The Face of Bargaining," *Operations Research,* IX, No. 6 (1961), 886–897; M. Deutsch and R. M. Krauss, "Studies of Interpersonal Bargaining," *Journal of Conflict Resolution,* VI, No. 1 (1962), 52–76; J. Loomis, "Communication, the Development of Trust and Co-operative Behavior," *Human Relations,* XXX, No. 3 (1959), 305–315; L. Solomon, "The Influence of Some Types of Power Relationships and Game Strategies on the Development of Interpersonal Trust," *Journal of Abnormal and Social Psychology,* LXI, No. 2 (1960), 223–239; L. A. Borsch, Jr., "The Effects of Threat in Bargaining: Critical and Experimental Analysis," *Journal of Abnormal and Social Psychology,* LXXVI, No. 1 (1963), 37–45; A. Rapoport, "Studies of Conflict and Cooperation in Small Groups" (Mental Health Research Institute, University of Michigan, 1963), Mimeographed; A. Rapoport and C. Orwant, "Experimental Games: A Review," *Behavioral Science,* No. 7 (1962), pp. 1–37; T. Schelling, *The Strategy of Conflict* (Cambridge: Harvard University Press, 1960).

great deal of historical and descriptive microstudies. Although there is sizable literature here, very few area experts discuss Soviet foreign policy specifically in terms of risk and risk-taking. Essentially, the general impression conveyed by the literature is that the USSR has tended to avoid major foreign-policy risks. Ranked on a continuum from the risk-taking to the risk-avoiding ends or poles, the Soviet foreign-policy experts tended to judge the Soviet risk-taking propensity to be relatively low rather than relatively high.[6]

The majority of Western writers on the subject perceive the USSR as past- and present- (rather than future-)oriented; with Soviet decision-makers viewing the horizon as relatively limited (rather than wide open); with greater reliance on national and interstate (rather than ideological, party and movement) ties; where restraint is perceived as prudence (rather than fear); where slow persuasion and agreement is preferred to rapid and risky force; and where in fact both tactics and goals (rather than tactics only) change over time.

The available literature evaluating Soviet risk-taking thus confirmed our initial assumption that the Soviet risk-taking propensity has been judged

[6] Vernon V. Aspaturian, "Dialectics and Duplicity in Soviet Diplomacy," *Air Force and Space Digest,* ILVI (1963), 50–54; Frederick C. Barghoorn, *Soviet Foreign Propaganda* (Princeton, N.J.: Princeton University Press, 1964); Raymond Bauer, *The New Man in Soviet Psychology* (Cambridge: Harvard University Press, 1952); Cyril E. Black and Thomas P. Thornton, eds., *Communism and Revolution: The Strategic Use of Political Violence* (Princeton, N.J.: Princeton University Press, 1964); Zbigniew K. Brzezinski, *Ideology and Power in Soviet Politics* (N.Y.: Frederick A. Praeger, Inc., 1962); Edward Crankshaw, "Dissension Inside the Kremlin," *Atlantic,* CCIX, No. 6 (June, 1963); Alexander Dallin, ed., *Soviet Conduct in World Affairs* (New York: Columbia University Press, 1960); David J. Dallin, *Soviet Foreign Policy After Stalin* (Philadelphia: J. B. Lippincott Company, 1961); Isaac Deutscher, *The Great Contest* (New York: Oxford University Press, 1960); George F. Kennan, *Russia and the West Under Lenin and Stalin* (Boston: Little, Brown & Company, 1960); Wladyslaw W. Kulski, *Peaceful Coexistence: An Analysis of Soviet Foreign Policy* (Chicago: Henry Regnery Company, 1959); Ivo J. Lederer, ed., *Russian Foreign Policy: Essays in Historical Perspective* (New Haven: Yale University Press, 1962); Elliott R. Goodman, *The Soviet Design for a World State* (New York: Columbia University Press, 1960); Richard Lowenthal, *World Communism; The Disintegration of a Secular Faith* (New York: Oxford University Press, 1964); J. M. Mackintosh, *Strategy and Tactics of Soviet Foreign Policy* (London: Oxford University Press, 1962); Philip E. Mosely, *The Kremlin and World Politics, Studies in Soviet Policy and Action* (New York: Vintage Books, 1960); Alvin Z. Rubinstein, *The Foreign Policy of the Soviet Union,* rev. ed. (New York: Random House, Inc., 1966); Frederick L. Schuman, *The Cold War: Retrospect and Prospect* (Baton Rouge, La.: Louisiana State University Press, 1962); Hugh Seton-Watson, *From Lenin to Khrushchev; The History of World Communism* (New York: Frederick A. Praeger, Inc., 1960); Marshall D. Shulman, *Stalin's Foreign Policy Reappraised* (Cambridge: Harvard University Press, 1963); Julian Towster, *Political Power in the USSR 1917–1947* (New York: Oxford University Press, 1948); Bertram D. Wolfe, "Communist Ideology and Soviet Foreign Policy," *Foreign Affairs,* XII, No. 1 (October, 1962).

low and Soviet attitude toward risk-taking conservative, defensive, and cautious. The authors consulted appear largely to agree with the validity of Andrei Vyshinski's statement at Potsdam in 1945 that the USSR is "conservative. . . . We want to keep what we have got."

CRISIS, RISK, PROBABILITY, AND RISK-TAKING: THOUGHTS, CONCEPTS, AND DEFINITIONS

Before proceeding any further, it may be convenient to explain what we mean by the principal terms—*crisis, risk,* and *risk-taking*—that we employ in the study.

A *crisis* in international relations is in our view an extraordinary situation which results from unusual extensive and intensive inputs to the international system—inputs accelerating paces, increasing tensions, unbalancing stabilities, and increasing the danger of war. Although there can be crises in which only one member of the international system perceives itself as seriously threatened, the most frequent and important crises are those in which two or more nations present each other with serious contingent threats. Multiple-contingent threats, whether implicit or explicit, real or imagined, tend to produce unstable situations if the opponents try to anticipate and thwart each other's action, thus introducing the possibility of second- and third-order escalations of conflict.[7]

In the face of a serious contingent threat, the time available for decisive action appears reduced and a level of psychological tension and uncertainty conducive to the outbreak of violence is approached.

A crisis may be compared to a situation of high fire hazard in which (1) lightning started a small fire (situational, environmental cause), (2) someone dropped a lighted match (attitudinal, behavioral cause), or (3) a fireman started a preventive controlled fire to burn a firebreak around a village located in the forest (functional cause). We thus speak of *fire hazard, sparking action* and *firehouse action:* (1) the pre-existing level of international tension is the degree of fire hazard; (2) the action which triggers the crisis (i.e., the lightning, the dropping of the match) is the action which, loosely, we refer to as having *caused* the crisis—the *sparking action* is the risk-taking action; (3) the action taken by various parties to lessen what they perceive to be an unacceptably high level of risk to themselves or their allies we call the

---

[7] The concepts of first-, second-, and third-order escalation are discussed in the Project Michelson report, *Human Communication and Deterrence* by Ithiel de Sola Pool, Technical Publication 2841 China Lake, California: U.S. Naval Ordnance Test Station, September, 1963.

firehouse action. Normally, the firehouse action may be expected to be symmetrical, i.e., proportionate to the perceived danger.

It is typical of sparking action that, were it to occur in a situation of no fire risk, it would cause little comment or even pass unnoticed. It is also typical that the sparking agent himself, being concerned about some minor local issue, may fail to perceive the wider fire risk latent in his action. Or the action may be accidental, or erroneous; or it may be of a habitual or semiautonomous sort, as when a man, in sheer anger, takes a swing at a member of an occupying army.

Risk[8] is a liability to error; it is a function of possible change. Risk involves a level of uncertainty. Where no prediction of the outcome is possible, pure change is involved; this, however, is not the usual situation in international relations. Here, one can at least broadly define the limits of possible gain or loss. When uncertainty is involved, it is a function of experience; if many cases are involved, a statistical probability may be calculated. Risk then becomes objectified uncertainty.

Foreign-policy decision-making has always involved an element of uncertainty for its participants. Machiavelli's advice and criticism concerning interstate relations, Bismark's classical statement concerning "the art of the possible," and contemporary treatises on game theory all focus on this element of uncertainty. Analytically speaking, we may assume that decision-makers cope with uncertainty in a twofold manner: first, they assign priorities to alternative courses of action in terms of their own estimates of the probable outcome (or outcomes) of each alternative; and second, they act on the basis of such priorities and probabilities. If a state perceives that its priorities are "at odds" with those of another state, it may nevertheless (1) estimate that the realization of such priorities is rather probable and (2) decide to achieve such priorities by engaging in a risk situation with the other state. Probability estimates and the willingness and capability to engage in risk situations permit decision-makers to cope with uncertainty.

The mathematical notion of probability has received much formulation

---

[8] According to *Webster's Unabridged International Dictionary,* "risk is (1) hazard, danger, peril, exposure to loss, injury, disadvantage or destruction, as, mountain climbing involves great *risks*; risk of assassination. (2) In forest-protection usage, any agency that may cause a fire. Cf. HAZARD. (3) *Insurance* (a) The chance of loss or the perils to the subject matter of insurance covered by the contract; also, the degree of probability of such loss. (b) Short for *amount at risk,* that is, the amount which the company may lose. In life insurance the risk at any given time equals the difference between the reserve and the face of the policy. (c) Loosely, a person or thing considered with reference to the risk involved in placing insurance upon him or it. (d) The character of hazard involved in insurance—usually with a qualifiying word; as, war *risk,* fire *risk,* catastrophe *risk.* Syn.—See DANGER."

and reformulation during the past century. Essentially, there are three schools of thought concerning the basic mathematical principles underlying probability theory. Some view probability in terms of an actor's "degree of belief" concerning the probable outcome of an event. Others adhere to the frequency interpretation of probability. And contemporary mathematical statisticians conceptualize probability theory as mathematical models of random phenomena. For our purposes it is only important to note the existence of these schools and remember that estimates of probable outcomes of events may be more or less subjective. Although it is conceivable that precise probability laws could be associated with each action hypothesis of a given alternative, it is empirically more plausible to assume that decision-makers merely view their external world in terms of whether possible outcomes are more or less likely. Whether their estimates are more objective rather than intuitive and subjective presumably depends on the length of time involved in a given decision-making period; the more time involved, the more objective the estimates.

If a state perceives that its priorities are "at odds" with those of another state, the combination of subjective- and objective-probability estimates may be such that the decision-makers will engage in a risk situation with the other state. We assume that the decision to initiate or respond to a risk situation occurs after such probability estimates have been made.

When we speak of the risk which a nation takes in acting in a certain way, we refer usually to the probability that the action would have involved the nation in question in war with another nation. In speaking of the Soviet Union and the United States at the present time, for example, we are normally referring specifically to the probability of a nuclear exchange between these powers.

We may regard the risk attached to any action as the potential result of the action in a particular situation. As an example, when a man drives a truck over a bridge, he always runs the risk that the bridge may collapse. If a man in a 3-ton truck drives over a bridge which is labelled unsafe for vehicles weighing more than 1 ton, the risk becomes considerable. Let us suppose the risk is .5, i.e., that the chances are equal that he comes across safely or that he descends into the depths. This risk remains at .5 whatever the driver's reason for taking the risk. The driver may not have seen the notice, and so be unaware of the risk. Or he may be driving away from a burning ammunition dump in the only available vehicle. If he doesn't cross the bridge, the risk of death from the imminent explosion is .9. If he does cross the bridge, the risk of death from the explosion drops to 0, but the risk that the bridge will collapse is .5. Rationally, he chooses the lesser risk. In every case, the probability that the bridge will collapse remains at .5.

The notion of *risk-taking* propensity as a stable pattern of behavior arises from the possibility that particular actors may respond to the imponderables of risk situations in fairly consistent, nonrandom ways. For example, a certain individual may prefer low-risk, low-profit alternatives to high-risk, high-profit alternatives, although it may be impossible to determine which would be more productive over a long period of time. Short-term risks may be preferred to long-term risks, or vice-versa.

Not only the immediate risk situation, but also its antecedents may influence risk-taking. Admittedly, *motive* influences risk-taking. An atom bomb dropped on New York by the Soviet Union as a measure of retaliation for something would have a very high risk. But if the bomb were dropped by accident, and if this information were to reach Washington in time, and in convincing form, the risk would be much less. Or the principal national decision-maker may be a known reckless gambler, a Hitler; chances are that he can get away with quite a bit if he plays his cards right and bluffs well. Or our driver may be a soldier whose job or *function* is it to drive over that unsafe bridge several times, whereby multiplying the risk to himself by the number of crossings. Or the driver may be forced by *circumstances* to drive over the bridge, e.g., his wife is about to have a baby and he drives her to the hospital.

For analytical purposes, then, we may define the level of risk-taking in terms of the *situation* in which an action is taken (risk *ad rem*), or in terms of the *motives* of the person taking the risk (risk *ad personam*). An actor may engage in a risk situation for reasons which are accidental (due to ignorance or lack of foresight), or conscious and purposive, or unconscious but functional. If the actor engages in risks that are unnecessary and not in his best interests, we may talk of risk-taking which is not rational.

As we knew of no way to measure motives, we decided to define levels of risk-taking according to the situations in which particular actions might occur. In seeking ways of quantifying risk and risk-taking, our task was to invent a measuring technique on the basis of which the risk situation would be assessed, so that different risk-taking levels could be compared.

A useful risk scale may range from -1 to $+1$. If war is the threat, an action of -1 risk is that which is certain to avert war. An action of $+1$ risk is that which is certain to cause a war. An action of 0 risk does not change the pre-existing probability of the occurrence of a nuclear war (level of international tension).[9]

Clearly, we had several factors to take into account. Four have already emerged: (1) the action itself, (2) the actor, (3) the pre-existing probability of war, and (4) the situation in which the action occurs.

If we make the assumption of rationality—and it is not certain when we are justified in making such an assumption—we assume that an agent nation, before acting, carefully assesses the risk attached to the proposed action and decides that the probable gains from the action make the risk worthwhile, pretty much in the same way that the man driving over the bridge rationally decided that a risk of death of .5 was better than a risk of .9.

Nobody consciously enters into a risk situation without calculating what to do if the situation worsens. These plans determine whether a situation of tension appears to be *self-intensifying, self-reducing,* or *stable.* A nation runs a risk in the interests of goal-achievement of some sort. If the risk gets too high, the nation can try to bring the risk level down again by a conciliatory act which sacrifices a measure of goal-achievement. Or it can attempt to bring the risk level down by becoming so much more threatening that the other side is forced into conciliatory and appeasing behavior.

No skillful strategist, in other words, ever enters into a calculated-risk

[9] As an example: (1) When the presence of Soviet long-range missiles in Cuba was definitely established by the U.S. government, the risk of war may have risen to, say, +.7. Putting the missiles in Cuba was a risk action—a higher risk action than the U.S. placing of missiles in Turkey. The risk was higher for at least two reasons: (a) it was the first communist missile base on the U.S. frontier; and (b) the U.S., not being used to powerful hostile forces just outside its frontier, could be expected to overreact to the sudden presence of such forces in a way the USSR would not. (2) The risk in the act of putting long-range nuclear weapons in Cuba by the USSR in 1963 would probably have to be assessed as high as +.5. If the pre-existing probability or war latent in the facts of ideological conflict plus the arms race was +.2, the putting of the weapons into Cuba would raise the probability to +.7. President Kennedy then had to act. If we assess the risk value of his blockade at +.2, the overall risk of a nuclear exchange rises to a new high level of +.9. This is far beyond the level of Soviet risk tolerance; so, Premier Khrushchev ordered his ships either to turn back and avoid the blockade or to submit meekly to inspection. This action may have had a risk value of, say, −.4, so that the probability of the new situation resolving itself by nuclear violence drops to +.5. Then President Kennedy's action in not insisting on on-site inspections may have had a risk value of −.2, dropping the overall tension to +.3. Actual troop and missile withdrawals by the USSR may have had a further risk value of −.2, dropping the final level of international tension to .1, lower than before the crisis. Possibly the U.S. blockade was the lowest risk action possible consistent with not acquiescing to the presence of weapons in Cuba. An outright invasion of Cuba at that time, such as some advocated, may have had a risk value of, say, +.5, making the probability of nuclear war rise to 1.2, i.e., more than a certainty. Logically, of course, a probability cannot rise to more than 1 (certainty); computed probabilities of more than 1 must be regarded as analogous to the concept of overkill.

situation without planning an emergency strategy for use in case the risk turns out to be considerably higher than expected. Two types may be adumbrated: *risk-reducing emergency strategy* and *risk-intensifying emergency strategy*—"we risk it and if they get through we pull out," and "we risk it and if they get tough we fight." It can be argued that a low-risk action combined with risk-intensifying emergency strategy will, in the long run, be much more dangerous than a high-risk action combined with risk-reducing emergency strategy. The reason is that the first, although perhaps obviating risk in the specific instance, leaves a residue which increases the risk-taking readiness of the opponent in future risk-taking situations, i.e., future conflicts will be entered into at a higher level of pre-existing tension. The second, however, can reduce the level of pre-existing tension. Putting long-range rockets in Cuba was a high-risk action on the part of the Soviet Union. But it was combined with the risk-reducing emergency strategy: If the U.S. gets tough, we pull out. The U.S. got tough, and the Russians did pull out, and the general level of U.S.-USSR tension was less than it had been before the crisis. The U.S. blockade was a low-risk action in a tension situation which depended for its effectiveness on the assumption that Soviet emergency strategy was of a risk-reducing sort.[10] President Kennedy said, in effect: If you show us that your emergency strategy is risk-reducing, we will adopt a risk-reducing course as well; but if you show us your emergency strategy is risk-increasing (i.e., if you see the blockade as the *casus belli*) we will fight.

Risk-taking is not merely a means to goal-achievement; it is also a form of *nonverbal communication*. It is characteristic of nonverbal communication in that positive statements can be made but negative ones cannot. As the story goes, one octopus can destroy another, and one often does, and every octopus is afraid of the aggressive powers of every other. Octopi nevertheless cooperate and live amicably with each other. But one octopus cannot *say* to another: "I will not attack you." So when an octopus wants amicable relations with another octopus, it chooses a chance to adopt a position of maximum threat to the other octopus, so that the second octopus wakes up to find itself completely at the mercy of the first. The first octopus maintains its threat posture for a time, then gradually withdraws, thus saying, in nonverbal language: "I could have killed you easily and I didn't, so you can trust me in the future." This is the start of amicable and cooperative relations between organisms that can, if they choose, destroy each other.

Under conditions where verbal communications are never regarded as sincere, risk-taking becomes in fact a form of communication between

[10] Nathan Leites, *A Study of Bolshevism* (New York: The Free Press, 1953), Chapter XIX.

nations. Game theory is based on the proposition that verbal moves are of lesser importance than action. A participant must signal his intentions with a concrete move, i.e., he must incur a risk to show that his demands are serious.

Finally, we assume that "spontaneous punitiveness," i.e., punitiveness intended to and in fact going beyond the normal, routine, symmetrical and reciprocal levels demanded by a "fitting" response to the initial transgression (crisis input) is aggressive; it is asymmetrical, overreacting and escalating. On the other hand, a response which underreacts to the risk-taking stimulus is cautious; this is the phenomenon known as *appeasement*. It is clear that a tendency toward "spontaneous appeasement" profoundly influences the characteristic risk-taking level of a nation. The League of Nations was in a mood of gross underreaction in the thirties, enabling Hitler and Mussolini to get away with monumental risks.

The causes of underreaction and overreaction on the part of nations are complex, obscure, and controversial. But the fact of the phenomena cannot be doubted and must be taken into account in our risk calculations. How do we decide whether a response is or is not fitting, indicating high or low propensity for risk and risk-taking?

ACTIONAL-SYMMETRY CONSTRUCT

As our yardstick by which to measure, at first roughly, the Soviet risk-taking propensity in individual crises—whether the Soviet behavioral stance in a crisis was a fitting response to the challenge or whether the USSR over-acted (was aggressive) or underacted (was placative)—we employed the symmetry construct used in criminal law and the law of torts (in common law since about 1400 and in civil law since the Roman law period) and known as the *theory of self-defense*. It stipulates that, to prevent harm to oneself where there is no resort to law, (1) autonomous reasonable steps may be taken (2) as long as reasonable belief exists that harm is about to be committed. As long as these two conditions are met, the law absolves such behavior from legal liability (such behavior is "privileged").

This construct has been universally recognized and is indisputable. The privilege extends to the use of all "reasonable" force to prevent any threatened act, whether intended or negligent. The actor is not liable where he acts under a "reasonable" but mistaken apprehension; he is not required to wait until a blow is struck. Though he is not required to behave with courage, he is not free to act with abnormal timidity. Most important, his self-defense is limited to the use of force which is "reasonably" necessary for protection against the threatened injury; to go beyond the necessity of the situation is not privileged by law.[11]

If the act of self-defense is "reasonable" as to the threatening harm—or, as we would put it, if the response is *symmetrical, proportionate,* or *reciprocal* to the challenge—it is "privileged" *because* it is fitting. If it goes beyond the necessity, i.e., if it contains "spontaneous punitiveness" going *beyond* the level demanded by a fitting response to the initial transgression, then the reaction is "risky," escalatory, and aggressive in its own right. If the actor retreats or underresponds or underreacts, on the other hand, his reaction is risk-avoiding, "appeasing," and "placative."

To be able to superimpose this self-defense/actional symmetry construct upon Soviet behavior in the twenty-nine international crises, we have first reduced the crises to a manageable typology consisting of seven categories as follows:

TYPOLOGY OF CRISES

Type I: USSR attempted to extend its influence over a *contiguous, noncommunist nation* in the post-World War II but pre-NATO period.
           a. Iran
           b. Czechoslovakia

Type II: Civil war in a noncommunist nation (contiguous to at least one Communist party-state) with material *aid given by both East and West to the opposing factions.*
           a. Greece—contiguous to Bulgaria, Yugoslavia, and Albania
           b. Indo-China—contiguous to China; theater of subversive and revolutionary warfare
           c. Korea—contiguous to China
           d. Laos—contiguous to China; theater of subversive and revolutionary warfare.

Type III: *Western diplomatic initiative* with long-term implications taken in *European* environment.
           a. Marshall Plan—economic alignment
           b. NATO—military alliance

Type IV: *USSR confronted with independent Communist party-state reaction* against Soviet control and/or policies.
           a. Yugoslavia—noncontiguous; no armed uprising; an "ideological" break

[11] *Restatement of the Law of Torts* (St. Paul: American Law Institute Publishers, 1934), I, 120–121. See also William L. Prosser, *Handbook of the Law of Torts,* 2nd ed. (St. Paul: West Publishing Company, 1955), pp. 88–90; and L. Oppenheim, *International Law* (London: Longmans, Green & Co., Ltd., 1935), I, 157–160, 243–245.

    b. East Germany—outbreak of violence due mainly to economic grievances; a Soviet-occupied nation

    c. Poland—no outbreak of violence except preliminary disturbances in Poznan

    d. Hungary—violence on the part of insurgents and massive Soviet repression

    e. Albania—noncontiguous; no violence, but an "ideological" break; part of Sino-Soviet dispute

    f. Finland—no violence; a noncommunist state under Soviet domination; rapid accommodation of Soviet desires

    g. China—other superpower of communist system; no violence but an "ideological" break

Type V: Crises involving *China and a noncommunist state* in a classic situation of generally short duration.

    a. Tibet, 1950—Chinese occupation and annexation of Tibet

    b. Tibet, 1959—violent revolt in Chinese satellites repressed

    c. India—violence along Sino-Indian border area; two giants of Asia

    d. Formosa—China involved with U.S. and Taiwan regime at time of Korean War; escalation danger

    e. Quemoy—China involved with U.S. and Taiwan regime; escalation danger

Type VI: Classic crisis of short duration involving *direct confrontation of East and West* (USSR and U.S. and its allies) with consequent high danger of escalation.

    1. Crises of Soviet initiative:

        a. Berlin blockade

        b. Berlin, 1958—verbal threats

        c. Berlin, 1961—high U.S. and Soviet troop concentration in Berlin

    2. Crises of U.S. initiative:

        a. U–2—U.S. violation of Soviet air space; plane shot down; ensuing crisis was verbal

        b. Bay of Pigs—U.S.-sponsored invasion of the only Communist party-state in Western hemisphere

Type VII: Armed intervention by West followed by *mise en place of UN police force* in previously Western colony in Middle East or Africa in reaction to threat posed by indigenous nationalism to Western interests.

    a. Suez—British, French, and Israeli troops vs. UAR; U.S. and USSR (paradoxically) both mediators

    b. Lebanon-Jordan—function of Iraq coup; U.S. and British troops landed in Middle East in close proximity to USSR

c. Congo—presence of Belgian and European mercenary troops in civil war-torn African state

Next, we have built into each of the seven categories of crises several alternative choices, ranging from low to high risk, *in addition* to the one selected by the USSR in a given crisis:

TYPOLOGY OF ALTERNATIVE SOVIET VERBAL OR ACTION MOVES

Note: (1) The numerical sequence of alternative moves indicates the risk element in each move *in relation to* the other alternative moves. When more than one move has the same number, this indicates that all moves bearing this number have an equal element of risk in relation to one another.

Note: (2) The ratings of *L*, *M*, and *H* indicate the amount of risk on *absolute scale*, which is based on an anticipated symmetrical response to the Soviet move on the part of the other party. The range of rankings is

Low:	*Medium:*	*High:*
L_1	M_1	H_1
L_2	M_2	H_2
L_3	M_3	H_3

Alternatives for Crises Type I:

L_1 1. *immediate ceasing* of all Soviet operations (and withdrawal of troops, if applicable) in face of Western verbal or action protests;

L_1 2. engineering of a *coup d'etat* from within without aid of external Soviet pressures;

L_3 3. keeping Soviet troops in the country (or province) beyond the withdrawal deadline and trying to install a communist-inspired regime;

L_2 4. engineering a *coup d'etat* from within with the aid of external Soviet pressures (such as the presence of Soviet troops on the borders, the presence of high-ranking Soviet officials in the nation, and so on);

H_1 5. sending Soviet troops into the state to ensure the consolidation of a communist-inspired regime.

Alternatives for Crises Type II:

L_1 1. giving support to the communist insurgents but avoiding material or physical involvement;

L 2. denunciation of Western aid to anti-communist elements and threat of war if such activities continue;

L_2 3. giving limited material and technical aid to the communist insurgents and letting the contiguous communist state(s), particularly where China is involved, serve as intermediary;

L_3 4. giving direct Soviet material and technical aid openly to the communist insurgents;

M₃ 5. dispatching Soviet military to the arena, but without its entering into the country involved;

H₃ 6. giving massive Soviet aid to the communist insurgents, including the dispatch of Soviet troops to the area (e.g., Spanish civil war);

Alternatives for Crises Type III:[12]

L   1. proposing concessions and applying external threats and pressures to discourage specific states from participating in the Western system;

L   2. creating a rival bloc from among the Communist party-states;

L   3. protesting against the Western action in the United Nations;

L   4. instigating internal agitation by communist and leftist elements in specific states to discourage their participation in the Western system.

Alternatives for Crises Type IV:

L   1. letting the dissident manifestations take their course without interference, and attempting reconciliation with the regime, whether the same or altered by the disturbances;

L   2. condemning the dissident party-state (with the support of other members of the communist system);

L   3. breaking off of diplomatic relations with the refractory state;

L   4. cutting off or substantially reducing all economic and technical aid to the rebellious country;

L   5. attempting to subvert internally the upstart regime;

L   6. applying an economic blockade to force the rebellious state back into line;

L₃ 7. alerting and massing Soviet (and/or other Communist party-states) troops on the borders to intimidate the rebellious state into submission;

M   8. physically smashing the rebellion and coercing the regime into acceptance of Soviet domination, if the state is already Soviet-occupied;

M–H 9. sending in Soviet troops to smash the rebellion and restore total subservience.

Alternatives for Crises Type V:

L   1. verbally supporting the Chinese position in public;

L   1. voting against anti-Chinese motions in the United Nations and/or verbally protesting against the Western action in the UN;

L   1. adopting a neutral attitude, neither supporting nor condemning the Chinese position;

L   1. verbally condemning the Chinese action;

---

[12] There is no ranking here since all alternatives amount to a low disposition toward risk-taking from the perspective of a short-term analysis.

L   1. continuing to give material aid (in the case of India) to China's adversary in accordance with a pre-existing agreement;

L_3 2. verbally supporting the Chinese position with a pledge, in some cases made solemn by revision or signing of a treaty, to go to war on the side of China if necessary;

L_3 3. offering and implementing increased military-aid pledge to China during the crisis;

M–H 4. sending Soviet military to the area to indicate a strong Soviet willingness to support the Chinese.

Alternatives for Crises Type VI:

(A) U.S.-USSR crises:

L   1. verbally threatening U.S. allies indirectly involved in crisis (Norway and Pakistan);

L   1. diplomatic protests and warnings transmitted to U.S.;

L   2. rupture of a forthcoming summit conference and/or refusal to participate in *ad hoc* international conferences in which the U.S. (and the USSR) have been taking part;

L_3 3. promoting members of Soviet international hierarchy favoring a more aggressive policy toward the U.S.;

L_3 4. calling up reservists and putting Soviet troops on alert;

M   5. dispatching symbolic Soviet military to areas in proximity to Western states indirectly involved.

(B) U.S.-initiated crises:

L   1. verbal protest and threat to U.S.;

L   1. recall of Soviet vessels with announcement by U.S. of *mise en place* of naval blockade;

L   2. symbolic immediate increase in Soviet material aid to the state which is also involved in the dispute with the U.S.;

L_3 3. placing of Soviet military forces on alert;

M_1 4. dispatching of a limited Soviet force to the area;

H_3 5. physically attempting to break the blockade.

(C) Soviet-initiated crises:

L   1. sending a note to Western powers threatening to turn over Soviet powers in Berlin to East German regime;

L_3 2. confronting West with a *fait accompli*—Soviet powers in Berlin turned over to East Germans;

L_3 2. periodically impeding Western physical access to Berlin on a symbolic level;

M_1 3. building a wall cutting East Berlin off from West Berlin;

M_2 4. suddenly building up the concentration of Soviet forces in the area;

M_2 4. placing Soviet and Warsaw Pact forces on a battle alert;

H   5. imposing a land blockade on Berlin;

H_3 6. imposing a total, ostensibly permanent blockade on Berlin.

Alternatives for Crises Type VII:

L₁ 1. verbal denunciation of Western action accompanied by threats of Soviet action;

L₃ 2. proposal to send Soviet volunteer troops to the area;

L₃ 3. limited dispatch of Soviet material aid and advisers;

L₃ 4. placing of Soviet forces on alert;

M   5. alerting of Soviet troops and manuevering of these troops on the Soviet borders closest to the disturbance;

M–H 6. dispatching of a limited Soviet military force to the area without sending the force into the disturbed nations;

H   7. dispatching limited number of Soviet forces into the area.

The result of this historical test via the self-defense/actional symmetry construct confirmed the collective judgment of Western scholars and experts in the field as well as our own initial assumptions theses: Soviet behavior in the post-World War II crises was either *symmetrical—or less than symmetrical—to the particular situational challenge*, it was not unreasonable and escalatory in its riskiness. It was symmetrical in Hungary in 1956; in the U-2 incident in 1960; in the Sino-Soviet conflict (up to 1963); and indirectly in the Czechoslovak *coup d'etat* in 1948. It was less than symmetrical or somewhat pacificatory in Iran in 1946; in Greece in 1946; in Berlin in 1948; in Korea in 1950; in East Germany in 1953; in Yugoslavia in 1948; in Lebanon-Jordan in 1959; in the Congo in 1960; in the Berlin Wall issue in 1961; in Albania in 1961; in Finland in 1961; and in Cuba in 1962; and it was decidedly cautious in the Marshall Plan installation in 1947; in the NATO establishment in 1949 and again in 1955; in Poland in 1956; in the Suez crisis in 1956; in the Quemoy incident in 1958; in Berlin in 1958; in Laos in 1959; and in the Bay of Pigs in 1961. (It was passive-indifferent in Tibet in 1950 and again in 1959; in the Formosa Straits conflict in 1950; and in the Sino-Indian clash in 1962.)

Restated, the above results lead to the conclusion that the more "serious" a crisis was perceived, the more cautious was the Soviet move (Cuba in 1962); conversely, the less "serious" the crisis, the less cautious the Soviet response (U-2 incident). Also, the less "concerned" in a crisis, the more cautious the Soviet stance (Tibet, Formosa, the Sino-Indian conflict), whereas conversely the greater the Soviet stake in a crisis, the less cautious the Soviet action (Hungary in 1956).

MODEL OF SOVIET RISK-TAKING

Soviet behavior in the post-World War II crises was then either proportionate or less proportionate to the dangers perceived as threatening the

USSR; but it was *not* overly punitive or aggressive, i.e., disproportionate.

The next and more difficult question to ask is, *how* cautious was the USSR? If its risk-taking index was low rather than high, *how low* in fact was it? In other words, we wish to measure the risk the USSR took—or avoided—in the various crises; to do so, we must somehow find ways and means to accomplish this task.

In our attempt to cope with this problem, we set up a model of risk-taking in crises: In every interacting crisis situation, we argued, there are at least two primary opposing parties. A crisis occurs when one party (A) takes the initial action (input, risk, R_1) which is likely to disrupt the equilibrium level (the pre-existing situation) between it and another party (B). (A) takes this action (and assumes the risk R_1) to obtain a benefit, i.e., secure a gain (increment in its capacity). Without the expectation of gain (Eg), the initial action would not be justified; this initial action is never taken to prevent a loss.

The crisis does not occur, however, unless the expected gain on the part of (A) is perceived as a significant loss on the part of (B). When (B), perceiving itself to be exposed to the ever-increasing loss (risk, R_2) resulting from its nonresponse [while (A) comes closer to achieving the gain] regards the situation as unbearable, (B) finally acts. The threshold of unbearable risk (cost) to (B) is thus approached at the same time as the threshold of a significant gain (benefit) for (A) draws nearer. Frustrated, (B) responds (output, risk, R_3). The crisis issue is joined; the crisis begins. (B) assumes a risk which is now related to his own action (rather than to his nonaction, as before) and is thus positive. If the response of (B) is proportionate or symmetrical to the initial action of (A), the initial expected gain of (A) has been reduced by the response of (B) to zero. (When we say *symmetrical* here, we mean that although in terms of *short-term* considerations one might conclude that R_3 was of a "higher" magnitude, a *long-term* evaluation would show that the magnitude of R_3 was justified in terms of the risk (R_2) of (A) obtaining a significant gain. Thus the Soviet dispatch of tanks into Hungary, although appearing rash at first, was symmetrical [i.e., "reasonable"] in terms of the long-term considerations involved. In general, $R_2 \cong R_3$.)

In each crisis, then, as (A) is perceived as reaching the threshold of a significant gain in capacity, (B) perceives itself to be attaining the threshold of intolerable loss (risk) due to its nonaction. When the crisis is finally engaged, a new kind of risk behavior emerges, this time dependent upon the type of mutual *communication* through various means (*verbal* to *violent*) by which the actors attempt to readjust their respective gains (benefits) and losses (costs) in order to return their relations to the previous, or at least a mutually agreeable, level of equilibrium. In most cases the entire process now reverses itself, and gains, losses, and risk return to zero. In an extraordinary situation, however, where one or both parties are unwilling to seek a downward accommodation, a situation of *escalation* takes place. In this case, the initial process repeats itself, starting with a new input of initial risk, which is normally much higher than R_3.

It is true that normally the initial action by (A) may be perceived, by (A) as well as by (B), as but a new development in the dynamics of international relations, an input which does not necessarily "dangerously" disrupt international relations. (Especially the party to whose advantage the development works, more often than not fails to perceive this development as likely to disrupt the equilibrium of the situation.) In fact, we have observed that the USSR tends so to interpret the initial action, its own as well as that of its adversaries: For the USSR, R_1 (R_{A1}) does not normally create the danger; R_1 (R_{B1}) does. We could have assisted nonmilitarily the Hungarian freedom fighters, for example, without incurring the risk of war with the USSR; and Premier Khrushchev may not have originally perceived the sending of missiles to Cuba as the war-like action it seemed to President Kennedy.

$R_3(R_{B1})$, the response of (B), is perceived by (A) as nullifying its own initial action: it is the loss of its original expected gain. If no escalation on either side takes place, then the circle is closed, the crisis is over. This is the normal crisis pattern.

Having superimposed the model upon several crises, we found that it was essential to identify the party that initiated the crisis, i.e., made the first move which seriously disturbed the balance. In some crises the initiator is much more difficult to determine than in others. Sometimes a gap in formation regarding the crisis immediately puts us on uncertain ground. Yet it is important to distinguish between those crises the Soviet Union perceived to be thrust upon it and those crises which, from what information is available, the Soviet Union initiated. This kind of grouping gave us consistent crisis patterns of action with which to compare crises, isolating the more basic behavioral similarities that persist (Figure IX-1 describes the risk-taking model).

Expectations determine risk-taking behavior. The initiator of a crisis will have more specific expectations than the respondent, at least in the early stages of the crisis. This differential in expectations can explain various levels of risk-taking at various points in the action-reaction pattern.

Initially, we analyzed two Berlin crises, the 1948 blockade and the 1961 Berlin Wall conflict. In each case we developed two alternative interpretations, trying to establish initial and proximate actions and the pattern of

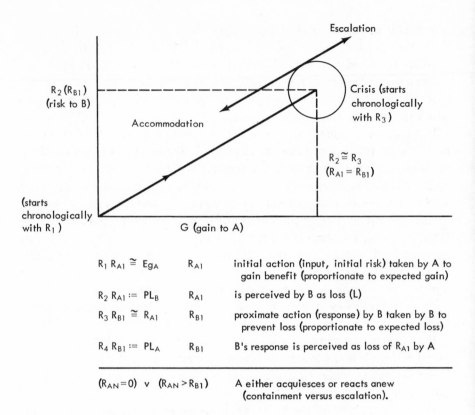

$R_1 \ R_{A1} \cong E_{gA}$	R_{A1}	initial action (input, initial risk) taken by A to gain benefit (proportionate to expected gain)
$R_2 \ R_{A1} := PL_B$	R_{A1}	is perceived by B as loss (L)
$R_3 \ R_{B1} \cong R_{A1}$	R_{B1}	proximate action (response) by B taken by B to prevent loss (proportionate to expected loss)
$R_4 \ R_{B1} := PL_A$	R_{B1}	B's response is perceived as loss of R_{A1} by A

$(R_{AN}=0) \ \lor \ (R_{AN} > R_{B1})$	A either acquiesces or reacts anew (containment versus escalation).

accommodation and/or escalation. Next we applied the risk model to Yugoslavia and Laos.

Three things became clear to us in the process: (1) Our attention should focus on the response in each crisis. This, after all, is the action which challenges the disadvantageous development, which "joins the issue," which causes the crisis to come into being. This action is perceived by its initiator as "likely" to disrupt the equilibrium. (2) The initiator of a crisis always seeks to gain benefit. By asking who is to gain from a crisis it is possible in most cases to identify the initiator. And (3) if we think we know the proximate action (response) but can not trace back to an initial action, chances are that this is an example of crisis being used strategically (for its own sake), e.g., the Khrushchev proposal on Berlin in 1958. The procedure then is to begin with the response and attempt to take one firm step backward in time.

An area which has been the scene of numerous crises, e.g., Berlin, can evolve its own factors of risk from any given action. The learning process of two regular dueling partners can be rather impressive. A Soviet demand for the "normalization" of the Berlin situation today does not create crisis; it did in 1958. The complete prohibition of movement between the East and West sectors would not create crisis today; a less severe step did in 1961.

On the basis of these considerations, we have attempted to identify initiators in the twenty-nine crises, as listed in Table IX-1.

Table IX-1

CRISIS	INITIATOR	ATTEMPTED GAIN BY USSR	THREATENED SOVIET LOSS
1. Iranian crisis, 1946	R*	x	
2. Greek crisis, 1947	R	x	
3. Marshall Plan, 1947	W**		x
4. Prague Coup, 1948	R	x	
5. Berlin blockade, 1948	R	x	
6. Soviet-Yugoslavia crisis, 1948	S†		x
7. Korean War, 1950–1953	R	x	
8. Invasion of Tibet, 1950	C‡		
9. Formosa Straits, 1950	W		
10. Indo-China, 1950–1954	C		
11. East Berlin riots, 1953	S		x
12. NATO, 1955	W		
13. Polish revolt, 1956	S		x
14. Hungarian revolution, 1956	S		x
15. Suez crisis, 1956	W		x
16. Lebanon-Jordan crisis, 1958	W		x
17. Quemoy crisis, 1958	C		
18. Proposal on Berlin, 1958	R	x	
19. Revolt in Tibet, 1959	S		
20. Laos crisis, 1959–1962	W		x
21. U-2 incident, 1960	R		x
22. Congo, 1960	W		x
23. Bay of Pigs invasion, 1961	W		x
24. Berlin Wall, 1961	R	x	
25. Soviet-Albanian dispute	S		x
26. Soviet-Finnish relations, 1961	R	x	
27. Sino-Indian dispute, 1962	C		
28. Cuban crisis, 1962	R	x	
29. Sino-Soviet conflict, 1963	C		x

* R—USSR.
** W—U.S. or other Western state.
† S—Other Communist party-state.
‡ C—China.

The risk-taking model was not only instrumental in refining our risk-taking analysis but helped us to define Soviet risk-taking propensity more explicitly. *The model showed that a crisis normally does not occur until both the initial action and reaction have taken place, i.e., that it obviously takes two to make a quarrel (a crisis).* It also suggests that the action of the initiator (its riskiness) might be judged against his anticipated *gain*, that the reaction of the responding party might possibly be most effectively judged against his anticipated *loss*, and that accommodation and/or escalation bids are best evaluated against other bids in a crisis.

We then applied the model to the remaining crises to test its capacity for describing, dissecting, and analyzing Soviet risk-taking behavior in crises. Up to this point, however, we applied only *certain features* of the model to the analysis of Soviet crisis behavior.

INTENSITY OF CRISES: INDEPENDENT VARIABLES

The problem of how to avaluate crises in terms of their respective intensity of riskiness is a complex one. Should we attempt to appraise riskiness via a single variable basic to all crises or should we consider crises a reflection of many intervening variables, which should be extracted, compared, scaled, and evaluated? The first alternative might be accomplished via a consideration of a key variable such as, for example, the number of nations involved. There are some theoretical inquiries available which suggest the relevance of the number of nations involved in determining the probability of a crisis escalating (becoming more intense). For example, this approach, relating the number of actors to the riskiness of the situation, finds theoretical justification in behavioral studies of conflict, both international and experimental. Dina Zinnes, in a study of hostility in international relations based on a content analysis of communications during the crisis period preceding the outbreak of war in 1914,[13] found that the more nations involved in a conflict, the more opportunities any one country will have to perceive the environment as hostile. Thus data on the number of nations and great powers involved are considered relevant to the amount of threat in a conflict situation. Zinnes found a significant correlation between a state's perception of the number of "persecutors" and its feeling of being "persecuted." One would presume that there would be a high chance of escalation when any one state feels "persecuted"; the risk of war would be increased.

A study using nonzero-sum games may also be mentioned. If we accept Zinnes' finding that the number of nations in a conflict affects the amount of threat perceived by the actors, an experiment by Morton Deutsch becomes relevant. Deutsch has shown that when threat is high it is more difficult for

[13] D. Zinnes, "Hostility in International Decision-Making," *Journal of Conflict Resolution,* XVI, No. 3 (September, 1962), pp. 236–244.

participants in a bargaining situation to reach a satisfactory solution than when threat is low or nonexistent.[14] Thus, when a large number of nations are involved in a crisis situation, high threat may increase the risk.

These studies lend a measure of validity to attempts to express crisis intensity simply on the basis of the numbers of nations involved. If, for example, all crisis participants were divided into essential and nonessential national actors (great powers and small countries), and only the number of essential national actors was considered—as a much more important determinant of crisis intensity than the number of small countries (these are taken into consideration only in the case of a tie)—the crude ranking of crisis as shown in Table IX-2 would be obtained.

Table IX-2 Ranking of Crisis Identity

CRISIS	DATE	RANK	ESSENTIAL NATIONAL ACTORS	NONESSENTIAL NATIONAL ACTORS
Berlin wall	1961	1	USSR, U.S., U.K., France, Germany	—
Berlin blockade	1948	2	USSR, U.S., U.K., France	—
Greece	1946	3.5	U.S., U.K., USSR,	Greece
Indochina	1950–51	3.5	U.S., France, China	Vietnam
Korea	1950	5.5	China, U.S.	N. Korea, S. Korea
Laos	1959	5.5	China, U.S.	North Vietnam, Laos
Formosa	1950	8.5	U.S., Red China	Nationalist China
Quemoy	1958	8.5	U.S., China	Taiwan
USSR-Albanian dispute	1961	8.5	USSR, China	Albania
Cuban blockade	1962	8.5	USSR, U.S.	Cuba
U-2 incident	1960	11.5	USSR, U.S.	—
USSR-China	1963	11.5	USSR, China	—
Iran	1946	↑	USSR	Iran
Czechoslovakia	1948		USSR	Czechoslovakia
Yugoslavia	1948		USSR	Yugoslavia
Tibet	1950	Tied for	China	Tibet
East Berlin riots	1950	18	USSR	East Germany
Poland	1956		USSR	Poland
Hungary	1956		USSR	Hungary
Tibet	1959		China	Tibet
Bay of Pigs	1961		U.S.	Cuba
Finland	1961		USSR	Finland
China-India	1962	↓	China	India

[14] Morton Deutsch, "The Face of Bargaining," *Operations Research,* IX, No. 6 (November-December, 1961), 886–897.

Compared with the preliminary ranking of crisis seriousness, based on intensity of force involved, either actual or potential, important differences appear:

Preliminary Ranking of Crisis Intensity

1st magnitude crises: Brink of war (nuclear) USSR-U.S.:
Cuban blockade, Berlin blockade, Berlin Wall

2nd magnitude crises: Strategic or local wars (limited):
Korea, Indochina, Congo-UN crisis, Bay of Pigs, Laos, Suez Canal, Greece, Iran

3rd magnitude crises: Brink of war (major Soviet ally):
Quemoy, Formosa

4th magnitude crises: Local and "internal" strife:
Hungary, East Berlin riots

5th magnitude crises: Diplomatic crises, USSR-U.S.:
U–2, Berlin (1958)

6th magnitude crises: Diplomatic maneuvers, USSR-U.S.:
Marshall Plan, NATO, Lebanon-Jordan

7th magnitude crises: "Internal" diplomatic crises:
USSR-China, USSR-Albania, Yugoslavia, Poland, (Finland)

8th magnitude crises: Local and "external" strife (major Soviet ally):
China-India, Tibet (1950), and Tibet (1959)

For example, the Cuban blockade is rated on the former scale as below the dispute over Laos in 1959; the Iranian crisis of 1946 is rated in thirteenth place on the latter scale; and different relative weights are given by the two models to the USSR and China. These different rankings suggest significant deviations between the two scales.

For this reason we selected the second alternative: a crisis, we argued, is determined by *several* key variables, not just one; its intensity of riskiness is perceived by the participants as a mix of those variables. This more rigorous approach should permit us to perform a linear regression analysis of the quantified varied categories, which could be run to see if improved predictions resulted from such a complex analysis.

The intensity or inherent riskiness of crises should be expressed, we decided, as a cumulative index of the following five key independent (non-behavioral) variables: (1) *geography* (i.e., distance from the Soviet Union and those states friendly to the Soviet Union, distance from the United States and those powers friendly toward the United States, distance from other participants, ease of access for the USSR, and so on); (2) *stakes* (what are the Soviet Union and its opponent really quarreling over, in political terms);

(3) *parties* (who are the primary actors in the crisis, what is the likelihood of hostility, what is the likelihood of aggressive action against the USSR if certain parties are involved); (4) *weapons-military factor* (at the time of the crisis, what was the degree of military-weapons superiority or inferiority of the Soviet Union's opponent); and (5) *developmental factor*, i.e., the stage of development within which the crisis took place (a) in the Communist party-state system [Soviet leadership and effectiveness of control], (b) in the East-West relations [in terms of the cold war or hostility-friendship dichotomy], and (c) in the relations between the Soviet Union and developing nations [political and economic transactions].

Using a nine-point scale based on rankings from low to high determined independently by five expert judges, a value was assigned to each independent variable in each crisis (as a function of risk accruing to the USSR) as follows (each independent variable has a scale of alternatives in ascending order [low to high] of risk *to* the Soviet Union):

I. Geographical location
1. Contiguous to the USSR and no Western state.
2. Contiguous to China and landlocked.
3. Contiguous to other Communist party-states.
4. Contiguous to China but open to the sea.
5. Contiguous to the USSR and noncommunist states.
6. Contiguous to other Communist party-states and non-Communist party-states.
7. Not contiguous to any Communist party-state—open sea.
8. Not contiguous to any Communist party-state—landlocked.
9. Contiguous to the U.S.
II. Stakes
1. Diplomatic embarrassment to the U.S.
2. Asia as characterized by indirect Soviet involvement.
3. Consolidation of the West against the USSR.
4. Extension of communism in Africa.
5. Middle East as part of historical decline of Western influence in the Arab world.
6. Soviet hegemony in Eastern Europe.
7. Preservation of a unified Soviet system.
8. Berlin as the key to anti-Soviet Germany.
9. Fate of the Communist party-state in the Western hemisphere.
III. Parties
1. China vs. Asian state.
2. Inside Communist party-state or Finland.
3. China vs. U.S.

4. USSR vs. Communist party-state.
5. Inside Asian or African state.
6. Inside noncommunist state in Europe or Iran.
7. Against ex-Western colonial nation.
8. USSR vs. Western state or states.
9. USSR vs. U.S.

IV. Weapons—Military Factor

A. *East–West*

1. ⎫
2. ⎬ 1958–1962
3. ⎭

4. ⎫
5. ⎬ 1949–1957
6. ⎭

7. ⎫
8. ⎬ 1945–1948
9. ⎭

B. *Inside Communist party-state system*

1. 1945–1963: Sustained overwhelming Soviet military superiority.

V. Developmental Factor

A. *Communist Party-State System* (Soviet leadership and effectiveness of control)

1. 1945–1947: Formulation of Communist party-state system.
2. 1949–1953: Consolidation of Communist party-state system.
3. 1953–1955: Period of system uncertainty.
4. 1948: Yugoslav secession.
5. 1958–1960: Informal Chinese challenge within context of formal system unity.
6. 1956–1958: Destalinization.
7. 1961: Overt Soviet reaction to Chinese challenge.
8. 1962: Widening of Sino-Soviet breach.
9. 1963: Overt Chinese response to Soviet criticism. Denunciations become mutual and open.

B. *East–West Relations* (in terms of hostility-friendship)

1. 1945: Postwar amiability.
2. 1963: Nuclear test-ban treaty.
3. 1959–1960: Camp David, Paris Conference.
4. 1955–1958: Hungarian revolution, Suez, sputnik, Lebanon, Quemoy, Berlin note.
5. 1959–1962: U–2, Berlin crisis, Cuban missile crisis.
6. 1953–1954: Uncertainty following Stalin's death.
7. 1946–1947: Peace treaty disputes, containment policy, Truman Doctrine.
8. 1948–1949: Czechoslovakia coup, Marshall Plan, NATO, Berlin blockade.

9. 1950–1952: Korean invasion, Chinese intervention.

C. *Soviet Union-Developing Nations Relations* (political and economic transactions)

1. 1962–1963	4. 1957–1959	7. 1954
2. 1961	5. 1956	8. 1953
3. 1960	6. 1955	9. 1945–1952

The resulting ratings, again independently determined by five expert judges, were then totaled for each crisis. These were the coefficients of inherent riskiness, as cited in Table IX-3, of the twenty-nine crises for the USSR.

The eleven most serious and risky of the twenty-nine crises, the model showed, were the following: (1) Berlin blockade, 1948; (2–3) Cuban crisis, 1962, and Iranian crisis, 1946; (4–5) Greek crises, 1947, and Czechoslovak coup, 1948; (6) Bay of Pigs, 1961; (7) Berlin, 1958; and (9–11) Suez crisis, 1956, Lebanon-Jordan crisis, 1958, and Marshall Plan, 1947.

INTENSITY OF CRISES: BEHAVIORAL VARIABLES

In Table IX-4, we found it useful to separate initiator and respondent, but we have not distinguished among the actions of each participant (i.e., between action—or "bids"—taken during the crises and those taken during the resolution—accommodation/escalation—stage). In the case of each participant, only his *maximum* bid—i.e., most aggressive action in terms of its character, as quantified by a six-point scale (low: verbal-diplomatic to high: open violence)—is given. The table compares the bids of each of the participants against those of their opponents, both individually and as a "side" (for example, the USSR and Egypt bid on the same "side" in the Lebanon-Jordan crisis). If the numerical difference is *positive*, it indicates that the USSR (or its crisis ally) was more aggressive and more inclined to take a risk than its opponent. *Zero* difference indicates that opposing bids were "symmetrical," or of equivalent magnitude. A *minus* difference indicates that the USSR (or its crisis ally) took less risky actions than its opponents. The results of this tabulation give us one kind of evaluation of Soviet risk *behavior*. These results should be compared[15] with the coefficients of inherent riskiness (intensity) of the crises; but they should also be compared with the individual variables of the intensity table in order to give the behavioral findings more meaning. Here we merely compare the *absolute values* of the

---

[15] Comparisons can be general, but they will probably be more meaningful if they are made by crisis category (direct, indirect, European, and Asian Communist party-states).

Table IX-3 Coefficients of Inherent Riskiness (Intensity) of Twenty-nine Crises

CRISIS	DATE	GEOG. LOCATION	STAKES	PARTIES	WEAP./MIL. FACTOR	DEVELOP. FACTOR	RELATIONSHIP	TOTAL	RANKING OF TOTALS	ELEVEN MOST SERIOUS CRISES
Iranian crisis	1946	5	5	6	8	9	c	33	2.5	2-3
Greek crisis	1947	6	6	6	7	7	b	32	4.5	4-5
Marshall plan	1947	3	3	8	6	7	b	27	10	9-11
Czechoslovak coup	1948	5	6	6	7	8	b	32	4.5	4-5
Berlin blockade	1948	6	8	8	7	8	b	37	1	1
Soviet-Yugoslav crisis	1948	6	7	4	1	4	a	22	18.5	—
Korean conflict	1950	4	2	5	6	9	b	26	12	—
Invasion of Tibet	1950	2	2	1	6	9	c	20	22	—
Formosa Strait	1950	4	2	3	5	9	b	23	15.5	—
Indochina	1950	4	2	7	5	7.5	b	25.5	13	—
East Berlin riots	1953	6	7	2	1	3	a	19	23.5	—
NATO	1955	3	3	8	5	4	b	23	15.5	—
Polish revolt	1956	1	7	4	1	6	a	19	23.5	—
Hungarian revolution	1956	5	7	4	4	6	a	23	15.5	—
Suez crisis	1956	7	5	7	4	4	b	27	10	9-11
Lebanon-Jordan crisis	1958	7	5	7	4	4	c	27	10	9-11
Quemoy crisis	1958	4	2	3	3	4	b	16	27.5	—
Proposal on Berlin	1958	6	8	8	3	4	b	29	7	7
Revolt in Tibet	1959	2	2	1	2	4	c	11	29	—
Laos crisis	1959	6	2	5	2	2.5	c	17.5	25	—
U-2 incident	1960	1	1	9	1	5	b	17	26	—
Congo	1960	8	4	5	1	3	c	21	20.5	—
Bay of Pigs invasion	1961	9	9	7	1	5	b	31	6	6
Berlin Wall	1961	6	8	8	1	5	b	28	8	8
Soviet-Albanian dispute	1961	6	7	2	1	7	a	23	15.5	—
Russo-Finnish relations	1961	5	6	2	1	7	a	21	20.5	—
Sino-Indian dispute	1962	4	2	1	1	8	a	16	27.5	—
Cuban crisis	1962	9	9	9	1	5	b	33	2.5	2-3
Sino-Soviet conflict	1963	1	7	4	1	9	a	22	18.5	—

Letter coding: a Communist party-states; b East-West; c USSR developing countries

Table IX-4 Bidding of Participants in Crises

Crisis	Date	Initiator	Maximum Bid	Initiator's Ally	Maximum Bid	Maximum Respondent	Respondent Maximum Bid	Respondent's Ally	Maximum Bid	Difference Between Maximum Bids (Sides)	Difference Between Maximum Bids — Primary	Difference Between Maximum Bids — Allies
Iranian crisis	1946	USSR	4	…	…	Iran	4	U.S., G.B.	1	0	0	+3
Greek crisis	1947	Gr. CP	6	USSR	3	Greece	3	U.S., G.B.	3	0	0	0
Marshall Plan	1947	U.S.	3	…	…	USSR	2	West	…	+2	+2	+1
Czechoslovak coup	1948	Cz. CP	4	USSR	2	Cz.	3	G.B., Fr.	1	+1	+1	+1
Berlin blockade	1948	USSR	4	…	…	U.S.	3	West (UN)	3	0	0	0
Soviet-Yugoslav crisis	1948	Yugo.	2	…	…	USSR	3	West	5	+1	+1	…
Korean conflict	1950–53	N. Korea	6	CPR, USSR	5/3	S. Korea	6	USSR	…	0	0	CPR, USSR: 0 / USSR, U.S.: –2
Invasion of Tibet	1950	CPR	6	…	…	Tibet	6	…	1	0	0	+5
Formosa strait	1950	U.S.	4	…	…	CPR	1	USSR	1	–3	–3	–3
Indochina	1950–54	V.M.	6	CPR, USSR	3	France	6	U.S., G.B.	3	0	0	0
East Berlin riots	1953	E. Germany	6	…	…	E. Germany	6	USSR	6	0	0	0
NATO	1955	U.S.	4	…	…	USSR	4	…	…	–2	–2	…
Polish revolt	1956	Poland	2	…	…	USSR	4	…	…	0	+2	…
Hungarian revolution	1956	Hungary	6	…	…	USSR	6	…	…	0	0	–5
Suez crisis	1956	Israel	6	Fr., G.B.	6	Egypt	6	U.S., USSR	1	0	0	…
Lebanon-Jordan crisis	1958	Iraq	4	Egypt, USSR	1	Lb., Jr.	1	U.S., G.B.	4	+2	+3	–3
Quemoy crisis	1958	CPR	6	USSR	1	Taiwan	4	U.S.	4	0	+2	–3
Proposal on Berlin	1958	USSR	1	…	…	West	1	…	…	0	0	…
Revolt in Tibet	1959	Tibet	6	…	…	CPR	6	…	…	0	0	…
Laos crisis	1959–62	Pa. Laos	6	USSR, DUR	3/6	RLA	6	U.S.	4	0	0	USSR, U.S.: –1 / DRV, U.S.: +1
U-2 incident	1960	USSR	1	…	…	U.S.	1	…	…	0	0	…
Congo	1960	Belgium	6	…	…	Congo	6	U.S., U.N.	3	0	0	0
		Lumumba	6	USSR	3	Kasavubu	6	USSR	1	0	0	–5
Bay of Pigs invasion	1961	U.S.	6	…	…	Cuba	6	USSR	1	+1	+1	+3
Berlin Wall	1961	USSR	4	…	…	U.S.	4	Fr., G.B.	…	+1	+1	…
Soviet-Albanian dispute	1961	Albania	2	…	…	USSR	3	…	…	…	+1	…
Russo-Finnish relations	1961	USSR	2	…	…	Finland	1	…	…	+1	+1	0
Sino-Indian dispute	1962	CPR	6	USSR	1	India	6	West	1	0	0	…
Cuban crisis	1962	USSR	4	…	…	U.S.	4	…	…	0	0	0
Sino-Soviet conflict	1963	CPR	3	…	…	USSR	3	…	…	0	0	…

Note + = USSR (or pro-USSR nation), aggressive
0 = symmetry
− = USSR (or pro-USSR nation), cautious

Bid Scale: 1. Verbal-diplomatic
2. Political
3. Economic-material
4. Force deployment
5. Indirect violence (subversion or UN intermediary)

341

USSR's bids, independent of their relationship to opponent's bids, the seriousness coefficient, and/or the separate variables making up this co-efficient. We rejoin the risk-taking model which measures the initiator's action against his anticipated gain and the responding party's reaction against his expected loss, if we compare the absolute bids with the *stakes* of a particular crisis.

The USSR made the highest bids in the following crises: (1–2) Czecho-slovak coup, 1948, and Polish revolt, 1956; (3–6) Berlin blockade, 1948; Soviet-Yugoslav crisis, 1948; Soviet-Albanian dispute: and Russo-Finnish relations, 1961.

Soviet behavior may also be analyzed in terms of *the character* of the overall Soviet action in each crisis, quantified on a nine-point scale (low risk: immediate withdrawal to high risk: protected conflict). The scale assumes that withdrawal—i.e., willingness to renounce gains and/or accept losses—is a less risky action than conflict—i.e., refusal to renounce gains or accept losses. Compromise lies between these two extremes and entails a willingness to adjust to both gain and loss without completely eliminating one or the other. Evaluation of Soviet behavior in terms of both bids and the overall action in each crisis gives us an important new dimension of Soviet behavior.

Relationship between Independent and Behavioral Variables

We have delineated a series of "independent" and "behavioral" conceptual categories or variables which we believe are related to each other in a systematic manner. Each crisis, therefore, has its nonbehavioral aspects, which can be defined as the situational or relatively static characteristics of the crisis. These are: (1) the geographical location of the crisis; (2) the stakes involved; (3) the parties involved; (4) the state of military or weapons parity; and (5) a developmental aspect which is defined as the level of hostility or tension existing between the actors at the time that the crisis occurred. The theoretical assumption underlying the fifth nonbehavioral variable is that the level of tension or hostility existing between the two actors operates as a type of threshold. Thus, a crisis occurring during a time of higher tension involves greater risk, because any given act is more likely to be interpreted as involving a greater threat to the perceiver than if the threshold were higher (i.e., the level of hostility lower). In the second type of situation there is a greater likelihood that a given act will be interpreted as being less hostile than if the tension level were higher. A similar reasoning lies behind each of the nonbehavioral variables: there is a scale of alternative states for each variable, with each state involving greater or lesser risk to the Soviet Union when it acts in the international system.

Therefore to each of these variables was assigned a scale of alternatives with an ascending order (low to high) of risk to the Soviet Union. The first three nonbehavioral variables (geographical location, stakes, and parties) use the same scale for all crises, but the last two variables employ different scales for different categories of crises: the military- and weapons-parity variable uses one scale for crises involving the USSR with the West and the developing nations, and another scale is assigned to those crises involving other members of the world communist system. The developmental variable employs three different scales for indicating level of tension: (1) for those crises within the communist system which are scaled according to levels of Soviet leadership and effectiveness of control over the communist system at a given time; (2) as general levels of hostility-friendship in crises involving the West at a given time; and (3) in terms of levels of political and economic interaction with the developing world in crises with nations of that grouping.

The behavioral aspects of Soviet risk-taking are categorized as (1) the maximum bid made by the initiator in the crisis, (2) the bid made by the responding party, and (3) the outcome of the crisis in terms of the behavior of the Soviet Union. The first two variables are scaled in terms of the greater or lesser violence of their bid (from verbal diplomatic to open violence); the act is scaled the same whether or not the Soviet Union or a pro-USSR nation is the initiator or the respondent in the crisis. The outcome is scaled according to the behavior of the Soviet Union in "terminating" the crisis. Outcomes, thus, are scaled in terms of the withdrawal (immediate, delayed, or protected). The lower end of the scale then is the more pacific, nonviolent crisis resolution, whereas the higher end of the scale represents more conflictual, violent behavior.

Within the theoretical framework we have developed for this investigation, the nonbehavioral aspects of crises are conceived of as independent variables and the behavioral aspects as dependent variables. In other words, we hypothesize that there are systematic relationships between the two sets of variables, and that "inputs" [(in terms of high or lower risk alternatives among the independent variables) (or nonbehavioral aspects)] are systematically associated with particular directional changes in crisis "outputs" (i.e., higher or lower bids or more or less violent crisis outcomes).

We also hypothesize that different relationships among the independent and dependent variables will be salient in different situational contexts. Three type of situational contexts were constructed, and all the crises were divided into categories within each of the situational contexts as well as on an all-crisis basis. Thus all the crises were grouped into three time categories: (1) 1945–1949; (2) 1950–1953; (3) 1954–1963. The first period represents that in which the Soviet Union did not possess atomic arms. The second period is that of Soviet possession of atomic, but not nuclear, arms. The third period is that of essential parity with the West.

All the crises were also divided into three categories, depending on whether they occurred within the communist system between the Soviet Union and the West or the communist system and the developing nations. A third dichotomous categorization of all the crises was made on the basis of whether the Soviet Union or its ally was the initiator or the respondent in the crisis.

The method of determining the relationship between the variables was that of rank-ordering the values of the variables for the crises included in each category and computing a Spearman rank-correlation coefficient. Thus, each dependent variable (initiator's maximum bid, respondent's maximum bid, and outcome for the USSR) was correlated with each independent variable (stakes, geographical risk, saliency of parties, weapons-military parity, and hostility level) to determine the direction and extent of the relationship between them for the purpose of discovering those variables which can best predict Soviet crisis behavior.

The numerical values for all independent variables and each dependent variable for each crisis in each situational context were punched onto IBM cards and then recorded onto tape. A program was written for computing the Spearman rank-correlation coefficient with the correction for tied ranks.[16] The computations were performed on the IBM 7090 computer, and results were recorded on paper from the tape by the IBM 1401 printer.

A total of 135 rank-correlation coefficients were computed (five independent variables with three dependent variables in nine situational contexts). We discuss those that are statistically significant, with some exceptions, in Appendix IX-1, but the reader should bear in mind that those relationships that are explicated represent only a part of the number possible. The remainder, therefore, are those for which our data show little or no significant association.

SUMMARY OF FINDINGS

Though the Soviet Union in terms of *bidding* either as initiator or respondent showed mixed tendencies in terms of risk-taking, the general trend was for the USSR to take less rather than more risk in higher bids put forth.

[16] See Sidney Siegel, *Nonparametric Statistics for the Behavioral Sciences*, (New York: McGraw Hill, Inc., 1956), pp. 202–213.

Table IX-5   Outcome of Crisis

CRISIS	SOVIET ACTION	MAGNITUDE	RISK
Iranian crisis	Delayed withdrawal	2	1
Greek crisis	Protracted withdrawal	3	2
Marshall Plan	Protracted conflict	9	3
Czechoslovak coup	Immediate conflict	7	4
Berlin blockade	Compromise (gain equal to loss)	5	3
Soviet-Yugoslav crisis	Protracted conflict	9	6
Korean conflict	Compromise (gain equal to loss)	5	1
Invasion of Tibet	Indifferent	—	—
Formosa Strait	Indifferent	—	—
Indochina	Compromise (gain greater than loss)	6	5
East Berlin riots	Immediate conflict	7	4
NATO	Protracted conflict	9	7
Polish revolt	Compromise (gain less than loss)	4	3
Hungarian revolution	Delayed conflict	8	5
Suez crisis	Compromise (gain equal to loss)	5	4
Lebanon-Jordan crisis	Compromise (gain less than loss)	4	3
Quemoy crisis	Indifferent	—	—
Proposal on Berlin	Compromise (gain equal to loss)	5	1
Revolt in Tibet	Indifferent	—	—
Laos crisis	Compromise (gain greater than loss)	6	3
U-2 incident	Immediate conflict	7	4
Congo	Protracted withdrawal	3	3
Bay of Pigs Invasion	Immediate withdrawal	1	1
Berlin Wall	Delayed conflict	8	4
Soviet-Albanian dispute	Protracted conflict	9	4
Soviet-Finnish relations	Compromise (gain greater than loss)	6	1
Sino-Indian dispute	Indifferent	—	—
Cuban crisis	Delayed withdrawal	2	2
Sino-Soviet conflict	Protracted conflict	9	7

But the tendencies for risk-avoidance or risk-taking seem much more pronounced when we consider *crisis output*. There is a definite difference in the chronological time groupings, with risk-avoidance predominant both in the immediate postwar period and the Khrushchev era, but with an ambivalent tendency in the intermediate, late Stalin period. Also, when controlling for groupings, we find striking variations. The Soviet Union was much more willing to approach conflict with another member of the communist system when it perceived stakes to be higher. However, if the West or a developing nation was involved, a more cautious pattern was followed. Crisis outputs here decreased as the stakes and geographical risk increased, and this pattern was consistent with a decrease (though not statistically significant) in risk alternatives of parties, weapons parity, and hostility levels in crises with the developing nations.

CONCLUSION

It is our conclusion that the multiple constraints superimposed on Soviet risk-taking throughout this time period have been such that the resulting level and pattern of Soviet risk assumed in the twenty-nine crises have been *low* and *narrow*. Soviet crisis behavior was found to be conservative rather than radical, cautious rather than reckless, deliberate rather than impulsive, and rational (not willing to lose) rather than nonrational.

Throughout our research, we have assumed that risk-taking and risk-calculation is a product of rational behavior. Relying on William Riker's definition of rationality—in politics rational men are men who would rather win than lose, regardless of the particular stakes[17]—we assumed that rational men may be misinformed, adventurous, primitive, reckless, overcautious, or appeasing, but they do not want to lose. This is why we do not agree that the lack of emotional investment in objectives produced a lack of readiness to take risks to achieve the objectives. Instead, we argue that, on the basis of the available empirical evidence, Soviet risk-taking is principally a function of perceived material *capability, not* (hostile, aggressive) *attitude*.

In addition, risk-taking is a form of *nonverbal communication*. This is how the U.S. views Soviet risk-taking ("their deeds matter, not their words") and how it assesses it. The Soviet Union must incur risk to communicate to us their seriousness of purpose.

The *overall formulas* of Soviet risk-taking we have derived from our study are as follows:

(1) *All crises.* The USSR tends to be more placative as a respondent than as an initiator (in terms of weapons and military parity) and more aggressive as initiator than as respondent. However, this second proposition was found to be so because the original challenge or stimulus, i.e., the initial risk-taking action—and input of new tensions into international relations (unless an actual act of war)—did not appear to be perceived by the USSR as a risk-creating mechanism, whether initiated by the USSR or its antagonist; but the response to it, the output, the joining of the issue by the oppon ent, did. As a consequence, Soviet antagonists appear to be in the position of being able to afford new stimuli, new challenges, and new initial risk-taking actions of their own without incurring a disproportionate risk. This is not in itself perceived by the USSR (irrespective of their verbal response) as "dangerous behavior." Furthermore, Soviet decision-makers are aware of and employ risk-reducing emergency strategy. Putting long-range rockets in Cuba was

[17] William Riker, *The Theory of Political Coalitions* (New Haven: Yale University Press, 1962), p. 22.

such a strategy—an initial risk action coupled with timed, automatic risk-reducing mechanism. When the U.S. got tough, the USSR pulled out. This coupling of attack with automatic readiness to withdraw under fire makes the initial challenge a useful political tool of little risk.

The difference between Stalin and Khrushchev as Soviet risk-takers had been minimal. True, in low-tension cases, Khrushchev was more active, flamboyant, ribald, imaginative, and inventive; however, in high-tension crises, he was as cautious, conservative, and circumspect as Stalin. Khrushchev was simply more sophisticated, and more aware of and better skilled in employing a risk-reducing emergency strategy mechanism coupled with the initial risk action.

The additional statements which can be made about Soviet risk-taking behavior are the following:

The less concerned with the crisis objective, the lower the Soviet risk-taking propensity (Tibet, Formosa, the Sino-Indian conflict), whereas conversely the greater the Soviet concern, the less cautious the USSR (Hungary).

The higher the stakes, the more reluctant the USSR as the risk-taker.

The higher the Soviet bid, the lower the Soviet propensity for risk-taking, i.e., the more force the USSR uses, the less the Soviet perception of the crisis as being risky for the USSR (e.g., Hungary).

The riskier (the more serious), the crisis, the more cautious the USSR.

The less risky (serious) the crisis, the more willing the USSR to acquire gain or engage in conflict (and vice-versa, with the USSR withdrawing or compromising).

The more risky (serious) the crisis, the more force the USSR tends to use (in all crises).

(2) *East-West crises.* The greater the Soviet weapons-military parity with the West, the lower the Soviet perception of risk in actual East-West conflicts.

The stronger the other party in crisis; the greater the geographical distance from the USSR; and the greater the stakes involved, the more cautious the Soviet crisis response.

(3) *Soviet crises with other Communist party-states.* The stronger the other party—the greater the stakes (and the farther the distance from the Soviet Union), the less cautious the USSR, and the more willing to assume risk and engage in conflict.

The less the Soviet control in "the socialist system," the greater the intensity of crises there.

The less the Soviet control of the "socialist system," the less the Soviet force used in crises there.

(4) *Time*. Soviet decisions in crises tend to take days rather than hours or minutes.

The more actively a Soviet decision invokes the change in the *status quo* and is directed against normal, routine expectations, the longer the time period to make that decision.

As an initiator of a crisis, the USSR tends to take much longer (on an average of six-and-one-half times more) to decide than when acting as a respondent.

Compromises and conflicts tend to involve more Soviet decisional time than withdrawals (r = 0.750).

The farther a crisis occurs from the USSR (r = 0.842), the greater the stakes involved (r = 0.853); the more important (essential, salient) the parties (r = 0.822), the greater the potential magnitude of the weapons-military involvement (r = 0.894); the more intense the cold war (r = 0.736), the less the Soviet affective control over the other Communist party-states (in Soviet crises with them); and the greater the tendency of the risk situation toward violence, the longer the Soviet decision-makers tend to delay action.

Assessing the Soviet *gains and losses* in the twenty-nine crises, we found that in nine crises, the USSR attempted to gain benefits (Iran, 1946; Greece, 1947; Czechoslovakia, 1948; Berlin, 1948; Korea, 1950; Suez, 1956; Berlin, 1958; Finland, 1961; and Cuba, 1962) but succeeded only twice—in Czechoslovakia in 1948 and in Finland in 1961. In both cases, it dealt from a position of strength with two small states. In eight crises, the USSR feared loss (the Marshall Plan in 1947 [and NATO in 1955]; Yugoslavia in 1948; East Germany in 1953; Poland in 1956; Hungary in 1956; Albania in 1962; and China in the last several years) but suffered what may be assessed as actual tangible loss in only four cases—Yugoslavia; freezing of West European borders (i.e., via the Marshall Plan and NATO); Albania; and China.

On this basis—and it is quite possible that other investigators may assess Soviet gains and losses differently—for all the hopes, frustrations, costs, and tensions in the seventeen crises, the USSR has little to show: it lost four and won only two cases. And, except for the hardening of the formerly soft East-West European borders, all the losses and gains took place in the Communist party-states and in Finland. To put it mildly, the Soviet batting average in the twenty-nine post-World War II crises has been very low.

According to Morton Kaplan, the attitude toward risk depends upon the needs of the system making the decisions;[18] undoubtedly this is so. But the *attitude* in turn depends on so many *other* considerations, we found, that a statement like this is almost meaningless; the needs, yes, but *when*, against *whom*, backed by *what* and *where*? These, we submit, must be the questions.

[18] Morton A. Kaplan, *System and Process in International Relations* (New York: John Wiley & Sons, Inc., 1957), p. 208.

THE SOVIET UNION AND INTERNATIONAL ORGANIZATION

International organization, one of the major twentieth-century stages for the conduct of foreign policy, is an institutionalized diplomatic arena in which members practice open diplomacy and, to a new extent, democracy in international relations. As new in the world as the USSR, general international organization, chiefly in the form of the League of Nations and the United Nations, has proved to be an important catalyst of Soviet foreign policy.

An international organization of states is an association of members who join together to facilitate cooperation among themselves for common purposes. *The League of Nations* tended to express the democratic principles of nineteenth-century Western liberalism. The organization was built on a pattern of thought which placed belief in human progress on a platform of natural law. The League's fundamental theoretical principle was the recognition of man's dignity and his right to personal freedom as a condition of universal peace and order. Constitutionalism, humanitarianism, freedom, equality, enlightenment, peace—ideas previously diffused but rooted in the heritage of Western civilization—were to be united under a common roof and elevated to legal expression of common interests.

Unfortunately, the various espectations of members, and especially of the powerful members, of what the League ought to be, created an ideological schism which prevented practical success. The French approach and attitude toward the League was from the beginning conservative. France simply viewed the League as a security system against Germany, which had invaded France three times in a century. Preservation and enforcement of the postwar *status quo* was thought essential to French security, and any change, even peaceful, of Germany's subordination might endanger it.

The British viewed the League in a different light. To them it was an important meeting ground, useful both for serving the needs of the world at large and for the perceived national interests of its members. Great Britain was ready to give Germany a chance and to allow it the League's facilities to improve its Versailles fate. But the British did not view the League as a parliament of the world or a supranational organization, as idealists in smaller nations and the vision of Woodrow Wilson characterized it. At the same time, the British did not share the narrow French attitude of building a monolithic European defense against Germany.

Some small European states tended to follow the French position. But the League never became a security organization even in the European theater where it was the strongest. After all, issues of war and peace could not be resolved by international organization but only by the courses which nation-states, and especially large nation-states, pursued. The League facilitated or hindered, but it did not determine these courses. "In the end it was just another institution, and nothing more."[1]

The League became neither a universal organization nor a homogeneous federation of states. Worse, it failed to realize that peaceful change was a *sine qua non* attribute of a condition of peace. Specifically, Article 19 of the League Covenant raised hope that any initial mistakes in the Versailles Treaty could be repaired; but, the League failed to invoke this article in practice.

It is unfair to attribute, as some observers have, the League's downfall to the evil plans of National Socialist Germany, Fascist Italy, Imperial Japan, and/or the Soviet Union. Undoubtedly, "the doctrine, aims and practices of the totalitarian states were in direct conflict with the purposes and action of the League [and] they rejected every restraining action because their success depended on surprise and intimidation."[2] It may be conceded that the four states shared considerably in blame for what happened, but the record of the League proves that the guilt was more widely distributed. Lack of effective procedure for the revision of treaties, failure to solve the disarmament problem, and reluctance to employ machinery for settlement of disputes can not simply be attributed to "the deliberate design of the totalitarian states . . . to divide, weaken, and immobilize the peace forces in the world."[3] The other members, especially France and Great Britain, must be blamed as well. And the great nonmember, the United States, must be viewed at least as responsible for the failure of the League of Nations as the several intimidated members.

The prevailing concept behind the *United Nations* deviated somewhat from the optimistic aspirations of the League of Nations. The experience of

---

[1] See Osten Unden's statement in the General Assembly, 443rd Plenary Meeting, *U.N. Official Records* (New York: UN, September 24, 1953), p. 118.

[2] Marcel Holden, "Europe Without the League," *Foreign Affairs*, XVIII (1939), 13.

[3] *Ibid.*, p. 14.

the League, in juxtaposition to the expectations, hopes, and beliefs of some of the League's founding fathers, impressed the architects of the post-World War II international organization. Conspicuously absent in planning for the United Nations was the belief that mankind is moving inexorably toward universal acceptance of the same type of government and thus toward a guarantee of peace for all time. No principle of the United Nations Charter indicated preference for a particular form of government, and there was no condition for admission to the United Nations stipulating a democratic form of government. The United Nations became more of a "center for harmonizing the actions of nations in the attainment of common good" (Article 1 of the Charter). Although not rejecting expressly all the optimistic assumptions essential to the League, the United Nations has been more modest in aspiration. The Charter merely "reaffirms faith . . . in the dignity and worth of the human person" (Preamble).

Communist doctrine is opposed to the idea that government founded on the recognition of man's dignity and his right to personal freedom can be a guarantee of universal peace. Marxist-Leninist theory professes goals which stipulate establishment of another type of international organization, quite different from the League of Nations or the United Nations. Such a new international organization presupposes radical changes in the internal affairs of its members, a *sine qua non* of their admission into the organization. This is why Soviet spokesmen would prefer, for example, a Soviet-sponsored international organization such as the World Peace Council to the United Nations. Such an "international organization," is "a truly universal and the most representative international organization in the whole world. The World Peace Council, at variance with the United Nations Organization, represents the nations themselves, not their governments. In this is its particular strength and its indisputable moral authority."[4] The capitalist governments allegedly do not represent their particular countries but only the ruling classes therein. They are therefore assumed to be unrepresentative of the wishes of their people. As a consequence, to follow the Marxist-Leninist argument, an organization composed of individuals is bound to be more representative than one composed of governments.

But Communist party-states do not join or remain in international organizations because they have common long-range goals with the noncommunist members. They join and remain in such organizations because they share some short-range interests with the other members and because they believe they can turn their participation to their own advantage. There is admittedly

[4] S. V. Molodtsov, "For the Prevention of War, For the Peace Pact," *Sovetskoe gosudarstvo i pravo*, VII (1951), p. 23.

a challenge to the freedom of action of a Communist party-state which becomes a member of an international organization across ideological frontiers. The noncommunist majority may shape the international organization in its image more successfully than the communist minority can. Undoubtedly this process would be even more true if the picture were reversed, as it was, for instance, at the Belgrade Conference on the Danube in 1948. It seems clear that any member in the minority position would insist, as a price for membership and participation, on minority rights for self-protection and self-expression.

A universal organization of states tends to acknowledge and preserve the *status quo*. Both the League and the United Nations neglected adequate provisions for peaceful change. Both relied on international law, as well as some new rules which they helped introduce and make acceptable. International law, like all law, is conservative; it protects the established order against change and favors the preservation of things as they are. True, "law and order can not be conceived as a negation of a healthy international evolution."[5] Yet both the Covenant and the Charter failed to emphasize such change.

A Communist party-state, member of an organized community of nations, can easily identify itself with international organization so far as it desires to preserve and maintain the *status quo*. It can not, however, identify itself with such an organization of states in its desire to change the *status quo*. Its attitude towards such an organization depends then, on the relationship of its aspirations for change to its aspirations for maintaining certain characteristics of the *status quo*. Consequently, a Communist party-state cannot help sharing some attitudes with the bulk of membership, for instance a fear of general war, but at the same time, it cannot avoid some misgivings about the organization over the indefinite future.

Another part of the Communist party-state attitude toward international organization is its tactical response to a minority position in the international community. A continually guarded and suspicious demeanor, the product of a fundamentally hostile regard for fellow members must be presumed. This caution may be expected to be exaggerated by the relative lack of domestic heritage of democratic norms.

The object of this chapter is then to examine how and why the USSR has cooperated with the League of Nations and United Nations. It may also be thought of as a study of one of the several channels of communication and

---

[5] *Documents of the United Nations Conference on International Organization* (San Francisco: UN, 1945), VI, 410.

interaction which the USSR has with the noncommunist international environment.

SOVIET UNION AND THE LEAGUE OF NATIONS

Lenin, before 1917, indicated (1) that a Socialist Russia could conceivably become a member of an international organization of free republics and nonmonarchial states. His concept of an international organization, similar to the concept of leading European statesmen at the time, was an organization of European states, a United States of Europe. To Lenin, however, such an organization would have been only a transitional arrangement for converting Europe to socialism. (2) He preferred an organization of socialist states, should that be possible.

Faithful to Marx, Lenin emphasized that socialism, not an international organization, would guarantee lasting peace: "Peace must be sought and fought for . . . not in a league of equal nations under capitalism, but in the future, in the socialist revolution of the proletariat."[6] Capitalism might attempt to prepare the world for world government; only under socialism, however, could this process come to fruition. Before the Bolshevik Revolution, then, Lenin was not opposed to an international organization in principle. He opposed basing such an organization on the capitalist system.

After the Revolution, Lenin showed preference for bilateral relations with other nations separately. The League of Nations, both in form and in content, was too rigid. Soviet Russia was too different, too new, too revolutionary to fit into the League and was bound to be misunderstood there. As People's Commissar of Foreign Affairs Chicherin put it, "Russia would prefer to see general congresses convene for the purpose, which would appoint their own executive organs with the duty of putting into effect such decisions as might be taken."[7] A permanent international organization with broad competence and with its functions in the hands of capitalist states seemed a formidable obstacle to Soviet plans. If there had to be a collective international agency, the Soviet government preferred *ad hoc* conferences without limitations on sovereignty, without sanctions, and without constraints.

Lenin and his friends could justify their original attitudes towards the

[6] V. I. Lenin, *Collected Works* (New York: International Publishers, 1942), p. 67. Cf. Dale C. Fuller, "Lenin's Attitude Toward an International Organization for the Keeping of Peace, 1914–1917," *Political Science Quarterly,* LXIV (1949), 245.

[7] Special note from Chicherin proposing a new kind of League of Nations in 1923. Quoted in Kathryn W. Davis, *The Soviets at Geneva, 1919–1933* (Geneva: Librairie Kundig, 1934), p. 21.

League of Nations and its members; their hostility was not unprovoked. France was instrumental in helping Poland, a League member, in her war against the Soviet Union. The League held its very first session during this war. It suggested various lines of demarcation but hardly attempted to gain Soviet confidence. England intervened in the Bolshevik Revolution and, assisted by the United States, supported the White Armies in their effort to bring about the downfall of the Bolshevik government. The League refused persistent private appeals for help during the 1921–1922 Russian famine. And Woodrow Wilson, the League's founding father, hoped out loud that the League would develop into "an antidote to communism" and would aid what the Soviets called counterrevolutionary tendencies.[8]

To Soviet leaders the League understandably seemed not an international organization for maintenance of world peace but rather an active coalition of anti-Soviet allies united to destroy the Soviet Union, "an alliance of world bandits against the proletariat" (Lenin), "a league of capitalist against the nations" (Chicherin), and "the fist of the Supreme Allied Council."[9] Before 1927, the Soviet attitude toward the League was founded on this claim of incompatibility with a bourgeois world united in the League of Nations against the Soviet Union. At the same time, however, Soviet leaders found it feasible to maintain contact with the League's technical agencies. They cooperated in some projects of the League, such as those combatting communicable diseases and narcotic drugs, promoting rehabilitation of refugees, and repatriation of prisoners of war.

At the League of Nation's Economic Conference in Geneva in 1927, which the Soviet Union attended, the Soviet delegation declared for the first time that a peaceful coexistence in the League of Nations between the Soviet Union and the capitalist world was possible. This step implied growing Soviet interest in the search for peace not only on a bilateral basis as in the past, but also on a multilateral level.

Peace for the Soviet Union was now at a premium. To build and modernize rapidly at home, peace was needed more than justice in the prevailing world order. A Soviet Union undisturbed by war would be of greater use to the workers of the world. Soviet foreign policy from 1927 to 1934 may be characterized as a determined search for security—a security which would permit pursuing the kinds of domestic policies dictated by "socialism-in-one-country." Peace for the Soviet Union seemed best realizable through

[8] Harold W. V. Temperly, *A History of the Peace Conference of Paris* (New York: Oxford University Press, 1924), VI, 580.

[9] K. W. Davis, *The Soviet Union and the League of Nations, 1919–1933* (Geneva: General Research Center, 1934), p. 4.

nonintervention, nonaggression, neutrality, and disarmament. With the exception of neutrality, Soviet tactics coincided with the efforts of the League.

Then, with deterioration of the interational situation, the USSR demonstrated a tendency to replace a project close to its heart, total disarmament, by the principle of collective security:

> The question is not that of disarmament itself, since that is only a means to an end, but that of guaranteeing peace. And since that is so, the question actually arises, could not the Conference (the 1934 Disarmament Conference) feel its way toward other guarantees of peace; or, at any rate, might it not increase the measure of security for at least those states which, cherishing no aggressive designs, were not interested in war and which, in the event of war, might become only the objects of attack?[10]

Finally, with the dangers emerging both in Europe and in the Far East, Stalin felt forced to alter Soviet foreign policies. Active alliances became attractive, even on multilateral basis. On September 18, 1934, a year after National Socialist Germany had withdrawn from the League, the Soviet Union entered.

After castigating the League for such a long time as a pious disguise of imperialism, the Soviet Union joined for compelling strategic reasons. On both sides it was a marriage of convenience; many members felt the League needed the Soviet Union as much as the Soviet Union needed the League. Common enemies, Japan and Germany, now lay outside the organization. The Soviet Union was on its way as the new protagonist of collective security.

France and England wished to strengthen the League of Nations in any fashion. Soviet membership would raise its prestige after Japanese and German withdrawal and while Fascist Italy pressed for debilitating revision of the League as an organization. Soviet membership might strengthen the support of the left-of-center parties in all democratic countries and counterbalance critics on the right.

Thus, common danger brought the League and the USSR together. As the Chairman of the Council of People's Commissars Molotov put it on January 28, 1935, contrasting the past with the future:

[10] Litvinov, summing up the two years' work of the Disarmament Conference, May 29, 1934: *Minutes of the General Commission of the Conference for the Reduction and Limitation of Armaments* (Geneva: League of Nations, 1936), III, 659.

It is known that the League of Nations in its time was created by states then still not desirous of recognizing the rights of the new worker-peasant state to exist, but instead, participating in anti-Soviet military intervention. Strong efforts were made in its time to transform the League of Nations into a weapon directing the mouth of the cannon on the Soviet Union. . . . Since then much water has flowed under the bridge. Events of recent times have emphasized these changes which have taken place in the situation of the League of Nations. The League of Nations has become for them, in the given circumstances, confining and inconvenient. But the majority of participants in the League of Nations are now for one or another consideration not interested in the unleashing of war.[11]

The Soviet Union did not join the League of Nations "in order to promote international economic and social cooperation"; it never regarded the League's economic and social activities as a stepping stone to political unity. Stalin wanted security for the Soviet Union. The League of Nations appeared to him a possible shield against external threat to the Soviet Union. This is why the Soviet Union joined, and this is why Stalin wanted to strengthen the League and build it up.

Between 1934 and 1938 Soviet spokesmen in the League of Nations were among the strongest supporters of the League as a collective-security organization. But they were steadily disillusioned by its failure of resolution. The League, they felt, did not make use of its resources.

The League of Nations' Covenant did not and could not provide for a harmonious and homogeneous system of international security. France, like the USSR, attempted to build up in the League a collective system that would guarantee French security; Great Britain saw the League primarily as a body to foster international cooperation and good will, without a direct responsibility for the enforcement of peace. Stalin's hopes were dashed. The League "did not prohibit aggression" and "it never made sanctions against aggressors effective."[12] Thus, in 1939, the Soviet Union left the League of Nations for exactly the same reason it had joined five years before: to seek a more promising path to Soviet national security.

After concluding the famous Hitler-Stalin pact of August 30, 1939, and thereafter embarking upon the "Winter War" with Finland, the Soviet Union

---

[11] "Report to the Seventh All-Union Congress in Moscow," *Documents on International Affairs* (London: Royal Institute of International Affairs, 1936), p. 405.

[12] Stalin in *Pravda,* No. 4, 1934, quoted in T. A. Taracouzio, *War and Peace in Soviet Diplomacy* (New York: The Macmillan Company, 1940), p. 194. See also S. B. Krylov in Ye. A. Korovin, *Mezhdunarodnoe pravo* (Moscow: Gosiurizdat, 1951), p. 425.

was officially expelled from the League for failure to fulfill its obligations under the Covenant.

The Soviet delegation, refusing to participate in the debate of the League of Nations on Soviet aggression in Finland, was censured and expelled *in absentia* for its action. But the League paid as well. With World War II under way, the European countries feared involvement and retaliation by the Soviet Union or by its new and aggressive ally, Nazi Germany. They either remained passive (the Scandinavian countries, Baltic states, Holland, and Denmark) or they did not even appear for the meeting. Switzerland, anxiously avoiding any act which might be interpreted by Germany as hostile, insisted on a passive attitude toward the Soviet-Finnish war. China preferred to stay out of trouble with the Soviet Union. Ironically, the South American representatives, far removed from potential attack by the Soviet Union or Germany, appeared the most militant defenders of the League of Nations' principles.

The Soviet reaction to the verdict of the Council was immediate; the League was condemned again as an instrument of a coalition of hostile states, an instrument of the imperialist Western bloc:

> Instead of terminating the war between Germany and the Anglo-French bloc, the present membership of the League of Nations is striving to fan the flames of war in the northeast of Europe. In the final analysis Russia can only gain as a result of this action: she is free from all moral responsibility for the infamous deeds of the League, and henceforth the Soviet Union will have full freedom of action.[13]

The League, its position precarious before, could not take another severe blow; the Soviets were right at least in this respect: The debate in which the Soviet behavior was censured and the USSR formally expelled from the League was the last official meeting of the League of Nations as an international organization.

SOVIET UNION AND THE UNITED NATIONS

In the waning days of World War II, Stalin treated the United Nations as he had the League of Nations in 1934. He showed interest in the new international organization as a bulwark against the resurgence of Germany and Japan and thus as a new collective-security agency which could protect

[13] Statement of Tass, quoted in David J. Dallin, *Soviet Russia's Foreign Policy, 1939–1942* (New Haven: Yale University Press, 1942), p. 173.

the Soviet Union against external danger. Both in Stalin's writings and in diplomatic discussions, the United Nations was described as an uninterrupted continuation of the wartime coalition under peacetime conditions. Stalin did express, even before the end of the war, apprehensions concerning the new security organization's following the path of the League of Nations in lining up some powers against others. But the distribution of power in the United Nations appeared to allay his apprehension. Remembering well the fate of nations which quit the League, Stalin also viewed the Soviet membership in the United Nations as a guarantee that the organization would not concert action against the Soviet Union.

In the eighteen months' period between the Moscow and San Francisco conferences, the Soviet Union had no reason for complaint. The Big Five presented a united front at San Francisco with respect to the Articles of the Chapter concerning security provisions (Articles 5–8 and 12). Three security concepts—namely, the responsibility of the great powers for peace and security, the elevation of the Security Council as a primary organ, and the Great Powers' unanimity principle—were readily accepted and defended by all the Great Powers. Even minor disagreements—concerning exclusion of a Great Power from discussing peaceful settlement of a dispute to which it is a party, unanimity of approval for discussion of matters in the Security Council, and the place of regional arrangements and organizations as bases for peace and security—were settled by compromise.

The first real disagreement among the Great Powers, although warnings had appeared in previous discussions, occurred at the London Conference of Foreign Ministers in the fall of 1945. In the United Nations, it burst out in the Security Council with a 1946 discussion of the Iranian question, having to do with the withdrawal of Soviet troops from the Iranian province of Azerbaijan. From that time the conflict continued—and intensified—with the Greek question, Berlin blockade, the Communist *coup d'etat* in Czechoslovakia, and the war in Korea.

In the Soviet view, the unexpected performance of the United Nations in Korea was a reconfirmation, if that was needed, of the United States' manipulation of the organization against the Soviet Union. Correspondingly, the Soviet effort in the United Nations sought to weaken the organization in order to weaken the United States, as well as to convince the UN membership that no major international problem could be solved without the direct and willing participation of the Soviet Union. Liberal use of its veto in the Security Council dramatized this assertion. In debate, Soviet delegates hammered away at the alleged United States attempt to monopolize the United Nations as its own agent, pointing out that Soviet cooperation in the

United Nations would be necessary for survival of the organization.

For Stalin, the United Nations thus became a security organization which failed just as had the League of Nations. The Security Council which had symbolized to him the embodiment of the principle of security lodged within the concept of unanimity of Great Powers—the meeting ground of powerful states capable of dealing with grave issues and a forum where the Soviet interests were to be protected by the veto—proved to be a mirage. The weakening of the primacy of the Security Council by the United States not only seemed illegal but attacked the very premises upon which the Soviet Union joined the organization. In terms of his hopes, the United Nations was a failure. It was not the kind of prophylactic organization to which the Soviet Union originally subscribed in 1945.

At that time the United States operated the majority principle in order to check the Soviet Union's undesirable moves much better than did the Soviet Union operate the minority principle. The balance has worked to the advantage of the United States in the United Nations. In a number of instances the Soviet opposition in the United Nations was unable to cope with determined actions of the Western powers. The Soviet minority tactics, although effective in using the veto as a check against the decisions of its capitalist partners, have proved less potent than the Western majority tactics. The veto could prevent—but it could not create. For the Soviet Union, the veto has been the most important principle of the Charter precisely because it offered in security matters a balance in procedural techniques between the protection of the minority and the imposition of rule by the majority. In the rich organizational experience of the Soviet leaders, procedure has proved to be very important. Without the veto, the Soviet Union would have left the organization a long time ago. It would have felt forced to leave. With the veto the United Nations was a failure but not dangerous. Without it the organization would have been both. As Vyshinsky put it in 1948,

> The veto is a powerful political tool. There are no such simpletons here as would let it drop. Perhaps we use it more, but that is because we are in the minority and the veto balances power. If we were in the majority, we could make such grandiloquent gestures as offering to waive the veto on this or that.[14]

And so while the United States was making grandiloquent gestures in the General Assembly, the Soviet Union used the veto in the Security Council.

[14] Speech by Vyshinsky in Paris, November 1948, to the *Ad Hoc* Political Committee, quoted in *The New York Times*, November 25, 1948.

Stalin's successors at first followed in Stalin's footsteps, as Stalin had first followed in Lenin's. The important change took place in December, 1955, when the Molotov proposal for a package admission of new members (after fifty-five Soviet vetoes on admission of new members) was finally accepted. The package consisted of sixteen new members, of which twelve were sponsored by the West (Austria, Italy, Finland, Spain, Ireland, and Portugal from Europe and Jordan, Libya, Laos, Cambodia, and Ceylon from among the Asian-African nations) and four by the Soviet Union (Bulgaria, Rumania, Hungary, and Albania). Japan, paired with Outer Mongolia, was vetoed by Nationalist China. The ratio of 3 to 1 in favor of the West was attractive, but the United States' loss of political dominance in the General Assembly was thereby sealed. The shift which had taken place was towards anticolonialism, neutralism, and a more functional and less security-conscious organization.

From then on the new Soviet leadership proved its versatility. Recognizing new opportunities, Khrushchev skillfully combined Stalin's defensive posture in the organization with an imaginative new offensive. He adopted a series of positions which closely resembled the attitude of a majority of members. Even more than before, the Soviet delegation emphasized anti-imperialism and anticolonialism; in this way, the USSR sought maximum support from Asian, African, and Latin American members of the United Nations. The Soviet delegation now adopted attitudes which would have been impossible for Stalin—such as proneutralism—and in fact it began to advocate plans previously defended by the United States *against* the Soviet Union. The Soviet representatives now argued that the center of gravity in the United Nations was and ought to be the General Assembly; that all members of the United Nations, large and small, are not only legally but also politically equal; that the Charter of the United Nations must be loosely rather than strictly construed; and that the veto in the Security Council should be reserved for emergency purposes. The Soviet delegates argued that there should be a greater alliance on majority vote in the General Assembly. They increasingly emphasized that the United Nations should not only perform a passive security function, but should become an active, universal organization for peace, proclaiming freedom from colonial oppression, neutralism, and equality for all. Not only ought the Asian-African members be represented in the Secretariat, but there should in fact be three legally represented blocs in the Secretariat and hence three Secretaries—one to represent the Western powers, one the Communist party-states, and the third the "nonaligned" members.

Khrushchev was the first Soviet leader to put the West and particularly the United States on the defensive in the UN. In the process he seemed to be returning to certain of Lenin's views, for instance those concerning the proper behavior of a communist minority in a parliamentary situation.[15]

The Party should not cut itself off from the masses, said Lenin; as a matter of fact, it should join those organizations to which the masses already belong or which represent them. Within these organizations the Party should form a solid core, a "fraction"—composed of all Party members in that organization—who then must act as a highly disciplined group making sure that the organization follows a maximum number of policies in accord with the Party's aims and directives. Because of its closely knit unity and obedience to orders, the "fraction" would become an effective device for achievement and then maintenance of minority control of the organization.

In the United Nations the Soviet Union and its eleven "fraternal socialist allies"—the Ukrainian and Belorussian SSR's, and Albania, Bulgaria, Cuba, Czechoslovakia, Hungary, Mongolia, Poland, Rumania, and often Yugoslavia—appear to follow the techniques of "the leading core" and "the vanguard" which "unites the most active and politically conscious" elements. The position of the Communist party-states in the United Nations dictates reliance on such minority tactics. The Parties' long minority experience offers a wealth of experience valuable for exactly such activity.

The Communist party-states in the United Nations have indeed acted as a fraction; they are closely knit, they attempt to guide as many policies of the organization as possible in accordance with Soviet aims, and they work constantly to win positions of leadership. Their effort is sustained and the group relies, just as the Party, on professional skill, specialization, hard work, and skill to master parliamentary procedures and turn them to advantage.

In the mid-1960's the obedience, discipline, and unity of the communist group is less pronounced than it was in the past. The Sino-Soviet conflict intrudes here as elsewhere. The Albanian delegation, for example, alone among the Communist party-states, voted against endorsement of the nuclear test-ban treaty; the Cuban delegation was bitterly opposed to the efforts of Brazil to denuclearize Latin America, while Poland supported them; and Rumania supported Israel in debate on the Arab-Israeli war settlement. But the conflicts are still muted and do not yet encroach effectively upon the formal leadership of the USSR among the Communist party-states in the United Nations.

The purpose of this sustained maneuvering for influence within the United

[15] See Chapter VIII.

Nations is dual. It is not, as some believe, simply to destroy or take over the organization. That would bring swift and almost certainly dangerous reaction and at the same time would destroy the usefulness of the organization for the minority. Instead, it is a persistent defense and promotion of the party-states' interests through organizational and procedural devices. The defense "cannot be static"; the accent is on actively strengthening the group's influence and prestige within the United Nations. Active defensive posture is thus synchronized with the group's initiative against those standing in the way of its influence. The attack on "colonialists" and "imperialists" is a pragmatic device employed both to weaken the West and at the same time to rally a cohesive, reliable bloc among newly admitted members from Africa and Asia.

On review, it must be said that the balance which used to work to the advantage of the U.S. and the Western powers in the United Nations has proved increasingly difficult to maintain. The relative effectiveness of Soviet methods in the United Nations, whether or not one agrees with them, is hard to deny. "Bold minority actions," viewed individually and separately, often appear to be just tedious obstructionism, at times even pathetic and transparently ridiculous. When projected against the whole life of the United Nations organization and viewed as parts of the whole, however, they are not to be discounted.

It is true that the USSR, one of the Great Powers of the Security Council, has failed to live up to the purposes and pledges asserted in San Francisco in 1945. But so, it may be argued, have the other Great Powers: the United States, Great Britain, France, and Nationalist China. They, and the smaller nations too, have all tried to use the United Nations for the defense and promotion of their parochial interests. The same thing happened in the League of Nations, and it would be fatuous to expect anything different while nation-states perceive parochial interests and the opportunity to serve them.

Both organizations were designed to be led, if not controlled, by the powerful members permanently seated in the League's Council and the United Nations' Security Council. In both organizations, however, the small members have tried collectively to assert themselves and have sought in numbers a substitute for individual power. The ultimate acquisition of prestige by the Assembly of the League of Nations was their success. The General Assembly of the United Nations, in view of the League's experience, was designed to have even less significance within the organization than the Assembly had under the League Convenant. The UN General Assembly was empowered to discuss "any question or any matter within the scope of the present Charter," but it was supposed to refer "any question on which action is necessary" to the Security Council. The Security Council found agreement increasingly difficult on measures touching the world's "peace and security." When in November, 1950, the United States-sponsored "Uniting for Peace" resolution was adopted, it provided the possibility of convening the General Assembly in emergency session on twenty-four-hour notice and of making recommendations for collective action against an aggressor, including the use of armed force. The new measure did not empower the Assembly to compel a member to do anything the member did not want to do; it did, however, increase the prestige of the Assembly, its opportunity to bring collective opinion into focus, and its significance vis-à-vis the Security Council.

With decreasing use and usefulness, the Security Council lost some of its power to the General Assembly, and in turn the Great Powers lost some of their prerogatives to the smaller and less powerful states in the United Nations. United States tactics, adopted to circumvent Soviet obstruction, proved to be a boost to the nonaligned states when membership burgeoned. It also made the effort to win friends among this group potentially decisive.

As a leader of a one-tenth minority in the United Nations, the USSR could be judged quite successful. After 1955 it weakened considerably the West and the United States in the United Nations; it continued to neutralize many United Nations' actions it disagreed with; it diluted the United Nations' tendency to be an organization to support the *status quo*; it weakened the organization especially in instances where its actions would encroach on the sovereignty of members; and it rode well the anticolonial waves which periodically resulted in sweeping emotional resolutions, whatever the wisdom behind them.

The United Nations is now a different organization from what it was twenty years ago; and it is so perceived and evaluated by the USSR. It may be a "useful" and "necessary" organization—because it is the most representative international organization ever, because it permits sustained and institutionalized airing of issues which otherwise may be avoided or neglected, and because its scope of activities have grown by leaps and bounds. It is no longer viewed by the USSR primarily as a security organization: major political issues, such as Vietnam, are often missing from the UN agenda. The Security Council, immobilized by disagreements among the Great Powers, ceased to play the political and security role for which it was created long ago; and the General Assembly, instead of undertaking the peacekeeping functions which the Council is unable to perform, tends to be engaged in a merry free-for-all of issues which the majority of the Assembly favor but which have little to do, directly and immediately, with issues of peace and security.

Soviet analysts say that "the glacier of history (in the UN) is moving in a direction that does not suit Washington at all."[16] That may be so, but probably the new directions does not entirely suit Moscow either. In the old days, the Communist party-state delegations in the United Nations may have been "but a tiny group of Jacobins" and may now "speak to an entirely different audience."[17] But the new audience is not easily moved unless it recognizes its own purposes. It may support resolutions calling for liquidation of military bases in colonial territories, or for national liberation of colonial territories, but it declined to recommend removal of military bases from small territories (including Guam, the big U.S. air base in the Central Pacific). The anticolonial majority has not proved a dependable Soviet ally.

Even Soviet observers admit "the limited positive aspects in the practical work of the United Nations" and the fact that "decisions of the United Nations are more declarative than imperative."[18] The United Nations can have decisive influence in crises—as in Cyprus or Suez or at the beginning of the Congo chaos—only when the USSR and the United States, whatever their motivations, find themselves on the same side. Separately, the going is difficult for both. And "parallelism" of Soviet and American interest is often difficult to discover.

The Soviet ascendancy in the United Nations consists almost exclusively in checking and weakening the United States' former position: the USSR has in effect pushed the United States toward the restrictive, defensive position which the Soviet Union formerly occupied, while the USSR has been challenging the United States for its position of moral leadership.

THE VETO

Both in the League and in the United Nations, the Soviet delegates insisted concurrently upon the legal equality of members *and* the political elitism of Great Powers, while rejecting any trend toward majoritarianism.

The equality of states has been hailed as an important principle of Soviet

[16] Boris Izakov, "The U.N., Past and Present," *New Times,* No. 49 (December 8, 1965), p. 5.

[17] K. V. Kiselev, in "The U.N., Past and Present," *New Times,* No. 49 (December 8, 1965), p. 4.

[18] M. Lvov, "United Nations: Results and Prospects," *International Affairs,* No. 9 (September, 1965), pp. 7, 9. See also G. I. Tunkin, "Organizatsia Obedinenykh Natsii: 1945–1965 gg. (Mezhdunarodnoe problemy)," *Sovetskoe gosudarstvo i pravo,* No. 10 (October, 1965), pp. 58–68.

foreign policy, "an instrument in the fight between the forces of progress and democracy and the forces of reaction and imperialism." In 1946 Stalin pointed out:

> I ascribe great importance to the United Nations Organization inasmuch as it is a serious instrument for maintaining peace and international security. The strength of this international organization lies in the fact that it is based on the principle of the equality of states and not on the principle of the domination of some over others. If the United Nations Organization succeeds in the future, too, in maintaining the principle of equality, then it will undoubtedly play a great positive role in guaranteeing universal peace and security.[19]

Stalin spoke about legal, not political, equality; an equality which had a protective connotation for the Soviet Union, which minimized any tendency for a more integrated international organization.

The Soviet attitude towards political equality, on the other hand, has been negative. Pointing to the given economic and social inequality among nations, the Soviet policymakers have stressed the difference between small and large nations and denied the validity of the "one nation, one vote" principle as artificial and illogical. To them, effective power was the corollary of the difference and must be so recognized in any workable international organization. They thus reinforced nineteenth-century distinctions between nations, accepting the assumption that major political problems should be dealt with by major nations. They accepted as self-evident that membership in the Council of the League was confined to the major powers, supporting the opinion that there is not nor can there be political equality between large and small nations; they sought, not always with success, to reserve the prerogative of major international problems to powerful nations. At the Dumbarton Oaks and San Francisco conferences, the Soviet representatives reiterated their position, against the heavy protests of smaller nations.

The principles of legal equality for all states but political predominance of the Great Powers appear to be direct applications of the Soviet domestic concept of equality to the community of nations. In a communist system efficiency, effectiveness, and speed matter a great deal; formal equality has no meaning where power problems are concerned. The Soviet Union rejected the League of Nations for its "pseudo-democratic principle of a formal equality of all members" both in the Council and in the Assembly, and

---

[19] Reply to question put by Eddie Gilmore, March 22, 1946, in I. V. Stalin, *On Post-War International Relations* (New York: International Publishers, 1947), p. 9.

praised the Security Council of the United Nations, designed to be "able to take quick and effective measures for the maintenance of international peace."[20]

Soviet jurists have argued that political inequality does not undermine the principle of legal equality in international relations but provides this principle with a stable foundation. The principle of unanimity among the permanent members of the Security Council not only affirms the sovereign equality of states but "it is a significant guarantee of sovereignty of small states and their rights. . . . The permanent members represent a minority of the members of the Security Council, and the principle of unanimity gives them opportunity to prohibit but not to initiate positive actions."[21]

Contempt for "formal majorities" has characterized the Bolshevik party ever since the Revolution: "It would be naïve to wait for a 'formal' majority on the side of the Bolsheviks; no revolution ever waits for *this*."[22] "Bold minority action" has been second nature to the Communists since their access to power: the Soviet Union accepted its minority position in international relations and applied its rich domestic minority experience to international dealings, both in the League and in the United Nations.

Insistence on majority rule in an international organization is "rather silly" according to Vyshinsky:

> Most of the criticism of the voting rule in the Security Council arises because it is forgotten that the United Nations is not a federation and is not a world superstate, and that the voting procedure of sovereign nations cannot possibly be considered on the same basis as the voting procedure in the Parliament or in the Congress of the United Kingdom or of the United States, respectively.[23]

In the League of Nations, the Soviet Union had advocated the idea that a state should not be judge in its own case; in the United Nations it reversed its position and insisted that in the Security Council the opposite principle

[20] S. V. Molodtsov, "The Rule of Unanimity of the Permanent Members of the Security Council—the Immovable Foundation of the United Nations," *Sovetskoe gosudarstvo i pravo,* No. 7 (1953), p. 46.

[21] I. D. Levin, *Suverenitet* (Moscow: Iuridicheskoe Izdat., 1948), p. 352. P. D. Morosov defended the permanent members of the Security Council before the Sixth Committee of the General Assembly, Nov. 2, 1953: General Assembly, Eighth Session, Sixth Committee, Summary Records of Meetings, *U.N. Official Records* (New York: UN, September 16 to November 28, 1953), pp. 93, 94.

[22] V. I. Lenin, *Will the Bolsheviks Retain State Power?* (New York: International Publishers, 1932), p. 4.

[23] Speech of November 21, 1947: *U.N. Documents,* No. A/P.V./122 (November 21, 1947), pp. 121, 122.

must be introduced. Stalin remembered well his experience in the League of Nations. At Yalta he reminded his colleagues of Soviet expulsion from the League, and, in 1947, Gromyko, justifying Soviet use of the veto before the First Committee of the General Assembly, recalled the "inglorious end" of the League.

Soviet policymakers realized well that their semi-isolation, their ideological difference with the noncommunist states, and their minority position made them vulnerable in any international gathering. Their insistence on rights of self-protection, both procedural and substantive, was the *sine qua non* of their participation in an international organization.

The Charter of the United Nations, at variance with the Covenant of the League, substitutes majority decision, simple or qualified, for the requirement of unanimity; the exception to this rule is the veto power held by the five permanent members of the Security Council over security problems and over the adoption of amendments to the Charter.

The principle of unanimity, Inis L. Claude, Jr. rightly pointed out, "is the best guarantee for a 'just' decision, but carries the danger of the imposition of 'no decision' by a minority" and may in fact mean *minority* rule: "It confers upon a minority of one the procedural competence and the moral authority to determine policy in a negative fashion."[24] For the Soviet Union the unanimity rule of the five permanent members of the Security Council has been the foundation of its Charter precisely because it offered, in security matters, an artificial symmetry between the USSR and the capitalistic nations.

Molotov said a number of times that the right of veto, although not a panacea, prevented the formation of aggressive blocs, discouraged intrigue, and provided an effective tool for better cooperation in the interests of all the powers, large and small. To the Soviet Union the veto became a "means of self-defense against pressure" and the weapon which protects Soviet "independence" and "sovereign equality" against "attempts to dictate in international affairs, (trying) to impose one's will by hook and crook."[25] It may be interesting to note that the Soviet Union places decisions of international organizations among the sources of international law, if these decisions are *truly binding*. For example, decisions (not recommendations) of the Security Council of the United Nations, if based on the unanimity of permanent members, are considered sources of international law.

The Security Council veto was not designed only to prevent the formation

[24] Inis L. Claude, *Swords into Plowshares* (New York: Random House, Inc., 1956), p. 137.
[25] Vyshinsky, speaking to the Political Committee of the General Assembly, Oct. 10, 1950: *Speeches by A. Y. Vyshinsky at the Fifth Session of the General Assembly of the U.N.* (Washington, D.C.: Embassy of the USSR, 1950).

of an anticommunist alliance; as a matter of fact, it was incorporated in the Charter as much in response to U.S. as Soviet wishes. True, the Soviet emphasis of the veto power became greater than that of the United States or any other power. Once East-West cooperation deteriorated to the point of cold war, the Soviet Union had, in the Security Council veto, means of coping with the situation. However, it is also true that at the insistence of the Western powers, the Soviet Union gave up its claim to veto the acceptance of disputes for discussion by the Security Council, and it ceased to consider abstention from voting as constituting a veto, although all the Great Powers agreed at San Francisco that it did.

The Soviet Union invoked its veto power over one hundred times in the UN's first twenty years[26] and has used it as a bargaining lever against the Western powers. But a careful look at the record suggests that the Soviet veto has not been as insuperable an obstacle to the United Nations as some observers suggest. It is more a symptom of the condition of the international system than a cause of it. Given the great reliance of the United Nations upon moral suasion and voluntary cooperation, the veto has undoubtedly avoided the passage of numerous unenforceable resolutions. It has thus helped preserve the stature of the organization as a reservoir of limited but usable international consensus rather than condemning it to ridicule as only the ineffectual bastion of irrelevant utopianism.

Lately, with the new "balance of forces" in the United Nations, the USSR has tended increasingly to de-emphasize its unequivocal stand on the difference between legal and political equality; it has even seemed to welcome Afro-Asian insistence on majority decisions in most matters. Not that it has reversed its stand on the Security Council and the veto power of permanent members there. But in the General Assembly and other United Nations bodies it has resisted any suggestion of weighted voting (apportioned by population, GNP, contributions to the United Nations, or otherwise) as a euphemistic term for American political control: "Such plans would immediately deprive the developing nations of all weight. . . . These reform plans are a measure of Washington's dissatisfaction with the way things have been going in the United Nations."[27] It cannot have escaped Soviet observation that the new complexion of UN membership, giving greater and greater weight to the developing nations, is a sword which cuts two ways.

---

[26] France had used the veto four times, and Great Britain and Nationalist China had exercised it twice. See "The Soviet Record in the United Nations," *Communist Affairs,* I, No. 3 (October, 1962), 7.

[27] Izakov, *op. cit.,* p. 5. See also M. Lvov, "United Nations: Results and Prospects," *International Affairs,* No. 9 (September, 1965), p. 9.

THE SOVIET UNION AND SPECIALIZED ECONOMIC AND TECHNICAL AGENCIES

In the ten-year period prior to its entry into the League of Nations, the USSR gradually joined in the technical work of the League in connection with various international problems. It cooperated with a number of quasi public organizations of an economic and technical nature operating under direction of the League following Article 24 of the Covenant. These Soviet relations with the various technical, social, and economic international organizations were motivated by the desire for markets and trade—both to hasten the program of building socialism and to forestall wars which might involve the Soviet Union.

Activities of the League of Nations which were of benefit to the USSR without involving it in political commitments were favored by the Soviet government. It not only participated in such international bodies but went so far as to solicit their assistance. At the same time, the Soviet delegates carefully stressed the eclectic Soviet attitude toward the functions of these organizations. They were explicit in their reservations against political commitments and emphasized retention of their right of withdrawal in case of disagreement: "From the international point of view, as well as from the point of domestic policies we find it in complete conformity with our purposes to participate in such preliminary undertakings which do not conflict with our aims."[28]

In 1938, the USSR was a member of nearly all the organizations dealing with health, of almost one-third of the arts and science organizations, of the Red Cross, of eight institutions dealing with communication and transit, and so on. All in all, it was participating in over one hundred and fifty international organizations and had participated in most of them even before joining the League of Nations.

The International Labor Organization considered Soviet participation essential in its program of ameliorating global labor conditions. After initial Soviet hostility, some cooperation and exchange of information was promised by Soviet officials. But in 1930 the Soviet Union officially denounced all earlier overtures of the ILO, replaced its official representative, who had a tendency to cooperate, and refused to discuss the matter further.

As a member of the League, the USSR automatically became a member of the International Labor Organization. In July, 1935 the Soviet government sent its representatives to attend the ILO's Nineteenth Conference. The

[28] Christian G. Rakovskii, *Liga Natsii i SSSR* (Moscow: Kommunisticheskaia Akademiia, 1926), p. 18.

Soviet decision to enter into the activities of the ILO was perhaps more significant than its membership in the League itself. Since the ILO was

> ... an organization believing in an illusory possibility of peaceful co-operation between classes (the exploited and the exploiting) and in the possibility of solving the social problems of a capitalistic economic order by an evolutionary process, it was nothing but a bridge between the bourgeoisie and the "heads" of the bureaucratic professional unions, and a means to overshadow the class consciousness of the toiling masses.[29]

However, time showed Soviet participation in the International Labor Organization was only nominal; the Soviet government did not ratify a single ILO convention, supplied no information, and did not appoint a permanent delegation. Its membership ceased automatically when the USSR was expelled from the League.

The Soviet Union played a leading part in the League of Nations only in regard to international security matters. Soviet officials were members of the main functional agencies of the League, such as the Financial Committee, Economic and Transit Organizations, Health Committee (which the Soviet Union joined before it entered the League), and a Soviet Deputy Secretary-General was added to the League Secretariat. However, the Soviet Union never consented to the nomination of a Soviet member on the Mandates Commission, and it refused to participate in the League's social agencies, such as the Child Welfare Committee. The Soviet representatives in the League tried to discourage all attempts to equalize the functional with the security duties of the League. Litvinov, in a speech to the League Assembly in 1935, explained his point of view this way:

> I do not dwell on the accessory, non-political work of the League. Far from denying the importance of such work, be it of an economic, social, or humanitarian character, I would not like to see too much League energy diverted in that direction at the expense of the fundamental task for which it has been founded.[30]

Originally, Soviet interest in the "accessory" activities of the United Nations was equally negligible. This was easy to understand. Soviet reluctance to impair its sovereignty; the possibility that active cooperation in social and economic matters might call for the exchange of information,

---

[29] T. A. Taracouzio, *The Soviet Union and International Law* (New York: The Macmillan Company, 1936), p. 278.

[30] League of Nations, *Official Journal,* Special Supplement No. 138 (1935), p. 71.

which would mean the revealing of secrets jealously guarded behind the iron curtain; and American predominance in the United Nations including the functional agencies—were equally serious obstacles to active Soviet co-operation.

The USSR participated in the Bretton Woods and Hot Springs conferences, became a member of the UN Relief and Rehabilitation Agency (UNRRA), and displayed interest in the discussions of the Economic and Social Council; it withdrew in 1949 from World Health Organization, allegedly because of the overly extravagant administrative expenses of the organization; it rejoined the Universal Postal Union and the International Telegraph Union; and it joined the World Meteorological Organization. But its cooperation in economic and social matters was generally lukewarm and hesitant, active only where its direct benefit was concerned, as in UNRRA. Gradually, the Soviet Union's attitude toward the specialized agencies grew more hostile, and it charged them with being instruments of American economic imperialism. Before Stalin's death, the Soviet Union did not customarily contribute funds for the relief, reconstruction, and development of war-devastated or underdeveloped countries.

In 1953, a change of Soviet attitude towards functional international cooperation became noticeable: first, the Soviet government, through its delegates at the Economic and Social Council, offered a financial contribution to the Southeast Asian nations of 4 million rubles for technical assistance in 1953. In April, 1954, the Soviet Union joined UNESCO and rejoined the International Labor Organization. In July, 1956, the USSR announced its intention to resume participation in the World Health Organization, to become a member of the International Bureau of Education, and to contribute 2 million rubles in kind and services to the United Nations Children's Fund.

Increasing Soviet interest in the United Nations Technical Assistance Program and the Soviet attempt to increase its economic assistance for the underdeveloped countries of Southeast Asia constituted similar reversals of the previous Soviet attitude. Up to then, the Soviet government was vocal but ineffective: it advocated development of Asian countries recently freed from colonial status but did not participate in a single United Nations program designed to aid those countries. It emphasized the exploitative policy of the West without supporting its own recommendations (e.g., the building of heavy industry) by deed. To make up for the lack of its own assistance, the Soviet Union minimized the significance of the United Nations Technical Assistance Program and stressed the direct consequences of capitalist expansion to the sensitive Asian nations.

The unexpected 1953 financial contribution and other Soviet pledges delivered comparatively small amounts of money but gained important psychological impact. The Soviet decision-makers seemed to realize that technical assistance to underdeveloped areas was an important new factor in international relations.

The above-mentioned Soviet entry into UNESCO was a significant departure. Previous determined Soviet rejection of the possibility of creating a philsophic synthesis which would transcend Soviet ideology was understandable:

> One would think that UNESCO would strive in its activities to uphold and propagate the ideas of peace, friendship, and cultural cooperation among the nations. But having come under the thumb of American imperialists, this humanitarian organization endeavors instead to undermine the struggle against the warmongers, to divert the masses from it by false abstract talk about "the intellectual and moral solidarity of mankind." In actual fact, this supposedly international agency is an auxiliary of the United States State Department.[31]

Attempts to secure political support from noncommunist countries and neutrals, the potential ability of UNESCO to influence world opinion, and the new drive for peaceful coexistence appeared sufficient to overbalance the reluctance of the Soviet Union to enter this "State Department nest." The USSR subsequently has contributed to UNESCO publications, participated in its conferences, and sponsored several seminars and congresses in the USSR.

Increasing Soviet activities in the United Nations economic, social, and humanitarian organizations have thus manifested a sharp contrast from former Soviet behavior. This is not to say that the USSR displayed a preference for a nonpolitical, technical, and consultative international organization, as is often claimed. Its primary criterion of evaluation remained Soviet security; its priority in both the League and the United Nations upon international security explains the Soviet initial attitude toward the specialized agencies of those two organizations.

Neither does the more recent approach mean that the Soviet objections against these international functional agencies have been erased. The present Soviet absence from agencies such as the International Refugee Organization, International Bank for Reconstruction and Development, and the International Monetary Fund probably will continue in the future, although

---

[31] N. Yevgenev in *New Times,* March 29, 1950, p. 11.

Soviet condemnation of the activities of those agencies may become less vocal.

What it does mean is that the Soviet concept of security has been changing: Soviet leaders have come to realize that while a large-scale war appears improbable in the near future, sole reliance on military and security forces in international relations is obsolete and economic, social, and cultural forces continue to gain importance in international relations. Active participation in economic, social-welfare, and humanitarian endeavors of international organizations was recognized as an important channel for Soviet foreign policy. The Soviet Union is better served within than without United Nations specialized agencies, and the danger of participation, as proved by the membership of other Communist party-states in many of these organizations in the past, has proved to be far smaller than the Soviet leaders feared. Economic, social, and cultural coexistence has been proven possible; for the USSR it also has become very desirable.

In the past, the Soviet policy of abstention from the functional agencies disclosed Soviet reluctance to compete with the United States, leader and director of those agencies, for a variety of reasons, not all altruistic. Soviet leaders were content with exposé and condemnation of the U.S. role in the specialized agencies.

It might be argued that the United States had politicized functional agencies of the United Nations. In a way, the United States had developed a tendency to view the economic, social, and cultural activities of the United Nations as one base for its anticommunist program. After initial hesitation, the Soviet Union accepted the challenge; compartmentalization into cultural, economic, and social matters on the one hand and political matters on the other was not realistic. In a sense, the USSR came to participate in international functional organizations for the same reasons Stalin had decided to join the League and the United Nations: it was apparently to the political interest of the Soviet Union.

Today, the USSR is represented in all the specialized agencies it joined earlier plus three new ones established since 1956: The Inter-Governmental Maritime Consultative Organization (IMCO-1958), the International Development Association (IDA-1958), and the International Atomic Energy Agency (IAEA-1957).

THE SOVIET UNION AND DISARMAMENT

Originally, the Communists stipulated that disarmament was possible solely in a socialist future because the mere existence of capitalist states made war inevitable—that it was

. . . necessary to destroy capitalism [in order] to eliminate the inevitability of wars. . . . The Communist Party emphatically rejects the reactionary illusions of *petit-bourgeois* democrats about achieving disarmament under capitalism. It sets against them . . . the slogan of crushing the resistance of exploiters, of a fight to victory over the bourgeoisie of the whole world, both in internal civil wars and international wars.[32]

Capitalist disarmament was nothing but maneuvering for a better position in the next war, an instrument of propaganda to quiet the rising proletariat in capitalist countries. This was Lenin's precept, and in it was the primary motivation behind Soviet support in the 1920's of immediate disarmament schemes calculated to expose in a grand style this capitalist hypocrisy. Still, universal disarmament would also mean lessening the danger to Soviet Russia from a hostile outside world and depriving bourgeois governments of their means to suppress socialist revolutions.

Before 1922, the Soviet Union did not exploit the idea of disarmament. Between 1922 and 1927, however, Soviet leaders began to explore the possibilities both of universal disarmament and regional disarmament: at Geneva, at Moscow in 1922, and at the League Naval Conference at Rome in 1924. Each of these attempts proved unsuccessful.

The Soviet proposal of November, 1927 for universal and total disarmament was a radical and far-reaching measure to limit state sovereignty. Presented by Litvinov at the Fourth Session of the Disarmament Preparatory Commission of the League, the Soviet proposal called for immediate, complete, and universal disarmament: dissolution of all Armed Forces on land, sea, and in the air; destruction of all arms, warships, military aircraft, fortifications, and armament plants; abolition of compulsory military services; suppression of appropriations for war purposes; abolition of war or Defense Ministries of governments; and prohibition of war propaganda. Instead, the Soviets proposed a national police force "employed by voluntary contracts of service, authorized in the territory of each of the contracting states for the purpose of customs and revenue, police supervision, internal police, and the protection of state property."[33]

Though compatible with the aims of Article 8 of the Covenant, this proposal (as well as the subsequent Soviet proposals of 1928) was incompatible with the platform previously adopted by the League members in the disarmament talks, namely, a disarmament-security-arbitration formula.

---

[32] Lenin, *Sochineniia,* 3rd ed. (Moscow: Gosizdat, 1935), XXIII, 97.
[33] *League Documents* (Geneva: League of Nations, 1927), Nos. C.667; M.225 IX; C.46; M.23.

Litvinov sarcastically reported to the XVth Congress of the Soviet Communist Party that the Soviet proposal "was received as a sacrilege, as an attack on the very foundations of the League of Nations, as a breach of all proprieties."[34]

To other states the Litvinov proposal had a different aspect. It was rejected summarily as only propaganda materials and the Soviet Union had not hindered such an interpretation:

> The aim of the Soviet proposals was not to spread pacifist illusions but to destroy them; not to support capitalism . . . but to propagate the fundamental Marxian postulate, that disarmament and the abolition of war are possible only with the fall of capitalism. . . . It goes without saying that not a single Communist thought for a moment that the imperialist world would accept the Soviet disarmament proposals. . . .[35]

The Soviet Union withdrew the proposal and submitted, in 1928, a new one calling for partial and gradual disarmament. The strongest powers were to reduce their armaments by 50 per cent, the weakest by 25 per cent, and those in the middle by 33 per cent. A fourth category included states disarmed by the World War I peace treaties. This draft included abolition of air warfare, poison gas, certain types of guns, and so on. A permanent international control commission, composed of representatives of legislatures and workers' organizations, would inspect the execution of this plan. The proposal contained rigid control measures:

> With a view to ensuring genuine control, the Permanent International Commission of Control shall be entitled to carry out investigations on the spot in the event of reasonable suspicion of a breach of the present Convention and of the subsequent supplementary Agreements on the reduction and limitation of armaments, and to appoint for this purpose special commissions of inquiry.[36]

The second Soviet proposal was less radical than the first, but the Soviet draftsmen knew well that it, too, would not be acceptable:

> The [Soviet] second scheme which provided for partial disarmament and for a gradual reduction of land and naval forces . . . was not a

---

[34] Quoted in Frederick L. Schuman, *Soviet Politics at Home and Abroad* (New York: A. A. Knopf, Inc., 1946), p. 230.

[35] *The Sixth Congress of the Communist International* (1928), p. 37.

[36] Article 43 of the Soviet Draft Convention, *League Documents* (1926), Nos. C.185; M.50 IX.

concession to pacifism; on the contrary, it served to expose more completely the attitude of the great powers toward the small and oppressed nations.[37]

After this the Soviet policymakers limited themselves to criticism of other nations' disarmament proposals. In fact, they subjected every such new proposal to scathing comment. Aligning themselves with the minority "anti-Versailles" group, they urged radical cuts in armament; in practice, they sided with Germany and, quite often, with Italy against France and her allies. The Soviet Union did however declare its adherence to the Briand-Kellog Pact (which provided that the signatory parties renounce war as an instrument of national policy and agree not to seek the solution of future disputes by other than pacific means) and was the first country to ratify it.

At the World Disarmament Conference in 1932, the Soviet Union revived its plans for disarmament with what appeared to be a less critical and cynical attitude. There, Litvinov re-emphasized Soviet adherence to the principle of disarmament, suggesting three fundamental points, agreement upon which could lead to partial disarmament and greater international security: (1) reduction of existing armed forces, (2) reduction of war materials and munitions, and (3) a reduction ratio proportionate to present military strength.[38]

All the Soviet proposals were rejected by the Conference, primarily on the grounds that peace might be secured better by standing armies than in any other way. Also, the old apprehensions of Soviet intentions lingered in the air. After all, if the army is one of the tools of suppression of the proletariat by the ruling class in a state, as Marx asserted, and if all capitalist armies were abolished or reduced, may not then the Red Army, "an instrument in the hands of the proletarian dictatorship . . . become a universal socialist militia," ready to take over and fill the vacuum?

These apprehensions were fortified by statements of Soviet leaders. The Soviet concept of the role of the Red Army—of its weapons and equipment, of the general preparations for increasing military strength, of the inevitability of war, of "revolutionary" peace—made the incompatibility seem clear. "While agreeing to cooperate with other states" said Litvinov in 1933,

we cannot forget that we are dealing with capitalist states. . . . Being thus forced to be on the offensive, we shall continue as of old and even more

---

[37] *The Sixth Congress of the Communist International, loc. cit.*

[38] Eugene A. Korovin, "The USSR and Disarmament," *International Conciliation,* No. 292 (September, 1933), pp. 18–20.

to strengthen and improve the basis of our safety—our Red Army, Red Fleet and Red Air Force.[39]

Further, the Red Army was supposed not only to solidify the dictatorship of the proletariat in one country, but also to be made use of as a starting point for the overthrow of imperialism in all countries.[40]

Disarmament was indeed perceived as part of that future towards which society is drawn like a magnet, a classless and stateless heaven. At the time of the Soviet disarmament proposals, however, Soviet disarmament would have caused grave problems for the Soviet Union. With Japan's leaving the League and Hitler's withdrawal from the General Disarmament Conference, Stalin became quite aware of the possible consequences of those events for Soviet security.The League's effort to achieve general disarmament had proven unsuccessful; the announcement of conscription by National Socialist Germany in 1935 effectively ended all further attempts. The Soviet government began to look for more effective safeguards of its security.

In essence, the post-World War II disarmament issues were similar to those the League of Nations wrestled with. The only difference was emphasis: while the League stressed *reduction* of armaments, exchange of information on armaments, and control over armaments, the United Nations sought primarily to *regulate* armaments in order to "promote the establishment and maintenance of international peace and security with the least diversion for armaments of the world's human and economic resources."[41] Supervision and sanctions for armament limitations were the two points the United Nations stressed more than the League.

In 1945 the Soviet government approved in principle the effective safeguards—inspections and other means—included in the Truman-Attlee-King Declaration, a statement initiating the program for dealing with peaceful uses of atomic energy. As a matter of fact, until the beginning of the actual negotiations in the United Nations Atomic Energy Commission, through all the official actions that preceded, "the Soviet attitude towards atomic energy control was passive and acquiescent."[42]

[39] Speech at the Fourth Session of the Central Executive Committee of the USSR, December 29, 1935; in *Izvestiia,* December 30, 1935.

[40] I. V. Stalin, "Ob osnovakh Leninisma," in *Voprosy Leninisma,* 11th ed. (Moscow: Gosizdat, 1945), p. 47.

[41] *United Nations Charter,* Article 46.

[42] Frederic Osborn (U.S. Deputy Representative on the United Nations Atomic Energy Commission, 1947-1950), "The USSR and the Atom," *International Organization,* No. 5 (1951), p. 483.

The Soviet Union had no nuclear weapons; their manifest possession by the United States was viewed as a considerable threat to Soviet security. The Soviet Union became, therefore, adamant about the need to outlaw atomic warfare. In 1946, when Bernard Baruch introduced his famous proposal for international control of all atomic products,[43] the Soviet reception was entirely negative. It could not have prevented use of the bomb sooner or later, in the event of a general war. Mr. Baruch implied as much when he called on the world to outlaw not merely the bomb, but war itself. But more importantly, the plan would have hampered Soviet efforts to close the military technological gap with the United States and would have opened Soviet territory to hostile, capitalist representatives.

In October, 1946, Molotov proposed a resolution to reduce armaments, including prohibition of the manufacture and use of atomic energy for military purposes. If all nations would follow, he argued, there could be no atomic war. It read like the scores of resolutions introduced since the early 1920's, which the USSR had attacked for their futility. Later in the fall, the Soviet Union submitted two more proposals to the General Assembly: one for the general reduction of armaments, which was adopted with modifications by the Assembly; and a second, requesting that information be transmitted to the Security Council concerning the size and disposition of members' Armed Forces, which was also adopted after extensive discussion.

It was clear from these proposals and from the discussion which followed that the USSR wanted all decisions on the disarmament problem concentrated in the Security Council. Also, the two resolutions had the additional effect of divorcing the regulation of atomic from conventional weapons—placing the latter in the Conventional Armaments Commission and the former in the Atomic Energy Commission. But in spite of Soviet protest, the two commissions were brought together to form one Disarmament Commission in 1951, pursuant to Western initiatives.

After two years of discussion and profound disagreement, the Disarmament Commission created a subcommittee of five members (the United States, Great Britain, France, Canada, and the Soviet Union) to seek in private discussions a solution acceptable to all. Fourteen sessions later (in London, May 13-June 22, 1954) and in spite of great effort on the part of Western powers, the Soviet views remained unchanged.

Then, later that year, in the Ninth Session of the Assembly, Vyshinsky caused a sensation by declaring that the Soviet Union was ready to accept,

[43] In the U.N. Atomic Energy Commission, June 14, 1946: *U.S. Department of State Bulletin*, XIV (1946), 1057.

as a basis for discussion, the Franco-British proposals just rejected in London. Vyshinsky's attitude became conciliatory; he even renounced the principle of subordination of all disarmament to the prior unconditional prohibition of atomic weapons, a stand heretofore advocated by the Soviet representatives.[44]

Consequently, the subcommittee resumed its talks in London in February, 1955. Before the first meeting, the Soviet government denounced the policy of the Western powers, described the danger of atomic war, and proposed (1) to destroy entirely the stockpiles of atomic and hydrogen weapons and utilize the atomic materials exclusively for peaceful purposes, (2) not to increase armaments and armed force above the January 1, 1955, level and not to increase expenditures for military purposes above the budgetary levels for 1955, and (3) to establish an international control for implementation of these proposals.[45]

In May, the Soviet Union submitted a further series of proposals. Their outstanding feature was a plan to combine the banning of nuclear weapons with ceilings on the number of troops and conventional armaments. The United States, Soviet Union, and Communist China would be limited to 1,500,000 men each, Great Britain and France to 650,000 men, and all other countries to 150,000–200,000 men.

Then came the 1955 Geneva Disarmament Conference. Western representatives each presented a plan as a basis for new disarmament talks. The Americans presented President Eisenhower's idea of aerial control, which included the Soviet suggestions on control of important strategic locations. The British proposed, as a starter, a creation of an intermediary zone in Germany, on both sides of the East-West dividing line, where control of armaments and military installations could be carried out. The French recommended a control system for reciprocal inspections; their idea was to utilize the budgetary savings created by reduction of military spending for rapid development of underdeveloped countries. The Soviet representative, Nikolai Bulganin, reiterated the latest Soviet subcommittee proposals.

But proposals were all that occurred. The subcommittee resumed meetings in New York in August, taking them as a starting point. Work was conducted behind closed doors, but the lack of progress was all too apparent. In September, Marshal Bulganin sent a direct message to President Eisenhower concerning disarmament, ostensibly to speed up the work of the subcommittee. The message was conciliatory in tone but insisted that aerial

---

[44] *U.N. Document* No. DC/53 (June 22, 1954), Annex 1, p. 1; see also *U.N. Documents,* No. DC/5.c.1./PV12 and 17 (June, 1954).

[45] *Chronique de Politique Etrangére,* No. 8 (1955), p. 756.

reconnaissance and information exchange would have to be established on a multilateral rather than a bilateral basis. The meetings droned on.

The following spring, Andrei Gromyko proposed another disarmament plan to the subcommittee, the emphasis of which rested almost entirely on limitations of military manpower and cuts in conventional weapons. The sole reference of the proposal to nuclear weapons suggested prohibition of further nuclear tests. For the first time, the Soviet plan did not mention control of nuclear weapons.

Then, in May 1956, Radio Moscow announced:

> Wishing to make a new contribution towards the course of disarmament and safeguarding the peace . . . the Soviet government has taken the following decision:
>
> 1. To carry out in the course of one year, i.e., by 1st May 1957, a new and still greater reduction in the armed forces of the Soviet Union, namely by 1,200,000 men in addition to the reduction of 640,000 carried out in 1955.
>
> 2. In conformity with this, to disband sixty-three divisions and independent brigades, including the disbanding of three air divisions and other military units numbering more than 30,000 men which are stationed on the territory of the German Democratic Republic. Also to disband a number of military schools of the Soviet Army. To put into reserve 375 warships of the Soviet Navy.
>
> 3. In conformity with the above, to reduce the armaments and military equipment of the Soviet armed forces, as well as Soviet military expenditure within the Soviet state budget.
>
> 4. The demobilized service men from the armed forces will be given the opportunity of obtaining employment in industry and agriculture.[46]

In addition, the announcement repeated the former Soviet proposals on nuclear weapons without appreciable changes.

Proportionately, the cut was not much larger than the previous strategic reductions of the Western Armed Forces; but it was announced to the world in circumstances which lent value to the professed new Soviet drive for "peaceful coexistence" with the West. And, as in the past, the Soviet leaders made no secret of their intention to embarrass the Western powers by their new unilateral reduction of Armed Forces, "so that all can see who is working for, and who is hindering the end of the armaments race."[47]

But controls were still the key issue. The West rejected all the Soviet

[46] *The New York Times,* May 15, 1956, p. 8.
[47] *Ibid.*

disarmament proposal on the grounds that controls were still inadequate.

The subcommittee reconvened in 1957 for its longest session. Two Soviet proposals were offered initially, neither containing anything new. Two more were submitted, each containing some compromise, but were still found unacceptable. Principle areas of professed agreement and disagreement could now be summed up as follows:

A 2,500,000-manpower level for the USSR and the U.S. with 650,000 for France and the United Kingdom was agreeable. The West continued to insist on settlement of political issues as a condition for further reduction, but the Soviets would not agree to this. There was agreement on the principle of exchange of information as a means of control, but not on how this was to be done. In principle, both sides favored a controlled suspension of nuclear tests, but there was no agreement on the nature of the controls; the USSR objected to the U.S. insistence that production of fissionable fuel must cease before a test ban could become permanent. Both sides agreed to the principle of ground and air inspection, but they could not agree on the area to be inspected.

For over two years following the 1957 sessions, the Disarmament Commission did not meet; negotiations were carried out informally by smaller groups and with more limited objectives. It was in the area of a proposed nuclear test ban that the most promising discussion developed. In June, 1957 the USSR offered for the first time to permit control posts on its own territory to supervise a test ban. Then in March, 1958 the USSR announced a voluntary unilateral test moratorium which put considerable pressure on the U.S. to follow suit, without waiting for an end to fissionable fuel production. It was agreed that wider discussions in meetings of the subcommittee should resume in 1960. But as so often in the past, these meetings again reached stalemate and were adjourned.

However, the twelve-nation conference on Antarctica, held in Washington in the fall of 1959, did bring a small but welcome bright spot into the gloom of disarmament impasse. The USSR, the U.S., and other contracting parties signed a formal treaty which provided that the continent of Antarctica should be used solely for peaceful purposes. (At the same time, the signatories resolved that the treaty, designed to advance the principles of the UN Charter, should be open for accession by any UN member.) The Soviet Union agreed to a right of inspection in Antarctica by duly accredited observers of the respective treaty signatories. This step, many hoped, might lead to ultimate Soviet acceptance of similar inspection arrangements elsewhere.

Although the treaty was relatively inconsequential in immediate effect, the precedent of regional demilitarization had been established. Thus it could also be viewed as a harbinger of future agreements to respect other territory and even the newly significant reaches of outer space similarly.

The years 1960–1962 were generally discouraging for proponents of disarmament, witnessing as they did the U-2 spy plane episode and the abortive Paris Summit Conference; then the Bay of Pigs invasion attempt, an end to nuclear test moratoria, and the building of the Berlin Wall; and finally the Cuban missile confrontation between the United States and the Soviet Union.

But new Soviet activities in 1963, though still peripheral to the real issue of effective arms control, nevertheless raised hopes that the USSR and the West would eventually find common ground on important matters.

First, the Soviet Union decided to conclude an agreement with the United State for a Washington-Moscow direct-communications link or "hot line" in order to reduce the danger of misreading the other power's signals. (The line was first used in emergency by Chairman Kosygin and President Johnson in the midst of the 1967 Arab-Israeli crisis.)

Second, the USSR agreed to conclude a tripartite (with the U.S. and Great Britain) treaty banning nuclear tests in the atmosphere, in outer space, and under water—which require no inspection to detect—while postponing the more difficult issue of underground tests. In the test-ban treaty, the signatories agreed not only to refrain from nuclear testing except underground, but also to render no assistance to others in such tests. The treaty, open to all states for accession, has now been signed by a majority of them. France, Communist China, and Cuba (to Soviet embarrassment) have refused to sign the document.

Third, Foreign Minister Gromyko proposed a Soviet-American agreement to ban the placing in orbit of objects carrying nuclear weapons. The Soviet proposal, cast as a United Nations resolution, was passed by acclamation in the General Assembly in October, 1963. In December, 1966 a multilateral treaty governing exploration and use of outer space, which included the prohibition on nuclear weapons in orbit, was unanimously endorsed by the General Assembly and subsequently ratified by both the U.S. and the Soviet Union.

Unfortunately, many of the hopes raised in 1963 have yet to be fulfilled. True, in 1964 the U.S., Great Britain, and the USSR each unilaterally decided on partial cutbacks in their planned production of fissionable materials, but there was no clear evidence of implementation. The Soviet Union also used the United Nations as a forum in which to reiterate most of the more general disarmament proposals it had made in past years, submitting them now to the General Assembly. But the proposals again failed to provide for inspections or other safeguards which would make them credible and acceptable to the West. Whether they dealt with a comprehensive test ban, measures to guard against surprise attack, reductions in military budgets, weapons, and manpower or whether they postulated more propagandist ends, such as an outright ban on the use of nuclear weapons, a declaration from each nuclear power that it would never be first to use such weapons, return of military forces stationed outside their own national frontiers, dismantlement of all foreign military bases, or establishment of "nuclear-free zones" in Central Europe and elsewhere—regardless, they met the same objection in the West, one which could be clearly foreseen by their Soviet initiators.

In June, 1965, the Disarmament Commission recommended an early convocation of a world disarmament conference (the Political Committee adopted it as a resolution in November, 1965) with the participation of all states. It also called on its eighteen-nation Committee to resume discussions, especially concentrating on a ban of underground tests and a nuclear nonproliferation treaty. By mid-1967 disagreement over the content of a nonproliferation treaty had been reduced appreciably, but an approved draft had not yet been achieved.

One must conclude that the perennial Geneva-based Disarmament Commission has accomplished little. It simply reflects the world of reality—and unless both sides want to negotiate, public debate in the Commission may be a fruitless loss of time. If the arms race and further nuclear proliferation are really to be halted, then a conference of willing nuclear powers, including China and France, as proposed by both Secretary-General U Thant and General de Gaulle, can not be delayed much longer.

Over twenty years have elapsed since the proposal of the Baruch Plan, but it seems only more certain now than ever that the one dependable way to prevent war is simply to agree not to go to war. It appears today that the United States does not really believe in prohibition of nuclear weapons, with or without effective controls. The Soviet position seems similar, if not identical. Yet both seem to realize that each possesses enough bombs to destroy the other for the price of self-destruction. Although the British and the French have essentially adhered to their 1955 stands for combining questions of nuclear control and general disarmament, including ceilings for Armed Forces of the Great Powers, the Soviet Union seems to have moved closer to the position of the United States.

The disarmament question is only one of the issues the Soviet Union is using against the Western world in Asia and in Africa; however, in Europe it is the chief weapon employed by the Soviet Union, reinforcing the pre-World War II Soviet theme aiming to show Soviet opposition to war of any kind and to increase European neutralism: Unless the Americans go home, Europe may be involved in war. American "interventionists" using military bases on European territory, are thus branded with responsibility for any new threat of war.

The fact remains that disarmament has, in spite of all the proposals, counterproposals, discussions, and resolutions which have since been put forward, proceeded little beyond the Anglo-Soviet-American Declaration on General Security of October 30, 1943, in which those three governments and Nationalist China declared their intention to "confer and cooperate with one another and with other members of the United Nations to bring about a practicable general agreement with respect to the regulation of armaments in the post-war period."[48]

On this issue before the League of Nations, the USSR sided with Germany and Fascist Italy against the West in the twenties. Later it deserted them and joined the West. And in time of national danger disarmament was entirely abandoned as fruitless and illusory.

After World War II the Soviet leaders approached the disarmament issue in very much the same spirit as before.

The situation began to change, however, not because the USSR, or the West for that matter, meant it to change but because of the *deus ex machina* of the nuclear bomb.

The possibility of mutual destruction altered the problem of disarmament: it made general war a prospect of unrelieved horror and brought new and unclear parameters into the disarmament discussions. In the forum of the United Nations endless rhetoric and exasperatingly small increments on changed behavior testify to the difficulty nations have finding and specifying the common ground among themselves—ground which without the burden of historical diversity and the imprisoning matrix of past commitments might seem readily apparent.

REFORM

In the United Nations, the attitude of the Soviet representatives toward amendments of the Charter has been as negative as if it was in the League of Nations, although for different reasons. The USSR, in a minority position, feared with some justification that any amendment of the Charter would strengthen the United Nations as a tool against the Soviet Union and deprive the organization of its usefulness to the USSR.

[48] *U.S. Department of State Bulletin,* XIII (1943), 307–311.

The opposition of the Soviet Union to the convocation of a General Conference on the Charter Review has been persistent. In 1953, when proposals to undertake preparatory work prior to convening such a conference were being debated in the General Assembly, the Soviet Union voted against both the placing of the matter on the agenda of the Assembly and against the proposals themselves.

In opposing efforts to revise the Charter, Soviet delegates emphasized their claim that the debates on revision illustrated the struggle between two schools of thought: one which desired international cooperation through the United Nations (the Soviet Union and its friends); the other which reflected a desire for world domination (the United States and its allies). The effectiveness of the United Nations could be increased through respect and a sincere desire for cooperation, claimed Soviet spokesmen. For that reason, it was not necessary to amend the Charter. The Soviet Union was opposed to any proposal for preparatory work in any form which would lead to any Charter review.

> Inasmuch as the Soviet Union and a number of other states do not agree to revision of the United Nations Charter, the ruling circles of the United States and Great Britain have apparently come to the conclusion that they will not succeed in fully adjusting the United Nations Organization to their aggressive policy, although they are striving to achieve this. The United Nations Charter proved to be inconvenient for them and they failed to achieve results from their attacks on the USSR for its defense of the very principles on which the United Nations Organization was established, since they could in no way shake the position of the Soviet government which is defending the sacred cause of the consolidation of universal lasting peace and is consistently exposing each and every aggressor and warmonger.[49]

The United Nations Charter was "fairly satisfactory," Vasily V. Kuznetsov told the General Assembly in the fall of 1955. What was needed was that all members, "and primarily the United States," really start observing it. He asserted that a Charter Review Conference would slow down considerably the "consolidation of trust among nations." And he repeated the standard Soviet arguments on the veto and accused the United States of Charter violations (in excluding the Chinese Communist representatives from the United Nations, in establishing the Little Assembly in 1947, and in setting

[49] Statement issued by the Ministry of Foreign Affairs of the USSR on January 29, 1941: *USSR Information Bulletin,* No. 3 (February 11, 1949), p. 86. See also the speech of P. D. Morozov, *op. cit.*

up the 1950 Collective Measures Committee). Mr. Kuznetsov assured the Assembly that the USSR was opposed to Charter revision and would fight suggestions to that effect with resolute determination.[50]

But in 1964, the Soviet Union sponsored alterations in the Charter all of its own: To "reinforce" the United Nations and to "enhance its efficacy," it proposed amendments extending the composition of the Security Council, the Economic and Social Council, and the office of the Secretary-General in order to give broader representation to the new Afro-Asian members. On Soviet initiative, the Eighteenth General Assembly adopted a resolution to increase the number of nonpermanent members of the Security Council from six to ten and the membership of the Economic and Social Council from eighteen to twenty-seven. The Soviet Union was the first Permanent Member of the Security Council to ratify those resolutions as amendments to the Charter, in December, 1964.

An international police force has appeared desirable to many since World War II. Article 43 of the Charter is a reflection of this desire. It provides, as a third cornerstone of security in the United Nations (the first two being reduction of armaments and regulation of atomic energy), that security forces be supplied by members. These would not be international nor even United Nations forces, but national contingents to be made available to the Security Council by special agreement.

The USSR has never agreed on a method for contribution of forces by members. As a matter of fact, the Soviet delegation has insisted on principles which, if adopted, would probably deprive Article 43 of its original meaning. The USSR has maintained that the permanent members of the Security Council must contribute equal components of the proposed forces in the air, at sea, and on the ground; that such forces must be stationed only in metropolitan territories or territorial waters of the contributing members; that after employment of such forces by the Security Council, they must return to the original stations within ninety days; and that "assistance and facilities" available to the Council should not include bases of the contributing members.[51]

Judging from the limitations, restrictions, and conditions which the USSR introduced in its plan for building up the forces of the Great Powers, the Soviet attitude toward internationally available forces in terms of Chapter

---

[50] *The New York Times*, Nov. 18, 1955, p. 5; see also U.N. General Assembly, *Official Records*, November 16, 1955, *passim*.

[51] See *U.N. Document*, No. S/336 (April 30, 1947), p. 80; and *Security Council Official Records, Second Year*, No. 44 (June 6, 1947), p. 963.

VII of the Charter has been cautious, almost negative. When the Secretary-General proposed a United Nations guard force, the Soviet delegates attacked the proposal as violating national sovereignty and the constitutional powers of the Security Council, and also as an instrument of United States imperialism. Underlying the Soviet attitude to any United Nations police force was probably the old fear that such a force could be manipulated by the "imperialists" and used against the USSR.

And yet, in the early period of the Congo chaos in 1960, the Soviet Union favored United Nations action in the Congo, voting in the Security Council for the United Nations Congo Force as that force was proposed by Secretary-General Dag Hammarskjold. As originally stipulated, this force would not intervene in the internal affairs of the Republic of the Congo but would merely protect the integrity of the new nation. But even when it became evident that the United Nations force would not restrict itself to that difficult injunction, Soviet support was not withdrawn. Only later on, in September, 1960, when Moscow began sending direct unilateral aid to some factions in the Congo, did the USSR reverse itself and withdraw support from the United Nations force. It then vetoed in the Security Council a resolution for military assistance to the Congo. The USSR not only now blamed the Secretary-General for the course of events but accused the United Nations force in the Congo of imperialist aggression. Many Asian and African nations were alienated by this new Soviet stand.

The discomfiture of the Soviet Union at the obstacle now posed to it by the United Nations, because of an unforseen shift of internal forces in the Congo, led to a wide-front attack on the UN structure and procedure. The change of the balance of forces in the United Nations, so the new Soviet argument went, required adjustments in United Nations machinery which would reflect this change. Not only should the Military Staff Committee resume its work, in accordance with "the introduction of order in peace-keeping operations," but "all the practical questions relating to the composition of United Nations forces . . . and the structure of the command of these forces" should be re-examined. This would be "a real way" to enable the United Nations to play a more effective part in the maintenance of peace and security in the world.[52]

Two persistent issues evolved from this Congo episode: a Soviet demand for a change in the personnel and structure of the United Nations administration, and a refusal to pay for UN expenditures of which it did not approve.

Actually, a part of the Soviet Union's complaint on personnel went back

---

[52] M. Lvov, "United Nations: Results and Prospects," *International Affairs,* No. 9 (September, 1965), p. 8.

before the Congo crisis. As early as 1958, Soviet delegates complained of discrimination against the USSR in selecting candidates for vacancies in the UN Secretariat. In 1958, only 1.6 per cent of the technical experts used by the United Nations were Soviet citizens. Of 3,700 members of the United Nations missions sent to underdeveloped countries in the 1955–1959 period, only forty came from the USSR (about 50 per cent emanated from the United States and its allies). The Soviet Union also claimed only 2.2 per cent of the UNESCO staff in 1958, while contributing 13 per cent to that organization's budget. Furthermore, of the top twenty-eight positions in the United Nations Secretariat, the USSR held only one as compared to seventeen held by citizens of NATO countries. At the secondary level in the supervisory ranks, the Western powers had twenty-eight men, the neutralist states five, and the Communists one.[53]

By 1960, the United Nations administrative structure was said to have become intolerable to the Soviet Union. This led Khrushchev, in September, 1960, to propose the *troika* amendment to the Charter. Referring to the Congo experience where, he charged, the Secretary-General had been able to ignore the will of the Security Council, the Soviet Premier demanded a thoroughgoing change. He proposed

> . . . a collective U.N. agency consisting of three persons, each representing a definite group of states [the West, the Communist states and the non-aligned nations]. This would provide a definite guarantee that activity of the U.N. executive agency would not prove detrimental to one of these groups of states.[54]

The *troika* device (with each group apparently possessing a veto) was to be applied to all branches of the United Nations and to all other international organizations.

The Soviet proposal did not stir a great deal of favorable response, even among the Afro-Asian members of the United Nations. It yielded only small parochial gains—three new Under-Secretaries to assist the Secretary-General. During the tenure of Secretary-General U Thant, there has been virtually no further discussion of the *troika* proposal.

Almost no change has occurred in the Soviet staff pattern at the United Nations since 1958. The USSR is still underrepresented—well below the

---

[53] Alexander Dallin, *The Soviet Union at the United Nations* (New York: Frederick A. Praeger, Inc., 1962), pp. 101–102.

[54] B. Dmitreyev, "Life Knocks at the Doors of the U.N.," *Pravda*, Sept. 28, p. 2, quoted in the *Current Digest of the Soviet Press*, XII, No. 39 (1960), 16–17.

quota desirable if the United Nations should truly have a balanced international administration. This is chiefly because the USSR, although complaining that it is underrepresented, has not offered comparably equipped candidates for existing vacancies and has favored short-term (two-year) appointments, a practice destructive to the United Nations career-service concept.

The second issue brought to a head by the Congo episode concerned Soviet financing of United Nations peace-keeping operations. In 1964, the United States demanded that members, including the USSR, share the cost of the United Nations peace-keeping operations, including those of the United Nations force in the Congo. The Soviet Union refused to pay the sum it had been assessed for the Congo forces (and for those in Cyprus and the Middle East), charging that these operations were initiated or conducted illegally, in violation of the UN Charter. As a consequence, a United States-British–sponsored UN Special Committee on Peace-Keeping was established by the General Assembly. The Soviet Union protested that only the Security Council, not the General Assembly, had power under the Charter to sponsor any peace-keeping action involving the use of Armed Forces. Therefore, the Soviet Union argued, exclusive power to initiate and arrange the financing for peace-keeping activities rested with the Security Council. But the United States insisted that the USSR either pay its debts, at least in part, or be deprived, under Article 19 of the Charter, of its voting rights. In its turn, the Soviet government reaffirmed its stand and warned that any effort to use Soviet refusal to pay to deprive the USSR of its voting rights in the United Nations would create "serious harm" to the United Nations.[55]

A confused state of affairs followed—a state of affairs which paralyzed the Nineteenth Session of the United Nations. Only the Security Council functioned. In spite of an advisory opinion from the International Court of Justice invalidating its position, the USSR maintained its refusal to pay and found support in a parallel refusal by France. The Special Committee on Peace-Keeping failed to agree on either principles or financing. Reflecting a serious constitutional crisis, the financial difficulties were a new evidence of the profound differences about the role of the UN; not only between the United States and the USSR, but among other members as well.

In August, 1965, the United States withdrew its objections. It hoped that if the USSR were not pressed, it might quietly meet the deficit (as implied by the Soviet Permanent Representative at a meeting of the Special Committee on Peace-Keeping in May, 1965). But nothing happened. As of this

[55] *Pravda,* August 27, 1964, p. 1.

writing, the Soviet Union still has not paid its share of the United Nations peace-keeping operations.

One answer to our initial query concerning the behavior and attitudes of the USSR toward an organized community of nations and more specifically toward problems posed by the United Nations is that the behavior and attitudes of neither the international organization nor the USSR are the same as they were even ten years ago. Both have changed a great deal.

The United Nations today no longer reflects accurately the power relationships of the world. Dominated by weak developing nations, the General Assembly often deals with issues which are largely tengential to, although they often reflect, major political decisions in international affairs. Exhibiting a significant lag between historical changes and its own structural pattern, the United Nations has yet to bring its Charter up to date. But perhaps the shaping of world order in our turbulent times can not be expected to be rapid; it certainly is not an easy task.

Always the realists, Soviet decision-makers have adjusted to the new United Nations. They find it "useful," "expedient," and even "necessary" for prosecuting their foreign policy. They have long accepted the fact that major political and security decisions are normally not made there. Vietnam shows the limitations of the United Nations' resources. The Pakistani-Indian negotiations at Tashkent in 1966 illustrated again that although Security Council resolutions may lead to nothing, comparable decisions may be effectively arrived at outside the UN framework. At the same time, the large membership of the General Assembly appears to preclude serious discussion and negotiation of delicate issues. From any national or international point of view, not least that of the USSR, the UN is no panacea. But the expenditure of effort by the Soviet representatives also testifies that they do not discount it as impotent or irrelevant either.

Soviet ascendance in the United Nations over the last twenty years is manifested in a present voting parity or near parity with the West. But in the process of gaining this degree of support, the USSR has been socialized into its new role in the UN too. Its present behavior is generally a far cry from the early post-World War II obstructionism. In the course of reaching specific compromises with noncommunist states—involving the growing scope of UN technical and functional activities in particular—the tacit recognition of a large body of common interests has built by accretion. These common interests cannot often be compartmentalized in "nonpolitical" categories.

The Soviet Union thus tries to use the UN to advance what it perceives to be its interests. Where these interests appear to include frustrating Western policies, Soviet delegates prove themselves accomplished at that art. Where these interests appear to include collaboration across ideological frontiers, as they frequently do, the Soviet delegates demonstrate a comparable capacity. In both cases, the USSR finds the United Nations an important instrument and arena.

Perhaps surprisingly, the preceding paragraph might be written almost identically to summarize the place of the United Nations in American foreign policy.

THE SOVIET UNION AND INTERNATIONAL LAW:
Soviet Treaties[1]

International treaties and agreements are important devices of states in their mutual relations. They are instruments of stability as well as change in international relations, catalysts and moderators of political forces in the international arena, and tools for integration or decentralization. For Soviet Russia, a state new and allegedly unique in the world, international treaties have proved to be especially significant, because they call for conscious and voluntary action founded on explicit consent and free will, binding the parties solely through the manifestation of their consensus based on un-abridged sovereignty. Through international treaties, Soviet Russia defined, maintained, and developed its independence and secured status as well as recognition of its "special" and "altogether different" organization and structure in the world. By means of international treaties, Soviet Russia clarified and made concrete its relations with other states at the various stages of its development. International treaties have helped the Soviet Union to accelerate its own pace of development. They helped to make Soviet Russia, originally an outcast, gradually acceptable and accepted in the world; in the process, they permitted the USSR to introduce, press for, and at times successfully defend radical innovations in international relations. At the same time, however, international treaties assisted other nations in curbing many excesses on the part of the USSR, either directly by their contents or through the understanding that there would be no treaty unless certain conditions of comity and reciprocity were met by the Soviet Union.

As the majority of Soviet treaties have been concluded with capitalist states, they have been concluded with the "exploiting classes" and thus

---

[1] This Chapter is based in part on material drawn from Jan F. Triska and Robert M. Slusser, *The Theory, Law, and Policy of Soviet Treaties* (Stanford: Stanford University Press, 1962), with the permission of the publisher, Stanford University Press, © 1962 by the Board of Trustees of the Leland Stanford Junior University ; and from Jan F. Triska, "Soviet Treaty Law: A Quantitative Analysis," *Law and Contemporary Problems*, XXIX, No. 4 (Autumn, 1964), 896–909, by permission.

helped to create and maintain a new stratum in the legal superstructure over the heads of the proletariat. They helped to guard the interests of the ruling classes in the capitalist states, which are allegedly destined to coerce or oppress the other classes. While treaties concluded by the Soviet state have helped to lead the Soviet population toward socialism, they have also been helpful to the ruling classes in the capitalist societies. Stalin noted the dual effect: "The highest development of governmental power for the purpose of preparing the conditions for the withering away of governmental power—this is the Marxist formula. Is this 'contradictory'? Yes, it is. But this contradiction is life, and it reflects completely the Marxist dialectic."[2]

The initial Soviet intent of no international treaties and no cooperation with capitalist countries was rapidly abandoned; Soviet leaders came early to realize the need for international treaties as an instrument of policy and as a specific and flexible regulator of Soviet foreign relations. Yet, the ideological views continually expressed about capitalist treaties as "tools of aggressive foreign policy," about the "imperialist essence" of such treaties and their "fictitious significance," could not produce any high respect for Soviet treaties concluded with such partners. Utility, in conflict with principles, could be at best accommodated.

Soviet treaties have thus represented a double standard ever since their inception: As instruments of practical policy, they have been viewed as significant and meaningful. As retreats from ideology, they have been considered unimportant and ephemeral. But because of the long-forced coexistence of these two incompatible standards, accommodation was found for both; just as in more basic Soviet concepts, such as state and law, policy needs here determined the ratio of coexistence. Doctrine depended on policy, not vice versa; cynics might even say that policy exploited ideology. At any rate, doctrine did not exclude the possibility of temporary coincidence of communist and bourgeois interests. The specific treaty subject to abrogation upon predetermined conditions could conveniently define the nature and limits of the coincidence.

An analysis of Soviet treaties is thus primarily an investigation of one instrumentality of Soviet foreign *policy*, ranging from the original brief and negative span to the "most positive" present attitude, not an investigation of the ideological ingredient mixed in individual Soviet treaties under the watchful guidance of Soviet foreign policymakers.

---

[2] I. V. Stalin, *Voprosy Leninizma,* 10th ed. (Moscow: Gospolihzdat, 1934), p. 427.

INTERNATIONAL TREATIES AS SOURCES OF INTERNATIONAL LAW AND ORDER

Ever since the first Soviet entry into foreign relations, international treaties and agreements have been claimed as the fundamental source and *prima facie* foundation of relations between Soviet Russia and other governments. Successive Soviet leaders have relied more on international treaties than on all other foundations of international order combined. They have made clear their view that treaties constitute the ideal vehicle for relations between the Soviet state and the outside, noncommunist world. As a widely cited Soviet Procurator General put it, while speaking on the significance of the trial of major German war criminals before the International Military Tribunal at Nuremberg:

> In the international sphere, the prime source of law and the only legal act is a treaty, an agreement of states. Just as on a national scale a law, if accepted by legislative departments and appropriately published, becomes an unconditional and ample legal basis for actions of organs of national justice, so in the international field a treaty, concluded between states, is an unconditional and sufficient legal basis for realization and activity of organs of international justice, created by these states.[3]

Nor has this reliance on treaties tended to slacken as the power of the Soviet state has increased; quite the contrary. Under Khrushchev, the Soviet state had stepped up the pace of its treaty activity. During the first two years of Khrushchev's economic and cultural offensive, the Soviet government concluded more than three hundred treaties with some forty partners, especially the leading Afro-Asian nations: 143 in 1955 (of which 135 were bilateral agreements) and 167 in 1956 (of which 142 were bilateral), the highest number of treaties ever concluded by the Soviet government in a two-year period.

Most Western students of Soviet law agree that Soviet international legal doctrine was elaborated according to Soviet state practice, in agreement with that practice, and to justify that practice. At first, Soviet treaties were couched in the semantic stereotypes of traditional bourgeois treaty practice and were based on principles of traditional international law. A minority of Soviet treaties contained Marxist ideological provisions, but these stipulations were isolated and lacked any unifying principle. If there was any consistency at all, it was the Soviet expectation of the benefits or at least the removal of danger a given treaty might bring about, and a given contracting party

[3] *Pravda,* February 9, 1946.

was therefore to a considerable degree the determinant of both the language and the principles emphasized.

As the Soviet scholar, Korovin, pointed out in 1924, this mixture of principles and motivations in early Soviet treaty practice, which "drew arguments in articles and paragraphs [both] from extracts of treaties concluded by the [Russian] Imperial Government" and from Marxist-Leninist ideology, "resulted in an entirely ambiguous situation."[4] Consequently, there was in the earliest period no clear Soviet theory of treaties.

Once the Soviet government had been recognized by the leading foreign powers and diplomatic relations had been regularized, Soviet theory of international treaties began to take form. Lagging behind Soviet practice in time, theorists now had certain governmental practices to follow, to systematize, to analyze, to justify, and to defend. Just as Soviet treaty practice during the 1917–1922 period can be characterized as a mixture of traditional and revolutionary principles, so Soviet scholars in the period 1923–1928 selected elements from this mixture in order to elaborate a more systematic Soviet doctrine.

For the Soviet theorists of this period and for those who have followed them, international treaties have retained the crucial significance they had in Soviet practice from the beginning. They saw in treaties signed by the Soviet government a bridge between the traditional and revolutionary systems which both could recognize. Relations between the USSR and the rest of the world were to be built on solid, business-like foundations; utility, expediency, and the Soviet criteria of security have been served well by the instrumentality of international treaties. And, given the limitations superimposed by Soviet ideological objectives, the Soviet concern for sovereignty and explicit consent, the exclusively reciprocal character of treaties, and the essential adaptability of treaties to fit particular, concrete situations, the Soviet preference for treaties as instruments of relations with other countries is understandable.

Although Lenin was the imaginative innovator, Stalin functioned chiefly as the cautious administrator. But it was Khrushchev, flexible, pragmatic, adapatable, and with the rich experience of the Soviet past to learn from, who plunged into treaty relations (bilateral, plutilateral, and multilateral) with all kinds of partners (capitalist, socialist, and Communist) on all kinds of subjects (political, military, economic, communication, legal, cultural, and health). Indeed, so have his successors.

International custom has been accepted by nearly all Soviet scholars only

[4] Ye. A. Korovin, *Mezhdunarodnoe pravo perekhodnogo vremeni*, rev. ed. (Moscow: Gosizdat, 1925), p. 5.

as a second, but still fundamental, source of international order. Professor Kozhevnikov's assessment of the value of international custom—"Regardless of the uncertainty, instability, and relativity of international custom, it would be incorrect to underestimate, let alone to ignore its significance as a source of law in international relations."[5]—became classic. Indeed, why should "the Soviet government be deprived of those rights which require no treaty formulation and derive from the very fact that normal diplomatic relations exist?"[6] Soviet practice found international custom useful; Soviet theoreticians approved and accepted international custom as the second foundation of order in relations between the Soviet Union and the rest of the world.

Soviet scholarship after World War II began to stress, as a third source of international law, basic *concepts and principles* of international law. These could be viewed as the Soviet interpretation of general principles of law. Variously understood as legal analogies, natural law, general principles of justice, and so on in the West, the general principles of law became for most Soviet theorists a series of "basic laws, norms, and concepts" of legal, political, social, and ethnical content. The great majority of these principles have their origins, in one way or another, either in traditional international law or in treaty law and thus have been accepted, or are acceptable, universally. However, while the *terms* in which the principles are formulated by Soviet writers may be similar to or identical with those employed in the West, the *content and significance* of the principles are sometimes given a different interpretation in the Soviet and non-Soviet worlds.

Decisions of international organizations such as the United Nations, international courts such as the International Court of Justice, and other "permanent and temporary" international organizations, conferences and agencies have been, more often than not, viewed by Soviet writers as "an important source of international law" for the member states, "provided that they were [so] recognized and applied in practice."[7] Such decisions "do not always receive proper attention, in spite of [their] great significance and the importance of the role that [they] play," complained Professor Krylov, out of his extensive judicial experience. This is true. Soviet scholarship, just as Soviet—and Western—practice, has viewed such decisions as subsidiary

---

[5] F. I. Kozhevnikov, "K voprosu o poniatii mezhdunarodnogo prava," *Sovetskoe gosudarstvo i pravo,* No. 2 (1940), p. 101.

[6] Ye. B. Pashukanis, *Ocherki po mezhdunarodnomu pravu* (Moscow: Gos. Izd-vo Sov. Zakonodatel'stvo, 1936), Chapter 2.

[7] S. B. Krylov, "Bor'ba SSSR za mir," in Durdenevskii and Krylov (eds.), *Mezhdunarodnoe pravo* (Moscow: Inst. Prava, Akad. Nauk SSSR, 1947), p. 25.

sources of international law; nor does Krylov's complaint appear to have had any practical effect in altering this situation.

Similarly, *decisions of national courts, domestic legislation, the codification of international law,* and occasionally other sources have been recognized by the USSR. *International morality and international comity,* on the other hand, have been generally rejected by Soviet theoreticians as impractical.

In the fifty-year period of the existence of the Soviet state, then, the metamorphosis of Soviet theory on sources of world order has been considerable. Theory evolved from the original position—international treaties *and very little else*—to the present point of view—international treaties *and* international custom, general principles (concepts and norms) of international law, decisions of international organizations, decisions of national courts, domestic legislation, and so on. As a consequence, and although there are differences, the Soviet hierarchy of sources has come to resemble quite closely the generally accepted Western pattern.

First, international conventions, both general and particular, still tower over other sources for Soviet theorists. Yet subtle differences in terminology may be distinguished. Although in the late Stalin period the usual formula was that treaties were the "basic" source, in later writings it is often said that treaties and custom are *both* basic sources but that treaties are the "principal" or more important source.[8]

Second, the difference in "motivations" leading to conclusion of international treaties has always been solemnly pointed out: ever since Lenin, Soviet writers claim, "The Soviet state viewed international treaties as a serious means in the struggle for peace, for the victory of communism. On the other hand, the imperialist states exploit international treaties to mask their aggressive goals to secure legally the dependence of small states. International treaties in the hands of the imperialists become new legal forms of colonialism (Baghdad Pact and SEATO) and a cover-up for aggression

---

[8] G. I. Tunkin, "Coexistence and International Law," *Recueil des cours,* XCV, No. 3 (1959), 22–23. The former Chief of the Treaty and Legal Department of the Ministry of Foreign Affairs of the USSR summed up the Soviet point of view on the subject in his 1958 Hague lectures as follows: "The concept according to which general international law is exclusively customary law, though quite correct in the time of Vattel, is obsolete; it does not reflect the real present-day situation as to the sources of international law. The existence of a considerable number of multilateral international treaties to which all or almost all states are parties (i.e., general or universal international treaties) and also extensive efforts in the field of codification of international law have led to a situation where international treaties become a direct means of changing, developing, and creating new norms of general international law."

(North Atlantic Pact). V. I. Lenin used to characterize such international treaties as 'treaty conspiracies.' "[9]

Third, selectivity and eclectism are applied to *all* sources under the criterion of "democratic" principles." In other words, the USSR accepts those norms as foundations of international order which it recognizes itself or which it views as not in opposition to Soviet foreign policy; such norms are made binding by the acceptance of the Soviet state.

Fourth, there is an old distinction which is still preserved in Soviet theory between substantive and formal sources of international law. *Substantive* (or material) sources of order are the "real foundations" which condition the origin and the development of all order, namely, the productive relations characteristic for each society. That class which controls the means of production in a society is the class which forms and determines order and its concrete content. In relations among states the substantive sources, because of the presence of both socialist and capitalist systems, are and must be struggle, coexistence, and competition. These are the material bases of international order, which is then manifested in the *formal*, external, legal sources: international treaties, international custom, general principles of international law, decisions of international organizations, and so on.

However, these and similar differences are primarily doctrinal and have had remarkably little impact on actual Soviet treaty practice.

On the other hand, the Western view on sources of international law has not stood still in the last fifty years either. International custom was universally viewed as "the most important source of international law" fifty years ago. Today it is regarded as one of the two most important sources and, in general, as perhaps the second one on the scale. This fact, at least partly, owes its origin to the presence of the Soviet Union in the world community. As Charles De Visscher aptly put it, "Acceleration of history, and above all *diminishing homogeneity in the moral and legal ideas that have long governed the formation of law*—such, in their essential elements, are the causes that today curtail the development of customary international law." International custom "is not adequate to the needs of a world that changes with unprecedented speed"; international treaties—flexible, decentralized, rational, specific, adaptable, innovating, and stabilizing—were bound to take over where international custom, surer but slower, was proved wanting.[10]

---

[9] A. N. Talalaev, "V. I. Lenin o mezhdunarodnykh dogovorakh," *Sovetskoe gosudarstvo i pravo*, No. 4 (1958), p. 24. The refererence is to Lenin, *Sochineniia*, 4th ed. (Moscow: Gospolitizdat, 1940–1960), XXIII, 116.

[10] Charles De Visscher, *Theory and Reality in Public International Law*, P. E. Corbett (trans.) (Princeton, N.J.: Princeton University Press, 1957), p. 156. Italics added.

We may conclude, then, that after fifty years of "struggle," "coexistence," and "competition," there is a fairly close similarity between Soviet and Western views on the sources of order in international relations, and that in both international treaties are of principal importance.

THE SOVIET LAW OF TREATIES

Soviet spokesmen contend that *Soviet* treaties are more important for orderly, peaceful, and just international relations than other treaties. This is so, they maintain, because both in form and in substance Soviet treaties differ profoundly from other international treaties.

Here we devote our attention to (1) Soviet, as contrasted with Western, treaty law and (2) the allegedly marked legal and procedural differences between Soviet and non-Soviet treaties, ranging from the definition of those treaties to the effect of war upon them. Our principal concern, while piecing together from the many varied Soviet sources what may fairly be termed the *Soviet law of treaties*, is the significance of those alleged differences for international cooperation: Are these differences of such magnitude as to parochialize *a priori* Soviet treaty relations?

Our findings are based on first, Soviet treaty doctrine, as elaborated by Soviet theorists, and, second, Soviet treaty practice, as it has evolved since 1917. The Soviet treaty network, which has been densest with the party-states (an exception is the case of Finland, with whom the Soviet Union has concluded more agreements than with any other state), covers virtually all the countries of the world.

In most cases Soviet treaty doctrine and Soviet treaty practice have been found in agreement, with practice apparently determining the theory. Since explicit Soviet treaty theory concerns itself primarily with political treaties (there are relatively few in number in Soviet treaty-making), we have brought in governmental practice with respect to trade and functional treaties for a more comprehensive view.

In the discussion that follows we adopt the traditional anthropomorphic pattern commonly used in both the Soviet Union and the West when dealing with the subject of treaty law. First, an international treaty is conceived and, if all goes well, born; this is the formation period. Second, once born, the treaty either lives or simply exists for a period of time; this is the treaty's operational period. And finally, a treaty dies, is killed, or even murdered; or it may be mercifully put to sleep for a period of time, to be revived—or not—later on. This is the termination and suspension stage.

Nature and Scope

Soviet treaties are "usually" formal, written documents; however, oral treaties have been entered into by the Soviet government as well. A Soviet-Mongolian People's Republic Mutual Assistance Pact, called a *gentleman's agreement,* was concluded orally on November 27, 1934, and the Agreement between the USSR and the Netherlands Government-in-Exile Concerning Reorganization of Diplomatic Missions into Embassies was negotiated orally in London on October 22, 1942 and November 4, 1942. Treaties do not necessarily have to be embodied in a single "instrument," with the signatures and seals of authorized personnel, divided into articles, and preceded by a preamble. Although this is the normal diplomatic practice, "less complicated agreements" may be concluded by a simple exchange of notes.

International treaties may be called *pacts, agreements, conventions, tractates, accords, declarations, exchanges of notes, protocols,* and so on. Legally speaking, names do not matter. Soviet authors have concluded: "Such designations are merely conventional in their distinction."[11]

The Soviet definition of a treaty includes both (1) traditional and (2) ideological elements, the latter appended to the traditional conception during the second half of the existence of the Soviet state. Thus a treaty is (1) an international agreement among states creating rights and obligations in international law of public-law character, usually embodied in a written instrument whatever its name, and (2) a typical and most widespread legal form of struggle or cooperation in the realm of political, economic, and other relations among states. It rests on basic legal principles of equality of the contracting parties, bilateral acceptability, and mutual benefit.

Capacity and Competence of Parties to Conclude Treaties

Only sovereign states have the "full" formal as well as substantive capacity to contract international treaties on all problems. It is true that Soviet doctrine also views nations and peoples actively fighting for their sovereign independence as subjects of international law. However, the capacity of such groups to enter into treaty relations has never been considered complete or equal to that of sovereign, independent states. Dependent peoples and nations conclude international treaties only within the framework of the international document defining their dependence.

The United Nations is regarded as a subject of international law, but an atypical one; the Advisory Opinion of the International Court of Justice of April 11, 1949, which recognized the United Nations as a "full" subject

---

[11] Pashukanis, *op. cit.,* p. 157.

of international law, is "incorrect and must be rejected." However, it is admitted that international organizations are endowed with some rights normally associated with the equality of subjects in international law: the right to conclude *some* international treaties—as defined in the multilateral treaties founding international organizations—is among them.

Normally, only authorized Soviet (and Union Republic) representatives may conclude international treaties on behalf of their respective competent Supreme Soviets. They must be properly issued plenary powers which empower them to conclude a given international treaty.[12]

Consent

At first, Soviet theorists denied that the USSR would ever recognize any means except free will and consent as legitimate foundations for the conclusion of international treaties; a defeated state was thus not considered obliged to observe the peace treaty forced upon it. Under changed conditions after World War II, however, coercion and force have been viewed as legal and have not been considered an invalidating factor in treaty obligations forced upon a Soviet treaty partner.

Purpose

A treaty must be capable of realization from both "the juridical and the factual" point of view. And the object of a treaty "must be admissible from the point of view of international law." If one party, for example, attempts to include a stipulation in a treaty permitting pillage of foreign merchant ships at sea, such a party proposes something outside the realm of treaty law and international law.

Otherwise, "everything belonging to the sphere of international relations" may be the object of treaties. However, "each state may obligate itself only in relation to that which legally or in fact is included in its authority or command."[13]

Language

Soviet treaty practice "strictly adheres" to the principle of "complete equality" of languages of the contracting parties. And the USSR "permits exceptions to the above principle on the basis of agreement with the other

---

[12] Soviet army and navy commanders have occasionally been authorized to conclude agreements of a military nature on behalf of Soviet Russia. Pashukanis, "Dogovor mezhdunarodnyi," in *Entsiklopediia gosudarstva i prava* (Moscow: Izd-vo Kom. Akademii, 1925), col. 976.

[13] V. I. Lisovskii, *Mezhdunarodnoe pravo* (Kiev: Gos. Universitet, 1955), p. 234.

contracting party of the treaty or in special cases." The Act of Unconditional Surrender of the German Armed Forces, signed in Berlin on May 8, 1945, for example, although drawn up in the English, Russian, and German languages, had only two authentic texts, English and Russian; similarly, the Peace Treaties with Italy, Rumania, Bulgaria, Hungary, and Finland of February 10, 1947 were drawn up in English, French, Russian, and in the languages of the defeated countries, but only the English and Russian (and French in the Italian Peace Treaty) texts were designated as authentic.[14]

The Russian language became one of the world's diplomatic languages after World War II, chiefly because of the radically altered Soviet power position. At the 1945 San Francisco Conference on the United Nations, Molotov put it differently: "I shall speak on this matter in Russian—a language that not all of you know. But I know that the Russian language is very well suited for a just cause and I hope that what I shall say will be both comprehensible and convincing."[15]

Signature and Ratification

Originally, under the 1936 Constitution, the conclusion of international treaties was the sole prerogative of the Union. By virtue of a 1944 amendment, however, the Union Republics as well received the right to conclude agreements with foreign states. The RSFSR Constitution read as follows: "The jurisdiction of the Russian Soviet Federated Socialist Republic, as represented by its higher organs of state power and organs of state administration, embraces establishment of representation of the RSFSR in international relations."

Identical language was employed in the other Constitutions of the Republics; however, no specific provisions concerning their treaty powers appeared in the Republican Constitutions. Thus the authority of the individual Union Republics to conclude international agreements rests solely on Article 18a of the Soviet (USSR) Constitution. The agencies competent to conclude treaties for the individual Union Republics are their respective Supreme Soviets and Presidia.

Should the signing of an agreed-upon treaty be delayed, the Soviet government may be expected to suggest initialing of the text by the plenipotentiaries who, instead of fully signing and affixing seals to the treaty, place their initials under the text. This denotes completion and approval of the

---

[14] F. I. Kozhevnikov, "Sovetskoe gosudarstvo i mezhdunarodnye dogovory," in Korovin (ed.), *SSSR i problemy mezhdunarodnogo prava* (Moscow: Akademiia Obschestv. Nauk, 1947), p. 86.

[15] Plenary Session, April 30, 1945, reported in *Pravda,* May 2, 1945.

coordinated and edited treaty next. Once the cause of the delay has been removed, the initialed treaty is formally signed. This initialing stage, of course, is not considered mandatory.

The ratification of international treaties has sometimes been regarded by Soviet scholars as an institution inherently alien to Soviet political and governmental concepts, resting as it does on a principle that is rejected by the Soviet system of "democratic centralism"—the principle, namely, of separation of powers, of checks and balances. On this view the problem of ratification is not one of "significance in principle, but primarily of state technique."[16]

From the Soviet point of view, there should be no internal political struggles over the ratification of important treaties—struggles that are familiar phenomena in the history of other states. Since the entire Soviet state structure is organized to carry out a single, unified policy, there is allegedly no place for the expression of views at variance with the government, either on the part of the public or of organized political opposition. Accordingly, it might well seem that the ratification of international treaties and the associated governmental processes of review and approval could either be eliminated entirely or drastically reduced in scope and significance.

In fact, however, practical considerations have prevailed over political doctrine. Initially for reasons of emergency (during the forced negotiations for a peace treaty with the Central Powers in 1918), and later for reasons of reciprocity and prestige, an elaborate technique of ratification and approval was developed by the Soviet government.

Article 14 of the 1936 Constitution entrusted the ratification of treaties to the supreme organs of the USSR: "The jurisdiction of the Union of Soviet Socialist Republics, as represented by its highest organs of state authority and organs of government, covers: (a) Representation of the Union in international relations, conclusion and ratification of treaties with other states; (b) Questions of war and peace." Article 31 provided that the Supreme Soviet of the USSR should exercise the powers referred to in Article 14, insofar as they do not, by virtue of the Constitution, come within the jurisdiction of other organs. Ratification of international treaties was, however, expressly made one of these exceptions, for Article 49 provided that the Presidium "ratifies international treaties."

In 1938, in addition, a special law, "On the procedure of ratification and denunciation of international treaties of the USSR," was enacted. It is this law that governs Soviet ratification today.

[16] Ye. A. Korovin, *Sovremennoe mezhdunarodnoe publichnoe pravo* (Moscow-Leningrad: Gosizdat, 1926), p. 94.

Article 1 of the law restated the 1936 constitutional provisions concerning ratification, making it the exclusive prerogative of the Presidium of the Supreme Soviet. Article 2 substantially modified the list of treaties subject to ratification previously; it made ratification necessary for peace treaties, but also for treaties of mutual assistance against aggression, treaties of mutual nonaggression, and treaties that the contracting parties agreed were to be ratified. This was thought sufficient to uphold the prestige of the socialist state and leave Soviet diplomats free to persuade foreign colleagues to agree to the ratification of treaties that were of particular interest to the Soviet Union.

The major change, however, consisted in adding two new categories of treaties to those subject to Soviet ratification: treaties of mutual assistance against aggression and treaties of nonaggression. This provision was designed to meet the challenge of the new international situation that the Soviet Union faced:

The international situation has essentially changed since 1925–27. Aggression, political banditry, and violence in all forms and shapes have entered upon the international arena. Correspondingly the struggle of the Leninist-Stalinist foreign policy has also been intensified for peace and security, for unification of the forces of progressive humanity against fascist aggression. The Soviet government has advanced new institutions of peace: pacts of non-aggression, pacts of mutual defense against aggression. These measures are reflected in the listing found in Article 2 of the new law.[17]

The 1938 law also provided that only the organ that ratified a treaty was authorized to annul or denounce it; only the Presidium of the Supreme Soviet could denounce international treaties it had ratified.

Ratification is defined in the USSR as the solemn approval of an international treaty concluded by the supreme organs of the state, followed by the exchange of ratification documents with the treaty partner or partners. As to the nature of ratification, Soviet legal doctrine considers "incorrect," and rejects, the theory that ratification is simply declaratory and does not create a treaty; instead, it views the act of ratification, by which "the head of a state realizes his will, and gives to the treaty the force of law," as a *constitutive* act.

Two examples may be given of Soviet failure to ratify. On June 8, 1922,

---

[17] M. Plotkin, "O sile mezhdunarodnykh obiazatel'stv (K izdaniiu novogo zakona o poriadke ratifikatsii i denontsiatsii mezhdunarodnykh dogovorov SSSR)," *Sovetskoe gosudarstvo,* No. 5 (1938), p. 74.

the Soviet government refused to ratify a provisional commercial agreement with Italy of May 24, 1922 on the grounds that it contained no explicit recognition of the Soviet government and that it was too advantageous to Italy. In 1923, the Soviet government, claiming that the Lausanne Straits Convention of July 24, 1923 "violated the sovereign rights of Turkey and was clearly directed against the Soviet Union," refused to ratify it.

Soviet theory does not view a treaty that is subject to ratification as having any legal force until (1) the ratification process has been completed or (2) the exchange or deposit of the documents of ratification has been completed, respectively, depending upon the stipulation concerning ratification in the treaty text. Then, however, the ratification is considered as validating the treaty from the moment of signature, and it has thus a retroactive effect. In consequence, no changes may be introduced in the interval between signature and ratification of a bilateral treaty.

Accessions and Reservations

Widespread accession of new parties to the 1963 Soviet-U.S.-British nuclear-testing treaty has drawn provisions for such expansion of treaty obligations into the limelight.

Over the past fifty years the Soviet government has acceded to many multilateral treaties, agreements, and conventions concluded before the Bolshevik Revolution. In addition, it has acceded to many more multilateral treaties, mostly of functional—but *also* of political—nature, concluded since 1917. Today the Soviet practice of formally joining valid international treaties has been well established.

A reservation to a multilateral or to a plurilateral treaty is "a declaration made by a state party to the treaty that the said state intends to exclude some provision from the treaty, to change its significance or to impart a special meaning to it." It is "a formal declaration" which determines "certain additional or limiting conditions of the validity of a treaty in the relation of a given state to the other treaty partners." It is "a unilateral act," added to the treaty but not entered in its text.[18]

The policy of the Soviet government concerning reservations to multilateral treaties crystallized with the submission of the Soviet reservations to the Genocide Convention, defended successfully by Soviet diplomats at the

---

[18] V. N. Durdenevskii, "K voprosu ob ogovorkakh v mezhdunarodnykh dogovorakh," *Sovetskoe gosudarstvo i pravo*, No. 4 (1956), p. 97. See also Durdenevskii, "Soglasie storon pri ogovorkakh v mezhdunarodnykh dogovorakh," *Vestnik Moskovskogo Universiteta*, No. 4 (1951), and S. Borisov, "Suverennoe pravo gosudarstvuchastnikov mnogostoronnikh dogovorov zaiavliat' ogovorki," *Sovetskoe gosudarstvo i pravo*, No. 4 (1952).

United Nations, at the International Court of Justice, and elsewhere between 1948 and 1951.

The Soviet Union (and Czechoslovakia, Poland, Bulgaria, Rumania, the Belorussian SSR, and the Ukrainian SSR) signed the 1948 Convention on the Prevention and Punishment of the Crime of Genocide with two reservations. The first one concerns Article 9 of the Convention, which provides for the compulsory jurisdiction of the International Court of Justice in disputes regarding the interpretation and application of the Convention. The second concerns Article 12 of the Convention, which stipulates that the Convention applies only to metropolitan territories of the signatories and not to their overseas and colonial territories (the USSR maintaining that it should apply to both).

Several states objected, asserting that the Soviet reservations concern the substance of the Convention and could not be accepted unless agreed upon by the signatories. (Also questioned was the right of states to object to a reservation before their own ratification of such a treaty, as well as the legal effect of an objection to a reservation.)

Consequently, at the Fifth Session of the General Assembly of the United Nations in the fall of 1950, the problem of permissibility of reservations to multilateral treaties, placed on the agenda by the Secretary-General, was discussed at length. At that time, Soviet representatives reiterated the view that a signatory to a multilateral treaty has an undeniable right to make such reservations to the treaty as it deems necessary, and that this right, which stems from the sovereignty of a state, can be limited only by the state itself.

The General Assembly, unable to cope with the several issues raised, asked the International Court of Justice for an advisory opinion on the matter. At the same time, the Assembly asked the International Law Commission of the United Nations to study the problem in general, without reference to the particular reservations to the Genocide Convention.

The International Court of Justice, in May, 1951, gave an advisory opinion confined specifically to the Genocide Convention. By seven votes to five, it stated that "if the reservation is compatible with the object and purpose of the Convention" and if at least some participants in the treaty have not objected to it, the state that made the reservation "can be regarded as being a party to the Convention."[19]

The International Law Commission, on the other hand, had questioned whether "the criterion of the compatibility of a reservation with the object

---

[19] *International Court of Justice Reports*, 1951 (Leyden: A. W. Sijthoff, annually), pp. 15, 29.

and purpose of a multilateral convention, applied by the International Court of Justice to the Convention on Genocide" can be applied to "multilateral conventions in general." In this way, the International Law Commission "had expressed itself in favour of the point of view defended by the Secretariat of the United Nations." The Commission recommended the inclusion in multilateral conventions of a rule on the permissibility or nonpermissibility of reservations and on consequences which might follow from this measure.[20]

Subsequently, Professor Durdenevskii suggested the universal adoption of this "expedient principle": A treaty should be considered "valid between the state that has made the reservation and all the other parties with the sole exception of that part to which the reservation pertains, unless the member opposing the reservation states directly that he is opposed to the employment of the entire convention [as] changed by the reservation in the relations between this member and the state that has made the reservation." This formulation, claimed Durdenevskii, would add flexibility and elasticity to the practice of treaty reservations: the reservation either would curtail the effect of the treaty for a state to a desired degree or would invalidate the treaty entirely between the state making the reservations and those states that protest it.[21]

According to a Soviet count, on January 1, 1959, the USSR was signatory to about two hundred multilateral treaties. On that date, the total number of Soviet reservations was more than sixty, attached to thirty-four multilateral treaties. With increased Soviet participation in multilateral treaties, the number of Soviet reservations has gone up.

In the final analysis, the practice of reservations to multilateral treaties is in the Soviet view "a product of the imperialist epoch," as anachronistic as imperialism. It is bound to pass "into oblivion" together with imperialism, as "there will be no place for it in the socialist international law of the future." But for the forseeable future it is an essential precondition for the growth of international law across ideological frontiers.

Legal Effect

Once an international treaty enters into force, it "authorizes and obligates" the contracting parties. On what grounds does the treaty obligation rest?

[20] *Report of the International Law Commission Covering Its Third Session* (New York: United Nations, 1949), pp. 2–8; F. Ivanov, "Chetvertaia sessiia Komissii mezhdunarodnogo prava," *Sovetskoe gosudarstvo i pravo*, No. 11 (1952), pp. 72–78. See also F. Ivanov and S. Volodin, "Piataia sessiia komissii mezhdunarodnogo prava," *Sovetskoe gosudarstvo i pravo*, No. 7 (1953), pp. 88–100.

[21] Durdenevskii, *op. cit.*, p. 100.

In bourgeois jurisprudence, on some "highly questionable premises," answered Pashukanis in 1925.

> In reality, the force of an international treaty lies in the existence of definite material interests and forces standing behind the interest. The treaty operates and is binding just so long as these interests and these forces exist. Never has any state signed nor will it sign an international treaty unless it has an interest in so doing and unless some force compels it to do so. On the one hand, no state undertakes obligations merely for the satisfaction of violating them forthwith. For this reason any international treaty, to the extent to which it reflects the vital interests of the parties and is dictated by these interests, and to the extent to which it reflects the political situation of the operative forces, represents a long-term formulation of specific relations. The conclusion of an international treaty, being merely the formulation of a correlation of forces that has actually come into being, in and of itself, introduces a new element, new qualities into the international environment which may be of fully realistic significance. For this reason both the overestimation of the importance of treaties in and of themselves and the denial that they play any role or have any real influence on the course of international relations are equally erroneous.[22]

This is the only explanation of the nature of obligation of international treaties that both is "acceptable" and "corresponds to reality." All states in their foreign policies "evaluate international treaties precisely in such fashion," Pashukanis concluded.

Despite the later purge and the official condemnation of Pashukanis, his theory survived in Soviet jurisprudence. Thirty years after Pashukanis had published his first exposition on the source of the binding force of international treaties, Lisovskii lamely repeated, in 1955, that the *pacta sunt servanda* principle rests "not at all on abstract principles but on the political and economic interests of states in the international arena. . . ."[23]

However, it has been universally admitted by Soviet doctrine that "without the recognition of the [*pacta sunt servanda*] principle, there can be no intercourse among nations. . . ." This principle, of course, applies solely to equal treaties, "concluded on the basis of [sovereign] equality of the contracting parties," not to "coercive, aggressive, and enslaving treaties": such treaties "contradict international law and consequently cannot enjoy its protection."[24]

---

[22] Pashukanis, *op. cit.*, p. 154.

[23] Lisovskii, *op. cit.*, p. 250.

[24] F. I. Kozhevnikov, ed., *Mezhdunarodnoe pravo* (Moscow: Gosiuridizdat, 1957), p. 243.

Treaties and Municipal Law

International treaties concluded by the Soviet Union are binding on the Soviet Union as a state in international law. Since they are already constitutional acts of the Soviet Union and have "normative significance," they become binding norms of Soviet municipal law merely by the publication of their texts. In other words, through promulgation within the Soviet Union "the boundary between [international treaties] and a [Soviet] municipal law becomes eradicated; the treaty, publicly announced, becomes a law, binding on the [Soviet] citizens. . . ." Except for actual promulgation, no special legislation is necessary. After an international treaty concluded by the Soviet Union has come into force, it is published; then, the treaty becomes Soviet domestic law, "mandatory for its citizens *as well as* its officials."[25]

It is entirely possible, of course, that an international treaty may contradict the municipal law of a contracting state. It may become necessary to enact specific legislation (e.g., to apportion funds from the state budget) in order that a treaty either may come into force or, if already in force, may be fulfilled. The Soviet Union stands for "meticulous" fulfillment of treaty obligations accepted by the contracting states, even if it means alteration of existing municipal law or enactment of new legislation.[26]

Interpretation

Soviet doctrine maintains that the following organs may interpret international treaties: (1) the contracting states (they may either agree on the interpretation by which they are then bound, or interpret the treaty separately, through their respective government organs, including their national courts. If another party, or parties, does not accept the interpretation, however, then only the party that intercepted the treaty is bound by that interpretation and carries full responsibility for the interpretation.); (2) the international Court of Justice, in consonance with Article 36 of the Statute of the Court (should the parties so agree, they may make the jurisdiction of the Court compulsory for all their disputes concerning interpretation of their treaty or treaties, or the parties may agree to accept the jurisdiction of the Court only in particular, concrete disputes, and thereby accept only optional jurisdiction of the Court.); (3) international organs, such as the Security Council and the General Assembly (with respect to the interpretation of the Charter) of the United Nations; (4) arbitration and courts of arbitration (these organs

---

[25] F. I. Kozhevnikov, "Nekotorye voprosy teorii i praktiki mezhdunarodnogo dogovora," *Sovetskoe gosudarstvo i pravo*, No. 2 (1954), p. 74.

[26] F. I. Kozhevnikov, "Sovetskoe gosudarstvo i mezhdunarodnye dogovory," in Korovin (ed.), *Mezhdunarodnoe pravo* (Moscow: Gosiurizdat, 1951), p. 95.

can be implemented when the contracting parties so agree either in the original treaty or later on when the need arises. The decision than is compulsory for the parties.); (5) conciliation commissions (these organs only can recommend how to solve a dispute rather than hand down decisions that are compulsory.); and (6) diplomatic missions of the parties concerned.

However, and this is all-important, only the contracting parties as a whole have the right to decide if any, or which one, of these organs may interpret their treaty or treaties.[27]

Soviet doctrine considers it imperative that interpretation of treaties be conducted, first, in strict consonance with "the basic principles of international law," namely, "principals of universal peace and security of nations," "state sovereignty," "equality and mutual advantage," *"pacta tertiis nec nocent nec prosunt,"* and *"pacta sunt servanda."* Second, treaties must be interpreted as bona fide agreements, concluded by the contracting parties with reference to both actual goals and conscientious fulfillment. Third, interpretation should take place without reference to the issue of the treaty as a source of law—whether the treaty itself is viewed as a treaty law or a treaty contract. All treaties are legal acts of sovereign states and as such express the wills of the contracting parties, irrespective of their possible broader or narrower meanings. Fourth, interpretation must pay attention to the latter *as well as to the meaning* of the treaty, with particular reference to the respective contracting parties. Fifth, interpretation must add effectiveness to the treaty and must make the treaty more—rather than less—effective. Sixth, a prohibitive rule of interpretation has precedence over an imperative one, and an imperative one has precedence over a permissive rule. Seventh, preference should be given to special over general provisions. Eighth, if possible, treaties should be interpreted *contra proferentem*, i.e., against that party which initiated the particular provision or provisions. And lastly, all doubts should be interpreted in favor of, rather than against, the obligated party. Of all these principles of interpretation, however, the most important is said to be the first one: "International treaties must be interpreted in strict consonance with the basic principles of international law."[28]

Termination

In addition to mutual agreement of the parties, international treaties may be lawfully terminated by (1) fulfillment of the treaty provisions, (2) termination of the time period stipulated in the treaty, (3) objective impossibility

[27] V. M. Shurshalov, *Osnovaniia deistvitel'nosti mezhdunarodnykh dogovorov* (Moscow: Akad. Nauk SSSR, 1957), pp. 459–461.

[28] *Ibid.*, pp. 383–402.

of realization of the treaty objectives ("for example, [realization] of a treaty of alliance, should war between the allies break out"), (4) "the consummation" of a treaty, (5) unilateral repudiation pursuant to the terms of the treaty, (6) extinction of one of the states "as a subject of international law," (7) extinction of the object of the treaty ("if the treaty was concluded in relation to some object—such as, for example, an island and its neutralization—and the object has vanished, the treaty ceases to be effective"), and (8) should "further fulfillment of the treaty contradict basic principles of international law."

In other words, Soviet doctrine accepts the methods for legitimate termination of international treaties normally propounded in international law.

If an international treaty is in contradiction with "the generally recognized norms of international law . . . [it] is not valid," the modern Soviet position holds. And as the "primary" norms of international law in the Soviet view are international treaties, the priority of conflicting treaty obligations is thereby resolved; a later treaty is null and void if it is in conflict with a prior treaty between one of the parties and a third state. The "time element" mentioned above in connection with the conflict of international treaties with municipal law and favoring the latter act, international or national, has not been applied here.

The signing of a treaty which the Soviet government views as being in conflict either with an existing Soviet treaty or with the UN Charter is "an illegal act which cannot have any legal consequences in favor of the lawbreaker," i.e., the non-Soviet power. Soviet doctrine of international law here claims the right to judge the validity and legality of international treaties from the standpoint of Soviet interest ("the Soviet aspiration to establish peace throughout the world") and to condemn as "invalid" those treaties which the Soviet foreign policymakers characterize as "illegal acts."[29]

Revision and Denunciation

The Soviet government has always been in favor of "progressive" revision of international treaties—treaties "that do not correspond to new requirements of international life from the point of view of interests of international peace, law, and justice." At the same time, it has been against "reactionary" revision of treaties—against "the tendencies of bourgeois diplomacy to utilize revision of treaties to the detriment of the vital interests of small and weak nations." And it has insisted on explicit "consent of all the signatories"

---

[29] Lisovskii, *op. cit.,* p. 244; I. S. Pereterskii, "Znachenie mezhdunarodnogo dogovóra dlia tret'ego (ne zakliuchivshego etot dogovor) gosudarstva," *Sovetskoe gosudarstvo i pravo,* No. 4 (1957), pp. 75, 79, 80.

to any treaty amendment; by this *sine qua non* condition it has meant consent of the RSFSR, and later the USSR, to revision of any treaty signed by *any* prerevolutionary Russian government.[30]

Although the Soviet constitutional practice of formal denunciation of international treaties has not been entirely consistent in the past, there has been a clear accord on the nature of the process among Soviet diplomats and writers ever since the early twenties: Denunciation of an international treaty means the unilateral termination of the treaty based on previous agreement between the contracting parties. Usually, though not necessarily, this agreement is expressed in the treaty itself, together with the manner in which and the time limit within which the denunciation may take place. Denunciation of international treaties is thus considered "a legally correct method of terminating treaties," and as such it has been copiously used by the Soviet government.

Effects of Violation or Changed Conditions

Soviet foreign policy, in practice as well as in theory, has never deviated from the rule that it is lawful for a contracting party unilaterally to terminate an international treaty if it regards the other contracting party or parties as having violated the treaty.

As Pashukanis put it in 1925 (and as many others have confirmed since), the failure to observe a treaty by one party gives the other party "the right to repudiate the treaty." Such a step by the wronged treaty partner has been considered a lesser evil than an attempt to compel the observance of the treaty by self-help, that is, war, and "must therefore be preferred."[31]

In his 1957 study, Shurshalov completed the considerable but labored developmental circle of the Soviet changed-conditions concept. First, he quoted Western and Soviet authorities. Second, as is customary, he enumerated past cases of claims of changed conditions. Finally, he concluded (1) that the changed-conditions clause (*rebus sic stantibus*) was a fundamental part of the law of treaties because it was, after all, "included in a number of important international treaties," but (2) that it could not be recognized as a general norm of international law "because all attempts to endow the clause with general applicability have remained up to now without success"; on the other hand, (3) that the clause is essential for economic and political progress in the world, which it supports against unconditional demands for the *status quo* frequently made on behalf of the *pacta sunt*

---

[30] F. I. Kozhevnikov, ed., *Mezhdunarodnoe pravo*, p. 274.

[31] Pashukanis, *op. cit.*, col. 982; Kozhevnikov, "Sovetskoe gosudarstvo i mezhdunarodnye dogovory," p. 109; Lisovskii, *op. cit.*, p. 257; Shurshalov, *op. cit.*, p. 215.

servanda principle, "as a cover-up for preservation of imperialist dominations in colonies." Therefore, although the *pacta sunt servanda* concept must be viewed as a general rule, the changed-conditions clause must be recognized as a particular exception to that rule, dictated by life and progress. The two, he decided, are compatible and could exist side by side. No unilateral repudiation on the basis of the changed-conditions clause should take place, Shurshalov echoed Lisovskii. However, unilateral repudiation, *if no agreement was possible*, was permitted by existing international practice.[32]

The strained development of the changed-conditions doctrine in the Soviet Union reflects the obvious difficulty Soviet theorists have faced throughout the existence of the Soviet state of keeping up with the changing needs and demands of the Soviet government. Since 1917, Soviet foreign policy has oscillated widely between the rule that treaties must be kept under all conditions and the particular exception to this rule when "life itself" so demands. Soviet doctrine has defended this oscillation and, like the Soviet government, has applied it especially to changes in government if brought about by "social revolution," the extinction of states (e.g., Poland in 1939), the progress of dependent and colonial nations, and treaties that, although "equal" at the time of conclusion, later contradict "the basic norms and principles" of international law and must therefore be abrogated. The clause of changed conditions has not been applied, on the other hand, to territorial changes per se or to the establishment of new states in the world (with the exception of states created by "social [or colonial] revolution").

Of the two contending claims—that the clause is a phenomenon of either law or fact—the latter has won in Soviet doctrine. Indeed, in his conclusion, Shurshalov is not far from modern Western writers on the subject: they agree that treaty law has to steer a course between the Scylla of impairing the obligations of good faith and the Charybdis of enforcing obsolete and oppressive treaties.

Effect of War on Treaties

Soviet policy with respect to the effect of war on treaties has moved from one polar position to another. After World War I, the Soviet government approved the Versailles Peace Treaties provisions stipulating that the Great War abrogated all bilateral treaties and suspended the operation of multilateral treaties; it disapproved of the victors' claims to the right to reinstate those bilateral treaties that it wished to revise. And in no case before World

---

[32] *Ibid.,* p. 128. See also Shurshalov, *Osnovnye voprosy teorii mezhdunarodnogo dogovora* (Moscow: Akad. Nauk SSSR, 1959).

War II did the Soviet government ask its treaty partners to reinstate any bilateral prewar treaties.

After World War II, however, when some of the delegations at the Paris Peace Conference agreed that the new peace treaties should follow, with respect to the provisions on the effect of war on prewar treaties, the example of the post-World War I Peace Treaties, the Soviet delegation opposed such suggestions. Conditions had changed, and the Soviet Union had acquired vested interest in preserving prewar treaties.

The present Soviet answer to the question of what is the effect of war on treaties runs as follows: As far as bilateral treaties are concerned, war abrogates some, suspends the operation of some, and makes some operative. The criterion for decision usually is, or should be, stipulated in the treaties. If it is not, "firmly established custom" is of great assistance. In all other cases, former belligerents should have an opportunity to reinstate or revise as many former treaties as they consider useful. With respect to multilateral treaties, they are suspended only in relation to the belligerents and merely to the extent to which the war prevents their full operation.[33]

Soviet treaty law, on the whole, is not widely different from Western treaty law. They both shared one cradle, and this common origin shows. In those several instances where Soviet treaty law does differ from the Western concept, however, the difference is politically oriented. This is especially observable in problems concerning unilateral termination of treaties.

In addition, the Soviet law of treaties is characterized by growing sophistication, by increasingly careful attention to detail, and by general meticulousness. In comparison with primitive beginnings in the early 1920's, the development since then has been remarkable.

Soviet treaty practice has almost without exception determined the general line of theory; the task was left to the theorists to comply. Under the limitations imposed, they did rather well.

At the same time, Soviet literature on international treaties has not been characterized by complete conformity. Disagreements among the Soviet authorities have appeared from time to time on many important issues.

SECRET TREATIES

By virtue of the Decree on Peace, issued immediately after the Bolshevik seizure of power and allegedly written personally by Lenin himself, the

---

[33] See A. N. Talalaev, "Prekrashchenie mezhdunarodnykh dogovorov v istorii i praktike Sovetskogo gosudarstva." *Sovetskii ezhegodnik mezhdunarodnogo prava, 1959* (Moscow: Izdat. "Nauka." 1960), pp. 144–155.

Soviet government claimed to be "the first in the world not only to declare its renunciation of the methods of secret diplomacy but also to practice this principle, literally from the first day of its existence." The Soviet government ostentatiously published over one hundred secret treaties as "acts of pilferage," "including the Secret Agreement on the Division of Asiatic Turkey between Russia, Great Britain, and France of September 1, 1916"; this Soviet action was "a considerable contribution to the cause of propaganda 'by deeds and not by words,' " said Lenin.[34]

During the Brest-Litovsk peace negotiations the Soviet representatives demanded the "right to publish their protocols" and to "transfer the negotiations to Stockholm." At later international conferences, from Genoa in 1922 to Paris in 1946, Soviet representatives have vociferously urged the abolition of secret diplomacy. Soviet theorists, citing this public record, have maintained that it was the Soviet government that "formulated and carried out this new principle in international relations," which has "developed into a new principle of contemporary international law."

But are secret treaties another "capitalist evil" from which the Soviet government has clearly and distinctly dissociated itself? No, answered Professor Kozhevnikov in 1947: "Under certain circumstances," the conclusion of secret treaties by the Soviet government "is not in contradiction with the general principles of Soviet foreign policy." As a matter of fact, "the simple conclusion of agreements that are not published" is a practice the Soviet government accepts and endorses in general, and especially "if future publication is presumed," once the reasons for secrecy have been eliminated. This was the case of the Yalta Agreement of February 11, 1945, with respect to questions concerning the Far East, as well as of other treaties concluded during the "Patriotic War" and dealing with such questions as the time and place for opening the Second Front, military supplies, and the Soviet entry into the war against Japan.[35]

Some secret treaties, then, are not viewed as incompatible with the

---

[34] Lenin, *Sochineniia,* 2nd ed. (Moscow-Leningrad: Gosizdat, 1926–1932), XXII, 102, as quoted by Kozhevnikov, "Sovetskoe gosudarstvo i mezhdunardonye dogovory," p. 90.

In a speech delivered at the First All-Russian Congress of the Navy on December 5, 1917, Lenin stated: "We have published secret treaties and we shall continue to publish them. No malice and no slander against us shall dissuade us from this policy. The lords and masters of the bourgeoisie are enraged over the fact that the people see the reasons why they were driven to the slaughter. We say that we must work hand in hand with the revolutionary class of the toilers of all countries. The Soviet government adopted this policy in publishing secret treaties to show that the rulers of all countries were scoundrels. This is propaganda not in word but in deed." Lenin, *Sochineniia,* 4th ed. (Moscow: Gospolitizdat, 1940–1960), XXVI, 310–311, also quoted by Kozhevnikov, *loc. cit.*

[35] *Ibid.*

principles of Soviet foreign policy; what is considered incompatible with these principles is secret diplomacy. Lenin, Kozhevnikov maintains, was never against all secret treaties—he was simply against secret diplomacy.

Soviet treaty doctrine attempts to differentiate secret diplomacy and "negative" secret treaties, which are both "bad," from state secrets and "positive" secret treaties, which are both "good" and therefore practiced by the Soviet government. "One-sided, unequal, coercive, and criminal" treaties that the Bolshevik government annulled and published must allegedly be distinguished from positive secret agreements that are not subject to publication until a certain future time (i.e., their content must be concealed from "inimically minded states").

This differentiation raises problems of logic, which are not clarified by the theorists or by Soviet practice. For example, was the Secret Protocol, supplementing the Soviet-Nazi Nonaggression Pact of August, 1939, a positive secret treaty, arrived at by open diplomacy? And how about the other secret agreements that the Soviet government concluded with Nazi Germany between August, 1939 and June, 1941 and that have never been published in the Soviet Union?

Soviet Russia is known to have been a party to many secret treaties and agreements, especially in the 1920's, just before World War II and in the middle 1940's.

Between 1921 and 1933, a number of secret Soviet-German military agreements concerning matters expressly prohibited by the Versailles Peace Treaties were concluded between the two governments, their agents, and various cover organizations. They provided for the establishment of German airplane factories in Soviet Russia; joint-stock companies (such as Bersol, which was to manufacture lewisite poison gas) in Soviet Russia; joint military bases, and in particular, joint tank-training centers in Soviet Russia; German aid and assistance to Soviet munition factories and plants; the delivery of Soviet munitions to Germany; the training of Soviet pilots, technicians, and officers by German pilots, technical experts, and instructors; exchanges of visits between staff officers of the Red Army and the Reichswehr; and so on.

With the advent of Hitler, the secret collaboration between Germany and the USSR came to a sudden standstill in 1933—to be resumed again in 1939. The Soviet-German Secret Protocol Concerning Spheres of Influence in Eastern Europe (the Baltic States, Finland, Poland, and Bessarabia) of August 23, 1939 inaugurated a series of Soviet-German secret agreements concluded between 1939 and 1941.

On October 9, 1944, Stalin and Churchill, meeting in the Kremlin, reached an oral, informal secret agreement on spheres of influence in the Balkans, with the United States government reserving its position. According to the secret agreement, as reported by Churchill, the USSR was to enjoy a 90 per cent predominance in Rumania, a 75 per cent predominance in Bulgaria, and a 50-50 share with the United Kingdom and "others" in Yugoslavia and Hungary; the United Kingdom, for its part, was allocated a 90 per cent of predominance in Greece.[36]

At Yalta, Stalin concluded on February 11, 1945 with Churchill and Roosevelt a secret Agreement Concerning Soviet Entry into the War Against Japan. His price included maintenance of the *status quo* in Outer Mongolia and the Soviet acquisition of Southern Sakhalin, Diaren, Port Arthur, the Manchurian Railway, and the Kuril Islands.

Since 1945, no new Soviet secret treaties have been verified, although several have been reported or surmised on good authority.[37] In view of the earlier Soviet *practice* in this matter, however, and the defense and rationalization provided for it by the authorities on Soviet treaty *doctrine*, it would be surprising indeed if Soviet policymakers had refrained from concluding new secret treaties since 1945. That they have engaged in secret diplomacy is a matter of public record.

TREATY VIOLATIONS

To many Western observers, the most important issue about the Soviet government's contractual obligations has been its apparent readiness to violate its own international commitments when it has considered its interests to be furthered by such action. Soviet spokesmen, on the other hand, paint an entirely different picture. They deny categorically the existence of any treaty violations on the part of the USSR and, instead, lay grave charges of treaty violations at the door of the principal Western powers.

Soviet leaders maintain that a government established as the result of a profound social, economic, and political revolution is not bound by the international agreements concluded by its predecessors and that the

[36] W. S. Churchill, *The Second World War* (Boston: Houghton Mifflin Company, 1953), VI, 72–81, 226–235.

[37] Those reported include the following: three protocols with Hungary of December 9, 1947 (Slusser and Triska, *op. cit.,* p. 240) and A Secret Protocol of January 24, 1949, concerning establishment of the Council of Mutual Economic Assistance (*ibid.,* p. 256).

A secret Soviet-Czechoslovak military agreement has been inferred from evidence pointing to Soviet military aid to the Czechoslovak army in May, 1950 (*ibid.,* p. 429). Other secret military agreements with the party-states can be regarded as highly probable, especially in the case of Soviet military aid to North Korean Armed Forces before the attack on the Republic of Korea on June 25, 1950. A similar secret military agreement may well have been at the base of Soviet aid to the East German Armed Forces.

annulment of such agreements by such a government is a legitimate act.

At the Genoa Conference in 1922, for example, Chicherin defended Soviet repudiation of the Tsarist government's debts to foreign creditors by citing historical precedent in support of "that principle of law according to which resolutions which are a violent rupture with the past carry with them new juridical relations in the foreign and domestic affairs of states." Chicherin continued: "Governments and systems that spring from revolution are not bound to respect the obligations of fallen governments." This view was employed by Soviet theorists in 1957 to justify repudiation by the communist government of China of treaty obligations entered into by the Chinese government before 1949.

More recently, however, Soviet spokesmen have maintained that the Soviet Union has observed all the international treaties concluded by pre-Soviet governments, provided that they did not contradict "the basic principles of Soviet foreign policy."[36]

The extinction of a state or government with which the Soviet government has signed a treaty constitutes grounds for annulment of the treaty by the Soviet government and its consequent release from all the ensuing obligations under the treaty. On the basis of this principle, on September 17, 1939, the Soviet government issued a statement claiming that "The Polish state and its government have virtually ceased to exist" and that therefore "Treaties concluded between the USSR and Poland have ceased to operate." With this note, the Soviet Union cleared from its path the contractual network that it had established with Poland, from the Peace Treaty signed at Riga on March 18, 1921 to the Nonaggression Treaty of July 25, 1932, reaffirmed as recently as November 26, 1938.

On this basis the Red Army proceeded to occupy those parts of Poland assigned to Russia under the Soviet-Nazi Agreement of August, 1939, and Soviet civilian administrators and the Secret Police carried through the incorporation of the newly acquired territories into the Soviet Union.

The Soviet government recognized the Polish government-in-exile in a treaty signed on July 30, 1941. In the treaty, the Soviet government stated that its agreements with Germany in 1939 concerning the partition of Poland were no longer valid; nevertheless, it insisted throughout the war on retaining the areas it had seized in 1939. A clash over this issue formed one of the major causes underlying the rupture of diplomatic relations between the Soviet government and the Polish government-in-exile in April, 1943.

[38] Pereterskii, *op. cit.*, p. 75.

Allegations of the violation of a treaty by a partner of the Soviet government has been used as a basis for Soviet denunciation of the treaty. This malleable principle was foreshadowed in September, 1918 when the Soviet government declared that Turkey, by seizing the city of Baku and by other "persistent violations" of the Soviet-Turkish treaty concluded at Brest-Litovsk on March 3, 1918, had shown that the treaty was "no longer in force."

A more significant use of the principle was the charge made by the Soviet government on November 28, 1939 that Finland had "systematically violated" its obligations under the Soviet-Finnish Nonaggression Treaty of January 21, 1932, that its actions showed that it had "no intention of complying with the provisions" of the treaty, and that the Soviet government accordingly regarded itself as "released from the obligations ensuing from" the treaty. Subsequently, the Soviet Union launched an attack on Finland, set up a puppet Finnish government on Soviet territory, and recognized this body as the legitimate government of Finland. Only stubborn Finnish resistance forced the Soviet government to modify its stand.

The procedure followed by the Soviet government in June, 1940 with regard to its nonaggression or mutual-assistance treaties with the Baltic States was more elaborate. Soviet charges of "gross violations" of the treaties by Lithuania, Latvia, and Estonia were duly made, but instead of using the charges as a basis for denouncing the treaties, the Soviet government demanded the formation in the three states of governments "able and willing to ensure" that the treaties would be "honestly put into operation" and that enemies of the treaties would be "vigorously restrained." Governments acceptable to the Soviet Union were promptly set up, and, under the close supervision of Soviet civilian and military representatives, these bodies proceeded at once to put into motion the legal and administrative machinery needed to convert their states into constituent republics of the Soviet Union.

In September, 1949, evidence was presented at the trial of the Hungarian communist leader Laszlo Rajk and a number of other defendants that purported to show that Yugoslavia had violated the Soviet-Yugoslav Treaty of Friendship, Mutual Assistance, and Post-war Collaboration of April 11, 1945. Soviet denunciation of the treaty, citing the evidence of the Rajk trial, followed on September 28, 1949.

The decision by the Soviet leaders after Stalin's death to heal the breach between Russia and Yugoslavia forced them to admit the falsity of the evidence on which denunciation of the 1945 treaty had been based, notwithstanding the damage this admission did to the arguments by which the Soviet government justified the denunciation. In March, 1956, Mátyás

Rákosi, First Secretary of the Hungarian Communist Party, announced the full rehabilitation of Rajk and his codefendants in the 1949 trial, following review of the trial by a special commission of the Hungarian Ministry of Justice in 1955 and the suicide of the judge who had presided over it.

On May 7, 1955, the same argument, violation of a treaty by the Soviet Union's treaty partners, was used as a ground for Soviet denunciation of its wartime treaties of alliance—those with Great Britain, of May 26, 1942, and with France, of December 10, 1944. Both treaties had been scheduled to run for twenty years. The Soviet government alleged violation of the treaties by the two powers through their signature in 1954 of agreements calling for re-establishment of German Armed Forces.

One of the more persistent subjects of dispute between the Soviet government and its treaty partners has been the charge that the Soviet government violated treaty pledges to refrain from revolutionary propaganda or subversive activity directed against its treaty partners. The standard Soviet reply to charges of treaty violation of this kind has been that a clear and valid distinction can be drawn between the actions of responsible officials of the Soviet government and actions of the same individuals in their capacity as leaders of the world communist movement.

It is clear that Soviet Russia has not thus violated or circumvented *all* its international treaties and agreements. As Pashukanis put it, "No state undertakes obligations merely for the satisfaction of immediately violating them." As might be expected, Soviet violations have affected primarily treaties on political subjects—treaties of alliance, peace treaties, and treaties of mutual assistance, regional security, nonaggression, and neutrality. In regard to economic, technical, and functional treaties, Soviet violations have been *infrequent*, and when they have occurred, political rather than economic considerations have determined the Soviet action.

QUANTITATIVE ANALYSIS OF TREATIES

It is true that an analysis based on quantitative or "hard" data does not necessarily possess greater evidential weight than an analysis based on qualitative or "soft" data. This depends upon the problem under investigation. A rigorous content analysis of Plato's writings, for example, may tell us little about Plato's philosophy, though it may yield less exalted information not obtainable otherwise. On the other hand, there are legitimate questions which can be answered through quantitative inquiry. For example, the question whether relations among states depend upon and are conditioned by the volume, scope, frequency, type, and speed of the interstate transactions can be answered quantitatively by an analysis of the transactional data correlated with other scaling of relationships between states.

In the five-year period between January 1, 1958 and December 31, 1962—the most stable domestic time span since Stalin—the USSR allegedly concluded 1,058 international agreements, 965 of them bilateral.[39] Compared with the 2,586 such agreements claimed in the first forty-one-year period of the regime's existence or the 702 agreements in the immediately preceding five-year period (1953–1957), this record emphasizes the simple fact that the Soviet Union has been substantially extending this aspect of its foreign relations. The greatest relative jump did come in the five years following Stalin's death, when the annual average number of agreements concluded tripled. Since 1962, the quantitative increase has continued, though at a less rapid rate of acceleration.

It is also notable that the greatest increase has been among bilateral agreements. The long-standing Soviet preference for this type of contractual relationship, rather than the less manipulable multilateral agreement, persists. In 1958–1962, the ratio of bilateral to multilateral treaties was over 10 to 1.

In this five-year period, the USSR entered into bilateral contractual engagements with sixty-two states. However, it concluded 922 or about 89 per cent of its agreements with only thirty-six of these states. Of these, 43.7 per cent were with the other thirteen Communist party-states (two-thirds of these involved East Europe), 27.6 per cent with the developing countries, 7.1 per cent with the leading Western states, and 5.1 per cent with Finland, Austria, and Japan.

Prior to 1958, the fifteen leading Soviet treaty partners had been (1) Finland, (2) Poland, (3) Germany (and West Germany), (4) Rumania, (5) Communist China, (6) and (7) Czechoslovakia and Bulgaria, (8) Hungary, (9) Yugoslavia, (10) East Germany, (11) France, (12) the United Kingdom, (13) Italy, (14) Norway, and (15) Albania. They were thus primarily geographically close neighbors of the Soviet Union, and secondarily the leading West European countries. The reshuffling which took place in the 1958–1962 period (see Table XI-1) manifested a clear change of salience.

[39] R. M. Slusser and G. Ginsburgs, "A Calendar of Soviet Treaties, January-December 1958," *Ost Europa Recht,* VII (1961), 100–131; "A Calendar of Soviet Treaties, January-December 1959," *Ost Europa Recht,* VIII (1962), pp. 137–164; G. Ginsburgs, "A Calendar of Soviet Treaties, January-December, 1960," *Ost Europa Recht,* IX (1963), pp. 120–159; "A Calendar of Soviet Treaties, January-December, 1961," *Ost Europa Recht,* X (1964), pp. 116–148; and "A Calendar of Soviet Treaties, January-December 1962," *Ost Europa Recht,* XI (1965), pp. 129–160.

Table XI-1   Soviet Bilateral Contracting Parties 1958–1962

RANK	CONTRACTING PARTY	TREATIES AND AGREEMENTS
1	Poland	61
2	Bulgaria	44
3	Hungary	39
4	Outer Mongolia	37
5–6	Czechoslovakia, Cuba	35
7	East Germany	34
8–9	Rumania, India	33
10	North Vietnam	32
11	North Korea	31
12–13	China, Afghanistan	30
14	Indonesia	28
15	Finland	27
16	Yugoslavia	25
17	Egypt	24
18	Ghana	21
19	Guinea	20
20	Albania	19
21	U.S.	18
22	U.K.	17
23	France	16
24	Iraq	15
25–28	West Germany, Cambodia, Austria, Ceylon	13
29–30	Italy, Japan	12
31	Norway	11
32–34	Iran, Ethiopia, Morocco	10
35	Tunisia	9
36–39	Nepal, Sudan, Brazil, Somalia	8
40	Iceland	7
41–42	Senegal, Laos	5
43	Mali	4
44–46	Turkey, Greece, Syria	3
47–50	Burundi, Burma, Cameroun, Uganda	2
51–62	Sweden, Algeria, Nigeria, Dahomey, Rwanda, Jamaica, Trinidad and Tobago, Denmark, Yemen, Canada, Samoa	1

The new matrix clearly favored the Communist party-states and the developing nations. The emphasis on treaty ties with geographical neighbors remained strong, but the ideological factor loomed stronger (see Cuba). And the Western capitalist nations collectively fell behind the third world.

We have categorized the Soviet treaties concluded over the 1958–1962 period by content as follows: trade and commerce (254 agreements); technical-economic aid in areas of industry and industrial production (150 agreements); diplomatic affairs—recognition of states and governments, exchanges of ambassadors, establishment of relations, diplomatic visits, consular conventions, and so on (133 agreements); cultural issues, including cultural and educational exchanges and assistance and collaboration in science (131); scientific questions and technical aid in scientific and cultural problems (107); economic aid, payments agreements, economic collaboration, and credit agreements (103); matters dealing with international waters, navigation, and fishing (35); matters of transportation, customs, travel, citizenship, and border demarcation (41); matters concerning peaceful uses of atomic energy and disarmament (20); issues of communication (21); technical-economic aid in areas of agricultural and/or geological development (21); health problems, social security plans, and aid in building hospitals (13); settlements of international claims (12); and military aid or other military issues (10).

The fourteen categories include both bilateral and multilateral engagements; of the latter, the highest number concerns matters dealing with diplomatic and consular affairs (17) and international waters, navigation, and fishing (16); economic aid and payments agreements (11); matters of transportation, customs, and travel (13); and trade and commerce (6).

Comparing the above classification with pre-1958 Soviet performance, we find that Soviet economic agreements showed a sharp rise; Soviet political agreements dived into decline (in fact "solemn" political treaties disappeared altogether); and Soviet functional agreements, shifted into new categories, gained mildly in number.

The Soviet propensity is to proliferate bilateral contractual engagements, chiefly in the economic and functional spheres, with states which politically, economically, and/or functionally are already relatively close to the USSR. What does this imply in terms of more enduring tendencies, conditions, and developments of Soviet treaty law and policy?

With respect to the Soviet treaty law, it tends to diminish dissimilarity to Western treaty law. The political-ideological orientation of Soviet treaty law noted above refers primarily to problems concerning unilateral termination of treaties, a problem disappearing with the decline of strictly political Soviet treaties. With the new Soviet tendency to pursue political and economic advantage chiefly via economic and functional utility, the trend has been from the ideological to the pragmatic and from the hegemonial to the consensual.

With respect to Soviet treaty policy, the de-emphasis of political treaties confirms that the USSR is more attracted by incremental improvements of her *status quo* than by dramatic or reckless challenges of it.

Finally, the trends of recent development in Soviet treaty practice pose a new problem for the USSR in the context of conflict among the Communist party-states. Soviet freedom of action has been somewhat circumscribed by the profusion of treaties interrelating the party-states. Rather than indignant imperialists, it is now Communist China which predominantly accuses the USSR of treaty violations, and on a large scale at that. According to an editorial in *Hung Chi*, the ideological journal of the Chinese Communist Party's Central Committee, and reprinted by *Jen Min Jih Pao*, the Chinese Communist Party daily on February 4, 1964:

> The leaders of the C.P.S.U. [Communist Party of the Soviet Union] have violated the Chinese Soviet treaty of friendship, alliance and mutual assistance, made a unilateral decision to withdraw 1,390 Soviet experts working in China, to tear up 343 contracts and supplementary contracts on the employment of experts, and to cancel 257 projects of scientific and technical cooperation, and pursued a restrictive and discriminatory trade policy against China.

CONCLUSION

We would suggest that the main reason for attempting to reach agreements with Soviet Russia and the states of the communist system is that these agreements, if wisely drawn and adequately safeguarded, *can* serve to advance mutual interests of mankind. No national leaders should abandon the vision of a world community of states joined voluntarily together under a rule of law and existing peacefully together in mutually beneficial collaboration. That cannot be achieved without the active participation of the Soviet Union.

As a means toward this goal, treaties concluded with the Soviet Union and the states of the communist system can serve a definite, but limited, function. They cannot by themselves create mutual trust and cooperation, but they can help to create conditions in which trust and cooperation can grow. They can reduce some causes of tension and distrust, and they can reinforce the substance of international collaboration. Perhaps, most important, they can serve to bring Soviet citizens into direct contact with non-Soviet ideas and values and, in this way, contribute to the evolution of Soviet policy toward a greater willingness to compromise and collaborate with other nations.

If the proposition is accepted that there are valid arguments in favor of concluding agreements with the Soviet Union, one may ask what types of agreements appear most likely to be useful.

Certain types of *economic* agreements with the Soviet Union may be regarded as reasonably safe bets. Trade agreements for limited periods of time, for specific commodities and with carefully worked out time schedules, specifications for quantity and quality of goods, and provisions for delivery have enjoyed a relatively high standard of performance on the part of the Soviet Union.

Agreements on *cultural exchange* appear reasonably likely to yield satisfactory results to both sides and to be observed within admittedly elastic but nevertheless realistic limits. The reason is simple: in an agreement of this kind the potential gains are greater than the risks involved. The Soviet leaders try, through the use of cultural agreements, to demonstrate the alleged advantages of the Soviet system and, thus, to strengthen its position in the forum of world public opinion.

The partner to a cultural agreement with the Soviet Union can legitimately hope for results just as valuable. It is in the interests of the other nations to supply as many Soviet citizens as possible with accurate information about their policies. Cultural agreements with the Soviet Union thus offer a definite opportunity to make direct contact with the mass of the inhabitants of the Soviet state. More effectively than any other medium, the cultural, scientific, and industrial exhibitions and performances which have been presented in the Soviet Union by states that have concluded cultural agreements with Russia have served to bring to Soviet citizens fresh concepts and a realization of the diversity and vitality of noncommunist countries.

In the period since Stalin's death in 1953 the Soviet Union has displayed an unusual degree of activity in adhering to international *functional* agreements. To take only one example, since 1953, the Soviet Union has ratified more than twenty conventions of the International Labor Organization, a body that Soviet spokesmen long denounced as a capitalist tool for the suppression of revolutionary spirit among the workers.

In our view, the adherence of the Soviet Union to agreements of this type is a development to be welcomed and encouraged. Adherence to them inevitably helps to bring the Soviet state, Soviet society, and Soviet citizens into the general stream of the political and economic life of mankind, and whatever does that, in our opinion, must be regarded as being of positive value.

During the two decades that preceded the outbreak of World War II, the statesmen of the Western powers attempted to establish a world order from which Soviet Russia was either totally or partially excluded. It can reasonably be argued that the rise of the fascist aggressor states was a direct consequence of this attempt and of a fracturing of the spiritual and political unity of mankind which it manifested. International functional agreements may be a small factor in the progress of global society toward peaceful unity, but they are not a negligible one; nor is Soviet adherence to them a factor of negligible significance.

The most difficult problem is that of negotiating major *political* treaties between noncommunist nations and the Soviet Union. Is it worthwhile concluding agreements of this kind, knowing that they may be subject to violation or evasion?

It is the hegemonial aspects of the Soviet system which have been responsible for the high degree of political antagonism that has characterized Soviet foreign policy. They have appeared to be impossible to eliminate and difficult to reduce. Attempting to do so on the plane of international agreements has seemed to mean persisting in dealing with the effects rather than the causes of the problem. Relaxation of political tensions ought to be preliminary, many feel, to political agreements, which formally and authoritatively proclaim such relaxation in concrete, applied terms.

Of the three alternatives—withdrawal from contact, compromise, and integration of interests—the first is unrealistic and the third is as yet unattainable. Compromise, the modification of the extreme alternatives, and renunciation or reduction of demands implies a degree of equality of interest in the bargain. This is the way the majority of Soviet treaties have actually worked: on the basis of a compromise that reduced the incompatibility of the points at issue, the area of agreement and satisfaction that allowed common interests (however minimal) to emerge helped to discover additional subordinate reasons for cooperation formerly not recognized, shifted somewhat the value-ordering, and supplied new, not entirely unsatisfactory, conditions. In other words, a treaty based on compromise made the new situation somewhat preferable to the past nontreaty situation.

We submit, therefore, that *political* treaties may serve as a potential means of specific compromise, leading to the general compromise that may contribute to a slow but steady step-by-step reduction of political antagonism. Political treaties, properly framed and provided with adequate safeguards, should in our opinion be viewed as one among several tools available for reducing tension in the world and thereby strengthening the prospects for peace.

CONCLUSION

Following our short historical overview of Soviet foreign policy in Chapter I, we devoted several chapters to the Soviet decision-making process and followed that by attention to patterns of Soviet international behavior by geographical area. Finally, we have examined Soviet behavior in international organization and the Soviet approach to the building of international order through treaty law. It is now time to draw together the findings of the separate chapters and to relate them a little more systematically than we have done so far.

Let us begin with the relations of the four complex variables—institutional structure, personalities, "objective" events, and Marxist-Leninist doctrine—upon which we focused in our effort to understand the process of Soviet foreign-policy decision-making.

Our examination of *institutional structure* yielded several major conclusions, in addition to a description of the legal and theoretical organization for foreign-policy decisions. There are *two parallel hierarchies of institutions*, one Party and one government, whose participation in foreign-policy decision-making are complementary. The two hierarchies are fused at the peak of authority, the Politburo of the Party Central Committee, and more specifically in the *leadership* of the Politburo. Although each hierarchy has a clearly defined line of authority, the relationship between the two hierarchies is such that at every level Party organs exercise control and guidance over the corresponding government organs.

In decisions respecting *Soviet relations with capitalist countries*, horizontal control by the Party is exercised chiefly through veto over personnel appointments, general oversight of government performance, and personal influence over the behavior of Party cadres holding government roles. The expertise of the government agencies is rarely challenged, and there is little or no overlap of function. The Foreign Ministry, for example, was established specifically to meet the need for implementing relations with capitalist governments

—a function that the Party remains institutionally unequipped to perform.

Relations between the *CPSU and communist and workers' parties in the capitalist countries* are the province of the International Department of the Party Central Apparatus. In decisions respecting Soviet relations with the party-states, there is, additionally, an overlap in function between Party and government. Circumstantial indicators affirm predominance here of Party roles (e.g., Party career men rather than professional diplomats as ambassadors to party-states).

In decisions respecting *Soviet relations with the newly independent and industrializing countries*, dual management of Soviet policy is evident in the simultaneous activity of the International Department in direct relations with the nonruling Parties and the activity of government agencies in direct relations with the respective governments. In cases of conflict the Party institutions probably take precedence.

The *lower echelons* in both the government and Party institutional hierarchies are important. Even when decisions are perceived to be critical, they control the information base for higher echelons. And in the case of decisions perceived as less vital, they exercise administrative discretion in implementation.

There are relatively *few instances of institutional fusion* between the Party and government hierarchies. One exception (aside from those specified above) is the Chief Political Directorate of the Soviet Army and Navy. A clear separation of function, however, appears generally to be the rule.

Prescription of new or changed goals for the USSR and initiation of changes in policies are functions of the *Politburo leadership*. This is true both in practice and as a consequence of Marxist-Leninist decision theory. Even a dictator's role, however, is limited by the scope and accuracy of information available and by the need to maintain authority granted by other members of the Party Politburo. The latter is the greatest apparent limitation, and it operates to ensure for some Politburo members a strong influence in recommending and modifying policy initiatives. It serves to mark Politburo sessions as the locus of Soviet foreign-policy initiatives.

In the ongoing foreign-policy process, *top government roles* are usually assigned the tasks of submission and analysis of information and recommendation of possible courses of action. *Top Party roles* are primarily assigned the tasks of evaluation of specific courses of action, and after policy has been set, elaboration, explanation, and interpretation of policies among the elite. Both Party and government roles assume the tasks of confirmation and ratification both of courses of action and the senior decision-makers themselves. Party-elite roles afford greater freedom of action than government-elite roles.

Within the Party hierarchy, the *Secretariat* and its appointed *Central Apparatus* influence foreign policy by framing the questions which the Politburo will answer. Thus they collectively set bounds upon the Politburo's alternatives. The role of *General Secretary* is particularly important for foreign-policy decision-making, because it can provide legitimation before Party and public so that its occupant can assume the role of dictator. Historically it has assured its occupant the power among the Soviet elite to establish dictatorial authority.

Although the established roles in which they perform define the nature and extent of the individual role players' participation in the foreign-policy decision process, the choices left to the individual are sufficiently open to make personality an important variable. Over a period of time the skills and attitudes with which an individual plays his role may reshape the role itself and its relations to others. The individual's skills and attitudes, conversely, are largely the product of the experiences associated with the various roles in which he spends his career. This interaction of roles and personalities yielded several major conclusions when we turned to individual members of the foreign-policy elite as our units of analysis.

Although the Party Politburo is an *institutional* fusion of Party and government hierarchies, *functional* fusion resulting from one individual fulfilling roles in both hierarchies simultaneously is the exception rather than the rule. For example, members of the Party Secretariat generally are not government Ministers at the same time. This fact emphasizes the distinction of the two parallel foreign-policy decision hierarchies identified earlier. From 1958 to 1964 Khrushchev as dictator was the most notable exception. Late in 1962 Aleksandr Shelepin, as chief of the Party-State Control Committee (itself a fused institution) temporarily became another. Below this top-authority level instances of personal fusion of Party and government foreign-policy roles became even less frequent. Propaganda-dissemination roles are a notable exception. Propaganda expertise is considered a Party sphere, and all propagandists are in effect Party spokesmen. On the government side, foreign-intelligence roles frequently find an individual fusing two government agencies. Otherwise, Party *rank* accompanying government *role* is as far as fusion progresses. At the lower levels of the foreign-affairs elite Party membership appears to be primarily a clearance for admission to government roles. One need not be and seldom is a Party activist.

The CPSU foreign-affairs elite is small in comparison with the domestic-affairs elite, although the latter also concentrates authority in a narrow pyramid by Western democratic standards. In 1967, only six of nineteen Politburo members and candidates showed a major foreign-affairs orientation.

On the government side, the foreign-affairs elite is larger. The two facts i dicate a *relatively greater influence for the personality variable in formulation of Soviet foreign policy than in its administration.*

The foreign-affairs elite in the Party Politburo show two distinctive *career patterns:* Party "line officer" and Party "staff officer." Within the Secretariat, the "staff" career pattern is more frequent among foreign affairs–oriented members. Among the government foreign-affairs elite, narrow professional specialization is the rule, with, as a notable exception, the higher percentage of career Party personnel representing government in other party-states.

Among both top Party and government elite, those concerned with foreign affairs have more experience in domestic affairs than those in domestic affairs have in foreign affairs. Particularly in the Party, careers in domestic "construction of socialism" have been the rule. This fact emphasizes the narrow concentration of foreign-affairs expertise in the Party elite and indicates the heavy reliance which the Politburo must place upon second-echelon advice from both the Central Apparatus and the government agencies.

Generalizations relevant to the impact of individuals on their roles in the Soviet foreign-policy decision process at the lower and intermediate levels must be based for the most part upon our knowledge of the educational and environmental backgrounds of these groups.

Some of our findings about these groups suggest that the *half-educated Bolshevik,* holding his office because of revolutionary zeal and personal loyalty to his superiors, *is a vanishing breed* in Soviet foreign-affairs agencies. He never was as prevalent in this domain as in domestic affairs. The further down one probes into the decision hierarchy, the greater formal training one encounters. While this is true for both the Party and government hierarchies, it is especially notable on the government side, where technical competence is the single most important qualification for entry and advancement into the intermediate bureaucratic elite.

In the mid-1960's, the majority of *senior foreign-affairs personnel* had entered upon their careers just before or during World War II. They differed from their juniors in two ways. First, they shared a more varied career background and were more often the product of on-the-job training than their Institute-trained juniors whose careers had not been disrupted by the war. Secondly, they had not only survived the zig-zags of the foreign-policy line during Stalin's last decade and then the trauma of de-Stalinization, but also they had proven their ability to adapt quickly and probably cynically. Their juniors had not been tested in this way. Education had left the latter rich in factual knowledge within a simple and relatively uncontradicted system of official values provided by the Party.

The *junior foreign-affairs personnel* are distinguished by the narrowness of their professional specialization (which dates from their late adolescence), whether they are military officers, ministerial bureaucrats, or intelligence personnel. Their professionalization is as evident as their thorough knowledge of their crafts. What all share is the dry and unloved courses in Marxism-Leninism and modern history cast in its framework. Even the sophisticated political apologetics which the future diplomats receive proceeds from these established points of reference.

In an effort to investigate systematically one controversial aspect of the subjective attitudes brought to the foreign-policy decision process by members of the Soviet elite, we derived a number of propositions about the place of *Marxist-Leninist doctrine* as a conditioner of the elite's world view and then subjected the hypotheses to tests utilizing verbal-content analysis. Eight propositions of a total fourteen appeared to be convincingly confirmed in the context tested. They may be summarized as follows:

The proportion of premises taken entirely from Marxist-Leninist doctrine and the incidence of doctrinal stereotypes are greater for purposes of concluding broad trends and general expectations for the future than for specific conclusions and expectations of tightly interrelated, specific events.

The impact of Marxist-Leninist doctrine, both by furnishing substantive premises and by influencing the interpretation of observed events, is greater in the context of long-range planning and expectation than in the context of short-range analysis and decision.

There is greater density of doctrinal stereotypes present in the foreign-affairs formulations of elite members whose primary role involves them only peripherally in foreign affairs than in the foreign-affairs formulations of elite members whose roles involve them directly and extensively in foreign affairs.

There is a greater overall density of doctrinal stereotypes present in the formulations of elite members directly and extensively involved in foreign affairs than in the formulation of elite members whose roles are primarily concerned with domestic affairs.

The density of doctrinal stereotypes in the formulations of older members of the Soviet foreign-affairs elite is greater than that among the younger members.

The investigation of the place of the doctrine in Soviet foreign-policy decison-making revealed that *in most cases doctrine is important only as a modifier of perceptions of events*. Shifting the analysis to events themselves in an effort to specify their place in the decision process, we found them the link between foreign-policy outputs and subsequent decisions. Defining events as *perceived instances of rapid change in the international system*, we found them over a protracted time period to be the basis for translating long-range goals into programmatic policies. It is the perception of the environment in company with the perception of historical process that provide the basis for positing specific courses of action for the state in the international system. Perceived changes in the environment thus produce modifications of those courses of action. We developed the following major conclusions about the place of events:

Events are conveyed into the Soviet foreign-policy decision process as perceptions of rapid change in the international system which demand a response by the Soviet Union. The evaluation stimulated by the event may be one of *success, failure, threat,* or *opportunity,* or a combination of perceptions of these elements.

Events which thus become inputs for Soviet foreign policy may result from the impact of Soviet programmatic policy upon nonreciprocating targets. In this case, the predominant affective perception is one of success-failure, and periodic inputs take the form of feedback information which leads to modification or continuation of the programmatic policy.

Events which become policy inputs may also result from the intersection of programmatic Soviet policy with the programmatic policy of other actors in the international system. Such interactions may be either antagonistic or reinforcing. It is the antagonistic collisions which have the greatest potential for becoming *crises,* in which grave consequences are perceived from a threatening situation and in which a very short decision time is perceived to be available.

Events which become policy inputs may also result from unreciprocated programmatic policy of other actors directed toward the Soviet Union. Such stimulus often generates a qualitatively new Soviet program to neutralize perceived threat.

Events may also result from the collision of third actors' programs, which do not at the outset involve the Soviet Union as a respondent; or they may result from changes within either another state or the Soviet Union, which cause a change in the international system. In these cases the perceptions may be of threat or opportunity or a combination of the two. The success-failure dimension will not initially be involved.

Events may stimulate either modification or initiation of Soviet action with respect to their immediate situations, or they may stimulate additionally a long-term modification of Soviet programmatic policy or goals. The former is much more frequently the case. *Soviet programmatic policy and goals appear to be unusually persistent.* Changes in the personnel composition of the Soviet decision elite appear more likely to result in radical modifications of program than any other type of events considered.

Relating the conclusions about events to those developed about the place of doctrine, we concluded that *Marxist-Leninist interpretation of events by the Soviet elite is most significant for the international system as the basis for setting persistent Soviet programmatic policy* which may predestine repeated collision crises. There is little reason to suppose, on the other hand, that contemporary Soviet-elite interpretations of particular events and their probable immediate consequences will be significantly different from noncommunist interpretations of the same events.

In examining each of the four factors—*men, roles, doctrine,* and *events*— we have found not only that each could be identified as an input for the Soviet foreign-policy decision-making process but that each is to some degree a function of the others. Thus, while policy is a function of personality, personality is a function of role, doctrine, and events. At any one moment in time a policy decision is dependent upon a unique arrangement of these four factors. The arrangement is the resultant of cumulative past effects of each factor in interaction with the other three. In this light it becomes absurd to consider any one factor decisive over a period of time. In a single given instance, say on October 27, 1962, our study points to the personality of the dictator Khrushchev as decisive for a Soviet-policy decision regarding the Cuban missile confrontation with the United States. But an understanding of that personality could only be gained by including examination of the cumulative effect of doctrine, role, and past events upon it. This is an extreme example for purpose of emphasis. Much less would it be reasonable to attempt to understand more routine Soviet foreign-policy behavior without analysis of each of the four factor inputs.

The Director of an International Relations Institute which serves the Foreign Ministry and the Communist Party Central Committee of an East European country was asked how new political decisions were taken in his country, what the process was. He replied, in effect, that the members of the top political organ would perceive a current situation as intolerable. A casting about for alternative courses of action which might alleviate the situation would ensue. Plausible alternatives would be evaluated by the top political organ collectively, and a decision would be taken to try one. From our study it appears that this description could well be applied to the Soviet foreign-affairs decision-making process. We would point out the inescapable interplay of our four key variables: role structure determining what individual personalities would be confronted with choices, events stimulating perception of an "intolerable situation," evaluation of alternatives by individual personalities whose expectation and values are in part conditioned by Marxism-Leninism. Additionally we would note that in his description this official referred only to the process in which a new line of policy is initiated. The preliminary collection, selection, and interpretation of information at subordinate institutional levels, and the subsequent elaboration, confirmation, and implementation processes (which we have posited as important elements of the total decision process) must be added.

The Soviet decision-makers have discovered no really effective alternative to the Stalinist integration-by-force in *the world communist system*. They have tried to shift the predominant basis of authority and to revise the structure of supranational decision-making, but the Stalinist empire has failed to become a Soviet-led community of nations and parties. Pursuit of a new ideal has deteriorated into an *ad hoc*, piecemeal effort to slow down an unmanageable disintegration which is constantly aggravated by the stubborn Sino-Soviet conflict. The party-states' institutions such as the COMECON, the Warsaw Treaty Organization, and the Joint Institute of Nuclear Research have failed to preserve Soviet leadership under changed conditions. The progressive erosion of the Communist party-states' coalition has spread to the nonruling Communist Party organizations, which face grave problems of their own, and has adversely affected the whole movement. *A process of disintegration has set in in the communist system.*

The demand for autonomy, voiced by some units and latent in others, makes the communist movement increasingly unstable as a system. It seems inconceivable, given this development, that the Communist Parties, ruling and nonruling, will function primarily as *communist* system units in the future. The expectations and aspirations of rank-and-file Communists for the first time are juxtaposed in many lands to a proliferation of alternatives and possibilities. They see a better world to win, and they are discovering that they can win it faster by joining, rather than avoiding or undermining, the rest of the international system. As a consequence, we would conclude that in the future characteristics shared with noncommunist states, e.g., stages of economic modernization, will render other systems of interaction more influential than that system defined by mutual deference to the symbols of Marxism-Leninism.

The post-Stalin approach to the *developing areas* loosened the cold-war stalemate by transferring a significant portion of the East-West conflict into a new arena: that of essentially economic and propaganda competition. This Soviet innovation, we concluded, is here to stay. The Soviet leaders, having embarked on this course, no longer have any attractive alternative. Cessation or sizable reduction of Soviet assistance would not only incur hostility among the recipients, but also might open new opportunities for both the West and the Chinese. As we said earlier, the struggle with China, and effective peaceful competition with the West, as well as the struggle for socialism in the "third world," heavily depend on the persuasiveness of Soviet programs in this area; and the Soviet leaders know it.

We have conceptualized *Soviet-American relations* as a multiple-symmetry model and have found the model useful both for orientation and analysis. Having tested its applicability in several dimensions of Soviet-American interaction, we are confident that it fairly approximates the ongoing relationship. The model is also useful when we think of the United States and the USSR not only as opposing powers but as two organizers of coalition. From this more complex conceptualization emerge certain additional propositions which have important implications for *Soviet policy toward the West:*

1. The lower the hostility between the opposing organizers of coalitions, the USSR and the United States, the more difficult the sustained maintenance of the respective coalitions. In turn, the more difficult the maintenance of opposing coalitions, the less polarized the hostility between the coalitions.

2. The lower the hostility between the opposing organizers of coalitions, the greater the emphasis on broadly competitive, rather than narrowly antagonistic, interaction. In this way the economic-technological home bases of the organizers are augmented, the side-payments to coalition members and nonmembers increase, and the interaction loses the character of a "zero-sum" game.

3. The reduction of hostility thus produces results which reinforce the reduction, and areas of agreement grow upon mutual perceptions of benefit.

4. The greater the resource base available to the coalition organizers, the greater the potential for prosecuting remaining conflicts between them. *But,* concurrently, the greater the material benefit of the economic-technological side-payments (and the appetite for it), the less attractive the direct allocation of scarce resources for military expenditures. We therefore would expect the process of lowered hostility and diffusion of coalitions to be accompanied by increased domestic-value conflict in the coalition organizers. Thus we might expect elite instability in the USSR to increase commensurate with

the persistence of doctrinaire perceptions of intransigent bourgeois-communist contradictions.

5. Limited violent conflicts between members of opposing coalitions during a generally competitive (rather than intransigently antagonistic) period, such as is the case with Vietnam, would, we think, tend either to increase or decrease the hostility between the coalitions and the cohesion of the respective coalitions, depending on the issues involved:

(a) If the conflict reaffirms the agreement of the members on the purpose of the respective coalitions, the cohesion of the coalition increases and the hostility between the coalitions also increases. The organizers act their original parts and support and are supported by coalition members.

(b) If, on the other hand, the conflict either does not affect the purpose of the coalition, violates that purpose, or feeds on a major disagreement (latent or expressed) among the respective coalition members, the cohesion of the coalition decreases. This, we conclude, is true of the Vietnam case.

We have found *Soviet crisis behavior* since World War II cautious rather than reckless, conservative rather than radical, temperate rather than impulsive, and relatively rational. Judged by the tangible pay-offs, the Soviet batting average in the crises of post-World War II period has been quite low; and the Soviet enthusiasm for provocation of crises as means to international advantage appears to have declined markedly.

In the *United Nations*, the Soviet Union has gained in some ways and lost in others. Its present voting parity or near parity with the West in the United Nations is a Soviet success. But this Soviet ascendancy has proved to be of little utility for propagation of communism. In the process, the USSR has been socialized into a new role in the United Nations and has lost much of its inclination to challenge the *status quo*, so evident in the early post-World War II era.

The Soviet Union, a relatively "satiated" power in the world, supports and upholds *international law and order,* which in turn favors the *status quo* and thus the maintenance of the Soviet position. Cautious incremental improvement upon, rather than a risky challenge of, the *status quo* has thus characterized recent Soviet foreign policy. For this purpose, international treaties and agreements—consensual, specific, adaptable, and flexible—have served the Soviet Union well—better than any other source or instrument of international law. The rapidly growing propensity of the USSR to use international treaties and agreements—principally economic, cultural, technical/functional —has been noted. Nor is there serious reason to doubt the ostensible Soviet posture of rectitude in international relations; it is the function of the heavy Soviet investment in the contemporary world order.

After five decades of stubborn experimentation, with severe setbacks as well as hard-won victories, the Soviet Union is approaching a period in which, more likely than not, the relationship between it and the rest of the world will change significantly in a number of respects. In spite of Soviet claims to the contrary, its non-Soviet environment has been changing and developing more rapidly than the USSR itself. In their separate ways, Eastern Europe, China, the developing nations, and even the West have been progressing rapidly along a path unforeseen even a short fifteen years ago. Ideologically this must be a shock to Communists; pragmatically, Soviet foreign-policy output, shaped to keep up with and fit this rapidly changing international environment, has been influenced greatly.

But even while seeking some sustained support of its foreign policy from abroad, the Soviet leaders had increasingly and unexpectedly to search for foreign-policy validation at home as well. Ways and means of informing the Soviet public rapidly and more or less accurately, such as the Khrushchev and Kosygin radio and TV reports to the nation, are niceties which Stalin did not need to bother about. Judging from the tenor of their speeches, the increasingly harassed Soviet leaders and bureaucrats tend to believe less in the deterministic communist future than in accommodation to a tolerable international and domestic equilibrium. Soviet actions abroad appear to be a confirmation of this state of affairs.

This is not to say that the Soviet leaders do not genuinely wish what they say must happen. They wish to have integrated, solid support from all the Communist Parties—ruling as well as nonruling—in the communist system. They wish to see the developing nations become "revolutionary democracies," their regimes affinitive to, and socialist allies of, the USSR. And they wish to put the West on the final defensive primarily by sheer growth of the communist system—an international system to include ultimately all states in the world built upon a uniform ideology and led by the Soviet Union.

But the dream-like qualities of these wishes, and the speeches built upon them, tend to run against a rapidly growing "credibility gap" shared by domestic and foreign validators of Soviet foreign policy alike. The dissipation and alienation of revolutionary fervor and the widely shared new pragmatism, expressed in the ascendancy of the young, the articulate, and the creative in the communist system, preclude a pure messianic persistence.

On the other hand, Western hopes for liberalization or "democratization" of Soviet foreign policy based on dissolution of the communist system in the near future and transformation of the structure of authority in the USSR are wishes which are equally unrealistic. By its sheer strength, the communist

Soviet Union is bound to continue to act, by hook or crook, as the political organizer of Eastern Europe. The relationship in the association may be more equitable, but leadership is bound to belong to the strongest in the region. This entails continued coalition rivalry with the Western powers.

The growth of China as a world power progressively complicates matters for the USSR, just as it does for the United States. As we pointed out in Chapter V, this was bound to happen where a would-be coalition organizer has the means to challenge the present organizer. But China's claim in Eastern Europe is weak and apparently weakening. Thus we conclude that competing efforts to organize international support will continue to engender big-power rivalry between the USSR and China and between the USSR and Western states. These rivalries will probably exercise a dampening effect on any tendencies toward liberalization of Soviet foreign policy.

A more complex Soviet Union thus faces a more complex world. Growing apart from some of the more extreme units in the communist system, and pushed by some of the more conciliatory units, the Soviet Union may find itself less alienated from the rest of the world community as time goes by. All governments wishing influence with others on a global scale need allies and friends. If Soviet foreign policy seeks global influence, rather than radical world transformation, the opportunity is not only open to it—it is the option we all wish the USSR would take.

A BIBLIOGRAPHY FOR FURTHER READING

All students of Soviet foreign policy are indebted to Thomas T. Hammond of the University of Virginia for his extensive annotated bibliography, *Soviet Foreign Relations and World Communism; a Selected Annotated Bibliography of 7,000 Books in 30 Languages,* published in 1965 by the Princeton University Press. This copious volume should be the starting point for any research on Soviet foreign policy. A more general and less extensive bibliography which also will be of use to students of this subject is *Books on Communism* (New York: Oxford University Press, 1964), first published in 1959 under the editorship of R. N. Carew Hunt and later updated by Walter Kolarz.

Below we list a selection of books, articles and documents, almost all of them in English, which will afford the student an opportunity to amplify aspects of Soviet foreign policy examined in our text. A wide variety of points of view are represented, but because of the language restraints we have observed Soviet statements and analyses are inevitably slighted. To supplement the Soviet translations which we have included, we strongly urge the student to make frequent use of the *Current Digest of the Soviet Press* (New York: Joint Committee on Slavic Studies, weekly). To this source of contemporary Soviet analysis and opinion, one may usefully add two English-language periodicals: *International Affairs* (Moscow: All-Union Society *Znanie,* monthly) and *New Times* (Moscow: *Trud,* weekly).

While we have duplicated a few entries below, we suggest that the reader pursuing one of the more specialized topics treated in Chapter II–XI be sure to consult also the more general references listed under Chapter I.

Some Primary Sources of Marxist-Leninist Theory

Marx, Karl. *Selected Works of Karl Marx and Frederick Engels.* Moscow: Foreign Languages Publishing House, 1950.

Lenin, Vladimir I. *Selected Works.* Moscow: Foreign Languages Publishing House, 1950.

Trotsky, Lev D. *The First Five Years of the Communist International.* New York: Pioneer, 1945.

_____. *Our Revolution; Essays on Working Class and International Revolution.* New York: Holt, Rinehart and Winston, Inc., 1918.

_____. *The Permanent Revolution.* New York: Pioneer, 1931.

_____. *The Revolution Betrayed.* Garden City, N.Y.: Doubleday & Company, Inc., 1937.

Stalin, Iosif. *Economic Problems of Socialism in the USSR.* New York: International Publishers, 1952.

_____. *Marxism and the National and Colonial Question.* New York: International Publishers, 1935.

_____. *Problems of Leninism,* rev. ed. Moscow: Foreign Languages Publishing House, 1940.

Khrushchev, Nikita S. *Crimes of the Stalin Era*. New York: The New Leader, 1956.
_____. *Communism, Peace and Happiness for the Peoples*. Moscow: Foreign Languages Publishing House, 1963.
_____. *For Victory in Peaceful Competition with Capitalism*. New York: E. P. Dutton & Company, Inc., 1960.
_____. *World Without Arms, World Without Wars*. Moscow: Foreign Languages Publishing House, 1960.
Statements by Khrushchev, Brezhnev, Kosygin, and most members of the Soviet foreign-policy elite are available in profusion in the *Current Digest of the Soviet Press,* which should be used in conjunction with the collections of "sacred texts" above.

Introduction. Problems of Analysis of Soviet Foreign Policy

Bell, Daniel. "Ten Theories in Search of Reality," *World Politics*, X, No. 3 (April, 1958).
Brody, Richard A. and John F. Vesecky. "Soviet Openness to Changing Situations: A Critical Evaluation of Certain Hypotheses about Soviet Foreign Policy Behavior." Forthcoming.
Brzezinski, Zbigniew K. "Communist Ideology and International Affairs," *Journal of Conflict Resolution,* IV, No. 3 (September, 1960).
Glaser, William A. "Theories of Soviet Foreign Policy," *World Affairs Quarterly,* XXVII, No. 2 (July, 1956).
"Ideology and Power Politics: A Symposium," *Problems of Communism,* IV, No. 2 (March-April, 1959).
Kennan, George F. ("X"). "The Sources of Soviet Conduct," *Foreign Affairs,* XXV, No. 4 (July, 1947).
Reshetar, John S. *Problems of Analyzing and Predicting Soviet Behavior*. Garden City, N.Y.: Doubleday & Company, Inc., "Doubleday Short Studies in Political Science," 1955.
Rubenstein, Alvin Z. *The Soviets in International Organizations*. Princeton: Princeton University Press, 1964.
Ulam, Adam B. "Soviet Ideology and Soviet Foreign Policy," *World Politics,* XI, No. 2 (January, 1959).

Chapter I. From Socialism in One Country to Socialism in One Region: An Interpretation of the Five Decades of Soviet Foreign Policy

A. GENERAL REFERENCES FOR THE HISTORY OF SOVIET FOREIGN POLICY.

Adams, Arthur E. (ed.). *Readings in Soviet Foreign Policy*. Boston: D. C. Heath and Company, 1961.
Alexander, Robert J. *Communism in Latin America*. New Brunswick, N.J.: Rutgers University Press, 1957.
Armstrong, John A. *The Politics of Totalitarianism; the Communist Party of the Soviet Union from 1934 to the Present*. New York: Random House, Inc., 1961.
Bailey, Thomas A. *America Faces Russia: Russian-American Relations from Early Times to our Day*. Ithaca, N.Y.: Cornell University Press, 1950.
Barghoorn, Frederick C. *The Soviet Cultural Offensive: the Role of Cultural

Diplomacy in Soviet Foreign Policy. Princeton, N.J.: Princeton University Press, 1960.

Beloff, Max. *The Foreign Policy of Soviet Russia 1929–1941.* London: Oxford University Press, 1947–1949.

Bishop, Donald G. (ed.). *Soviet Foreign Relations: Documents and Readings.* Syracuse, N.Y.: Syracuse University Press, 1952.

Brandt, Conrad, Benjamin Schwartz, and John K. Fairbank (eds.). *A Documentary History of Chinese Communism.* Cambridge: Harvard University Press, 1952.

Carr, Edward H. *A History of Soviet Russia.* New York: The Macmillan Company, 1950.

Communist Party of the Soviet Union, Central Committee. *History of the Communist Party of the Soviet Union (Bolsheviks); Short Course.* New York: International Publishers, 1939.

Dallin, David J. *The Rise of Russia in Asia.* New Haven: Yale University Press, 1949.

Dean, Vera M. *The United States and Russia.* Cambridge: Harvard University Press, 1941.

Degras, Jane (ed.). *The Communist International, 1919–1943; Documents.* London: Oxford University Press, for the Royal Institute of International Affairs, 1956–1960.

_____. *Soviet Documents on Foreign Policy.* London: Oxford University Press, for the Royal Institute of International Affairs, 1951–1953.

Deutscher, Isaac. *Stalin; a Political Biography.* New York: Oxford University Press, 1949.

Fischer, Louis. *The Soviets in World Affairs, 1917–1929.* London: Jonathan Cape, 1930. 2nd ed. Princeton: Princeton University Press, 1951.

Goldwin, Robert A., with Gerald Stourzh and Marvin Zetterbaum (eds.). *Readings in Russian Foreign Policy.* New York: Oxford University Press, 1959.

Goodman, Elliott R. *The Soviet Design for a World State.* New York: Columbia University Press, 1960.

Gromyko, A. A. *et al.* (eds.). *Diplomaticheskii Slovar,* 2nd ed. Moscow: Gozizdat, 1960–1963.

Gurian, Waldemar (ed.). *Soviet Imperialism—Its Origins and Tactics.* Notre Dame: Notre Dame University Press, 1953.

Hilger, Gustav and Alfred G. Meyer. *The Incompatible Allies; a Memoir-History of German-Soviet Relations, 1918–1941.* New York: The Macmillan Company, 1953.

Isaacs, Harold R. *The Tragedy of the Chinese Revolution,* 2nd rev. ed. Stanford: Stanford University Press, 1951.

Kennan, George F. *Russia and the West under Lenin and Stalin.* Boston: Little, Brown & Company, 1960.

_____. *Soviet Foreign Policy, 1917–1941.* Toronto: Van Nostrand, 1960.

Kennedy, Malcolm D. *A History of Communism in East Asia.* New York: Frederick A. Praeger, Inc., 1957.

Kolarz, Walter. *Russia and Her Colonies.* New York: Frederick A. Praeger, Inc., 1953.

Laqueur, Walter Z. *Russia and Germany.* Boston: Little, Brown & Company, 1965.

Lederer, Ivo J. (ed.). *Russian Foreign Policy; Essays in Historical Perspective.* New Haven: Yale University Press, 1962.

Lenczowski, George. *Russia and the West in Iran, 1918–1948; a Study in Big-Power Rivalry.* Ithaca: Cornell University Press, 1949.

Librach, Jan. *The Rise of the Soviet Empire.* New York: Frederick A. Praeger, Inc., 1964.

Lukacs, John. *A History of the Cold War.* New York: Doubleday & Company, Inc., 1961.

Mackintosh, J. M. *Strategy and Tactics of Soviet Foreign Policy.* New York: Oxford University Press, 1963.

McKenzie, Kermit E. *Comintern and World Revolution, 1919–1943.* New York: Columbia University Press, 1964.

McVey, Ruth T. *The Soviet View of the Indonesian Revolution; a Study in the Russian Attitude towards Asian Nationalism.* Ithaca: Cornell University Press, 1957.

Moore, J. Barrington. *Soviet Politics: The Dilemma of Power.* Cambridge: Harvard University Press, 1950.

Mosely, Philip E. *The Kremlin and World Politics.* New York: Vintage Books, 1960.

North, Robert C. *Moscow and Chinese Communists,* 2nd ed. Stanford: Stanford University Press, 1963.

Ponomaryov, B. N. *et al. History of the Communist Party of the Soviet Union.* Moscow: Foreign Languages Publishing House, 1960.

Possony, Stefan T. *A Century of Conflict: Communist Techniques of World Revolution.* Chicago: Henry Regnery Company, 1953.

Rubinstein, Alvin Z. *The Foreign Policy of the Soviet Union.* New York: Random House, Inc., 1966.

Seton-Watson, Hugh. *From Lenin to Khrushchev: The History of World Communism.* New York: Frederick A. Praeger, Inc., 1960.

Strausz, Robert *et al. Protracted Conflict.* New York: Harper & Row, Publisher, Inc., 1959.

Toynbee, Arnold J. *et al.* (eds.). *Survey of International Affairs.* London: Oxford University Press, under auspices of the Royal Institute of International Affairs, annually since 1925.

von Rauch, Georg. *A History of Soviet Russia.* rev. ed. New York: Frederick A. Praeger, Inc., 1958.

Wolfe, Bertram D. *Six Keys to the Soviet System.* Boston: The Beacon Press, 1956.

Zinner, Paul E. *International Communism: Ideology, Organization, Strategy.* New York: Frederick A. Praeger, Inc., 1963.

Zorin, V. A. *et al.* (eds.). *Istoria Diplomatii.* Moscow: Izdatelstvo Politicheskoi Literatury, 1959.

B. STUDIES FOCUSED ON THE PERIOD 1917–1921.

Bunyan, James T. (comp.). *Intervention, Civil War, and Communism in Russia, April–December 1918: Documents and Materials.* Baltimore: Johns Hopkins University Press, 1936.

Chamberlin, William H. *The Russian Revolution, 1917–1921.* New York: The Macmillan Company, 1935.

Deutscher, Isaac. *The Prophet Armed: Trotsky, 1879–1921.* New York: Oxford University Press, 1954.

Draper, Theodore. *The Roots of American Communism.* New York: The Viking Press, Inc., 1957.

Francis, David R. *Russia from the American Embassy, April 1916–November 1918.*
New York: Charles Scribner's Sons, 1921.

Gankin, Olga H. and Harold H. Fisher. *The Bolsheviks and the World War: The
Origin of the Third International.* Stanford: Stanford University Press, 1940.

Hulse, James W. *The Forming of the Communist International.* Stanford: Stanford
University Press, 1964.

Kennan, George F. *Soviet-American Relations, 1917–1920.* Princeton, N.J.:
Princeton University Press, 1956.

Morley, James William. *The Japanese Thrust into Siberia, 1918.* New York:
Columbia University Press, 1957.

Pipes, Richard. *The Formation of the Soviet Union: Communism and Nationalism,
1917–1923.* Cambridge: Harvard University Press, 2nd ed., 1964.

Smith, Clarence J. *Finland and the Russian Revolution, 1917–1922.* Athens, Ga.:
University of Georgia Press, 1958.

Ullman, Richard H. *Anglo-Soviet Relations, 1917–1921.* Princeton: Princeton
University Press, 1961.

U.S. Department of State. *Papers Relating to the Foreign Relations of the United
States, 1918–1929; Russia.* Washington, D.C.: Government Printing Office,
1931–1937.

Warth, Robert D. *The Allies and the Russian Revolution: From The Fall of the
Monarchy to the Peace of Brest-Litovsk.* Durham, N.C.: Duke University Press,
1954.

Wheeler-Bennett, John W. *Brest-Litovsk; the Forgotten Peace.* London: Macmillan
& Co., Ltd., 1938.

White, John A. *The Siberian Intervention.* Princeton, N.J.: Princeton University
Press, 1950.

Whiting, Allen S. with Gen. Sheng Shih-Ts'ae. *Soviet Policies in China, 1917–1924.*
New York: Columbia University Press, 1954.

Wrangel, Peter N. (Baron). *Always with Honor.* New York: Speller, 1957.

Zeman, Z. A. B. (ed.). *Germany and the Russian Revolution, 1915–1918: Documents
from the Archives of the German Foreign Ministry.* New York: Oxford University
Press, 1958.

C. STUDIES FOCUSED ON THE PERIOD 1921–1928.

Barghoorn, Frederick C. *Soviet Russian Nationalism.* New York: Oxford University
Press, 1956.

Brandt, Conrad. *Stalin's Failure in China, 1924–1927.* Cambridge: Harvard University Press, 1958.

Draper, Theodore. *American Communism and Soviet Russia; the Formative Period.*
New York: The Viking Press, Inc., 1960.

Eudin, Xenia J. and Robert C. North. *Soviet Russia and the East, 1920–1927: A
Documentary Survey.* Stanford: Stanford University Press, 1957.

Eudin, Xenia J. and Harold H. Fisher. *Soviet Russia and the West, 1920–1927:
A Documentary Survey.* Stanford: Stanford University Press, 1957.

Fischer, Ruth. *Stalin and German Communism: a Study in the Origins of the State
Party.* Cambridge: Harvard University Press, 1948.

Freund, Gerald. *Unholy Alliance: Russian-German Relations from the Treaty of*

Brest-Litovsk to the Treaty of Berlin. New York: Harcourt, Brace & World, Inc., 1957.

Kochan, Lionel. *Russia and the Weimar Republic.* Cambridge: Bowes and Bowes, 1954.

Mills, John S. *The Genoa Conference.* New York: E. P. Dutton & Co., Inc., 1922.

North, Robert C. and Xenia J. Eudin (eds.). *M. N. Roy's Mission to China: the Communist-Kuomintang Split of 1927.* Berkeley: University of California Press, 1963.

Rosenbaum, Kurt. *Community of Fate: German-Soviet Diplomatic Relations, 1922–1928.* Syracuse, N.Y.: Syracuse University Press, 1965.

Stalin, Joseph V. *Marxism and the National and Colonial Question.* New York: International Publishers, 1936.

D. STUDIES FOCUSED ON THE PERIOD 1928–1939.

Borkenau, Franz. *World Communism.* New York: W. W. Norton & Company, Inc., 1939.

Browder, Robert P. *The Origins of Soviet-American Diplomacy.* Princeton, N.J.: Princeton University Press, 1953.

Budurowycz, Bohdan B. *Polish-Soviet Relations, 1932–1939.* New York: Columbia University Press, 1963.

Carr, Edward H. *German-Soviet Relations between the Two Wars.* Baltimore, Md.: Johns Hopkins University Press, 1952.

Cattell, David T. *Communism and the Spanish Civil War.* Berkeley: University of California Press, 1955.

_____. *Soviet Diplomacy and the Spanish Civil War.* Berkeley: University of California Press, 1957.

Cole, G. D. H. *Socialism and Facism, 1931–1939.* London: Macmillan & Co., Ltd., 1960.

Davies, Joseph E. *Mission to Moscow.* New York: Simon and Schuster, Inc., 1941.

Harper, Samuel N. (ed.). *The Soviet Union and World Problems.* Chicago: University of Chicago Press, 1935.

Litvinov, Maksim M. *Against Aggression.* New York: International Publishers, 1938.

Schwartz, Benjamin I. *Chinese Communism and the Rise of Mao.* Cambridge: Harvard University Press, 1951.

The Soviet Union and the Cause of Peace. New York: International Publishers, 1936.

Taracouzio, T. A. *The Soviet Union and International Law.* New York: The Macmillan Company, 1935.

_____. *War and Peace in Soviet Diplomacy.* New York: The Macmillan Company, 1940.

United States Department of State. *Papers Relating to the Foreign Relations of the United States, 1933–1938; the Soviet Union.* Washington, D.C.: Government Printing Office, 1952.

E. STUDIES FOCUSED ON THE PERIOD 1939–1945.

Armstrong, John A. *Ukranian Nationalism, 1939–1945.* New York: Columbia University Press, 1955.

Churchill, Winston S. *The Second World War*. Boston: Houghton Mifflin Company, 1948–1953.

Clark, Alan. *Barbarossa: The Russian-German Conflict, 1941–1945*. New York: William Morrow & Company, Inc., 1964.

Dallin, Alexander. *German Rule in Russia, 1941–1945; A Study in Occupation Policies*. New York: St. Martin's Press, 1957.

Dallin, David J. *Soviet Russia's Foreign Policy, 1939–1942*. New Haven: Yale University Press, 1942.

Deane, John R. *The Strange Alliance; the Story of our Efforts at Wartime Co-operation with Russia*. New York: The Viking Press, Inc., 1947.

Documents and Materials Relating to the Eve of the Second World War. Moscow: Foreign Languages Publishing House, 1948.

Feis, Herbert. *Churchill, Roosevelt and Stalin; the War They Waged and the Peace They Sought*. Princeton, N.J.: Princeton University Press, 1957.

Rossi, Amilcare. *The Russo-German Alliance, August 1939–June 1941*. Boston: The Beacon Press, 1951.

Rothstein, Andrew (ed. and trans.). *Soviet Foreign Policy during the Patriotic War: Documents and Materials*. London: Hutchinson & Co., Ltd., 1946.

Rozek, Edward J. *Allied Wartime Diplomacy: A Pattern in Poland*. New York: John Wiley & Sons, Inc., 1958.

Sherwood, Robert E. *Roosevelt and Hopkins*. New York: Harper & Row, Publishers, Inc., 1950.

Snell, John L. (ed.). *The Meaning of Yalta; Big Three Diplomacy and the New Balance of Power*. Baton Rouge, La.: Louisiana State University Press, 1956.

Sonntag, R. J. and J. S. Beddie (eds.). *Nazi-Soviet Relations, 1939–1941; Documents from the Archives of the German Foreign Office*. Washington, D.C.: U.S. Department of State, 1948.

Stalin, Joseph V. *War Speeches, Orders of the Day, and Answers to Foreign Press Correspondents during the Great Patriotic War*. London: Hutchinson & Co., Ltd., 1946.

Stalin's Correspondence with Churchill, Attlee, Roosevelt and Truman, 1941–45. New York: E. P. Dutton & Co., Inc., 1958.

Stettinius, Edward. *Roosevelt and the Russians; the Yalta Conference*. Garden City, N.Y.: Doubleday & Company, Inc., 1949.

Tanner, Väinö A. *The Winter War; Finland against Russia, 1939–1940*. Stanford: Stanford University Press, 1957.

Timasheff, Nicholas S. *The Great Retreat*. New York: E. P. Dutton & Co., Inc., 1946.

United States Department of State. *Foreign Relations of the United States; Diplomatic Papers. The Conference of Berlin (The Potsdam Conference) 1945*. Washington, D.C.: Government Printing Office, 1960.

———. *Foreign Relations of the United States; Diplomatic Papers. The Conferences at Malta and Yalta, 1945*. Washington, D.C.: Government Printing Office, 1955.

F. STUDIES FOCUSED ON THE PERIOD 1945–1953.

Barghoorn, Frederick C. *The Soviet Image of the United States; a Study in Distortion*. New York: Harcourt, Brace & World, Inc., 1950.

Beloff, Max. *Soviet Policy in the Far East, 1944–1951*. London: Oxford University Press, 1953.

Borkenau, Franz. *European Communism*. London: Faber and Faber, 1953.

Byrnes, Robert F. (general editor). *East Central Europe under the Communists*. New York: Frederick A. Praeger, Inc., 1956–1957.

Clay, Lucius D. *Decision in Germany*. New York: Doubleday & Company, Inc., 1950.

Dennett, Raymond and Joseph E. Johnson (eds.). *Negotiating with the Russians*. Boston: World Peace Foundation, 1951.

Eagleton, William. *The Kurdish Republic of 1946*. London: Oxford University Press, 1963.

Haines, Charles G. (ed.). *The Threat of Soviet Imperialism*. Baltimore, Md.: Johns Hopkins University Press, 1954.

Kautsky, John H. *Moscow and the Communist Party of India: A Study of Postwar Evolution of International Communist Strategy*. New York: Technology Press of M.I.T., 1956.

Kennan, George F. *American Diplomacy, 1900–1950*. New York: New American Library, 1952.

Laqueur, Walter Z. *Communism and Nationalism in the Middle East*. New York: Frederick A. Praeger, Inc., 1956.

Meyer, Peter *et al*. *The Jews in the Soviet Satellites*. Syracuse, N.Y.: Syracuse University Press, 1953.

Mosely, Philip E. *The Soviet Union since World War II. Annals of the American Academy of Political and Social Science*. (May, 1949.) CCLXII.

Roberts, Henry L. (ed.). *The Satellites of Eastern Europe. Annals of the American Academy of Political and Social Science*. (September, 1950.) CCCXVII.

Seton-Watson, Hugh. *The East European Revolution,* 3rd ed. New York: Frederick A. Praeger, Inc., 1956.

Shulman, Marshall D. *Stalin's Foreign Policy Reappraised*. Cambridge: Harvard University Press, 1963.

Smith, Walter Bedell. *My Three Years in Moscow*. Philadelphia: J. B. Lippincott Company, 1950.

The Soviet Takeover of Eastern Europe. Center for International Studies, M.I.T. Cambridge: M.I.T. Press, 1954.

Stalin, Joseph V. *Economic Problems of Socialism in the USSR*. Moscow: Foreign Languages Publishing House, 1952.

Ulam, Adam B. *Titoism and the Cominform*. Cambridge: Harvard University Press, 1952.

G. STUDIES FOCUSED ON THE PERIOD 1953–1965.

Allen, Robert L. *Middle Eastern Economic Relations with the Soviet Union, Eastern Europe and Mainland China*. Charlottesville, Va.: Woodrow Wilson Department of Foreign Affairs, University of Virginia, 1958.

———. *Soviet Influence in Latin America; the Role of Economic Relations*. Washington, D.C.: Public Affairs Press, 1959.

The Anti-Stalin Campaign and International Communism: A Selection of Documents. The Russian Institute, Columbia University. New York: Columbia University Press, 1956.

Brzezinski, Zbigniew K. *The Soviet Bloc; Unity and Conflict,* rev. ed. New York: Frederick A. Praeger, Inc., 1961.

Bulganin, Nikolai A. and Nikita S. Khrushchev. *Visit of Friendship to India, Burma, and Afghanistan: Speeches and Official Documents (November-December 1955).* Moscow: Foreign Languages Publishing House, 1956.

Burks, Richard V. *The Dynamics of Communism in Eastern Europe.* Princeton, N.J.: Princeton University Press, 1961.

Cheng, Chu-Yuan. *Economic Relations between Peking and Moscow, 1949–1963.* New York: Frederick A. Praeger, Inc., 1964.

Crankshaw, Edward. *The New Cold War: Moscow v. Pekin.* Baltimore, Md.: Penguin Books, Inc., 1963.

Dallin, Alexander (ed.). *Diversity in International Communism: A Documentary Record, 1961–1963.* New York: Columbia University Press, 1963.

_____. *Soviet Conduct in World Affairs.* New York: Columbia University Press, 1960.

Dallin, David J. *Soviet Foreign Policy after Stalin.* Philadelphia: J. B. Lippincott Company, 1961.

Deutscher, Isaac. *The Great Contest.* New York: Oxford University Press, 1960.

Feld, Warner. *Reunification and West-German–Soviet Relations.* The Hague: M. Nijhoff, 1963.

Fischer-Galati, Stephan (ed.). *Eastern Europe in the Sixties.* New York: Frederick A. Praeger, Inc., 1963.

Floyd, David. *Mao against Khrushchev.* New York: Frederick A. Praeger, Inc., 1963.

Griffith, William E. *Albania and the Sino-Soviet Rift.* Cambridge: M.I.T. Press, 1963.

_____ (ed.). *Communism in Europe.* Cambridge: M.I.T. Press, 1964–1965.

_____. *The Sino-Soviet Rift.* Cambridge: M.I.T. Press, 1964.

Grzybowski, Kazimierz. *The Socialist Commonwealth of Nations.* New Haven: Yale University Press, 1964.

Hudson, G. F., Richard Lowenthal, and Roderick MacFarquhar. *The Sino-Soviet Dispute.* New York: Frederick A. Praeger, Inc., 1961.

Kardelj, Edvard. *Socialism and War: A Survey of Chinese Criticism of the Policy of Coexistence.* London: Methuen & Co., Ltd., 1960.

Kaznacheev, Aleksandr. *Inside a Soviet Embassy: Experiences of a Soviet Diplomat in Burma.* Philadelphia: J. B. Lippincott Company, 1962.

Kertesz, Stephen D. (ed.). *East Central Europe and the World: Developments in the Post-Stalin Era.* Notre Dame, Ind.: Notre Dame University Press, 1962.

Khrushchev, Nikita S. *Conquest Without War; an Analytical Anthology of the Speeches, Interviews, and Remarks of Nikita S. Khrushchev.* Compiled and edited by N. H. Mager and Jacques Katel. New York: Simon and Schuster, Inc., 1961.

_____. *The Crimes of the Stalin Era: Special Report to the 20th Congress of the Communist Party of the Soviet Union.* New York: The New Leader, 1956. Annotated by Boris I. Nicolaevsky.

Kulski, Wladyslaw W. *Peaceful Coexistence; an Analysis of Soviet Foreign Policy.* Chicago: Henry Regnery Company, 1959.

Laqueur, Walter Z. *The Soviet Union and the Middle East.* New York: Frederick A. Praeger, Inc., 1959.

Leonhard, Wolfgang. *Child of the Revolution.* Chicago: Henry Regnery Company, 1958.

Lippmann, Walter. *The Communist World and Ours.* Boston: Atlantic Monthly Press, 1959.

London, Kurt (ed.). *New Nations in a Divided World.* New York: Frederick A. Praeger, Inc., 1963.

————. *Unity and Contradiction; Major Aspects of Sino-Soviet Relations.* New York: Frederick A. Praeger, Inc., 1962.

Mehnert, Klaus. *Peking and Moscow.* New York: G. P. Putnam's Sons, 1963.

Pentony, DeVera E. (ed.). *Soviet Behavior in World Affairs: Communist Foreign Policies.* San Francisco: Chandler, 1962.

Schuman, Frederick L. *The Cold War: Retrospect and Prospect.* Baton Rouge, La.: Louisiana State University Press, 1962.

Seton-Watson, Hugh. *Neither Peace nor War; the Struggle for Power in the Postwar World.* New York: Frederick A. Praeger, Inc., 1960.

Thornton, Thomas P. *The Third World in Soviet Perspective.* Princeton, N.J.: Princeton University Press, 1964.

Váli, Ferenc A. *Rift and Revolt in Hungary; Nationalism vs. Communism.* Cambridge: Harvard University Press, 1961.

Warth, Robert D. *Soviet Russia in World Politics.* New York: Twayne, 1963.

Zinner, Paul E. (ed.). *National Communism and Popular Revolt in Eastern Europe; a Selection of Documents on Events in Poland and Hungary, February-November, 1956.* New York: Columbia University Press, 1956.

————. *Revolution in Hungary.* New York: Columbia University Press, 1962.

H. Some Major Journals in English Which Focus on Soviet Foreign Policy.

Asian Survey. Institute of International Studies, University of California. Berkeley, California. Monthly.

Bulletin. Institute for the Study of the USSR. Munich. Monthly.

China Quarterly. Congress for Cultural Freedom. London. Quarterly.

Current Digest of the Soviet Press. The Joint Committee on Slavic Studies. N.Y. Weekly.

East Europe. Free Europe Committee, Inc. N.Y. Monthly.

International Affairs. The Soviet Society for the Popularization of Political and Scientific Knowledge. Moscow. Monthly.

Mizan. The Central Asian Research Centre. London. Bimonthly.

New Times. Published by *Trud.* Moscow. Weekly.

Problems of Communism. U.S. Information Agency. Washington. Bimonthly.

Survey. Congress for Cultural Freedom. London. Quarterly.

World Marxist Review. Prague. Monthly.

Chapter II. Institutions of Soviet Foreign Policy

Armstrong, John A. *The Soviet Bureaucratic Elite.* New York: Frederick A. Praeger, Inc., 1959.

Aspaturian, Vernon V. "Internal Politics and Foreign Policy in the Soviet System," in R. Barry Farrell (ed.). *Approaches to Comparative and International Politics.* Evanston, Ill.: Northwestern University Press, 1966.

————. "Soviet Foreign Policy," in Roy C. Macridis (ed.). *Foreign Policy in World Politics*. Englewood Cliffs, N.J.: Prentice-Hall, Inc., 1958.

————. *The Union Republics in Soviet Diplomacy*. Geneva: Librarie E. Droz, 1960.

Avtorkhanov, Abdurakhman. *The Communist Party Apparatus*. Chicago: Henry Regnery Company, 1966.

Barghoorn, Frederick C. *Soviet Foreign Propaganda*. Princeton, N.J.: Princeton University Press, 1964.

Barmine, Alexander. *One Who Survived*. New York: G. P. Putnam's Sons, 1945.

Baykov, Alexander M. *Soviet Foreign Trade*. Princeton, N.J.: Princeton University Press, 1946.

Busek, Antony. *How the Communist Press Works*. New York: Frederick A. Praeger, Inc., 1964.

Cattell, David T. "Formulation of Foreign Policy in the U.S.S.R.," in Philip W. Buck and Martin W. Travis (eds.). *The Control of Foreign Relations in Modern Nations*. New York: W. W. Norton & Company, Inc., 1957.

Conquest, Robert. *Power and Policy in the USSR*. London: Macmillan & Co., Ltd., 1961.

Constitution of the USSR. Moscow: Foreign Languages Publishing House, 1962.

Crankshaw, Edward. "Dissension Inside the Kremlin," *Atlantic*. CCIX, No. 6 (June, 1962).

————. *Khrushchev's Russia*. Baltimore, Md.: Penguin Books, Inc., 1959.

Denisov, A. and M. Kirichenko. *Soviet State Law*. Moscow: Foreign Languages Publishing House, 1960.

Deriabin, Peter and Frank Gibney. *The Secret World*. Garden City, N.Y.: Doubleday & Company, Inc., 1959.

Deutsch, Karl W. *The Nerves of Government*. New York: The Free Press of Glencoe, 1963.

Fainsod, Merle. *How Russia is Ruled*. Cambridge: Harvard University Press, 1963.

————. *Smolensk under Soviet Rule*. Cambridge: Harvard University Press, 1958.

Fischer, Louis. *The Soviets in World Affairs*. London: Jonathan Cape, Ltd., 1930.

Granick, David. *The Red Executive*. Garden City, N.Y.: Doubleday & Company, Inc., 1960.

Hendel, Samuel (ed.). *The Soviet Crucible*. Princeton, N.J.: D. Van Nostrand Company, Inc., 1960.

Hermens, F. A. "Totalitarian Power Structure and Russian Foreign Policy," *Journal of Politics*, XXI, No. 3 (August, 1959).

Huszar, George B. de (ed.). *Soviet Power and Policy*. New York: Thomas Y. Crowell Company, 1955.

Juviler, Peter H. and Henry W. Morton, eds. *Soviet Policy-Making*. New York: Frederick A. Praeger, Inc., 1967.

Kaznacheev, Aleksandr. *Inside a Soviet Embassy; Experiences of a Russian Diplomat in Burma*. Philadelphia: J. B. Lippincott Company, 1962.

Khrushchev, Nikita S. *Crimes of the Stalin Era*. New York: The New Leader, 1956.

Kozhevnikov, F. I. (ed.). *International Law*. Moscow: Foreign Languages Publishing House, n.d. [1961].

Kruglak, Theodore E. *The Two Faces of Tass*. Minneapolis, Minn.: University of Minnesota Press, 1962.

Kuusinen, O. W. *et al. Fundamentals of Marxism-Leninism (Manual)*, rev. ed. Moscow: Foreign Languages Publishing House, 1963.

Lee, Asher (ed.). *The Soviet Air and Rocket Forces*. New York: Frederick A. Praeger, Inc., 1959.

Leonhard, Wolfgang. *The Kremlin since Stalin*. New York: Frederick A. Praeger, Inc., 1962.

Lowenthal, Richard. "The Nature of Khrushchev's Power," *Problems of Communism*, IX, No. 4 (July-August, 1960).

Nemzer, Louis. "The Kremlin's Professional Staff: the 'Apparatus' of the Central Committee of the Communist Party of the Soviet Union." *American Political Science Review*, XLIV, No. 1 (March, 1950).

Neyman, Alexei F. "The Formulation and Administration of Soviet Foreign Policy," in Samuel N. Harper (ed.). *The Soviet Union and World Problems*. Chicago: University of Chicago Press, 1935.

Ploss, Sidney I. *Conflict and Decision-Making in the Soviet Union*. Princeton, N.J.: Princeton University Press, 1965.

_____. *Recent Alignments in the Soviet Elite*. Princeton, N.J.: Center of International Studies, March, 1964.

Rigby, T. H. "How Strong is the Leader," *Problems of Communism*, XI, No. 5 (September-October, 1962).

Saikowski, Charlotte and Leo Gruliow (eds.). *Current Soviet Policies IV*. New York: Columbia University Press, 1962.

Schapiro, Leonard. *The Communist Party of the Soviet Union*. New York: Random House, Inc., 1960.

Scott, Derek J. R. *Russian Political Institutions*, 2nd. ed. New York: Frederick A. Praeger, Inc., 1961.

Simon, Herbert A. *Administrative Behavior*, rev. ed. New York: The Macmillan Company, 1957.

Slusser, Robert M. "The Role of the Foreign Ministry," in Ivo J. Lederer (ed.). *Russian Foreign Policy*. New Haven: Yale University Press, 1962.

Snyder, Richard C., H. W. Bruck, and Burton Sapin (eds.). *Foreign Policy Decision-Making*. New York: The Free Press of Glencoe, 1962.

Sokolovskii, V. D. (ed.). *Soviet Military Strategy*. Englewood Cliffs, N.J.: Prentice-Hall, Inc., 1963.

Sprout, Harold and Margaret Sprout. "Environmental Factors in the Study of International Politics," in James N. Rosenau (ed.). *International Politics and Foreign Policy*. New York: The Free Press of Glencoe, 1961.

Spulber, Nicholas. *The Soviet Economy: Structure, Principles, Problems*. New York: W. W. Norton & Company, Inc., 1962.

Towster, Julian. *Political Power in the USSR, 1917–1947*. New York: Oxford University Press, 1948.

Triska, Jan F. "A Model for Study of Soviet Foreign Policy," *American Political Science Review*, LII, No. 1 (March, 1958).

_____ (ed.). *Soviet Communism: Programs and Rules*. San Francisco: Chandler Publishing Co., 1962.

Tucker, Robert C. "Autocrats and Oligarchs," in Ivo J. Lederer (ed.). *Russian Foreign Policy*. New Haven: Yale University Press, 1962.

United States Department of State, Bureau of Intelligence and Research, Biographic Information Division. *Directory of Soviet Officials*. Washington, D.C.: Dept. of State, 1960–1961.

United States Senate, Committee on Government Operations, 86th Congress, 2nd Session. *National Policy Machinery in the Soviet Union*. Washington, D.C.: Government Printing Office, 1960.

––––––, Committee on Government Operations, 87th Congress, 1st Session. *Staffing Procedures and Problems in the Soviet Union*. Washington, D.C.: Government Printing Office, 1963.

von Laue, Theodore H. "Soviet Diplomacy: G. V. Chicherin, People's Commissar for Foreign Affairs, 1918–1930," in Gordon A. Craig and Felix Gilbert (eds.). *The Diplomats, 1919–1939*. Princeton, N.J.: Princeton University Press, 1953.

Vyshinsky, Andrei Y. (ed.). *The Law of the Soviet State*. New York: The Macmillan Company, 1948. (Soviet publication in 1938.)

Wolfe, Thomas W. *Soviet Strategy at the Crossroads*. Cambridge: Harvard University Press, 1964.

Wolin, Simon and Robert M. Slusser (eds.). *The Soviet Secret Police*. New York: Frederick A. Praeger, Inc., 1957.

Chapter III. The Men Who Make Soviet Foreign Policy

Alexandrov, Victor. *Khrushchev of the Ukraine*. New York: Philosophical Library, Inc., 1957.

Armstrong, John A. *The Soviet Bureaucratic Elite*. New York: Frederick A. Praeger, Inc., 1959.

Bereday, George Z. F. and J. Penner (eds.). *The Politics of Soviet Education*. New York: Frederick A. Praeger, Inc., 1960.

Bialer, Seweryn. "The Men Who Run Russia's Armed Forces," *The New York Times Magazine,* February 21, 1965.

Bol'shaia Sovetskaia Entsiklopediia, 2nd ed. Moscow: Gosudarstvennoe nauchnoe izdatel'stvo, 1954–1958.

Conquest, Robert. *Power and Policy in the USSR*. London: Macmillan Co. Ltd., 1961.

––––––. *Russia after Khrushchev*. New York: Frederick A. Praeger, Inc., 1965.

Counts, George S. *The Challenge of Soviet Education*. New York: McGraw-Hill Book Company, Inc., 1957.

Crankshaw, Edward. *Khrushchev: A Career*. New York: The Viking Press, Inc., 1966.

Deutscher, Isaac. *The Prophet Armed: Trotsky, 1879–1921*. London: Oxford University Press, 1954.

––––––. *The Prophet Unarmed: Trotsky, 1921–1929*. London: Oxford University Press, 1959.

––––––. *The Prophet Outcast: Trotsky, 1929–1940*. London: Oxford University Press, 1963.

––––––. *Stalin*. London: Oxford University Press, 1949.

DeWitt, Nicholas. *Education and Professional Employment in the USSR*. Washington, D.C.: National Science Foundation, 1961.

Djilas, Milovan. *Conversations with Stalin.* New York: Harcourt, Brace & World, Inc., 1962.

Ezhegodnik Bol'shoi Sovetskoi Entsiklopedii. Moscow: Izdatel'stvo bol'shoi sovetskoi entisiklopedii, annually.

Fischer, Louis. *The Life of Lenin.* New York: Harper & Row, Publishers, Inc., 1964.

Frankel, Max. "Moscow's Man Intrigues Washington," *The New York Times Magazine,* July 29, 1962.

Gehlen, Michael P. "The Educational Background and Career Orientations of the Members of the Central Committees of the CPSU," *The American Behavioral Scientist,* IX, No. 8 (April, 1966).

Gromyko, A. A. *et al.* (eds.). *Diplomaticheskii Slovar'.* Moscow: Gosudarstvennoe izdatel'stvo, 1960–1964.

Kaznacheev, Aleksandr. *Inside a Soviet Embassy; Experiences of a Russian Diplomat in Burma.* Philadelphia: J. B. Lippincott Company, 1962.

Kellen, Konrad. *Khrushchev: A Political Portrait.* New York: Frederick A. Praeger, Inc., 1961.

Korol, Alexander. *Soviet Education for Science and Technology.* Cambridge, Mass.: Technology Press of M.I.T., 1957.

Kruglak, Theodore E. *The Two Faces of Tass.* Minneapolis, Minn.: University of Minnesota Press, 1962.

Leonhard, Wolfgang. *The Kremlin since Stalin.* New York: Frederick A. Praeger, Inc., 1962.

Merzalow, Wladimir S. (ed.). *Biographic Directory of the U.S.S.R.* New York: Scarecrow Press, 1958.

Meyer, Frank S. *The Moulding of Communists.* New York: Harcourt, Brace & World, Inc., 1961.

Middleton, Drew. "The New Man in Soviet Diplomacy," *The New York Times Magazine,* December 7, 1958.

Paloczi-Horvath, Gyorgy. *Khrushchev.* Boston: Little, Brown & Company, 1960.

Parry, Albert. *The New Class Divided.* New York: The Macmillan Company, 1966.

Pistrak, Lazar. *The Grand Tactician.* New York: Frederick A. Praeger, Inc., 1961.

Ploss, Sidney I. *Conflict and Decision-Making in the Soviet Union.* Princeton, N.J.: Princeton University Press, 1965.

————. *Recent Alignments in the Soviet Elite.* Princeton, N.J.: Center of International Studies, March, 1964.

Pope, A. U. *Maxim Litvinoff.* New York: L. B. Fisher, 1943.

Rush, Myron. *The Rise of Khrushchev.* Washington, D.C.: Public Affairs Press, 1958.

Schatunowski, George. "The Training of Personnel," in Asher Lee (ed.). *The Soviet Air and Rocket Forces.* New York: Frederick A. Praeger, Inc., 1959.

Scheuller, George K. *The Politburo.* Stanford: Stanford University Press, 1951.

Schulz, Heinrich E. and Stephen S. Taylor (eds.). *Who's Who in the USSR 1961–62.* New York: Intercontinental Book and Publishing Company, Ltd., for the Institute for the Study of the USSR, 1962 (rev. ed. 1966).

Shub, David. *Lenin.* Garden City, New York: Doubleday & Company, Inc., 1951.

Shumilin, I. N. *Soviet Higher Education.* Munich: Institute for the Study of the USSR, 1962.

Souvarine, Boris. *Stalin*. New York: Alliance Book Corporation, 1939.

Stalin, Joseph V. *Mastering Bolshevism*. New York: Workers Library Publishers, 1937.

Trotsky, Lev D. *My Life*. New York: Charles Scribner's Sons, 1930.

―――. *Stalin*. New York: Harper & Row, Publishers, Inc., 1941.

Tucker, Robert C. "Autocrats and Oligarchs," in Ivo J. Lederer (ed.). *Russian Foreign Policy*. New Haven: Yale University Press, 1962.

United States Department of State, Bureau of Intelligence and Research, Biographic Information Division. *Directory of Soviet Officials*. Washington, D.C.: Department of State, 1960–1961.

United States Senate, Committee on Government Operations, 86th Congress, 2nd Session. *National Policy Machinery in the Soviet Union*. Washington, D.C.: Government Printing Office, 1960.

―――, Committee on Government Operations, 87th Congress, 1st Session. *Staffing Procedures and Problems in the Soviet Union*. Washington, D.C.: Government Printing Office, 1963.

von Laue, Theodore H. "Soviet Diplomacy: G. V. Chicherin, People's Commissar for Foreign Affairs, 1918–1930," in Gordon A. Craig and Felix Gilbert (eds.). *The Diplomats, 1919–1939*. Princeton, N.J.: Princeton University Press, 1953.

Wolin, Simon and Robert M. Slusser (eds.). *The Soviet Secret Police*. New York: Frederick A. Praeger, Inc., 1957.

Chapter IV. Doctrine and Events in Soviet Foreign Policy

Barghoorn, Frederick C. *Soviet Russian Nationalism*. New York: Oxford University Press, 1956.

Berelson, Bernard. *Content Analysis in Communication Research*. New York: The Free Press of Glencoe, 1952.

Boersner, Demetrio. *The Bolsheviks and the National and Colonial Question, 1917–1928*. Geneva: Droz, 1957.

Boulding, Kenneth E. *The Image*. Ann Arbor, Mich.: University of Michigan Press, 1956.

Bowles, Chester. "Is Communist Ideology Becoming Irrelevant?" *Foreign Affairs*, XL, No. 4 (July, 1962).

Brinkley, G. "Foreign Policy and the Transition to Communism," *Survey*, No. 38 (October, 1961).

Brzezinski, Zbigniew K. *Ideology and Power in Soviet Politics*. New York: Frederick A. Praeger, Inc., 1962.

Bukharin, Nikolai I. and E. Preobrazhenskii. *The A.B.C. of Communism*. London: Communist Party of Great Britain, 1922.

Burin, Frederick S. "The Communist Doctrine of the Inevitability of War," *American Political Science Review*, LVII, No. 2 (June, 1963).

Burns, Emile (ed.). *A Handbook of Marxism*. New York: Random House, Inc., 1935.

Cole, George D. H. *A History of Socialist Thought*. London: Macmillan Co. Ltd., 1953–1960.

Communist Party of the Soviet Union, Central Committee. *History of the Communist Party of the Soviet Union (Bolsheviks); Short Course*. New York: International Publishers, 1939.

Dallin, Alexander (ed.). *Soviet Conduct in World Affairs*. New York: Columbia University Press, 1960.

Daniels, Robert V. (ed.). *A Documentary History of Communism*. New York: Random House, Inc., 1960.

_____. *The Nature of Communism*. New York: Random House, Inc., 1962.

Diplomaticus. "Stalinist Theory and Soviet Foreign Policy," *Review of Politics*, XIV, No. 4 (October, 1952).

Drachkovitch, Milorad M. (ed.). *Marxism in the Modern World*. Stanford: Stanford University Press, 1965.

_____. *Marxist Ideology in the Contemporary World; its Appeals and Paradoxes*. New York: Frederick A. Praeger, Inc., 1966.

Festinger, Leon *et al*. *A Theory of Cognitive Dissonance*. Stanford: Stanford University Press, 1962.

Fisher, Harold H. *The Communist Revolution; an Outline of Strategy and Tactics*. Stanford: Stanford University Press, 1955.

Friedrich, Carl J. and Zbigniew K. Brzezinski. *Totalitarian Dictatorship and Autocracy*, rev. ed. Cambridge: Harvard University Press, 1966.

Goodman, Elliott, R. *The Soviet Design for a World State*. New York: Columbia University Press, 1960.

Gurian, Waldemar. *Bolshevism: Theory and Practice*. London: Sheed and Ward, Ltd., 1932.

Historicus. "Stalin on Revolution," *Foreign Affairs*, XXVII, No. 2 (January, 1949).

Holsti, Ole R. "The Belief-System and National Images, a Case Study," *Journal of Conflict Resolution*, VI, No. 3 (September, 1962).

_____ with Joanne K. Loomba, and Robert C. North. "Content Analysis," in Gardner Lindsay, and Elliott Aronson (eds.). *The Handbook of Social Psychology*, 2nd ed. Reading, Mass.: Addison-Wesley Publishing Company, forthcoming.

Hook, Sidney. *Marx and the Marxists: The Ambiguous Legacy*. Princeton, N.J.: D. Van Nostrand Company, Inc., 1955.

Hunt, R. N. Carew. *A Guide to Communist Jargon*. New York: The Macmillan Company, 1957.

_____. *The Theory and Practice of Communism*, 5th ed. New York: The Macmillan Company, 1957.

_____, Richard Lowenthal, Samuel L. Sharp and J. L. H. Keep. "Soviet Ideology and Politics—A Symposium," *Problems of Communism*, VII, No. 2 (March-April, 1958).

Jacobs, Dan N. (ed.). *The New Communist Manifesto and Related Documents*. New York: Harper & Row, Publishers, Inc., 1961.

Kennan, George F. ("X"). "The Sources of Soviet Conduct," *Foreign Affairs*, XXV, No. 4 (July, 1947).

Khrushchev, Nikita S. *For Victory in Peaceful Competition with Capitalism*. New York: E. P. Dutton & Co., Inc., 1960.

Kohn, Hans. *Pan-Slavism; Its History and Ideology*. Notre Dame, Ind.: University of Notre Dame Press, 1953.

Kristof, Ladis K. D. "The Origins and Evolution of Geopolitics," *Journal of Conflict Resolution*, IV, No. 1 (March, 1960).

Kulski, Wladyslaw W. *Peaceful Co-existence: An Analysis of Soviet Foreign Policy.* Chicago: Henry Regnery Company, 1959.

Kuusinen, O. W. *et al. Fundamentals of Marxism-Leninism (Manual),* rev. ed. Moscow: Foreign Languages Publishing House, 1963.

Labedz, Leopold (ed.). *Revisionism.* New York: Frederick A. Praeger, Inc., 1962.

Lasswell, Harold D. with Daniel Lerner and Ithiel de Sola Pool. *The Comparative Study of Symbols, an Introduction.* Stanford: Stanford University Press, 1952.

Leites, Nathan. *The Operational Code of the Politburo.* New York: McGraw-Hill Book Company, Inc., 1951.

_____. *A Study of Bolshevism.* New York: The Free Press of Glencoe, 1953.

Lenin, Vladimir I. *On Peaceful Coexistence.* Moscow: Foreign Languages Publishing House, n.d. [1962].

Lichtheim, George. *Marxism: An Historical and Critical Study.* New York: Frederick A. Praeger, Inc., 1961.

Lowenthal, Richard. *World Communism: The Disintegration of a Secular Faith.* New York: Oxford University Press, 1964.

Marcuse, Herbert. *Soviet Marxism.* New York: Columbia University Press, 1958.

Mehnert, Klaus. *Stalin Versus Marx.* London: George Allen & Unwin, Ltd., 1953.

Meyer, Alfred G. *Communism.* New York: Random House, Inc., 1960.

_____. *Leninism.* Cambridge: Harvard University Press, 1957.

Moore, J. Barrington, Jr. *Soviet Politics: The Dilemma of Power.* Cambridge: Harvard University Press, 1950.

Mosely, Philip E. *The Kremlin and World Politics, Studies in Soviet Policy and Action.* New York: Vintage Books, 1960.

Niemeyer, Gerhart. "The Ideological Motivation of Communists," *Modern Age,* V, No. 4 (Fall, 1961).

_____ with John S. Reshetar, Jr. *An Inquiry into Soviet Mentality.* London: Atlantic Press, 1956.

North, Robert C. "Two Revolutionary Models: Russian and Chinese," in A. Doak Barnett (ed.). *Communist Strategies in Asia.* New York: Frederick A. Praeger, Inc., 1963.

_____ with Ole R. Holsti, M. George Zannovich, and Dina A. Zinnes. *Content Analysis, a Handbook with Applications for the Study of International Crisis.* Evanston, Ill.: Northwestern University Press, 1963.

Osgood, Charles E. with George J. Suci, and Percy Tannenbaum. *The Measurement of Meaning.* Urbana, Ill.: University of Illinois Press, 1959.

Plamenatz, John P. *German Marxism and Russian Communism.* London: Longmans, Green & Co., Ltd., 1954.

Ponomaryov, B. N. *et al.* (eds.). *History of the Communist Party of the Soviet Union.* Moscow: Foreign Languages Publishing House. 1960.

Pool, Ithiel de Sola. *The "Prestige Papers," a Survey of Their Editorials.* Stanford: Stanford University Press, 1952.

_____. *Symbols of Democracy.* Stanford: Stanford University Press, 1952.

_____. *Symbols of Internationalism.* Stanford: Stanford University Press, 1951.

_____ (ed.). *Trends in Content Analysis.* Urbana, Ill.: University of Illinois Press, 1959.

Possony, Stefan T. *A Century of Conflict; Communist Techniques of World Revolution.* Chicago: Henry Regnery Company, 1953.

Radzinski, John M. *Masks of Moscow: A History of Russian Behavior Patterns.* Chicago: Regent House, 1961.

Riefe, R. H. "Moscow and the Changing Nature of Communist Ideology," *Journal of International Affairs.* XII, No. 2 (1958).

Rokeach, Milton. *The Open and Closed Mind.* New York: Basic Books, 1960.

Shulman, Marshall D. "The Real Nature of the Soviet Challenge," *The New York Times Magazine,* July 16, 1961.

Triska, Jan F. (ed.). *Soviet Communism: Programs and Rules.* San Francisco: Chandler Publishing Co., 1962.

Ulam, Adam B. "Soviet Ideology and Soviet Foreign Policy," *World Politics.* XI, No. 2 (January, 1959).

_____. *The Unfinished Revolution.* New York: Random House, Inc., 1960.

United States Senate, Committee on Foreign Relations, 86th Congress, 2nd Session. *Ideology and Foreign Affairs.* Washington, D.C.: Government Printing Office, 1960.

Wetter, Gustav A. *Dialectical Materialism; A Historical and Systematic Survey of Philosophy in the Soviet Union.* New York: Frederick A. Praeger, Inc., 1958.

Whiting, Allen S. *China Crosses the Yalu.* New York: The Macmillan Company, 1960.

Williams, Bernard. "Democracy and Ideology," *The Political Quarterly,* XXXII, No. 4 (October-December, 1961).

Wolfe, Bertram D. "Communist Ideology and Soviet Foreign Policy," *Foreign Affairs,* XLI, No. 1 (October, 1962).

_____. *Marxism: One Hundred Years in the Life of a Doctrine.* New York: The Dial Press, Inc., 1965.

Zinner, Paul. "The Ideological Bases of Soviet Foreign Policy," *World Politics,* IV, No. 4 (July, 1952).

Chapter V. The Soviet Union and the World Communist System

Armstrong, H. F. *Tito and Goliath.* New York: The Macmillan Company, 1951.

Barnett, A. Doak (ed.). *Communist Strategies in Asia: a Comparative Analysis of Governments and Parties.* New York: Frederick A. Praeger, Inc., 1963.

Bass, Robert and Elizabeth Marbury (eds.). *The Soviet-Yugoslav Controversy, 1948–1958; a Documentary Record.* New York: Prospect Books, 1959.

Beck, Carl. "Party Control and Bureaucratization in Czechoslovakia," *The Journal of Politics,* XXIII, No. 2 (May, 1961).

Black, Cyril E. (ed.). *Challenge in Eastern Europe.* New Brunswick, N.J.: Rutgers University Press, 1954.

Boersner, Demetrio. *The Bolsheviks and the National and Colonial Question 1917–1928.* Geneva: Droz, 1957.

Boorman, Howard L. *et al. Moscow-Peking Axis; Strengths and Strains.* New York. Harper & Row, Publishers, Inc., 1957.

Borkenau, F. *European Communism.* London: Faber & Faber, Ltd., 1953.

Brant, Stefan. *The East German Rising: 17th June, 1953.* New York: Frederick A. Praeger, Inc., 1957.

Bromke, Adam and Milorad Drachkovitch. "Poland and Yugoslavia: The Abortive Alliance," *Problems of Communism,* X, No. 2 (March-April, 1962).

Broz-Tito, J. "On Certain International Questions," *Foreign Affairs,* XXXVI, No. 1 (October, 1957).

Brzezinski, Zbigniew K. "Peaceful Engagement in Communist Disunity," *China Quarterly,* No. 10 (April-June, 1962).

———. *The Soviet Bloc: Unity and Conflict,* rev. ed. New York: Frederick A. Praeger, Inc., 1961.

Burks, R. V. *The Dynamics of Communism in Eastern Europe.* Princeton, N.J.: Princeton University Press, 1961.

Busek, Vratislav and Nicholas Spulber (eds.). *Czechoslovakia.* New York: Frederick A. Praeger, Inc., 1957.

Byrnes, Robert F. (ed.). *Yugoslavia.* New York: Frederick A. Praeger, Inc., 1957.

Dallin, Alexander (ed.). *Diversity in International Communism; a Documentary Record, 1961–1963.* New York: Columbia University Press, 1963.

———. "Long Divisions and Fine Fractions," *Problems of Communism.* XI, No. 2 (March-April, 1962).

Dedijer, Vladimir. *Tito.* New York: Simon and Schuster, Inc., 1953.

Dellin, L. A. D. (ed.). *Bulgaria.* New York: Frederick A. Praeger, Inc., 1957.

Djilas, Milovan. *Conversations with Stalin.* New York: Harcourt, Brace & World, Inc., 1962.

———. *The New Class.* New York: Frederick A. Praeger, Inc., 1957.

Duchacek, Ivo. *The Strategy of Communist Infiltration: the Case of Czechoslovakia.* New Haven: Yale Institute of International Studies, 1949.

Fischer-Galati, Stephen (ed.). *Eastern Europe in the Sixties.* New York: Frederick A. Praeger, Inc., 1963.

———. *Romania.* New York: Frederick A. Praeger, Inc., 1957.

Floyd, David. *Mao against Khrushchev; a Short History of the Sino-Soviet Conflict.* New York: Frederick A. Praeger, Inc., 1963.

Gibney, Frank B. *The Frozen Revolution; Poland: A Study in Communist Decay.* New York: Farrar, Straus and Cudahy, 1959.

Griffith, William E. *Albania and the Sino-Soviet Rift.* Cambridge: M.I.T. Press, 1963.

——— (ed.). *Communism in Europe; Continuity, Change, and the Sino-Soviet Dispute.* Cambridge: M.I.T. Press, 1964–1965.

———. *The Sino-Soviet Rift.* Cambridge: M.I.T. Press, 1954.

Grothe, Peter. *To Win the Minds of Men: The Story of the Communist Propaganda in East Germany.* Palo Alto, Calif.: Pacific Books, 1958.

Gsovski, Vladimir (ed.). *Church and State behind the Iron Curtain.* New York: Frederick A. Praeger, Inc., 1955.

Halecki, Oscar (ed.). *Poland.* New York: Frederick A. Praeger, Inc., 1957.

Helmreich, Ernest (ed.). *Hungary.* New York: Frederick A. Praeger, Inc., 1957.

Ignotus, Paul. "Hungary: Existence and Co-Existence," *Problems of Communism,* X, No. 2 (March-April, 1961).

Ionescu, Ghita. *Communism in Rumania, 1944–1962.* London: Oxford University Press, 1964.

Kennedy, Malcolm D. *A History of Communism in Asia.* New York: Frederick A. Praeger, Inc., 1957.

Kertesz, Stephen D. (ed.). *The Fate of East Central Europe.* Notre Dame, Ind.: Notre Dame University Press, 1956.

Korbel, Josef. *The Communist Subversion of Czechoslovakia: the Failure of Co-existence, 1938–48.* Princeton, N.J.: Princeton University Press, 1959.
_____. *Tito's Communism.* Denver, Colo.: University of Denver Press, 1951.
Kracauer, Sigfried and Paul L. Borkman. *Satellite Mentality: Attitudes and Propaganda Susceptibilities of Non-Communists in Hungary, Poland and Czechoslovakia.* New York: Frederick A. Praeger, Inc., 1956.
Labedz, Leopold (ed.). *International Communism after Khrushchev.* Cambridge: M.I.T. Press, 1965.
Laqueur, Walter and Leopold Labedz (eds.). *Polycentrism: the New Factor in International Communism.* New York: Frederick A. Praeger, Inc., 1962.
Lasky, Melvin J. (ed.). *The Hungarian Revolution.* New York: Frederick A. Praeger, Inc., 1957.
Lattimore, Owen. *Nationalism and Revolution in Mongolia.* New York: Oxford University Press, 1955.
_____ et al. *Pivot of Asia; Sinkiang and the Inner Asian Frontiers of China and Russia.* Boston: Little, Brown & Company, 1950.
Lewis, Flora. *A Case History of Hope; the Story of Poland's Peaceful Revolution.* Garden City, N.Y.: Doubleday & Company, Inc., 1958.
London, Kurt. "The Socialist Commonwealth: Pattern for Communist World Organization," *Orbis,* III, No. 4 (Winter, 1960).
Lowenthal, Richard. *World Communism; the Disintegration of a Secular Faith.* New York: Oxford University Press, 1964.
Lukacs, John A. *The Great Powers and Eastern Europe.* Chicago: Henry Regnery Company, 1954.
McLane, Charles B. *Soviet Policy and the Chinese Communists, 1931–1946.* New York: Columbia University Press, 1958.
McNeal, Robert H., ed. *International Relations Among Communists.* Englewood Cliffs, N.J.: Prentice-Hall, Inc., 1967.
McVicker, Charles P. *Titoism; Pattern for International Communism.* New York: St. Martin's Press, 1957.
Modelski, George. *The Communist International System.* Princeton, N.J.: Woodrow Wilson School of Public and International Affairs, Princeton University, Research Monograph No. 9, 1960.
Mosely, Philip E. "The Chinese-Soviet Rift: Origins and Portents," *Foreign Affairs,* XLII, No. 1 (October, 1963).
Neal, Fred Warner. *Titoism in Action: the Reforms in Yugoslavia after 1948.* Berkeley: University of California Press, 1958.
North, Robert C. *Moscow and Chinese Communists,* 2nd ed. Stanford: Stanford University Press, 1963.
Pentony, DeVere E. (ed.). *Red World in Tumult: Communist Foreign Policies.* San Francisco: Chandler Publishing Co., 1962.
Riker, William H. *The Theory of Political Coalitions.* New Haven: Yale University Press, 1962.
Rubinstein, Alvin Z. *Communist Political Systems.* Englewood Cliffs, N.J.: Prentice-Hall, Inc., 1966.
Scalapino, Robert A. (ed.). *The Communist Revolution in Asia; Tactics, Goals, and Achievements.* Englewood Cliffs, N.J.: Prentice-Hall, Inc., 1965.

Schmidt, Dana Adams. *Anatomy of a Satellite*. Boston: Little, Brown & Company, 1952.

Seton-Watson, Hugh. *From Lenin to Khrushchev*. New York: Frederick A. Praeger, Inc., 1960.

_____. *Nationalism and Communism; Essays 1946–1963*. New York: Frederick A. Praeger, Inc., 1964.

Shoup, Paul. "Communism, Nationalism and the Growth of the Communist Community of Nations after World War II," *American Political Science Review*, LVI, No. 4 (December, 1962).

Skendi, Stavro (ed.). *Albania*. New York: Frederick A. Praeger, Inc., 1956.

Skilling, H. Gordon. *Communism National and International; Eastern Europe after Stalin*. Toronto: University of Toronto Press, 1964.

_____. *The Governments of Communist East Europe*. New York: Thomas Y. Crowell Company, 1966.

Slusser, Robert (ed.). *Soviet Economic Policy in Postwar Germany*. New York: Research Program on the USSR, 1953.

Stehle, Hansjakob. *The Independent Satellite; Society and Politics in Poland since 1945*. New York: Frederick A. Praeger, Inc., 1965.

Syrop, Konrad. *Spring in October: The Story of the Polish Revolution of 1956*. New York: Frederick A. Praeger, Inc., 1958.

Taborsky, Edward. "The Revolt of the Communist Intellectuals," *Review of Politics*, XIX, No. 3 (July, 1957).

Toma, Peter A. "Revival of a Communist Party in Hungary," *The Western Political Quarterly*, XIV, No. 1, Part 1 (March, 1956).

United Nations General Assembly. *Report of the Special Committee on the Problem of Hungary*. New York: Columbia University Press, 1957.

United States Department of State, Bureau of Intelligence and Research. *World Strength of the Communist Party Organizations*. Washington, D.C.: Dept. of State, annually.

Whiting, Allen S. and Shih-Ts'ai Sheng. *Sinkiang: Pawn or Pivot?* East Lansing, Mich.: Michigan State University Press, 1958.

Zagoria, Donald S. (ed.). *Communist China and the Soviet Bloc. The Annals of the American Academy of Political and Social Science*, CCCILIX (September, 1963).

_____. *The Sino-Soviet Conflict, 1956–1961*. Princeton, N.J.: Princeton University Press, 1962.

Zinner, Paul E. (ed.). *National Communism and Popular Revolt in Eastern Europe*. New York: Columbia University Press, 1956.

Chapter VI. Institutions and Processes in the World Communist System

Brown, J. F. "Albania, Mirror of Conflict," *Survey*, No. 40 (January, 1962).

_____. "Rumania Steps Out Of Line," *Survey*, No. 49 (October, 1963).

Brzezinski, Zbigniew K. *The Soviet Bloc: Unity and Conflict*, rev. ed. New York: Frederick A. Praeger, Inc., 1961.

Burks, R. V. *The Dynamics of Communism in Eastern Europe*. Princeton, N.J.: Princeton University Press, 1961.

Cattell, David T. "Multilateral Co-operation and Integration In Eastern Europe," *Western Political Quarterly*, XIII, No. 1 (March, 1960).

Chamberlin, William Henry. "Communist Basic Tactics: Rule or Ruin," *Russian Review,* XX (January, 1961).

Deutsch, Karl W. *Political Community at the International Level.* New York: Doubleday & Company, Inc., 1954.

_____ et al. *Political Community and the North Atlantic Area.* Princeton, N.J.: Princeton University Press, 1957.

Dewar, Margaret. *Soviet Trade with Eastern Europe, 1945–1949.* London: Royal Institute of International Affairs, 1951.

Drachkovitch, Milorad M. (ed.). *The Revolutionary Internationals, 1864–1943.* Stanford: Stanford University Press, 1966.

Eckstein, Alexander. *Communist China's Economic Growth and Foreign Trade.* New York: McGraw-Hill Book Company, Inc., 1966.

Etzioni, Amitai. "The Dialectics of Supranational Unification," *American Political Science Review,* LVI, No. 4 (December, 1962).

Fischer-Galati, Stephen (ed.). *Eastern Europe in the Sixties.* New York: Frederick A. Praeger, Inc., 1963.

Gamarnikow, Michael. "Comecon Today," *East Europe,* XIII, No. 3 (March, 1964).

Garthoff, Raymond L. "The Concept of the Balance of Power in Soviet Policy-Making," *World Politics,* IV, No. 1 (October, 1951).

Ginsburgs, George. "Soviet Atomic Energy Agreements," *International Organization,* XI, No. 1 (Winter, 1961).

Griffith, William E. *Albania and the Sino-Soviet Rift.* Cambridge: M.I.T. Press, 1963.

_____. "An International Communism," *East Europe,* X, No. 7 (July, 1961).

Grzybowski, Kazimerz. *The Socialist Commonwealth of Nations.* New Haven: Yale University Press, 1964.

Holubnychy, V. "Soviet Economic Aid to North Korea," *Bulletin of the Institute for the Study of the USSR,* IV, No. 1 (January, 1957).

"Integrating the Satellites: The Role of COMECON," *East Europe,* VIII, No. 11 (November, 1959).

Jaster, Robert S. "CMEA's Influence on Soviet Policies in Eastern Europe," *World Politics,* XIV, No. 3 (April, 1962).

Kaser, Michael. *COMECON.* London: Oxford University Press, 1965.

Kecskemeti, Paul. *The Unexpected Revolution,* Stanford: Stanford University Press, 1961.

Kemeny, George. "Hungary and COMECON," *Survey,* No. 40 (January, 1962).

Kent, Nikolai. "Soviet Plans for Developing Heavy Industry in the Satellite Countries," *Bulletin of the Institute for the Study of the USSR,* VIII, No. 2 (February, 1961).

Kertesz, S. D. (ed.). *East Central Europe and the World.* Notre Dame, Ind.: University of Notre Dame Press, 1962.

Khrushchev, Nikita S. "Vital Questions of the Development of the World Socialist System," *World Marxist Review,* V, No. 9 (September, 1962).

Korbonski, Andrzej. "The Evolution of COMECON," *International Conciliation,* No. 549 (September, 1964).

Kulski, Wladyslaw W. "The Soviet System of Collective Security Compared with the Western System," *American Journal of International Law,* XLIV, No. 3 (July, 1950).

Lawson, Ruth C. *International Regional Organizations: Constitutional Foundations.* New York: Frederick A. Praeger, Inc., 1962.

Lenin, Vladimir I. *The Communist International.* Issued as Vol. 10 of Lenin's *Selected Works.* Moscow: Foreign Languages Publishing House, 1938.

London, Kurt L. "The 'Socialist Commonwealth'—Pattern for Communist World Organization," *Orbis,* III, No. 4 (Winter, 1960).

Miles, Edward L. with John S. Gillooly. *Processes of Interaction among the Fourteen Communist Party-States: An Exploratory Essay.* Stanford, Calif.: Stanford Studies of the Communist System, Research Paper No. 5 (March, 1965).

"The Military Strength of the USSR and the NATO Powers," *The Political Quarterly,* XXXI, No. 1 (January-March, 1960).

Mitchell, R. J. *A Theoretical Approach to the Study of Communist Organizations.* Stanford, Calif.: Stanford Studies of the Communist System, Research Paper No. 3, 1964.

———. *World Communist Community Building.* Stanford, Calif.: Stanford Studies of the Communist System, Research Paper No. 6, August, 1965.

Modelski, George. *Atomic Energy in the Communist Bloc.* London: Cambridge University Press, 1959.

Morris, Bernard S. "The Cominform: A Five-Year Perspective," *World Politics,* V, No. 3 (April, 1953),

Nollau, Gunther. *International Communism and World Revolution.* New York: Frederick A. Praeger, Inc., 1961.

Peaselee, Donald. *International Governmental Organizations.* The Hague: M. Nijhoff, 1956.

Pinder, John. "EEC and COMECON," *Survey,* No. 58 (January, 1966).

Pryor, Frederick L. *The Communist Foreign Trade System.* Cambridge: M.I.T. Press, 1963.

———. "Forms of Economic Co-Operation in the European Communist Bloc: A Survey," *Soviet Studies,* XI, No. 2 (1959).

Schenk, Fritz and Richard Lowenthal. "Politics and Planning in the Soviet Empire," *New Leader,* XLII, Nos. 1–3 (January, 1959).

Seton-Watson, Hugh and Zbigniew K. Brzezinski, *et al.* "The Communist Bloc— How United Is It?" *East Europe,* X, No. 11 (November, 1961).

Sievers, Bruce. *A Decision-Making Approach to the Study of the Communist System.* Stanford, Calif.: Stanford Studies of the Communist System, Research Paper No. 2, September, 1964.

Slusser, Robert M. and Jan F. Triska (eds.). *A Calendar of Soviet Treaties, 1917– 1957.* Stanford: Stanford University Press, 1959.

Sokolovski,, V. D. (ed.). *Soviet Military Strategy.* New York: Prentice-Hall, for the Rand Corporation, 1963.

Spulber, Nicholas. *The Economics of Communist Eastern Europe.* New York: John Wiley & Sons, Inc., 1957.

Staar, Richard F. "The East European Alliance System," *United States Naval Institute Proceedings,* XC, No. 9 (September, 1964).

Triska, Jan F. "Conflict and Integration in the Communist Bloc," *The Journal of Conflict Resolution,* V, No. 4 (December, 1961).

_____ and Robert M. Slusser. *The Theory, Law and Policy of Soviet Treaties.* Stanford: Stanford University Press, 1962.

United Nations, Economic Commission for Europe. *Economic Survey of Europe.* Geneva: United Nations, annually.

Wandycz, P. S. "The Soviet System of Alliances in East Central Europe," *Journal of Central European Affairs,* XVI, No. 2 (July, 1956).

Winston, Victor. "The Soviet Satellites—Economic Liability?" *Problems of Communism,* VII, No. 1 (January-February, 1958).

Wszelaki, Jan. *Communist Economic Strategy: The Role of East Central Europe.* Washington, D.C.: National Planning Association, 1959.

_____. "Economic Development in East-Central Europe, 1954–1959," *Orbis,* IV, No. 4 (Winter, 1961).

Zagoria, Donald S. (ed.). *Communist China and the Soviet Bloc. Annals of the American Academy of Political and Social Science,* CCCXLIX (September, 1963).

Zauberman, Alfred. "The CMEA (Council of Mutual Economic Aid), A Progress Report," *Problems of Communism,* IX, No. 4 (July-August, 1960).

_____. "Economic Integration: Problems and Prospects," *Problems of Communism,* VIII, No. 4 (July-August, 1959).

Zyzniewski, Stanley J. "Soviet Foreign Economic Policy," *Political Science Quarterly,* LXXIII, No. 2 (June, 1959).

Chapter VII. The Soviet Union and the Developing Areas

Alexander, Robert J. "Soviet and Communist Activities in Latin-America," *Problems of Communism,* X, No. 1 (January-February, 1961).

Allen, Robert L. *Soviet Economic Warfare.* Washington, D.C.: Public Affairs Press, 1960.

_____. "United Nations Technical Assistance: Soviet and East European Participation." *International Organization,* XI, No. 4 (Autumn, 1957).

Armstrong, John A. "The Soviet Attitude Toward UNESCO," *International Organization,* VIII, No. 2 (Spring, 1954).

Ball, William M. *Nationalism and Communism in East Asia,* rev. ed. London: Cambridge University Press, 1956.

Barghoorn, Frederick C. *The Soviet Cultural Offensive.* Princeton, N.J.: Princeton University Press, 1960.

_____. *Soviet Foreign Propaganda.* Princeton, N.J.: Princeton University Press, 1964.

Barnett, A. Doak (ed.). *Communist Strategies in Asia.* New York: Frederick A. Praeger, Inc., 1963.

Beim, David O. "The Communist Bloc and the Foreign Aid Game," *Western Political Quarterly,* XVII, No. 4 (December, 1964).

Berliner, Joseph. *Soviet Economic Aid.* New York: Frederick A. Praeger, Inc., 1958.

Bjelajac, Slavko N. "Soviet Activities in Underdeveloped Areas," *Military Review,* XLI, No. 2 (February, 1961).

Black, Cyril E. and Thomas P. Thornton (eds.). *Communism and Revolution: The Strategic Use of Political Violence.* Princeton, N.J.: Princeton University Press, 1964.

Brzezinski, Zbigniew K. (ed.). *Africa and the Communist World.* Stanford: Stanford University Press, 1963.

Conolly, Violet. *Soviet Economic Policy in the East*. London: Oxford University Press, 1933.

_____. *Soviet Trade from the Pacific to the Levant*. London: Oxford University Press, 1935.

Dinerstein, Herbert S. "Doctrines on Developing Countries: Some Divergent Views," in Kurt London (ed.). *New Nations in a Divided World*. New York: Frederick A. Praeger, Inc., 1963.

_____. "Rivalry in Underdeveloped Areas," *Problems of Communism*, XIII, No. 2 (March-April, 1964).

Eagleton, William, *The Kurdish Republic of 1946*. London: Oxford University Press, 1963.

Eudin, Xenia J. and Robert C. North. *Soviet Russia and the East, 1920–1927*. Stanford: Stanford University Press, 1957.

Eytan, Walter. *The First Five Years; Israel between East and West*. London: Weidenfeld and Nicholson, 1958.

Galay, N. "Zhukov in India," *Bulletin of the Institute for the Study of the USSR*, IV, No. 4 (April, 1957).

Goldman, Marshall I. "A Balance Sheet of Soviet Foreign Aid," *Foreign Affairs*, XLIII, No. 2 (January, 1965).

Gruliow, Leo (ed.). *Current Soviet Policies II*. New York: Columbia University Press, 1956.

_____. *Current Soviet Policies III*. New York: Columbia University Press, 1960.

Hammer, Ellen J. *The Struggle for Indochina*. Stanford: Stanford University Press, 1954.

Harrison, Selig S. *India: The Most Dangerous Decades*. Princeton, N.J.: Princeton University Press, 1960.

Hostler, Charles W. *Turkism and the Soviets*. New York: Frederick A. Praeger, Inc., 1957.

Jackson, D. Bruce. "Whose Man in Havana?" *Problems of Communism*. XV, No. 3 (May-June, 1966).

James, Daniel. *Red Design for the Americas: Guatemalan Prelude*. New York: The John Day Company, Inc., 1954.

Kolarz, Walter. *Communism and Colonialism*. New York: St. Martin's Press, 1964.

Kulski, Wladyslaw W. *Peaceful Coexistence*. Chicago: Henry Regnery Company, 1959.

Laqueur, Walter Z. "Communism and Nationalism in Tropical Africa," *Foreign Affairs*, XXXIX, No. 4 (July, 1961).

_____. *The Middle East in Transition*. New York: Frederick A. Praeger, Inc., 1958.

_____. *The Soviet Union and the Middle East*. New York: Frederick A. Praeger, Inc., 1959.

_____. "Towards National Democracy: Soviet Doctrine and the New Countries," *Survey*, No. 37 (July-September, 1961).

Lenczowski, George. *Russia and the West in Iran, 1918–1948; a Study in Big-Power Rivalry*. Ithaca, N.Y.: Cornell University Press, 1949.

Lenin, Vladimir I. *The National-Liberation Movement in the East*. Moscow: Foreign Languages Publishing House, 1957.

Mackintosh, J. M. *The Strategy and Tactics of Soviet Foreign Policy*. London: Oxford University Press, 1962.

McVey, Ruth T. *The Soviet View of the Indonesian Revolution: a Study in the Russian Attitude Towards Asian Nationalism.* Ithaca, N.Y.: Cornell University Press, 1957.

Madariaga, Salvador de. *Latin America between the Eagle and the Bear.* New York: Frederick A Praeger, Inc., 1961.

Morison, David L. *The USSR and Africa.* London: Oxford University Press, 1964.

Mosely, Philip E. "Soviet Policy in the Developing Countries," *Foreign Affairs,* XLIII, No. 1 (October, 1964).

Nollau, Gunther and Hans J. Wiehe. *Russia's South Flank: Soviet Operations in Iran, Turkey and Afghanistan.* New York: Frederick A. Praeger, Inc., 1963.

Overstreet, Gene D. and Marshall Windmiller. *Communism in India.* Berkeley: University of California Press, 1959.

Padmore, George. *Pan-Africanism or Communism? The Coming Struggle for Africa.* New York: Roy, 1956.

Pye, Lucian W. *Guerrilla Communism in Malaya; Its Social and Political Meaning.* Princeton, N.J.: Princeton University Press, 1956.

————. "Soviet and American Styles in Foreign Aid," *Orbis,* IV, No. 2 (Summer, 1960).

Ra'anan, Uri. "Moscow and the 'Third World'," *Problems of Communism,* XIV, No. 1 (January-February, 1965).

Randall, Francis and Laura Randall. "Communism in the High Andes," *Problems of Communism,* X, No. 1 (January-February, 1961).

Ravines, Eudocio. *The Yenan Way; the Kremlin's Penetration of South America.* New York: Charles Scribner's Sons, 1951.

Rubinstein, Alvin Z. *The Foreign Policy of the Soviet Union,* rev. ed. New York: Random House, 1966.

————. *The Soviets in International Organization.* Princeton, N.J.: Princeton University Press, 1964.

Saikowski, Charlotte and Leo Gruliow (eds.). *Current Soviet Policies IV.* New York: Columbia University Press, 1962.

Schneider, Ronald M. *Communism in Guatemala, 1944–1954.* New York: Frederick A. Praeger, Inc., 1958.

Shapiro, Samuel. "Selling Oil and Influencing People," *Problems of Communism,* X, No. 1 (January-February, 1961).

Simon, Maurice D. "Communist System Interaction with the Developing States, 1954–1962: A Preliminary Analysis." Stanford, Calif.: Stanford Studies of the Communist System, Research Paper No. 10, January, 1966.

Smith, Howard K. *et al. The Ruble War: A Study of Russia's Economic Penetration vs. U.S. Foreign Aid.* Buffalo, N.Y.: Smith, Keynes and Marshall, 1958.

Swarup, Ram. *Communism and Peasantry: Implications of Collectivist Agriculture for Asian Countries.* Calcutta: Prachi Prakashan, 1954.

"Text of Statement by Leaders of 81 Communist Parties After Meeting in Moscow," *The New York Times,* December 7, 1960.

Thornton, Thomas. "Peking, Moscow and the Underdeveloped Areas," *World Politics,* XIII, No. 4 (July, 1961).

Toynbee, Arnold. "Impressions of Afghanistan and Pakistan's North-West Frontier In Relation To The Communist World," *International Affairs,* XXXVII, No. 2 (April, 1961).

United States Department of State, *Intervention of International Communism in Guatemala.* Washington, D.C.: Government Printing Office, 1954.

Van Wagenen, Richard W. *The Iranian Case, 1946.* New York: Carnegie Endowment for International Peace, 1952.

Wolf, Charles Jr. "Soviet Economic Aid in Southeast Asia, Threat or Windfall?" *World Politics,* X, No. 1 (October, 1957).

Young, Cuyler T. "The Race Between Russia and Reform in Iran," *Foreign Affairs,* XXVIII, No. 2 (January, 1950).

Zagoria, Donald. "Sino-Soviet Friction in Underdeveloped Areas," *Problems of Communism,* X, No. 2 (March-April, 1961).

Chapter VIII. The Soviet Union and the West

Abel, Elie. *The Cuban Missile Crisis.* Philadelphia: J. B. Lippincott Company, 1966.

Albrecht, Andrze. *The Rapacki Plan—New Aspects.* Warsaw: Zachodnia Agencja Prasowa, 1963.

Angell, Robert C. with Virginia S. Dunham and J. David Singer. "Social Values and Foreign Policy Attitudes of Soviet and American Elites," *Journal of Conflict Resolution,* VIII, No. 4 (December, 1964).

Australia, Royal Commission on Espionage. *Report of the Royal Commission on Espionage,* 22nd August 1955. Sidney: Commonwealth of Australia, 1955.

Barghoorn, Frederick C. *The Soviet Image of the United States; a Study in Distortion.* New York: Harcourt, Brace & World, Inc., 1950.

_____. "The Soviet View of America," *Orbis,* II, No. 1 (Spring, 1958).

Bechhoefer, Bernhard G. *Postwar Negotiations for Arms Control.* Washington, D.C.: Brookings Institution, 1961.

Beim, David O. "The Communist Bloc and the Foreign Aid Game," *Western Political Quarterly,* XVII, No. 4 (December, 1964).

Bishop, Donald G. *The Roosevelt-Litvinov Agreements.* Syracuse: Syracuse University Press, 1965.

Boulding, Kenneth E. *Conflict and Defense: a General Theory.* New York: Harper & Row, Publishers, Inc., 1962.

Bronfenbrenner, Urie. "The Mirror Image in Soviet-American Relations: A Social Psychologist's Report," *Journal of Social Issues,* XVII, No. 3 (1961).

Canada, Royal Commission to Investigate Disclosures of Secret and Confidential Information to Unauthorized Persons. *The Report of the Royal Commission to Investigate Disclosures of Secret and Confidential Information to Unauthorized Persons.* Ottawa: E. Cloutier, 1946.

Carr, Edward H. *The Soviet Impact on the Western World.* New York: The Macmillan Company, 1949.

Dallin, Alexander *et al. The Soviet Union and Disarmament; an Appraisal of Soviet Attitudes and Intentions.* New York: Frederick A. Praeger, Inc., for the School of International Affairs, Columbia University, 1964.

Dallin, David J. "Methods of Soviet Diplomacy," *Modern Age,* V, No. 4 (Fall, 1961).

_____. *Soviet Espionage.* New Haven: Yale University Press, 1955.

Davidson, W. Phillips. *The Berlin Blockade.* Princeton, N.J.: Princeton University Press, 1958.

De Gramont, Sanche. *The Secret War; the Story of International Espionage since World War II.* New York: G. P. Putnam's Sons, 1962.

Dennett, Raymond, and Joseph E. Johnson (eds.). *Negotiating with the Russians.* The Hague: Martinus Nijhoff for the World Peace Foundation, 1951.

Dulles, Allen W. *The Craft of Intelligence.* New York: Harper & Row, Publishers, Inc., 1963.

Galay, Nikolai. "The Lessons of Vienna," *Bulletin of the Institute for the Study of USSR,* VIII, No. 7 (July, 1961).

Garthoff, Raymond L. *Soviet Strategy in the Nuclear Age,* rev. ed. New York: Frederick A. Praeger, Inc., 1962.

Gehlen, Michael P. *The Politics of Coexistence.* Bloomington, Ind.: Indiana University Press, 1967.

Ginsburgs, George. "Neutrality and Neutralism and the Tactics of Soviet Diplomacy," *American Slavic and East European Review,* XIX, No. 4 (December, 1960).

Iklé, Fred Charles. *How Nations Negotiate.* New York: Harper and Row, Publishers, Inc., 1964.

Ingram, David. *The Communist Economic Challenge.* New York: Frederick A. Praeger, Inc., 1965.

Joy, Charles Turner. *How Communists Negotiate.* New York: The Macmillan Company, 1955.

Kahn, Herman, *On Escalation; Metaphors and Scenarios.* New York: Frederick A. Praeger, Inc., 1965.

_____. *On Thermonuclear War.* Princeton, N.J.: Princeton University Press, 1961.

Kaznacheev, Aleksandr. *Inside a Soviet Embassy.* Philadelphia: J. B. Lippincott Company, 1962.

Kennan, George F. "America and the Russian Future," *Foreign Affairs,* XXIX, No. 3 (April, 1951).

_____. *Russia, the Atom and the West.* New York: Harper & Row, Publishers, Inc., 1958.

_____ ("X"). "The Sources of Soviet Conduct," *Foreign Affairs,* XXV, No. 4 (July, 1947).

Kertesz, Stephen D. "Reflections on Soviet and American Negotiating Behavior," *Review of Politics,* XIX, No. 1 (January, 1947).

Korovin, E. A. "The USSR and Disarmament," *International Conciliation,* No. 292 (September, 1933).

Kovner, Milton. *The Challenge of Coexistence: a Study of Soviet Economic Diplomacy.* Washington, D.C.: Public Affairs Press, 1961.

Krivitsky, Walter (pseud.). *In Stalin's Secret Service.* New York: Harper & Row, Publishers, Inc., 1939.

Kulski, W. W. "Soviet Diplomatic Techniques," *Russian Review,* XIX, No. 3 (July, 1960).

Laserson, Max M. "Russia and the World: A Soviet Review of Diplomacy," *International Conciliation,* No. 429 (March, 1947).

Liska, George. *International Equilibrium.* Cambridge: Harvard University Press, 1957.

Mazour, Anatole. *Finland between East and West.* Princeton, N.J.: D. Van Nostrand Company, Inc., 1956.

McClelland, Charles A. "The Acute International Crisis." *World Politics,* XIV, No. 1 (October, 1961).

————. "General Systems in the Study and Control of Conflict," in Elton B. McNeil (ed.). *The Nature of Human Conflict.* Englewood Cliffs, N.J.: Prentice-Hall, Inc., 1965.

McNeill, William H. *America, Britain and Russia: Their Cooperation and Conflict, 1942–1946.* N.Y.: Oxford University Press for the Royal Institute of International Affairs, 1953.

Mosely, Philip E. "Is It Peaceful or Coexistence?" *The New York Times Magazine,* May 7, 1961.

Noel-Baker, Philip J. *The Arms Race: a programme for World Disarmament.* London: Stevens, 1958.

North, Robert C. with Howard E. Koch, Jr., and Dina A. Zinnes. "The Integrative Function of Conflict," *Journal of Conflict Resolution,* IV, No. 3 (September, 1960).

Osgood, Charles E. *An Alternative to War or Surrender.* Urbana, Ill.: University of Illinois Press, 1962.

Roberts, Henry L. *Russia and America; Dangers and Prospects.* New York: Harper & Row, Publishers, Inc., 1956.

Schelling, Thomas C. and Morton H. Halpering. *Strategy and Arms Control.* New York: Twentieth Century Fund, 1961.

Scott, Andrew M. "Challenge and Response: A Tool for the Analysis of International Affairs," *Review of Politics,* XVIII, No. 2 (April, 1956).

Standley, William H. and Arthur A. Ageton. *Admiral Ambassador to Russia.* Chicago: Henry Regnery Company, 1955.

Strausz-Hupé, Robert *et al. Protracted Conflict.* New York: Harper & Row, Publishers, Inc., 1959.

Taracouzia, Timothy A. *War and Peace in Soviet Diplomacy.* New York: The Macmillan Company, 1940.

Truman, Harry S. *Memoirs.* Garden City, N.Y.: Doubleday & Company, Inc., 1955–1956.

United Nations Secretariat. *Historical Survey of the Activities of the League of Nations Regarding the Question of Disarmament 1920–1937.* New York: United Nations, 1951.

Vatcher, William H. *Panmunjom; the Story of the Korean Military Armistice Negotiations.* New York: Frederick A. Praeger, Inc., 1958.

Wheeler, Harvey. "The Role of Myth Systems in American Soviet Relations," *Conflict Resolution,* IV, No. 2 (June, 1960).

Whelan, Joseph G. "The U.S. and Diplomatic Recognition: The Contrasting Cases of Russia and Communist China," *China Quarterly,* No. 5 (January-March, 1961).

Wilcox, Francis O. "Soviet Diplomacy: A Challenge to Freedom," *Annals of the American Academy of Political and Social Science,* CCCXXIV (July, 1959).

Wise, David and Thomas B. Ross. *The U-2 Affair.* New York: Random House, Inc., 1962.

Wolfe, Thomas W. *Soviet Strategy at the Crossroads.* Cambridge: Harvard University Press, 1964.

Zinnes, Dina A. with Robert C. North, and Howard E. Koch, Jr. "Capability, Threat and the Outbreak of War," in James N. Rosenau (ed.). *International Politics and Foreign Policy*. New York: Free Press of Glencoe, 1961.

Chapter IX. The Soviet Union: Reckless or Cautious?

Aspaturian, Vernon V. "Dialectics and Duplicity in Soviet Diplomacy," *Journal of International Affairs*, XVIII, No. 1 (1963).

Atkinson, J. W. "Motivational Determinants of Risk-Taking Behavior," in J. W. Atkinson (ed.). *Motives in Fantasy, Action and Society*. Princeton, N.J.: D. Van Nostrand Company, Inc., 1958.

Barghoorn, Frederick C. *The Soviet Cultural Offensive: The Role of Cultural Diplomacy in Soviet Foreign Policy*. Princeton, N.J.: Princeton University Press, 1960.

Bauer, Raymond. *The New Man in Soviet Psychology*. Cambridge: Harvard University Press, 1952.

Borch, L. A., Jr. "The Effects of Threat in Bargaining: Critical and Experimental Analysis," *Journal of Abnormal and Social Psychology*, LXVI, No. 1 (January, 1963).

Carter, Charles Frederick *et al.* (eds.). *Uncertainty and Business Decisions: The Logic, Philosophy and Psychology of Business Decision-Making under Uncertainty: A Symposium*, 2nd ed. Liverpool: Liverpool University Press, 1957.

Cohen, John and Mark Hansel. *Risk and Gambling; the Study of Subjective Probability*. New York: Philosophical Library, Inc., 1956.

Cramer, Harold. *Collective Risk Theory: A Survey of the Theory from the Point of View of Theory of Stochastic Processes*. Stockholm: Nordiska bokhandein, 1955.

Dallin, Alexander. *The Soviet Union and the United Nations: An Inquiry into Soviet Motives and Objectives*. New York: Frederick A. Praeger, Inc., 1962.

Deutsch, Morton. "The Effect of Motivational Orientation Upon Trust and Suspicion," *Human Relations*, XIII, No. 2 (May, 1960).

Egarton, R. D. *Investment Decision under Uncertainty*. Liverpool: Liverpool University Press, 1960.

Ekeblad, Frederick R. *The Statistical Method in Business*. New York: John Wiley & Sons, Inc., 1962.

Farrar, Donald. *The Investment Decision under Uncertainty*. Englewood Cliffs, N.J.: Prentice-Hall, Inc., 1952.

Festinger, Leon. "A Theory of Social Comparison Processes," *Human Relations*, VII, No. 2 (May, 1954).

Good, Isidore J. *Probability and the Weighing of Evidence*. London: Charles Griffin & Co. Ltd., 1950.

Hardy, Charles. *Risk and Risk-Bearing*. Chicago: University of Chicago Press, n.d. [c. 1931].

Kneale, W. *Probability and Induction*. Oxford: Clarendon Press, 1949.

Knight, Frank. *Risk, Uncertainty and Profit*. Boston: Houghton Mifflin Company, 1921.

Loomis, James L. "Communication, the Development of Trust and Cooperative Behavior," *Human Relations*, XII, No. 4 (August, 1959).

Lowenthal, Richard. "After Cuba, Berlin?" *Encounter,* XIX, No. 6 (December, 1962).

McDonald, John. *Strategy in Poker, Business and War.* New York: W. W. Norton & Company, Inc., 1950.

Mackintosh, J. M. *Strategy and Tactics of Soviet Foreign Policy.* London: Oxford University Press, 1962.

Rapoport, A. and C. Orwant. "Experimental Games: A Review," *Behavioral Science,* VII, No. 1 (January, 1962).

Scodel, Alvin with J. S. Minas, P. Ratoosh, and M. Lipetz. "Some Descriptive Aspects of Two-person, Non-Zero-Sum Games," *Journal of Conflict Resolution,* III, No. 2 (June, 1959).

Shackle, George L. S. *Decision, Order and Time in Human Affairs.* Cambridge: Cambridge University Press, 1961.

———. *Expectations in Economics,* 2nd ed. Cambridge: Cambridge University Press, 1952.

Shulman, Marshall D. *Stalin's Foreign Policy Reappraised.* Cambridge: Harvard University Press, 1963.

Social Science and Research Council, Committee on Business Enterprise and Research. *Expectations, Uncertainty and Business Behavior.* New York: Social Science Research Council, 1958.

Solomon, Leonard. "The Influence of Some Types of Power Relationships and Game Strategies on the Development of Inter-Personal Trust," *Journal of Abnormal and Social Psychology,* LXI, No. 2 (September, 1960).

Von Neumann, John and Oskar Morgenstern. *Theory of Games and Economic Behavior.* Princton, N.J.: Princeton University Press, 1947.

Chapter X. The Soviet Union and International Organization

Allen, Robert L. "United Nations Technical Assistance: Soviet and East European Participation," *International Organization,* XI, No. 4 (Fall, 1957).

Armstrong, John A. "The Soviet Attitude Toward UNESCO," *International Organization,* VIII, No. 2 (Spring, 1954).

Armstrong, Hamilton F. "U.N. On Trial," *Foreign Affairs,* XXXIX, No. 3 (April, 1961).

Dallin, Alexander. *The Soviet Union at the United Nations.* New York: Frederick A. Praeger, Inc., 1962.

Davis, Kathryn (Wasserman). *The Soviets at Geneva: the U.S.S.R. and the League of Nations, 1919–1933.* Geneva: Librarie Kundig, 1934.

Emerson, Rupert and Inis L. Claude, Jr. "The Soviet Union and the United Nations: An Essay in Interpretation," *International Organization,* VI, No. 1 (Winter, 1952).

Fleming, D. F. "The Soviet Union and Collective Security," *Journal of Politics,* X, No. 1 (February, 1948).

Frankel, J. "The Soviet Union and the United Nations," in *Yearbook of World Affairs,* VIII (1954).

Fuller, C. Dale. "Lenin's Attitude Toward an International Organization for the Maintenance of Peace, 1914–1917," *Political Science Quarterly,* LXIV, No. 2 (June, 1949).

———. "Soviet Policy in the United Nations," *Annals of the American Academy of Political and Social Sciences.* CCLXIII (May, 1949).

Gardner, Richard N. *In Pursuit of World Order*. New York: Frederick A. Praeger, Inc., 1964.

Garthoff, Raymond L. "War and Peace in Soviet Policy," *Russian Review,* XX, No. 2 (April, 1961).

Goodman, Elliott R. "Cry of National Liberation: Recent Soviet Attitudes Toward National Self-Determination," *International Organization,* XIV, No. 1 (Winter, 1960).

_____. *The Soviet Design for a World State*. New York: Columbia University Press, 1960.

_____. "The Soviet Union and World Government," *Journal of Politics,* XV, No. 2 (May, 1953).

Gross, Leo. "Was the Soviet Union Expelled From the League of Nations?" *Yale Law Journal,* LV (1946).

Jacobson, Harold K. "The USSR and ILO," *International Organization,* XIV, No. 3 (Summer, 1960).

_____. *The U.S.S.R. and the UN's Economic and Social Activities*. Notre Dame: University of Notre Dame Press, 1963.

Johnson, Joseph E. "The Soviet Union, the United States, and International Security," *International Organization,* III, No. 1 (Winter, 1949).

Juviler, Peter H. "Interparliamentary Contacts in Soviet Foreign Policy," *American Slavic and East European Review,* XX, No. 1 (February, 1961).

Korovin, E. A. "The USSR and Disarmament," *International Conciliation,* CCCXCII (September, 1933).

Kozhevnikov, F. I. (ed.). *International Law*. Moscow: Foreign Languages Publishing House, n.d. [1961].

Litvinoff, Maxim. *Against Aggression*. London: Lawrence and Wishart, 1939.

Osborn, Frederick. "The USSR and the Atom," *International Organization,* V, No. 3 (August, 1951).

Prince, Charles. "Current Views of the USSR on the International Organization of Security, Economic Cooperation and International Law, a Summary," *American Journal of International Law,* XXXIX, No. 3 (July, 1945).

_____. "The USSR and International Organizations," *American Journal of International Law,* XXXVI, No. 3 (July, 1942).

Rubinstein, Alvin Z. *The Soviets in International Organizations: Changing Policy toward Underdeveloped Countries, 1953–1963*. Princeton, N.J.: Princeton University Press, 1964.

_____. "Soviet Policy in ECAFE: A Study of Soviet Behavior in International Economic Organization," *International Organization,* XII, No. 4 (Autumn, 1958).

_____. "Soviet Policy Toward Under-Developed Areas in the Economic and Social Council," *International Organization,* IX, No. 2 (Spring, 1955).

Rudzinski, Alexander W. "Soviet Peace Offensives," *International Conciliation,* No. 490 (April, 1953).

Chapter XI. The Soviet Union and International Law: International Treaties

Baade, Hans W. (ed.). *The Soviet Impact on International Law. Law and Contemporary Problems,* XXIX, No. 4 (Autumn, 1964).

Chakste, Mintauts. "Soviet Concepts of the State, International Law and Sovereignty," *American Journal of International Law,* XLIII, No. 1 (January, 1949).

Florinsky, Michael T. "The Soviet Union and International Agreements," *Political Science Quarterly,* LXI, No. 1 (March, 1946).

Ginsburgs, George. "A Calendar of Soviet Treaties, January-December, 1960," *Ost Europa Recht,* IX (1963).

———. "A Calendar of Soviet Treaties, January-December 1961," *Ost Europa Recht,* X (1964).

———. "A Calendar of Soviet Treaties, January-December 1962," *Ost Europa Recht,* XI (1965).

———. "Soviet Atomic Energy Agreements," *International Organization,* XV, No. 1 (Winter, 1961).

Hazard, John N. "Cleansing Soviet International Law of Anti-Marxist Theories," *American Journal of International Law,* XCI, No. 1 (January, 1946).

———. "The Soviet Conception of International Law," *Proceedings, American Society of International Law* (1939).

———. "The Soviet Union and International Law," *Soviet Studies,* I, No. 3 (January, 1950).

Kelsen, Hans. *The Communist Theory of Law.* New York: Frederick A. Praeger, Inc., 1955.

Korovin, Eugene A. "The Second War and International Law," *American Journal of International Law,* XL, No. 4 (October, 1946).

Kozhevnikov, F. I. (ed.). *International Law.* Moscow: Foreign Languages Publishing House, n.d. [1961].

Kulski, Wladyslaw W. "Soviet Comments on International Law and International Relations," *American Journal of International Law,* XIV–XLVIII, L (1951–1954).

Lapenna, Ivo. *Conceptions Sovietiques de Droit International Public.* Paris: Pedone, 1954.

Levin, D. B. "Foreign Policy of the USSR and International Law," *USSR Information Bulletin* (January 14, 1948).

Lissitzyn, Oliver J. "Recent Soviet Literature on International Law," *American Slavic and East European Review,* IX, No. 2 (April, 1952).

Margolis, Emanuel. "Soviet Views on the Relationship Between National and International Law," *International and Comparative Law Quarterly,* IV, No. 1 (January, 1955).

Schapiro, L. B. "The Soviet Concept of International Law," in *Yearbook of World Affairs.* London: Stevens, for the London Institute of World Affairs, 1948, II.

Schlesinger, Rudolph. "Soviet Theories of International Law," *Soviet Studies,* IV, No. 3 (January, 1953).

Slusser, Robert M. and George Ginsburgs. "A Calendar of Soviet Treaties, January-December 1958," *Ost Europa Recht,* VII (1961).

——— and ———. "A Calendar of Soviet Treaties, January-December 1959," *Ost Europa Recht,* VIII (1962).

——— and Jan F. Triska. *A Calendar of Soviet Treaties, 1917–1957.* Stanford: Stanford University Press, 1959.

——— and ———. "Professor Krylov and Soviet Treaties," *American Journal of International Law,* LI, No. 4 (October, 1957).

Taracouzio, Timothy A. "The Effect of Applied Communism on the Principles of International Law," *Proceedings, American Society of International Law* (1934).

_____. *The Soviet Union and International Law: A Study Based on the Legislation, Treaties and Foreign Relations of the Union of Soviet Socialist Republics.* New York: The Macmillan Company, 1935.

Triska, Jan F. "The Soviet Law of Treaties," *Proceedings, the American Society of International Law* (1959).

_____ and Robert M. Slusser. "Ratification of Treaties in Soviet Theory, Practice and Policy," *The British Yearbook of International Law,* XXXIV (1959).

_____ and _____. *The Theory, Law and Policy of Soviet Treaties.* Stanford: Stanford University Press, 1962.

_____ and _____. "Treaties and Other Sources of Order in International Relations: The Soviet View," *The American Journal of International Law,* LII, No. 4 (October, 1958).

Tucker, Robert C. "Russia, the West and World Order," *World Politics,* XII, No. 1 (October, 1959).

Tunkin, Grigori I. *Co-existence and International Law. Recueil des Cours* (Academie de Droit International), XCV (1958).

United States Senate, Committee on the Judiciary, Subcommittee to Investigate the Administration of the Internal Security Act and Other Security Laws, 84th Congress, 2nd Session. *Soviet Political Agreements and Results.* Washington, D.C.: Government Printing Office, 1956.

appendix # THE CHARTER OF THE COUNCIL
VI–I   ON MUTUAL ECONOMIC AID

(*Vedomsti Verkhovnogo Soveta SSSR,* No. 15, April 21, 1960, pp. 162–170; translated from *Current Digest of the Soviet Press,* published weekly at Columbia University by the Joint Committee on Slavic Studies, XII, No. 23 (July 6, 1960), 9–11; copyright 1960 by the Joint Committee on Slavic Studies, reprinted by permission.)

The governments of the People's Republic of Albania, the People's Republic of Bulgaria, the Hungarian People's Republic, the German Democratic Republic, the Polish People's Republic, the Rumanian People's Republic, the U.S.S.R. and the Czechoslovak Republic,

Taking into account that successful economic cooperation among their countries fosters the most rational development of the national economy, an increase in the population's living standard and a strengthening of the unity and solidarity of these countries;

Fully determined to continue developing comprehensive economic cooperation on the basis of the consistent implementation of the international socialist division of labor in the interests of building socialism and communism in their countries and ensuring a stable peace throughout the world;

Convinced that the development of economic cooperation among their countries contributes to the achievement of the aims defined by the Charter of the United Nations;

Affirming their readiness to develop economic ties with all countries, regardless of their social and state systems, on the basis of equality, mutual benefit and noninterference in one another's internal affairs;

Recognizing the ever growing role of the Council on Mutual Economic Aid in the organization of economic cooperation among their countries;

Hereby agree, with these aims, to adopt this Charter.

Article I. AIMS AND PRINCIPLES

1. The Council on Mutual Economic Aid shall have the aim of contributing, through the unification and coordination of the efforts of the member countries of the Council, to the planned development of the national economies and an acceleration of economic and technical progress in these countries; to increasing the level of industrialization of countries with a less developed industry; to an uninterrupted rise in labor productivity; and to a steady advance in the well-being of the peoples of the member countries of the Council.

2. The Council on Mutual Economic Aid shall be based on the principles of the sovereign equality of all the member countries of the Council.

The economic and scientific-technical cooperation of the member countries of the

Council shall be carried out in accordance with the principles of complete equality of rights, respect for sovereignity and national interests, mutual benefit and comradely mutual aid.

Article II. MEMBERSHIP

1. The charter members of the Council on Mutual Economic Aid shall be the countries signing and ratifying this Charter.

2. Admission to membership in the Council shall be open to other countries of Europe that share the ideas and principles of the Council and have agreed to assume the obligations contained in this Charter.

Admission of new members shall be carried out by decision of a session of the Council on the basis of official requests by countries for admission to membership in the council.

3. Any member country of the Council may withdraw from the Council by notifying the depositary of this Charter. This notification shall enter into force six months after its receipt by the depositary. The depositary shall inform the member countries of the Council upon receiving such notification.

4. The member countries of the Council agree:

(a) to ensure the fulfillment of the recommendations of agencies of the Council adopted by them;

(b) to give the Council and its officials the necessary assistance in the fulfillment of the functions stipulated in this Charter;

(c) to provide the Council with materials and information necessary for accomplishing the tasks entrusted to it;

(d) to inform the Council of the progress of fulfillment of recommendations adopted in Council.

Article III. FUNCTIONS AND POWERS

1. In accordance with the aims and principles stipulated in Article I of this Charter, the Council on Mutual Economic Aid:

(a) shall organize:

the comprehensive economic and scientific-technical cooperation of the member countries of the Council with a view to the most rational utilization of their mutual resources and to acceleration of the development of production forces;

the preparation of recommendations on major questions of economic ties stemming from the plans for development of the national economies of the member countries of the Council, with a view to coordinating these plans;

the study of economic problems of interest to the member countries of the Council.

(b) shall help the member countries of the Council in working out and implementing joint measures in the following spheres;

the development of the industry and agriculture of the member countries of the Council on the basis of consistent implementation of international socialist division of labor and specialization and cooperation in production;

the development of transport with the aim, first and foremost, of ensuring increased shipments of export-import and transit freight of the member countries of the Council;

the most effective utilization of the capital investments allocated by the member countries of the Council for the construction of projects being built on the basis of joint participation;

the development of trade and the exchange of services among the member countries of the Council themselves and with other countries;

the exchange of scientific-technical achievements and advanced production experience;

(c) shall undertake other activities necessary for achievement of the aims of the Council.

2. In the person of its agencies acting within the limits of their competence, the Council on Mutual Economic Aid shall be empowered to adopt recommendations and decisions in accordance with this Charter.

Article IV. RECOMMENDATIONS AND DECISIONS

1. Recommendations shall be adopted on questions of economic and scientific-technical cooperation. Recommendations shall be communicated to the member countries of the Council for their consideration.

The member countries of the Council shall carry out the recommendations adopted by them upon the decisions of the governments or the competent agencies of these countries in accordance with their legislation.

2. Decisions shall be adopted on organizational and procedural questions. Decisions shall enter into force, if not otherwise stipulated in the decisions themselves, on the day of the signing of the protocol of the meeting of the corresponding agency of the Council.

3. All recommendations and decisions of the Council shall be adopted only with the concurrence of the member countries of the Council concerned, and each country shall have the right to declare its interest in any question being considered in the Council.

Recommendations and decisions shall not extend to countries that have expressed their disinterest in the given question. However, any of these countries may subsequently subscribe to the recommendations and decisions adopted by the other member countries of the Council.

Article V. AGENCIES

1. In order to carry out the functions and powers stipulated in Article III of this Charter, the Council on Mutual Economic Aid shall have the following basic agencies:

a Session of the Council,

a Conference of Representatives of Countries in the Council,

Permanent Commissions,

a Secretariat.

2. Other agencies that may prove necessary shall be established in accordance with this Charter.

Article VI.   THE SESSION OF THE COUNCIL

1. The Session of the Council shall be the highest agency of the Council on Mutual Economic Aid. It shall be empowered to discuss all questions falling within the competence of the Council and to adopt recommendations and decisions in accordance with this Charter.

2. The Session of the Council shall consist of delegations from all the member countries of the Council. The composition of the delegation of each country shall be determined by the government of that country.

3. Regular Sessions of the Council shall be convened twice a year, rotating among the capitals of the member countries of the Council and presided over by the head of the delegation of the country in which the Session is meeting.

4. An extraordinary Session of the Council may be called at the request or with the agreement of at least one-third of the member countries of the Council.

5. The Session of the Council:

(a) shall examine:

proposals on questions of economic and scientific-technical cooperation submitted by the member countries of the Council and also by the Conference of Representatives of Countries in the Council, the Permanent Commissions and the Secretariat of the Council;

the report of the Secretariat of the Council on the work of the Council;

(b) shall determine the direction of work of the other agencies of the Council and basic questions of the agenda for the subsequent Session of the Council;

(c) shall carry out other functions that prove necessary for achieving the aims of the Council.

6. The Session of the Council shall be empowered to establish such agencies as it considers necessary for carrying out the functions entrusted to the Council.

7. The Session of the Council shall establish its own rules of procedure.

Article VII.   THE CONFERENCE OF REPRESENTATIVES OF COUNTRIES IN THE COUNCIL

1. The Conference of Representatives of Countries in the Council on Mutual Economic Aid shall consist of representatives of all member countries of the Council, one from each country.

The representative of a country in the Council shall have, at the seat of the Secretariat of the Council, a deputy, the necessary number of advisers, and other staff workers. Upon authorization of the respresentative, the deputy shall carry out the functions of the representative in the Conference.

2. The Conference shall hold its meetings as the need arises.

3. The Conference shall have the right, within the limits of its competence, to adopt recommendations and decisions in accordance with this Charter. The Conference may also submit proposals for the consideration of the Session of the Council.

4. The Conference:

(a) shall examine the proposals of member countries of the Council, the Permanent Commissions and the Secretariat of the Council on ensuring implementation of the recommendations and decisions of the Session of the Council and also other questions of economic and scientific-technical cooperation requiring decisions in the period between Sessions of the Council.

(b) Shall, when necessary, discuss in advance proposals of the member countries of the Council and also of the Permanent Commissions and Secretariat of the Council on questions of the agenda for the subsequent Session of the Council;

(c) shall coordinate the work of the Permanent Commissions of the Council and shall examine their reports on work done and on future activities;

(d) shall approve:

the staffs and budget of the Secretariat of the Council and also the report of the Secretariat of the Council on execution of the budget;

the Regulations on the Permanent Commissions and the Secretariat of the Council;

(e) shall establish control agencies for checking on the financial activity of the Secretariat of the Council;

(f) shall carry out other functions stemming from this Charter, and also the recommendations and decisions of the Session of the Council.

5. The Conference may create auxiliary agencies for the preliminary preparation of questions.

6. The Conference shall establish its own rules of procedure.

Article VIII. THE PERMANENT COMMISSIONS

1. The Permanent Commissions of the Council on Mutual Economic Aid shall be established by the Session of the Council with the aim of contributing to the further development of economic ties between the member countries of the Council and to organizing comprehensive economic and scientific-technical cooperation in individual branches of the national economies of these countries.

The Regulations on the Permanent Commissions shall be approved by the Conference of Representatives of Countries in the Council.

2. Each member country of the Council shall appoint its representatives to the Permanent Commissions.

3. The Permanent Commissions shall have the right, within the limits of their competence, to adopt recommendations and decisions in accordance with this Charter. The Commissions may also submit proposals for examination by the Session of the Council and the Conference of Representatives of Countries in the Council.

4. The Permanent Commissions shall work out measures and prepare proposals on implementation of the economic and scientific-technical cooperation stipulated in point 1 of this article, and shall also carry out other functions stemming from this Charter and from the recommendations and decisions of the Session of the Council and the Conference of Representatives of Countries in the Council.

The Permanent Commissions shall submit annual reports on work done and on their future activities to the Conference of Representatives of Countries in the Council.

5. Meetings of the Permanent Commissions shall be conducted as a rule at their permanent seats, which shall be determined by the Sessions of the Council.

6. The Permanent Commissions may, when necessary, create auxiliary agencies. The composition and competence of these agencies, as well as the place of their meetings, shall be determined by the Commissions themselves.

7. Each Permanent Commission shall have a secretariat, headed by the secretary of the Commission. The apparatus of the secretariat of a Commission shall be a part of the Secretariat of the Council and shall be maintained at the expense of its budget.

8. The Permanent Commissions shall establish their own rules of procedure.

Article IX. THE SECRETARIAT

1. The Secretariat of the Council on Mutual Economic Aid shall consist of a Secretary of the Council, his deputies and such personnel as may be needed for carrying out the functions entrusted to the Secretariat.

The Secretary and his deputies shall be appointed by the Session of the Council and shall direct the work of the Secretariat of the Council. The personnel of the Secretariat shall be recruited from among citizens of the member countries of the Council in accordance with the Regulations on the Secretariat of the Council.

The Secretary of the Council shall be the chief official of the Council. He shall represent the Council before the officials and organizations of the member countries of the Council and of other countries, and also before international organizations. The Secretary of the Council may empower his deputies, and also members of the Secretariat staff, to act on his behalf.

The Secretary and his deputies may take part in all meetings of agencies of the Council.

2. The Secretariat of the Council:

(a) shall present a report on the work of the Council at the regular Session of the Council;

(b) shall assist in the preparation and conduct of the Session of the Council, the Conference of Representatives of countries in the Council, meetings of the Permanent Commissions of the Council, and conferences convened upon the decision of these agencies of the Council;

(c) shall prepare, upon the instructions of the Session of the Council or the Conference of Representatives of Countries in the Council, economic surveys and studies based on materials of the member countries of the Council, and also shall publish materials on questions of economic and scientific-technical cooperation of these countries;

(d) shall prepare:

Proposals on questions of the work of the Council for consideration by the appropriate agencies of the Council;

informational and reference materials on questions of the economic and scientific-technical cooperation of these countries;

(e) shall organize, jointly with the Permanent Commissions of the Council, the preparation of drafts of multilateral agreements on questions of economic and scientific-technical cooperation on the basis of recommendations and decisions of the Session of the Council and the Conference of Representatives of Countries in the Council;

(f) shall undertake other activities stemming from this Charter, from recommendations and decisions adopted in the Council, and from the Regulations on the Secretariat of the Council.

3. The Secretary of the Council, his deputies and the personnel of the Secretariat shall act as international officials in carrying out their official duties.

4. The seat of the Secretariat of the Council shall be in Moscow.

Article X. Participation by Other Countries in the Work of the Council

The Council on Mutual Economic Aid may invite countries that are not members of the Council to take part in the work of agencies of the Council.

The conditions under which representatives of these countries may participate in the work of agencies of the Council shall be determined by the Council in agreement with the respective countries.

Article XI. Relations with International Organizations

The Council on Mutual Economic Aid may establish and support relations with economic organizations of the United Nations and with other international organizations.

The character and form of these relations shall be determined by the Council in agreement with the respective international organizations.

Article XII. Financial Questions

1. The member countries of the Council on Mutual Economic Aid shall bear the expenses incurred in the maintenance of the Secretariat and the financing of its work. The share of each member country in these expenses shall be determined by the Session in Council, and other financial questions shall be determined by the Conference of Representatives of Countries in the Council.

2. The Secretariat of the Council shall present to the Conferences of Representatives of Countries in the Council a report on execution of the budget for each calendar year.

3. The expenses incurred by the participants in the Session of the Council, the Conference of Representatives of Countries in the Council, meetings of the Permanent Commissions of the Council and conferences conducted within the framework of the Council shall be borne by the countries represented at these meetings and conferences.

4. The expenses incurred in connection with the meetings and conferences mentioned in point 3 of this article shall be borne by the country in which these meetings and conferences are held.

Article XIII. Various Enactments

1. The Council on Mutual Economic Aid shall enjoy on the territory of each member country of the Council the capacity necessary for carrying out its functions and achieving its aims.

2. The Council, as well as the representatives of the member countries of the Council and officials of the Council, shall enjoy on the territory of each of these

countries the privileges and immunities that are necessary to carry out the functions and achieve the aims stipulated by this Charter.

3. The capacity, privileges and immunities mentioned in this article shall be determined by a special Convention.

4. The regulations of this Charter shall not affect the rights and duties of the member countries of the Council stemming from their membership in other international organizations or from international agreements concluded by them.

Article XIV. LANGUAGES

The official languages of the Council on Mutual Economic Aid shall be the languages of all the member countries of the Council.

The working language of the Council shall be Russian.

Article XV. RATIFICATION AND ENTERING INTO FORCE OF THE CHARTER

1. This Charter shall be subject to ratification by the signatory countries in accordance with their constitutional procedures.

2. The instruments of ratification shall be deposited with the depositary of this Charter.

3. The Charter shall enter into force immediately upon deposit of the instruments of ratification by all the countries signatory to this Charter, which fact the depositary shall communicate to these countries.

4. With respect to any country that, in accordance with point 2 of Article II of this Charter, may be accepted in the Council on Mutual Economic Aid and ratifies this Charter, the Charter shall enter into force on the day of deposit by this country of the document on ratification of the Charter, which fact the depositary shall communicate to the other member countries of the Council.

Article XVI. PROCEDURE FOR AMENDING THE CHARTER

Any member country of the Council on Mutual Economic Aid may submit a proposal on amending this Charter.

Amendments to the Charter approved by the Session of the Council shall enter into force immediately upon deposit with the depositary of the documents on ratification of these amendments by all the member countries of the Council.

Article XVII. CONCLUDING ENACTMENTS

This Charter shall be drawn up in one copy in the Russian language. The Charter shall be deposited with the government of the U.S.S.R., which shall distribute certified copies of the Charter to the governments of all the other member countries of the Council and shall also inform these governments and the Secretary of the Council of the deposit of the instruments of ratification with the government of the U.S.S.R.

In witness thereof, the representatives of the governments of the member countries of the Council on Mutual Economic Aid have signed this Charter.

Concluded in Sofia on December 14, 1959.

A. KELLEZI, by authorization of the government of the People's Republic of Albania.

R. DAMYANOV, by authorization of the government of the People's Republic of Bulgaria.

A. APRO, by authorization of the government of the Hungarian People's Republic.

B. LEISHNER, by authorization of the government of the German Democratic Republic.

P. JAROSIEWICZ, by authorization of the government of the Polish People's Republic.

A. BIRLEDEANU, by authorization of the government of the Rumanian People's Republic.

A. KOSYGIN, by authorization of the government of the U.S.S.R.

O. SIMUNEK, by authorization of the government of the Czechoslovak Republic.

***

In accordance with Article IV of this Charter, the Charter of the Council on Mutual Economic Aid entered into force on April 13, 1960.

appendix

VI–II

THE CONVENTION ON CAPACITY, PRIVILEGES AND IMMUNITIES OF THE COUNCIL ON MUTUAL ECONOMIC AID

(*Vedomsti Verkhovnogo Soveta SSR,* No. 15, April 21, 1960, pp. 170–173; translated from *Current Digest of the Soviet Press,* published weekly at Columbia University by the Joint Committee on Slavic Studies, XII, No. 23 (July 6, 1960), 11–12; copyright 1960 by the Joint Committee on Slavic Studies, reprinted by permission.)

The governments of the People's Republic of Albania, the People's Republic of Bulgaria, the Hungarian People's Republic, the German Democratic Republic, the Polish People's Republic, the Rumanian People's Republic, the U.S.S.R. and the Czechoslovak Republic,

taking into account Article XIII of the Charter of the Council on Mutual Economic Aid, which stipulates

that the Council shall enjoy on the territory of each member country of the Council the capacity necessary for carrying out its functions and achieving its aims,

that the Council, as well as the representatives of the member countries of the Council and officials of the Council, shall enjoy on the territory of each of these countries the privileges and immunities that are necessary for carrying out the functions and achieving the aims stipulated in said Charter, and

that the aforementioned capacity, privileges and immunities shall be determined by a special Convention,

have agreed on the following:

Article I. CAPACITY

The Council on Mutual Economic Aid is a legal person and shall be empowered:
(a) to conclude agreements;
(b) to acquire, lease and alienate property;
(c) to appear in court.

Article II. PROPERTY, ASSETS AND DOCUMENTS

1. The premises of the Council on Mutual Economic Aid shall be inviolable. Its property, assets and documents, regardless of where located, shall enjoy immunity from any form of administrative or court interference, except when the Council itself shall waive immunity in any specific case.

2. The Council on Mutual Economic Aid shall be exempt from the payment of all direct taxes and dues, both statewide and local. This regulation shall not apply with respect to payments for communal and similar services.

3. The Council on Mutual Economic Aid shall be exempt from the payment of customs duties and from restrictions on the import of goods intended for official use.

Article III. PRIVILEGES AS REGARDS COMMUNICATIONS

The Council on Mutual Economic Aid shall enjoy, within the territory of each of the member countries of the Council, no less favorable conditions with respect to priority, tariffs and rates in postal, telegraph and telephone communications than those enjoyed by the diplomatic representatives of the respective countries.

Article IV. REPRESENTATIVES OF THE MEMBER COUNTRIES OF THE COUNCIL

1. In carrying out their official duties in agencies of the Council and also at conferences conducted within the framework of the Council, representatives of the member countries of the Council shall be granted the following privileges and immunities within the territory of each member country of the Council:

(a) immunity from personal arrest or detention and also from the jurisdiction of legal institutions with respect to all acts that might be committed by them in the capacity of representatives;

(b) inviolability of all papers and documents;

(c) the same customs privileges regarding personal baggage as are granted to staff members of equivalent rank of diplomatic representations in the given country;

(d) exemption from conscription and from the payment of direct taxes and duties with respect to salaries paid to the representatives by the country that has appointed them.

2. In addition to the privileges and immunities stipulated in point 1 of this article, the representatives of countries in the Council and their deputies shall enjoy the privileges and immunities granted to diplomatic representatives in the given country.

3. The privileges and immunities stipulated in this article shall be granted to the aforementioned officials solely in official interests. Each member country of the Council shall have the right and shall be obligated to withdraw the immunity of its representatives in all cases in which, in the opinion of this country, immunity interferes with the administration of justice and withdrawal of immunity does not impair the aims in connection with which it was granted.

4. The provisions of points 1 and 2 of this article shall not apply to the relations between a representative and agencies of the country of which he is a citizen.

5. The concept "representative" in this article shall include representatives of the countries in the Council and their deputies; heads, members and secretaries of delegations; and advisers and experts.

Article V. OFFICIALS OF THE COUNCIL

1. Upon the representation of the Secretary of the Council, the Conference of Representatives of Countries in the Council on Mutual Economic Aid shall determine the categories of officials to whom the provisions of this article shall apply.

The names of such officials shall be periodically reported to the component agencies of the member countries of the Council by the Secretary of the Council.

2. On the territory of each member country of the council, officials of the Council:

(a) shall not be legally or administratively liable for any acts they may commit in their capacity as officials;

(b) shall be exempt from conscription;

(c) shall be exempt from the payment of direct taxes and duties with respect to salaries paid to them by the Council;

(d) shall have the right to the same customs privileges with respect to their personal baggage as are granted to staff members of equivalent rank of the diplomatic representations in the given country.

3. In addition to the privileges and immunities stipulated in point 2 of this article, the Secretary of the Council and his deputies shall enjoy the privileges and immunities granted to diplomatic representatives in the given country.

4. The privileges and immunities stipulated in this article shall be granted to the aforementioned persons solely in the interests of the Council and independently of the execution by these persons of their official functions. The Secretary of the Council shall have the right and shall be obliged to withdraw immunity granted to any official in cases in which, in his opinion, immunity interferes with the administration of justice and can be withdrawn without impairing the interests of the Council. With respect to the Secretary of the Council and his deputies, the right to withdraw immunity shall rest with the Conference of Representatives of Countries in the Council.

5. The provisions of point 2(b) and (c) of this article shall not apply to officials of the Council who are citizens of the country in which the agency of the Council in which these persons work is located.

Article VI. CONCLUDING ENACTMENTS

1. This Convention shall be subject to ratification by the member countries of the Council in accordance with their constitutional procedures.

2. The instruments of ratification shall be deposited with the depositary of this Convention.

3. The Convention shall enter into force immediately upon deposit of the instruments of ratification by all the member countries of the Council signatory to this Convention, which fact the depositary shall communicate to these countries.

4. With respect to any country that in accordance with point 2 of Article II of the Charter of the Council on Mutual Economic Aid, may be admitted to the Council, this Convention shall enter into force on the day of deposit by this country of the document on ratification of the Convention, which fact the depositary shall communicate to the member countries of the Council.

5. This Convention shall be drawn up in one copy in the Russian language. The Convention shall be deposited with the government of the U.S.S.R., which shall distribute certified copies of the Convention to the governments of all the other member countries of the Council and shall also inform these governments and the Secretary of the Council of the deposit of the instruments of ratification with the government of the U.S.S.R.

In witness thereof, the representatives of the governments of the member countries of the Council on Mutual Economic Aid have signed this Convention.
Concluded in Sofia on December 14, 1959.

A. KELLEZI, by authorization of the government of the People's Republic of Albania.

R. DAMYANOV, by authorization of the government of the People's Republic of Bulgaria.

A. APRO, by authorization of the government of the Hungarian People's Republic.

B. LEISHNER, by authorization of the government of the German Democratic Republic.

P. JAROSIEWICZ, by authorization of the government of the Polish People's Republic.

A. BIRLEDEANU, by authorization of the government of the Rumanian People's Republic.

A. KOSYGIN, by authorization of the government of the U.S.S.R.

C. SIMUNEK, by authorization of the government of the Czechoslovak Republic.

***

In accordance with Article VI of this Convention, the Convention on the Capacity, Privileges and Immunities of the Council on Mutual Economic Aid entered into force on April 13, 1960.

TREATY OF FRIENDSHIP, CO-OPERATION AND MUTUAL ASSISTANCE (THE WARSAW TREATY), 14 MAY 1955

(Reprinted from *Documents on International Affairs,* published by Oxford University Press under the auspices of the Royal Institute of International Affairs (London: Oxford University Press, 1958), pp. 193–197, by permission.)

The contracting parties,

Reaffirming their desire for the organization of a system of collective security in Europe, with the participation of all the European states, irrespective of their social and state systems, which would make it possible to combine their efforts in the interests of securing peace in Europe,

Taking into consideration at the same time the situation obtaining in Europe as the result of ratification of the Paris agreements, which provide for the formation of a new military grouping in the shape of the 'Western European Union' together with a remilitarised Western Germany, and for the integration of Western Germany in the North Atlantic bloc, which increases the threat of another war and creates a menace to the national security of the peaceloving states,

Convinced that, under these circumstances, the peaceloving states of Europe should take the necessary measures for safeguarding their security, and in the interests of maintaining peace in Europe,

Guided by the purposes and principles of the United Nations Charter,

In the interests of further strengthening and promoting friendship, co-operation and mutual assistance, in accordance with the principles of respect for the independence and sovereignty of states, and also with the principle of non-interference in their internal affairs,

Have resolved to conclude this Treaty of Friendship, Co-operation and Mutual Assistance, and have appointed as their authorised representatives:

The Presidium of the People's Assembly of the People's Republic of Albania—Mehmet Shehu, Chairman of the Council of Ministers of the People's Republic of Albania,

The Presidium of the People's Assembly of the People's Republic of Bulgaria—Vylko Chervenkov, Chairman of the Council of Ministers of the People's Republic of Bulgaria,

The Presidium of the Hungarian People's Republic—Andras Hegedus, Chairman of the Council of Ministers of the Hungarian People's Republic,

The President of the German Democratic Republic—Otto Grotewohl, Prime Minister of the German Democratic Republic,

The State Council of the Polish People's Republic—Joseph Cyrankiewicz,

Chairman of the Council of Ministers of the Polish People's Republic,

The Presidium of the Grand National Assembly of the Rumanian People's Republic—Gheorghe Gheorghiu-Dej, Chairman of the Council of Ministers of the Rumanian People's Republic,

The Presidium of the Supreme Soviet of the Union of Soviet Socialist Republics —Nikolai Alexandrovich Bulganin, Chairman of the Council of Ministers of the U.S.S.R.,

The President of the Czechoslovak Republic—Viliam Siroky, Prime Minister of the Czechoslovak Republic,

Who, having presented their credentials, found to be executed in due form and in complete order, have agreed on the following:

Article 1

The contracting parties undertake, in accordance with the Charter of the United Nations Organisation, to refrain in their international relations from the threat or use of force, and to settle their international disputes by peaceful means so as not to endanger international peace and security.

Article 2

The contracting parties declare their readiness to take part, in the spirit of sincere co-operation, in all international undertakings intended to safeguard international peace and security and they shall use all their energies for the realisation of these aims.

Moreover, the contracting parties shall work for the adoption, in agreement with other states desiring to co-operate in this matter, of effective measures towards a general reduction of armaments and prohibition of atomic, hydrogen and other weapons of mass destruction.

Article 3

The contracting parties shall take council among themselves on all important international questions relating to their common interests, guided by the interests of strengthening international peace and security.

They shall take council among themselves immediately, whenever, in the opinion of any of them, there has arisen the threat of an armed attack on one or several states that are signatories of the treaty, in the interests of organising their joint defence and of upholding peace and security.

Article 4

In the event of an armed attack in Europe on one or several states that are signatories of the treaty by any state or group of states, each state that is a party to this treaty shall, in the exercise of the right to individual or collective self-defence in accordance with Article 51 of the Charter of the United Nations Organisation, render the state or states so attacked immediate assistance, individually and in agreement with other states that are parties to this treaty, by all the means it may consider necessary, including the use of armed force. The states that are parties to this treaty shall immediately take council among themselves concerning the necessary joint measures to be adopted for the purpose of restoring and upholding international peace and security.

In accordance with the principles of the Charter of the United Nations Organisation, the Security Council shall be advised of the measures taken on the basis of the present article. These measures shall be stopped as soon as the Security Council has taken the necessary measures for restoring and upholding international peace and security.

Article 5

The contracting parties have agreed on the establishment of a joint command for their armed forces, which shall be placed by agreement among these parties, under this command, which shall function on the basis of jointly defined principles. They shall also take other concerted measures necessary for strengthening their defence capacity, in order to safeguard the peaceful labour of their peoples, to guarantee the inviolability of their frontiers and territories and to provide safeguards against possible aggression.

Article 6

For the purpose of holding the consultations provided for in the present treaty among the states that are parties to the treaty, and for the purpose of considering problems arising in connection with the implementation of this treaty, a political consultative committee shall be formed in which each state that is a party to this treaty shall be represented by a member of the government, or any other specially appointed representative.

The committee may form the auxiliary organs for which the need may arise.

Article 7

The contracting parties undertake not to participate in any coalitions and alliances, and not to conclude any agreements the purposes of which would be at variance with those of the present treaty.

The contracting parties declare that their obligations under existing international treaties are not at variance with the provisions of this treaty.

Article 8

The contracting parties declare that they will act in the spirit of friendship and co-operation with the object of furthering the development of, and strengthening the economic and cultural relations between them, adhering to the principles of mutual respect for their independence and sovereignty, and of non-interference in their internal affairs.

Article 9

The present treaty is open to be acceded to by other states—irrespective of their social and state systems—which may express their readiness to assist, through participation in the present treaty, in combining the efforts of the peaceloving states for the purpose of safeguarding the peace and security of nations. This act of acceding to the treaty shall become effective, with the consent of the states that are parties to this treaty, after the instrument of accedence has been deposited with the government of the Polish People's Republic.

Article 10

The present treaty is subject to ratification, and the instruments of ratification shall be deposited with the government of the Polish People's Republic.

The treaty shall take effect on the date on which the last ratification instrument is deposited. The government of the Polish People's Republic shall advise the other states that are parties to the treaty of each ratification instrument deposited with it.

Article 11

The present treaty shall remain in force for 20 years. For the contracting parties which will not have submitted to the government of the Polish People's Republic a statement denouncing the treaty a year before the expiration of its term, it shall remain in force throughout the following ten years.

In the event of the organisation of a system of collective security in Europe and the conclusion of a general European treaty of collective security to that end, which the contracting parties shall unceasingly seek to bring about, the present treaty shall cease to be effective on the date the general European treaty comes into force.

Done in Warsaw, on May 1, 1955, in one copy each in the Russian, Polish, Czech, and German languages, all the texts being equally authentic. Certified copies of the present treaty shall be transmitted by the government of the Polish People's Republic to all the parties to this treaty.

In witness whereof the authorised representatives have signed the present treaty and have affixed thereto their seal

    By authorisation of the Presidium of the People's Assembly of the People's Republic of Albania—Mehmet Shehu,

    By authorisation of the Presidium of the People's Assembly of the People's Republic of Bulgaria—Vylko Chervenkov,

    By authorisation of the Presidium of the Hungarian People's Republic—Andras Hegedus,

    By authorisation of the President of the German Democratic Republic—Otto Grotewohl,

    By authorisation of the State Council of the Polish People's Republic—Joseph Cyrankiewicz,

    By authorisation of the Presidium of the Grand National Assembly of the Rumanian People's Republic—Gheorghe Gheorghiu-Dej,

By authorisation of the Presidium of the Supreme Soviet of the Union of Soviet Socialist Republics—Nikolai Alexandrovich Bulganin,

By authorisation of the President of the Czechoslovak Republic—Viliam Siroky.

A CALENDAR OF SOVIET ECONOMIC AID TO THE DEVELOPING STATES, 1954—1962*

Developing States-Dates	*Details*	*Sources*
AFGHANISTAN		
1/54	$3.5 million credit, 3% interest, five years repayment for two grain elevators, three electric—four grinding—mills, bread-baking factory.	Mikesell, Appendix II. Berliner, p. 198. Billerbeck, p. 116. State 6632, p. 83.
7/54	$1.2 million loan for a 60–mile gasoline pipeline, oil-storage tanks.	Berliner, p. 198. Billerbeck, p. 116. Mikesell, Appendix II.
8/54	$2.0 million credit for road-building equipment.	Mikesell, Appendix II. Berliner, p. 198.
12/54	$1.0 million estimated loan for cotton-processing equipment.	Berliner, p. 198. Mikesell, Appendix II.
5/55	$2.1 million, no interest for construction of asphalt factory, cement plant, paving of streets of Kabul.	Mikesell, Appendix II. Berliner, p. 198. State 6632, p. 83. Billerbeck, p. 116.
1/56	$100 million loan, 2% interest for building of two hydroelectric plants, three motor-repair shops, a physical-chemistry laboratory, chemical-fertilizer plant, highway over Hindu Kush, three irrigation dams, construction of airport.	Berliner, p. 198. Mikesell, Appendix II. State 145, p. 25. UN, p. 233. Billerbeck, p. 116. State 6632, p. 83.
1959	$129.0 million grant to assist in building a 470-mile road.	State 43, p. 21. Billerbeck, p. 115. State 145, p. 25.
1961	$196.0 million loan for use during Second Five-Year Plan; petroleum exploitation and power development.	State 43, p. 21. State 145, p. 25. USIA.

* Modified from Simon, "Communist System Interaction with the Developing States, 1954–1962: A Preliminary Analysis" (Stanford, Calif.: Stanford Studies of the Communist System, 1966), pp. 59–75. Mimeographed.

A Calendar of Soviet Economic Aid (*cont'd.*)

Developing States-Dates	*Details*	*Sources*
BURMA		
1/57	$29.8 million as interest loan to build an institute of technology, a hospital, and a polyclinic, a theater, and a sports center. To be repaid over twenty years by rice deliverie.	Billerbeck, p. 119. State 6632, p. 70.
1/58	$7.0 million credit, $2\frac{1}{2}\%$ interest, twelve years repayment. To build two irrigation dams and a farm-implement factory.	Billerbeck, p. 119. Mikesell, Appendix II. State 6632, p. 71. State 43, p. 24.
CAMBODIA		
1957	$6.0 million estimated gift to assist in the building of a hospital.	Billerbeck, p. 121. State 145, p. 27. State 43, p. 24.
1961	$30.0 million credit, repayable in twelve years at $2\frac{1}{2}\%$ interest for exploratory work and planning of irrigation and hydroelectric projects; equipment for, and technical assistance in, building of iron and steel plant, tire plant, and so on.	UN, p. 233.
ETHIOPIA		
1959	$1.8 million grant for the construction of a technical school, completed and dedicated in 1963.	State 43, p. 30. State 145, p. 34. Billerbeck, p. 154.
7/59	$100 million credit, twelve years repayment for the construction of an oil refinery, a gold-processing plant, geological and mineral surveys, and a feasibility study for a metallurgical plant.	State 43, p. 30. UN, p. 233. Ebert, p. 13. Billerbeck, p. 154. State 145, p. 33.
GHANA		
8/60	$42.0 million credit, twelve years repayment for construction of industrial enterprises, power stations, prospecting, vocational training.	UN, p. 233. Hamrell & Widstrand, p. 116. Ebert, p. 13. State 145, p. 34.
11/61	$42.2 million credit for the construction of plants for the production of building material, cotton, and paper factories.	Hamrell & Widstrand, p. 116.

A Calendar of Soviet Economic Aid (*cont'd.*)

Developing States-Dates	*Details*	*Sources*
GUINEA		
1959	$35.0 million for construction of factories, a polytechnical institute, agricultural production development, prospecting. Twelve years repayment, 2½% interest.	UN, p. 233. Billerbeck, p. 77. Ebert, p. 13. State 145, p. 33. State 43, p. 30.
1960	$21.5 million credit to aid river projects.	State 43, p. 30. State 145, p. 33.
INDIA		
2/55	$115.5 million credit repayable in twelve years at 2½% interest for Bhilai steel works.	Billerbeck, p. 129. Berliner, p. 200. State 6632, p. 90. State 145, p. 25.
1955	$2.0 million estimate for file-manufacturing plant.	Berliner, p. 200.
12/55	$.5 million for twenty drilling rigs for coal mining.	Mikesell, Appendix II.
4/56	$16.8 million for Bhilai steel works at 2½% interest and repayable in twelve years.	Billerbeck, p. 130. State 6632, p. 90. Berliner, p. 200. Mikesell, Appendix II.
6/56	$3.6 million for equipment for oil industry.	Billerbeck, p. 130. Berliner, p. 200. State 6632, p. 91. Mikesell, Appendix II.
6/56	$5.0 million for Bhilai steel plant.	Mikesell, Appendix II.
6/56	$10.0 million for equipment for diamond mine, geological survey, and training of Indian personnel.	Berliner, p. 200. Mikesell, Appendix II.
9/57	$20.0 million credit for development of pharmaceutical industry.	Billerbeck, p. 131.
11/57	$125.0 million for five development projects: engineering works for heavy machinery in Ranchi, engineering works for mining machinery, a power station, optical-lens factory, development of Korba coal mine. Repayment in twelve years at 2½% interest.	State 43, p. 22. State 145, p. 25. UN, p. 233. Ebert, p. 13. Berliner, p. 200. State 6632, p. 90.
9/59	$25.0 million for a petroleum refinery in Barauni.	Billerbeck, p. 132.

A Calendar of Soviet Economic Aid (*cont'd.*)

Developing States-Dates	*Details*	*Sources*
2/60	$375.0 million credit; twelve years repayment at 2½% interest for Third Five-Year Plan.	Billerbeck, p. 130. UN, p. 233. Ebert, p. 13. State 43, p. 22. State 145, p. 25. UN, p. 234.
1961	$125.0 million credit for Third Five-Year Plan; twelve-year repayment.	UN, p. 233. State 145, p. 25. State 43, p. 22. UN, p. 233.

INDONESIA

9/56	$100.0 million to build a metallurgical works, a superphosphate factory, highways, organization and equipment of rice plantations. Twelve years repayment, 2½% interest.	Billerbeck, p. 134. State 43, p. 23. UN, p. 233. Ebert, p. 13. Berliner, p. 200. State 145, p. 26. Mikesell, Appendix II.
1957	$8.0 million for the supply of 4,000 jeeps. To be repaid within five years.	Billerbeck, p. 133. Ebert, p. 13. State 6632, p. 78.
6/59	$17.5 million for a sports stadium and a navigation school; 2½% interest repayable within twelve years.	Billerbeck, p. 134. UN, p. 233. Ebert, p. 13.
1960	$250 million for industrial plants, especially for the iron and steel industry, metallurgical works, plant for the chemical and textile industries, and atomic-energy establishments; 2½% interest repayable in seven years.	Billerbeck, p. 234. State 43, p. 23. UN, p. 233. Ebert, p. 13. State 145, p. 26.
1961	$367.0 million for industrial development including enterprises in iron and steel, nonferrous metals, chemicals, and textile industries, development of agriculture, utilization of atomic energy for peaceful purposes.	UN, p. 233.
1962	$1.4 million for industrial development.	UN, p. 233.

A Calendar of Soviet Economic Aid (*cont'd.*)

Developing States-Dates	Details	Sources
IRAQ		
3/59	$137.5 million credit for economic development.	Billerbeck, p. 135. State 43, p. 27. State 145, p. 20. UN, p. 233. Ebert, p. 13.
1960	$45.0 million credit for a major rehabilitation of the Basra-Baghdad Railway.	State 43, p. 27. State 145, p. 30. UN, p. 233. Ebert, p. 13.
MALI		
3/61	$44.5 million for geological prospecting work, improvement of navigation of Niger River, sports stadium, building of Mali-Guinea railway, cement works, and a school. Twelve years repayment.	Hamrell & Widstrand, p. 116. Ebert, p. 13. State 145, p. 34.
NEPAL		
1959	$6.4 million for hydroelectric power station, a sugar factory, a cigarette factory, and a hospital. Specialists from USSR to aid in preparatory work for road-building.	Billerbeck, p. 146. State 375. Ebert, p. 13.
1961	$8.0 million credit.	UN, p. 233.
PAKISTAN		
1961	$30 million credit for oil exploration; twelve years repayment, $2\frac{1}{2}\%$ interest.	State 43, p. 25. State 145, p. 28. UN, p. 233. Ebert, p. 13.
SOMALI REPUBLIC		
6/61	$52.0 million credit for the establishment of a seed-production and plant-breeding center, a deep-water harbor in Berbera, building of a dairy and a meat-production collective.	Hamrell & Widstrand, p. 117. Ebert, p. 13. UN, p. 233. State 145.

A Calendar of Soviet Economic Aid (*cont'd.*)

Developing States-Dates	*Details*	*Sources*
SUDAN		
11/61	$22.0 million for construction of four canning factories and an asbestos cement works, for geological research work, and for schools for vocational training.	State 43, p. 32. State 145, p. 35. Hamrell & Widstrand, p. 117. UN, p. 234. Ebert, p. 13.
SYRIA		
3/56	$3.0 million estimated loan for grain-storage facilities, oil tanks, a cement plant.	Berliner, p. 201. Mikesell, Appendix II.
10/57	$150 million credit, $2\frac{1}{2}\%$ interest, twelve years repayment; nineteen projects representing all of Syria's important development projects.	Billerbeck, p. 147. State 43, p. 26. UN, p. 234. Ebert, p. 13. Berliner, p. 201.
TUNISIA		
8/61	$27.8 million credit for construction of hydroengineering works and the building and equipment of an institute of technology at the University of Tunis.	Hamrell & Widstrand, p. 117. UN, p. 234. State 43. State 145, p. 135. Ebert, p. 13.
TURKEY		
7/57	$10.0 million credit for a sheet-glass factory.	State 145, p. 31. State 6632, p. 64.
9/57	$5.0 million estimated credit for a caustic soda and calcium plant.	Berliner, p. 201.
UAR (EGYPT)		
2/56	$2.0 million estimated credit for nuclear-physics laboratory.	Berliner, p. 199. Mikesell, Appendix II.
1956	$2.8 million gift.	State 6632, p. 45.
1/58	$175.0 million credit at $2\frac{1}{2}\%$ interest, to be repaid in twelve years in goods or cash for sixty-five development projects.	Billerbeck, p. 152. Berliner, p. 200. Mikesell, Appendix II. State 6632.
2/59	$100.0 million loan at $2\frac{1}{2}\%$ interest, twelve years repayment for first stage of Aswan Dam construction.	Billerbeck, p. 152. UN, p. 233. State 43, p. 25. State 145.

A Calendar of Soviet Economic Aid (*cont'd.*)

Developing States-Dates	Details	Sources
1960	$225.0 million to assist in latter stages of Aswan Dam project. Twelve years repayment, $2\frac{1}{2}\%$ interest.	State 43, p. 25. State 145, p. 28. UN, p. 233. Billerbeck, p. 152. Ebert, p. 13.
1962	$170.0 million, twelve years repayment for construction and expansion of enterprises in metallurgical, machine-building, oil, electric power, food, and other industries, prospecting, vocational training, Aswan Dam project, development of communications.	UN, p. 233.

YEMEN

1956	$25.0 million credit for port construction, fifteen years repayment at $2\frac{1}{2}\%$ interest.	State 43, p. 26. State 145, p. 30. Berliner, p. 201. Billerbeck, p. 150. Mikesell, Appendix II. Ebert, p. 13.
1958	$25.0 million for road-building, construction of irrigation plants, a nationwide geological survey, fifteen years repayment, $2\frac{1}{2}\%$ interest.	Billerbeck, p. 150. State 6632, p. 60.

ABBREVIATIONS

Berliner: Joseph S. Berliner, *Soviet Economic Aid, The New Aid and Trade Policy in Underdeveloped Countries* (New York: Frederick A. Praeger, Inc., 1958).

Billerbeck: Klaus Billerbeck, *Soviet Bloc Foreign Aid to Underdeveloped Countries, An Analysis and a Prognosis* (Hamburg: Hamburg Archives of World Economy, 1960).

Ebert: Freidrich-Ebert Institute, *The Soviet Bloc and the Developing Countries* (Hanover, Germany: The Freidrich-Ebert Institute, 1962).

Hamrell and Widstrand: Sven Hamrell and Carl G. Widstrand, eds., *The Soviet Bloc, China, and Africa* (Uppsala: The Scandinavian Institute of African Studies, 1964).

Lewin: Pauline Lewin, *The Foreign Trade of Communist China* (New York: Frederick A. Praeger, Inc., 1964).

Mikesell: Raymond F. Mikesell and Jack N. Behrman, *Financing Free World Trade with the Sino-Soviet Bloc* (Princeton: Princeton Studies in International Finance, 1958).

State 43: U.S. Department of State, *The Communist Economic Offensive Through 1963* (Washington, D.C.: Bureau of Intelligence and Research Memorandu.n RSB–43, June 18, 1964).

State 145: U.S. Department of State, *The Sino-Soviet Economic Offensive Through June 1962* (Washington, D.C.: Bureau of Intelligence and Research Memorandum RSB–145, 1963).

State 375: U.S. Department of State, *Communist China's Economic Offensive in the Less Developed Countries* (Washington, D.C.: Department of State Publication 6632, May, 1958).

UN: United Nations Economic Conference, *Trade between the Centrally Planned Economies and Developing Countries* (Geneva: United Nations Conference on Trade and Development, 1964), Appendix Table V.

appendix

VII–II

Communist Exports to Selected Less Developed Countries, 1961–1963[a]* (in millions of current U.S. dollars)

Area and Country	Total Communist 1961	1962	1963	USSR 1961	1962	1963	East European Countries 1961	1962	1963	Communist China 1961	1962	1963
Total	1,132.5	1,241.0	1,410.4	354.9	428.2	481.5	560.7	577.4	651.0	210.7	235.5	274.4
Latin America	*140.9*	*110.6*	*115.7*	*31.1*	*40.4*	*41.0*	*108.7*	*68.4*	*72.6*	*1.8*	*1.8*	*2.1*
Argentina	47.6	23.4	15.5	11.9	8.2	3.5	37.8	15.0	11.9	.1c	1.2	0.1
Brazil	70.3	65.3	75.6	19.2	31.8	37.1	51.1	31.1	37.7	.1	.4	0.9
Chile	1.5	2.7	3.4	c	c	0.1	1.5	2.6	3.3	c	c	c
Colombia	5.0	4.7	5.0	c	c	c	4.9	4.7	4.9	.1	c	c
Ecuador	.7	.1	n.a.	—	—	n.a.	.6	c	n.a.	.1	—	n.a.
Guiana	1.4	.6	n.a.	—	—	n.a.	1.4	.5	n.a.	—	.06	n.a.
Honduras	—	1.3	1.7	—	—	—	—	1.3	1.7	—	—	—
Jamaica	—	.6	.1	—	—	—	—	.6	.1	—	—	c
Mexico	3.1	1.2	2.5	.3	c	0.1	1.7	1.1	2.4	1.1	c	c
Peru	1.2	1.5	1.4	c	c	c	1.2	1.5	1.4	c	c	c
Surinam	—	1.0	1.2	—	—	c	—	.3	.3	—	.7	.9
Uruguay	4.1	3.0	1.8	.9	.3	0.2	3.2	2.7	1.6	c	c	c
Venezuela	5.7	5.3	4.8	c	c	c	5.3	5.0	4.6	.4	.3	0.2
Middle East	*400.6*	*406.9*	*439.3*	*153.7*	*131.2*	*139.1*	*205.1*	*241.8*	*261.8*	*37.4*	*33.9*	*38.0*
Aden	2.7	3.9	4.5	c	c	0.6	2.6	3.8	3.7	c	.07	0.1
Cyprus	3.2	6.2	5.1	1.7	1.7	2.0	1.5	4.5	3.1	—	—	—
Greece	50.4	54.8	68.5	19.9	20.3	28.4	30.4	34.4	40.0	.1	.06	0.1
Iran	42.1	22.4	30.8	18.3	13.8	14.5	15.3	8.6	16.3	8.5	c	0.1
Iraq	43.0	58.8	62.2	12.0	24.3	26.2	21.6	25.2	23.5	6.3	9.2	12.5

	1	2	3	4	5	6	7	8	9	10	11	12
Middle East (cont'd.)												
Israel	6.7	8.5	13.4	.3	.2	0.3	5.8	8.3	13.1	.6	°	°
Jordan	7.4	8.6	14.2	.1	.4	1.7	6.2	6.9	10.4	.9	1.3	2.0
Lebanon	13.0	—	n.a.	4.0	—	n.a.	9.0	—	n.a.	.7	—	n.a.
Libya	4.9	6.2	10.4	1.5	1.5	3.4	2.1	4.7	6.7	.2	.06	0.3
Malta	2.6	3.8	5.0	°	.4	1.6	1.8	3.4	3.3	1.1	.05	0.1
Syria	19.2	30.0	21.5	8.1	3.8	2.4	10.0	22.5	16.2	°	3.7	3.0
Turkey	39.5	37.6	50.2	8.4	6.4	8.9	30.6	31.1	41.3	18.9	—	—
United Arab Republic	165.9	165.3	153.5	79.4	58.3	49.1	67.6	87.5	84.2	18.9	19.3	19.9
Africa	*170.2*	*167.3*	*183.5*	*47.3*	*49.1*	*48.3*	*91.9*	*85.0*	*105.2*	*33.3*	*33.2*	*30.2*
Algeria	7.7	5.2	n.a.	.6	3.9	n.a.	6.1	1.2	n.a.	.8	°	n.a.
Angola	.4	.5	.5	—	—	—	.4	.5	.5	—	—	°
Cameroon	1.2	1.0	1.1	—	°	°	1.2	.9	.9	n.a.	.1	.2
Congo (Braz)	n.a.	n.a.	n.a.	n.a.	n.a.	n.a.	n.a.	n.a.	n.a.	n.a.	n.a.	n.a.
Congo (Leo)	.6	.2	.2	°	°	°	2.1	.2	.2	.1	°	°
Ethiopia	4.1	5.6	6.8	.9	1.0	1.1	2.9	3.4	4.1	.3	1.1	1.6
Fed of Rhodesia & Nyasaland	1.9	1.7	1.2	.05	°	°	1.6	1.5	1.0	2.4	.3	.2
Ghana	21.1	22.1	33.9	6.2	5.1	9.1	12.5	13.2	22.7	4.6	3.8	2.1
Guinea	29.8	23.8	17.9	16.5	13.2	8.2	16.7	10.1	5.6	4.6	.5	4.1
Ivory Coast	n.a.	2.1	.2	n.a.	°	°	n.a.	.3	.1	n.a.	1.7	°
Kenya	.6	1.0	1.8	—	—	—	.6	.8	1.5	.2	.1	.3
Mali	6.4	12.3	8.7	5.4	9.3	5.2	.8	2.1	2.3	8.6	.8	1.2
Morocco	26.9	28.5	32.6	4.1	5.2	7.1	14.2	14.4	18.8	6.4	8.9	6.8
Nigeria	20.8	19.7	21.8	°	.1	.3	14.4	15.1	17.1	3.2	4.4	4.4
Senegal	3.4	5.3	2.5	°	°	°	.2	.1	.2	.5	5.1	2.3
Sierra Leone	2.6	3.1	2.7	°	°	°	2.1	2.6	2.4	4.7	.5	.3
Sudan	24.5	26.7	33.8	8.9	8.4	12.6	9.9	14.6	16.9	n.a.	3.8	4.3
Tanzania	n.a.	n.a.	1.6	n.a.	n.a.	—	n.a.	n.a.	1.4	n.a.	n.a.	.3
Togo	—	n.a.	1.2	—	n.a.	.3	—	n.a.	.7	1.3	n.a.	.3
Tunisia	10.1	6.7	13.5	2.7	2.2	4.4	6.1	3.9	8.2	1.3	.6	.9
Uganda	.1	.2	1.3	—	—	—	.1	.1	.4	°	°	.9

Communist Exports (*cont'd.*)

Area and Country	Total Communist			USSR			East European Countries			Communist China		
	1961	1962	1963	1961	1962	1963	1961	1962	1963	1961	1962	1963
Asia	*380.9*	*512.0*	*596.3*	*110.7*	*195.0*	*225.8*	*130.6*	*150.7*	*164.8*	*138.0*	*166.3*	*202.4*
Afghanistan	32.0	40.1	50.1	32.0	39.4	44.9	n.a.	.6	5.2	n.a.	n.a.	—
Burma	29.7	39.9	46.7	4.5	5.9	9.2	4.6	5.5	10.9	20.6	28.6	26.9
Cambodia	12.3	17.3	19.9	1.6	2.3	3.2	3.8	4.9	5.6	6.1	8.3	9.8
Ceylon	18.2	27.6	53.6	2.0	7.2	12.7	8.9	11.8	11.9	7.3	8.6	29.0
India	134.3	215.3	223.6	53.4	122.5	127.8	77.3	89.6	95.4	3.6	2.5	.3
Indonesia[b]	69.2	69.2	70.8	8.8	8.8	16.7	20.4	20.4	18.1	39.2	39.2	35.9
Malaya & Singapore	67.0	76.2	109.4	2.8	3.3	5.2	7.9	6.4	8.7	56.3	65.9	94.0
Pakistan	10.6	16.4	15.7	3.8	4.6	4.4	3.2	8.0	5.4	3.6	4.2	5.9
Taiwan	1.3	1.1	1.1	—	—	—	—	c	—	1.3	1.1	1.1
Thailand	6.3	4.4	5.4	1.8	1.0	1.7	4.5	3.4	3.6	—	c	—
Europe	*39.2*	*44.1*	*75.6*	*13.9*	*12.5*	*27.3*	*25.0*	*31.5*	*46.6*	*.3*	*.3*	*1.7*
Iceland	17.4	17.2	19.5	11.0	10.4	11.9	6.4	6.8	7.6	c	c	c
Portugal	8.5	4.6	4.9	1.6	—	.4	6.6	4.5	4.3	.3	.1	.2
Spain	13.3	22.4	51.2	1.3	2.1	15.0	12.0	20.1	34.7	—	.2	1.5

a These data are based on official trade statistics of the free world countries involved—that is, the communist exports indicated are the free-world trading partner's reported imports. Totals are derived from unrounded data and may not agree with the sums of the rounded components.

b Estimated for 1962–1963.

c Less than $50,000.

* Source: *The Communist Economic Offensive Through 1964*, U.S. Department of State, Bureau of Intelligence and Research, Unclassified Research Memorandum RSB–65 (Washington, D.C.: Government Printing Office, August 4, 1965), pp. 24–31.

Communist Imports from Selected Less Developed Countries, 1961–1963ᵃ* (in millions of current U.S. dollars)

Area and Country	Total Communist			USSR			East European Countries			Communist China		
	1961	1962	1963	1961	1962	1963	1961	1962	1963	1961	1962	1963
TOTAL	1,125.5	1,173.8	1,401.4	418.2	505.0	582.2	497.8	515.8	636.5	178.6	153.0	179.2
Latin America	*165.1*	*186.5*	*180.7*	*32.8*	*66.7*	*60.4*	*109.7*	*93.3*	*116.9*	*21.1*	*26.6*	*3.4*
Argentina	56.9	74.0	55.1	12.7	8.5	13.5	38.5	39.9	38.5	4.2	25.8	3.1
Brazil	74.8	73.2	92.5	19.2	39.0	40.1	55.6	34.2	52.2	°	°	0.2
Chile	1.2	1.6	3.0	—	.4	0.2	1.2	1.3	2.8	—	n.a.	°
Colombia	2.1	3.4	5.8	—	—	—	2.1	3.4	5.8	—	n.a.	°
Ecuador	.2	.6	1.3	—	—	—	.2	.06	1.3	—	—	—
Jamaica	—	1.0	n.a.	—	.5	n.a.	—	.5	n.a.	—	—	n.a.
Mexico	14.6	6.3	3.6	—	5.6	2.9	.1	.6	0.8	4.5	—	°
Peru	.4	2.1	8.1	°	°	°	.4	2.1	8.1	°	°	°
Uruguay	14.9	24.2	11.1	.9	12.8	3.7	11.6	10.7	7.3	2.4	.7	0.1
Venezuela	—	°	0.1	—	—	°	—	°	0.1	—	n.a.	—
Middle East	*380.3*	*318.6*	*437.3*	*124.0*	*109.1*	*168.3*	*228.0*	*182.0*	*228.0*	*28.2*	*27.5*	*40.9*
Aden	°	.3	°	—	—	—	—	.3	°	°	°	°
Cyprus	2.4	3.1	3.7	1.4	1.8	1.4	.9	1.4	2.3	—	n.a.	—
Greece	52.3	50.4	57.7	18.8	19.2	22.4	33.5	31.2	35.3	°	°	°
Iran	40.7	18.5	31.8	17.7	11.0	15.3	23.0	7.4	16.5	°	°	°
Iraq	4.9	9.5	12.5	2.2	3.3	5.8	1.2	2.3	2.1	2.0	4.0	4.5
Israel	7.0	8.4	9.6	.4	.3	0.6	6.6	8.1	9.0	°	—	—
Jordan	.9	1.1	1.0	—	—	—	.9	1.1	1.0	°	—	—
Lebanon	3.5	—	n.a.	2.0	n.a.	n.a.	1.5	—	n.a.	—	—	n.a.

Communist Imports (cont'd.)

Area and Country	Total Communist			USSR			East European Countries			Communist China		
	1961	1962	1963	1961	1962	1963	1961	1962	1963	1961	1962	1963
Middle East (cont'd.)												
Libya	.7	.4	0.4	.7	.2	0.4	c	.2	c	—	—	c
Syrian Arab Republic	27.0	40.5	61.4	3.3	5.3	13.6	11.6	30.8	27.9	12.1	4.4	19.9
Turkey	29.9	26.6	35.4	4.5	5.5	7.1	25.4	21.1	28.3	c	—	—
United Arab Republic	211.0	160.0	223.7	73.0	62.5	101.7	123.4	78.1	105.5	14.6	19.1	16.4
Africa												
Algeria	106.5	130.0	179.8	35.3	43.7	56.7	42.3	66.7	77.4	26.0	19.5	45.4
Angola	2.0	.2	n.a.	1.0	.1	n.a.	1.0	.1	n.a.	—	—	n.a.
Cameroon	.8	1.6	.5	—	—	—	.8	.5	.5	c	n.a.	—
Congo (Braz)	.4	.5	.1	—	—	—	.4	.5	.1	—	n.a.	n.a.
Congo (Leo)	n.a.	n.a.	n.a.	n.a.	n.a.	n.a.	n.a.	n.a.	n.a.	n.a.	n.a.	n.a.
Ethiopia	1.3	1.3	1.7	.4	.8	1.4	.9	.5	1.1	c	c	.6
Fed of Rhodesia & Nyasaland	12.0	15.0	15.4	n.a.	8.3	6.0	n.a.	4.2	8.3	c	2.5	0
Ghana	10.5	25.1	34.6	8.6	10.4	20.6	5.6	10.4	13.5	n.a.	2.5	1.1
Guinea	16.4	12.4	13.4	5.3	2.5	2.4	9.0	9.3	10.1	2.1	.6	.9
Ivory Coast	3.0	.2	.3	3.0	n.a.	—	—	.2	.3	—	n.a.	—
Kenya	n.a.	n.a.	1.7	n.a.	n.a.	—	n.a.	n.a.	.7	n.a.	n.a.	1.0
Mali	—	3.9	.1	—	1.4	.1	—	2.5	—	—	c	—
Morocco	17.6	23.7	31.1	4.7	4.7	8.1	9.3	14.8	16.8	3.6	4.2	6.2
Nigeria	6.9	4.4	4.4	—	.1	c	3.1	4.4	3.5	3.8	c	1.0
Senegal	n.a.	n.a.	.1	n.a.	n.a.	c	n.a.	n.a.	.1	n.a.	n.a.	—
Sudan	21.2	31.2	43.3	9.8	10.0	15.3	7.4	11.1	15.4	4.0	8.8	12.5
Tanzania	n.a.	n.a.	11.9	n.a.	n.a.	0.2	n.a.	n.a.	1.3	n.a.	n.a.	10.4
Tunisia	7.7	6.3	7.6	2.5	2.3	2.6	4.7	3.7	5.0	.5	.2	—
Uganda	9.4	1.7	11.7	—	n.a.	—	—	1.7	.5	9.4	—	11.2

Asia	*444.6*	*502.1*	*554.9*	*218.0*	*274.4*	*285.5*	*119.3*	*148.5*	*177.1*	*105.9*	*79.2*	*89.3*
Afghanistan	17.0	25.8	26.6	17.0	25.3	19.6	n.a.	.5	7.0	n.a.	n.a.	—
Burma	41.3	33.3	27.8	c	10.1	9.1	4.1	4.3	6.4	37.2	18.9	12.3
Cambodia	3.5	6.8	12.0	.9	1.0	0.5	.7	2.3	9.4	.7	3.5	1.5
Ceylon	33.9	47.9	38.5	9.5	7.8	6.9	7.0	12.1	10.4	17.4	28.0	21.1
India	113.5	163.9	192.1	65.2	75.3	101.3	47.9	88.0	90.2	.4	.4	—
Indonesia	77.4	72.5	70.9	31.5	36.2	25.2	9.5	10.7	10.1	36.4	26.1	35.6
Malaya and Singapore	128.9	133.1	152.4	89.9	110.6	111.5	35.2	20.6	33.9	3.8	.8	5.4
Pakistan	27.0	13.4	30.8	3.4	3.7	9.4	13.6	8.1	8.3	10.0	1.6	12.9
Thailand	2.1	6.3	3.8	.6	4.4	1.9	1.3	1.7	1.4	—	—	0.4
Europe	*30.0*	*36.8*	*48.7*	*8.1*	*11.1*	*11.3*	*20.8*	*25.3*	*37.1*	*.1*	*.1*	*0.2*
Iceland	10.1	15.6	16.3	5.1	10.9	10.7	5.0	4.7	5.7	c	—	—
Portugal	4.9	5.5	6.5	c	—	c	4.8	5.3	6.3	.1	.1	0.2
Spain	15.0	15.6	25.8	3.0	.4	0.7	12.0	15.3	25.2	c	c	—

[a] These data are based on official trade statistics of the free-world countries involved—that is, the communist imports indicated are the free-world trading partner's exports. Totals are derived from unrounded data and may not agree with the sums of the rounded components.

[b] Estimated for 1962–1963.

[c] Less than $50,000.

* Source: *The Communist Economic Offensive Through 1964*, U.S. Department of State, Bureau of Intelligence and Research, Unclassified Research Memorandum RSB-65 (Washington, D.C.: Government Printing Office, August 4, 1965), pp. 24–31.

In discussing the findings, we have repeatedly used the words *increase* and *decrease* to denote the relationship between the variables. In all cases the language is explicit in discussing the variables' relationships in terms of greater or lesser risk to the Soviet Union. However, as a form of mental shorthand, the reader is advised to look at the direction of the correlation coefficient (whether the actual number is a positive or negative one), for this denotes whether the relationship involves greater or lesser risk for the Soviet Union. Because of the manner in which the variables were scaled, all correlation coefficients having a positive direction involve greater risk-taking, whereas those correlation coefficients having a negative direction for the relationship of the variables indicate risk-avoidance.

A. THE INITIATOR'S MAXIMUM BID

The initiator's maximum bid (whether that of the Soviet Union or another party) correlated with different independent variables during the three time periods. In the 1945–1949 period, the initiator's bid increased as weapons parity decreased ($r_s = .74$, significant at .10 level). However, in the 1954–1963 period, the initiator's bid increased as the level of hostility between the actors *decreased* ($-.42$ significant at .10). Thus the initiator's bid in the Khrushchev era increased when tension levels between the Soviet Union and its opponent were generally lower.

When the crises were divided into the intrasystem or intersystem groupings in which they occurred, we found that in those crises involving East-West relations the initiator's maximum bid *increased* as the saliency of the parties *decreased* ($-.65$, significant at .01), involving less risk for the Soviet Union. A definite pattern of risk-avoidance is found with those crises involving the emerging nations. The initiator's maximum bid *increased* as the stakes involved *decreased* ($-.84$, significant at .05), as the saliency of parties *decreased* ($-.83$, significant at .05) and as weapons parity *increased* ($-.64$, significant at .10). The fact that we found significant relationships in East-West and communist-developing nations crises, but none in those involving only the communist system, indicates that the initiator's maximum bid is permitted to go higher, given the same level of risk to the Soviet Union in intrasystem crises, than in those involving the West or the developing countries.

When the crises are categorized for Soviet or non-Soviet initiation, we see a mixed tendency for an alternative of decreased risk to be chosen. Consequently, when the Soviet Union is the *initiator* in a crisis (no matter what grouping is involved, which explains why the propensity here is ambivalent), the bid of the USSR will *increase* as the saliency of the parties *decreases* ($-.52$, significant at .05). On the other hand, the Soviet bid (as the crisis initiator) *increased* as the level of weapons parity with the United States *decreased* (.41, significant at .10). When the Soviet Union is the *respondent* in a crisis, the initiator's maximum bid *increases* as the geographical risk to the Soviet Union *increases* (.49, significant at .10). Thus, the opponent of the Soviet Union is willing to increase his bid when the risk to the Soviet Union is higher, at least in terms of the geographic variable.

For *all* crises as a group, we found that the initiator's maximum bid *increased* as the geographical risk to the Soviet Union *decreased* (− .32, significant at .05).

B. THE RESPONDENT'S MAXIMUM BID

We found that the responding party's maximum bid was affected by different variables when the crises were divided according to the bloc groupings in which they occurred. When East-West relationships were involved, the respondent's bid *increased* as the geographical risk to the Soviet Union *increased* (.36 significant at .10). When the crisis involved Soviet-developing nations relations, the respondent's bid *increased* as the stakes *decreased* (− .82, significant at .05), as the saliency of the parties *decreased* (− .84, significant at .10). When the respondent's bid is then considered in the three groupings, we again find that the independent variables of risk to the Soviet Union seem to have no statistically significant relations with the respondent's bid in intracommunist system crises and that the respondent's bid in crises with the West (no matter who the respondent is) increased with geographical risk to the USSR; however, in crises involving the developing nations, a definite pattern of *increase* in the respondent's bid was found to be associated with a *decrease* in the risk for the Soviet Union in the stakes and saliency of parties involved and in the level of weapons parity.

When the Soviet Union is the crisis initiator, the respondent's maximum bid *increases* with the level of hostility (.44, significant at .10). If the Soviet Union was the respondent, its bid would *increase* as the stakes *increased* (.48, significant at .10), no matter what bloc was involved, but that its bid as the respondent would *increase* as levels of tensions decreased (− .45, significant at .10). This again shows an ambiguous tendency, since we did not control for system grouping (too few cases). Thus both the Soviet bid as the initiator or respondent, independent of time period or grouping, shows a mixed tendency toward risk-taking and risk-avoidance with different variables being associated with different levels of bidding, depending, apparently, on the particular bloc grouping in which the crisis occurs.

C. THE OUTCOME

When we grouped the crises according to time period, we found that in the 1945–1949 period the crisis outcome approached the conflictual end of the dimension (and moved away from compromise and withdrawal) when weapons parity *increased* (− .92, significant at .05) and when levels of tension *decreased* (− .70, significant at .10). Both, then, indicate a tendency for risk-taking in terms of the manner of crisis resolution when the riskier elements of the situation are minimized. Conversely, if the elements of risk are high, the outcome for the Soviet Union approaches compromise and withdrawal. This is during the period when the United States had a monopoly of atomic weapons.

The relationships of the variables change during the following period, which are the last years of Stalin's rule as well as the period when the Soviet Union had atomic, but not nuclear, arms (which the United States did possess). We found in this transitional period a mixed tendency in risk-taking. The crisis-outcome levels *increased* as stakes *increased* (.79, significant at .10) and as geographic risk *increased* (.75, significant at .10). However, at the same time crisis outcomes are higher when weapons parity *increases* ($-.82$, significant at .10) and when levels of hostility *decrease* (-1.00, significant at .01).

During the third period, that of essential nuclear parity (and coinciding with the leadership of Khrushchev), the pattern changes, reverting to one of a lesser tendency to approach conflict when risk factors are high. We found that as geographical risk *decreased,* the crisis-outcome level decreased ($-.52$, significant at .05).

When we consider crisis outcomes in terms of the bloc groupings involved, we find a great variation. Crisis-outcome levels involving the communist system *increase* as stakes *increase* ($-.53$, significant at .10). Though the correlation coefficients are not statistically significant, we found the same relationship of risk to outcome in intrabloc crises in terms of the increase in geographic risk ($-.46$) and in saliency of parties (.32) with an increase in crisis levels.

INDEX